DISOBEYING HITLER

DISOBEYING HITLER

GERMAN RESISTANCE
IN THE LAST YEAR OF WWII

RANDALL HANSEN

FABER & FABER

First published in Canada in 2014 by Doubleday Canada,
a division of Random House of Canada Limited,
a Penguin Random House company

First published in the UK in 2014
by Faber & Faber Limited
Bloomsbury House
74–77 Great Russell Street
London WC1B 3DA

Printed and bound by CPI Group (UK) Ltd, Croydon, CR0 4YY

A CIP record for this book
is available from the British Library

ISBN 978–0–571–28451–1

2 4 6 8 10 9 7 5 3 1

For Kieran

Hitler's Germany has neither a past nor a future.
Its only purpose is destruction, and destroyed it shall be.

THOMAS MANN

CONTENTS

Introduction | 1

INTRODUCTION

I N 1943, THE SOVIETS forced the German army to make multiple retreats in Russia. Adolf Hitler, Chancellor of Germany and leader of the National Socialist German Workers' Party (NSDAP), had to decide what to do with territories evacuated by the German military. His answer was clear: the retreating Wehrmacht was to destroy everything in its wake. The enemy would recover only an "unusable, uninhabitable wasteland" in which "mines would continue to explode for months."[1] Vast swathes of Europe and Russia would be left blackened, desolate, and lifeless. Hitler's original vision of racial domination was replaced by a similarly horrendous one: scorched earth.

As the Wehrmacht staggered backward on all fronts, Hitler transformed these musings into a series of concrete orders: to poison, block, and wreck all ports across Europe; to destroy Paris; to blow up industry, railroads, bridges, utilities supplies, and archives, museums, and other cultural institutions in Germany; and to defend every German city, street by street, house by house, all intended to cause massive destruction and loss of life. From September 1944, Hitler issued a death sentence for Germany. On September 7, he had an editorial published in the Nazi mouthpiece, the *Völkischer Beobachter*. "Not a German stalk of wheat," it thundered, "is to feed the enemy, not a German mouth to give him information, not a German hand to offer him help. He is to find every footbridge destroyed, every road blocked—nothing but death, annihilation and hatred will meet him."[2] Hitler, his minister for propaganda, Joseph Goebbels, and Heinrich Himmler, head of the SS, all agreed that "nothing that could be of any service to the enemy could be allowed to fall into his hands."[3]

Most German field marshals, generals, and Nazi Party officials were all too ready to obey Hitler. They sent tens of thousands of young men to their deaths; wilfully destroyed industry, bridges, and buildings; and launched a defence of cities and towns that resulted in their complete destruction. A small but morally and militarily important minority of soldiers and civilians, however, said no. As most other soldiers and party members fought on to the awful end, these officers, soldiers, and—above all—civilians chose to disobey. They sought to spare industry, electrical and gas installations, ports, bridges, and roads. And, as Allied armies pushed deep into the heart of Germany in 1945, they sought to prevent a pointless and wholly destructive military defence of their cities against British, American, French, and Soviet armies. If they failed, the price of disobedience was death.

This book tells their stories. It explores what resistance in Germany meant after the influential figures around Claus von Stauffenberg had been killed or were on the run following the failure on July 20, 1944, of his plot, codenamed "Valkyrie," to assassinate Hitler. It examines how German officers lower down the chain of command responded to Hitler's nihilistic orders for the destruction of Germany and Europe. And, above all, it shows how ordinary people—workers, architects, doctors, and priests—possessed the conviction, bravery, and guile necessary to throw themselves into a final act of resistance against the National Socialist regime.

CHAPTER 1

WAR, ATROCITIES, RESISTANCE

O N SEPTEMBER 1, 1939, German planes appeared over the central Polish city of Wieluń. Their bomb bays opened. The synagogue, church, hospital, and houses below exploded. Horrified residents streamed out of the city. They found little respite: Stuka dive-bombers, which would terrify civilians across Europe, strafed them. Bodies littered the roads. The operation was repeated in dozens of cities across the country.

As the bombers laid waste to Poland's cities, 1.5 million German soldiers poured across its borders from the west, north, and south. While Germany's air force swept from the skies the few modern airplanes the Poles could muster, fast-moving German tanks burst through Polish positions, surrounded them, and destroyed them.[1] The Polish government desperately hoped that the British and French would honour their guarantee to intervene. On September 17, foreign troops indeed arrived, but they were not Anglo-French: Stalin had ordered his forces to attack Poland from the east. The Poles put up a resistance that can only be described as heroic and managed to inflict 45,000 casualties on the Germans, but the outcome could not be doubted. By October, it was over. The Germans, at this point "enthusiastic advocates of unconditional surrender," had utterly crushed Poland; more than a hundred thousand Polish soldiers were dead.[2]

During and after the campaign, Wehrmacht tactics were uncompromisingly brutal. Over the course of a three-week campaign, German forces burned 531 towns and villages (with Warsaw and the province of Łódź suffering particularly heavy damage) and killed 16,376 people.[3] As Polish towns and Polish divisions fell, German soldiers murdered thousands of prisoners of war, male civilians, women, and children.

As awful as their techniques were, Wehrmacht officers might have been able to justify them as tactical: any form of actual or potential resistance was crushed with the aim of subjugating Poland to German authority. The burning of villages, the shooting of prisoners, and the murder of civilians are hardly uncommon in the history of warfare, even if the German combination of new technology with old martial methods led to a far greater loss of life.[4] But murder was more than tactical: it was an end in itself. Over the course of the campaign, mass, systematic murder displaced tactical killing by the German army, "renegade" murders by Waffen-SS units, and revenge killings by ethnic Germans.[5] The Führer and his generals had redefined warfare. Civilians would not be killed in order to win a war; rather, the war would be waged and won so that the murder of civilians could be perfected. The National Socialist vision, which is difficult to comprehend in the scale of its horror, was one of endless domination, violence, and death.[6]

The executions were primarily carried out by the SS units that participated in Poland's occupation: the Einsatzgruppen der Sicherheitspolizei (special task forces of the Security Police, or Sipo, but, in reality, death squads). Organizationally, the SS, led by Heinrich Himmler and Hitler himself, was divided into the Party Secret Service (Sicherheitsdienst, or SD) and the Secret Police (Geheime Staatspolizei, or Gestapo), which together made up the broadly investigative and policing wings of state security. The apparatus also included the Criminal Police (Kriminalpolizei, or Kripo) and the Order Police (Ordnungspolizei, or Orpo); the latter included police services such as fire, water, and air protection, among others. The SS also had military (Waffen-SS) and paramilitary wings; it was under the latter that the Orpo's police battalions murdered massive numbers of civilians. The Orpo also supplied five hundred men to the Einsatzgruppen.[7]

Men from the Gestapo, the SD, and the Kripo were formed into five Einsatzgruppen, and one was attached to each of the invading armies.[8] Later, two more Einsatzgruppen and one Einsatzkommando (from Danzig/

Gdańsk) were added, with a detachment of Orpo forming part of a seventh Einsatzgruppe.[9] Together, they totalled almost three thousand men.[10] The targets of these Einsatzgruppen were Polish nationalists, intellectuals, Roman Catholic clergy, and, of course, Jews.

In a typical operation, SS Sturmbannführer (Major) Kurt Eimann, commander of an SS regiment in the Free City of Danzig, recruited several thousand SS members into an auxiliary police force, the Eimann Battalion.[11] In November, the battalion met a trainload of disabled people from Pomerania, who were loaded into trucks and driven into the forest. They were met by Polish political prisoners digging a pit. The first victim, a fifty-year-old woman, was led to the edge. Eimann pulled out a pistol, placed it at the base of her skull, and pulled the trigger. The murder of the other disabled people followed. The SS then killed the political prisoners, threw them on top of the pile of bodies, and covered the graves with dirt.[12] That month, some 3,500 people would be shot and dumped into mass graves. During the Polish campaign, the Einsatzgruppen, backed up by other SS units and 100,000 ethnic Germans, murdered tens of thousands of Polish intellectuals, Jews, mental patients, prostitutes, Roma, and Sinti.[13] They singled out Jews for particularly brutal treatment.

Although the SS committed the majority of the murders, the German army was hardly innocent. It worked with the Einsatzgruppen in pushing tens of thousands of Jews over the demarcation line into the Soviet zone, and its units sometimes shot civilians. But above all, the German army divided responsibilities between itself and the SS in a manner that provided the latter with carte blanche to commit mass murder.[14] Led by General Quartermaster Eduard Wagner, the army negotiated agreements with the SS designed to contain, if possible, SS murder but above all to shield the German army from direct involvement in it.[15] The effort failed on both counts. The German army tolerated in some cases the deliberate execution of civilians; in others, it provided indirect assistance through the provision of logistical support; and in still others, it directly participated in the executions. The German army, writes Holocaust historian Raul Hilberg, "went out of its way to turn over Jews to the Einsatzgruppen, to request actions against Jews, to participate in killing operations, and to shoot Jewish

hostages in 'reprisal' for attacks on occupation forces."[16] The army gave
the SS a free hand to launch a genocidal campaign on an unimaginable
scale while ensuring its own complicity. The SS tested these techniques in
Poland. They perfected them farther east, in the Soviet Union, where millions of Jews stood in the path of the invading German army.

[WAR]

On June 22, 1941, over three million German troops—twice the number
thrown at Poland—attacked the Soviet Union: it was Operation Barbarossa.[17]
Supported by the now familiar artillery barrage and aerial bombardment,
three army groups (Heeresgruppen) moved into Soviet territory. Army Group
North, commanded by Feldmarschall Wilhelm Ritter von Leeb, cut northeast through the Baltics and on toward Leningrad. Feldmarschall Fedor von
Bock's Army Group Centre, the most heavily armed and formidable of the
three concentrations, pushed east through the Soviet Union toward Moscow.
Finally, Army Group South, under Feldmarschall Gerd von Rundstedt,
advanced southeast toward Odessa and Sevastopol. The Wehrmacht's strategy relied on the overwhelming combination of mobility and power: rapidly
moving divisions, particularly panzer divisions, would outmanoeuvre and
surround the enemy as the blunt force of artillery, air, and infantry power
destroyed it.[18] The strategy was immensely effective: German forces repeatedly landed devastating blows on their dazed enemy. In just over two weeks,
they captured some 400,000 Soviet soldiers, and Army Group Centre pushed
on to Smolensk, the gateway to Moscow. These initial successes threw both
Soviet High Command and Stalin himself into a state of shock.

In the southern theatre, Rundstedt's Army Group South encountered
the fiercest early resistance, although its gains look limited only in compari-
son to the rapid advances of the two army groups to the north. Early in the
campaign, Army Group South captured 100,000 Soviet troops near Uman.
Then, Army Group Centre's Panzer Group 2 under Generaloberst Heinz
Guderian advanced south to assist General der Infanterie Carl-Heinrich
Stülpnagel's Seventeenth Army in a successful encirclement of Kiev.[19]
Another 650,000 men fell into captivity.

The Seventeenth Army contained two of the most enigmatic officers of the Second World War: Stülpnagel himself, and Oberstleutnant Dietrich von Choltitz. Stülpnagel was a humanist, almost philosophical officer and a longtime opponent of Hitler. He had been intimately involved in 1938 coup preparations designed to overthrow Hitler after the Allies' expected rejection of German claims on the Sudetenland. In the Polish campaign, he opposed SS crimes against civilians.[20] Yet, less than two years later, he participated in those crimes. During the early days of Operation Barbarossa, the Seventeenth Army reached Lviv (German: Lemberg). As it did, retreating Soviet troops killed several thousand Ukrainian nationals imprisoned in the city. In response, German forces, both Wehrmacht and Einsatzgruppen, incited a retaliatory pogrom that killed four thousand Jews. According to one Soviet source, Stülpnagel planned the incitement and reported back to Berlin that it could be used as a model elsewhere.[21] Such *Selbtsreinigungsaktionen*, or "self-cleaning actions," would allow the Germans to spare manpower otherwise assigned to the murder of Jews while shifting responsibility for the killings onto the local population.[22]

Although he resisted orders to shoot Soviet generals in reprisal for the killing of POWs, Stülpnagel also took part in German anti-partisan warfare, which resulted in the widespread revenge killing of innocents from July 1941.[23] Anti-partisan warfare was bound up with the National Socialist equation of Judaism and Bolshevism, an equation that Stülpnagel took as read. On June 30, 1941, he signed the following anti-partisan order: "when the perpetrators of sabotage or attacks on soldiers cannot be identified, then Jews or Communists, particularly Jewish Komsomols [members of a Soviet youth league], should be shot as revenge."[24] In August, he noted that "Draconian measures" against the Jews led some Ukrainians to take pity on them. It was necessary, therefore, to educate the Ukrainian population in order to "obtain a resolute and more uniform rejection" of Jews.[25] Stülpnagel saw no contradiction between this hardened anti-Semitism and a humanitarian concern for other civilians: in August 1941, he called for the "appropriate treatment and care of the civilian population in the occupied territories."[26]

Stülpnagel worked with the SS to implement anti-Jewish measures. In late September, he approached Sonderkommando 4b (part of Einsatzgruppe

C) with the request to annihilate the Jews of the central Ukrainian city of Kremenchuk in response to three cases of cable sabotage.[27] By November, the Sonderkommando had killed thousands of Jews.[28] In early October 1941, Stülpnagel requested a transfer away from the eastern front. He knew then—as he would for the rest of his life—that he was deeply implicated in National Socialist crimes.[29] When his son asked him if Jews were being killed, Stülpnagel's reply was: "You must remain pure."[30]

Stülpnagel's crimes were hardly the only ones committed by the army, and in some cases officers did not wait for sabotage or suspected sabotage. Apparently hoping to have the whole awful business done with, commanders urged the Einsatzgruppen to get on with the killing, sometimes even providing men and materiel to make the SS's job easier.[31]

For his part, Dietrich von Choltitz made his mark in an early campaign that, thanks to Hitler, owed much more to classical warfare than it did to Blitzkrieg. After Kiev and Kharkiv, Rundstedt ordered the Romanian Fourth Army to capture the port of Odessa, which it did after a three-month siege. As Odessa fell on October 8, Army Group South pushed farther east, occupying most of the Crimean Peninsula by the end of the month. Only the important port city of Sevastopol held out. General Erich von Manstein, who had taken over command of the Eleventh Army after Generaloberst Eugen von Schobert's death in early September, wished to bypass the city and make a dash for the oil-rich Caucasus. Hitler, however, never resisted the urge to attack a fortress, and he ordered Manstein to take the city. Hitler's logic was that an attack would allow his forces to seize the port and protect its southern flank from naval assault as it advanced into the Caucasus.

In addition to his Eleventh Army, Manstein had the support of the Romanian Third Army and a regiment commanded by Choltitz. Sevastopol was a fortress guarding the approaches to the city's great port, home to the Russian Black Sea Fleet. With Manstein's army literally at its gates, Sevastopol remained under siege all winter. On June 2, Manstein ordered an artillery and aerial bombardment of the city. As the Luftwaffe hammered the city from the skies, great mortar guns shelled it below. Over one thousand tons of shells landed in the city, destroying it block by block. A single shell could pulverize anything in its path. On June 7, Manstein's troops began moving in. It was during this period that Choltitz acquired a reputation for brutality and unquestioning obedience to orders.

Despite the hammering they had taken, the Soviets put up a bitter resistance. When they ran out of ammunition, they attacked the Germans with their bare hands. But the combination of air, artillery, and infantry strength overcame the Soviets. On July 4, the Germans took Sevastopol. The Soviet Black Sea Fleet evacuated the port and retreated to the Caucasus. When the city fell into German hands, it looked like the face of the moon.[32] The Soviets suffered appalling casualties. The agonies experienced by the citizens and defenders of Sevastopol deserve a much more prominent place in the collective memory than they currently enjoy.

The concentration of Germany's heaviest guns on Sevastopol meant that they were unavailable for a siege upon another city: Leningrad. The first units of Leeb's Army Group North reached the city by September 4. Soon, Leningrad and fully thirty Soviet divisions were encircled, waiting for the hammer's blow.

It never fell. Rather than ordering his forces into the city, which they most likely would have taken, Hitler decided that they would remain outside it. Subjected to a heavy conventional artillery barrage, one without the concrete-busting super-artillery that was then being used on Sevastopol, the city would be starved into submission. Leningrad's residents suffered terribly, and the plague of starvation would haunt them for two years. Soviet internal security reported its first case of cannibalism in December.[33] By the time the siege was fully lifted in early 1944, approximately one million people had starved to death.[34] Only the refusal of the Finns to close off all access points to the north of the city, which allowed the Soviets to provide a minimum of supplies, kept the situation from becoming worse still.[35]

As the siege of Leningrad began, the bulk of the German forces in Army Group Centre had their eye on a bigger prize: Moscow itself. A staggering array of forces—almost two million men, two thousand tanks, and 1,390 aircraft—prepared for the assault on the Soviet capital: Operation Typhoon. On September 30, 1941, Bock ordered the attack. In a replay of the summer campaign, his troops at first surged forward, sending the eight Soviet armies standing in the path of the German advance reeling.[36] German troops were intoxicated with success. As in the summer, however, early victories were deceptive. Heavy autumn rains slowed the advance, and by the end of October, German equipment was lumbering slowly through the mud. The weather then switched: rain became ice, and German machines and German men froze. But above all, Germany had reached the limits of its material strength at precisely the moment when the greatest prize seemed so tantalizingly close. As historian Gerhard Weinberg argues: "What needs to be understood is that [by the first week of December 1941] the Germans were at the end of their offensive strength, that they had not mobilized their society as thoroughly for war as the Soviet Union, and that the Soviet leadership not only remained in effective control of the unoccupied portions of the country but mustered its human and materiel resources for a devastating blow at the invaders."[37]

That blow came on December 5. General Georgy Zhukov's forces smashed German salients north and south of the city, and then turned to thrust westward. They crushed the German forward units and made deep cuts toward the rear.[38] The Germans staggered backward, leaving abandoned vehicles, burned villages, and dead or dying soldiers in their wake. Against loud cries from his generals for withdrawal, Hitler brought in General Walter Model, a fanatical Nazi with a reputation for personal bravery and brutal discipline (he would harangue and at times shoot his men). But even Model's talents might not have been enough had Stalin not lent a helping hand: against Zhukov's wishes, Stalin ordered a series of offensives up and down the length of the front in early January. These moves were designed to free Leningrad, encircle Army Group Centre, and cut off German armies in the south.[39] They went ahead, but they were largely a failure because they diverted essential forces away from the key objective: destroying Army Group Centre. That army group survived, and Model was able to stabilize the front more or less where it was before Operation Typhoon.

Despite Model's success, the war had irrevocably changed course. The Soviets inflicted on the Germans a defeat from which they never fully recovered. In the wake of the disaster, Hitler sacked all three army group commanders on the eastern front.[40] World War II at this point had become on that front much like Germany's situation in World War I. The strategy of concentrating the overwhelming force of panzer divisions on a single decisive point broke down over the vast spaces of the Soviet Union. The front had widened as German troops went forward and the supply lines following them failed to keep up.[41] Short on supplies, Europe's most technologically advanced army reverted to trench warfare. Hungry men with lice and skin infections crowded themselves into damp, fetid bunkers, trying to keep themselves warm by using their frostbitten hands to shove newspapers down their thin clothing.[42] The Germans, like the Soviets on whom they had imposed such misery, were in for a long, awful winter.

As summer arrived, the mood in German High Command (Ober-kommando der Wehrmacht, or OKW) improved. As Stalin drew forces away from other positions to reinforce Moscow, Hitler caught him off guard by ordering the next major movements toward the north and the south. In preparation for it, fully one half of all German formations on the eastern front were attached to Army Group South. Hitler split this new, enlarged army group into Army Groups A and B. The original plan involved the two army groups pushing east to create a shield for a later surge south-ward into the Caucasus.[43] The Caucasus would provide the Germans with much-needed oil while denying it to the Soviets, and open the possibility of a thrust into Iran and Iraq, creating the tantalizing prospect of hooking up with Erwin Rommel's Afrikakorps.[44] The Germans could then drive the Allies out of the Middle East, sever Western Europe's southern supply route to the Soviets, and, with the support of the Grand Mufti of Jerusalem, slaughter all the Jews in that region.[45] A murder squad attached to Rommel's army, an Einsatzgruppe for the Middle East, would organize and imple-ment the murders.[46] As Rommel's army cut north to meet German forces moving southeastward through the Caucasus, the two great death scythes slicing through Eurasia and the Middle East would meet.

The British would put an end to Rommel's ambitions in the south. In the north, Hitler changed his mind and instead ordered the bulk of the two army groups to move immediately south and on toward the Caucasus, with the exception of the remnants of the Eleventh Army sent north to Leningrad. Meanwhile, a single army—the Sixth—was tasked with taking

Stalingrad.[47] Following a brutal battle in which both sides gave no quarter, General Friedrich Paulus surrendered and marched his beaten and dismal men into Soviet captivity. By February 1943, an army that just two months earlier had totalled 225,000 men was reduced to merely 90,000.

By early 1943, the Germans had lost Stalingrad; the siege of Leningrad had been partially broken through the opening of a land corridor on Lake Ladoga's southern shore; and the Soviets (temporarily) retook Kharkiv (in northeastern Ukraine) and Belgorod (forty kilometres north of the Ukrainian-Russian border). During first half of the year, the situation calmed a little, and the Germans enjoyed some successes. Tactical withdrawals in the south stabilized the front there; the Germans retook Ukraine's second-largest city, Kharkiv, and they pulled divisions out of a salient near Leningrad. With the front thus stabilized, Hitler prepared once again to throw everything he had at the Soviets.

For three months, Manstein marshalled men and equipment for an assault on the Kursk salient, running roughly from Oryol to Kharkiv. Soviet intelligence picked up the preparations, and Stalin decided to let the attack go ahead in the hope that Germany would exhaust its material and human strength. On July 5, the two greatest armoured forces the world has ever seen threw themselves directly at each other.[48] Bombers screamed across the sky. Tanks smashed into each other. Infantrymen riddled the enemy with gunfire. Casualties on both sides were immense, and the earth beneath them turned black as blood mixed with dust and soil. Like so many battles on the eastern front, it was a conflict in which two great, pitiless, and murderous dictators smashed against each other like mad gods with such brutality and force that the rest of the war appeared to be a sideshow.

Germany's Ninth Army made some progress in the north, advancing some eighteen miles, but in the centre, the battle became a body-strewn war of attrition. Manstein wanted to continue, but Hitler called it off on July 13. Germany had thrown its best units, its best equipment, and its best commanders—Manstein and Model—against the Soviets and nonetheless suffered a stunning defeat.[49]

Hitler had wanted to send a powerful message to the world through the battle at Kursk. He did so, though it was not the one he had anticipated.

The message instead told of "the triumph of the Red Army over the Wehrmacht in a slugging match of enormous size and ferocity."[50] The war was by no means decided, but the advantage had shifted to the Soviets. Over the next year, they would drive the Germans and their allies out of their positions west of Kiev and northern Ukraine, Odessa and the Crimea, and Leningrad.[51] In desperation, Hitler sacked Manstein and Kleist and promoted Nazi enthusiasts Model (Army Group South) and Schörner (Army Group A), but it made little difference. In January 1944, the Soviets liberated Leningrad. These victories were unquestionably impressive, and Soviet strength awed all participants in the conflict. But between the Red Army and victory lay a great obstacle, one which constituted the heart of the forces that had invaded, occupied, and ravaged the Soviet Union for three years: Army Group Centre, positioned roughly in the middle of a front stretching two thousand miles from the Gulf of Finland to the Black Sea.[52]

Three years to the day after the German invasion of the Soviet Union, the Soviets removed that obstacle. On June 22, 1944, following a massive buildup, the Red Army attacked: they unleashed Operation Bagration. On the first day, the Soviets encircled most of an entire army, sent another staggering backward, and generally sent waves of panic shooting through the rear areas of Army Group Centre.[53] A week into the offensive, Soviet attacks had killed 130,000 German troops, or an incredible 18,500 each day. A further 66,000 were taken prisoner.[54] Feldmarschall Busch, the commander in chief of Army Group Centre, collapsed into panic. "What can I do? What can I do?" he asked his chief of staff.

There was little he could do. The Soviet offensive was unstoppable. Hitler fired Busch on June 28 and replaced him with the dynamic and ruthless Model, but this superior commander was also overwhelmed. The Red Army, demonstrating that there was no German monopoly on Blitzkrieg tactics, surged forward and passed through Belorussia's ruined villages and broken towns.[55] The last major city in Belorussia was Minsk, which too fell on the night of July 2–3.[56] From there, Soviet forces plunged toward Lithuania and Poland. Following an artillery barrage of 170,000 shells, Marshal Konstantin Rokossovskii's armies pushed toward Lublin on July 17. Six days later, Lublin was liberated and, with it, the Majdanek concentration camp.[57] The Soviets took the first pictures of huge heaps of shoes and human hair and of machines designed to grind bones into fertilizer.[58] Between 80,000 and 110,000 people had died at the camp; the vast majority—between 59,000 and 72,000—were Jews.[59] After Lublin, the Red Army turned northwest toward the Vistula and Warsaw.[60]

The destruction of Army Group Centre was the single greatest defeat suffered by Hitler's armies over the course of the war, far greater than the better-known battle at Stalingrad. In one campaign, the Soviets obliterated twenty-eight divisions. The Germans lost 589,425 men on the eastern front between June and August 1944.[61] The Soviets' own losses were also immense. Stalin estimated them at 178,000, but they were probably much higher. He could, however, afford these losses; Hitler and Model could not. Fought over the same battlefields and in and around the same cities, Operation Bagration was Operation Barbarossa in reverse, with Berlin rather than Moscow the ultimate symbolic prize.

[ATROCITIES]

Throughout the first three years of the German-Soviet conflict, the Wehrmacht treated both soldiers and civilians with unimaginable cruelty. As Germany smashed through one position after another in 1941, hundreds of thousands of Soviet troops fell into captivity. The Germans beat them, herded them into open pens, taunted them with scraps of food, and then allowed them to starve. Over the course of the war, some three million POWs, or almost 58 percent of Soviet troops, would die, most of starvation and disease.[62] Others—an unknown figure—were shot.[63]

Starvation had both a passive and an active role. The passive: German soldiers, perhaps subject to noble exceptions whose stories have been lost, were utterly indifferent to the fate of the millions of supposedly racially inferior Slavs dying in captivity.[64] The active: hunger was a powerful political and tactical weapon throughout the war.[65] Politically, mass starvation was basic to Hitler and Himmler's plan for the East: a brutal colonization and demographic reordering that would see the starvation of its population (between 30 million and 45 million people would eventually die of hunger), the razing of its cities, the transformation of vast agricultural spaces into German farming communities, and the enslavement of the surviving civilians.[66] This demographic revolution was to be launched after a quick German victory. As the war dragged on toward winter, starvation assumed an immediate tactical purpose: millions of German troops needed food, and they were ordered to take it from the local population. Advancing troops stole as much as they could. Finally, on Hitler's orders, the Germans hoped to starve Leningrad into submission rather than capturing it through a siege and assault. The deliberate starvation of millions of people thus served three purposes: it made them disappear, it fed German armies, and it aided those armies' advance across the Soviet Union.

Only war would fill in all the details, but the broad picture had long been clear to German High Command.[67] In contrast with Poland, the relationship between the army and the SS in the Soviet Union was specified with greater clarity, and the murder was more extensive. On March 26, 1941, SS-Gruppenführer Reinhard Heydrich and the quartermaster general, Wagner, agreed that "within the framework of their instructions and upon their own responsibility, the Sonderkommandos are entitled to carry out executive measures against the civilian population."[68] German Army High Command (Oberkommando des Heeres, or OKH) adopted the agreement as an official regulation on April 28, 1941.[69]

The army gave the SS a free hand to commit unlimited murder within the rear of areas held by Wehrmacht forces. "Despite the high degree of verbal camouflage in the definition of the tasks of the SS," writes Jürgen Förster, "there could be no doubt among the army command, after Hitler's numerous public and private remarks on the connection between Bolshevism and Jewry, after the measures taken in the Reich, and after the murders in Poland, that along with the Communist leadership stratum the Jews in the occupied Soviet territories were also to be exterminated."[70] The lack of restraint and discipline that characterized these killings, rather than the principle of ethnic cleansing itself, would eventually push Wagner into joining the anti-Hitler conspiracy.[71]

The March 26 agreement between the SS and the army was followed by others on the treatment of civilians and of the Soviet political leadership.

On May 24, 1941, a decree, only slightly amended by the army, was distributed that removed civilians from military jurisdiction, meaning that officers and soldiers would face no punishment for executing civilians suspected of guerrilla activity or for the collective punishment, including murder, of civilians in order to quell that activity.[72] The decree provided the framework for another measure: on June 8, 1941, armies and army groups received the Commissar Decree.[73] The decree, once again modified in the details on implementation but not in overall intention by the army, ordered the immediate execution of Soviet political commissars captured in hostilities.[74] The most recent research concludes that the "vast majority" of commanders passed the order on, and that the overwhelming majority of frontline units implemented it.[75]

Following the June 22, 1941, German invasion of the Soviet Union, a war of conquest became a war of annihilation.[76] The Einsatzgruppen, having tested their techniques in Poland, followed German armies into the Soviet Union. They committed mass murder up and down the front. By the end of July, the Einsatzgruppen had killed 63,000 civilians—90 percent of them Jews.[77] By August, the SS introduced two changes. First, Einsatzgruppen and other SS units began systematically murdering women and children, whose treatment had been until then little discussed.[78] Second, the murder squads developed a standard method.[79] They brought large numbers of Jews to an open area. The SS forced those near the front to dig a large pit. They ordered the Jews to undress and stand at its edge. They then shot them, watching them fall into the pit, or forced them to lie on the rows of bodies below before firing from above. Many of the SS men shot wildly, and large numbers of their victims writhed in the pits, dying slowly of their wounds or being buried half alive. During the executions, Germans of all sorts took photographs; in the evening, there was food and drink for the SS recruits. "The Jews," wrote one recruit from Reserve Police Battalion 105, "are being totally eradicated."[80]

Anti-partisan warfare, conducted under the shield of the jurisdiction decree, was similarly brutal. In one example, Army High Command East (covering the Baltic states, eastern Poland, and West Belarus) reported in March 1943 that the army had aided police battalions in killing 3,300 Jews,

2,074 "bandits," and 7,344 "bandit helpers," the last of which included those only suspected of having provided assistance.[81]

[RESISTANCE]

The atrocities, and the treatment of the civilian population generally, had two effects: they radicalized the majority and alienated a minority of the German officer corps. For many officers, their culpability in tolerating or executing the atrocities hardened their will to fight on, above all when it seemed that Germany would lose the war. They knew they were war criminals and that defeat meant prosecution. For others, the atrocities led to shock, shame, and, gradually, a determination to distance themselves from the policies and those who promoted them. It is fair to say that the atrocities rekindled the military resistance that had been moribund since 1940, when Germany's stunning victory over France showered Hitler in glory as it covered the resisters in despair.

Before developing this point, a few words on other forms of German resistance are necessary. Since the 1960s, the general public has mostly associated resistance in Nazi Germany with military resistance and above all with Claus von Stauffenberg. The military resisters were, in fact, the last to organize against Hitler. There had been opposition even before 1933, but these opponents hailed largely from the extreme ideological left. Despite their insistence that Social Democrats—the major left-centre political party during Weimar as well as today—were "social fascists" who had eased the National Socialists' ascent to power, the Communists were among the first to act. After Hitler became chancellor, organizations flooded Germany with anti–National Socialist pamphlets. Within two years, Communist networks were riddled with informants, and, in 1935, a wave of arrests tore those resistance networks to shreds.[82] When the Nazi-Soviet pact was signed in August 1939, Communist resisters in and outside of concentration camps were thrown into a state of utter confusion. Communist resistance nonetheless reorganized in the run-up to Operation Barbarossa. The "Red Orchestra," an anti-Nazi and anti-democratic group led by Harro Schulze-Boysen (a Luftwaffe staff officer) and Arvid Harnack (a lawyer), passed information on to the Soviet Union, including warnings about German intentions to invade.[83] The group also launched leaflet campaigns drawing attention to Nazi atrocities across Europe. The Gestapo caught up with them in 1942. The majority of the group was arrested and many of its members, including Harnack, Schulze-Boysen, and their wives, were executed. Communist resistance was smashed.

The Social Democrats had also long warned of the dangers of National Socialism, and they were able to arrive at this conclusion without reference to an ideological high command in Moscow. They suffered particularly severely during the first wave of terror immediately after the Nazis came to power (most early concentration camps were for Communists and Social Democrats) but rallied sufficiently to organize early campaigns against National Socialism. Active Social Democratic resistance groups sprang up across the country. They distributed propaganda, organized meetings, and urged opposition. At the shop level, there were also islands of immovable working-class opposition to the Nazis, such as the dockers in Bremen.[84] Their resistance was of the daily, passive sort—for example, refusing to give the Hitler salute. The union leadership provided some of the most active opposition, with figures such as Wilhelm Leuschner (a Social Democratic politician and union leader) and Jakob Kaiser (a Roman Catholic unionist and Centre Party member), along with Julius Leber (editor of a Social Democratic newspaper), forging contacts with the conservative and military resistance. Profoundly scarred by conservatives' denunciations of them as traitors after they formed the Weimar Republic in 1918–1919, the Social Democrats made it clear they would bring the workers onto the streets only after a successful military coup.[85]

These early resistance activities were important not so much for their effect, which was minimal, but for their role in keeping the flame of resistance alive in Germany and for projecting the image of "another Germany" to a justifiably skeptical outside world. In this sense, there was some commonality between the German resistance and the equally brave but then small and ineffectual French resistance. Unlike the French, however, the Germans could rely on nothing from the Allies. Good Germans could only complicate the war effort.

The Social Democrats were drawn into an unlikely relationship with the conservative and military leaders who had connived to bring Hitler to power because the socialists' closest ideological neighbours—the aristocratic Kreisau Circle of Adam von Trott zu Solz, Helmuth James Graf von Moltke, and Peter Graf Yorck von Wartenburg—were not prepared to act. The Kreisau Circle, a broad group of Christian resisters who, in Berlin and Kreisau, debated and wrote about their plans for a Germany after National Socialism, contained those, like Moltke and Trott, who had opposed Hitler since 1933.[86] The Circle played an important role in signalling to the Allies the existence of an internal opposition, but their chief task, as they understood it, involved planning for life after Germany's total defeat. Similarly, the Protestant and Roman Catholic churches provided little active resistance to Hitler. The Catholic bishop Clemens August Graf von Galen and the Protestant pastor Martin Niemöller (author of "First they came for the Communists . . .") publicly criticized National Socialism, and Niemöller paid for it with seven years in a concentration camp. But the churches' main resistance consisted of protecting their own work from National Socialist interference.[87] Christianity, as distinct from the Christian churches, did play a role: it informed the conscience of individual resisters, creating a conflict between their religious and secular commitments that could be resolved only through action.

Added to this mix were resisters within the Abwehr (the intelligence arm of the German military). Under its head, Admiral Wilhelm Canaris, the Abwehr became, in the words of historian Hugh Trevor Roper, "not only a nest of spies but a nest of conspirators."[88] Canaris was a monarchist, a nationalist, and a Franco sympathizer but also a Christian who viewed the atrocities with horror.[89] Some of the most famous names in the resistance—Dietrich Bonhoeffer, Hans von Dohnanyi, Hans Bernd Gisevius, and Hans Oster—were associated with the Abwehr.[90]

A final group of resisters was the "White Rose," consisting of university students and professors in Munich who, drawing again on Christianity, distributed anti-regime leaflets in the city until their February 1943 arrest and executions.[91] The group was entirely civilian, had no contact with the military, and operated largely in isolation.[92] In this, the White Rose members were much like the post–July 20 civilian resisters whom we will encounter again in subsequent chapters.

In developing their plans, all German resisters except, eventually, the military made a fatal error: they made their plans contingent on someone else's actions. The Abwehr figures who warned the British of Hitler's rush to war depended on Chamberlain and Daladier's willingness to stop him. The Kreisau Circle depended on the firepower of Allied armies; the Social Democrats depended on the German army.

The Social Democrats, at least, did so out of necessity. The military resisters were the only ones with the access and the power to remove Hitler, and the army was the only institution that had any hope of controlling events in a post-Hitler Germany and of initiating contacts that the Allies might take seriously. The military had helped bring Hitler to power, and without the military, war, empire, and genocides were impossible. Conversely, only the military could remove the dictator that it had helped install. "It was a paradox," writes military historian Winfried Heinemann, "that the only system-threatening resistance emerged from precisely the organization that played such a decisive [*tragenden*] role in creating that system in the years between 1933 and 1939."[93] The army had made Hitler, partially in 1933 and wholly between 1939 and 1941; only the army could stop Hitler.

Many military resisters came not from the top of the German army but from the middle ranks of the officer corps.[94] For some military resisters, plans to remove Hitler predated the war and might well have prevented it had Daladier and Chamberlain not acquiesced at Munich. The resisters' differences with Hitler were partly strategic. They were prepared to contemplate the use of military force to achieve Germany's aims.[95] As they were soldiers, this should not be surprising. But their understanding of war as an instrument of politics differed greatly from Hitler's. Their conception of war was Bismarckian: military force was applied until it achieved specific and limited ends, such as the recovery of "lost" territory, the elimination of the Polish Corridor, the securing of land and coastal positions in Eastern Europe capable of breaking a British blockade, and even the defeat of Bolshevist Russia. Once these aims were achieved, that force was removed. Hitler's understanding of war, on the other hand, was nihilistic and genocidal: the

slaughter of whole peoples, world domination, and, it seems, war and violence without end. For all that, and apparently oblivious to Hitler's hatred
of church and monarchy, most older military resisters were initially support-
ive of Hitler and intoxicated by the promise of a reinvigorated, militarized,
and autocratically stable country. There was no contradiction between this
early support and their later scorn for Hitler. On the contrary: it was akin to
the hatred a man can feel for his ex-wife (and vice versa).

The military resisters, like people of their education, class, and experience, held complex attitudes regarding Jews (and much else). At one
extreme, General Carl-Heinrich von Stülpnagel was an anti-Semite who
readily accepted the equation of Judaism with Bolshevism and who encouraged a pogrom in Galicia.[96] At the other, Ulrich von Hassel, a conservative
diplomat, condemned the Nuremberg laws as the "end of our country" and
Kristallnacht as "an unequivocal disgrace."[97] Others were located at many
points in between. Carl Goerdeler, the former mayor of Leipzig and close
friend of Ludwig Beck, argued that the "Jewish question" would never be
safely settled until Jews established a state of their own. As basis for this,
Goerdeler accepted the prevailing assumption that Jews clearly belonged
to "another race."[98] He hastily drew up a memorandum in 1941–42 that presented a rather utopian plan in which Jews would receive citizenship from
a new Jewish state but would nonetheless be eligible to work in Germany
and, under a number of intentionally broad exceptions, would be entitled
to dual German citizenship. The plan would have overturned the bulk of
the Nuremburg racial laws as well as earlier restrictions barring certain
categories of Jews from German citizenship.[99] In addition, Goerdeler could
be uncompromising in his opposition to violent anti-Semitism: he went
in full formal dress in April 1933 to Leipzig's Jewish quarter to protect its
residents from SA (Sturmabteilung, or Storm Division, the Nazi Party's
earliest paramilitary organization thugs), and that same year ordered the city
police to free Jews arrested by storm troopers.[100] Goerdeler resigned in 1936
when composer Felix Mendelssohn's monument was removed, against the
mayor's orders, from the Leipzig Gewandhaus concert hall.[101]

Johannes Popitz, the Prussian minister of finance, offered his resignation to Hitler over Kristallnacht and was horrified by the Final Solution.

He did, however, support the right of the government to remove Jews from the civil service if it wished to.[102] Popitz, it seems, also supported anti-Jewish restrictions along the lines of the Nuremberg laws as long as that restriction was the extent of anti-Jewish legislation and not a prelude to further action.[103] Like thoughtful people generally, the best among them struggled in their attitudes and changed them over time, making historians' selection of any one statement as evidence of their unchanging worldviews highly problematic.[104] It is a reasonable generalization to say that most military resisters viewed Jews as distinct from Germans, wanted to reduce Jewish influence in postwar German life, and in most cases would not have been sorry to see many of Germany's Jews voluntarily leave if the Zionist dream of a Jewish homeland were realized. But they were nonetheless horrified by the wholesale murder of the Jews.

The reasons informing the military resisters' turn against Hitler were similarly varied. As Gerhard Weinberg has remarked, "different straws break the backs of different camels."[105] The military resisters who first turned against Hitler—Ludwig Beck and Carl-Heinrich von Stülpnagel, with Franz Halder, as ever, equivocating—did so on largely strategic grounds: the war Hitler tried to provoke would bring disaster on Germany. Those who broke with Hitler last—Wolf-Heinrich Graf von Helldorf, a longstanding SA man and enthusiastic Jew-basher; Feldmarschall Erwin Rommel; and General Erich Hoepner, who wished to crush Russia and Jewish Bolshevism—did so because Hitler had brought military disaster on Germany.[106] Had Hitler succeeded, they would have continued to support him. Still others defy comprehension: the resistance activities of Arthur Nebe, a senior SS officer and commander of Einsatzgruppe B, involved passing information to Hans Oster in the Abwehr regarding his *own* order to murder over forty thousand Jews.[107]

For all the variation, it is possible to generalize about the resisters' motivations. The core of the military resistance—Henning von Tresckow and, from 1942, Claus von Stauffenberg—turned against Hitler for three reasons that, though separate, were by no means mutually exclusive. First, Hitler's centralization of army power in his hands and those of his lackeys (Wilhelm Keitel and Alfred Jodl) had decimated the army's command structure (through the dismissing of generals and a lack of army control over the eastern front) and resulted in an inefficient and often disastrous prosecution of the war.[108] Second, Hitler's meddling command, combined with his constant orders to hold untenable positions, was leading to great losses of life among German troops.[109] Third, he was conducting a ruthless war of extermination against local populations in German-occupied territory.[110] In short, Hitler was wrecking the army, sending hundreds of thousands of soldiers to their deaths, and slaughtering millions of innocent civilians in the process. Relatively few turned against the Nazis solely out of concern for Hitler's victims (Henning von Tresckow was one), but the atrocities deeply offended German officers' sense of honour. This offence, combined with the effect of Hitler's leadership on the German army and its soldiers' lives, helped push many more into the resistance column.[111]

Tresckow, the earliest anchor of the wartime German resistance, turned against Hitler after the murders committed during the 1934 Röhm putsch, Kristallnacht, and, above all, after the early 1939–41 atrocities in Poland and elsewhere on the eastern front.[112] He then used his institutional position as chief of operations for Army Group Centre to draw in a widening group of predominantly young resisters.[113] In addition, no fewer than nineteen members of Tresckow's previous unit, Infantry Regiment 9 in Potsdam, would be involved in the July 20 attempt on Hitler's life.

Like military resisters generally, Tresckow hoped that Hitler would lead Germany to military disaster and that Tresckow could then persuade the army to turn against the regime. "It would be impossible," notes historian Peter Hoffmann, "to persuade a victorious German Army to revolt against Hitler."[114] When Hitler's wars in France and initially in the Soviet Union led not to defeat but to stunning victories, it wrecked the resisters' plans.

Ever a man of action, Tresckow was quick to regroup. He began by trying to win over major field commanders: Commander in Chief Bock, later Kluge, and Feldmarschall Georg von Küchler, who was commander in chief of Army Group North.[115] When these efforts failed, he looked instead to the home front: in late 1942 or early 1943, Tresckow met General Friedrich Olbricht of the General Army Office in Berlin, who promised to use the Replacement Army in Berlin, Vienna, Cologne, and Munich to launch a coup.[116] The Replacement Army (*Ersatzheer*) was made up of some two million troops stationed within the Reich for training and as reserves. As Olbricht, with frequent vacillations, drew up these plans, Tresckow devoted himself to the nitty-gritty work of acquiring explosives through his intelligence officer, Gersdorff.[117]

They then launched their first attempt. On March 13, 1943, Hitler visited Kluge at Smolensk, and Tresckow and Schlabrendorff handed an officer a package to be taken back to Berlin; it was a bomb, but it did not go off.[118] Tresckow refused to be thrown by this setback, and plans—given new impetus as Claus von Stauffenberg moved toward the centre of the conspiracy—continued through 1943. Stauffenberg, who first struggled to reconcile the demands of military duty with those of Roman Catholicism and his hybridized aristocratic-romantic sense of honour,[119] was a relative latecomer to resistance. But unlike Halder, Kluge, or even Olbricht, when he joined, he joined resolutely. He had concluded in early 1942 that Hitler had to be killed; by early 1943, he was actively lobbying senior army figures to join a coup; and by October 1, 1943, he was chief of staff at the General Army Office in Berlin, serving under Olbricht. He was also the anchor of the coup plans in Berlin. By February 1944, the political and military infrastructure from which a coup could be launched was in place, and it included some of the most illustrious names in Prussian military history: Tresckow, Moltke, and Yorck.[120] On the twentieth of July, they acted.

CHAPTER 2

THE COUP AGAINST HITLER

O N JULY 20, under the blazing East Prussian sun, a dashing colonel, Claus von Stauffenberg, entered a war conference room with Adolf Hitler at his eastern headquarters, the Wolf's Lair (*Wolfsschanze*). Twenty-four men, including Hitler, stood around the large table. Stauffenberg left his briefcase under the table. In the windowed hut (a last-minute change of location from an airtight bunker), Generalleutnant Adolf Heusinger outlined for a furious Hitler the scale of the military disaster befalling Germany. An aide then stepped into the room and told Stauffenberg that there was a call for him. Leaving his briefcase, Stauffenberg departed.

At 12:45, a bomb in the briefcase exploded.[1] The heavy table shattered, and the men were thrown back by the force of the blast.[2] Oberst Heinz Brandt's leg was blown off. Regierungsrat Heinrich Berger, who had been standing just across from the briefcase, lost both legs. Flying wood splinters struck and seriously injured Generallutnant Rudolf Schmundt and General Günther Korten of the Luftwaffe. All four men would die as a result of their injuries.[3]

As the bomb exploded, Stauffenberg made a dash for his car, where his adjutant, Oberleutnant Werner von Haeften, was waiting. Ordering the driver on, they managed to exit the compound and made for a waiting plane bound for Berlin. Operation Valkyrie was under way. Led by Stauffenberg, the resisters would announce an SS plot to overtake the government. They would then use the army to lock down the SS, to arrest Goebbels, Göring, and the rest of the senior National Socialist leadership, and to install a civilian government that would open negotiations with the Allies. Stauffenberg would both plant the bomb and lead the operation, but his Allies in Berlin would launch Valkyrie as soon as they got word of Hitler's death.

In Berlin, General der Infanterie Friedrich Olbricht, in charge of the military district headquarters within Germany, was responsible for initiating the Valkyrie orders. Unsure of Hitler's fate, however, he dithered and failed to initiate the coup during the crucial hours during which communications between Berlin and Hitler's headquarters were cut off (by General Erich Fellgiebel).

When the coup was finally launched, it was too late. Stauffenberg arrived in Berlin to take charge just as the first Valkyrie orders were going out. Keitel, meanwhile, having identified Stauffenberg as the likely organizer of the coup, was in touch with General Friedrich Fromm, head of the Replacement Army, assuring him of Hitler's safety. Fromm was of central importance because the resisters had only three military formations at their disposal: Fromm's Replacement Army, the Twenty-Third Infantry Division, and most important, that division's Ninth Infantry Regiment stationed in Potsdam.[4] These troops could move on Berlin, but a successful coup required sufficient numbers of senior German commanders to side with Stauffenberg.

Urged on by Stauffenberg's friend and chief of staff Oberst Albrecht Mertz von Quirnheim, Olbricht finally launched Operation Valkyrie just before 16:00.[5] Two sets of announcements went out from the Bendlerblock, the massive office complex in the Bendlerstraße that housed the German army's headquarters in Berlin. The first said that Hitler was dead and that "an irresponsible clique of Party leaders divorced from the front" had tried to "stab the army in the back"—the latter phrase could not have been a coincidence—and to seize power.[6] The Reich government was, therefore, declaring a state of emergency and granting Feldmarschall Erwin von Witzleben supreme command of the armed forces and full executive power.[7] The second announcement, containing Fromm's forged signature, issued a series of orders to the armed forces to protect all telecommunications and postal facilities; arrest all senior Nazi officials; occupy all concentration camps and detain their commandants and guards; arrest all Waffen-SS commanders suspected of disloyalty; and occupy all Gestapo and SD offices.[8] A young major and another Tresckow protégé, Hans-Ulrich von Oertzen, sent out the first orders.[9]

As Oertzen was sending out those orders, Stauffenberg and his adjutant, Oberleutnant Haeften (who had helped him prepare the bomb for detonation), arrived at the Bendlerblock. "He's dead," Stauffenberg reported. He and Olbricht then went to see Fromm, who outranked all the conspirators at the Bendlerblock. When Fromm refused to join the conspirators, they placed him under arrest. Stauffenberg had him locked into an office and kept under guard.[10] It was 17:00, and the coup in Berlin was on the cusp of its greatest success.

Generalleutnant Paul von Hase, the commandant of Berlin and a valued associate of Olbricht and Beck, summoned Major Otto Ernst Remer to his offices at Unter den Linden No. 1. Hase gave Remer the Bendlerblock line: the SS had launched a putsch; the army was assuming plenary powers; and he, Remer, was therefore to cordon off the government quarter in Berlin. Remer, a fanatical Nazi and obedient soldier, replied, "Very good."[11] By 18:30, central Berlin was locked down and in the hands of the resisters.

Elsewhere, troops began to mobilize. Following Valkyrie orders, army commanders seized key radio stations, road junctions, and bridges outside Berlin.[12] From 18:00, Oertzen received reports confirming that the operations were going well.[13]

In Krampnitz, in the northern outskirts of Potsdam, Oberst Harald Momm, commander of the Riding and Driving School, shouted when he received the news, "Orderly, a bottle of champagne; the pig's dead!"[14] Against the better judgment of his senior officer, Momm led an armoured infantry training group to the Victory Column in Berlin's Tiergarten. They were there to check SS troops advancing from the Lichterfelde barracks on Himmler's order. The SS troops never moved: Himmler was waiting to see which way the wind blew.[15]

From here, the coup began to fall apart. With no definitive confirmation of Hitler's death, orders sent out under Olbricht's name were questioned, only partially implemented, or refused. Although the Berlin wing of the conspiracy was probably doomed by Hitler's survival all along,[16] the decisive moment occurred in the government quarter that had been locked down by Remer. On Hase's orders to arrest, Remer reluctantly entered Goebbels's rooms. He was far more suspicious of the propaganda minister than he was of the army.[17]

Goebbels quickly allayed those suspicions: he put a call through to Hitler. Hitler asked Remer if he recognized his voice, confirmed that he was unharmed, and entrusted Remer with the security of the capital.[18] He was to use all means available to crush any resistance. Remer ordered the cordons around the government quarter to be removed immediately.

If things were going badly outside the Bendlerblock, they were going at least as badly within. When Witzleben arrived from Zossen around 19:00 to take command of the Wehrmacht, he went first to General Eduard Wagner's office, where Wagner told him that the assassination attempt had failed.[19] Witzleben was furious; he called the entire coup a "screw-up"[20] and left with Wagner.

To make matters worse, Fromm, with the help of a sympathetic officer, began to initiate countermeasures. They made little difference to the coup, which had by then failed, but they were decisive for the fate of the resisters. The assisting officer knew of a little-known exit in the room leading to a dark passage and a staircase to the upper floor.[21] He used it to slip out and warn other officers in the building who, somewhat incredibly, did not realize a coup was being conducted in their midst. A senior officer, Oberstleutnant Franz Herber, put a telephone call in to another officer. "Is Wagner part of this?" Herber demanded to know. "Whose side is he on? We want to make a clean sweep here. We will not be forced to join Stauffenberg's regime."[22] Herber and others decided to demand an explanation from Olbricht. Olbricht gave none, and instead ordered that the building be prepared for a final defence.[23]

The coup was now collapsing. Olbricht's orders were never implemented. Herber and the other officers seized arms designed for the defence of the Bendlerblock and instead used them to put down the coup.[24] Shots were heard. Fromm was retrieved, and when the general returned to his office, he found Stauffenberg, Mertz von Quirnheim, Haeften, and Olbricht held at gunpoint by armed staff officers.[25]

Seeking to save his own skin, Fromm then took countermeasures well after the coup had failed. He arrested Stauffenberg, Haeften, Olbricht, and Mertz. After ordering a subordinate officer to finish off Ludwig Beck after his failed suicide attempt, Fromm declared: "In the name of the Führer, a court martial convened by me has pronounced [its] sentence: Oberst von Mertz, General Olbricht, the Oberst whose name I will not mention, and Oberleutnant von Haeften are condemned to death."[26]

Stauffenberg, Mertz, Haeften, and Olbricht walked down the stairs into the courtyard calmly, with only Haeften briefly trying to tear himself free. It was almost 00:30. Fromm ordered his assistant to set up a firing squad of ten men under an officer. The courtyard was flooded with car lights. When Stauffenberg stood before the firing squad, Haeften threw himself in front and died first. As he did, Stauffenberg shouted, "Long live holy Germany!" The next salvo killed him. Fromm climbed atop a military vehicle, gave a rousing speech to the troops, and called for three thunderous cheers of "Sieg Heil." He left the conspirators to be buried and drove off to ingratiate himself to Goebbels.[27]

One of Stauffenberg's last acts before his execution was to urge Fromm's secretary to make a phone call to Paris. He had failed in Berlin, but there was still hope for the resistance in the French capital. "Hopefully," as General Wagner had more directly put it a few hours earlier, "Paris sees it through."[28]

CHAPTER 3

FROM FAILING HANDS

The Coup in Paris

B Y JULY 1944, Paris had been under German occupation for just over four years. The occupation of the city divided into roughly three phases. The first, coinciding mostly with the leadership of Otto von Stülpnagel, military commander of France (*Militärbefehlshaber*), lasted from approximately June 1940 until his resignation in February 1942.[1] During these years, the capital suffered inflation and unemployment, but it was a relatively stable period. Indeed, for those who did not flee the capital as German tanks approached it, the initial period of the occupation was anticlimactic. Rather than an army of marauding vandals, the first occupying troops were mostly young men who were wide-eyed and excited about being in the famous city. They viewed the French with neither hatred nor condescension.[2] The image of these young, clean-cut soldiers lining up for the Eiffel Tower, insisting on paying for everything, and displaying smiles for young women and respect for old ones was so beguiling that a resistance pamphlet felt obliged to remind Parisians, "these are not tourists!"[3]

It was during this period that a German officer knocked on the apartment door of a group of French civilians who may have had some connection to the resistance. They froze. The officer politely asked if one of the Frenchmen, the uncle of Madame Talbot, could accompany him to the Grand Hotel in order to tune a piano.[4] Though fearing a trap, they both went along. The Germans fed them well, and after the piano was tuned, the officer paid the uncle generously. He added that the soldier who would play the piano wanted to thank him in person. A young soldier, no more than twenty years old, sat down seriously, tested a few keys, and then played Chopin superbly. Despite herself, Madame Talbot melted. "Time disappeared," she later wrote. "The music enveloped [envoûter] it. The Polish composer, the German artist, the French listener shared an emotion without borders. I realized that the soldier from an arrogant country and the man of a crushed nation shared . . . an extraordinary communion, one that spoke of something greater than cannons, bombs, and the force of humiliation."[5] Her uncle was left shaken by the experience.

Other, more robust forms of intimacy continued to vex the German military administration. Despite non-fraternization policies, French prostitutes enjoyed a very good defeat: German soldiers filled brothels across the city. The military appealed to honour (sleeping with prostitutes was unworthy of a German soldier), fear (whores were plagued by venereal disease), and racism (liaisons with "Jewess" or "Negress" prostitutes would be severely punished), but nothing worked.[6] After this effort—neither the first nor the last in human history to shut down the world's oldest profession—the military gave up and settled on twenty-four brothels for German soldiers (which soon proved insufficient).[7]

The relative tranquility characterizing this first period did not last. On August 21, 1941, a young German naval cadet named Alfons Moser was getting off the train at the Barbès-Rochechouart metro station. An equally young activist, Pierre Georges, came up behind him, shouting, "Tyszelman is avenged!" and shot Moser in the back, killing him. (Samuel Tyszelman was a twenty-year-old Communist who had been executed two days earlier for taking part in an illegal demonstration.) In reprisal, the Germans shot three "Communists." De Gaulle condemned the metro assassinations as costly, premature, and therefore pointless, but they continued.[8] They proved to be the beginning of a cycle of assassination and retribution that would result in the execution of some five hundred French hostages.[9] As horrible as these were, they were a small fraction of what Hitler wanted. On February 15, 1942, Otto von Stülpnagel resigned in protest.[10]

The second phase of the occupation had begun. The executions coincided with another new development in occupation policy: the increasingly brutal exploitation of French agriculture, natural resources, industry, and labour driven by Fritz Sauckel and Albert Speer. At the time of Stülpnagel's resignation in 1942, work programs for French citizens sent to Germany became forced, and France would soon become the third supplier, after Russia and Poland, of forced labourers to Germany.[11] Two months later, on March 27, 1942, the first convoy of (non-French) Jews was deported to Auschwitz. On May 7, Reinhard Heydrich appointed Carl Oberg his new Statthalter (governing representative), thus putting the SS and police in France under his purview.[12] Heydrich, who was about to be killed by Czech partisans, and Oberg were convinced that Stülpnagel's military administration was indulging French partisans. Oberg soon put an end to it. On July 10, he issued an order declaring that any assassins, saboteurs, and troublemakers (*Unruhestifter*) who did not turn themselves in within ten days would see all their male relatives shot, including cousins and brothers-in-law, and all female relatives and children would be imprisoned.[13]

That same month, the SS intensified its persecution of Jews in Paris. On July 16, 1942, nine thousand police officers, under orders from Oberg and the head of the French police, Réné Bousquet, spread out across the greater Paris region. They arrested 12,884 Jews and kept them crowded for days in the Vélodrome d'Hiver under intolerable conditions.[14] From there, with children separated from their parents, they were transported to assembly centres outside Paris (most to Drancy, northeast of the capital), where they were then loaded onto trains to Auschwitz.[15] The head of the SD in France, Helmut Knochen, had no staff in the capital, and he relied on the Parisian police to identify, round up, and deport the Jews. There were examples of individual disobedience, such as policemen who showed up at a Jewish residence to announce in advance that they would be back in an hour or so to deport everyone.[16] But in the main, the French police cooperated thoroughly in the operation, and Vichy officials, led by Pierre Laval, added their own stamp to it by insisting on the deportation of Jewish children, whom even the Germans were prepared to spare.[17]

Unsurprisingly given his history of anti-Semitism, Otto von Stülpnagel's successor and cousin, Carl-Heinrich von Stülpnagel, did nothing to stand in the way of these deportations. But he also did little to support them: the SS had taken over control of the police in the spring of 1942, and the police implemented the deportations.[18] The area for which Stülpnagel had responsibility was the policy on shooting French hostages in reprisal for attacks on German soldiers. He continued it: some 500 to 550 such persons were shot over the course of the German occupation.[19] Stülpnagel signed the orders for the execution of often young resisters, and he generally left the SS in Paris to get on with its awful work. "Stülpnagel," writes the author of an early study, "for all his plotting, did nothing, absolutely nothing, to stand in the way of the torture cellars and shooting walls of the Paris Gestapo."[20]

Not standing in the way, of course, is not the same thing as joining in. One of the noteworthy features of the Holocaust in France is that, relative to other countries in Europe, far fewer Jews were deported and murdered.[21] Whereas two-thirds of Dutch and Belgian Jews were exterminated, two-thirds of Jews in France survived. The majority of those deported, moreover, were not French but, rather, foreign Jews residing in France. Despite four years of military occupation, some 75 percent of Jews with French citizenship survived.[22]

They did so because of the way in which French citizenship interacted with Roman Catholic resistance. In both occupied and unoccupied France (and all of occupied France after 1942), the Vichy regime showed a particular reluctance to denaturalize French Jews as a precondition for turning them over to the Germans. This reluctance can only be understood with reference to the particular power of national citizenship: the Germans took it essentially as a given that French Jews could not be deported until they had been denaturalized.[23] And for other reasons—opposition of the French public and above all the Roman Catholic Church—Vichy balked at a mass denaturalization. Following the July 1942 deportations, both general public and Roman Catholic opposition ratcheted up further.[24] The decisive moment came in August 1943. Rumours of an intended mass denaturalization and an immediate roundup made their way to Rome, and Pope Pius XII dispatched Monsignor Chapoulie to see Vichy Chief of State Philippe Pétain on August 5, 1943. The pope, Chapoulie told Pétain, was "very upset" about the proposed anti-Jewish measures and was worried about the effect they would have on the marshal's eternity.[25] The pope's message left Pétain shaken, and he withdrew his support for mass denaturalization. On August 7, in a heated exchange with Knochen, "for the first time in the history of the Final Solution in France," Laval said "no."[26]

The Allied landings in North Africa in November 1942 (Operation Torch) initiated the third phase of the occupation.[27] As the Allies seized North Africa, writes historian Allan Mitchell, "German troops rushed to the southern coast and pointed their binoculars across the sea. In effect, they thereby annexed Vichy France to the occupied zone and assumed command everywhere from Roubaix to Marseille."[28] They held it, against no serious internal threat from either France's citizens or its sycophantic politicians, until the summer of 1944.

By then, the signs of a regime under threat were there for everyone to see. The Vichy regime had given up any pretense of offering a new vision of France and became a police state, clinging to power and promising only order over anarchy.[29] The SS showed its most monstrous side: screams of the tortured, emanating from Gestapo headquarters on the avenue Foch in Paris, became louder and more frequent.[30] Oberg, throwing aside all restraint, ordered the ripping open of genitals, the gouging of eyes, the smashing of hands, and the amputation of fingers with hammers and knives.[31] Food shortages were widespread. Meanwhile, the Allies moved ever closer. Allied bombing destroyed the rail and road networks supplying the capital and hit uncomfortably close targets in the suburbs. Above all, the Allies, who had struggled onto the beaches at Normandy on June 6, 1944, were preparing to push out of their bridgeheads and to move on toward the Seine. It was time to act.

JULY 20, 1944 was a hot and humid day in the French capital. Stuffy air clogged Paris's streets, and thunder cracked above them. That morning, Oberst Eberhard Finckh, deputy chief of General Staff West in Paris, was in his offices in the rue de Surène, not far from the Place de la Concorde and the Champs-Élysées. The telephone in Finckh's office had been ringing nonstop all morning, and the voice on the other end always demanded the same: "Send us more munitions, more parts, more ammunition, more gasoline.

Immediately!"[32] With a weary voice, he answered the telephone once again in his strong Swabian accent: "This ish Finckh." This time, a voice said, after a pause, only one word: "*Übung*"—"exercise."[33] The line went dead.

The call was from Quartermaster General Eduard Wagner's office in Zossen.[34] Finckh laid down the receiver, walked to his safe, opened it, and retrieved a set of documents.[35] They contained the plotters' detailed plans for seizing Paris within hours of Hitler's death. Finckh picked up the phone again and called Luftwaffe Oberstleutnant Cäsar von Hofacker, Stauffenberg's cousin and a close confidant of the military governor of France. "Is everything ready for the exercise?" Finckh asked. "Of course," Hofacker replied.[36] Finckh signed off, occupied himself with his morning tasks, and waited.

Around 14:00, the phone rang again. "It's done . . . It's done [*abgelaufen*]," the caller said and hung up.[37] Finckh slowly replaced the phone's receiver. "It's actually happening," he said to himself.[38] Finckh left his offices, got into his car, and drove through Paris's familiar streets: along the Bois de Boulogne, across Neuilly, past the old Fort Mont-Valérien, then along the Seine until the car reached Saint-Germain-en-Laye, stopping on a street lined with villas housing the General Staff West and its adjutants.[39] German troops with machine guns patrolled the streets.

After a short inspection, Finckh stopped in front of a large villa partially concealed by its garden. He got out of his car and reported to a large and jovial Bavarian, General der Infanterie Günther Blumentritt, who had helped in the planning of the Polish and French occupations and had taken part in Operation Barbarossa. After the war, he would be one of the few generals who conceded that Hitler, for all his faults, had a capacity for instinctively seeing the dangers in a given military plan that were overlooked by the General Staff.[40]

Finckh told Blumentritt about what had happened in Berlin and claimed, somewhat disingenuously, that he had the information from Stülpnagel.[41] Blumentritt then put in a call to Feldmarschall Günther von Kluge, who was at La Roche-Guyon. Kluge was both Rommel's successor as commander of Army Group B and overall commander of German forces in the west.[42] Kluge's chief of staff, Generalleutnant Hans Speidel, a close confidant to Rommel, answered. Speaking in a whisper and using vague phrases ("something has happened in Berlin") and context-free words ("dead"), Blumentritt tried to tell the story to Speidel. Speidel either did not or pretended not to understand. Blumentritt put down the phone and headed to the front to find Kluge.[43]

At 16:00, after Blumentritt left, the phone rang at the Hotel Majestic on avenue Kléber in Paris, which housed Stülpnagel's staff. Hofacker, a cultured and educated Swabian, went to answer it. Like many in the resistance, Hofacker had emerged from the trenches of World War I as a nationalist, passed through a period of bitter anti-democratic and anti-Semitic sentiment, and initially welcomed the arrival of Adolf Hitler.[44] Witnessing Hitler's brutal exploitation of occupied France (he had naively believed in meaningful Franco-German cooperation in a new German Europe) transformed Hofacker into an anti-Hitler resister. Hofacker and his boss, Stülpnagel, were the anchors of the resistance in Paris, though they were different men. Stülpnagel was of an introspective, intellectual bent.[45] Hofacker was a man of action. The day before the coup was launched, on July 19, he confided to Stülpnagel and others that the coup had only a 10 percent chance of success, but that it had to be launched as it promised to end the slaughter.[46]

When Hofacker picked up the phone, it was his cousin, Claus von Stauffenberg. "Hitler," Stauffenberg told him, "is dead."[47] Hofacker placed the phone on the receiver and summoned his friend, Friedrich Freiherr von Teuchert, a civilian advisor to the administration, from a meeting.[48] With lit-up eyes, Hofacker told his friend, "Hitler is dead. Maybe Himmler and Göring too. The explosion was massive. The putsch is under way; the government quarter in Berlin is being occupied as we speak."[49] Teuchert ran to give the news to a lawyer and administrator, Walter Bargatzky, who was on staff at the Hotel Majestic. When Teuchert found him, Bargatzky had already heard; the two threw their arms around each other.[50]

Their joy was short-lived. When they turned on the radio to hear Witzleben's address to the nation, what they heard instead was that Hitler was slightly hurt but very much alive.[51] Teuchert recovered quickly: the news could only mean that the Nazi regime was at the point of collapse; otherwise, they would not have reported the attempt at all. It was, Teuchert continued, only another reason to act quickly in France.[52]

Stülpnagel, meanwhile, was doing just that. He told his orderly officer, Oberleutnant Dr. Baumgart, to summon his principal officers.[53] One by one, they arrived in his rooms: Oberst Hans Otfried von Linstow, Stülpnagel's chief of staff; Generalleutnant Eugen Oberhäußer, Stülpnagel's chief communications officer; Dr. Elmar Michel, head of economic affairs (one, with administrative affairs, of the two civilian subdivisions in the occupation structure); and Generalleutnant Hans Reichsfreiherr von Boineburg-Lengsfeld, Commander of Paris.[54] One after another, he gave them the code word, and they knew what to do. All the details had been prepared well in advance. Baumgart, who watched the men come in and then leave looking shaken, finally asked: "What's going on here?"[55]

What was going on was nothing less than the total occupation of Paris by the resisters. Stülpnagel ordered Oberhäußer to block all communications except his own with Berlin.[56] He then gave his most important order to Boineburg and handed him, along with his chief of staff, Oberst Karl von Unger, a map that had been updated in the previous few days.[57]

Boineburg had his orderly officer, Dankwart Graf von Arnim, summon Oberstleutnant Kurt von Kraewel, a boisterous commander who led the First Regiment, 325th Security Division (the division being under Boineburg's command).[58] Kraewel was not to be found. He had slipped into civilian clothing in a large housing block and informed his driver that he would call him when he wanted to be picked up.[59] One could imagine what he was up to. When Arnim reported this to Boineburg, the general choked and looked like he would suffocate. Arnim then fetched Kraewel's adjutant, who also had no idea where his commander was. Boineburg, no doubt ready to court martial Kraewel, ordered the adjutant to alert the regiment, to prepare barricades, and to distribute ammunition to the men.[60] Kraewel appeared two hours later, once again in uniform.

After a tense meal, Kraewel saw Stülpnagel again and received new orders. Then, at 20:00, Kraewel and the entire regiment prepared to march. Accompanied by Boineburg and Arnim, they were moving under the cover of darkness toward the grand avenue Foch, the residential and professional home of the SS and SD in Paris.[61]

CHAPTER 4

PARIS, JULY 20, 1944

The SS Locked Down

AVENUE FOCH, running southwest from the Arc de Triomphe, is one of Paris's most expensive streets. It is also one of Paris's widest, and it is often loud and congested. There are, however, long parks on either side of it, which lend privacy along two additional one-way streets that run parallel to the avenue and provide secluded access to the expensive houses that line them. Had such people marked their doors, names such as Onassis and Rothschild would have once graced the street. In 1944, a far more thuggish and disreputable set of characters occupied the avenue's houses: Dr. Helmut Knochen, the head of the SD, had his headquarters at No. 84, and SD officers occupied Nos. 82 and 86.

Avenue Foch terminates at its southwest end as it begins at the opposite end, in a roundabout, albeit a considerably less grand one. One of the streets extending from the roundabout, at basically a ninety-degree angle from the avenue Foch, is the boulevard Lannes. Carl Oberg, Knochen's boss and head of the SS and security police in France, had his offices at No. 57, while SD recruits were billeted in newly constructed buildings on the same street. Together, the two thoroughfares formed a rough L that made up the core of the Nazis' terror organization in Paris: the SD, the Gestapo, and the Sipo were all within a few minutes of each other. On the night of July 20, 1944, the German army in Paris descended upon them from all sides.

At 21:30 that evening, trucks transporting the men of Kraewel's First Regiment, 325th Security Division drove quietly up avenue Foch. The convoy stopped near the end of the street, and the men climbed out and took cover behind the parks' thick bushes and the large, leafy trees running along the street. SS guards were posted in front of several of the doors, but the soldiers, mostly foreign recruits from Ukraine, southern Russia, or the Danube region, had fallen asleep in the warm summer evening.[1]

As Kraewel's men took their positions along the avenue Foch, shock troops under Generalmajor Walther Brehmer moved slowly through the thick bushes of the Bois de Boulogne, the large park that abuts the western side of the roundabout connecting avenue Foch and boulevard Lannes. Boineburg himself was among them.[2] From where they stood, they could see the Gestapo billets. The lights were on, the buildings quiet, a few sentries pacing to and fro in front of them.[3] Their occupants expected nothing.

At 22:30, Brehmer gave the order. A whistle pierced the night. Cars and trucks moved into position along the street. Another whistle. Hundreds of troops hit the street at once and rushed the buildings. The surprise was total.[4] The sentries, confused and disorientated, laid down their weapons.[5] Only a single machine gun went off, the product of an SD sentry's clumsy effort to salute an army officer, but it hit no one.[6]

The operation continued with absolute precision. Weapons drawn, the officers and their shock troops burst into the Gestapo billets. They dashed up the stairs, kicked open doors, and screamed, "Hands up!"[7] With orders from Stülpnagel to open fire on any who resisted, the troops searched the men for weapons, ordered them into the courtyard, and loaded them into waiting trucks.[8] One set of vehicles made for the prison at Fresnes, south of Paris, which had been cleared for the new guests; the other rolled on toward the old fortifications of the Fort de l'Est in Saint-Denis, north of the capital.[9]

As the men under his command stormed the billets, Brehmer moved toward No. 57. He had undertaken to arrest Oberg personally.[10] The SS leader was at his desk, in shirtsleeves and on the telephone, when Brehmer entered the room. Brehmer pointed a gun at him. The SS leader jumped up and asked Brehmer what this "nonsense" (*Unfug*) was supposed to mean.[11] The SS in Berlin, Brehmer replied, had launched a putsch and Oberg was therefore under arrest. Oberg, claiming the whole thing had to be a misunderstanding, handed over his weapon and gave himself up.[12]

This operation occurred simultaneously with another. As Boineburg and Brehmer's troops moved into position along boulevard Lannes, Kraewel commanded units that were hiding among the trees along avenue Foch. He organized the arrests differently. Rather than immediately storming the three grand houses holding the SD officers, Kraewel first occupied the rooms of the officer on duty.[13] On Kraewel's order, the SD commander summoned his men into the office, where Kraewel disarmed them. As he arrested the SD officer corps, Kraewel's troops poured into the building, arrested all other SD men and locked the three buildings down.[14]

The entire SS and SD in Paris—some twelve hundred men—had been arrested without a shot being fired in anger. All that was left was the senior SD officer, Dr. Knochen. A junior officer said that Knochen was at a Paris nightclub and offered to retrieve him.[15] Kraewel put him under arrest as soon as he returned, and Knochen joined the other senior SS officers in the Hotel Continental in the rue Castiglione.[16] As the clock approached midnight, members of the army's First Security Regiment piled sandbags in the courtyard of the École Militaire, its headquarters. They were to act as butts for the executions-by-shooting that would follow summary courts martial.[17] Bargatzky, himself a lawyer by training, had advised Hofacker to shoot Oberg, Knochen, SS-Sturmbannführer Hagen, and Dr. Maulaz (the SD staff member foisted onto the military governor's staff) and to avoid any distracting legal proceedings.[18]

In the span of a few hours, Stülpnagel, Hofacker, and Boineburg had surrounded and neutralized the Nazi military and political machinery in Paris. The most famous city in the world, and by far the most important in France, was in the hands of the German resistance.

When Boineburg and his adjutant, Arnim, returned to Stülpnagel's rooms on the fourth floor of the Hotel Raphael, the general had already left.[19] Speidel had called at 19:00, summoning Stülpnagel, who left for La Roche-Guyon, headquarters of Army Group B, with Hofacker.[20] Linstow, Stülpnagel's chief of staff, had stayed behind and taken charge, and he set up a makeshift office in one room with a billiard table. Officers streamed into the adjoining room. The atmosphere was festive, and the alcohol flowed. The men, mostly older officers, spoke of the end of the war, returning home, and the end of Nazism. In Linstow's adjacent room, the mood was entirely different. He had known for hours that Hitler had most likely survived. Yet he decided, following the urging of his fellow officers in Paris, to launch the coup in Paris anyway.[21] Stauffenberg had believed that to take Berlin was to take Europe; Linstow hoped to revise that logic: take Paris, take the west, and let the Allies overrun the front and take Berlin.

At midnight, everyone went quiet. The Führer was about to speak. Goebbels's shrill, grating voice cracked through the radio.[22] As it did, Arnim looked up to see Stülpnagel, back from his appeal to Kluge, quietly entering the room. The general said nothing, but the meeting with Kluge had not gone well. Over the course of the evening, Kluge had oscillated between embracing the putsch and condemning it. The decisive factor was Hitler. When a message arrived insisting Hitler was dead, Kluge spoke sternly about the "historic hour" and talked with General Blumentritt, who had been with him since around 18:00, about detailed plans for achieving a ceasefire on the western front.[23] When a telex from Keitel arrived, Kluge immediately changed his tune, muttering about "a bungled assassination attempt."[24]

Stülpnagel, Hofacker, Boineburg, and Linstow moved toward the radio. Hitler spoke of the "small clique of ambitious, unconscionable, and criminally stupid officers." Stülpnagel stood expressionlessly as he listened, though the way he was slowly wringing his gloves behind his back betrayed something of his emotions to those who saw it.[25] Few people, least of all Stülpnagel himself, believed that the general could save his command or his life. The only question now was who would go down with him.

Stülpnagel's first move, bowing to the inevitable, was to order the release of those arrested. He ordered Boineburg to do so and to bring Oberg to him.[26] While Boineburg approached Oberg with feigned casualness and an affected smile, his men released the prisoners in Saint-Denis and Fresnes.[27] A good number of the SS prisoners refused to leave their cells out of fear that they might be shot.

When Oberg arrived at the Hotel Raphael there was, to put it mildly, a certain tension in the room. It was broken somewhat unexpectedly by

Otto Abetz, the German ambassador. He was a fully paid-up Francophile, a looter of Jewish property, and a co-organizer of the Final Solution in France. He was also, by this point, unconvinced of Hitler's merits. Without consulting Stülpnagel, Abetz said to Oberg, "Do you want to know why the general arrested you and the SD? He thought [the coup in Berlin] had something to do with some ambitious scheme of Himmler's and wanted to keep you out of it . . . You cannot accuse the general of having broken his oath of loyalty. He simply, and in good faith, did what he thought was his duty." He then appealed for unity in the face of a cracking western front, and everyone raised their champagne glasses as Stülpnagel stared dumbfounded at Abetz.[28]

Blumentritt left La Roche-Guyon for Paris well after midnight. He visited naval headquarters, shook hands, patted a few backs, and casually dismissed the whole affair.[29] Blumentritt told Admiral Theodor Krancke, the commander of Naval Group West who was threatening to use his men to free the SS and SD prisoners, that he, Krancke, had been the "victim of a misunderstanding."[30] Blumentritt then visited Knochen, who, with vengeful satisfaction, told him that Oberg was on his way to the Hotel Majestic. In an inspired stroke, Blumentritt immediately replied, "I'm just going there. Come with me."[31] Blumentritt, Knochen, and a Standartenführer Hagen got into the car. Ten minutes into the drive, Knochen turned to Blumentritt: "We must get our stories straight!"[32] It was just what Blumentritt wanted to hear.

When Blumentritt and Knochen entered room 405 at the Hotel Raphael, the heads of the SS and the army were there together. Stülpnagel, Oberg, Boineburg, Linstow, and Finckh, along with Abetz, sat at the table, while other men stood in groups chatting.[33] Everyone was well lubricated.[34]

The only one missing was Hofacker, who had slipped into an adjoining room to destroy documents. Oberg, who had since learned that his prison cell had been prepared on July 19, repeated Knochen's words: "We *must* get our stories straight."[35] In hushed tones, Blumentritt and Oberg outlined an agreement to present a united front to the outside world and, above all, to Himmler's security apparatus.[36] This agreement in hand, Blumentritt urged both sides to put the whole matter behind them. For their part, Oberg and

Knochen made a point of appearing forgiving and made it clear, through their behaviour if not their words, that they would be good sports about the whole matter.[37] During the dinner, Blumentritt took Stülpnagel aside and gently informed him of Kluge's order to "keep away from your headquarters for three of four days until things have cleared up a bit." It was an invitation to flee, and showed that Kluge was a better man than Fromm: there would be no face-saving executions in Paris.

But it could not end there.[38] The arrest of the entire SS, SD, and Gestapo apparatus in Paris could not go completely unnoticed, and both sides needed to get on the same page. Blumentritt again took charge and had a text drawn up, which was to be read to all troops in the capital the next morning. It stated: "The SS and army units in Greater Paris organized a surprise exercise with live ammunition [*mit scharfer Munition*]. The exercise went well. I extend my thanks to all participants. Signed Oberg and Boineburg." The ruse partially worked: the arrests made by the army in Paris were far more limited than those in Berlin, and the majority of those involved in the coup—Boineburg, Brehmer, Kraewel, and Arnim, among others—survived.

Oberg and Knochen's seemingly magnanimous behaviour merits comment. A contemporary observer suggested they acted as they did out of some sense of larger soldierly solidarity or shared vulnerability in a foreign country.[39] These factors may have played a role; motivation is always complex. But of likely greater effect was the simple fact that Oberg and Knochen had been made to look like complete asses. A single security regiment, hardly the cream of the German army, had arrested the whole of Hitler's finest men in France before they could get a single shot off. The SS and SD had as much of an interest as the army did in covering the whole thing up. The more that came out about July 20, the more likely it was that suspicion would fall on Oberg.

LIKE THAT OF BERLIN, the story of July 20 in Paris is fascinating for what might have been. Unlike Berlin, however, the decisive matter was not the position of Stauffenberg's bomb or the relocation of the conference from a bunker to a hut. The decisive matter was one of political and military choice. Had the coup occurred five days earlier, as originally planned, or had an RAF low-level strafing attack on one particular German vehicle not occurred, that choice would have partly been in the hands of Feldmarschall Erwin Rommel. As fate, so thoroughly unkind in July of 1944, would have it, the decision fell entirely to a very different character.

CHAPTER 5

THE RESISTANCE'S LAST HOPE

Rommel against Hitler

O N July 17, 1944, Feldmarschall Erwin Rommel, as was his habit, was touring the Normandy front in his staff car.[1] By this point in the war, the Allies had, thanks to American attacks on the Luftwaffe, total air superiority,[2] and the sky above the battlefield was swarming with Allied aircraft. On his return around 18:00, Rommel's car was near the village of Livarot, approximately fifty miles south of Le Havre. The main road was blocked by burning vehicles hit by Allied aircraft, and Rommel could see a group of enemy planes. Seeking safety, his driver left the main road for a secondary one. The car rejoined the main road two and a half miles from Vimoutiers and began making its way toward the town. Holke, a spotter, kept a watchful eye on the sky. Suddenly, he saw them: two aircraft, flying low, coming up the road behind them. Rommel or his aide, Hellmuth Lang, ordered the driver to step on it. He did, and made for a side road three hundred yards ahead. Rommel looked back.

The side of the car exploded. Shards of glass cut into Rommel's face. The windshield pillar smashed into his left temple and cheekbone, knocking him unconscious. A fragmentation shell shattered the driver's left shoulder and arm. The car struck a tree, skidded over to the left side of the road, and then rolled into the ditch on the opposite side. As it did, Rommel was thrown from the car.

The vehicle stopped about twenty yards from a bleeding Rommel. Lang and Holke jumped out and dove for cover. After the second aircraft made a last attack and flew on, the two ran to Rommel, who was bleeding severely.[3] Lang could not get another car for forty-five minutes, at which point he and Holke took the wounded Rommel and the driver, Daniel, to a religious hospital. A French doctor tended to Rommel's wounds, which he described as "severe."[4] There was little hope, he said, of saving Rommel's life. The two wounded men were transferred to an air force hospital at Bernay some twenty-five miles away. Daniel died that night, and Rommel was transferred again to a hospital near Saint-Germain. Against expectations, he survived, but it was obvious that his tenure as commander of Army Group B was over.

AS IS THE CASE with many World War II figures, the myth and mystique of Rommel have been so thoroughly built up that it is often difficult to distinguish fact from fiction. Hitler and Goebbels, with much help from Rommel himself, constructed the original Rommel myth. Hitler wanted to satisfy the public's craving for glorious military heroes by offering them two—"one in the sun and one in the snow"—whose exploits would take place on the periphery of the main continental battle.[5] Rommel was the first, and Generaloberst Eduard Dietl of the Norwegian and Finnish campaigns was the second.[6] There is certainly nothing unusual about the active construction of military myths such as these. The odd thing in the case of Rommel is the participation of the Allies in the process. Warring nations usually only mythologize those on their own sides.

It is clear that Rommel fit the mould of a German officer neither in his background nor in his approach to war. Whereas most German officers were products of the aristocracy, Rommel's background was thoroughly middle class: his father was a school principal in Heidenheim, in the heart of provincial Swabia.[7] He was thus distant from both the Prussian centre of power within the German army and from the southern German aristocracy (which produced both Stauffenberg and Hofacker) that claimed a place within it.[8] Rommel's father married a bit above himself, taking as his wife the daughter of a senior local dignitary. Otherwise, Rommel was raised in a household largely indistinguishable from a dour middle-class family in England or America. The rules were strict, the parents were distant, and the emphasis was on thrift, honesty, plain speaking, and hard work.[9] Rommel exhibited all these characteristics, along with a certain social puritanism (two glasses of wine was one too many for him), throughout his life.

As a military strategist, however, he was anything but conformist. During World War I—a war in which progress was tracked by inches, not miles—Rommel distinguished himself in the Battle of Caporetto, immortalized by Ernest Hemingway in *A Farewell to Arms*. He placed himself at the front and, without regard to his own safety, pushed his men deep into the Italian position.[10] With just two hundred men under his command, he captured nine thousand Italians, a military triumph for which he was awarded, after much lobbying on his part, Imperial Germany's highest honour, the *Pour le mérite*.[11] It was during the Second World War that his fame reached its height, paradoxically, through a series of battles in North Africa that he ultimately lost. Part of Rommel's notoriety can be attributed to the way in which he conducted battle. Military historian Liddell Hart describes the field marshal's rise:

> Rommel's fame continually grew, owing to the way he baffled successive
> British offensives, and, above all, through his startling ripostes whenever
> his annihilation was prematurely announced. In the process, the troops
> of the British Eighth Army came to think much more highly of him than
> they did of their own commanders, and his Jack-in-the-box performance
> so tickled their sense of humour that their admiration became almost
> affectionate.[12]

When the Eighth Army finally had Rommel cornered, the British appreciation for unlikely pluck seamlessly transformed into an equally strong British appreciation for last stands.

In other ways, English admirers constructed Rommel into a romanticized version of how they liked to see themselves: a man of few words and simple tastes (the English diet would have suited Rommel perfectly) who demonstrated bursts of incredible, reckless bravery and yet maintained the utmost modesty regarding his accomplishments.[13] As with so many constructions, fact overlaps seamlessly with fiction.

Taciturn Rommel might have been, but modest he was certainly not. He was immensely vain, ambitious, and self-promoting. His superiors found him brutal, tactless (if not rude), and prone to going over his commanders' heads.[14] No Prussian, he had a marked disobedient streak. He could be equally brutal with his men. But he was also a meritocrat. He gave dynamic junior officers opportunities to prove themselves in battle that would have been inconceivable under seniority-bound generals.[15]

Rommel's bravery, his egalitarianism (he evidently insisted on receiving the same rations as his men), and his personal commitment to battle (he was always metaphorically and almost always literally leading his men from the front) inspired among his men a love and loyalty that was unusual even in the patriotic fervour of war.[16] Many of these traits surely facilitated the development of a rapport with Hitler: both had strong roots in southern Germany, both had been soldiers at the front during World War I, and, as a result, both were outsiders to the mostly aristocratic and Prussian generals who surrounded Hitler at the Wehrmacht's helm.[17]

Rommel's fame also rests on the fact that the war in the desert was as close to a "clean fight" as there was in World War II.[18] There were few civilians — and even fewer Jews — in the North African Desert. Until El Alamein, Rommel was a Hitler loyalist who devoted all his energies to furthering the interests of the Nazi regime. But as far as we know, he was never guilty of committing war crimes against either civilians or Allied soldiers. Some evidence, although it is not conclusive, indicates that Rommel might have either modified or disobeyed entirely orders from Hitler that amounted to such crimes.[19] This distinction is rarer among Wehrmacht officers than some once believed.[20]

In assessing Rommel's legacy, it is important to view his actions throughout the entire duration of the war. Rommel had been brought in to North Africa by Hitler to rescue the Italians from yet another military disaster and managed to recapture the entire Cyrenaica (eastern and coastal) region of Libya from British forces by mid-April 1941. In addition, he succeeded in taking Tobruk from the British in late June 1942, an impressive coup that temporarily shook British morale at home and on the front.[21] "We have," Winston Churchill told the House of Commons, "a very daring and skilful opponent against us, and, may I say across the havoc of war, a great general."[22] With his now customary audacity, Rommel, by then named a field marshal, pushed his forces deep into Egypt. They made it to El Alamein, 150 miles northwest of Cairo. There, General Bernard Montgomery bested Rommel's men while the field marshal himself was on health-related leave. The German forces were overwhelmed, and by the time Rommel made it back to the front on October 25, it was too late. Rommel, after launching one last counterattack, knew that he had to break out or see the annihilation of his troops.

Hitler, in effect, ordered their annihilation. In the midst of this chaos, an order from Berlin arrived on November 3. "The [situation] requires that the El Alamein position be held to the last man. There is to be no retreat, not so much as one millimetre! Victory or death!"[23] It was signed by Adolf Hitler.

Rommel first tried to fudge the matter. He ordered two Italian corps and one division to hold firm, while he had his Afrikakorps retreat six miles west that evening to hook up with another Italian corps. He then sent a telegram to Hitler indicating that he had held his position.

By the next day, Rommel had to make a more resolute choice: he had eighty tanks facing six hundred British, and the RAF had command of the skies. If he did not break out, his forces would be surrounded and destroyed. Receiving no reply to his request for a breakout, he moved—clearly in defiance of the order to hold his ground.[24] Taking advantage of heavy rain on the night of November 6, Rommel ordered the retreat. He led his men on a 1,500-mile move west, harassed by the British Eighth Army every step of the way. At the end of it, Rommel ran right into the Allies again in the Atlas mountain range in northern Tunisia. Hitler called the field marshal back to Germany on March 6 and, on May 13 1943, the Allies overwhelmed the Germans and their Italian allies, taking 275,000 soldiers into captivity—at this point, the largest Axis capitulation of the war.[25]

Rommel returned to Germany an ill man (he suffered chronic stomach pain) and a broken one, telling his teenage son, Manfred, that he expected no further assignments.[26] The field marshal felt the exhaustion not only of years of war but also of a new rift with his Führer. The military senselessness of Hitler's obsession with never ceding an inch of territory had finally clashed against Rommel's soldierly insistence on adapting to changing military circumstances. Indeed, the El Alamein order "became a turning point" at which Rommel began to withdraw from his relationship with Hitler.[27]

As the Axis position deteriorated further, however, Hitler decided he wanted Rommel back. The dictator sent him briefly to Greece in expectation of an Allied invasion that never happened and then to northern Italy to defend against the encroaching Allies as commander of the newly re-formed Army Group B (Heeresgruppe B). There, Rommel tussled with Feldmarschall Albert Kesselring of the Luftwaffe over strategy.[28] Kesselring argued for a forward defence south of Rome, whereas Rommel countered that Rome could not be held and that the real danger was amphibious landings north of Kesselring's proposed defensive line.[29] The matter came to a head at an October 17 meeting with Hitler. The Führer offered Rommel command of Italy but ordered him to follow Kesselring's strategy. Rommel refused, arguing that he had to inspect the front for himself, retain operational flexibility, and could only submit his military plan *after* his appointment.[30] Hitler was disinclined to take orders from his field marshals at any point in the war. Rommel probably did not help his case by calling OKW Operations Chief Keitel and his deputy, Alfred Jodl, "assholes,"[31] although there is little reason to dissent from the judgment. But after two weeks of hesitation, Hitler nonetheless ordered Rommel and Army Group B to northern France to strengthen German defences against the expected invasion.

Rommel threw himself into the job but almost immediately fell into another strategic argument, this time with his superior, Feldmarschall Gerd von Rundstedt, who was the Oberbefehlshaber West (OB West, or Commander in Chief West) and, therefore, Rommel's superior. Rundstedt was a conservative Prussian of the old school who followed orders unflinchingly—including those to kill women and children as punishment for partisan activity—and had the curious distinction of being fired and then recalled by Hitler three times.[32] The two disputed whether defences against an Allied invasion should be concentrated on the coast (Rommel's preference) or inland (Rundstedt's).[33] Hitler sided with both and therefore neither of them: defences would be established both inland and on the coast. Hitler split Panzer Group West, allotting three divisions each to Rommel and Rundstedt, with the proviso that Rundstedt's could not be moved without Hitler's approval.[34]

Despite shortages of materiel and competent men, Rommel quickly produced results.[35] His efforts saw the rate of mine-laying increased from forty thousand a month to one million, and by early May, he had a half-million obstacles installed on the beaches and potential airborne landing grounds.[36] "I am more confident than ever before [of victory]," Rommel told his secretary on the fifth. "If the British give us just two more weeks, I won't have any more doubt about it."[37]

They would, but Rommel's frantic efforts were undermined by two developments. First, the Allies used false intelligence briefings to delude both Rundstedt and Rommel, like most other German commanders, into thinking that the main assault would be on the port of Calais, across the strait from Dover, rather than on the beaches of Normandy.[38] Second, the splitting of forces between Rundstedt and Rommel meant that only one of the six divisions under Rundstedt's command, the Twenty-First, was anywhere near Normandy; Rommel's strategy of using concentrated force to prevent an Allied landing was undercut from the start.[39] Furthermore, these strategic divisions among land forces were exacerbated by a lack of coordination with the other services: the army could not order in support from the navy or from the few Luftwaffe airplanes available over France.[40] "After five years of war," Rommel bitterly remarked, "it should be clear to even German High Command that the extent of Luftwaffe and army coordination will be decisive for the battle's outcome."[41]

ON THE NIGHT OF JUNE 5, three airborne divisions with paratroopers took off from England. They were followed by vast convoys of troops accompanied by six battleships, twenty-three cruisers, and eighty destroyers.[42] Churchill, given at the best of times to dark moods, went to bed in the blackest of glooms. "Do you realise," he said to Clementine, "that by the time you wake up in the morning, twenty thousand young men may have been killed?"[43] Eisenhower prepared his resignation, drafting a speech explaining why the operation had failed.

Around 6:30 on the morning of June 6, the German Seventh Army witnessed the full force of Allied air, naval, armoured, and infantry power unleashed on them. The skies thundered as six thousand planes drenched the German positions with bombs. Hundreds of ships bombarded the beaches, large stretches of which vanished in bursts of smoke and dust.[44] The bombing stopped ten minutes before Allied troops began disembarking in the water and making for the beaches under enemy fire. The operation applied a core principle underlying American military strategy since the US Civil War: the application of overwhelming power in the form of a headlong assault against the enemy.[45]

And it caught the Germans entirely by surprise. As the first paratroopers landed, Rommel was on leave at his home in Herrlingen (near Ulm), Rundstedt was sleeping, and Hitler was preparing for bed. Hitler himself would not be presented with firm evidence that the invasion had begun until noon, six hours after the first assault troops hit the beaches.[46] By that time, the moment during which a massive, coordinated German defence might have repelled the numerically smaller Allied forces had passed.[47] The Germans recovered some of their poise by the afternoon of D-Day, but even then German High Command refused to call in reserves from the Fifteenth Army.[48]

The confusion would not end that day. It was only toward the end of July that the Germans realized that there would be no landing in the Pas-de-Calais area at all.[49] But by then, it was too late to move reinforcements from there to the invasion front, which was on the verge of being ruptured by an American breakout.[50]

With the Allies on French soil, British and US fighters blackening the skies, and the Soviets launching in late June their great offensive in the east, only the most delusional and sycophantic of Hitler's generals (Keitel and Jodl topped the list, but there were others) believed the war would end in anything but Germany's defeat. Legend has it that, as the Allies broke out of their beachheads and repulsed German attempts at counterattacks, Rundstedt screamed at Hitler and the General Staff, "Make peace, you idiots!"[51] Not one for constructive criticism, Hitler fired Rundstedt (again!) and replaced him with Feldmarschall Günther von Kluge, widely regarded as one of Germany's more reliably Nazi commanders.

Rommel, too, was gradually growing impatient in the face of the crumbling western front. At a June 29 meeting at Hitler's Berghof alpine retreat, Rommel, speaking truth to power, stated that Germany's military situation in the west was utterly precarious. There was no military solution left that could lead to German victory on the western front. Rommel urged, therefore, that a "political alternative" be found. Germany should reach an armistice on the already lost western front and then transfer its western armies to the eastern front.[52]

Hitler was furious. He snapped back, "You look after your divisions," and ordered Rommel to leave the room.[53] In searching for a solution beyond total military victory, Rommel had committed the gravest of sins.[54] Kluge, waiting in the wings, acerbically remarked that the field marshal would "now have to get accustomed to obeying orders."[55]

Within two weeks, Rommel had the grim satisfaction of seeing his predictions come true. On July 15, he summarized for Hitler Germany's disastrous military situation: "We must expect that in the foreseeable future the enemy will succeed in breaking through our thin front. . . . The troops are everywhere fighting with heroic bravery (*heldenmütig*), but their fate is sealed. It is time to draw the necessary conclusions. As commander in chief of the army group, I believe it is my duty to make these facts clear."[56] That same day, he told another colleague that he, with Kluge's blessing, had presented Hitler with an "ultimatum."[57]

As Rommel slowly moved toward a definitive break with his Führer, the resisters began to look to him. Rommel possessed real, albeit limited, military appeal. He was a frontline commander and a very effective one. He did not, however, command rear positions near Paris, and he was not Stülpnagel's superior; that position was occupied by Kluge.[58] Rommel nonetheless presided over of an entire army group that was directly confronting the Allies' most ambitious undertaking of the war in Europe. Rommel's greatest value, however, was reputational. He commanded complete loyalty among his troops, enjoyed respect and admiration from other commanders and their men, and was immensely popular with the German people. The July 20 plotters thus saw Rommel's function more as political than military: both the coup and their efforts to open negotiations with the Allies would have broader support if they enjoyed the blessing of Germany's most famous field marshal. In 1944, the resisters decided to put out feelers to him. On July 9, Cäsar von Hofacker met with Rommel at the latter's headquarters at La Roche-Guyon, northeast of Paris.

The specifics of their conversation—and, most important, the views Rommel might have expressed regarding a coup—are difficult to verify because only those two men were present for it. The details available come in part from Stuttgart mayor Karl Strölin's own postwar accounts.[59] Strölin was a longtime member of the Nazi Party and was involved in the deportation of Jews from his city to death camps, so his recollections must be treated with caution. Nonetheless, it is certain that the two men met and that Rommel, at the very least, was made aware of preparations under way for some form of regime change.

This does not, however, mean he knew about, much less supported, the resisters' plan to assassinate Hitler in order to effect that regime change. The evidence is inconclusive. The strongest indication suggesting Rommel's support for an assassination is likely a secretly recorded conversation between General Heinrich Eberbach, who in summer 1944 served in the staff of Rommel's Army Group B, and his son. Both were imprisoned at Trent Park (a stately home in North London). In a private conversation in September 1944, Eberbach said: "Even when we were out at the front Rommel said to me, 'Germany's only possible hope of getting off reasonably well lies in our doing away with [umgelegt] Hitler and his closest associates as soon as possible.'"[60] This view was further supported in the 1950s by Generalleutnant Alfred Gause, who had served as chief of staff to Rommel for several years as well as to Eberbach in Normandy and who maintained that Rommel knew about the attack on Hitler.[61]

Among historians, Maurice Philip Remy makes the strongest case in favour of Rommel's knowledge of and support for killing Hitler, citing the meeting between Rommel and Hofacker at Rommel's headquarters. Remy maintains that Hofacker informed Rommel of all details of the plot, including the assassination plans.[62]

Against all of this, much evidence suggests the opposite: that Rommel neither knew nor approved of assassination plans. The meeting itself does not carry the argument. As Ralf Georg Reuth notes, Hofacker almost certainly maintained "'need to know' principles" as they were "entirely consistent with the approach of the conspirators."[63] For all its obvious problems as a source, the SD's own post-mortem of the failed conspiracy concluded that only a "very small circle" actually knew about the assassination plot (as distinguished from the overall coup plans).[64] For her part, the field marshal's widow, Lucie, insisted after the war that "although she was aware of her husband's acute disdain" for Hitler, "she refused to believe that he would have agreed to the attempt on the Führer's life."[65]

A further issue concerns Remy's sources. He bases his conclusions on the postwar accounts of Rommel's chief of staff, Hans Speidel, who was not present at the meeting.[66] Moreover, Speidel is hardly a model of clarity or reliability: he is on record saying exactly the opposite: that Rommel's "plan" was to seize Hitler and put him on trial in a German court.[67] Speidel is equally inconsistent in his subsequent publications.[68]

Other sources are even less reliable. Hans Bernd Gisevius and Wilhelm Keitel, who also knew Rommel, claimed in postwar testimony at Nuremberg that the field marshal supported the assassination attempt.[69] Gisevius was driven to resistance by frustrated ambition, was an apologist for Einsatzgruppe commander Arthur Nebe, and wrote highly unreliable postwar memoirs.[70] Keitel was a war criminal who would eventually hang at Nuremburg. In addition, these comments need to be contextualized in the postwar era in which they were made. The German public at large has viewed Stauffenberg and July 20 positively only since the 1960s. Linking Rommel with the coup in the late 1940s was opprobrium, not approbation. Most people in Germany then regarded the conspirators as "traitors and outcasts."[71] In this context, it would make sense that Rommel's enemies would have sought to besmirch his legacy by implicating him in the coup. Other, similar sources used to buttress the view that Rommel was on side with the assassination are also from the immediate postwar period[72] or state only that Rommel had knowledge of the coup generally and do not specifically mention the assassination attempt.[73]

The question of whether Rommel knew about and supported the assassination of Hitler is distinct from the question of what he would have done following the assassination attempt. Would he have lent his support to the coup once it was under way? The most reliable, though not conclusive, evidence comes from the secret tapes made of German generals' conversations among themselves while in captivity at Trent Park. According to General Eberbach, Rommel told the General that "there was nothing else to be done but to make an armistice, at once if possible, and if necessary take steps against [Hitler's] government, in case they weren't sensible enough to give the order."[74] Rommel also asked SS Obergruppenführer and Waffen-SS Generaloberst Sepp Dietrich whose side he would be on if the army surrendered in the west. "Yours," Dietrich replied.[75] In all these cases, Rommel's desire to end the war was based squarely on military judgment: the German army was finished.

And that is the central point. Rommel was not a resister in any reasonable definition of the term. Indeed, he was sympathetic to at least some elements of National Socialism, and his personal loyalty to Hitler was significant.[76] He finally turned against Hitler because there was, in his eyes, no hope after Normandy that Germany could win the war. This was not an instantaneous turn but, rather, a "process" that "began slowly" and did not follow a smooth, linear course; as weeks and months passed, it became clear to Rommel that the war was lost and that the madman at Germany's helm was determined to wrench the nation into the abyss.[77] His fidelity to military principle over political goals and his track record of disobedience paint a picture of a man willing to seek the most sensible solution for the senselessly desperate situation that Hitler and his cronies had created in the west. In Rommel, we can see how conflicting motivations and loyalties led individuals to disobey, even if their actions did not rise to the level of full resistance. Rommel may well have opposed the assassination of Hitler, but he was wholly in favour of making peace on the western front.

As so often, answering one question serves only to raise another: would Rommel's move to open the western front have succeeded? What would have happened if Rommel and Sepp Dietrich had urged surrender, while Kluge, overall commander in the west and Rommel's superior, retained his loyalty to Hitler and ordered the men to keep fighting? To whom would junior commanders have listened? Would a civil war, of which there is precious little tradition in Germany, have broken out?

It is certainly possible that Rommel, Dietrich, and Eberbach (commander of the Panzer Group West, later named Fifth Panzer Army) would have ordered their men to surrender.[78] It is less likely, but also possible given his history of incessant vacillation, that Kluge too would have agreed to open the front. Since Kluge was Kluge, it would have depended entirely on events. Had Rommel, Dietrich, and Eberbach laid down their arms, and had Rommel's prestige inspired widespread admiration among commanders in France, and had this portended a great Allied rush toward Germany and thus an early end to the war, Kluge just might have opted for Rommel, Stülpnagel, Hofacker, and the Allies over Hitler, Goebbels, Himmler, and Göring.

This is of course highly speculative, but in either event—Rommel, Dietrich, and Eberbach acting alone, or with Kluge's support—the result would have been that significant elements of the Wehrmacht in the west would have laid down their arms and gone en masse into captivity as they later did in the Ruhr pocket in April 1945. Mass surrenders on the western front would not have ended the war alone, but would have been an immense boon to the Allies. Multiple divisions would have entered captivity, and the Allies could have made an immediate break north and east toward Germany, possibly even jumping the Rhine as remaining divisions, confused and denuded by a sharp increase in desertions, staggered backward. Hitler would have faced the choice of allowing them to advance or transferring divisions from the eastern front. In either case, the result would have been an earlier end to the war. In the end, all this is naturally conjecture, as we cannot know how Rommel would have reacted to the actual surrender opportunity and how knowledge of Hitler's assassination would have shaped his judgment. But we can say that the ultimate outcome of the July 20 plot may have been determined not only by the unsuccessful attack on Hitler but also, at least in part, by the *successful* one on Rommel.

Rommel's story is most fascinating for what might have been. What in fact happened was an altogether sorrier affair. The task that would have been Rommel's, had his car not been strafed, fell to the Commander in

Chief West and Rommel's replacement as commander of Army Group B: Feldmarschall Günther von Kluge. In his hands lay the opportunity to contact the Allies or even to surrender by opening the front, thus allowing the Allies to move through France and on to Germany.[79]

Over the course of July 20, Kluge's position was driven not by any principle beyond coming down on the safe side: if Hitler were dead, he would support Hofacker and Stülpnagel; if not, he would not. He was hardly alone: on July 20, and indeed well before it, there were many people who tried to run with the foxes and hunt with the hounds.[80] But Kluge's failings ran deeper than this. For years, he had played the role of the opportunist perfectly: listening to Beck's appeals, leaving the general with the impression that Kluge was a man of the resistance but balking when it came to any concrete action. In one breath he would curse Hitler; in the next, he would gladly accept a bribe of 250,000 reichsmarks, an enormous sum in its day (Hitler, doubtful of their loyalty, regularly bribed his field marshals). Once it became clear that Hitler survived, the coup for Kluge—and thus for Germany and Europe—was over. Its final chance slipped away with Kluge's words: "If only the pig were dead [*Ja, wenn die Sau tot wäre*]."

In the end, perhaps the only redeeming thing that could be said about him was that he was not entirely without self-knowledge. A few days before Kluge's suicide on August 19, 1944, the chief of staff of the Seventh Army, Oberst (Colonel) Rudolf-Christoph von Gersdorff, came to visit the field marshal. Gersdorff urged Kluge to display some courage, pressing him to withdraw his troops to Germany's prewar borders, to overthrow the Nazi regime, and to try to negotiate with the Allies.[81] When Kluge argued that failure would make him "the biggest swine in world history," Gersdorff responded with eloquence. "Every great man in world history" faces a decision, the outcome of which commits him to posterity as either a criminal or "a savior in times of dire need."[82] Kluge laid his hand on the colonel's shoulder and replied, "Gersdorff, Feldmarschall Kluge is no great man."

Chance had once again come down on Hitler's side. With Rommel out of the picture; Kluge in retreat; Stauffenberg, Olbricht, and Mertz dead; Stülpnagel under arrest; and Hofacker on the run, all the resisters could do was face the full and awful fury of Hitler's wrath.

CHAPTER 6

HITLER'S REVENGE

A S THE EVENING LIGHT began to fade in Berlin on July 20, 1944, Stauffenberg's coup had failed. Between 20:00 and 21:00, Remer, who had telephoned Hitler from Goebbels's office, had his men withdraw the roadblocks and guards from the city's government district.[1] By 21:30, Generaloberst Heinz Guderian, the famous panzer leader who later condemned the coup as a violation of Christian values (the bombing of Polish cities, the strafing of its citizens, and complicity in SS slaughter evidently posed no difficulties for Christianity), had thrown every effort into countering Olbricht's orders.[2] Guderian in fact knew about the coup, had waited to see if it would succeed before joining it, and was engaged in a great effort of tracks-covering.[3]

At the Bendlerblock itself, a detachment of the SS "Großdeutschland" Guard Battalion, which had earlier sealed the government quarter, arrived as Fromm was pronouncing a death sentence on Stauffenberg, Mertz, Olbricht, and Haeften. The army itself, not the SS, had put down the coup. Throughout the building, chaos reigned. The luckiest conspirators got out, though many were arrested later. Others were less lucky, at least immediately: Leutnant Ewald-Heinrich von Kleist, who had worked with Hase to secure the government quarter that night, made a daring escape. He struck an officer, took down a guard while dodging his bayonet, and dashed out looking for a window from which to jump. He chose one in a room full of

SS men.[4] In the end, it might have been the better choice: Kleist survived the war and died in 2013.

Those who managed to flee from the Bendlerstraße, and those who were never there in the first place, secured themselves time but little else. The Gestapo hunted them down relentlessly.

Fellgiebel, who cut off communications at the Wolf's Lair, was among the first arrested. He left the Wolf's Lair unmolested, but was soon called. His aide, Leutnant Dr. Helmut Arntz, asked him if he would like a pistol. "One stands," Fellgiebel replied. "One does not do that."[5] As he left, Fellgiebel said to Arntz, "If I believed in another world, I would say 'Auf Wiedersehen' [until we see each other again]." Fellgiebel's driver returned that evening "alone and in tears."[6]

Over the next three weeks, the Gestapo tortured Fellgiebel in vain. The general revealed nothing, insisting that he had acted alone.[7] The claim was incredible and the Gestapo knew it, but they could not make him talk. Fellgiebel's men repaid their fallen chief's loyalty. When his successor, co-plotter Generalleutnant Fritz Thiele, tried to hide his own involvement in the coup by denouncing Fellgiebel as a stain on the German army and the signal corps to anyone who would listen, his staff shunned him.[8] Their loyalty may have in the end inspired him. When Thiele was finally arrested (he had been at the Bendlerblock on July 20), he gave none of them away. The other members of the signal corps, both those who had participated in the coup and those who had not, closed ranks, and the Gestapo got nothing out of them. Thiele's successor, Generalleutnant Albert Praun, made the ingenious argument that the cycle of accusations, arrests, and releases was wrecking his ability to keep communications functioning.[9] The Gestapo gave up by mid-August.[10] Their efforts had been fatally undermined by the signal corps' discretion, by Fellgiebel's studied habit of telling people no more than they needed to know,[11] and above all by the general's fortitude under torture. Fellgiebel is one of the great and, to some degree, unsung heroes of July 20.[12]

A few hours after Fellgiebel was called back to the Wolf's Lair, the Gestapo arrested Generalmajor Hellmuth Stieff, the head of the Organization Section of the Army General Staff. Stieff had helped Stauffenberg secure the explosives for his bomb and had also done the same during a 1943 attempt on Hitler's life. It took the Gestapo six days of torture to secure any useful information from Stieff; by then, the names he gave were of those dead or already incriminated.[13]

The Gestapo also came for Major Hans-Ulrich von Oertzen, who had passed on the first Valkyrie orders and had been designated to take over part of Berlin on July 20.[14] Before being picked up, he managed to get a call in to his young wife. He said, "You will have heard what happened. I won't be coming home tonight."[15] Under interrogation, he incriminated himself by denying easily verifiable facts, such as his posting to Wehrkreis III (Berlin) in 1943.[16] One of his interrogators told Oertzen he was under arrest and disarmed him.

The next morning, July 21, Oertzen was able to place another call to his wife. "I've been linked with the assassination attempt. I had nothing to do with it. Go to your father's."[17] Oertzen then asked permission to use the bathroom. He burned and flushed down the toilet documents that would have incriminated other conspirators. On the way back, he hid one hand grenade in each of two sandbags in the passageway. Around 10:00, he asked if he could take a "breath of fresh air" in the passage.[18] Oertzen reached into the first bag, retrieved the hand grenade, and held it over his head. An officer lunged toward him. Oertzen detonated it. The officer was wounded, and Oertzen collapsed. Presuming him dead, the other guards cordoned off the area and called a doctor for the wounded officer. As they did, a still-alive Oertzen, bleeding severely from the head, crawled a couple of yards to the next bag and took out the second grenade.[19] This time, the officers dove for cover. Oertzen placed the grenade in his mouth. It blew his head off.[20] He was twenty-nine years old.

As Oertzen was destroying the documents, the man who tirelessly insisted that overthrowing Hitler was a moral duty to mankind,[21] Generalmajor Henning von Tresckow, was walking in the bright Soviet sunshine toward Hauptmann Eberhard von Breitenbuch, another conspirator.[22] Tresckow smiled at the young captain, though his smile faded when Breitenbuch told him that official duties meant that he could not accompany the general to the front. "That is too bad," Tresckow replied. "I would have liked you to witness my death."[23] Against a distraught Breitenbuch's protests, he remained unmoved. Tresckow shook his friend's hand and said, "Good-bye. We will see each other in a better world."[24] He then drove alone to the front, near Ostrów in Poland,[25] feigned an exchange of fire, and detonated a hand grenade under his chin.

That morning, Tresckow had spoken to his cousin and co-conspirator, Oberleutnant Fabian von Schlabrendorff. Tresckow shared with his cousin the last words on his life, his actions, and the German resistance to Hitler:

> Now everyone will turn upon us and cover us with abuse. But my convic-tion remains unshaken—we have done the right thing. Hitler is not only the archenemy of Germany; he is the archenemy of the whole world. In a few hours' time I shall stand before God, answering for my actions and for my omissions. I think I shall be able to uphold with a clear conscience all that I have done in the fight against Hitler.
>
> God once promised Abraham to spare Sodom should there be found ten righteous men in the city. He will, I trust, spare Germany because of what we have done, and not destroy her. None of us can complain of his lot. Whoever joined the resistance movement put on the shirt of Nessus. A man's moral worth begins only at the point where he is ready to lay down his life for his convictions.[26]

MANY MORE OF THE CONSPIRATORS would be captured by Nazi thugs. Witzleben was arrested at his aide's country house on July 21, the same day that Oertzen and Tresckow killed themselves. Other arrestees had long been opponents of the regime: Dr. Hjalmar Schacht, a former president of the Reichsbank and economics minister; Generaloberst Franz Halder, Beck's successor following his 1938 resignation and the author of the 1939 coup plans; Dr. Johannes Popitz, a former Prussian finance minister; and Oster and Canaris from the Abwehr. Halder and Schacht survived the war; the others were murdered.

General Eduard Wagner, who had provided Stauffenberg with an air-craft on the twentieth and received Witzleben the same day, knew they were coming for him.[27] Late on the twentieth, around 23:00, he learned that the

SS had been to his headquarters in Zossen and had made some arrests.[28] On July 23, Wagner shot himself at Zossen. It seems that one of his closest friends betrayed him. Wagner's diary, about which he had spoken to his wife days before his death, had been delivered to the Gestapo.[29]

At 9:00 on July 21, Stülpnagel received a summons to Berlin. Declining the offer of an airplane, he asked to be driven.[30] The car drove east out of Paris and on toward Germany. The car passed Verdun and crossed the Meuse — the killing fields of World War I on which Stülpnagel had fought. Half a mile out of Vaucherville, eight kilometres north of Verdun, Stülpnagel ordered his driver to stop, saying he needed a walk. He ordered the car to drive on and then walked toward the Meuse canal. The general kneeled, put a gun to his head, and fired. The bullet sliced through the optic nerve behind the right eye and exited through the left eye. The soldiers accompanying Stülpnagel, who had paused at the side of the road shortly after driving off, heard the shot and raced back. They found Stülpnagel floating in the canal. He was rushed to hospital, where doctors revived him and then transferred him to Berlin.

The arrests of Linstow and Hofacker quickly followed. They came for Linstow on July 24, Hofacker the next day, and Finckh on the day after that.[31] Under questioning, Hofacker was defiant. The Gestapo interrogated him brutally: "What were you thinking? You have a wife and five children." A patriot to the very end, Hofacker replied, paraphrasing Heine, "What's a wife and child to me? This is about my Fatherland!" ("*Was schert mich Weib und Kind, jetzt geht es um mein Vaterland*").[32] He and Linstow were among the ninety resisters executed at the Berlin-Plötzensee prison.[33]

On the same day they came for Finckh, another officer, Oberst Wessel Freiherr Freytag von Loringhoven, took matters into his own hands.[34] The colonel had supplied Stauffenberg with explosives and fuses in June and, in 1943, had flown with Canaris to Rome to warn the Pope of rumours that his kidnap and murder were being planned by Hitler. Fearing arrest by the Gestapo, however, he fled into an East Prussian forest and killed himself. His body was found that night. His last letter to his wife and four sons, with his blood spattered over it, is on display in the Bundeswehr Military History Museum in Dresden, courtesy of the family.[35]

As the conspirators were executed or committed suicide, Hitler's thirst for revenge was far from satiated. He then looked to the resisters' families. Himmler promised that "the Stauffenberg family will be exterminated down to its last member."[36] *Sippenhaft*, the arrest of kith and kin, was official National Socialist policy. The Gestapo arrested 140 family members, mostly wives and children of the July 20 resisters.[37] Himmler sent the youngest children to orphanages while moving wives and older children from one concentration camp to another.[38] But he never ordered their murder. In one case, he seemed even to behave with a mystifying humanity. At the end of September, he replied to a letter sent by Loringhoven's mother-in-law to Hitler appealing for the release of her grandchildren. The children, Himmler assured her, would be with her in a few days and the case against her daughter settled by the courts.[39] Loringhoven's four sons were released in October. Gerald Reitlinger suggests that Himmler was "strangely amenable to private correspondence," but this personal quirk seems insufficient as an explanation.[40] Rather, Himmler wanted to use the families as a bargaining chip in possible negotiations with the Allies. In late August, Himmler made a first contact with Churchill via a telegram, though the contents are unclear.[41] Had Himmler known that the Allies viewed the possibility of an agreement with him with utter contempt, he would likely have had the families slaughtered.[42]

While the resisters' families were being delivered to concentration camps, the resisters themselves faced National Socialist justice. The first step was to expel the resisters from the German army: Keitel, Rundstedt, and Guderian presided over the meetings of the Wehrmacht Ehrenhof (Court of Honour) at which these decisions were made.[43] Once expelled from the Wehrmacht, suspects could then be made to face a criminal court. Guderian claims in his memoirs, without specifying a single soul that benefited from his kindness, that he helped as many as he could.[44] Rather than a series of courts martial, Hitler ordered obscene public trials in the People's Court, which had been set up in April 1934 to punish political offences quickly and according to National Socialist principles.[45] The trials were presided over by Roland Freisler, a former Communist who, like a few others of his ilk, became a Nazi fanatic.[46] In 1943, he had ordered the beheading of Hans and Sophie Scholl and Christopher Probst for distributing anti-Nazi leaflets in Munich, and he had represented the Ministry of Justice at the Wannsee conference on the "Final Solution to the Jewish Question in Europe." The trials began on August 7, 1944.[47]

Freisler, cloaked in red with arms flailing, his face contorted with hatred and rage, screamed at the defendants.[48] He intended, and indeed the trial was largely conceived, to intimidate and humiliate them. The tactic was an utter failure. The accused conducted themselves with a dignity that impressed all those watching. When Freisler cut off Hofacker during his trial, Hofacker snapped back, "Be silent, Herr Freisler! Today it is my head that is at stake. In a year it will be yours!"[49] Knowing his sentence would be death, Hofacker ended his speech in defiance: "I immensely [*außerordentlich*] regret that I could not take the place of my cousin Stauffenberg, who failed to do the job because of his severe war injuries."[50] If he had done so, Hofacker meant, Hitler would already be dead. Yorck, one of the few resisters whose condemnations of Nazi genocide was complete and unqualified,[51] was fearless and steadfast throughout the proceedings.[52] "The vital point," he insisted in the face of Freisler's abuse, "running through all [your] questions is the totalitarian claim of the state over the citizen to the exclusion of his religious and moral obligations towards God."[53] Hans-Bernd von Haeften—the brother of Werner (who had thrown himself in front of Stauffenberg), a member of the Kreisau Circle, and one of the resisters within the Foreign Office[54]—was even more to the point: "According to the view I have of the role of the Führer in world history, I assume that he is a powerful instrument of evil."[55]

As the resisters laid into Freisler, many of them haggard from their agonies and often deliberately dressed by their accusers in shabby clothes, Nazi observers shifted uneasily in their seats. They watched the moral authority they had hoped to parade with the show trial slip irretrievably away. Even Reich Justice Minister Otto Georg Thierack, "a fanatical Nazi who in his ideological ardour had . . . surrendered practically the last vestiges of a completely perverted legal system to the arbitrary police lawlessness of the SS," complained about Freisler's behaviour.[56]

The resisters' final acts of bravery meant that they, rather than the Gestapo, had the last word.[57] But those acts made not a bit of difference to the trials' outcome; there was never any chance that they would. Before the court began its first hearing, Hitler vowed to "wipe out and eradicate" the resisters: "they must hang immediately, without any mercy."[58] Hitler personally chose Freisler, partly because he thought—not without irony, as it turned out—that he would be able to silence the accused. Freisler sentenced them all to death by hanging: Finckh, Hoepner, Fellgiebel, Hofacker, Linstow, Berthold von Stauffenberg, Stieff, Stülpnagel, Witzleben, and many others. Among those killed was Erwin Planck, the son of the world-famous physicist Max Planck. As the net closed on the conspirators, one man remained unharmed but very much in the Gestapo's sights: Rommel.

On October 14, they came for him. That day, Erwin Rommel's fifteen-year-old son, Manfred, returned home from duty as an anti-aircraft auxiliary for a short holiday.[59] He arrived early in the morning, and his father was waiting for him. After breakfast, Rommel told his son that two generals would be visiting him that day.[60] They had told him that they were coming to discuss his further war service, but Rommel doubted that this was the real reason. "Today will decide what is planned for me," he said to Manfred, "whether a People's Court or a new command in the East." The latter, Rommel added, he would take: "Our enemy in the East is so terrible that every other consideration has to give way before it. If he succeeds in overrunning Europe, even only temporarily, it will be the end of everything which had made life appear worth living."[61]

At noon, they arrived. Rommel asked his son to leave the room.[62] Manfred saw him again forty-five minutes later, coming out of his mother's room.[63] Rommel explained to him that he had said his last goodbyes to his wife. "I have just had to tell your mother," Rommel said slowly, "that I will be dead in a quarter of an hour."[64] The generals had claimed that both Speidel and Stülpnagel named him as an accomplice in the July 20 plot and that Goerdeler had left documentation naming Rommel as president in post-Hitler Germany.[65] "In view of my 'services in Africa,'" Manfred's father continued, quoting the generals with contempt, "I am to have the chance of dying by poison. . . . If I accept, none of the usual steps will be taken against my family, that is, against you. They will also leave my staff alone."[66] He was promised a state funeral, and his death would be officially attributed to an automobile accident that occurred on the western front.[67]

Rommel said goodbye to his son and to his adjutant. In full uniform and carrying his marshal's baton, he walked toward a car with an SS man in the driver's seat.[68] He took the seat in the back, and the two generals got in the car after him. Manfred looked at his father for the last time as the car drove east, in the direction of Blaubeuren and Ulm.

A short distance from the house, the car stopped. One of the generals led the driver away from the car; the other handed Rommel a cyanide capsule.[69]

Twenty minutes later, the telephone at Rommel's home rang. It was a reserve military hospital in Ulm.[70] The Desert Fox was dead; two generals had delivered his body.

THE CIRCUMSTANCES LEADING UP to Rommel's death are complex and disputed. Suspicion had long fallen on Rommel by the time the trials of the July 20 conspirators began. As Stülpnagel gained consciousness after being operated on after his failed suicide attempt, he shouted out "Rommel! Rommel!" either in front of Gestapo officials or a doctor who reported it to them.[71] Goerdeler's papers listed the field marshal as future president.[72] Were this not enough, Rommel was allegedly implicated by Hofacker through Rommel's own chief of staff, Hans Speidel, and by Kluge's nephew, Karl Rahtgens, who was a another resister.[73]

As incriminating as these pieces of evidence were, they were only part of the material viewed by Hitler and his associates in the weeks following the failed plot. The ultimatum that Rommel had written on July 15 did not reach the Führer until July 23; Kluge had kept it to himself for several days before passing it further up the chain of command.[74] The effect when it did arrive must have been great: dictators have little tolerance for disobedience or ultimatums at the best of times, and Rommel's must have seemed especially egregious in the immediate aftermath of the assassination attempt.

As this was going on, Rommel's enemies in the Wehrmacht and Nazi Party leadership conspired to bring down the field marshal. Keitel and Jodl in the OKW took the lead. They deeply resented Rommel's meteoric rise, and they had long feared that "Hitler's favourite" might be made commander in chief of the army.[75] They had both been in the room at the Wolf's Lair when the bomb went off, and they saw at close range Hitler's fury at the betrayal. The opportunity to attribute even a shred of responsibility to their nemesis was not to be missed. In this effort, they had a powerful—indeed, the most powerful—figure in the Nazi Party bureaucracy: Martin Bormann. Bormann, like Keitel and Jodl, resented the field marshal's unusually close relationship with Hitler.[76] Throughout August, these figures built up a case to the dictator that Rommel was a "defeatist."[77]

The Gestapo gathered more intelligence about Rommel over the month of September, and the field marshal's penchant for sometimes overly frank honesty did not serve him well. Historian Desmond Young reports in his early biography of the Desert Fox that the local party boss in Ulm, Kreisleiter Wilhelm Maier, visited Rommel in early September. Casting himself as a friend, Maier reported to Rommel that he had heard from the head of the SS in Ulm that the field marshal no longer believed in victory. With a frankness that worried Rommel's teenage son, the field marshal replied, "Victory! Why don't you look at the map? The British are here, the Americans are here, the Russians are here: what is the use of talking about victory?" When Maier mentioned Hitler, Rommel replied, "That damned fool!" Maier responded with a word of caution. "You should not say things like that, Feldmarschall. You will have the Gestapo after you—if they are not already."[78]

Desmond Young, the source of these quotations, wrote in 1952 about an Italian journalist who accused Maier of going home after this visit with Rommel and drafting a thirty-page report, which he then took to Berlin and handed personally to Bormann the next day. Maier was for a time in a French prisoner-of-war camp with Manfred Rommel at Landau, and he denied the story. Assuring Rommel's son of his friendship, Maier swore that he knew nothing of the field marshal's murder.[79] The journalist's story, Young concluded long before the archives were opened, "may very well be true."[80]

It is. The claim that the report had been "handed personally" to Bormann was a bit of journalistic embellishment, as was the estimate of thirty pages. But Maier, who had in fact visited Rommel under instructions from Gauleiter Wilhelm Murr, sent a report to Berlin after his meeting with Rommel, though possibly not on the following day.[81] In it, he stated that Rommel had spoken with extreme pessimism about the military situation and had criticized Hitler for not coming to see Normandy himself. Maier evidently then reported the conversation to Heidenheim's mayor, Dr. Meier. Meier, citing his concern for Rommel's "constitution" (*innere Haltung*), passed the information up to Bormann.[82] Bormann, convinced that Stauffenberg had drawn Rommel into the resistance during his time in Africa, informed Hitler, Keitel, and Himmler.[83]

Bormann dispatched Heinrich Walkenhorst to see Gauleiter Murr and Maier.[84] Maier was now himself in danger, as Bormann had described him as "pessimistic"—the same adjective applied to Rommel and one that could cost a man his life.[85] During the meeting, Maier might have retreated a bit: he attributed doubtful claims to Rommel (for example, that he was positively predisposed toward Hitler and had expressed concern about the Führer's health) along with highly plausible ones (that Rommel was bitterly critical of Göring and the Luftwaffe).[86] Rommel was hardly alone in the latter: the Gestapo and the Party, watching German cities turned to rubble, also viewed Göring with contempt.[87]

The meeting seemed to go well for Maier. Walkenhorst found Maier to be an "absolutely positive person," and Murr spoke in glowing terms about Maier's work in Ulm.[88] But this all confirmed the party and the Gestapo's conclusion that Rommel no longer backed the regime. As Walkenhorst put it, Maier's confirmation and above all his report to the SD "made my job much easier."[89] It did not, despite Walkenhorst's endorsement, save Maier: Bormann had already ordered him fired. The Reich could not have pessimistic local party bosses.[90]

Although the Italian journalist was right about Maier's having played a role, he exaggerated the effect. Walkenhorst met Maier and Murr on October 13, midday, and he drafted his report on October 16. By then, Rommel had been dead for two days, and the report was a bit of bureaucratic tidying up.

If Walkenhorst's report did not get Rommel killed, Maier's September 19 report to Murr, which found its way quickly to Bormann, certainly helped to that end. By this date, the Nazi elite was turning on Rommel from all sides: Hitler's increasing suspicions, Hofacker's mutterings under torture, Stülpnagel's postoperative mention of the field marshal's name, and Maier's report all pointed toward Rommel's complicity in the events of July 20, 1944. The information from Maier was simply more ammunition for Bormann, who continued to pursue his vendetta against Rommel in his presentations to Hitler. Bormann's hatred of the field marshal reached dizzying heights of pettiness: he criticized Rommel for his "vanity" in refusing to wear eyeglasses.[91]

Rommel's apparent guilt was compounded even further, perhaps unintentionally, by his own former chief of staff, Hans Speidel. Under torture from the Gestapo, Hofacker had allegedly confessed that he had told Speidel about the entire assassination plot. Speidel was questioned and put before the Wehrmacht Court of Honour that would decide if he should be expelled from the military and handed over to the always-bloodthirsty People's Court. Speidel told the court that he had dutifully informed Rommel, his superior, of Hofacker's disclosure. It was Rommel, therefore, who was the guilty party for having failed to pass the information up the chain of command.[92] The court, led by Guderian and Keitel themselves, concluded that Speidel had done his duty and was therefore "not guilty" though not "free from suspicion." This decision shifted the blame to Rommel.[93]

But the factor of perhaps greatest importance in damning Rommel was the evidence that Rommel himself had generated in his own pattern of disobedience: his retreat from El Alamein, his refusal to follow Hitler's wishes in Italy, his protestations to the Führer at the Berghof in June 1944, and his unapologetically pessimistic view expressed in his July 15 ultimatum. These acts were known to all parties, who likely viewed them as in line with the goals of the conspirators even if not made in concert with them. Indeed, Bormann noted in late September that Rommel's criticisms of the generals surrounding Hitler "absolutely correspond" to the nature of allegations (*Unterstellungen*) against the "Stauffenberg-Goerdeler-Clique."[94] In the regime's eyes—or, at least, in Bormann's—Rommel's pattern of disobedience was not a result of the field marshal's professional military objections to Hitler but, rather, was a sign of his involvement in the July 20 conspiracy.

In addition, Rommel had made one final plea to Hitler on October 1, in order to vouch for the incriminated Speidel and to emphasize that he had always done all in his power to ensure German victory.[95] This in itself might well have seemed suspicious to the dictator. A few days later, and in a final act of disobedience, Rommel refused an order from Hitler on October 7 to report to Berlin for an audience with the Führer. He did so on the basis of his health being too fragile to make such a journey, but the official doctor's excuse was exaggerated at Rommel's own request,[96] and the Gestapo, who had long had Rommel under surveillance, knew it.[97] For Hitler, "this refusal from the otherwise ambitious general was the last piece of circumstantial evidence of his guilt."[98]

It is difficult to say which of these facts Hitler regarded as the smoking gun or, indeed, if there was one. But collectively, this evidence was more than Hitler needed to act. On his order, Keitel gave two subordinates two documents: a letter informing Rommel that he was charged with treason and a statement by Hofacker that he had met Rommel.[99] Two generals left for Rommel's home in Herrlingen.

In the end, Rommel's greatest advantage—the pragmatic tenacity that earned him so much early military glory—turned out to be his greatest liability. Rommel viewed the military and political situations with the same cold objectivity as he always had. When reason pointed to victory, Hitler showered his commander with praise and patronage. But when reason led to the clear conclusion that Germany could not win after June 1944, Hitler no longer wished to listen. Rommel's repeated refusal to toe the line and to tell Hitler what he wanted to hear increased the divide between the two men. When implications stemming from July 20 subsequently came to light—whether they were genuine, coerced, or simply fabricated matters little in this context—it was enough to tip the balance. Resistance did not get Rommel killed, as he was not part of the July 20 German resistance. But disobedience did.

STAUFFENBERG, OERTZEN, Hofacker, Tresckow, and, indirectly, Rommel, as well as many others, paid the ultimate price for the failure of the coup, but the rest of the German army and the German home front were also affected by its failure. The public prosecutions greatly stiffened the army's resolve to fight on as they demonstrated that opposition meant death. Hitler was convinced that "providence," a favourite term of his, had saved him again, and the assassination attempt confirmed his long-held belief that treachery among the General Staff, a new stab in the back, had robbed Germany of a quick and easy victory.[100] Hitler's suspicions of the army—always present and intense since the failure to take Moscow in late 1941—increased further still, and the National Socialist Party and the SS saw their power increase relative to the army, though the Nazi regime remained "polycratic," made up of multiple, mutually jealous centres of power.[101] Above all, for Hitler the only way to answer the treachery of the coup, and to silence the "babble" of foreign propaganda following the coup, was through the "totalization of the war effort in Germany . . . and in the parts of Europe under her control."[102] Among the first testing grounds for this total war would be the French capital.

CHAPTER 7

DID A PRUSSIAN SAVE PARIS?

I N THE LATE 1950S, two reporters who had met during the war, Larry
Collins and Dominique Lapierre, were working in Paris—Collins for
Newsweek, Lapierre for *Paris Match*. In the early 1960s, they wrote a history
of the liberation of Paris titled *Is Paris Burning?* and placed the German
commandant of the capital, General Dietrich von Choltitz, at the centre
of the narrative.

The story was the ideal stuff of rip-roaring journalistic history: cannons
trained on Paris's monuments, bridges wired with explosives, and a block-
busting howitzer—a siege mortar—with the menacingly Teutonic name of
Karl making its way to French capital.¹ As it did, Choltitz was transformed.
A hardened supporter of Hitler handpicked by the dictator for his ruth-
lessness, he was said to have gone through a moral transfiguration as he
contemplated his Führer's order to blow the City of Light to pieces before
the Allies could occupy it. His eye distracted by pretty gardens and pretty
girls, he set out to save the French capital. Against all odds, a Prussian saved
Paris from ruin.

It was quite a story. The problem is that the book is filled with unref-
erenced claims, distortions, and half-truths. As a scholarly account of the
liberation of Paris, it is almost useless. The book attributed to Choltitz a
military capability that he lacked. Upon closer, source-based inspection,
it becomes clear that he could command neither the artillery and infantry

divisions, which were mostly fighting elsewhere, nor the tactical bombers, which had been blown out of the sky by the Americans, that would have been necessary to devastate the capital.[2] Almost pathetically, all he could manage to do was hold down a civilian uprising and await the end. The most critical interpretation of Choltitz holds that the so-called saviour of Paris, who was feted by French politicians and a literary public in the last years of his life, was a fraud.[3]

As so often, the truth lies between the extremes. Choltitz was not a Stauffenberg, a Stülpnagel, or a Hofacker. He was not a man who, whatever his earlier sympathies for National Socialism, eventually set his face firmly against Hitler and Nazism and threw his energies into ensuring their overthrow. Yet, he was something more than an accomplished headline grabber, a media-friendly self-promoter who convinced gullible journalists to transform his military weakness into heroism of the highest order. He was a complex, morally ambiguous, and, in the end, brave and pragmatic man who used his position to ensure the near-bloodless surrender of one of the world's most beautiful cities. Paris was never at risk, as Collins and Lapierre would have us believe, of becoming a Dresden—or, more aptly, a Warsaw—under Choltitz's command. But a more obedient, stubborn, and fanatical man could have handed over to the Allies a scarred city, littered with many more bodies.

The story of Paris's salvation, however, is much more than the story of Choltitz. As in the case of Speer, the relentless focus on this one man by journalists and Hollywood filmmakers searching for heroes obscures the role of other German officers. Many of them were veterans and, rather against the odds, survivors of July 20. And most, if not all, of them had developed a deep love for this most lovable of cities. They had set in place efforts to minimize damage to Paris even before Choltitz arrived to assume command, and they gladly extended essential aid to Choltitz in disobeying Hitler's orders. Finally, flexibility in Allied policy allowed a quick capture of the city.

The story of Choltitz is nonetheless central to disentangling fact from fiction in understanding Paris's last days under German occupation. That story begins not in the French capital but in Rotterdam. Choltitz, whose career in the German army extended all the way back to his enlistment in

1914, was by 1940 an Oberstleutnant and commander since 1937 of the Third Battalion, Sixteenth Airborne Infantry Regiment (Luftlande Infanterie-Regiment 16) that took part in the May 1940 attack on Rotterdam. His actions there and, later, in Sevastopol suggested a reputation for brutality and nearly blind obedience.

A further, contested foundation of Choltitz's reputation may have been laid near Sevastopol. After Choltitz's ultimate surrender in August 1944, the Allies placed him with other generals at Trent Park, North London. Unknown to the generals, the British taped and transcribed their conversations. In one conversation, Choltitz is quoted as referring, rather out of context, to Hitler's order on the Jews: "The worst job I ever carried out—which however I carried out with great consistency—was the liquidation of the Jews. *I carried out this thoroughly and entirely [bis zur letzten Konsequenz].*"[4]

Historians have rushed to judgment. Choltitz's son, with a rather obvious horse in the race, pointed out that no audio recording of the conversation has surfaced.[5] As the transcribers could not see who was speaking, it is possible that another general made the comment. It is even possible, though less likely, that the copy is a forgery. As yet, no corroborating evidence of Choltitz's involvement in the massacre has been found. Many German generals committed atrocities, so it is possible, perhaps probable, that Choltitz ordered the action. There simply is not yet enough evidence to know with certainty.

It is easier to believe that Choltitz was the sort of unreflective anti-Semite that one would expect, given his age, class, and profession. In reaction to Churchill's speech on September 28, 1944, he said to Generalleutnant Karl-Wilhelm von Schlieben (who had surrendered Cherbourg): "Have you read Churchill's speech? *Appalling* beyond all words! A Jewish brigade to go to Germany! Then the French will take the west and the Poles the east. The hate in that speech! I am completely shattered."[6]

Choltitz was cast as a player in the events of August 1944 by Hitler himself. On August 7, the dictator summoned Choltitz to the Wolf's Lair. There, still bearing injuries from the July 20 explosion and seething with rage at the generals who had betrayed him, Choltitz was given new orders: he was to take over the command of Paris and defend it to the last bullet.[7]

Hitler was not alone in viewing Paris as decisive. No less a figure than Rommel was convinced that the Allies would see the capture of Paris as "operationally, politically, economically, and psychologically decisive."[8] They would then use it as a base for launching an invasion of the Reich. Hitler, however, would add his own twist: if Choltitz could not defend Paris, he was to destroy it. The meeting with Hitler has often been written up as the defining moment when Choltitz realized that Hitler was insane.[9] It might have been, but Choltitz, like all German generals, had more than enough information before August 1944 to support that proposition.[10]

Choltitz was a monarchist who had served as a child page to the Queen of Saxony, a descendant of a Prussian aristocratic military family, and a veteran of the Wilhelminian army. Contemporary accounts suggest that the monocled general was a bit pompous and somewhat of a snob.[11] None of this recommended him to Hitler. Hitler chose him rather because of his reputation as an unquestioning follower of orders. Choltitz had proved himself in Hitler's eyes while fighting the Allies during the Normandy breakout, not to mention his record of unstinting loyalty over almost five years of war. Although Choltitz found it convenient after the war to express regret over his campaign at Normandy, he fought it at the time with determination, skill, and great willingness to tolerate large numbers of German casualties. As his future orderly officer put it, "We knew, and could even understand given the context [presumably of July 20], that Hitler wanted to trust a 'Nazi general' who could act drastically [*scharf durchgreift*] when defending Paris. As Paris had been declared a fortress, the plan was already in place: Paris would be defended, as it was so wonderfully put [by Hitler], 'from the rubble.'"[12]

As a first step to transforming Paris into a fortress, Hitler had allowed all non-essential administrative personnel, the SD, and Gestapo to leave the city.[13] Trucks parked outside the various German headquarters across Paris were being loaded with papers, records, and equipment. Smoke and ash from burning documents once again filled the summer sky. In the rue Royale, which links La Madeleine to the Place de la Concorde, busloads of German soldiers prepared to depart. Some of them waved handkerchiefs in a sad, silent farewell to the city.[14]

When Choltitz arrived in Paris on the tenth, he made his way to a handsome building at boulevard Raspail No. 26, across the river from the Louvre and the Tuileries. It was the house of Generalleutnant Hans von Boineburg-Lengsfeld, who had led the arrest of the Gestapo, SS, and SD on July 20. Boineburg had been sacked, though he would survive the war, and Choltitz was to replace him. If Collins and Lapierre are to be believed, Choltitz's arrival at Boineburg's residence was met with only resignation and despair.[15] Choltitz, in their account, was harshly dismissive of Boineburg's plans for defending Paris, which involved forming a defensive ring around the city. Such a plan provided a line of defence, but it also—not without reason—ensured that the bulk of fighting would occur outside the capital. Boineburg's plea that Choltitz do "nothing that could bring irreparable destruction to Paris" met only silence. In a final, dramatic gesture, Choltitz is said to have implicitly cast scorn on Boineburg's decadence by eschewing his boulevard Raspail house in favour of a relatively simple room at the Hotel Meurice. He then turned to Boineburg and added laconically, "For the days ahead, Herr General, I shall need a headquarters, not a residence."

Choltitz indeed stayed at the Hotel Meurice, but the rest of this story is fiction. More reliable evidence shows that Choltitz had a long after-dinner conversation with Boineburg and Oberst Unger, who was, like Boineburg, connected to the July 20 conspiracy. It was during this conversation that Boineburg, along with Unger, appealed to Choltitz to spare the city. They did so on strategic grounds: destroying Paris would serve no military purpose.

Dankwart Graf von Arnim, Boineburg's orderly officer (*Ordonnanzoffizier*), was also at boulevard Raspail No. 26 that evening. Arnim was a young, soft-spoken aristocrat from Brandenburg who had served on the eastern front before being transferred to Paris. He had worked under Boineburg for a year and, like most staff officers in Paris, was connected to the events of July 20. He had heard about them from family members involved in the planning, but he only learned of the coup's launch as it occurred. The coup's failure would cost him a great deal: the National Socialists hanged one cousin on the day that Choltitz arrived in Paris; two more of his cousins would be hanged in September.[16] In Arnim's far more reliable account, following the chat, "it was clear that Boineburg and Unger were on the very best of terms with Choltitz. . . . There was clearly an agreement to focus exclusively on military and administrative matters, and that the most important issue at stake was the fate of Paris."[17]

Arnim took Choltitz to his rooms at the Hotel Meurice. The orderly had asked to be transferred to the Panzer Lehr Division in Normandy, presumably to avoid being party to the destruction of Paris. To this, Choltitz replied that he had already spoken with Boineburg about Arnim's further employment. Choltitz needed an orderly officer whom he could trust, one who understood the complexities of Paris; the general really had to insist, therefore, that Arnim stayed.[18] (It was further evidence that the distance between Boineburg and Choltitz was, from the beginning, not great.)

As it was an order, Arnim had little choice, but the conversation had also revealed that the two men were distant relatives.[19] The fact that Choltitz both consulted Boineburg, an officer so deeply implicated in the July 20 plot, and made a point of hiring a support officer so close to Boineburg, hardly made him the general of Hitler's fantasies. In fact, given that Choltitz had long had ties to the German military resistance and held Stauffenberg in the highest regard, this common address book is unsurprising.[20] The important point here is that Choltitz did not go through a moral transformation *during* his tenure in Paris. Though possibly at a later meeting rather than this one, Choltitz commented on Hitler's order to destroy Paris: "I cannot implement this insane order."[21] He made the decision not to defend Paris *before* that tenure and without reference to the military means at his disposal. The Collins-Lapierre thesis *and* the counterclaim that Choltitz did not destroy Paris because he lacked the means both get it wrong.

Had Choltitz wished to launch a robust defence of the city, German reports in August 1944 would not have made happy reading for him. The core of German defences in Paris was the 325th Security Division (used on July 20 to arrest the SS), made up of four regiments of mostly older troops.[22] Security divisions were weaker than field divisions, given the age of the soldiers and the fact that they had less artillery and motor transport.[23] The division had a small number—as few as four—of small tanks.[24] Their job was to mop things up, to come in after the advancing field divisions had defeated the enemy, to occupy the area, and to put down any efforts at last-ditch resistance. The division had some five thousand troops. According to postwar French military estimates, Choltitz also had at his disposal some twenty-three 105 mm and 150 mm cannons, thirty-six 75 mm and 88 mm guns, around nineteen Mark V-VI tanks and as many as fifty-nine Mark III-IV tanks.[25] After the war, Choltitz deliberately played down the number of tanks he had, claiming it was only four.[26] Finally, Choltitz could give orders to Generalmajor Hubertus von Aulock, who commanded battle troops positioned by Boineburg outside the city: the 48th and 338th Infantry Divisions, a storm battalion of the First Army, and the batteries of the First Flak Brigade. This brigade, however, was not very mobile and consisted largely of seventeen-year-olds with little military training.[27] Altogether, Choltitz had 17,000 to 20,000 troops under his direct command: 5,000 attached to the 325th Security Division and the rest in units positioned outside the city's perimeter, as well as the authority to commandeer any units passing through the city.[28] Choltitz could thus directly or indirectly command some 25,000 to 30,000 men.[29]

Beyond this, Choltitz could call on limited air support. On August 17, the Luftwaffe was ordered to destroy all the airbases around Paris and moved its headquarters to Reims. Across France, it had only sixteen fighter groups with around 150 serviceable fighters.[30]

Military shortages were not Choltitz's only problem. Paris's restless inhabitants, having suffered arrogance, humiliation, and hunger since 1942 (the time of Otto von Stülpnagel's resignation), smelled blood. News of the July 20 coup, of Allied military triumphs in Normandy, and of bombing raids outside the capital all combined to suggest a picture of German weakness. On August 10, Parisians struck. Exactly 152 years after the Paris mob assailed the Tuileries and massacred the Swiss Guard, the railway men, defying the strictest German orders, went on strike.[31] The strike was conducted with a militancy that would command an anarchist's respect (those who wavered were won over at gunpoint)[32] and was a great success. Within two days, the capital was cut off to rail transport. The Germans, who had been so keen to get into the city four years earlier, were now equally keen to get out of it. As an early historian of the liberation put it, the mob of Germans trying to get out of town from the Gare de l'Est was almost as great as it was at the same station when they herded the Jews eastward to death. Old Luftwaffe generals, the more strikingly platinumed of the stenographers at the Majestic, telephone operators, administration officials small and great, naval officer candidates, . . . old superannuated sergeants major, liaison officers and interpreters, cooks and mess waiters, Gestapo small fry in gabardine raincoats, and all these followed by their wives, sisters, cousins, maids-of-all-work, and mistresses, were trying to pile into any sort of train or vehicle that would carry them east.[33]

At least in partial response to the strike and the unrest it reflected, the Germans sought to take out those Parisians with the greatest material ability to harm them: the police. On Kluge's orders, the Germans began disarming them by the hundreds on August 13, starting in the tough working-class district of Saint-Denis.[34] The plan backfired: on August 14, the local police, who had served the Germans so efficiently in suppressing the population and rounding up the Jews, streamed into the arms of the resistance. Three resistance organizations—Honneur de la Police, Police et Patrie, and Front National de la Police (the first two were moderately socialist, the last was Communist)—used the German action to call for a general strike on the sixteenth.[35]

Two days before the strike was launched, the three wings of what would become the French uprising in Paris met. They were the Communists, the Gaullists, and the police. For the Communists, there was Henri Rol-Tanguy ("Colonel Rol"), a thirty-eight-year-old sheet-metal worker, Communist Party member, and experienced soldier who had served in both the Spanish Civil War and the French army in 1940 (winning the Croix de Guerre).[36] He evidently saw no contradiction between his service to France and his membership in the Communist Party, though that party had denounced the war during the period 1939 to 1941 as "an imperialist-capitalist conspiracy."[37] In June 1940, the Communist party newspaper, l'Humanité, welcomed the arrival of German troops in Paris and called on French workers to fraternize with them.[38] Whatever conflict of loyalties he suffered up until June 1941, Rol was the leader of the Parisian wing of the Communist resistance and the undisputed leader of the planned uprising against the Germans.[39] André Tollet and André Carrel served directly under him.[40]

Marching at times in step but never in spirit with the Communists was the second wing, consisting of de Gaulle's men in France. De Gaulle's representative was Alexandre Parodi. Parodi was the general delegate for the Provisional Government of the French Republic, itself a creation of de Gaulle, who upgraded the umbrella French Committee for National Liberation into a government-in-waiting.[41] He also led a Gaullist General Delegation in the capital. The military equivalent of Parodi was Jacques Chaban-Delmas, head of the National Military Delegation. De Gaulle had promoted the athletic twenty-nine-year-old to the rank of general on May 1, 1944.[42] As civilian authority superseded the military, Chaban-Delmas in principle answered to Parodi.[43] Parodi's job was to prevent a premature insurrection that could result in a bloodbath and to ensure that, when the Allies took Paris, neither the Communists nor the Pétainists were sufficiently powerful to claim the right of government in postwar France.[44] The members of the delegation were few and, despite the honour of having been handpicked by de Gaulle, they could not at this point match the prestige of the Communists.[45] As de Gaulle later said to Mendès France with some hyperbole, "We only had on our side Jews, negroes, hunchbacks, cripples, failures, and cuckolds."[46] Léo Hamon, a Christian Socialist resister from Toulouse, was vice president of the Communist-leaning Parisian Liberation Committee.[47] Despite this title, as a Christian Socialist, Hamon was closer to the general than the Communists.

In principle, de Gaulle and Chaban-Delmas controlled the armed wing of the resistance: the French Forces of the Interior (FFI). On April 4, de Gaulle appointed General Marie-Pierre Kœnig, who had joined him in London, as overall commander of the FFI, while Chaban-Delmas was to direct forces on the ground in Paris. In practice, however, it did not work that way.[48] Communists made up the largest single bloc among FFI fighters—and overall amounted to something like 50 percent of the FFI in Paris—and Rol was determined to exercise his authority over the FFI. Under great pressure from the Communist leadership, Parodi sought instructions from Algiers. Receiving no reply, he made a call: he agreed that the Parisian Liberation

Committee would direct the FFI and "lead the national insurrection."[49] De Gaulle was furious ("there can be no question of divesting ourselves of any power"), but his reply never made it to Parodi.[50] The result was that, in the last days of the German occupation, the Communists would direct the FFI, while Parodi attempted to prevent a national insurrection that could lead to the loss of much blood and treasure while allowing the Communists to seize power.

The final wing in the Parisian resistance was made up of very recent converts: the police. There were Communists among the police, but their sympathy lay in the main with de Gaulle. Every police officer that refused to hand over his arms to the Germans went over, with weapons, to the resistance. After four years of collaboration they, unlike Rol or Parodi, had a great deal to prove.

The main argument at the meeting of these three factions was whether the police should go on a general strike. As a sign of things to come, Parodi and Rol had a spirited argument, with the former arguing against and the latter in favour. Parodi, as another sign of things to come, agreed to compromise for the sake of unity: better perhaps an ill-advised general strike than a situation in which some police went on strike while others did not.[51] And the Communists certainly had a point when they argued that, in the absence of a strike, the Germans would continue to disarm the police, robbing the capital of the closest thing it had to an army.[52] As the ranks closed, the FFI issued a strike order:

> The hour of liberation has arrived. Today it is the duty of the whole body
> of the police to join the ranks of the FFI . . . you will do nothing further
> to help the enemy maintain order. . . . You will refuse to arrest patriots . . .
> to check identities, to guard prisons and so forth. You will aid the FFI in
> putting down anyone who continues to serve the enemy in any way . . .
> Police who do not obey these orders will be considered traitors and col-
> laborators. . . . On no pretext allow yourself to be disarmed. . . . March
> with the people of Paris to the final battle.[53]

It was in this city that the new commandant of Greater Paris, General Dietrich von Choltitz, arrived on August 10. Denuded of troops and equipment, and armed with orders to defend or destroy the capital, he faced a population seething with anger and possibly on the verge of open rebellion. The view outside Paris was no better. In Baden Baden were his wife and children, all of whom would be arrested in accordance with the Sippenhaft policy if he failed to carry out his orders. In the north and west of France were the Allies, fully prepared to charge him as a war criminal if he did. It was in this unappealing environment that the new commandant issued his first orders.

CHAPTER 8

TO DESTROY THE CITY OF LIGHT

WITHIN DAYS OF assuming his command, Choltitz found himself under sharply increased political pressure. On August 15, General Walter Warlimont ordered a 38 cm assault howitzer to be mounted on a Tiger chassis, then beginning to come off the assembly line, to be dispatched to Feldmarschall Walter Model. Model was to send the assault howitzer to Paris "to smash internal disorder" there.[1]

Pressure emanated not only from German High Command but from Paris itself, though in the latter it was the civilians rather than his superiors that Choltitz had to fear. Parisians had been anything but indifferent to the very obvious German administrative pullout from the city. For the first time in four years, they sensed the faint light of freedom over the city as well as a theretofore unknown flicker of fear among their German captors. People became less respectful and restrained toward Wehrmacht soldiers, who found themselves verbally and even physically abused if they were foolish enough to move through the city alone. Others—the French resistance—began to organize.

Choltitz responded by playing good cop/bad cop. Bad cop: he ordered a parade of troops and tanks around the Opéra, and he had notices posted warning Parisians that acts of violence against German troops would be met with uncompromising force.[2] Good cop: Choltitz met city officials on August 16. Speaking self-consciously in French, he appealed for calm and the security of his troops.³ This required order. In exchange, Choltitz promised to ensure that "Paris would be neither defended nor destroyed, nor delivered to looting and arson."⁴

It is doubtful that either of his two actions was very effective. The prefect of police, Amédée Bussière, replied that German troops were responsible for their own security, and that the French police would have no means to maintain order without arms.⁵ The meeting ended without any clear conclusions but also without Choltitz issuing any imperious ultimatums.⁶ It also had positive effects. Afterwards, the French commented on Choltitz's moderate tone and the complete absence of the brutality that had characterized previous governors.⁷ "He seemed like a jolly fat man [*un bon gros*]," someone remarked.⁸

The next day, Choltitz had another problem on his hands. A portly Swedish businessman and consul general to France, Raoul Nordling, came to see him about political prisoners.⁹ Accompanying him was Emil Bender, a somewhat obscure figure who seems to have been one of Canaris's anti-Nazis in the Abwehr responsible for counterespionage in Paris.¹⁰ He was also a fluent French speaker and translated for Choltitz.

Nordling wished to speak about the thousands of prisoners held in concentration camps, prisons, and hospitals in and around the city. He feared that the SS would take the pullout from the city as a pretext to liquidate them. As if on cue, Oberg—head of the SS and security police in France—arrived in the middle of the meeting and declared that he had orders to evacuate the prisons and camps.¹¹ After Oberg left, Choltitz asked Nordling for his opinion. "It is of the utmost importance," the Swede replied, "that we prevent the massacre of the prisoners, as the responsibility for such a catastrophe would rest with the German army [and not merely the SS]."¹² Choltitz replied, "I am a military man; I know nothing of civilians. If they are *franc-tireurs*, I execute them; if they are not, I leave them alone. I ignore entirely the category of political prisoners. I can't let them go as they are [Hotel] Majestic's"—that is, the Military Commander of France's—"responsibility."¹³ Choltitz, silently expressing his contempt for Oberg, gave Nordling a letter urging (*prescrivait*) the prisoners' release.¹⁴ He was to take it to a Major Huhm at the Hotel Majestic.

"You better hurry," Choltitz added. "Major Huhm leaves Paris at noon."[15] It was 11:30.

Nordling and Bender rushed to the Hotel Majestic.[16] Barricades surrounded the building, trucks drove constantly to and from the hotel, and Germans inside were frantically burning documents. Huhm met them immediately and, thanks to Choltitz's letter, was willing to cooperate.[17] But he wanted something in return. "We must establish a convention. If we liberate French prisoners, we need something in return, for instance twenty-five German POWs for each French civilian."[18] Reacting with unhelpful honesty, Nordling replied that he did not have a single German POW. That might have been the end of it, but Huhm replied, "It's only a formality."[19] Nordling got him down to five POWs for each French civilian and then left to meet a lawyer named Mettetal with connections to the resistance.[20] Mettetal grabbed a typewriter and paper, drew up a contract, and they left for the Hotel Majestic at 12:20. The contract transferred responsibility for hospitals, camps, and prisons to Nordling, to be assisted by the Red Cross. The clause regarding the prisoner exchange, however, was meaningless: the contract provided for the immediate release of the political prisoners but no date for the release of German POWs.[21] "The details of [the Germans' release]," the contract stated, "cannot be fixed by the present accord and will be specified subsequently with the agreement of the Red Cross." Choltitz agreed to the contract immediately.[22]

Within days, over three thousand prisoners were freed in Greater Paris.[23] At Fresnes, the operation was a great success, with one exception. A young woman refused to leave her cell. Guards had earlier announced the execution of twenty-five prisoners, so she thought her time had come.[24] She clung to her cell as her liberators tried to coax her out.[25] At Romainville, early efforts failed. The camp's commander, Major Achenbach, claimed that it was outside Choltitz's jurisdiction, and he added that the orders of all German generals in Paris were worthless as they were involved in the July 20 plot.[26] When argument failed, Nordling and Bender responded with the one thing the SS understood: force. They returned with a member of Choltitz's staff, an Oberst Heigen. Heigen threatened to send Achenbach and his largely Georgian troops to the eastern front.[27] Achenbach backed down, insisting only on a written order from Choltitz, which Choltitz provided. Bender, Heigen, and Nordling were able to secure the prisoners' release, though not before the Georgian troops under Achenbach's command opened fire on them.[28] At Compiègne, Nordling and Bender failed to prevent a trainload of 850 prisoners from leaving, but a Wehrmacht general at Péronne, having received a copy of the contract, ordered the prisoners' release.[29] An earlier trainload from Compiègne had received no such last-minute reprieve: 1,800 prisoners were transported to Germany under intolerable conditions; several hundred died along the way.[30] Himmler himself overruled Choltitz and insisted that a further trainload of hundreds of prisoners from Fresnes be delivered to Germany.[31]

On August 18, as Nordling was negotiating prison releases, the key leaders of the resistance met to agree on a common strategy.[32] The Communists wanted a full-scale revolt, regardless of the human cost. "Two or three hundred thousand dead Parisians are of no consequence," one of them, possibly Rol, exclaimed.[33] The hard part would be securing the agreement of non-Communist, chiefly Gaullist resisters. Looking with a suspicious eye on the few men and arms that Rol could call his own, they were opposed. "You do not launch an insurrection with six hundred arms," remarked Léo Hamon.[34] Such a force was pitifully small for the liberation of the capital, but it was just large enough to provoke a "bloody and destructive" German reprisal.[35] As the Gaullists resisted, the Communists began to rant. They would do it with or without the Gaullists, and the consequences be damned.

In the middle of the argument, someone gave Parodi important news.[36] The police hoped to press home the advantage they gained in launching a strike on August 10 by seizing the Prefecture.[37] With this information, Parodi urged the Gaullists to come to his side. If the strike was to go ahead regardless, they had to join it in the hope that they could control it. Like any good negotiator, Parodi knew when to retreat, and he gave the operation his blessing. But he did not leave it at that. After the meeting, he sent a message to French General Marie-Pierre Kœnig: the Allies should be prepared to make a rush on Paris.[38] As he did, Model ordered that Paris be defended "at an unspecified blocking position," to which all available forces would be brought.[39]

On August 16, two days before Rol pushed through agreement to the insurrection, Herbert Eckelmann, Stadtkommissar for Paris (roughly, a deputy mayor), went with a French officer to Choltitz's headquarters at the Hotel Meurice. They, and the French resistance, had long known of explosives laid around the city. German engineers had knocked holes in the walls of power plants and prepared them to hold explosives; they had prepared central telephone exchanges, electricity works, gas installations, and even museums for destruction.[40] The Germans were to set off all these charges in the event of a German retreat.[41] The two appealed to Choltitz to spare the installations. After a few routine protests about the duty of a soldier and civilians' inability to understand military matters, Choltitz agreed with a condition. Feigning ignorance about the French resistance, he said there were "foreign elements" in the city. If the French could keep those elements in check, and be sure that "terrorists" did not occupy the installations, Choltitz would spare the gas, electricity, and telephone facilities. The German kept his word: he had the explosives removed from the power plants and gas installations and gave orders that the telephone exchanges be spared; only the military exchange would later be blown up.[42]

Two days after his meeting with the French, Choltitz received another order from Feldmarschall Walter Model, by then commander of both German High Command West and Army Group B: "Central Paris will be defended. All available forces are to be transferred to the city."[43] Army Group B sent a further order, to Choltitz and all troop formations around Paris: "the planned destruction and paralysis" should begin.[44]

AT 8:00 ON AUGUST 19, some two thousand police officers gathered on and around the great square in front of Notre Dame, which stands directly opposite the Prefecture.[45] They stood around aimlessly, for no one knew what to do. Then their leaders arrived in small trucks from which a few rifles and machine guns were distributed.[46] At 8:30, the men crossed the street to the Prefecture.[47] Someone knocked. A single sentry opened the door and saw two thousand men surging toward him. He put up no fight as they pushed him aside and scrambled into the building. With thousands of people crammed inside, the Prefecture felt more like an air-raid shelter than the seat of the most significant insurrection in France since 1848. To make matters worse, new groups of resisters, many of them young men, would periodically arrive and announce that *they* had seized the Prefecture.[48] The scene anticipated Monty Python, but, for the first time in four years, the French flag flew above Paris.[49] More importantly, it was the Gaullists, not the Communists, who made the decisive first strike. On August 17, Charles Luizet, a fierce Gaullist loyalist designated as the new prefect of the police, had arrived in Paris with the goal of blocking an uprising if he could, and of controlling it if he could not.[50] In the midst of all of this, a hapless German Unteroffizier walked across the parvis in front of Notre Dame and found himself arrested.[51]

To thin out the ranks and give the surplus men something to do, parties were ordered to cross the boulevard du Palais and to occupy neighbouring buildings: the Palais de Justice (home to the police courts, as well as the treasured Gothic glass chapel, the Sainte-Chapelle) and the Tribunal de Commerce.[52] Rol, who happened to cycle past and stopped when he heard the French national anthem being sung, was furious that he had not been informed of the mission and attempted to take charge.[53] Around 11:00, Rol and Luizet had what the official police record of the events calls a "veritable council of war."[54] Rol most likely yelled some more. In any case, the two of them went outside to meet Parodi in order to discuss "points of order" and "methods."[55] Whatever these were, the men were unable to relay them back to those in the Prefecture: shots fired from an unknown source cut them off from the entrance. Instead, Senator Edgar Pisani, whom Luizet had run into by chance and deputized on the spot, was in charge.[56] There in the Prefecture, with sandbags at windows and guns pointing toward Notre Dame, he waited with his men for the Germans.

Among the first to arrive—possibly the very first—was Arnim. Choltitz had earlier put through a call to the Prefecture. Amédée Bussière, the prefect of police who was confined to his office and who was desperately trying to position himself as an intermediary between the resistance and the Germans, assured the general that all was well.[57] Choltitz did not believe a word of it, and he sent Arnim in an open jeep with two sergeants to see what was going on.[58] The vehicle drove through the hot summer sun along the Seine, over the Île de la Cité past the Palais de Justice, and on toward Place Saint-Michel on the Left Bank.[59] The streets were almost entirely empty. Then, suddenly, the NCO next to Arnim screamed: a bullet had hit his upper arm. Arnim and the unwounded sergeant grabbed their machine pistols and fired back. Another bullet went through the wounded NCO's chest, spraying blood everywhere. Yet another bullet pierced one of the front tires. Arnim slapped the driver's back and shouted, "Drive! Drive!" Despite the blown-out tire, they sped to safety. Choltitz had his answer. He now needed to decide how to respond.

At 14:00, exactly one German military vehicle appeared in the boulevard du Palais behind the Prefecture while small numbers of infantrymen tried to sneak across the Petit Pont toward the parvis across from the front of the structure.[60] Machine-gun fire from the vehicle raked the Prefecture. It was war: the police on both sides of the building opened fire on the vehicles and infantrymen. Another vehicle, probably driving east along the Seine on the south side of the Prefecture, took a direct hit and exploded in flames. The Germans inside were killed, and the resisters were able to scurry out, recover some arms, and retreat to the relative safety of the Prefecture.[61]

The Germans then sent in tanks, but not many: only two lumbered into position.[62] At 14:30, one trained its turret on the southern wing of the building overlooking the Seine, while the other took up a position in front of Notre Dame.[63] The second tank fired a single shell.[64] It exploded in the great archway in front of the Prefecture, tearing off half of the great door's left side and exposing the inner courtyard. The battle was almost over. The police panicked, and some men attempted to flee the building.[65] They were stopped, and calm was only restored, by Léo Hamon, who appealed for order.[66] It worked: a bus was wheeled over to block the shattered door, and sandbags were piled in to close the gap.[67] The event was a microcosm of French politics: while the Communists could bring thousands into the streets, the Gaullists could govern.

The resisters braced themselves for the next blow. It never came. The tanks withdrew. For the rest of the day, military vehicles and infantry engaged the Prefecture in a firefight. The boulevard du Palais was, as one early historian of the day put it, "like a shooting gallery, with Resistance riflemen pouring bullets into it from the Prefecture on one side and the Palais de Justice on the other."[68] Yet most Parisians had little if any idea of what was going on near Notre Dame, and even the Germans themselves continued to stumble ignorantly into the fight. At 14:40, almost three-quarters of an hour into the worst fighting the capital had seen since 1940, a tanker truck filled with 5000 litres of highly explosive liquid drove right into the middle of it. But the truck did not explode. The resisters captured it and thereby secured a large supply of fuel for their Molotov cocktails. At 15:15, the Germans launched a second attack on the Prefecture. The fighting was relatively severe: three military vehicles destroyed, six German soldiers killed, and another four taken prisoner.[69]

While this was going on, three SS officers pulled up to the Hotel Meurice in an armoured vehicle. Arnim greeted them and took them up to see Choltitz.[70] They told him that the Führer had sent them to "secure" the Bayeux Tapestry, stored in the cellars of the Louvre, by taking it back to Germany.[71] Choltitz had been expecting them: Oberg had called him the night before about the tapestry, saying he would send trucks over to retrieve it.[72] Before they arrived, Choltitz had agreed with the German army's art curator—previously the director of the Goethe Museum archives in Weimar—that they would "lose" the keys to the Louvre.[73] As the SS men stood in Choltitz's office, bullets from the museum were flying across the Tuileries. Anyone seeking the tapestry would have to take them out first. Promising a machine gun and a tommy, Choltitz remarked: "Surely, you'll manage to fetch the tapestry from the cellar; it's a trifling job . . . [for] the Führer's best soldiers."[74] After a two-hour attempt to sum up the courage, the SS men, declaring the tapestry no longer in the Louvre, withdrew.[75]

Back in the Prefecture, the resisters fought bravely, and the relative safety of the building's solid stone walls—which were unlikely to be penetrated given the Germans' reluctance to fire shells—meant they imposed more losses on the Germans than they themselves sustained. A few German soldiers were cut down in the streets, and passing vehicles were ambushed. But their position was an essentially defensive one, and the overall military plan did not extend much beyond holding the building; the resisters hoped, at that moment against the odds, that the Allies would not bypass Paris.

By the early evening, the steady spray of bullets against the Prefecture was wearing its occupants down. The Germans were unwilling or unable (most likely, whatever patriotic histories suggest, the former) to force the insurgents out of the Prefecture. But by the end of the day, the insurrectionists were short on ammunition and morale.[76]

And they were getting on Choltitz's nerves. Even more ominously, they were testing patience in Berlin. When Hitler heard of the insurgency, he ordered the "ruthless defence of Paris."[77] German High Command knew it lacked the means to contain millions of people in revolt, and was convinced that the best way to prevent a large-scale insurgency was to crack down brutally on any manifestation of opposition.[78] However limited the military means at Choltitz's disposal were, blasting the resisters out of the Prefecture was certainly within his capabilities. A few more tanks armed with proper shells could blow large holes in the building, wrecking the structure and the morale of the men inside—after all, a single shell had almost sent two thousand men scurrying. But above all, an air attack before the assault could take care of most of the resistance. Luftflotte 3 (Air Fleet 3 of the Luftwaffe), responsible for northern France, had only had about 150 fighter-bombers at its disposal, but that was more than enough to destroy a neighbourhood (recall that eight hundred bombers could destroy an entire city). The Americans had air superiority, but a night attack could allow the Germans to dodge any American fighters, who themselves had no stomach for a dogfight over Paris. The Luftwaffe, for its part, was keen to launch such a night raid.[79]

Choltitz was at least tempted. Seeking perhaps absolution, he spoke with Nordling. "I was told," Choltitz said, "that Parisians were terrorists. I saw them as peace-loving [*paisable*]. . . . I released prisoners, and what happened? Terrorists took the Prefecture, and they are shooting just under my windows. The French are impossible! I have to maintain order, and I will maintain order. I will destroy the Prefecture."[80] His tone then switched from the bellicose to the melancholy: "I was at Stalingrad. Since then, I have done nothing but manoeuvre to avoid encirclement. Retreat after retreat, defeat after defeat. And here I am now in Paris. What will happen to this marvellous city?"[81] As Choltitz seemed to weaken, Nordling jumped in: "If you destroy the Prefecture, you will also destroy Notre Dame and the

Sainte-Chapelle . . . and to what end?"[82] The insurrection, he continued ingeniously, was against Vichy rather than the Germans.[83] He urged the general to imagine future historians writing about the German devastation of Paris, or even the transformation of some of its monuments to dust.[84] Choltitz, standing with a view of the Tuileries, the Louvre, and the banks of the Seine, was moved. "If there were only leaders [*chefs*] among the insurgents, we could find a modus vivendi, but with whom am I supposed to negotiate?" Choltitz had agreed to nothing, but he had admitted the possibility of negotiations; it was enough for Nordling.[85]

As Nordling returned to his offices at 18:00, German tanks returned to the Prefecture. An hour and a half later, someone inside it made a phone call. All the senior figure resisters would later disclaim responsibility for it, but one of them requested a "suspension of arms."[86] Nordling put the idea to Bender, who in turn passed to Nordling information about German defence points across the city.[87] Displaying the dexterity behooving a secret service agent, Bender slipped through Paris's dangerous streets back to the Hotel Meurice, where he impressed upon Choltitz the danger of launching another attack on the Prefecture.[88] There is some debate on what happened next. Choltitz later denied ever agreeing to a formal ceasefire, and Nordling may well have played the two sides off each other, suggesting to Choltitz that the resisters wanted a ceasefire and vice versa.[89] In any case, when Nordling told the resisters of a ceasefire offer, he knew how to frame the proposal, embellishing the offer and flattering the resisters' newfound sense of soldierly prowess.[90] Choltitz, Nordling told them at 20:30, "was ready to recognize the combatants in the Police Prefecture as the civil authorities responsible for Paris, to treat those captured as prisoners of war, to respect all the local occupied administrations, and to aid in supplying food and water to Paris, all on the condition that a truce was respected."[91] They had thirty minutes to think about it.

The truce offer was a godsend for the resisters. They had at their disposal thirty-nine automatic weapons, a few dozen pistols, and only an hour's worth of ammunition left.[92] The German army was being reinforced, albeit weakly: Model made available two battalions of the Sixth Parachute Division to Paris along with two mobile artillery units, and the Ninth Panzer Division was ordered to reconstitute itself in the Paris area.[93] The resisters may have been unaware of the details of these reinforcements, but they were fearfully aware that SS soldiers were on their way to the city.[94] Pierre Taittinger, president of the Paris Municipal Council under Vichy, tried to direct the negotiations, but he was by this point irrelevant. The most important conversations occurred between the Gaullist Hamon, who urged that the truce spare Paris unnecessary destruction, and Nordling.[95] The argument that won over the Gaullists Hamon, Roland Pré, and Chaban-Delmas was one of time: a truce would allow them to regroup and gather more arms.[96] Rol-Tanguy remained adamantly opposed, but by approximately 21:00, the majority of resisters had agreed to a truce — in principle.[97] The question was how to work it out in practice. Doing so would take much time and never fully succeed. But for the moment, a beautiful corner of an exceedingly beautiful city had been saved.

IF THE COMMUNISTS WERE concerned with barricades, the Gaullists were concerned with buildings: they wanted to be sure that city hall and the main ministries were occupied by men loyal to de Gaulle.[98] At 5:00 on the morning of August 20, 1944, Léo Hamon, who had steeled nerves after the Germans attacked the Prefecture, took advantage of the truce and led seventy-five police officers (*gardiens de la paix* — police officers on the beat), twenty-five men of the Gaullist delegation's *corps francs*, twenty-five female auxiliaries, and twenty-five FFI to the Hôtel de Ville.[99] Taittinger was waiting for them. Three days earlier, Taittinger, as ever trying to make himself relevant, worked feverishly with Nordling to try to have Paris declared an open city; the two men contacted consuls general from the neutral states of Switzerland and Spain, urging them to place pressure on the German authorities.[100] Hamon would not reward Taittinger's efforts. At gunpoint, five FFIs arrested Taittinger, while Hamon himself went on to arrest the prefect of the Seine, René Bouffet. Bouffet was not in his office when Hamon arrived. Hamon decided to make a dramatic gesture anyway. Hammering his fist on Bouffet's unoccupied desk, he announced, "In the name of the Parisian Liberation Committee and on behalf of the Provisional Government, I take possession of the Hôtel de Ville!" Pointing to a bust of

Pétain, he added: "Take that thing away! It's got no business here."[101] He then waited for Bouffet to return.

When the prefect returned, he was indignant. "Do you have any idea what you are doing?" Bouffet asked Hamon. "You are behaving like children. . . . I am working to save Paris, which the Germans are threatening to transform into fire and blood, and you start playing a game whose consequences could well be terrible."[102] Unmoved by Bouffet's warning, Hamon arrested him. FFI led Taittinger across to the Prefecture. The resistance, and above all the Gaullists, held the administrative heart of Paris—a city that politically, economically, intellectually, and culturally dominates the country of which it is the capital.[103] Under the cover of the truce, the Gaullists would go on to occupy the ministries of the interior, finance, labour, and health.[104] While Rol-Tanguy and his men wasted lives on an unnecessary street battle, the Gaullists quietly slipped into power. It was a coup within a coup.

The truce that would serve the French so well was, however, showing cracks even before its details were worked out. In the hours before the terms of the truce could be agreed, dozens if not hundreds of skirmishes broke out across the city. At 8:00, FFI combatants opened fire on a group of Germans at Sully-Morland, killing three, wounding five, and taking one prisoner.[105] The same group attacked German barges on the Seine, killing four Germans; return fire shot one of the resisters through the heart, killing him instantly.[106]

As the morning wore on, more and more Frenchmen joined the fight. They were often boys, no more than eighteen or so, for whom the romantic appeal of the street battle was irresistible. For many, perhaps most, this final act of violent resistance against the Germans was sincere. But for others, youthful vigour, testosterone, a very human desire to be part of something bigger than themselves—and likely a little alcohol—played their customary roles. They returned home for supper that night, tired, dirty, and reticent about what they had done that day. "Where have you been and what have you been up to?" anxious parents asked. The boy would reply evasively: "Oh, nothing really."[107]

As ever in war, there were many scenes of horror for all those involved. Most have been forgotten, as if they never happened. But some were recorded. One involved five unknown French boys who were tasked with searching a car for arms. They were warned to avoid the rue la Fayette, as the Germans were covering it. On the way to the car, they followed the instructions; on the way back they did not. Trying to make time, they rushed across the street. The Germans opened fire. As the boys lay bleeding on the ground, the Germans stomped on them until they were dead. Only one managed to escape to tell the tale.[108]

Another man involved was destined to become France's most famous postwar philosopher. Jean-Paul Sartre had joined the street fighters for reasons that remain disputed to this day. In a later article in *Combat*, he recorded what he saw from the barricades: resisters spraying a passing German truck with bullets. It veered dangerously down the street and crashed into a shop-front, exploding instantly in flames. As the FFI approached the truck, the flames climbed up its driver, slowly burning him to death. His agonized cries filled the street: "Comrades!" (in German), "Mercy, mercy!" (in French). The enemy's suffering provoked contrasting human reactions that neither history, nor philosophy, nor psychology is ever able to explain. Some FFI enjoyed his tortures: "Let him roast like the pig he is," they remarked. Others took pity. One FFI moved as close to the vehicle as the ever-rising heat would allow. He took aim through the inferno and fired directly into the driver's seat. The cries stopped.[109]

While gunfire filled the streets, three resisters—the Gaullists Jacques Chaban-Delmas, Roland Pré, and Léo Hamon—met Nordling and the Germans. Nordling acted in his customary role as intermediary between the French and the Germans, and by noon or so, a truce had been hammered out. According to it:

- troops would be evacuated by the outer boulevards, avoiding the centre of Paris;
- the FFI were soldiers to be treated according to the laws of war;
- the Germans accepted the occupation of the Prefecture, the Hôtel de Ville, the suburban town halls, and would neither attack nor interfere with personnel occupying them; and
- the FFI would not attack Germans within their strongholds and headquarters.[110]

At 14:00, members of the Gaullist resistance drove through the streets of Paris circulating the following notice: "In light of the German High Command's agreement to refrain from attacking public buildings occupied by French troops and to treat French prisoners in accordance with the laws of war, the Provisional Government of the French Republic and the National Committee of Liberation ask you to cease firing on the occupier until Paris has been entirely evacuated. The greatest calm is recommended, and the population is urged to avoid the streets."[111]

Choltitz refused to announce the truce by radio because he did not want news of it, and the willingness to surrender that it implied, to get back to Berlin.[112] Instead, French police cars and German military vehicles drove through the city and announced the truce from loudspeakers.[113] A communiqué also went out from the Police Prefecture ordering, on behalf of the Provisional Government of the French Republic and the National Resistance Committee (both Gaullist organizations), a suspension of arms.[114] Parisians welcomed the truce openly and warmly: they rolled out French flags, danced in the streets, and even protected a German vehicle under attack at Aubervilliers.[115]

The joy was short-lived. The Communists reacted to the truce with contempt and the fighting continued unabated. On August 20, resisters in the seventeenth arrondissement, in the northwest of the city, near the Arc de Triomphe, held the town hall (*mairie*). At 16:30, German tanks opened fire.[116] Fifteen minutes later, a similar scene played out on the opposite end of town, in the twentieth arrondissement (home to the famous Père Lachaise cemetery): German tanks sprayed the town hall with bullets. In other parts of the city, the roles were reversed. German soldiers had set up positions in the "Central Gutenberg," the centre of the capital's telephone network right in the heart of Paris, not far from the Louvre and closer still to Les Halles. Under fire from the FFI, the pinned Germans refused to surrender and turned the building into a hostage: if the siege continued, they would set it on fire. It is not clear why these skirmishes started. Some attacks may have been deliberate; others likely occurred when trigger-happy Germans or French misread the local situation and opened fire. But in any case, the shooting continued. Over the next several hours, the pattern continued. German tanks and foot soldiers fired on occupied buildings and set up defensive positions for themselves in others. Paris was sprayed with bullets.[117]

Bullets—but not shells. A point that can be lost in these details is the relative restraint with which the German attacks were conducted.[118] With the exception of the single shell fired on the Prefecture (shattering the left side of its great door and the insurrectionists' nerves with it), they responded only with small-arms fire.[119] Though deadly for people, bullets cause little lasting damage to buildings or infrastructure.

Paris was, moreover, nothing like a city under siege: stores were open, and people strolled through the streets and sat in cafés.[120] The question on everyone's mind was whether the Germans would continue to show such restraint over the coming days. On August 20, another order arrived from Hitler: "the Paris bridgehead (with a switch line along the Seine across Paris) [is] to be held at all costs, if necessary without regard to the destruction of the city."[121] The question was of particular concern to the Gaullists, who watched with dread as the Communists did everything they could to provoke the Germans.

CHAPTER 9

PARIS IN REVOLT

T HE BARRICADES, and the street more generally, enjoy a prominent place in the French memory. Erected throughout Paris during the revolutions of 1789 and 1848, barricades have both enabled and nostalgized a tendency by the French people for mass protest in the streets. Inspiration was found specifically in the Spanish Civil War, but given this intellectual and cultural background, it was inevitable — or "overdetermined" as professors like to say — that barricades would once again spring up throughout the streets of Paris in August 1944.[1]

They did so on the morning of August 21. Prodded on by Communist leaflets, Parisians took to the streets. They began cutting down trees and digging up cobblestones. They piled sandbags and pushed trucks without gasoline into the streets. On Rol-Tanguy's instructions, the trucks were filled with cobblestones.[2] Trees, parapets from the quay, and tram tracks were piled up, creating a barricade.[3] Armed resisters then set up positions behind them, waiting for unsuspecting Germans to come by. A particularly robust barricade was set up in front of the fountain on Place Saint-Michel, but they also appeared along the quays and at multiple, not always strategically comprehensible points across the city.[4] They served, it must be said, no useful military purpose. A single 88 mm shell could have destroyed the most solid among them.[5] But that did not really matter. The barricades held symbolic value and encouraged Parisians of all ages to take part in winning back their city all the while creating the impression that the resistance controlled the streets.

At first, it went well. As Parisians became aware that resistance did not mean sudden death, the ranks of resisters started to swell by the hour. More and more people joined existing barricades, and others set up new ones. In the Prefecture, the atmosphere was almost festive: cooks prepared meals with food requisitioned daily from the marketplace at Les Halles, and access to the building was so safe that people would come by throughout the day looking for something to eat. Even the combatants' perpetual shortage of ammmunition appeared to improve: that morning, an expedition set out for the sixteenth arrondissement and returned with three tons of ammunition, mostly grenades and bullets.[6] But for those who wished to see them, there were signs that not all was well.

The first of these appeared in the afternoon. Brimming with youthful confidence, a troop of FFI set out to free French prisoners detained at one of the most important German positions in the city: the Hotel Continental, across the street from the Hotel Meurice and connected to it by an underground passage.[7] The Germans easily repulsed them; the hotel, the French noted, was "seriously protected."[8] That should not have come as a surprise.

As the French resisters were retreating from the streets around the Tuileries, Choltitz decided once again to make a show of force. Irritated that the truce had been so consistently flouted, he sent out the tanks.[9] Germans at three positions in the city launched separate attacks at exactly 11:45. In the seventeenth arrondissement, tanks opened fire on a public building. On the avenue d'Italie, five tanks fired on a crowd, but it is not clear if there were any casualties as a result.[10] Finally, on the Pont au Double, infantry or tanks or both opened fire on a group of French police, injuring seven men.[11]

These attacks may not have been coordinated, but their simultaneity showed that the Germans meant business at least to some extent. And they continued to do so. At 12:40, the Germans launched an assault on the Charonne post office in the twentieth arrondissement.[12] Within forty minutes, all French resistance had been overcome, several policemen were dead, and the post office was in German hands. Several hours later, at 17:15, they launched their most determined attack of the day. Ten tanks

opened fire on the prominent barricade at Saint-Michel.[13] In the heart
of the city, it blocked one of the main access points to the Île de la Cité
and the Prefecture. Frantically calling on support, the French were able
to hold out.

In doing so, they set the pattern that would prevail over the next day.
The Germans' success in the twentieth arrondissement would not be followed up: they would launch attacks on French positions, including the
Prefecture, but they did not succeed in dislodging any of them.[14] There
were, unsurprisingly, acts of cruel brutality: shortly before the failed attack
on the Prefecture on August 21, a German tank crew picked up a *gardien*.
Possibly acting on their own orders, they tortured him to extract information
about the defences in and around the Prefecture and then killed him.[15] Yet
there were also acts of kindness. Despite their losses, the French responded
with soldierly grace when the Germans requested to retrieve their fallen
soldiers from the area around the Panthéon.[16] It might have been a sense
of magnanimity in victory that inspired French accord, for things seemed
to be going their way. Over the course of the twenty-second, the Germans
abandoned a number of positions across the city, leaving the French large
stores—over two tons in one case—of ammunition.[17] The resisters in the
Prefecture, looking back on the day, concluded that it had been a "good"
one for the resistance.[18] Such confidence (or hubris—the two are never far
apart) inspired them to issue a further call to arms at 15:40, which was broadcast though loudspeakers mounted atop vehicles: "The Commanders of the
FFI and the Provisional Government of the Republic call on the population of Paris to make every possible effort [to resist the Germans]. Impede
the movement of armoured vehicles throughout the city and immediately
reinforce the barricades. As in 1830, as in 1848, protect the renaissance of
the French republic, and the Parisian way of life."[19]

CHOLTITZ SURVEYED THE EVENTS of August 21 and 22 from his
comfortable rooms in the Hotel Meurice. They gave him no reason to
be sanguine. As attacks on his troops multiplied, the pressure from Berlin
ratcheted up once more. At 17:45 on the twenty-first, he received an order
to "come down brutally on the FFI in Paris."[20] "The battle in Paris," OKW

ordered, "must be conducted mercilessly, and the city's bridges are to be blown up."[21] Another, even clearer order from Hitler followed on August 22: "Paris is to become a heap of rubble. The commanding general is to defend the city to the last man, and, if necessary, to go down with the city."[22] Choltitz replied that he had only two battalions to defend Paris—an understatement or outright lie—and he requested the transfer of a military police division and artillery to the capital.[23] Model replied, as he had to Hitler, that no troops could be sent. The type of unit Choltitz requested was not a coincidence: military police were trained to keep order, prevent panic, and round up deserters. They were neither regular soldiers trained in defence nor engineers trained in demolition. Army Group B instead ordered an engineer (*Pionier*) battalion and an artillery battalion into the city, though even Model thought that not all of Paris's bridges could be destroyed.[24]

Yet another group in Paris made trouble for both Choltitz and the FFI: the SS. There were several thousand SS troops in the city, and they were hardly under Choltitz's control, even at the best of times. Indeed, they treated the truce with a contempt not unlike that of the Communists.[25] As the situation in the capital deteriorated, they acted increasingly as a force unto themselves.

Sometimes they used terror. Just before 11:00 on August 21, around a hundred SS soldiers occupied the Lycée Lakanal. They took four Jewish hostages and threatened to execute them if there were any incidents in the street.[26] That evening, just after 18:00, French resisters reported ten times that number—a thousand SS soldiers—in the area between the Pont de la Folie in Bobigny (northeast Paris outside the ring road) and the Porte de la Villette (in the nineteenth arrondissement); they sprayed machine-gun fire.[27]

More often they resorted to murder. On August 16, the SS killed thirty-five resisters in the Bois de Boulogne; most were young and the majority from the FFI, though members of other resistance organizations were among the dead.[28] Five days later, just before 15:00, German (most likely SS) troops picked up six police officers who had been arrested earlier in the day on the boulevard des Invalides and drove them to the École Militaire to be shot.[29] The resisters sent men to rescue them, but to no avail: their bodies were exhumed a week later.

It is pointless to rank them in this respect, but one case was particularly brutal. Early on in the insurrection, the SS arrested eight police officers. They held the arrestees against a wall and acted as if they were about to execute them—but that would have been too quick. The SS lowered the men's arms and forced them into a truck. The truck took them to Vincennes, where a second simulated execution took place. The next day, the SS forced the men to view the mutilated bodies of eleven comrades. They had been tortured to death; flesh was hanging from the corpses' limbs, and their chests were smashed in (*défoncé*). The SS then performed yet another mock execution. The Germans then forced the men to carry heavy stones and beams under the hot sun until they collapsed with exhaustion. Finally, ignoring their pleas for mercy, the SS forced them to dig their own graves, and then murdered them. The sadism had lasted a full five days. When their bodies were eventually exhumed, the evidence of their final torture was clear: bruises, distended eyes, and flayed hands.[30]

MARAUDING SS WERE NOT the only units beyond Choltitz's control. On the morning of August 23, a German column made up of two armoured cars, three tanks, two flat wagons, and thirty other vehicles made their way past the Arc de Triomphe, down the Champs-Élysées, and toward one of Paris's most famous buildings: the Grand Palais, a vast exhibition hall with a great, glass-domed roof built for the Universal Exhibition of 1900.[31] The column, which was not under Choltitz's command, had heard of the truce and was attempting to pass through the city.[32] When the troops reached the Grand Palais, French police opened fire from an adjacent position, killing one German soldier.[33] The Germans responded not merely with gunfire but by preparing two small, toy-like tanks. They looked almost harmless: four feet long, two feet wide, and one foot high.[34] They were in fact Goliath tracked mines, containing some fifty kilograms of explosives. Around 10:30, operated by a remote-controlled device, the little "toy" tanks approached the Palais.[35]

The building exploded. The great glass roof shattered instantly, and shards showered down on anyone below.[36] For blocks around the structure, buildings shook, and the sound of the explosion echoed across Paris. In the

Palais, lions, tigers, and horses—all being kept there by a would-be Swedish profiteer planning a celebratory circus for after the liberation—joined a band of prostitutes—imprisoned there by the police—in an attempt to escape. Screaming lions and screaming prostitutes ran through the building.[37] Outside, the Germans surrounded the structure and waited.[38] A column of black smoke rose slowly up into the Paris sky.[39] By 11:25, the building was burning on all sides. The Paris firemen attempted to reach it, but the Germans blocked them until it was too late.[40] By 11:55, it was all over: led by the police commissariat's only German prisoner, a "dignified little baron," forty policemen came out, holding a white flag.[41] The German officer delivered them to Choltitz, who agreed to treat them as regular prisoners of war.[42] This show of force gave the French resistance the first real shock of the past four days, and it demonstrated the capabilities of a German general less inclined to tolerate the insurgency.

Less tolerance, to put it no more strongly, was of course precisely what Hitler wanted. On the morning of the Grand Palais attack, Hitler issued his firmest order yet: "[The] defense of Paris is of decisive military and political significance. Its loss would tear open [the] whole coastal front north of [the] Seine and deprive Germany of bases for very long-range warfare. Defense [is] to be conducted from [a] blocking belt in front of the city . . . The sharpest measures to quell [the] insurrection inside the city must be taken. Never, or at any rate only as a heap of rubble, may Paris fall into Allied hands."[43]

Other German officers were glad to help. The same day, Luftwaffe Generaloberst Otto Deßloch, commander of Luftflotte 3, telephoned Choltitz. He had orders, Deßloch told Choltitz, to bomb Paris, and he intended to use his fleet. Choltitz, arguing that his troops would otherwise be at risk, insisted that the attack take place by day. Deßloch argued that the attack could only take place at night, citing Allied fighters around Paris. As Choltitz knew all too well, given poor visibility, night raids by a few hundred airplanes could inflict substantial damage, particularly if the wind cooperated in creating large fires in a city made up of narrow streets. He therefore played his last card: if the Luftwaffe bombed the city, Choltitz would pull his troops out of any bombed areas and place blame on the Luftwaffe for compelling the retreat. Deßloch backed down, and the raid was called off.[44]

Deßloch's offer was not the only support refused by Choltitz. A week earlier, Army Group B approved a request for Panzer Lehr Division to be prepared to divert troops into Paris in the event of an uprising.[45] High Command also ordered General der Infanterie Erwin Vierow, Commander of North-West France, to ready his forces for the defence of Paris. Another commander offered a platoon of tanks to reinforce Paris's defences.[46] Choltitz declined all these offers, and he informed OB West that he personally would ensure order in Paris (*"hat die Aufrechterhaltung der Ordnung in Paris selbst übertragen erhalten"*).[47]

Choltitz also left the right paper trails. According to the *Lagebericht* (status report) of Army Group B, "local resistance that has flamed up [*örtlich aufflammender Widerstand*] has thus far been brutally crushed."[48] This could be nothing but a deliberate exaggeration, and it was part of a pattern. A few days earlier, as Rol-Tanguy was ordering Parisians to the barricades, Choltitz called Generalleutnant Hans Speidel, who had served as chief of staff to Rommel, Kluge, and now Model. Choltitz planned, he told Speidel, to blow up the Eiffel Tower, the Arc de Triomphe, and the Opéra, among other landmarks. A few weeks before, the two men had agreed that Hitler was deranged; the conversation was a ruse to fool the Gestapo wire tappers.[49]

At the same time that he let Berlin know how much he was doing, Choltitz told those closer to him — including Feldmarschall Walter Model on the western front — the opposite: there was nothing he could do. "For days," he replied on August 23 in direct response to Hitler's order to destroy Paris, "the mob has ruled this city, and my men have suffered great losses. We do not have the forces to put down this resistance. Terrorists have occupied the Louvre. The Grand Palais is burning. From the twenty-fifth, there will be no more food supplies."[50] Choltitz failed to mention that German forces, not "terrorists," had set the Grand Palais alight. He noted on the same day that he had written to General Günther Blumentritt of Chief of General Staff, OB West. Probably because he expressed such early sympathy for Stauffenberg and Stülpnagel, Blumentritt was now and would remain a firmly obedient commander ready to expend the last drop of blood in fighting the Allies. Choltitz told Blumentritt that he could not guarantee the general's passage into the city, as barricades in the city's outer districts made this impossible.[51]

And this, in turn, meant that he could not follow precisely the Führer's order: "The police are loyal [!], but powerless. Supplying the defence strongholds and the outer quartiers is barely possible anymore. There's shooting everywhere."[52] This was hardly an accurate description of the stalemate that had developed in Paris. In many parts of the city, people could have been forgiven for thinking that nothing was happening. Choltitz continued: "The shootings and other retaliatory actions called for by the Führer can no longer be implemented. In order to blow up bridges, we need to battle our way to them; in the case of 75 bridges, this is no longer possible. Any such measure could drive the majority of the still-passive population into the hands of the enemy."[53] The number seventy-five was carefully selected, as Berlin had ordered Choltitz to blow up seventy-two of Paris's bridges.[54] All of these claims were lies, or at least terrific exaggerations: Paris was not a battlefield, the resistance controlled nothing like seventy-five bridges, and the population's horrified but largely passive reaction to the destruction of the Grand Palais hardly suggested that it was made up of armed resisters-in-waiting. And Choltitz seems not to have mentioned the large store of explosives within easy reach. The Kriegsmarine had a large torpedo depot near Paris in Saint-Cloud to support the navy bases on the French coast, and it possessed enough explosives to inflict some serious damage. Boineburg had refused to deploy them. Choltitz lacked the engineers to prepare them, and he made no effort to acquire any.[55]

As much as Choltitz deceived Berlin, and as moderate as he was in his reaction to the FFI, Paris could not be liberated until he surrendered.[56] And he refused to surrender to the "terrorists". Nordling knew this all too well and decided to get in touch with the FFI again. Aware that Choltitz had no intention of evacuating the city, Nordling called Parodi and urged him to meet in order to discuss the modalities of a German evacuation. On August 23, Parodi sent a young finance inspector named Colonel Cruse to meet, with or without Choltitz's knowledge, Emil Bender at the Swiss consulate.[57]

At first, Bender stalled for time. He held meandering conversations with Cruse throughout Wednesday night and into Thursday, all the while hoping that Nordling would return with definitive news of Allied move-ments. When he did not, Bender had to come to the point: all the German garrisons in the city would defend themselves. The outcome of a battle with the Allies was not in doubt, but the road to it could still be cluttered with many bodies. He decided to tell Cruse the truth: "General von Choltitz cannot capitulate without an exchange of fire. His family is threatened; they are hostages to Hitler. He is a soldier bound by the requirements of military honour. He simply cannot surrender without a fight."[58] Bender stopped. He hesitated. Then, fighting back tears, he decided to commit treason. "So, it's necessary for you to fight. But why attack on all sides? The key to Paris's defences is the Hotel Meurice where the General is based. . . . The General will defend himself . . . [but] once he's defeated, all the other points of resistance will collapse."[59] It could not have been clearer: Choltitz would not surrender to the FFI; he would surrender only after a fight; and fighting him was the key to freeing Paris. Cruse had to get a message to General Jacques-Philippe Leclerc, head of the French Second Armoured Division.[60]

CHAPTER 10

PARIS LIBERATED, PARIS SPARED

A MERICAN OPPOSITION TO occupying Paris reflected two considerations. The first, already mentioned, was material: supplying the city
would starve the advance of the Western Allies' armies into Germany. The
second was political: the Americans suspected, rightly, that entering Paris
was about fighting a French civil war rather than an Allied-German war.
It was no secret that de Gaulle and the leading French general, Leclerc,
viewed a Communist takeover with horror. Added to all of this was a dispute
about the Allied chain of command. Major General Leonard T. Gerow,
commander of the American V Corps, believed correctly that Leclerc was
to take orders from him. Leclerc, backed up by de Gaulle, who had ignored
British orders and disembarked at Cherbourg, could not have cared less
what the Americans thought.

On August 21, Leclerc sent reconnaissance units numbering some one
hundred men to Paris; they were in fact intended to be the first Allied forces
in the city. When V Corps called about the movement, Leclerc's man on the
other end of the line denied there was any. The next day, Gerow personally
saw Repiton-Préneuf, the Second Division's chief of intelligence. Gerow
produced a note reminding Leclerc that his units were under American
command, ordered a recall of the reconnaissance units, and accused him
of "violating given orders." When Repiton, casting himself as a diplomat,
suggested that more moderate terms might be preferable, Gerow replied

that the language had nothing excessive in it.[1] De Gaulle, meanwhile, sent a letter to Leclerc to give his full support to the French general's disobedience: "I agree with your plan. We must make at least some contact with Paris without delay."[2] The always tense, sometimes explosive relationship between Gerow and Leclerc anticipated much in Franco-American relations after 1945.

Events soon overtook both Gerow's and broader American opposition to an assault on Paris. On August 22, as the truce between the Germans and the insurrectionists collapsed, Choltitz summoned Raoul Nordling and hinted that he should travel to the US side to urge the Americans to proceed to Paris as quickly as possible. He revealed that he had received orders from Hitler to destroy the city and would do so in a day or two or would otherwise likely be sacked.[3] Choltitz was exaggerating both his ability and willingness to destroy the city, but he hoped that doing so would bring the Allies in more quickly. Nordling suffered an ill-timed minor heart attack, but his brother, Rolf, led a delegation out of the city.[4] Choltitz refused to give Nordling a letter, for fear of leaving a paper trail for the SS, but he instructed Nordling to have any German troops denying them passage call the Hotel Meurice.[5] Choltitz also ordered Bender to accompany the Swede.[6] The emissaries first reached Lieutenant General George S. Patton but were sent by him on to Lieutenant General Omar N. Bradley.[7] (Patton had already received a similar appeal by Commander Roger Gallois, dispatched by Rol-Tanguy.)[8]

As it happened, Eisenhower was already softening his stance against taking the city after hearing exaggerated stories of four to five thousand children and old people dying daily and of the metro and sewage systems being mined.[9] This might have accurately described Warsaw in August 1944 but not Paris, even if Parisians were unquestionably suffering. By the time Nordling told Bradley of conditions in the capital and of Choltitz's willingness to cooperate with the Allies, Eisenhower had largely made up his mind. "What the hell, Brad," he said, "I guess we'll have to go in."[10] The Americans decided to allow a French division to enter the city first, though apparently one without any black troops. At 19:30, Bradley gave the news to Leclerc. "Well, you win," the American general said. "They've decided to send you to Paris."[11] Leclerc had of course already sent forces toward the capital, but now the full strength of the Second Armoured Division could be put into action.

The Second Division marched on Paris from the southwest, approaching from the village of Sées, moving toward Rambouillet, and cutting up from there into the capital itself.[12] For the assault on the city, Leclerc assigned the job to two of his three tactical groups: Tactical Group T under Colonel Paul de Langlade and Tactical Group V under Colonel Pierre Billotte.

In executing his move on Paris, Leclerc once again ignored Gerow's instructions. Gerow had specified western Paris—the Eiffel Tower, the sixteenth arrondissement across the Seine, and the industrial areas farther west—as the focus of the attack. This plan possibly reflected the very American idea that the Eiffel Tower is the centre of Paris.[13] In any case, Leclerc chose a better route into the city: Billotte's column would approach through the Porte d'Orléans on the southern edge of Paris, while Langlade's would move on the Porte de Saint-Cloud on its southwestern periphery. The two would converge on the Place de la Concorde, from where the rue de Rivoli could be followed directly to the Hotel Meurice. They did not in fact follow this exact route, but the Hotel Meurice and surrounding area remained the target.

Before moving into Paris, both Billotte and Langlade split their groups into two, creating smaller forces that could take advantage of Paris's back streets. The plan was to bypass the various strongholds within the city: Luftwaffe headquarters at the Palais du Luxembourg, the army Kommandantur at Place de l'Opéra, the Senate, the Chamber of Deputies, and the École Militaire. Instead, the division would move directly on the Hotel Meurice. Once Choltitz was neutralized, German resistance elsewhere would, they hoped, melt away. Gaullist resisters, it will be recalled, had already seized the Hôtel de Ville and the buildings of key French ministries. Following the split, Billotte's tactical group divided into forces under Lieutenant Colonel Joseph Putz and Colonel Louis Warabiot.[14] Langlade's tactical group split into two task forces headed by Lieutenant Colonel Pierre Minjonnet and Lieutenant Colonel Jacques Massu (who would later admit to systematic torture in Algeria).

Gerow urged a later departure, but Leclerc again ignored him. Leclerc's forces left the forest at Rambouillet at 6:30 on August 24. Billotte's

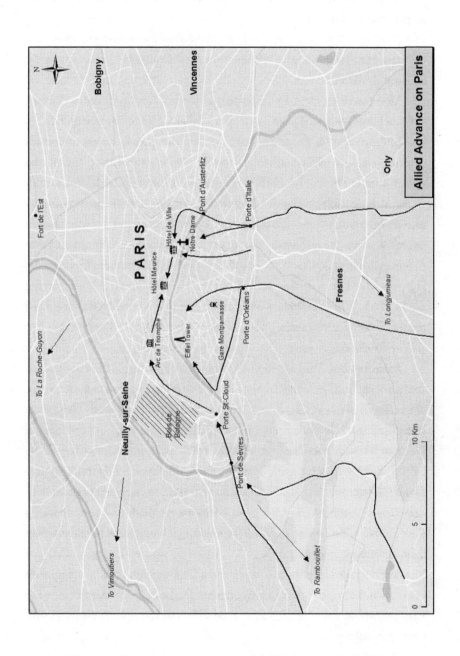

Allied Advance on Paris

two columns moved directly north into Paris, while Langlade's moved west toward the Pont de Sèvres, on Paris's western edge. Colonel Putz, leading one of the two forces under Tactical Group V, moved forward along the Orléans road in the lead. Putz encountered the first serious resistance at Longjumeau.[15]

After moving out of Longjumeau, Putz led the forces up to Antony, just over a mile to the southwest of Fresnes. In order to avoid fighting within the capital itself, Boineburg had concentrated the most important defences outside the city, creating a battle group under the newly promoted Generalmajor der Reserve Hubertus von Aulock.[16] As they did, Choltitz sent out the first of a series of orders designed to give the impression of ceaseless activity when, in fact, he was doing little more than waiting for the Allies to arrive. At noon on the twenty-fourth, Choltitz reported that his enemy was making strong advances to the southwest of the city despite all manpower at his disposal being deployed; he declared that he nonetheless was staying put in Paris.[17] Choltitz presumably hoped that this formulation would later provide cover for his failure to implement the Führer's orders on defence and destruction of the city.

It was against Aulock's forces, rather than anything within Paris, that the Second Division faced the greatest opposition. The flak batteries at the prison in Fresnes, and ten kilometres to the east on the edge of Orly, were particularly well defended. It took Putz until 18:00 on August 24 to clear the German forces at Fresnes. The inmates were imprisoned German soldiers, but this did not prevent them from fighting well. Indeed, their tenacity and canvas prison uniforms led desert veterans of the Second Division to believe that they were members of Rommel's Afrikakorps.[18] After Fresnes and Orly were secured, Putz opted to spend the night in Antony, near Fresnes, rather than advancing into the capital.[19]

As French forces were pushing toward Orly on August 24, another order came through from Berlin: German signals installations in the city were to be blown up with "no heed . . . paid to buildings in the vicinity."[20] The same day, and possibly in direct response to this order, Choltitz assured Blumentritt of his will to fight on: I want to emphasize "how serious the situation in Paris becomes with every passing hour. . . . [I nonetheless] wish to use the remaining strength of Aulock's forces, make a push for the east, establish contact with [German] troops and above all to receive instructions on how to fight on."[21] This was all nonsense; Choltitz had long given up. The only reply from Berlin was a reaffirmation of the order to defend Paris at all costs.[22]

As Billotte's men prepared to bed down outside Paris, Gerow was furious. He had not forgiven Leclerc for ignoring his orders, and he now suspected the French general of dawdling his way into Paris in order to enjoy the adoration of the civilian population. This was not the case: Leclerc was desperate to seize Paris.[23] But the delay inspired Bradley, who also wanted troops in the city, to order Gerow in. "To hell with prestige," he is said to have told his chief of staff, General Lev Allen, "tell the 4th to slam on it and take the liberation."

As it happened, neither Americans nor French but, rather, Spaniards would be the first into Paris. General Leclerc shared Gerow's frustration with the slow advance on the capital, but he was determined to get French troops into it first. He first sent a message to central Paris via a reconnaissance plane: "Hang on, we're coming."[24] He then ordered the Ninth Company, serving under Putz and Billotte, to make a dash for the city. Leclerc held the company commander, Captain Raymond Dronne, in particularly high regard.[25] As Billotte's Tactical Group V prepared to stay the night at Antony, Leclerc ordered Dronne into the city. "Slip straight into Paris," he told the ruffled and unshaven Dronne, "to the very heart of Paris!"[26]

Dronne's hastily organized column, backed up by a platoon of Gaullist loyalists, began making its way through the back streets of suburban Paris.[27] Across the capital, German units abandoned their positions and slipped out of the city.[28] By 20:00, Dronne reached the Porte d'Italie, the entry point to southeastern Paris. Civilians—first tentative, then ecstatic—poured into the streets. Young women scurried onto the vehicles and tanks to kiss the soldiers.[29] Led by Dronne's jeep, and followed by three tanks and a few other vehicles, the column stealthily crossed the Place d'Italie in southeast Paris, moved on to cross the Seine, and then turned left, following the north side of the river toward the Hôtel de Ville.[30] They arrived around 21:20 as night was falling.[31]

At that point, Langlade's tactical group was finally taking the approaches to the city from the southwest. The forces made good progress out of Rambouillet, but then ran into exactly the same Boineburg flak belt that had caused Putz so much trouble.[32] It took until late that evening for Langlade's men to fight their way through to the—thanks to Boineburg and Choltitz— intact bridge at Sèvres. By this point, the worst fighting was over, and it had, just as Boineburg wanted, all occurred outside Paris. It was now up to Choltitz to surrender.

As DRONNE'S COMPANY pulled up to the Hôtel de Ville at 21:20 on August 24, the portly captain descended from his jeep, dashed into the building, and reported to Gaullist resistance leader Georges Bidault. A wave of emotion swept over both men, rendering them mute.[33] Outside, young women surged toward the tanks and covered the grimy and unshaven men in kisses.[34] There must have been some young men there as well, but they seem not to have captured the soldiers' attention sufficiently to merit a mention in the archives.

Spontaneously, civilians made for nearby churches and rang the bells.[35] Then, far louder and more impressive bells rang out, drowning out the other churches. They were the bells of Notre Dame. Madeleine Quintaine from Normandy was in a Parisian apartment with her mother when she heard the bells ring out. She thought, "The bourdon of Notre Dame! They're here!" Just then, deafening cries of joy and waves of applause echoed through Paris's streets.[36]

At the Hotel Meurice, the reaction was very different, though it too contained an element of relief. Dietrich von Choltitz was drinking champagne from the hotel's cellar with his officers. The conversation was about the Saint Bartholomew's Day massacre of 1572; they drew parallels with their present situation and constructed a number of gory scenarios.[37] Choltitz got up, went to the phone, and called Hans Speidel. Choltitz held the telephone to the window. Implicitly referencing Sippenhaft, he asked Speidel to look out for his family. He then ordered Aulock's battle group, which the Second Division had engaged outside Paris, to withdraw behind the Seine.[38] At 23:30, he sent his last communication of the day to OB West: "Battles rage in all parts of the city. I am staying where I am [*sitze am alten Fleck*] and defending the Seine. . . . Neutral states have urged me to withdraw from the city. That is out of the question."[39]

The next day, August 25, Choltitz received another order from Hitler reiterating his August 23 order to defend the city "to the utmost."[40] Revealing clear and detailed knowledge of the forces at Choltitz's disposal, Hitler ordered that all tanks and motorized transportation be used to crowd the insurgents into small sections of Paris. Then, the security division was to be brought in. As the Luftwaffe pasted Paris with high explosives and incendiaries, the security division would blast the insurgents with howitzers and assault tanks. "The parts of the city which are in revolt," the order ended, "may be destroyed."[41] Jodl sent the order to Model, who passed it on to Choltitz; Choltitz paid little attention to it.[42] He instead negotiated the placement of the fifteen or twenty secretaries still in the hotel under the authority of the Swiss Consulate.[43] The Germans needed to get them out of the building before the firing began. Then, at 11:00, Choltitz sent his last communication to Model. "I have ordered bridges across the Seine on the eastern side of the city blown up, but destruction of bridges in the city centre proved impossible because our own troops were south of the river. Our situation remains unchanged. Paris is burning in multiple locations. The enemy is attacking our positions with tanks. I have been asked to capitulate three times, and I have refused it each time."[44]

Choltitz certainly had not ordered the bridges destroyed, Paris was not on fire, and the Allies were deliberately ignoring German strongpoints, but Allied troops were indeed moving into central Paris from all directions. Colonel Langlade's troops moved toward the Étoile and down the Champs-Élysées. Billotte's men made a faster journey up through the Porte d'Italie, following more or less the path taken by Dronne the night before, and ended up at the Prefecture. Leclerc followed in an armoured car and met Jacques Chaban-Delmas, and the two drove together to the Gare Montparnasse, Leclerc's designated command post.[45] Choltitz was given a surrender ultimatum, but he refused to give up without at least a token fight.

As Allied vehicles moved into the city, they were swept over by ecstatic Parisians. Advancing tanks were frequently slowed or even stopped by boys and girls who climbed onto them and clung to them, oblivious to the dangers of being pulled underneath the deadly tracks.[46] The girls were fairly indiscriminate about their targets. Father Roger Fouquer, divisional chaplain, found himself showered in hugs and kisses, to the immense amusement of his charges.[47]

In organizing the final assault, Langlade's men received the second prize: rooting the Germans out of the Hotel Majestic and the Hotel Raphael off the Champs-Élysées, Stülpnagel's old residence and that of senior German officers. As the head of the Protestant church in France looked on in horror, four German soldiers from the hotel were dragged off to be shot.[48] Only Édith Piaf's intervention prevented a young FFI resister from killing more by tossing a grenade into a truck full of German prisoners.[49]

The big prize went to detachments under Billotte: taking the Hotel Meurice. Billotte divided his attacking force into two columns under the command of Jean de la Horie: a tank company under Captain Branet and an infantry company under Lieutenant Henri Karcher. Branet had been taken prisoner in 1940 and then had, as it turned out, the good fortune of being interned in the Soviet Union. Once the Germans invaded, the Soviets repatriated him.[50] Both columns moved down the rue de Rivoli, the tanks on the street and the infantry under the cover of the arcade on the northern side of the street.

Once they arrived at the Hotel Meurice, tank fighting broke out on the street. Karcher and his infantrymen surged toward the Meurice, taking positions inside. Upstairs, one of Choltitz's staff whispered to him, "*Sie kommen, Herr General*" ("They're here").[51] Downstairs, a token exchange of gunfire and hand grenades followed, and then the Germans surrendered. Karcher dashed upstairs to find Choltitz and his men waiting for him, their guns laid out on the table.[52] The best Karcher could muster, at the most dramatic moment in France since June 1940, was "*Sprechen Sie Deutsch?*" ("Do you speak German?")[53]

Choltitz looked at him incredulously. "Probably better than you do."[54]

Just then, Commandant Jean de la Horie burst in and asked Choltitz if he was prepared to surrender. The Prussian general replied that he was prepared to discuss terms. French soldiers escorted Choltitz, Arnim, and the other senior staff into the street. The French soldiers struggled to protect the Germans from the crowds, who mobbed their former occupiers, managing sometimes to pull a German out of the column, punching and trampling on him.[55] As further proof that instant justice is rarely just, a bearded, tall Frenchman jumped forward, put a gun to the head of a man marching just in front of Arnim, and pulled the trigger.[56] The man killed was Dr. Otto Kayser, a prewar professor from Hagen and a Francophile.[57] A French nurse held Kayser's head as he died.[58]

Choltitz was then delivered to Gare Montparnasse. With Rol-Tanguy hammering at the door and demanding entry, Choltitz discussed surrender terms with General Leclerc. After Leclerc wearily granted entry to Rol-Tanguy, Choltitz formally surrendered. He agreed to a complete capitulation across Paris and to send his emissaries out to the strongholds to tell the units fighting there to lay down their weapons.[59] OB West, playing its part, put together a series of daily briefings for Keitel's attention. Drawn up over several days, they were meant to give the impression that Paris was a blood-soaked battleground, that the city was aflame, and, therefore, that Hitler's "rubble order" was being implemented.[60] Even the old Nazi Model, it seems, was prepared to lie to Hitler. What was in fact happening in Paris was the final surrender of isolated units. On the boulevard Saint-Germain, German soldiers who were holed up in two hotels gave themselves up to the Americans. As they moved the Germans through the street, thick crowds of civilians hurled abuse at them in a spectacle that Madeleine Quintaine, who had suffered years of German occupation, found deeply unedifying.[61]

French women accused of horizontal collaboration suffered worse fates. Inevitably, they were a mixed group. Some had found the powerful German soldiers desirable, especially given that many French were on forced labour duty in any case. Others consorted with Germans, with or without offering sex, in order to protect and feed their families. Some may have been convinced Pétainists, National Socialists, or both. Some had no doubt fallen in love. Others were simply the victims of malicious rumour. And still others were in the trade, and Germans were simply clients. Self-appointed avengers beat, shaved the heads of, and paraded all these types of women through the streets of Paris and provincial France. "I shall never forget," wrote Quintaine, "the woman whose head was shaved because she had slept with Germans."[62] As Parisians inundated the streets it was, as Father Roger Fouquer observed, "difficult to distinguish the true resisters from the *milice* and collaborators of yesterday."[63]

The purges would cast a long shadow over postwar French history, and they would complicate the memory of liberation. But all that lay in the future. For the moment, the French capital was free—and intact. Paris's largely preserved condition owed something to the German officers occupying it. Choltitz did not have the men or the materiel to destroy Paris. He could, however, have seriously scarred it and killed many more people in the process. But the central point is this: Choltitz made no effort to try. Shells were almost never used, there was no effort to use gasoline to set the city afire (fire destroys cities more effectively than bombs or shells), and Choltitz frustrated the Luftwaffe's bombing plans. Before Choltitz arrived in Paris, preparations for the sabotage of gas installations, power plants, and telephone exchanges had begun.[64] Choltitz made no effort to continue them. After the war, the bureau responsible for administering bridges and roads concluded that Choltitz had done nothing to mine the bridges, despite the arrival in the city of a battalion of engineers with three hundred naval torpedoes.[65] And although he expressed great anger at the insurgency in the city, he was measured and controlled in his response. In July 1944, Heinrich Himmler had suspended all court martial proceedings against indigenous populations in the occupied territories and authorized commanders to "crush" terrorists and saboteurs "on the spot."[66] Choltitz did nothing to implement such a policy in Paris. Rather, over the course of a week, he had played a triple game: he deployed just enough force to keep the FFI at bay while offering olive branches and truces to buy time; he assured Berlin directly and indirectly that he was still Hitler's man; and he entered into covert negotiations with the Allies to hand over the city. In all of this, he had the support of the officer corps in Paris, which was the almost intact infrastructure of the July 20, 1944, coup. As they had tried to end the war a month earlier, it was unsurprising that they were happy to ignore Hitler's calls for mass destruction.

For reasons that are understandable, scholars wish to assign the French uprising a decisive role in ensuring the surrender of Choltitz and the salvation of the capital.[67] The insurgents were undeniably brave, and they certainly spooked German army soldiers in the capital who, more than anything, simply wanted it to be over.[68] But their actions had little effect on the outcome, for it had been decided well in advance of the uprising: Choltitz—with the strong support of Boineburg—and Karl von Unger had decided by August 10 to ensure the safety of Paris.[69] That Choltitz appointed Boineburg's orderly officer, Arnim, as his own was further evidence of his basic agreement with his predecessor. There is a further logical flaw in those arguments crediting the uprising with such an important role: Choltitz lacked the means to defend, much less destroy, Paris—a point on which there is now a consensus. If Choltitz was not able to destroy Paris, the insurgents could not have prevented him from destroying Paris; if Choltitz could not defend Paris, then the insurgency was not needed to free Paris.

And what this means is that the uprising resulted in large numbers of unnecessary deaths. Had Rol-Tanguy followed Gaullist urgings and remained quiet, the German garrison either would have surrendered after token resistance to the invading Allies or would have waited the war out. The uprising might have hastened the liberation of Paris by forcing the Allies to come in, but probably not: the undeniable appeal of Paris to the Americans, de Gaulle and Leclerc's pressure, and above all their unilateral action (they sent troops *before* Bradley agreed to take the city) would likely have brought the Allies in with or without the insurrection. Even if we assume that the insurrection forced the Allies' hand, we have to ask whether an early liberation was really worth lives of thousands of French citizens, including many young people. It is very easy for authors to wax lyrical about the symbolic importance of the uprising when neither they nor their sons or daughters paid for it with their lives.

THE QUESTION OF WHETHER the uprising was worth it is distinct from the central question of Choltitz's intentions in Paris. There is one last piece of evidence on this point. Almost two months to the day after Paris's liberation, in late October 1944, Choltitz was imprisoned at Trent Park. There, he was secretly recorded speaking with General Hermann-Bernhard Ramcke, who had been ordered to defend Brest against the Allied advance.[70]

DC: "Did you destroy Brest?" he asked ". . . The town and everything? . . . Why on earth did you destroy the town?"

HBR: "The Americans bombarded the town ruthlessly too, and I said to myself: It's as much their blame as ours; those pigs must not be allowed to base themselves here on any account; they mustn't be allowed to use the town as a harbour and must be prevented from quickly establishing quarters for reconstruction personnel. Well, I set fire to [the town] and burned it down."

DC: "Did you really destroy the town completely?"

HBR: "I obliterated it entirely!"

DC: "But that is a *war-crime*!"

HBR: "No, I demolished the electric railway . . ."

DC: "No one worries about that, that's obvious. But why did you destroy civilian houses?"

"I told you the reason," Ramcke replied impatiently. "I blew them up whenever they were an obstruction and whenever military necessity called for it."

"But Ramcke," Choltitz said in response, "*that* is of course a war crime!"[71]

These words are hardly those of a man who would have destroyed Paris even with the most plentiful supplies of men and materiel.

CHAPTER 11

NORMANDY SOUTH

The Invasion of Southern France

THE SOUTHEASTERN COAST OF France stretches over 640 kilome-tres from the Spanish border to Italy. The landscape encompasses a seductively beautiful coastline, rugged hills, and two of Europe's most important ports, at Toulon and Marseille. In the summer of 1944, Army Group G was charged with defending it. The group's commander was Johannes Blaskowitz, a Prussian patriot with haunting eyes and a deep sense of German military honour. Blaskowitz had earned Hitler's undying enmity by protesting the murders of Jews on the eastern front by Himmler's Einsatzgruppen. He spent most of the war in military obscurity. He was the only Generaloberst not to be promoted to Feldmarschall in July 1940 (though Hitler had the nerve to invite him to the promotion ceremony for the others) and, indeed, was the only senior German general not to be promoted over the course of the war. Only Feldmarschall Gerd von Rundstedt retrieved him from obscurity. Possibly seeking a counterweight to Rommel, Rundstedt appointed him commander of Armeegruppe G in May 1944.[1] Two armies served under Blaskowitz: the First Army commanded by General der Infanterie Kurt von der Chevallerie, which defended south-western France, and the Nineteenth Army under General der Infanterie Friedrich Wiese, which defended southeastern France. Wiese had under his command seven infantry divisions and one reserve division, which were controlled by three corps headquarters. These were concentrated along the coast.[2] Wiese could also call on Generalleutnant Wend von Wietersheim's Eleventh Panzer Division, positioned west of the Rhône but en route to Avignon. Wietersheim was a forty-four-year-old Silesian veteran of the eastern front.[3]

The most important defensive points on the coast were Toulon and Marseille. The port cities' commanders had much in common. Both Johannes Baeßler (at Toulon) and Hans Schäfer (at Marseille) were born in 1892, both joined the Prussian Army at roughly the same time (1914 and 1912, respectively), and both served at the front during the First World War. And both men would play a defining role in the campaign. The 242nd and 244th Infantry Divisions they commanded were, with the Eleventh Panzer Division under Wietersheim, the strongest in southern France.

German coastal defences in southern France were extensive, though less impressive than those in the north of the country. Defence troops were concentrated near the water in strongholds, often several kilometres apart, occupied by an infantry group of, at most, platoon strength.[4] The strongholds were furnished with heavy weapons, including artillery capable of firing 220 mm shells; the Germans often camouflaged them with trees and shrubbery. On average, there was one stronghold every 800 metres, and the area between them was covered by machine-gun fire. There were more landmines on the beaches than anywhere else on the European continent, although according to Blaskowitz's postwar account, some of them were duds.[5] Underwater mines and obstacles, inspired by Rommel in Normandy, were especially effective impediments.[6] This thin crust of defence spread along roughly 650 kilometres of coastline, partly because the Germans remained uncertain to the end about the likely landing spot (and, indeed, viewed the area around Saint-Tropez as the least likely).[7]

The German troops lining up along the coast and in the port strongholds stared out across the Mediterranean. Across the sea in Naples was the headquarters of Lieutenant General Lucian Truscott's VI Corps, part of Lieutenant General Alexander M. Patch's Seventh Army. Truscott was among the ablest American commanders. He was never a glory-seeker in the vein of Generals Mark Clark or George Patton, but his description of the perfect commander owes something to the latter: "Wars aren't won by gentlemen. They are won by men who can be first-class sons of bitches. . . . It's as simple as that. No son of a bitch, no commander."[8] Truscott also shared Patton's passion for mobility, a trait that would serve well an army that was poised to chase the Germans across France. After a long and typically acrimonious debate between the Americans and de Gaulle, Truscott agreed that his initial assault on France's southern coast would be backed up by General Jean de Lattre de Tassigny's French II Corps, which would deal with any straggling resisters before moving on to Toulon and Marseille. Taking the two Allied corps together, 250,000 soldiers stood ready to attack 200,000 defending Germans.

On August 9, they moved. Great US transport ships and battleships sailed out of Naples, the Gulf of Taranto, Sardinia, and Algeria, and moved toward five beaches along the southern coast of France. The next day, XII Tactical Air Command, supported by the RAF and French Air Force, took out what was left of German air forces in the area, destroyed road and railway bridges and airfields, disrupted communications, and attacked the main coastal defence batteries.[9] The bombing was the culmination of a plan that had been implemented since April: as in northern France, the Allies hit transportation targets throughout the south in the run-up to the invasion.[10] Again as in northern France, they deliberately spread the bombing across the southern coast in order to confuse the Germans about the true landing point. The raids continued right up until D-Day, with special attention given to bridges crossing the Rhône.

At half past midnight on the morning of August 15, Operation Dragoon was formally launched. The airborne assault was led by Major General Robert T. Frederick's First Special Service Force, a joint US-Canadian commando unit that Frederick had created. The first targets were the islands of Levant and Port Cros. Within six hours, the Special Force had neutralized opposition: the Germans on Levant surrendered, and although those on Port Cros withdrew into old forts that proved impervious to bombing, they were effectively quarantined and posed no further threat to the invasion. The Germans, however, showed that the Allies had no monopoly on diversionary tactics. One of the Allied force's main targets, a seemingly great heavy battery on Levant, turned out to be a dummy.

The full airborne assault began at 3:30. Paratroopers were to seize bridges, block roads, and capture key towns.[11] Frederick himself, clothed in a white scarf made from a parachute, two stars on each shoulder, and a .45 automatic on his hip, boarded the first plane.[12] Approaching the coast, the pilot miscalculated the wind direction, and Frederick and his men jumped off target.

So did everyone else. All other airplanes followed the lead aircraft, and almost five thousand infantrymen, artillerymen, and engineers were scattered up to thirty miles off target.[13] They were the lucky ones: some did not reach the shore at all. As each plane followed the one ahead of it in ordering a jump, the last parachutists came down in the Mediterranean. Struggling against the full weight of their pack, and often tangled in their parachutes, most who landed in the water drowned. Those landing on the mainland had varying fates. Some landed in trees, suffering gashes and broken limbs, and they became easy targets for (mercifully rare) enemy gunfire.

As the parachutists struggled to pull their units together, a second wave of airplanes was approaching the beaches. Below them, great columns of water shot hundreds of feet into the air as shells landed near the beaches.[14] The aircraft were towing gliders containing jeeps, heavy mortars, and anti-tank weapons; each glider was usually manned by a pilot, co-pilot, and two men in the jeep. As the planes approached the beach, they released the gliders, which struggled to land their great weight safely. It often did not work. Some smashed into trees, ditches, and each other. Wood splintered, and jeeps—and soldiers—were sent flying.[15] Technical Sergeant Ralph Wenthold, who landed with the first assault, watched a glider come down in an orchard.[16] The trees tore its wings off, and it sailed headlong into a large tree. The fuselage shattered on impact, and the bodies flew in all directions. In other crashes, soldiers survived, impaled on stakes or with broken legs.[17] Medics hurried between shattered gliders, setting broken legs and sewing gashes, sometimes without anaesthetic. For those who could not be saved, parachutes were used as shrouds.[18]

Crashing gliders naturally threatened men as much as they did other gliders: parachutists often had to make a desperate dash across open fields, dodging crashing and landing gliders. Still other gliders landed smoothly and safely, but this was often no salvation. Others crashed into those already on the ground, killing everyone.[19] In one case, a soldier found himself joining would-be German POWs in a dash for their lives.[20] Sergeant "Hedy" Lamar came down unhurt but right in front of two German soldiers. They helped him out of a harness and then surrendered. Then the gliders came in and all three ran, never seeing each other again.[21]

For all the carnage, however, a medic who survived the jump rightly concluded that the casualty rate was relatively low:[22] there were 230 jump and glider casualties, or 2.5 percent of the nine thousand airborne troops involved in the operation.[23]

Those who survived the jump uninjured first tried to gather their units together and then looked for their firearms, which had been dropped in bundles ahead of the parachutists. After that, they began moving into the backcountry, blocking roads and moving on five vital crossroads towns from Fayence to Le Muy.[24] The move was also designed to bring them to safety, for the full force of Allied firepower was about to come down on this small corner of France.

At 5:50, the air forces struck again. First heavy bombers, then fighter-bombers drenched the beaches with explosives. Fifty kilometres of beach shook under the force of the barrage. Wooden buildings exploded into splinters, and concrete ones became powder; German soldiers in pillboxes went mad as the force of these impacts made blood gush from their ears, eyes, and noses. Then came the naval barrage: four hundred naval guns launched sixteen thousand shells within just sixteen minutes. "How can anything live under such a bombardment?" Truscott asked the chief of the French navy.[25]

Not much did. Under the pitiless assault, "German" defenders—many were Russian and Armenian—pulled back, abandoning their motorized antitank guns.[26] US forces were onshore with few casualties. For their part, French forces, to de Gaulle's bitterness, landed on the beaches a day after the Americans, on August 16. Brigadier General Jean de Lattre de Tassigny's II Army Corps prepared to liberate the great port cities of Toulon and Marseille.

With the Americans ashore and the French landing, the Germans—in Berlin and in southern France—considered how to respond.

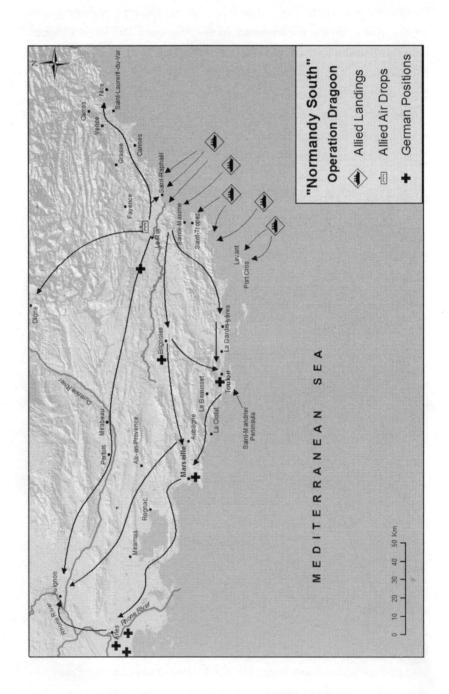

"Normandy South"
Operation Dragoon

◈ Allied Landings

▭ Allied Air Drops

✚ German Positions

MEDITERRANEAN SEA

N

Saint-Laurent-du-Var
Nice
Vence
Cairos
Grasse
Cannes
Fayence
Saint-Raphaël
Le Muy
Sainte-Maxime
Saint-Tropez
Levant
Port Cros
La Garde-Hyères
Digne
Bargoles
Durance River
Toulon
Le Beausset
Aubagne
La Ciotat
Saint-Mandrier Peninsula
Mirabeau
Pertuis
Aix-en-Provence
Marseille
Rognac
Miramas
Rhône River
Avignon
Arles
Rhône River

0   10   20   30   40   50 Km

LATE IN THE MORNING of August 15, Generaloberst Blaskowitz was on the phone at his headquarters in Rouffiac, not far from Toulouse. Communications, constantly ravaged by Allied bombers, were poor, but he had received word of the invasion and was trying to launch a counterstrike. In the midst of his planning, however, the line went dead.

In the field, responsibility fell to the Nineteenth Army under Wiese, according to one account an experienced commander and "ardent Nazi."[27] His immediate reaction was to order Generalleutnant Richard von Schwerin, commander of the 189th Infantry Division, to move to the invasion area.[28] These troops arrived, however, in "bits and pieces," so the airborne forces, and then elements of the American Forty-Fifth and Thirty-Sixth Divisions, were able to make short work of them.[29] By August 16, Truscott's forces had established a firm beachhead, and they held a corridor running from Toulon to Saint-Raphaël.[30] General Neuling's LXII Army Corps staff was surrounded, and within two days, they would be in captivity. With the bridgehead secure, the Americans were thinking of their next move north.

So were the Germans. Although he had failed to predict the location of the US landing, by the next day, Blaskowitz anticipated American movements almost perfectly. He wrote on the sixteenth: "The enemy will presumably thrust forward from the beachhead in a west-northwest direction in order to cut off first Toulon and later Marseille, and then advance in the general direction of the Rhône valley. The destruction, which has just taken place, of the Durance bridges at Pertuis and Mirabeau may also indicate that the enemy, after creating a useful bridgehead . . . will thrust via the area Digne toward the Central Rhône valley, particularly as this attack will soon bring him in full contact with the strong guerrilla forces [in] that area."[31]

This is exactly what the enemy did, and the Germans were unable to stop it. But they were able to bring one more division into play: the Eleventh Panzer Division under Wietersheim, known as the "Ghost Division" because its rapid mobility enabled it to appear suddenly in battle.[32] On August 13, guessing from the sharp increase in Allied bombing that an attack was imminent, Blaskowitz ordered the Eleventh Panzer Division to move from near Toulouse to Nimes-Arles on the eastern side of the Rhône near the river's mouth and within striking distance of the southern beaches.[33] The journey would take at least four to six days.[34] Wietersheim was moving his men, and still well west of the Rhône, when the Americans hit the beaches at Saint-Tropez. After dodging Allied bombers for hundreds of kilometres down secondary roads, Wietersheim reached the east bank of the Rhône. All the bridges as far as sixty miles upstream were gone: Allied bombing had already taken them out.[35] Mercilessly bombed and strafed by the Allied fighters that he had until that point avoided, Wietersheim was forced to ferry his men across the river "in driblets."[36] He would cross the Rhône only on August 23.[37] By the time he did, exhausted and with little fuel, his tanks were no use on the beaches. Army Group G's best division had missed the fight. As Blaskowitz predicted, the German army's ability to move sufficient forces eastward across the Rhône would be decisive for the outcome.[38] But movement was distinctly out of the question. American precision bombing of bridges in the run-up to the campaign had delivered Truscott's men an early and decisive advantage. It was tactical bombing at its best.

As Wietersheim began his long journey to the Rhône, Hitler was receiving reports in Rastenburg. They could not have been worse. The Red Army was sweeping across Poland. Army Group Centre was destroyed. General Bernard L. Montgomery and General Omar Bradley were pressing home their advantage in northern France. Army Group B was encircled in the Falaise, and two divisions were lost in two days.[39] Patton was dashing for the Seine. In southern France, the First and Nineteenth Armies were about to be smashed. Blaskowitz, against Hitler's orders, prepared for a withdrawal; he ordered the first units north toward the Rhône. Should Hitler challenge him, he would be able to argue that he was concentrating forces for a counterattack.[40]

Blaskowitz did not need to. Hitler—who was more willing to allow tactical withdrawals than self-serving German generals' postwar memoirs suggest—authorized an immediate withdrawal.[41] Army Group G was to be pulled north in order to make contact with the southern flank of Army Group B.[42] Hitler's headquarters issued three related orders. First, late on August 16, he ordered Blaskowitz's troops to retreat directly north, cutting

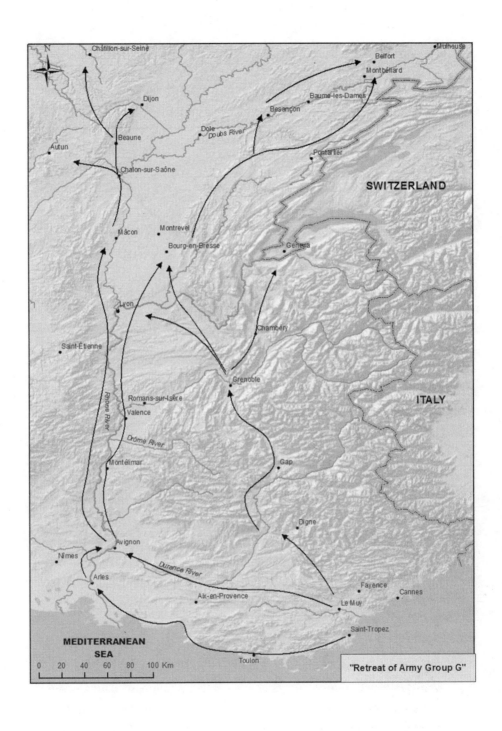

MEDITERRANEAN
SEA

0   20   40   60   80   100 Km

"Retreat of Army Group G"

right up the Rhône valley. Two days later, Hitler ordered them to re-establish the front some 160 kilometres southeast of Paris.[43] This new position
would, it was thought, allow them to link up with the Seventh Army pulling
back from western France. In a pattern that would soon become familiar,
Hitler added a scorched-earth order for the south of France: "The destruction of all objects so as to hinder the pursuit by the enemy is of the highest
importance. No locomotive, no bridge, no power station, no repair shop
[may] fall intact into the enemy's hands."[44]

Following Hitler's withdrawal orders, the chase was on. Wiese ordered
four divisions from the Nineteenth Army—the 198th Infantry, the 158th
Reserve, the 11th Panzer, the 338th Infantry—to organize a headlong
retreat up the Rhône valley. They were to reach Avignon by August 24.
Blaskowitz then ordered Wietersheim, still on the wrong side of the Rhône,
to cut across toward Aix, southeast of Avignon, and to protect the retreating Nineteenth Army's rear and to prevent its encirclement.[45] Finally, in
keeping with Hitler's order to transform harbour cities into fortresses, the
242nd and 244th Infantry Divisions were ordered to withdraw into Toulon
and Marseille, respectively. Baeßler was ordered to establish a blocking position east of Toulon, preventing Allied troops from entering the city.[46] Hitler
ordered that both Toulon and Marseille be defended to the last bullet and
to destroy the cities' ports if they could not hold them.[47]

Wietersheim's forces, having finally crawled up the east bank of the
Rhone, met the Americans on August 24 at Montélimar, eighty kilometres north of Avignon. There, the Americans attacked forward units of the
Eleventh Panzer Division. Truscott's goal was to encircle three German
divisions—the 198th and 338th Infantry Divisions, as well as the Eleventh
Panzer Division—from the south and the east. With only two of its divisions
left at Toulon and Marseille, the action would have all but destroyed the
Nineteenth Army. The Germans, however, fought back fiercely. Blaskowitz
ordered portions of the Eleventh Panzer Division to defend the rear mercilessly. "The utmost," he wrote, "must be demanded of the rearguards."[48]
Taking personal charge of the operation, Wietersheim pushed the two divisions, armed with tanks, armoured personnel carriers, and mobile guns,
straight north into US troops.[49] The Americans responded with force. The

operation lasted four hours, and the Eleventh Panzer Division suffered many casualties, but they managed to clear the road along the Rhône riverbank, seizing the approaches to La Coucourde (between Montélimar and Valence) from the east, with the heights north of it in German hands too.[50] Blaskowitz immediately sent the 338th Division north through the gap.[51]

By August 26, Wietersheim's men were approaching the Drôme River, which runs perpendicular to the Rhône. Then the retreat took a biblical turn. Despite the hot weather, the river's waters had risen, making passage northward impossible.[52] The Nineteenth Army appeared trapped against two rivers. All the bridges across the Rhône, its exit westward, had been destroyed.[53] The Drôme River, its exit northward, had overrun its banks, and artillery fire had left any potential crossing points wrecked and burning. To the south and the east, only the 198th Infantry and the Eleventh Panzer Divisions, deep in battle with Truscott's tanks, stood between the Americans and the retreating Germans. The 198th Infantry Division pushed south against the Americans, giving up the blocking line and establishing a new position along a six-kilometre front northeast of Montélimar.[54] As it did, the Eleventh Panzer Division threw itself into the American Fourth Division, protecting the Germans' east flank and keeping open the Nineteenth Army's only hope of escape.[55] Truscott responded by sending in the tanks, attacking northward.[56]

As the Eleventh Panzer Division first defended the eastern flank and the 198th Infantry Division held the south, German sapper troops went to work on the Drôme west of Loriel, creating an improvised bridge that allowed men and materiel to cross the river.[57] As the 11th and the 198th held a perimeter south of the river, the Germans abandoned tanks, vehicles, and weapons and pulled themselves slowly over the Drôme. All the while, Truscott's forces sprayed them with artillery fire.

On the other side, the chase continued. Again trying to encircle the Germans, Truscott moved units toward Bourg-lès-Valence, fifty kilometres north of Montélimar and just north of Valence, and captured the town.[58] Other units began threatening bridges over the Isère, the Germans' only escape north. As they did, Allied bombers swept in overhead. Some pounded Tain-l'Hermitage, through which the Germans would have to pass, while others attacked the Rhône near its bend just north of Lyon. If the Americans could hold it and establish a firm position, the Germans would once again be encircled. Wietersheim gathered together the strongest armour group he could and threw it directly north at the Americans. It managed to capture the town. With the Eleventh Panzer Division guarding the right flank at Romans-sur-Isère, twenty kilometres northeast of Valence, and two panzer grenadier regiments holding off the Americans eight kilometres to the south of Valence, the LXXXV Corps moved north onto the Isère River and from there on toward Lyon.[59] With fires from Allied bombings lighting the night, Wietersheim's units rolled past Tain-l'Hermitage on the twenty-ninth.

The next great hurdles were the Rhône (which runs roughly east–west from Switzerland to Lyon) and Doubs Rivers. With fierce, sometimes house-to-house fighting, Wietersheim pushed his men north toward Beaune, and from there he hoped to turn right toward Besançon.[60] Pivoting eastward at Beaune, the Eleventh Panzer Division then found, to its surprise, bridges that were under constant air attack but largely unscathed at Dôle, some fifty kilometres from Besançon.[61] Over the next five days, the Americans chased the Germans on both sides of the Doubs toward Belfort.[62] With sappers felling trees to block the Americans, Wietersheim and his men turned north at Montbéliard (where troops south of the Doubs crossed the one available bridge) and travelled twenty kilometres to Belfort.[63]

The chase continued, but it was largely over. Although written up as a failure, both sides could credibly claim victory. Blaskowitz had nominally evacuated Army Group G, but he had lost one town after another to Truscott's troops, and the Americans had ravaged his forces. Army Group G suffered over 130,000 casualties on the chase through France, including 7,000 killed, 20,000 wounded, and 105,000 captured.[64] Another 25,000 soldiers had been left behind at Toulon and Marseille. With the exception of Wietersheim's Eleventh Panzer Division, all infantry divisions and combat groups were shadows of their former selves. The Americans, for their part, had suffered few casualties—about 4,500. Truscott had chased the Nineteenth Army 1500 kilometres across rough terrain, harassing it almost every step of the way. At four points, Truscott came very close to encircling and destroying Army Group G.[65] His VI Corps nonetheless failed to deliver the decisive blow.

On September 10, Seventh Army forward units met up with forward patrols from Patton's Third Army, and four days later, Mediterranean command was folded into the West European chain of command.[66] Patch remained in charge of the US Seventh Army, but General Jacob Devers took over the Sixth Army Group to which it was subject. With most of western and southern France cleared of the Germans, the fight was now for Alsace, Lorraine, the Low Countries, and the Reich itself.

As the Americans and Germans bitterly fought each other up the Rhône valley, two other battles of arguably greater consequence for the Allied war effort raged along the southern coast, for Hitler had ordered something more than a simple withdrawal. Instead, he left one division each in Toulon and Marseille.[67] They had orders to transform these cities into fortresses. German troops were to defend Toulon and Marseille "to the last man" and, could they not be defended, to destroy their harbours.[68] Such destruction had ample precedent: the Germans had destroyed Brest, Cherbourg, Nantes, and Saint-Malo in the north, and on August 15, forces of the Nineteenth Army demolished the ports of Cannes and Nice.[69] When the order applying to Toulon arrived on Wiese's desk, he passed it on to Generalleutnant Johannes Baeßler.[70] The lives of tens of thousands of Allied and Axis soldiers, as well as the Allies' ability to supply their troops in northern France, turned on the willingness of these cities' commanders to obey.

CHAPTER 12

FORTS AND FORTRESSES

Toulon

B OTH NATURAL AND MILITARY defences made the port city of Toulon a formidable position. Toulon grew up around a bay surrounded in the north and east by hills and forests. Saint-Mandrier, a thumb-like peninsula, juts out into the sea, flanking the harbour with tall, natural barriers. Three great hills—Monts Caumes, Faron, and Coudon—rise into the heights just above the city.

The Germans had used these natural barriers to great advantage. All three hills had been made into heavily fortified strongholds.[1] While the Germans struggled elsewhere to implement Hitler's order to transform cities into fortresses, they thoroughly succeeded in Toulon. Within a two-square-mile area on the Saint-Mandrier Peninsula, jutting out in a wide hook from the coast, the Germans placed eighteen batteries with fifty-four guns and seventeen anti-aircraft guns.[2] They connected the batteries to a maze of tunnels with electric power plants and ammunition depots. In anticipation of being cut off, troops in both Toulon and Marseille had been directed to stockpile large amounts of ammunition and to secure water supplies sufficient to withstand a long siege. However, the guns suffered from one weakness: many pointed out to the sea and could not be turned fully inward to face a land invasion.[3]

Nonetheless, the defences on the approaches to the city were similarly impressive: antitank obstacles, pillboxes, and minefields waited for troops moving on Toulon. The Germans had established multiple artillery batteries across the city (though two of them had not been completed by August) with some 150 artillery pieces in total and protected them with mines and barbed wire.[4] The city's ancient forts were transformed into modern fortresses.[5] When Baeßler withdrew his 242nd Infantry Division toward the city, he had eighteen thousand German soldiers and sailors in the city.[6] They were not the best troops, but Baeßler, a veteran of Stalingrad who had successfully held off a Red Army encirclement of the city before being wounded, knew how to get the best out of them.[7] Finally, on August 16, large block-ships waited with steam up for the order to proceed into position for sinking.[8] Baeßler established his headquarters just east of the city in anticipation of an Allied attack on that side. On the seventeenth, Blaskowitz ordered Toulon's destruction.[9]

These were the forces that General Jean de Lattre de Tassigny faced when he sought to liberate Toulon and its important harbour. American planners had long agreed that a land attack on both Toulon and Marseille was the best option: toward the sea, both ports were far better defended than the beaches between them. Once the Allies had landed and quickly secured their beachheads, de Lattre ordered the First French, the Ninth Colonial, and part of the Third Algerian Divisions, with the help of crack rifle and shock battalions as well as a commando group, to encircle, isolate, and then capture Toulon.

The first job for French forces was to deal with German resistance at Hyères, a fortified port east of Toulon.[10] With Allied ships bombarding the port south of the town, French forces rooted out the mostly Armenian troops over two days, seizing complete control of the town and the roads from it to Toulon on August 21.[11] By that day, the town as well as German positions to the north and east, including the fort on Mont Coudon, had fallen. Among those captured was Baeßler himself.[12] Command passed from him to Konteradmiral (Rear Admiral) Heinrich Ruhfus, who was based on the Saint-Mandrier Peninsula.

Two days later, the French attacked. General de Lattre bravely moved advance forces into the city. As French forces attacked, Großadmiral Karl Dönitz, commander in chief of the German navy, ordered Ruhfus to put up the fiercest resistance; Toulon was to be defended "to the last cartridge." It was, he emphasized, crucial that the harbour not fall into Allied hands.[13] As in Marseille, Nice, and Cannes, the Germans had used the second half of July to mine the harbours and attempted to block them by sinking ships. Depth charges were laid along all the quays to prepare them for demolition.[14]

As the French troops moved on Toulon, they expected fierce German resistance, street-by-street fighting, and the possible creation of a German defence perimeter behind which the port of Toulon could be destroyed. Then, on August 24, the unexpected happened: when French forces reached the Fort Sainte-Marguerite in La Garde, perched on sea cliffs to the east of the city centre and port, an officer—Korvettenkapitän (Lieutenant Commander) Franz—agreed to surrender.[15] Asking for a delay in order to destroy his weapons, he told the French: "There have been too many deaths, too many injuries. I cannot continue." The French worked with Franz in leaving the right paper trail: they agreed to sign an attestation that the German commander had defended himself to the limit of the means available to him. Franz, 20 officers, and 571 NCOs (sous-officiers) and soldiers walked into captivity at 15:45.[16] Three further forts capitulated: Colle-Noire and Gavaresse at the same time, Carqueiranne a few hours earlier.[17] All were located some fifteen kilometres east of the city, on the way to Hyères, on a cape between the towns of Le Pradet and Carqueiranne. At the Carqueiranne fort, the commanding officer, Kapitän zur See (a naval rank that corresponds to an army colonel/Oberst) Müller, surrendered two officers and 121 airmen without a fight.[18] French forces had secured the area east of Toulon.

In the north of the city, the position was much the same. French General Joseph Magnan's Ninth Colonial Infantry Division made two lunges at the city: the first along a reverse arc running from La Valette to Valbourdin, just south of Mont Faron, and the second against the forts of Artigues and Sainte-Catherine, east of the harbour.[19] In the northern sector, over eleven hundred German soldiers walked into captivity, with all the officers claiming to have no knowledge of Ruhfus or his position.[20] At the same time, the Ninth Colonial units were moving on Fort Sainte-Catherine. The French commander, Gauvin, led a reconnaissance unit toward the fort and, rather than attacking, decided to attempt a negotiation with the Germans.[21] As fate would have it, Gauvin's Alsatian chauffeur spoke German, and he urged the lookout guards to see that struggle was pointless and that the battle was lost.[22] The guards referred the matter up his chain of command, and a few minutes later, a Luftwaffe major came out. Accompanied by Gauvin, the major went back into the fort and asked his men if they would surrender. They hesitated but, following his appeal, raised their arms in agreement. Another sixty-five men marched into captivity.[23]

As was generally the case in the last year of the war, the willingness to surrender against orders varied by commander. Despite the entreaties of Gauvin and a German captain who accompanied him brandishing a white flag, the commander at the Artigues fort, Major Fleischhut, refused to give up without a fight.[24] The Germans held out—showing as ever they could fight when they chose to—under three hours of shelling while both imposing and sustaining losses. At 20:00, the French called off the assault until the next morning; they had by then cleared a position to the sea, leaving the fort for the night as an isolated, but determined, point of resistance.[25]

By the evening of August 24, resistance had collapsed to the north and the east of the city, and new forces were approaching from the west. At Sanary-sur-Mer, ten kilometres west of Toulon, the commander of the artillery battery accepted French entreaties to discuss surrender terms.[26] A Kapitänleutnant Kaiser courteously welcomed the Seventh Chasseurs d'Afrique (a light cavalry corps) to the Hôtel de la Tour, now a shabby yet elegant hotel at the edge of the town's pretty port. Kaiser judged the conditions presented by the French delegation very reasonable, and the formal surrender was set for 20:00 that evening.[27] At that hour, soldiers from a battery at La Cride with those from two local observation posts joined the men from Kaiser's battery on the chemin de Sanary, where they handed over their weapons.[28]

Toulon was now surrounded and thoroughly infiltrated by French forces. Only isolated forts, both inside and outside the city, held out. Major Fleischhut at Fort Artigues, who had refused to surrender on August 25, did so out of a sense of honour that the German army had long ago squandered on the killing fields of Eastern Europe and Russia. After their surrender offer had been rebuffed, the French had no choice but to launch an attack the same day. To the cheers of onlooking civilians, shelling of the fort began again at 16:00, but most bounced harmlessly off the imposing structure.[29] After two hours, French patience was wearing thin. At 18:00, Colonel Raoul Salan, the battle-hardened commander of the Sixth Regiment of Senegalese Infantry (Tirailleurs) decided to up the ante and threaten the Germans with a massacre.[30] The question was how to convey this threat.

Captain Pate, commander of 71/84 Command Support Company (*compagnie de transmissions*), had a suggestion.[31] Arriving earlier that day to install communications, he had been shown a trench the Germans dug in order to disinter a cable linking the forts Sainte-Catherine and Artigues in eastern Toulon. Sixty centimetres down was a switchboard (*boîte de junction*). Staring at the fourteen switches, the captain chose one at random, connected it, and turned a handle. A surprised voice replied immediately, "*Wer ist denn da?*" ("Who's that, then?"). Pate explained that he was speaking in the name of the colonel commanding the attacking troops and that he wished to speak with Fleischhut. The German demanded to know how Pate had accessed the telephone line, but the Frenchman said nothing. Then Fleischhut came on the line. After verifying the provenance of the call and seeking assurances on the absence of "terrorists" (that is, partisans), Fleischhut agreed to surrender. Over a table laden by the Germans with beer and cigarettes, terms were settled at a quarter past seven that evening: the fort would be delivered intact, its supplies and electricity would be left undisturbed, the wounded would be cared for, and honours would be accorded to Fleischhut.[32] On August 28, at 7:00, the garrison buried its dead and de-mined the approaches to the fort.[33] An hour later, 27 officers, 399 soldiers, and 62 wounded (five gravely wounded had already been evacuated) marched into captivity.[34] A high price had been paid for Fleischhut's honour(s), but it could have been much worse.

A few hours after the August 25 assault on Fort Artigues began, French forces launched another against a German holdout west of the city, at Malbousquet.[35] At 19:50, the French opened an artillery barrage. For ten minutes, thirty cannons pounded the fort with everything they had. Seven minutes into it, a small French detachment made a dash toward the structure, a white flag flying. Unarmed German soldiers converged on the two men and took them to the fort's commander. With the sun setting, the detachment returned from the fort. The Germans would surrender the next morning at 7:00, some 150 wounded would be evacuated, and three officers would be given the usual honours for their bravery. The next morning, fully 1,450 walked into captivity. As a mark of respect to the man who had dodged his own artillery in his dash for the fort, they lay their arms before the captain who led the charge. Kapitän zur See Hellhoff, commander of the port of Toulon, marched out last.

From then, the dominoes began to fall. Remaining defences west of Toulon collapsed. At the fort at Six-Fours, two Swiss emissaries had made contact with the commander. Despite heavy shelling, the interior of the fort was intact. A German officer guiding the Swiss negotiators to his superior remarked, "If you know who constructed this fort, extend to them my compliments. They did an outstanding job!"[36] At noon on August 26, the soldiers manning the fort, along with batteries at Brégaillon and Mar-Vivo, gave up the fight. As they did, the commander at the Six-Fours fort addressed his men for the last time. "Soldiers, we have honoured ourselves through combat. We have attempted the impossible. Over three months, our battery has brought down 102 airplanes. Today, surrounded on all sides, we are powerless. As your commander, I am obliged to avoid a pointless massacre. You are from this moment forward prisoners. Conduct yourselves with dignity. Heil Hitler!"[37] With tears running down their faces, some men raised their arms, while others shook hands. Then almost five hundred soldiers walked into captivity.[38]

Three hours later, a French unit on the outskirts of Sanary stumbled across five German sailors. The Germans told them that two hundred of their comrades were occupying a battery close to the sea at Pointe Gueulois. The French sent one of the sailors to speak with the battery's commander; at 17:15, three officers and 212 marine artillery surrendered.[39] Around an hour later, a French squadron led by Captain Couturier approached the fort at Peyras. A German officer explained that he had ceased all firing at 22:00 the night before and that he had agreed to surrender to a Colonel Huck at noon on the twenty-seventh.[40] Couturier consulted his superiors and then demanded an immediate surrender. Firing off flak guns in a final salute, 205 soldiers and five officers surrendered.[41] As a warm, calm summer evening descended on Toulon, only the port itself remained in German hands.

On the Saint-Mandrier Peninsula—actually an island attached to the mainland by a centuries-old, man-made isthmus—Ruhfus defended the port with some eighteen hundred men.[42] He was under a full siege. As French units descended on the port, the Americans shelled it from sea. German naval personnel, charged with destroying the harbour, began to scurry. On August 27, the Americans captured one vessel and sank another four trying to escape the harbour (a sixth got away). At the same time, the French hit them from land. General Magnan opened a heavy artillery barrage on the five batteries guarding the peninsula. After pounding German positions, he ordered a ceasefire at 17:45.[43] He gave the Germans time to ponder their fate. At 19:00, he sent two officers to negotiate. A further two hours later, the two officers returned with a German lieutenant from the Second Battalion, 918th Grenadier Regiment, which was also based on Saint-Mandrier. His superior, Major Werth, was ill but had authorized him to offer the surrender of the entire regiment, including 20 officers and 650 soldiers.[44] Werth, a known anti-Nazi, argued that Ruhfus had no more authority; in leaving his command post at La Valette to retreat to the port, he constituted a deserter.[45]

This argument spoke well of Werth, but it nonetheless left Ruhfus in de facto command of almost two thousand men. But even this stubborn commander had now accepted that he was out of options. Trapped by enemies on both sides, he faced a choice. He could fight to the last bullet, imposing losses on the Allies by sending all of his men to their deaths.[46] Or he could surrender. He was inclined to the latter, but, a stickler to the very end, he sought some means for doing so in a manner that technically avoided the sort of open disobedience of orders that Werth was prepared to commit. A German propaganda broadcast offered him one. The day before, OKW had announced that "the fierce defence of the fortress Toulon has allowed German troops to escape across the Durance."[47] The Eleventh Panzer Division deserved much more credit than Ruhfus for this escape, but that hardly mattered at the time. Ruhfus had his out, and he reinterpreted his orders. They were not to defend the harbour of Toulon. Rather, they were to tie down the Americans long enough to allow Nineteenth Army to escape to northeastern France.[48] That objective achieved, Ruhfus could then throw in the towel. At 23:45, he surrendered on the same terms as Werth, delivering eighteen hundred men safely into French captivity.[49]

By early morning on August 28, seventeen thousand German soldiers and officers in Toulon and vicinity were prisoners. Huge quantities of weapons, including artillery, had been handed over. The French had suffered 2,700 casualties, the Germans 1,000.[50] Against Hitler's orders, not a single position in the city had fought to the last man, and multiple positions surrendered after only a token fight, or none at all. Moreover, several German soldiers had, unprovoked, offered their services to the French in identifying remaining German military strongholds. Collectively, these actions, combined with Ruhfus's willingness to call it off, contributed greatly to an early surrender. Beyond saving lives, the surrender—a week earlier than the Allies had expected—had cut short the demolition of the port. It fell damaged, but eminently repairable, into Allied hands. Just over two weeks later, on September 13, the French fleet sailed back into the great harbour that it had abandoned to the Germans twenty-one months earlier.[51]

One great port was in Allied hands; they had their eyes on another.

CHAPTER 13

EUROPE'S LIFELINE

Marseille

JUST OVER SIXTY KILOMETRES from Toulon, in the larger and strategically still more important city of Marseille—Toulon was a military
harbour, Marseille a commercial one—a parallel battle was playing out.
Marseille contained not one port but two: the small Old Port, a rectangu-
lar harbour around which the city's Old Town was built, and the massive,
modern harbour to the northwest of it. The newer harbour stretches north
up the coast, whereas the Old Port cuts inland just below it. The city possesses slightly less impressive natural barriers than Toulon: hills to the
southeast and a mountain chain to the north-northeast shelter it, and two
ancient forts guarded the approach to the Old Port.

Marseille's military defences, by contrast, were just as impressive as
those in Toulon: roadblocks and antitank mines outside the city, large
numbers of coastal batteries, minefields and antisubmarine nets around
the islands, and extensive defences at the harbour itself.[1] In addition, block-
ships and empty hospital ships rested in the harbour, waiting to be sunk.[2]
Some ten to twelve thousand troops formed the 244th Infantry Division,
along with four to five thousand naval gunners and riflemen.[3] German
artillery was superior to the French—150 to 200 cannons capable of firing
75 mm to 200 mm shells.[4] Reports on the troops' ages conflict, with different sources claiming they were both disproportionately young and
disproportionately old (perhaps they were both).[5] The Allies were prepared

for a long battle; planners assumed that it would take forty-five days to occupy Marseille.[6]

The defences were divided into a strong inner ring and a less thoroughly defended outer ring that traced the circle formed by mountains and hills around the city.[7] Outer defences were concentrated around the large settlement of Aubagne, some twenty kilometres inland east of the city, and at the castle of Saint-Marcel, guarding the route directly north toward Aix-en-Provence; multiple antitank obstacles blocked routes into Marseille.[8] These defences nonetheless had four disadvantages. First, although the mountainous terrain around Marseille formed a natural defence, there were multiple entry points to the east, north, and southeast of the city, meaning that defences were spread over a forty-kilometre area.[9] A concentrated Allied attack at any one point would enjoy numerical superiority.[10] Second, the great distances between defence points prevented the rapid transfer of units between them. Third, with the exception of Aubagne, to the east of the city, the defence points had weak artillery support.[11] Finally, as everywhere else at this point in the war, the Germans could call on little if any air power.[12]

The defence of Marseille was assigned to General Hans Schäfer, a highly respected veteran of Operation Barbarossa, who had the 244th Infantry Division under his command from August 14. The division was made up of *Volksdeutschen*, ethnic Germans from Eastern Europe, and many were older. They had, however, experience on the eastern front, which gave them battle-worthiness that, in their commander's eyes, cancelled out the disadvantages of age and nationality.[13] Morale was high, and the troops were physically fit and well fed. As another indication of fragmented structures, the commander of Marseille, Oberst Haustein, was under Schäfer's command, but the navy was not.[14] Schäfer had two related orders. First, the army and the navy were under orders to destroy the harbour if it could not be defended.[15] Second, *"the defensive zone of Marseille was to be held to the last man and last cartridge."*[16]

To prepare the defence of the city, Schäfer ordered his 244th Infantry Division to withdraw on the night of August 18–19 from positions between Cassis and Bandol (east of Marseille) toward outer defences of the city, with orders to check the French advance toward Marseille.[17] Destroying their guns, the troops moved into outer Marseille. As they did, Kapitän zur See Stoss, the harbour commander, reported that he had completed preparations for the demolition of the great harbour and the Old Port.[18] The harbour basin was to be poisoned (although sources are unclear as to how this would have been accomplished), all entrances blocked by the scuttling of ships, and all quays, sheds, cranes, and other installations blown up.[19] It would take, Stoss reported, four to six days to do so. By this point, according to Schäfer's (possibly self-serving) account, the great transport bridge had already been destroyed by an overeager demolition team.[20] On August 20, French authorities appealed directly to Foreign Minister Joachim von Ribbentrop, begging him to prevent the harbour's destruction.[21] He ignored the appeal, and another order to destroy the port went out. The navy signalled its agreement.[22]

As the 244th Infantry Division concentrated itself in the city for the final battle, many citizens of Marseille joined the fight. Armed ad hoc groups took to the streets, fired on any Germans they encountered, and had effective control of the streets at night.[23] The FFI in Marseille proved to be a more effective fighting force than in Paris, and they possessed an asset as important as skill: the capacity to instill fear. The FFI spooked Schäfer by turning the streets of the city into a guerrilla battleground, thus making easy movement between defensive positions impossible.[24] Marseille became a chain of defended islands, with the strongest concentration of troops located at the harbour.

And that harbour was very much under threat. On August 20, the German consul general, Freiherr Edgar von Spiegel, phoned Schäfer. Spiegel urged the commander to spare the harbour, as it was the "nerve centre" of the city.[25] Schäfer refused on military grounds but offered two concessions.[26] First, he delayed the start of demolition work for sixteen hours. Doing so would give Spiegel enough time to ask OKW to cancel the demolition order. Spiegel never got a reply, but the delay would be decisive. Second, Schäfer asked Stoss (the harbour commander) to spare the Old Port. This decision, in turn, spared the road that ringed the edge of the port, which would have been lost in the planned destruction. The road was one of the busiest in Marseille.

What would happen to the harbour itself partly depended on French designs. Under de Lattre's original orders, General Jean de Goislard de Monsabert, the mustachioed and kind-looking commander of the Third Algerian Infantry Division, was to move into the city's suburbs and hold them.[27] The bulk of French forces would move north, and Marseille, and the FFI within it, would be left to the Germans.[28] De Monsabert, however, forced de Lattre's hand. Going around his superior, he told a colonel serving under him: "If you see an opportunity [to capture the city], seize it. I can assure you that, by the day after tomorrow, I'll be drinking a *pastis* in Marseille."[29]

On the evening of August 20, the assault on the outskirts of Marseille began. That night, the Seventh Algerian Infantry Regiment (7e régiment de tirailleurs algériens), with tanks from the First Division and two Moroccan battalions (*tabors*), reached the approaches to Aubagne.[30] On de Monsabert's orders, they launched an attack on artillery batteries and an infantry battalion the next morning.[31] "Aubagne," reported the defending commander, "is afire."[32] The Germans put up serious resistance, and the first assault failed.[33] Then all communication went dead, and surrender rumours filtered back to Schäfer. "It is hard to make out," he wrote after the war, "what really happened at Aubagne! It seems scarcely conceivable that, in the face of [German] antitank weapons . . . a tank assault could have such a quick and thoroughgoing success!"[34]

What in fact happened at Aubagne was a skilful French reaction to the initial German rebuff. De Monsabert ordered in Moroccan reinforcements, and they steadily wore down German opposition. Pushing aside antitank obstacles, they attacked the defending Germans with bayonets, knives, and hand grenades.[35] One battalion seized six pieces of artillery. Seeing nothing but death awaiting his young recruits, the commanding German colonel surrendered on the evening of August 22. "How," he asked somewhat petulantly, "can you expect my poor young boys to measure up to your hardened and agile African troops?"[36]

When Schäfer got no word from Aubagne, he ordered a battalion to Camp de Carpiagne, in the mountains, about one kilometre southwest of Aubagne, to counterattack. The battalion was never heard from after it moved out; its commander most likely surrendered.[37] By the end of the twenty-second, the road to Marseille was open.

That same evening, other units were on the verge of entering Marseille as well. On August 21, before Aubagne fell, de Monsabert had ordered the Second and Third Battalions of the Seventh Algerian Infantry Regiment to launch two assaults from the north.[38] Rather than attacking a defensive position at the inner defence right at Saint-Marcel, on a major artery, they pushed their way through the northerly mountain range, climbing cliffs as great as seven hundred metres high, and then came down through La Valentine and Les Olives.[39] At the latter, they thoroughly surprised German forces; some one hundred of them were shirtless and enjoying the southern French sunshine.[40] The French now occupied Aubagne to the east and all the suburbs north of the city.[41]

That city seemed increasingly like a war zone. Inspired by events unfolding in Paris, FFI forces had taken to the streets on the nineteenth. They ambushed German supplies and sprayed the streets with bullets from buildings above them. They fired at a German navy ambulance and entirely encircled the navy hospital in the south of the city; doctors appearing at windows were greeted with gunfire.[42] At the same time, "civilians" (most likely FFI fighters) stormed the main post office with hand grenades, ordering the telephone operators out. The operators hung on while the Germans fired flak guns over the FFI, dispersing most of them.[43]

On the morning of August 23, French forces moving directly into Marseille were met—as so often in newly liberated areas of France—with cheers, flowers, and kisses. Then the battle took a more unconventional turn. Captain Jean Croisa, a priest from Lorraine who saw war as a just crusade against Nazism but who remained horrified by the unnecessary bloodshed, was guiding the Seventh Algerian Infantry Regiment down La Canebière, a grand boulevard leading to the Old Port.[44] As they moved toward the port, shells landed around them; the Germans had opened fire from the Saint-Jean and Saint-Nicolas forts that guarded the northern and southern exits to the sea.[45] Then, dodging cannon fire, cars approached Croisa's men. They were from the liberation committee—the Communist-dominated French resistance. After speaking, the French commander either agreed to or suggested a bluff: they would pretend that the liberation committee had taken the German consul general hostage at the Prefecture. With bullets flying about them, Croisa had Spiegel brought to him. With the French commander in the room, Croisa called Schäfer and persuaded him to meet the French. Schäfer agreed, "in order to spare the civilian population."[46] Schäfer agreed to meet at 16:00.[47]

To Schäfer's surprise, Croisa brought de Monsabert himself behind German lines to meet Schäfer. This in itself was unusual and is evidence of the degree to which the battle for Marseille was nothing like from the fight-to-the-death struggle demanded by Hitler. In postwar reports, both Croisa and Schäfer claimed that the other side asked for an armistice.[48] What they did agree on is that Schäfer raged against the insurgents in the city.[49] The Germans, the general argued, could not recognize them as a military force, and through their actions, Marseille had become a combat area and a legitimate target for shelling.[50] From a legal point of view, Schäfer was right, but de Monsabert was also right on the more important issue: the battle was going to end in a French victory. The only question was when.

De Monsabert left abruptly (and unmolested—this was still a gentlemen's battle), and the attacks continued.[51] On August 24, de Monsabert gave the order to take the hill leading up to the Notre Dame de la Garde cathedral, an imposing structure built on a fort and rising above the city with a massive gilded statue of the Virgin Mary on its steeple. French forces, coming under heavy German fire, at first made little progress.[52] But then, a young Roman Catholic civilian, Pierre Chaix-Bryan, took them to an apartment, through which they could access a narrow corridor leading to a little-known staircase that would lead them safely to the cathedral. Moroccan troops scurried up the steps.[53] At the cathedral, they found the monsignor, some Franciscans, and seventy-four German soldiers who, fearing the civilian population, had sought and received sanctuary.[54]

The port was now surrounded, and elsewhere units were surrendering. On August 25, at Peypin, some twenty-five kilometres north of the Old Port, French forces surrounded a battalion guarding the entrance to the mountain passes. After several calls for ammunition went unanswered, Schäfer received what he regarded as a "surprising" message from the Peypin battalion: "Assemble with remaining forces for our last counterattack." Having fired this off, the commander at Peypin most likely surrendered and marched his troops into captivity. The same evening, the so-called southern sector around Saint-Tropez came under intense mortar fire. The commander attempted a breakout, which failed. He radioed Schäfer for permission to surrender; all communication then ended.[55]

The harbour, meanwhile, remained very much under threat. Earlier that day, mortar and machine-gun fire raked the area, killing among others the harbour commander, Kapitän zur See Stoss. It came from the direction of the cathedral. Stoss's company sent repeated requests to Schäfer to open up an artillery barrage on French positions at Notre Dame. Schäfer refused, as it would have obliterated the cathedral.[56] In his account, Schäfer wrote to de Monsabert in protest the next morning. "I take the liberty of informing you that the German cps [companies] located in the vicinity of the cathedral of Notre Dame of Marseille, had been subject[ed] to repeated mortar and MG fire *from the church*. Up until now, I have rejected all [artillery requests] to shell the structure. However, should this fire continue, I shall be forced, much to my regret, to hold you responsible for the fate of Marseille's sacred shrine."[57] Still in Schäfer's version of events, de Monsabert wrote back immediately. He thanked Schäfer for sparing the cathedral and urged him not to revoke the order. His division, he continued, had not occupied the cathedral and had nothing to do with the fire coming from it.[58] This could only mean that the French resistance had occupied the church, and the French army had no control over it.

De Monsabert offered another version of events: that he told Schäfer that the fire was coming from near the cathedral but not from it, that men were only entering it for prayer and mass, and that Schäfer should "draw the logical consequences and accord to a basilica venerated around the world the respect it deserves."[59] In any case, the machine-gun and mortar fire continued, forcing the evacuation of the company from the harbour and the isolation and capture of an anti-artillery battalion and its commander.[60] Despite this, Schäfer declined to shell the cathedral.[61]

Elsewhere, the end was drawing near. In the north of the city, the battery at Merlan capitulated following a bombardment. Croisa, once again

playing the role of diplomat, urged the Germans to see the futility of continued struggle. When they did, the first soldier who emerged from the
battery, shaking with fear and extremely thirsty, asked Croisa for something
to drink. The captain provided it to him and to all the other men. "The
poor things," Croisa commented with striking generosity.[62] The Germans,
in turn, handed out cigarettes to French soldiers and civilians.

In the northern section of the city, Haustein continued a pointless battle
against French forces along the mountain range at Saint-Antoine. On August
26, the French tore through the defensive position there, isolated a heavy
battery, and engaged the Germans in a stubborn, close-combat battle.[63] The
Germans sustained heavy casualties, and Haustein repeatedly had to request
temporary ceasefires to collect the wounded.[64] The French regimental commander chivalrously granted them, but his efforts to convince Haustein of
the pointlessness of continued struggle failed until the twenty-seventh.[65]
Then, with his forces virtually annihilated, Haustein gave up.

So did everyone else. On the twenty-sixth, twelve hundred Germans
at a garrison in the Parc Borély, south of the Old Port, with or without
permission, had surrendered. The next day, Toulon fell, which opened the
possibility for transferring thousands of Allied troops to Marseille. Multiple
German positions in Marseille surrendered.[66]

Schäfer was now increasingly isolated. At the harbour, light 37 mm anti-
aircraft gun companies guarded its outer breakwaters.[67] Tank troops stood
at the main harbour road that Schäfer had refused to destroy. Some four
hundred naval personnel crowded into underground shelters; eighty were
wounded. Smoke from the battle drifted into the dank tunnels, choking
the men. Mortar fire rained down on the eastern sections of the defences
from positions at nearby factories.[68] Schäfer had lost contact with battalions
at Chaine and Saint-Cyr, between Marseille and Toulon, and Haustein
was surrendering the remnants of his units. At Cap Janet, in the northern
section of the great harbour at Marseille, an anti-aircraft battery had suffered substantial damage from shelling, which in turn had caused the local
civilian population to flee into a railroad tunnel.[69] In an odd turn of events,
German personnel took up responsibility for feeding them, maintaining
order, and protecting them from French shells and artillery.[70] Smoke from

the latter, however, filled these tunnels as well, and the Germans struggled to avoid a panic. Surveying this rapidly deteriorating situation, Schäfer concluded that a continued struggle would only lead to thousands of casualties. Ignoring Hitler's order to fight to the finish, he decided on the evening of August 27 to surrender.[71] He wrote to de Monsabert, making veiled reference to his commanders' often unilateral decision to surrender: "The situation confronting my forces has changed entirely since our August 23 conversation. The majority of positions have surrendered after an honourable resistance. In light of the superior forces engaged against us, the continuation of the struggle will have no result beyond the total annihilation of the forces remaining under my command. I therefore request for this evening, at 21:30, an armistice that will allow the agreement of honourable surrender conditions for the morning of August 28. In the absence of such agreement, we will fight to the last man."[72]

De Monsabert led the negotiations at 8:00 the next day. The most pressing matter was the de-mining of the harbour.[73] With Harbour Commander Stoss dead, however, the chain of command had broken down. Schäfer disavowed responsibility, as did both the next in command after Stoss. Stoss, it seems, had planned all demolitions himself and destroyed all documentation.[74] Demolitions continued that morning until they were stopped definitively at noon. From then, German engineers began removing all mines and explosives while German troops guarded arms depots until they could be handed over to the French. Not unusually in such situations, pockets of resistance continued fighting until Schäfer ordered them to stop.[75]

When the French entered the harbour, it was peppered with mines, and the great transport bridge had been destroyed. Some seventy-five sunken ships and much destroyed equipment blocked the port. Fully forty-one out of forty-two wrecking cranes had been destroyed.[76] Photos taken at the time show a catalogue of destruction along the quays and breakwaters, littered with great hunks of smashed concrete and twisted metal.[77] Like so much else in the last year of the war, the harbour was in part the victim of the failure of July 20. The admiral responsible for the French southern coast had been open to French appeals to spare the port, but he killed himself in Aix-en-Provence after it emerged that Hitler had survived.[78]

Despite the extent of destruction, the harbour was in better shape than that of Cherbourg, to say nothing of the one in Brest. Marseille's Old Port and the road over which supplies would be transported remained fully intact. In the great port, unexploded mines would delay the use of its port but posed no physical danger if properly defused. The glass was half full. General Schäfer is owed qualified credit for this relatively satisfactory state of affairs, as is Consul General Spiegel for urging him on. Schäfer spared the Old Port and the road leading from it into the city; he delayed demolition by a crucial sixteen hours; and he refused to sacrifice hundreds, if not thousands, of men so that demolition could be completed (Generalleutnant Karl-Wilhelm von Schlieben made such a sacrifice at Cherbourg). The rapid French advance also played a decisive role here: had de Monsabert's forces not advanced so quickly into the city, Stoss could have continued with the destruction of the port. An indication of Schäfer's willingness to continue a battle he was losing is given by his August 23 refusal of an armistice, even if we accept his claim that he was more concerned with securing the retreat of Army Group G up the Rhône valley. As so often in the last months of the war, commanders lower down the chain of command may have aided the French advance: at least one French commander wondered why the Germans failed to exploit their numerical superiority with a determined defence of the city.[79]

Finally, something is owed to a corruptible Austrian who saved a giant floating crane, the *Goliath*.[80] The director of technical services of the Marseille Chamber of Commerce came to see him with 200,000 francs in coins and pleaded with him to save the crane. Claiming it needed repairs, the Austrian arranged for it to be towed out of the harbour. Shortly after Marseille's capture, the crane was busy unloading 700 American vehicles.[81]

It is clear that Schäfer was no Hofacker or Stülpnagel—he was not eager to open an entire front to hasten an end to the war. Nonetheless, given the situation as it was, Schäfer refused to sacrifice more men than necessary to a lost battle. In doing so, he marched the majority of his forces—fully eleven thousand of the original force of thirteen thousand—into captivity. The French forces, for their part, behaved very decently, and de Monsabert later justly described the battle as "humane."[82] The great harbour, though damaged, was, thanks to Schäfer's delay, not completely destroyed and far easier to repair than ports in northern France. And above all, he took the crucial decision to spare the city's Old Port. His concern was more for the survival of the city than the supplying of the Allies, but the outcome was the same. The Allies had a key port—indeed, *the* key port at this point in the war—in their hands. Whereas Brest (though its weak connections to the hinterland made it a dubious port anyway) was beyond repair and Cherbourg could not be used until October, Marseille was receiving substantial shipments by early September. From then until March 1945, the southern French ports offloaded the largest tonnage of Allied supplies.[83] In October and November, southern ports supplied 40 percent of the western armies' supplies.[84] The vast majority of these supplies was offloaded at Marseille; at the end of October, the Americans handed Toulon back to the French for the landing of civilian supplies, and only small craft landed at the ports of Saint-Raphaël, Sainte-Maxime, and Saint-Tropez.[85] The Allied success in their armed struggle against the German military would have been unthinkable without the great harbour of Marseille.

The longstanding and, in some cases, continuing controversy over Operation Dragoon is curious in the light of this statistic.[86] National rivalries might have played a role here; the postwar British literature has been notably more critical of Dragoon than the American.[87] There might also be a visceral tendency to sympathize with a figure as sympathetic as Winston Churchill, although writers would do well to realize that the great man's mastery of the big picture—German intentions in the 1930s, Soviet intentions in the 1940s, the importance of the United States throughout—was tempered by some serious weaknesses in his thinking: a desire to micromanage strategy, an obsession with military diversions, and a capacity for erratic reversals of opinion on matters of immense geopolitical importance. Whatever the reasons, the basic facts speak for themselves: in insisting on an invasion of southern France, the Americans destroyed half a German army, allowing only the battered remnants to reform on the edge of the Reich, and they captured not one port but two. This last point would prove to be of crucial importance in supporting their next move: the invasion of Germany itself.

CHAPTER 14

VIOLENCE COMES HOME

Preparing the Defence of the Reich

B Y SEPTEMBER 14, 1944, Allied troops had reached a line that their quartermasters had not expected to see before May 1945. The front ran from north of Ostend through Ghent, Antwerp, cutting south and just east of Liége, through Malmédy, Bastogne, Luxembourg, and then just west of Metz and Nancy. The Allies also had German forces trapped at Dunkirk, Calais, Boulogne, and Le Havre. Combined with the even more impressive collapse of the Wehrmacht on the eastern front—where the Germans had suffered 1.2 million casualties and lost 250,000 horses—the German army appeared to be suffering its death throes.[1]

It was not. All along the front, running approximately from Belfort in northeastern France to Nijmegen in the Netherlands, the Allies' rapid advance came to a grinding halt. Up and down the length of the front, they were only a short drive from the Rhine. Yet it would be six months before they would cross the famous river, and during those months, they fought hard, costly, and at times vicious battles for every kilometre of territory. The fight would never quite match the cruel savagery of the eastern front, and the troops never dug themselves into First World War–style trenches, but the Western Allied advance bore more resemblance to these two types of conflict than its commanders could ever have imagined in the heady days of August 1944.

Patton's Third Army, driven on by the ever more daring general, had pushed through France toward Metz. From the south, General Truscott chased Blaskowitz's rapidly retreating Army Group G up the Rhône valley, providing eventual cover for Patton's southern flank. P-47 fighters shattered German troops' morale in front and on both flanks of Patton's advance. By August 26, the Third Army had advanced 640 kilometres and liberated nearly 340,000 square kilometres of France. The speed of the advance and lengthening supply lines led to fuel shortages, and Patton literally ran out of gas. But he, and the Allies generally, had made stunning progress: in France, Patton had moved an average of thirty kilometres a day.

After refuelling, and intensely frustrated that the delay had allowed Lieutenant General Courtney Hodges's First Army and Montgomery's Twenty-First Army Group to pull abreast of his troops, Patton pushed the Third Army on to the fortress city of Metz, on the Moselle River south of Luxembourg. Armed with his Michelin map, Patton's goal was to blast through Metz, "plunge to the Rhine at Mainz," cross the great river, and then drive on to Frankfurt.[2] The plan was partly founded on weak intelligence: his rapid drive across France had left G-2s (intelligence) scrambling, and they could not disseminate what information they did have about the forts at Metz.[3] But culture also played a role: the Americans viewed ancient forts with a certain modernist disregard. The Germans shared none of it, and they reinforced the great chain of forts, built up over centuries, with men and materiel.[4] Patton, ignorant of all of this but possessed of an obsession with the ancient battleground matching that of Hitler, confidently threw his forces against these defences in early September 1944. It did not go well. Patton faced supply shortages, strong natural defences, and German positions hastily reinforced with Volkssturm troops (more on these in the next chapter). And, finally, there was the weather, which was particularly atrocious, pelting the Americans with rain and turning the roads into mud. "I hope that in the final settlement of the war," Patton wrote to US Secretary of War Henry L. Stimson, "you insist that the Germans retain Lorraine, because I can not imagine a greater burden than to be the owner of this nasty country where it rains every day and where the whole wealth of the people consists in assorted manure piles."[5]

The result of these constraints was clear enough: Patton was not able to march, in his usually triumphant way, into Metz until November 25, and the last of the forts held out until December 13. As the bulk of Patton's forces encircled Metz, others—the XII and XX Corps—pushed on toward the Saar. As the December campaign came to a close, Patton's forces were finally up against the West Wall, and tentative bridgeheads were established across the Saar River.[6]

To the south in Alsace, covering Patton's flank, General Jacob Devers's Sixth Army Group brilliantly used that great advantage in war: being underestimated. Facing an admittedly greatly weakened Nineteenth Army (its best division, the Eleventh Panzer, had been transferred out), Devers's Sixth, with much help from French forces, cleared the Germans out of much of Alsace. On November 23, Strasbourg was in French hands.[7] Over the next three days, the final pockets of resistance surrendered. The tricolour fluttering in the wind atop the cathedral tower, French forces overlooked the Rhine.

There were still nonetheless considerable numbers of Germans to the west of them. The rush on Mulhouse and Strasbourg had left a large concentration of German troops around the city of Colmar that lay between them. There, in what came to be known as the Colmar pocket, the German Nineteenth Army created a tight, defensive mass that repulsed Leclerc's efforts to capture it.[8] It would take a major Allied effort to eliminate the pocket.

That effort would not be made until 1945. In the autumn of 1944, the Allies had far more pressing concerns. North of Patton, General Hodges's First Army ran into great and immediate trouble. The first significant city in Germany the Americans attacked was Aachen, positioned between Allied forces, on the one hand, and the Rhine River and Cologne on the other. Generalleutnant Gerhard von Schwerin, seeing the city abandoned by the police and the Nazi Party, ignored a Führer order to organize a mass evacuation of the city's terrified citizens.[9] He then left a note for the Americans: "To the commanding officer of the U.S. Forces occupying the town of Aachen. I stopped the stupid evacuation of civil population and ask you to give her [i.e., the population] relief."[10] Historians interpreted this as an effort to surrender the city without a fight, but more recent research suggests that Schwerin had a quick change of heart.[11] He ordered portions of his troops to defend the city, and he attempted to retrieve the note he had left for the Americans.[12] Schwerin failed, he was sacked, and the defence of Aachen continued.

It was a long and brutal fight. It took forces from Major General Charles H. Corlett's XIX Corps, with support from Major General J. Lawton Collins's VII Corps, two battles and six weeks to capture Aachen. And even then, it required a savage artillery barrage, an aerial bombardment, and brutal house-to-house fighting. As the infantry and tanks pushed in following the barrage and bombardment, machine-gun fire swept the streets ahead while tanks moved from building to building, spraying them with fire to cover the infantry.[13] Riflemen then rooted out the Germans, who had retreated to the buildings' cellars, with hand grenades and flamethrowers. It was not until October 21 that headquarters, garrisoned at the Hotel Quellenhof in west Aachen, raised the white flag. By then, Aachen was completely destroyed.[14]

After Aachen, Bradley's First and Ninth Armies were meant to jump the Roer (Rur) River and move toward Cologne, but they met fierce German resistance at the West Wall. They encountered further resistance when Hodges, fearing an attack on their flank, decided to push through the Hürtgen Forest, directly east of Aachen, and on to Düren. The thick forests proved to be inhospitable terrain, and the ever-tenacious German forces defied the Allies' hopes of breaking out. The forests prevented the use of tanks, slowed the advance under the best of circumstances, and limited American firepower, while at the same time easing the Germans' ability to cover every point with gunfire.[15] American infantrymen were exposed to a brutal double assault: German artillery burst overhead, cutting down through the thick trees and sending both German fire and tree splinters raining down on American soldiers.[16] Meanwhile, the weather was terrible, even by Germany's sorry autumnal standards. The result for three US Army Corps—the V, VIII, and XIX—was utter misery. Upon relieving soldiers of the Fourth Division, one young recruit of the 83rd Infantry Division observed that the men he was replacing looked like a "collection of ghosts . . . hollow-eyed from the constant pounding of gunfire, and fear of impending death."[17] The Americans broke through only after a late-November offensive named Operation Queen, in which American units took one small town after another in brutal, house-to-house fighting. On December 5, after the town of Bergstein fell, the V Corps's Second Ranger Battalion stormed Castle Hill, just beyond the town, against ferocious German counterattacks.[18] By the time the Americans seized it, only twenty-five men were standing. Overall, the Americans had suffered 25,000 casualties blasting through a forest that they could have easily bypassed.[19] For all of that, the American effort may not have been entirely in vain: it cost the Germans 12,000 troops, which they could ill afford, and denied them the use of the Hürtgen Forest in the preparation for the last great offensive in the west, one launched almost immediately after the fighting in the forest ended.[20]

When the Allies finally emerged from the woods, the open Roer plain stood tantalizingly in front of them. The Germans, however, could use the Roer dams to flood the plain at will, bringing down a biblical revenge on the advancing Americans. British Bomber Command made three attempts to destroy the dams, but Sir Arthur Harris, whose determination to destroy precision targets was invariably a fraction of his determination to destroy German cities, called the operation off. The Americans were stuck.[21]

North of the First US Army was Montgomery's Twenty-First Army Group. After Caen and the Falaise, Montgomery had pushed the Twelfth and Twenty-First Army Groups northeast, enjoying the same rapid advance as the Americans and planning to thrust into Germany with what he called the Schlieffen Plan in reverse.[22] Then, as everywhere else along the front, it began to go wrong. Montgomery, who had distinguished himself at Caen by rhetorical bravery and actual caution, launched one of the most daring or foolhardy operations of the western campaign—Operation Market Garden— on September 17.[23] On its eve, a personal message was read from Montgomery to all the troops. Referring to events since Normandy, he announced:

> The enemy has suffered immense losses in men and materiel; it is becom-
> ing problematical how much longer he can continue the struggle. . . . The
> Nazi leaders have ordered the people to defend Germany to the last and
> to dispute every bit of ground. . . . But the mere issuing of orders is quite
> useless; you require good men and true to carry them out. The great mass

of the German people know that their situation is already hopeless, and they will think more clearly on this subject as we advance deeper into their country; they have little wish to carry the struggle . . . The triumphant cry is now "Forward into Germany."[24]

Bradley laconically noted, "Had the pious teetotaling Montgomery wobbled into SHAEF with a hangover, I could not have been more astonished than I was by the daring adventure he [had] proposed."[25] Montgomery greatly underestimated both the strength of the German army and its commanders' willingness to resist. Allied airborne divisions successfully took bridges at Eindhoven and Nijmegen. But the landing of the British First Airborne Division north of the Rhine bridges at Arnhem, which did not receive the planned support from the "Garden" ground forces in time, was doomed: SS panzer divisions, aided by reinforcements, destroyed the British division, killing 1,130 airborne troops and capturing 6,000 more.[26]

Montgomery's early and failed attempt to jump the Rhine came at the cost of arguably more important objectives. British forces liberated Belgium, including the port of Antwerp, in early September. In anticipation, Model had ordered the demolition of all harbour installations on August 28, but Montgomery ultimately took the important harbour at Antwerp largely intact.[27] As Allied supply lines were seized, access to the harbour presented a golden opportunity, but Montgomery squandered it. He launched Market Garden rather than clearing the Scheldt estuary, the expanse between Antwerp and the North Sea. This decision had two consequences, both of which were damaging to the Allies. First, the bulk of the Fifteenth Army was able to escape, bringing to safety 82,000 men, 530 guns, 4,600 vehicles, 4,000 horses, and other equipment.[28] Second, once the Fifteenth Army had regrouped, it reinforced the Scheldt estuary. Montgomery ordered the Scheldt cleared only in early October. He gave the job to the First Canadian Army, led by Lieutenant General Harry D. G. Crerar, who had the most influence on the "raising, fighting, and eventual disbanding of the greatest army Canada has ever known."[29]

It took over a month of intense fighting for the Canadians to reach their goal. The Germans did not surrender the Scheldt estuary until November

9, after the Canadians launched a bloody amphibious assault on Walcheren Island. The Germans had planned a few days before to send self-propelled, exploding motorboats against the Western Scheldt—a measure that has all the marks of Hitler's obsession with technological wonder weapons.[30] The operation was cancelled owing to weather, and nothing seems to have come of it. After the November 9 surrender, Montgomery's men began clearing the waters approaching Antwerp of German mines, more than a month later than necessary.[31] The majority of almost thirteen thousand casualties, half of them Canadian, could have been avoided. Bradley viewed his British counterpart with seething resentment.[32]

Others viewed him, and the campaign generally, with a dark gloom. In mid-December, General Hastings Ismay sat down to pen a letter: "I cannot escape a sense of disappointment. Things were going so fast in August and September that I had good hopes that coherent opposition in Europe would cease by the end of the year. Nor was I the only one, by a long chalk, who indulged in these daydreams. Alas, they could not come true, and we find ourselves stuck or, at best, only just moving everywhere."[33] There were, in fact, more cracks in German morale than Ismay's dismal portrayal suggests. By early November, German High Command was increasingly worried about illegal surrender and desertion. On the fifth, Rundstedt warned that the initiation of any negotiation, other than temporary armistices to retrieve the wounded, was "strictly forbidden."[34] Once again showing his penchant for Nazi methods, this supposedly honourable Prussian invoked the Sippenhaft policy.[35]

Cracks, however, cannot been seen from a distance, so the Western Allies' main impression was one of mystifying, continuing, and often fierce German resistance. And, equally importantly, the German army's morale improved on the back of its relative successes in the autumn. Army generals and field marshals who had seemed to be living on borrowed time were able to regroup. They used Allied delays to reinforce the western front, taking full advantage of the natural and man-made barriers on and around the West Wall. They exploited their soldiers' natural desire to view the defence of their fatherland as a particularly noble call. And above all, for all their protestations after the war, they used every bit of the skill, ingenuity, and determination that had made the German army the world's premier fighting machine. As they did, however, those commanders faced another dilemma: they, along with party officials, industrialists, civil servants, and even average citizens, had to decide if they were to be complicit in the destruction of a country from within that they were supposedly defending against attacks from without.

CHAPTER 15

TO DESTROY GERMANY

Hitler and Scorched Earth

A s the Allies approached Germany in September 1944, Hitler ordered two responses: defend and, failing that, destroy. The problem with the former was that the German army had already led — and put — exponentially more of its own soldiers to death than it had in World War I; it was running out of manpower.[1] Hitler responded by increasing the Nazi Party's control over military strategy and by raising a militia. A September 20, 1944, decree announced that in the event of enemy forces reaching Reich territory, executive power would be transferred from the military commanders to the Reich Defence Commissioners (Reichsverteidigungskommissare), a position previously created by Hitler.[2] These were the Gauleiter, who were appointed by Hitler and answered to his secretary and chief of the Nazi Party Chancellery, Martin Bormann. In bestowing the title and authority of the Reich Defence Commissioner on most of his Gauleiter, Hitler hoped to establish them as rival commanders to the army. This was a further attempt to extend party influence over the army, and the army leadership was determined to resist it.[3]

A further Führer decree, on September 25, 1944, authorized the creation of what came to be known as the Volkssturm, a militia organized by the Nazi Party from men who were not actively in military service.[4] The suggestion first came from Heinz Guderian, Chief of the Army General Staff, who wanted permission for the Wehrmacht to form a large militia in eastern Germany to raise manpower to the point where a long, defensive battle against the Soviets could be sustained.[5] Bormann convinced Hitler that a militia under army control would lack the necessary zeal.[6] The September 25 Führer decree granted Bormann control over administrative and organizational matters and Himmler control of military matters.[7] In practice, however, the Volkssturm came under Bormann's control. Partly through exploiting the ambiguity in "organization," and partly through pure guile and determination, Bormann sidelined the SS.[8] Himmler gave up by December 1944 and noted that the organization had become "an instrument of power for Bormann . . . and the SS had no interest in it."[9] The matter was actually not that clear: although Bormann had the most power, the Gauleiter and Kreisleiter (who answered to Bormann but also retained some independence of action), the Wehrmacht, the SS, and—insofar as he protected labourers from conscription—even Albert Speer had some influence on the deployment of the Volkssturm.[10] What was clear was that all civilian men between the ages of sixteen and sixty were to be called up, and these ill-trained, badly equipped "soldiers," who had not been drafted into the army for good reasons, were ordered to defend the fatherland. Army commanders generally thought little of them.[11] Most Volkssturm fired only enough ammunition to get themselves, and less often Allied soldiers, killed, to take out the occasional enemy tank, and to anger the Allies enough to launch an artillery barrage.[12] The latter often heralded the total destruction of Germany's already ravaged cities.

It was, perversely, a prospect that Hitler welcomed. On those occasions when he would entertain the possibility of defeat, "scorched earth"—the destruction of all public, industrial, and military infrastructure by a retreating army—had been Hitler's backup plan for all fronts.[13] This continued to hold true even when those fronts withdrew into Germany itself. On September 7, 1944, Hitler ordered that a ruthless scorched-earth policy be applied to German territory. Everything was to be destroyed: industrial facilities, bridges, gas distribution systems, waterworks, power plants, museums, theatres, opera houses, and all records.

According to the account of Hitler's former architect and armaments minister, Albert Speer, one man blocked these plans: Speer himself. In the fifteen years that separated Speer's release from prison and his 1981 death, Speer devoted himself to shaping the historical record with the same determination, tirelessness, and precision that marked his efforts to build public architecture, clear houses of Jews, increase armaments production, and enslave hundreds of thousands of forced labourers.[14] According to Speer, he alone saved Germany from its Wagnerian fate. Racing back and forth across the country, he spared bridges, saved industry, preserved coal stocks, and rescued the Netherlands from massive flooding. He even stopped to feed the hungry along the way. One gets the impression that, had Speer been in Dresden on February 13, 1945, he would have raised his arms to the skies and turned the bombers around.

Speer's claims have been uncritically reproduced by some authors, mostly famously by his biographer, Joachim Fest. Others have been scathing. As journalist Dan van der Vat, approvingly quoting John Galbraith, put it: "Speer's claims to have frustrated Hitler's scorched-earth decree almost single-handed[ly]" were a story that "had gained much in the telling and contained 'major elements of fantasy.'"[15] As in the case of Choltitz, the truth falls short of Speer's construction of it, but he is not, for all that, quite the charlatan that van der Vat makes him out to be. Speer did act against Hitler, and documents presented in this book confirm Hitler's orders and Speer's willingness to disobey them.

The first scorched-earth orders went out as the Allies closed in on the Reich from the east, south, and west. On September 7, Hitler had an editorial published in the Nazi mouthpiece, the *Völkischer Beobachter*, calling for the widespread application of scorched-earth policies on German soil. "Not a German stalk of wheat," thundered the newspaper, "is to feed the enemy, not a German mouth to give him information, not a German hand to offer him help. He is to find every footbridge destroyed, every road blocked—nothing but death, annihilation and hatred will meet him."[16]

Speer had been entirely willing to tolerate a scorched-earth policy on the eastern front beyond the borders of Germany.[17] But he began to draw the line when it came to the western front and, above all, to Germany itself. His first response to Hitler's September order was to argue. He turned Hitler's professed belief in ultimate victory against him: given Germany's supposedly inevitable victory, any Allied occupation of German positions could only be temporary.[18] As Germany would soon recover those positions, it made little sense to turn them into industrial wastelands. Speer's next response was to act. He dictated a telegram making this argument, rescinding the implicit scorched-earth order and replacing it with a direct order that industry was to be "paralyzed" just before the Allies captured it.[19] What this meant in practice was that essential mechanical parts would be removed from weapons and industrial equipment. Without these parts, the equipment was useless, but it could be quickly and easily rendered functional again by replacing the missing components.

What was unclear, however, was who should receive these orders. The obvious choice was the Wehrmacht, as it possessed the explosives and weapons needed to set Germany alight in accordance with Hitler's order. The army was, however, less independent of the party following Stauffenberg's July 20 assassination attempt, and it was, in any case, not the only institution capable of implementing scorched earth. The Nazi Party's power spread out from Berlin to all reaches of the Reich through the Gauleiter, the Nazi regional governors who controlled the Volkssturm. Speer therefore needed to work through the Gauleiter, and this, in turn, meant that Speer had to involve his rival and Hitler's secretary, Martin Bormann.

In the middle of September, Speer prepared a letter for the main Gauleiter in western Germany: Wagner in Baden, Hoffmann in Westphalia South, Meyer in Westphalia North, Schleßmann in Essen, Florian in Düsseldorf, Bürckel in Westmark (Palatinate/Saar area), Simon in Moselland (Koblenz-Trier-Luxembourg), and Grohé in Cologne-Aachen. It stated: "The Führer has decided that he can shortly re-conquer the territories now lost. Since the Western areas are vital for the armaments and war production needed to continue fighting, all evacuation measures must be geared to the possibility of quickly restoring the industry of these areas to full operation. We must therefore avoid any extensive destruction. . . . Not until the last moment are the industrial installations to be rendered useless for a considerable time through 'paralysis.'"[20]

It was a clever move. To express anything approaching realism about Germany's prospects in 1944 and 1945 was to risk death; "pessimism" was a charge frequently levelled by Hitler, the SS, and Wehrmacht generals in the last year of the war. Rommel's supposedly pessimistic comments first brought suspicion down on him, and in the end, they contributed to his murder. Under Speer's formulation, victory was still possible, perhaps inevitable. And as he noted after the war, "unless [Hitler] cancelled his order for destruction, he was admitting that the war was lost. By such an admission he undercut the whole basis for total resistance."[21]

Speer framed his arguments in terms of military considerations. Any large-scale disassembly and transportation of industry would cost weeks of production; the destruction of electricity, gas, and water supplies would cut off troops; and the flooding of electricity works would put them out of operation for months.[22] He made no mention of the human costs of such destruction. This might have been strategic: neither Hitler nor Bormann possessed great reservoirs of sympathy for the German people, though it seems that even the thuggish Bormann was capable of an iota of compassion.[23] But an intervention a few days later betrayed Speer's belief in victory: on September 19, he complained bitterly and widely that a munitions factory near Aachen had been paralyzed two to three days too early. Factories, he insisted, were to keep operating until the last possible moment.[24]

Speer sent his order to Bormann on September 15, asking him to obtain Hitler's approval of the document; Speer also asked that Bormann include a note when forwarding the order, presumably to give at least the appearance of Bormann's own blessing of Speer's directives.[25] Speer phoned headquarters to see if it had been presented to Hitler; it had been, and the dictator had made only a minor change.[26] This satisfied Bormann, who passed the order directly on to the Gauleiter.[27] Striking while the iron was hot, Speer also urged Bormann to look east as well as west: "[I]t is necessary," he wrote to Bormann on the sixteenth, "that the letter sent to the western Gauleiter be forwarded, with a note from you, to Gauleiter Koch, Forster, Greiser, Bracht and Hanke."[28] Within a few days, Speer informed the Gauleiter of East Prussia, Danzig, the Warthegau, Upper and Lower Silesia, the Sudetenland, the Lower Donau, Vienna, Steiermark and Kärnten in Austria, and Tirol that Hitler's initial destruction orders had been rescinded.[29]

Over the next two weeks, orders countermanding scorched earth were distributed across the country as well as up and down the Nazi Party and Wehrmacht hierarchies. They all said basically the same thing: industry was not to be evacuated, production was to keep going until the last moment, and in the event of immediate Allied occupation, equipment was to be disabled but not destroyed. Willy Liebel, the mayor of Nuremberg whom Speer had appointed head of his Central Planning Board, passed the order on to Generalleutnant Max Schindler, head (*Beauftragter*) of the Armaments Inspectorate West, as well as to his Armaments Commissioners in the Wehrkreise (Military Districts) V (Stuttgart), VI (Münster), XII (Munich), and XIII (Breslau).[30] The choice of Schindler was not without irony. Liebel, a Nazi fanatic who had enthusiastically deported Nuremberg's Jews to their deaths, was writing to a contact, but not relative, of Oskar Schindler (the officer may have helped the more famous civilian Schindler in his efforts to employ and protect Jews).[31] On September 18, Speer forwarded Bormann's order on to Goebbels.[32] Two days later, Speer wrote to the army, navy, and Luftwaffe in Berlin, demanding that the transportation of industry from threatened areas on the western front be halted and reminding them that only the director of the Armaments Commission (Rüstungskommission) could decide which production would be moved.[33] Günther Schulze-Fielitz, General Inspector for Water and Energy and a senior figure under Speer, sent out the same orders to the Economics Ministries in Bremen, Münster, Düsseldorf, Cologne-Aachen, Koblenz, Wiesbaden, Saarbrücken, and Karlsruhe; to the western Gauleiter; to Generalleutnant Schindler; and to the Armaments Commissioners.[34]

The Armaments Commissioners were Speer's men: he set up the Armaments Commissions in 1942 in order to centralize control over regional economic institutions.[35] They were the regional anchors of Speer's Armaments Ministry, and their creation and institutionalization gave Speer, more than anyone else in the Third Reich, centralized control of industrial production across the country.[36] They gave him both formal power over and a close working relationship with the men now charged with implementing, and more importantly blocking, scorched-earth measures. And they played along brilliantly. Hörner, for example, the commissioner in Military District VI

(Westphalia, northern Rhineland, and eastern Belgium) instructed coal-mine operators on the left side of the Rhine to prevent "under all circumstances" the destruction of the mines and to prepare to bring them back on line as soon as the enemy was expelled from German territory.[37] Whether Hörner, the mine operators, or anyone else believed that the Allies were about to be expelled from Germany was unclear, but it did not matter. Speer thus sought to (a) secure control over the order's implementation, (b) neutralize it as much as possible, and, to the degree that this was not fully possible, (c) grant veto power to the Armaments Commissioners—that is, to himself.

The next day, Speer moved to soften further the "paralyzing order" Bormann had sent out to the western Gauleiter. The complex nature of Germany's electricity grid meant that it could not be shut down for a speci-fied, limited area; any shutdown would necessarily affect a large area and would, moreover, knock out water and food supplies.[38] Untold numbers would be without food or water and without any means to secure them. To check this, Speer ordered the Armaments Commissioners to follow complex sets of procedures before paralyzing the electricity grid. Before it could go ahead, Dr. Richard Fischer, the Reich's Electricity Load Administrator (*Reichslastverteiler*), a central government figure responsible for energy dis-tribution across Germany, had to agree. If he agreed, then permission still needed to be sought from the *Bezirkslastverteiler*, his local counterparts.[39] The order was then relayed on to the western Gauleiter. These bureaucratic layers may have provided necessary safeguards. But they did more than this: they slowed the decision-making process, introduced multiple veto points, and in so doing bought time. This, in turn, made it highly likely that advanc-ing Allied forces would capture the electricity grid intact.

Having largely succeeded in blocking the first scorched-earth orders, Speer then sought to locate control over the implementation of dismantling or destruction orders in the hands of his ministry, the factory owners, and the Wehrmacht—that is, away from the party apparatus. On October 2, he urged Gauleiter across the Reich to leave the final decision on whether and when industry would be destroyed or paralyzed up to the factory directors.[40] In making their decision, they were not to consult the Gauleiter but, rather, Speer's Armaments Commission. It did not take a great gift of imagination to see that factory directors were the actors least likely to implement destruction or even paralysis orders to the detriment of their own facilities. Speer also implemented extra measures to protect Germany's electricity supply, a source of enduring concern to him. On October 5, he ordered that all local electricity authorities refer all paralysis and destruction orders to Fischer.[41] Fischer was a close associate of Speer, having been awarded an Iron Cross at Speer's suggestion. Two weeks later, on the seventeenth, he wrote again to the western Gauleiter, reminding them that all decisions on the evacuation of industry were not to be made at the local level but, rather, had to go through Speer and his Armaments Commission.[42]

With the Gauleiter largely sidelined, the Wehrmacht proved an easier sell: on October 21, an order passed from Model down through the chain of command: electricity and gas supplies would only be paralyzed, water supplies would be preserved, and industry would be kept running up to the last moment.[43] Following Speer's instructions (*Anordnungen*), the order continued, neither plants nor parts were, as a rule, to be destroyed. In the event that destruction proved necessary, the decision was to be made by the army, in close consultation with local officials responsible for electricity distribution, with the companies themselves, and with the Armaments Commissioners. All military decisions, furthermore, needed to be subject to four key considerations:

1) provision for the remaining population;
2) adequate supplies of water;
3) water levels in the mines; and
4) supplies for essential services such as food and milk providers, hospitals, waste collection, and essential communications.

By the end of October, Speer had in place a command structure that gave his subordinates, working with the Wehrmacht, the last word on whether industry was dismantled or destroyed, and he had created a complex system of checks and balances that all but ruled out the destruction of the electricity grid. These revocation orders had passed to all corners of the Reich.[44]

Throughout all of this correspondence, Speer had two overriding concerns: that industrial infrastructure be preserved, and that production be maintained at the highest level until the latest possible moment. The goals of protecting Germany from Hitler and continuing the fight against the Allies were, at this point, complementary. Speer was also clearly and genuinely concerned about the fate of civilians caught up in the battle, despite what his critics have since said.[45]

No other senior National Socialist could have done the job. Speer was one of very few people in the Reich—perhaps even the only one—with such power to influence actors' willingness/unwillingness to destroy. He had access to and influence over industry, manpower, and above all, Hitler himself. No single Gauleiter, and not even a figure such as Bormann, had such power. Speer organized the campaign against the destruction, and the many orders to disable rather than destroy were sent by him or, importantly, cited his authority.[46]

The battle over scorched earth was far from over. Indeed, it would go on well into 1945, reaching its peak in March, when even Hitler found unconvincing the argument that the German army would soon reoccupy lost territory. In early December, Speer had to fight his battle over coal mines anew with Feldmarschall Keitel. On the sixth, Keitel, citing the "will of the Führer," wrote to Speer and urged him to revise his order to "disable, not destroy" coal mines.[47] As the Allies could put such coal stocks to excellent use, particularly in the Saar, it was essential to destroy them completely (*restlos*). Speer acted with his usual speed: as soon as he received the letter, he fired his own off to the Armaments Commissioner in Saarbrücken, instructing him that "all orders to destroy rather than to disable coal mines are null and void. The Führer has today again declared that he desires that coal mines be only disabled in the manner we have specified."[48] Thanks to Speer, it seems he had. On December 12, Keitel, who never had an opinion distinct from those of Hitler, sent an order to the head of Army Group G stating that all industries, including coal mines, were to be disabled but not destroyed.[49] Speer used his most recent victory to further strengthen the case against scorched earth. On the same day that Keitel wrote to the army, Speer wrote to the navy: he outlined his argument in favour of paralysis rather than destruction, and all but begged Großadmiral Karl Dönitz to reverse a late-November order for the navy to destroy shipyards before withdrawing.[50]

This frenetic burst of activity did the job. Hitler did not revisit his scorched-earth order for the rest of 1944. Speer's actions were clever, and—importantly in the paranoid, post–July 20 context—they were brave. They were also designed to help win the war. In his memoirs, Speer gives the impression that he had given up on victory as early as May 1944, that he saw then the madness of Hitler's plans, and that almost humanitarian reasons drove him to act in the autumn of 1944.[51] Speer did show humanitarian concern, but these claims are terrific exaggerations. He remained committed to victory far longer than he would admit, and, importantly, he first sought to save German industry because it served the cause of war.[52] Speer had flirted with the idea of a negotiated settlement of the war following the Allies' landing at Normandy, but these doubts had no effect on his commitment to the production of armaments for the prosecution of a war that was killing millions of people.[53]

In late 1944, it was a war effort that still had life in it. Part of the reason that Hitler abandoned scorched earth at this point was that the pessimism underpinning it gave way to a new optimism. Hitler had a plan for pushing the Allies back by unleashing a vast counteroffensive on the western front in the Ardennes. After a devastating blow had been dealt to the Western Allies, he would then be able to transfer divisions to the eastern front and push the Soviets back.

The idea was to assemble twenty-five divisions of Wehrmacht soldiers over a seventy-mile stretch of the front in the heavily wooded Ardennes.[54] In a surprise attack, two armies—the Fifth and Sixth Panzer Armies—would break across the Maas River around Liége and Dinant, push toward Brussels, split Allied forces in two, and eliminate the supply port at Antwerp.[55] The Fifteenth Army, meanwhile, would launch an attack toward Aachen, pinning Hodges's First US Army there. Two factors evidently underpinned Hitler's thinking.[56] First, the element of surprise, which had served him so well in 1940 and 1941, would again work its wonders. Second, the need to coordinate a response between Churchill and Roosevelt, whom he evidently saw as strategic heads of armies in the Hitlerian mould, would delay an Allied response until it was too late.

Generaloberst Alfred Jodl presented Hitler's plan to senior western commanders on November 3. They thought it hopeless.[57] The army had too few tanks, too little fuel, and too few men to manage it. They could forget about taking Antwerp. At best, German divisions might reoccupy Aachen and use it as a base for a subsequent westward push.[58] More importantly, it would be suicide to decrease troop concentrations on the eastern front, where the Russians were likely preparing their own offensive. Jodl rejected the generals' more modest strategic objectives out of hand. The result had to be so stunning that it would "make the western powers ready to negotiate."[59] Despite their objections, the generals quickly fell in line and soon touted, and in some cases perhaps shared, Hitler's delusions.[60] The problem of Allied air superiority would be solved by putting five thousand German planes in the air (the Germans could barely manage five hundred at this point) and the armies would reach Antwerp within four days.[61] By December 16, Rundstedt was calling for a holy war against the Anglo-Americans.[62]

The effort failed. The Germans enjoyed the advantage of surprise and cloud cover for a few days, but by Christmas Eve the clouds cleared. A vast armada of American bombers pitilessly hammered German troops. The German formations were smashed, and bridges, rail lines, and airfields were destroyed.[63] American ground forces then counterattacked. Suffering the torments of ice and snow and bitterly fighting to take one small town after another, the men of the American First and Third Armies slowly began to push the Germans back.[64] The Americans had suffered considerable losses: 80,987 were killed, wounded, or missing.[65] But these losses were either equal to German ones (if we believe German estimates) or 20,000 greater (if we believe the highest Allied one).[66] Most important in the overall strategic context, the Germans had committed their main strategic reserves in the west and left themselves still more exposed to the far greater threat facing the Wehrmacht: the Soviets' great push westward.[67]

CHAPTER 16

FIGHTING TO THE LAST MAN

The Allies at the Rhine

O N JANUARY 1, 1945, with the Ardennes counterattack effectively over but the Germans still in possession of the bulge created by it, Feldmarschall Model drew up an order for his men. It was pure bravado:

Beneath the thunder of the fierce winter battle in the West, we march over the threshold into the new year.

A year of the most difficult trials lies behind us. The German people withstood them all [as] you all stood guard on the Rhine.

Soldiers of the Eifel and Aachen! As the year turned, the Führer gave the order to attack. Your proven [*bewährte*] bravery and your incomparable worth as soldiers for Greater Germany have, despite all the difficulties of terrain, weather, and the enemy's material superiority [*Feindüberlegenheit*], achieved great success under the most trying of conditions. . . .

In 1945, you must once again, with boldness and steadfastness, seize the . . . sword of vengeance and raise it in our defence [*in der Abwehr erfolgreich führen*], and strike the enemy wherever you face him.

For the New Year, then, a new call:

The Front for the homeland!

The Homeland for the Front!

Adolf Hitler's Germany shall fight until victory![1]

Neither Bradley nor Eisenhower drew up a similar memorandum, and not only because American communiqués throughout the war were distinguished by uninspiring rhetoric. The Ardennes counterattack had caught them off guard, and, combined with stiffening resistance on the borders of the Reich, had seriously shaken Eisenhower's nerves. He wrote to Marshall on January 7:

> Due to the comparatively low scale of effort that the enemy is compelled to make on other fronts, an extremely high proportion of his personnel and material is pouring into the Western Front. Enemy units that have been badly cut up . . . are persistently and quickly built up. Replacements in tanks and men reach the front in a matter of days. . . . There is a noticeable and fanatical zeal on the part of nearly all his fighting men as well as the whole nation of 85,000,000 people, successfully unified by terror from within and fear of consequences from without. The Germans are convinced they are fighting for their very existence and their battle action reflects their spirit.[2]

All of this weighed heavily on Eisenhower as he considered the Allies' strategy for a counterattack.

In organizing it, they faced four challenges. First, they had to push the Germans back to the lines of December 1944 and thus flatten the bulge created by the Germans' unsuccessful drive for Antwerp. Second, they had to eliminate the Colmar pocket in Alsace. Third, they had to push through the dense fortifications of the West Wall, itself situated in a web of twisting rivers. Finally, they had to cross the Rhine River.

The question was where, at how many points, and what to do afterwards. Montgomery wanted a single northward thrust, a crossing of the Rhine north of Cologne, followed by a dash toward Berlin. Allied troops, led of course by Montgomery himself while the Americans did the dirty work of tying the Germans down in western Germany, would march triumphantly into the capital of the Third Reich. Bradley, by contrast, argued for a thrust through the Saarland, across the Rhine, and east toward Frankfurt.[3] Several calculations informed Bradley's position. Montgomery's proposal would involve crossing soggy ground and multiple waterways, the bridges over which the Germans would surely blow up. Advancing directly eastward would carry the Allies over friendlier terrain, allow them to seize both the Ruhr as well as the industrially important area around Leipzig, and cut off any German effort to withdraw forces southward and create an Alpine fortress—a very real, if unwarranted, fear at the time. Finally, the fact that Montgomery authored the Berlin plan was itself an argument against it. The Americans had long found grating the British tendency to combine imperiousness with a begging hand, and by early 1945, they were disinclined to indulge it. As Eisenhower put it after the war, "Montgomery had become so personal in his effort to make sure that the Americans . . . got no credit, that, in fact, we hardly had anything to do with the war, that I finally stopped talking to him."[4] Eisenhower, who had originally backed Montgomery, switched to a broad-front strategy. By pushing into Germany along a line stretching from Bonn in the north to Mannheim in the south, the Allies would prevent the Germans from concentrating their full force on a devastating counterstrike.[5] Two US corps would support Montgomery's advance north, but the bulk of the American forces moved east toward Frankfurt.

Montgomery fought the Americans every step of the way, and at points he would win small tactical victories (the vetoing of a bridgeless Rhine crossing, for instance) that would intensely annoy Patton, Hodges, and Bradley. But in the end, his resistance was as futile as that of the Germans. From the Normandy landings, the Americans, backed up by immense wealth and firepower, were to determine the course of the war on the western front. The British were becoming ever more marginalized. Churchill was a master at covering British weakness in a thick blanket of inspirational oratory, but neither he nor anyone else in his bankrupt nation could reverse or even limit that decline. The British century had given way to the American, and it was the American politicians and American generals who would determine military strategy in the western theatre.

The die was cast. A combination of British and Canadian armies would move northeast toward Bremen, Hamburg, and Lübeck, while other Canadian forces were to cut directly north in order to liberate Holland. The massive American Twelfth Army Group would move directly east into

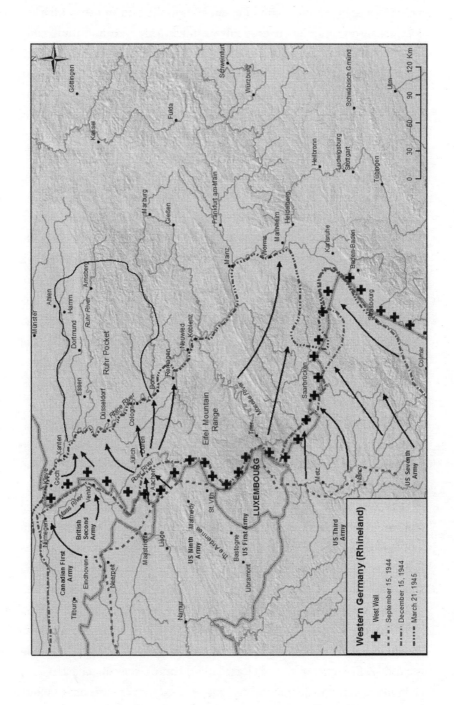

Western Germany (Rhineland)

＋ West Wall
－ ・ ・ September 15, 1944
－ ・ ・ ・ December 15, 1944
－ ・ ・ ・ ・ March 21, 1945

Canadian First Army

British Second Army

US Ninth Army

US First Army

US Third Army

US Seventh Army

LUXEMBOURG

Ruhr Pocket

Eifel Mountain Range

The Ardennes

Nijmegen

Tilburg

Eindhoven

Weert

Maastricht

Namur

Liège

Libramont

Bastogne

St. Vith

Malmedy

Goch

Xanten

Kleve

Venlo

Meuse River

Roer River

Jülich

Aachen

Düren

Cologne

Bonn

Rhine River

Remagen

Neuwied

Koblenz

Düsseldorf

Essen

Dortmund

Hamm

Ahlen

Münster

Ruhr River

Arnsberg

Moselle River

Trier

Metz

Nancy

Saarbrücken

Marburg

Gießen

Frankfurt am Main

Mainz

Worms

Mannheim

Heidelberg

Karlsruhe

Baden-Baden

Strasbourg

Colmar

Heilbronn

Ludwigsburg

Stuttgart

Tübingen

Schwäbisch Gmünd

Ulm

Würzburg

Schweinfurt

Fulda

Kassel

Göttingen

0 30 60 90 120 Km

central Germany, where it would encircle, isolate, and capture the Ruhr, and then move onward to the Elbe. Meanwhile, Patton's Third Army would move to the south through Metz and over the Moselle before heading to Jena and then cutting south into Austria and Czechoslovakia.

The restoration of the pre-December Allied position took until the last week of January. By the end of the month, the Allies were on Germany's western edge, right up against the West Wall. Montgomery's Twenty-First Army Group was the farthest north, with the Canadian First Army on top and the British Second below it. Just south of the British Second was the US Ninth Army, which was temporarily under Montgomery's command. He held an area running from Arnhem in the north, across the Waal and Maas (Meuse) Rivers, and along the Roer River to the dams near Jülich. The First US Army was in the middle section, in an area running from Liège in the north down past Bastogne in the south. Finally, Patton's Third Army was in Lorraine, while Devers's Sixth Army Group was in Alsace. In front of the Allies lay the Moselle and the small, twisting rivers of the Eifel; the great Roer dams; the dense Hürtgen Forest; and, running north–south, the belt of concrete pillboxes, minefields, entrenchments, and antitank obstacles that made up the West Wall.[6] And of course the bulk of the Reich lay behind that great natural and psychological barrier: the Rhine River.[7]

In late January, in three well-orchestrated operations, the Allies attacked. General Devers's Sixth Army Group, made up of French and American troops, launched a series of assaults on the German front in Alsace. Devers's forces were on the edge of Colmar itself by February 2, when the 109th Infantry Regiment, which could have easily taken the town, stood aside to let the French Fifth Armoured roll in and enjoy the local population's ecstatic welcome. De Lattre then ordered his men to cut south-west toward Rouffach; US General Allen's Twelfth Armored took the town while the French I Corps troops met other tasks. The Colmar pocket was cut in two, and German forces surrounded the Vosges Mountains. The US Third Division's Thirtieth Infantry Regiment, meanwhile, moved on Neuf-Brisach. A French civilian guided the Americans through a "secret" tunnel into the town. There, seventy-six German soldiers calmly awaited captivity. Their officers, shortly before fleeing, had ordered them to the resist to the last man.[8] Finally, de Lattre attempted a second encirclement, trapping the Germans between Neuf-Brisach and the Rhine. He just missed. The 708th Volksgrenadier Division led a desperate evacuation across the Rhine against orders; it escaped intact, and remnants of other units followed. By February 9, American and French troops had, after bitter, sometimes hand-to-hand fighting, destroyed German resistance in the Colmar pocket. Alsace was liberated, and Allied troops had reached the upper Rhine, the gateway to southern Germany and Austria.

The day before, at the northern end of the front, Montgomery's Twenty-First Army Group had launched a coordinated operation from positions around Nijmegen. In the early hours of February 8, 769 aircraft of Bomber and Fighter Command launched devastating tactical raids on German towns southeast of Nijmegen. Then, over a thousand guns opened fire in a massive artillery assault. "The concentration of fire," concluded the official Canadian history of the war, "which fell on the German 84th Division that day was probably not equalled on a similar front during the entire war in the west."[9] The results for the division, hardly one of Germany's best, were severe: collapsed communications, dazed gun crews unable to offer any resistance, and everywhere "an impression of the overwhelming force opposed to them."[10] In what must have been a stunning contrast, the battlefield suddenly fell silent as the Canadians laid out a smokescreen across the entire front. Under the thick cover, four divisions emerged slowly from the woods behind Groesbeek (south of Nijmegen) and pulled up to their start lines. The First Canadian Army was preparing its advance into Germany.

These forces faced the West Wall fortifications, roads blocked with concrete and steel, strongpoints at every farm and village, and the forest itself.[11] They would soon face a further obstacle: rising water. On February 9, the Germans set off charges on the Roer dams, flooding the surrounding area.[12]

Patton, meanwhile, made a plunge from the south toward Trier while his men cleared the Germans out of the "Orscholz switch," the area created by the confluence of the Moselle and the Saar. After persuading Bradley to allow him to retain Eleventh Armored Division longer than SHAEF instructions allowed, Patton drove triumphantly into Trier along Caesar's road, smelling "the sweat of the legions."[13] The quick capture of the city may have spared its utilities: German soldiers, dressed in civilian clothing, had placed naval limpet bombs and plastic explosives in a generator bearing house (supplying electricity to the city) and two hundred pounds of explosives in the city's waterworks generator house.[14] Not everyone was obeying Speer.

On February 23, one week before Patton entered Trier, US General William Simpson's Ninth Army launched Operation Grenade, designed to bring the Americans then in the area near Aachen to the northeast in order to meet the Canadians, who were moving southeast. They faced a similar set of obstacles: two forests, the flooded Roer, the Erft River connecting the Roer and Rhine, and German fortifications.[15] The greatest challenge was jumping the flooded Roer; Simpson was able to get his men across in boats, but the Germans proved adept at wrecking the Americans' efforts to establish bridges over which armour could cross. The strong current also certainly did not help. The result was often that infantry on the eastern side had to face the Germans without tanks.

After the tough Roer crossing, the Americans met pockets of determined resistance, but the advance was rapid. American forces reached the Rhine but still had to cross it. And to cross it, they needed bridges. At multiple points—in Düsseldorf, Krefeld-Uerdingen, Rheinhausen (not far south of Duisburg), and Wesel—the Americans came close to and sometimes within a hair's breadth of intact bridges only to see them collapse under the force of German explosives. Other units heard the distant sound of exploding bridges up and down the Rhine. In the face of repeated disasters, Simpson proposed crossing the Rhine without a bridge between Düsseldorf and Uerdingen, turning right down the bank of the river to secure other crossings, making for open country on the northern edge of the Ruhr, and moving east to capture Hamm.[16] Montgomery vetoed the operation on the ostensible grounds that the crossing would make the industrial Ruhr into a battleground (it would not have), but in truth, he wished to deny the Americans a crossing and claim maximum glory for his own set-piece Rhine crossing.[17] Montgomery's vanity possibly denied the Allies an early Rhine crossing and Ruhr envelopment, but fortune conspired to deny him the fame associated with the first Rhine crossing.

As the Ninth Army moved northeast across the Roer in late February, and while Patton's Third Army launched the southward "probes" that would eventually take Trier, Hodges's First Army moved toward Cologne.[18] By March 5, Collins's VII Corps reported that the city was almost within his grasp, and by March 7, General Hodges visited Cologne's imposing cathedral, rising relatively unscathed over the smouldering shell that remained of the ravaged city.[19] Rhinelanders almost immediately began approaching American soldiers, calling them "liberators," and taverns offered GIs free beer and wine. A few civilians nervously asked, "They're not coming back, are they?"[20]

As Collins approached Cologne and the Rhine, disintegrating German units staggered backward, retreating over the river in boats and over temporary bridges. Up and down the river, they continued to destroy bridges, which fell into the water like dominoes. As they did, one of Speer's men vented his frustration in writing. "It is madness," he wrote on March 7, "to sink our towboats [Schlepper] and most essential bridges, which we need most urgently. This amounts to abandoning voluntarily the entire territory west of the Rhine. These actions . . . must be prevented in the future."[21]

One bridge, a traditionally not very important one, remained. As the US VII Corps eliminated the last pockets of opposition around Cologne, US First Army's III Corps under Major General John Millikin moved toward the Ahr River, which flows perpendicularly into the Rhine on the latter's west side. On March 7, the Corps's Ninth Armored Division ordered one column from its Combat Command B — its primary fighting units — to jump the Ahr near its confluence with the Rhine while the other moved toward Remagen.[22]

The Thirty-Ninth Infantry Regiment, meanwhile, moved on Bad Godesberg, just south of Bonn. When the Second Battalion approached the city, Colonel Lunn, the battalion commander, and a Major Carrier reached a Roman Catholic orphanage on the Godeshöhe.[23] There, a Sister Elisabethine offered to help Major Carrier, who wanted to give Bad Godesberg the opportunity to surrender. Undeterred by several failed attempts, he reached a professor of medicine, Hans Schulten. Schulten, in turn, reported the surrender offer to Bad Godesberg's acting mayor,

Heinrich Ditz. (The town's actual mayor had fled across the Rhine.) Ditz was already on side. The person who mattered was the local army commander (Stadtkommandant), but he had already packed up and left town. On the same day, however, a Generalleutnant Richard Schimpf had led his Third Parachute Division—about six thousand men—into the vicinity of Bad Godesberg.

Fortunately for Bad Godesberg, Schimpf had little intention of keeping them there. Ignoring Model's order to defend the city, he started withdrawing his entire division to the right side of the Rhine, denuding Bad Godesberg of Wehrmacht soldiers. He then went to the Swiss consul general, Dr. Franz-Rudolph von Weiss, hoping to place himself under the neutral state's protection. He had come to the right place. Weiss could not offer him protection, but he could offer assistance. The consul general had befriended another local doctor, Paul Pies, and Pies had urged him to negotiate with the Americans. Weiss declined, saying he had no authority to do so.

On March 8, these disconnected efforts converged. Pies repeatedly called city hall, where someone finally told him, "Do whatever you want!" Meanwhile, Heinrich Ditz was already driving out to meet Colonel Lunn at the orphanage; he was harassed by scornful German soldiers shouting "traitor!" at him along the way. Ditz told Lunn that the city's commander, Schimpf, had not authorized his visit but that the commander was prepared to hand the city over without a fight. Ditz had derived this conclusion from the sort of conversation typical among resisters: nothing was said directly, but hints, meaningful silences, and coded language had made it clear that the commander would not do anything to endanger a peaceful surrender. Weiss, who had arrived in the meantime, tried his best to support Ditz's efforts and intervened enthusiastically in French, which Lunn did not understand and found more grating than helpful. The American asked an interpreter to tell Weiss to shut up, which she did with sufficient diplomacy to keep the conversation intact.

Although his diplomatic skills at the orphanage left something to be desired, Weiss helped arrange the crucial meeting between Schimpf and Lunn in a city hall bunker. Oddly, chemistry developed between them: the two officers learned that their divisions had met on the battlefield at Normandy, a fact that engendered mutual respect rather than hostility. Major Carrier even requested a souvenir; Schimpf retrieved and handed over his battle knife. In the middle of the discussions, General Manteuffel called from Bonn for a report on the defence measures in Bad Godesberg. Weiss, without giving his name and without handing the phone to Schimpf, replied, "The city is surrendering." Manteuffel assured Weiss that he, Manteuffel, would "hang on" (that is, hold the front). Bad Godesberg would not: Schimpf had already officially capitulated around noon that day, March 8, 1945. Not a shot had been fired, and—unusually for a Rhine city—it emerged from the war (almost) intact. Military personnel on both sides played the decisive roles: Lunn and Carrier did not tire in their efforts to offer the surrender of the city, and Schimpf withdrew his forces. With civilians, keen as almost ever to surrender, and Weiss playing an important mediating role, all cylinders were firing. Had more German commanders been of Schimpf's ilk, the war in western Germany might have had a very different outcome. As it was, most fought on, leading to terrible loss of life and the utter ruination of a once beautiful country they were ostensibly protecting.

As the war drew to a relatively happy close for Bad Godesberg, US Lieutenant Colonel Leonard Engeman's task force, containing an infantry and a tank platoon, was en route to Remagen. At 13:00 on March 7, the infantry platoon emerged from the woods overlooking the town. Second Lieutenant Emmet J. Burrows looked down at the spectacular view over the Rhine and Remagen—and at an intact bridge.

Burrows reported immediately to his company commander, who in turn reported to Engeman. The Combat Command B operations officer radioed the news to the commander, General William M. Hoge. Hoge rushed to Remagen, turning the risks and benefits over in his mind. The benefit: an intact bridge over the Rhine. The risks: an entire platoon blown into the air while crossing the bridge, or an entire battalion destroyed by the Germans waiting on the other side.[24] By 15:00, he had made up his mind. Hoge ordered Engeman to take the bridge immediately. As he did, a report arrived: a German, likely an unknown civilian from Remagen seeking to save a lifeline to his city, swore to the Americans that the bridge was to be blown up at 16:00.[25] Remagen lies on the west bank of the Rhine, so the Americans would first have to fight their way through the town in order to reach it. First Lieutenant Karl H. Timmerman pushed his infantry and tanks through Remagen against scattered resistance, reaching the bridge just before 16:00.[26] His infantrymen opened fire as they dashed for the bridge, trying to prevent the Germans from setting off charges.[27] The Germans returned fire from the towers, and the ground exploded in front of the Americans' feet: the Germans were trying to create a tank obstacle.[28] As Timmerman's men reached the bridge, Hauptmann Karl Friesenhahn, the bridge engineer officer, dashed across it under American fire, igniting reserve charges at the bridge's supports.[29] The air cracked with the sound of an explosion, the great bridge rose from its supports, and smoke filled the air. As the smoke and dust settled, the Americans strained their eyes to survey the damage. The bridge remained intact. Why it did so remains unclear to this day: the Germans attributed it to a lucky American shot that severed the main cable needed for the demolitions, but a German soldier or foreign labourer might well have sabotaged the explosives.[30] Whatever the reason, the bridge stood, and Timmerman ordered his men forward. Under machine-gun fire, they dashed from cover to cover under the girders, cutting every wire they saw as they went. From the banks, American tanks took out German infantry firing from a river barge and returned enough fire against other German machine-gun positions to make the crossing possible. The bridge was theirs.

Omar Bradley was with Major General Harold R. Bull, the head of operations at SHAEF, when Hodges called in the news. "Brad," Hodges breathed into the phone, "Brad, we've gotten a bridge."

"A bridge?" Bradley replied. "You mean you've got one intact on the Rhine?"

"Yep," Hodges replied. "Leonard nabbed the one at Remagen before they blew it up."[31]

Bradley was elated. He ordered Hodges to keep pushing men across and to secure the bridgehead.

General Harold Bull was not. He informed Bradley that there were no plans for a crossing at Remagen. Furious, Bradley replied, "What in the hell do you want us to do, pull back and blow it up?"[32] Bull's position was not quite as absurd as Bradley suggests in his memoirs. It reflected both a pedant's conviction that the original plan for a first crossing in Montgomery's sector had to be respected *and* the more reasonable argument that a Cologne-to-Koblenz crossing would run into less friendly terrain than either a northern or a Mainz-to-Karlsruhe one.[33] But his argument of course missed the larger picture. The point, insisted Bradley's chief of staff, was that the only bridge the Allies controlled just happened to be between Cologne and Koblenz: "a bird in the hand is worth two in the bush."[34]

The Germans certainly feared the Americans would see it that way. They were incandescent at the loss of the bridge. Rundstedt ordered its immediate destruction, and he launched an official investigation into dereliction of duty. He then ordered that the bridge be attacked at once through a coordinated assault by all elements of the Eleventh Panzer Division, backed up by transfers from Army Group G and the Luftwaffe.[35] It had little effect, either in stopping the Americans or in saving his job: Hitler sacked him on March 8 and replaced him with Kesselring.

As German artillery and bombs pelted the area around the bridge, Major General John Millikin ordered two new ones built, and reinforcements streamed across the three bridges, continually expanding the bridgehead on the east bank.[36] By March 9, Bradley had placed huge concentrations of new troops along the entire west bank of the Rhine, with a particularly heavy concentration between Krefeld and Cologne. By the tenth, German troops on the other side faced a wall of American foot soldiers and American firepower stretching from Cologne in the north to Koblenz in the south, and the Remagen bridgehead itself was some twelve kilometres wide.[37]

The Germans did everything they could to destroy it. They wrecked every craft that reached the east side of the river, and they ordered every possible means of destroying the bridge itself: swimming saboteurs and torpedoes, floating mines, conventional air attacks, and, increasingly desperate, even suicide attacks.[38] The bridge eventually fell, though nothing it seems was owed to German efforts: their forces were nowhere near the bridge at the time. On March 17, some two hundred American engineers were working on the bridge. They heard one sharp, short crack. Then another.

The deck of the bridge trembled, and dust rose from the shaking planks. "It was," remarks the US Army's official historian, "every man for himself": the men scrambled for the edges, and "with a grinding roar of tearing steel," the Remagen bridge "slipped, sagged, and with a convulsive twist plunged into the Rhine."[39] The bridge collapsed too soon for the twenty-eight Americans consumed by the Rhine but too late for the Germans: sufficient American forces had already crossed to hold the bridgehead, including the First Division of Collins's VIII Corps, which absorbed on its arrival the Seventy-Eighth Division. The Americans opened a second bridge the day the bridge at Remagen collapsed, and three more quickly followed.

As the Americans secured the bridgehead, the National Socialist regime and the Wehrmacht radicalized further. Within the army, there were signs of disintegration. Trains across the Reich were overflowing with deserters hiding among the legions of refugees fleeing the east.[40] Both groups were fleeing not only Soviet but also German brutality: the SS regularly shot soldiers and civilians trying to flee and massacred concentration camp victims wholesale. Throughout the country, stragglers became separated or, increasingly often, slipped away from their units. In many if not most cases, they were deserters. The regime's response to this flight was predictably brutal. On March 6, Rundstedt signed an order commanding all stragglers to attach themselves immediately to the nearest unit on the fighting front. From the fifteenth, the order continued, all unwounded soldiers found away from their units on roads, in villages, in civilian houses, on trains, or in civilian clothes were to be tried by a regimental court martial.[41] A guilty verdict meant death.

On the day the order took effect, Kesselring, who had assumed command in the West on March 10, ordered the execution of five officers for failing to destroy the Remagen bridge. Casually reproducing Nazi bombast, Kesselring added the following pearl of wisdom: "he who will not live in honour shall die in shame."[42] He ordered that the decision be made known to all the troops.[43] Dönitz, for the navy, sent out an equally zealous appeal to commanders in chief in all services: "[C]apitulation means suicide . . . Let us fanaticise our troops. Let us show hatred against our enemies. . . . Let us trust blindly . . . the leadership of Adolf Hitler. . . . However the situation may develop, we must stand four-square, embattled, unbowed. We shall never bend our backs to the enemy yoke."[44]

Once German High Command accepted that they were not going to push the Americans back over the Rhine, they launched efforts to contain the Remagen bridgehead. It ordered the under-strength 198th Infantry and 559th Grenadier Divisions to move immediately toward the American bridgehead.[45] The same day, the Germans ordered on their own cities the sort of area "terror attacks" that their propaganda had denounced for three years. Using a mix of one-third high explosive, one-third incendiary, and one-third fragmentation bombs, Army Group B's Fifteenth Airborne Division (Fliegerdivision) was to wipe out a clutch of towns around the Remagen bridgehead: Bad Honnef, Unkel, Erpel, and Linz am Rhein.[46] No mention was made of the civilian population in these towns, or the fact that fragmentation bombs in particular would have led to extensive casualties. The attacks either were not launched or were aborted not because of any humanitarian concerns but because the headquarters of Fifteenth Fliegerdivision in Flammersfeld, forty kilometres to the east of Remagen, had disintegrated a week earlier. Its men abandoned their equipment and fled eastward.[47]

These increasingly frantic efforts had no effect on the bridgehead and, if anything, served the Americans well by keeping German attention focused on what was to be a limited affair, the symbolism of the crossing notwithstanding. Hodges expressed great frustration with the steady but slow expansion of the bridgehead, and he sacked Millikin on March 17. In the end, however, American forces barely advanced beyond lines envisaged by Millikin. Collins's men launched a strong thrust north, reaching the southern outskirts of Königswinter.[48] On the eighteenth, patrols from the III Corps's Ninety-Ninth Division reached the Wied River due east of Remagen, while other contingents of the same division moved south to a point across Andernach. An enraged Hitler ordered the transfer of artillery from Army Group B.[49] As the army group was staring destruction in the face, such a transfer was hardly possible. Model, a human being whose manifest failings did not include an unwillingness to speak truth to power, had said as much on March 14.[50] What Hitler could not have known was that Eisenhower had by then decided to limit his forces to the goal of holding the bridgehead; it would not be the basis for a great thrust south and east toward Frankfurt. Bull had persistently resisted Bradley's efforts to see the transfer of a large number of Allied forces in order to exploit the Rhine crossing to the fullest, and, like a slow drip on hard stone, these arguments may have worn Eisenhower down. The ghosts of the Ardennes were also looking over his shoulders: conscious of limited Allied reserves, he was highly reluctant to concentrate his forces on any one crossing, be it British or American, lest the Germans launch another great counterattack. And, finally, Eisenhower had committed the necessary divisions to Montgomery's great set-piece crossing in the north, a crossing that the imperious field marshal was about to launch.

German positions in front of the Allies were beginning to disintegrate. Hitler, for a time, stuck as ever to his orders against withdrawal. Overwhelmed by a new-found American aggression in attack, combined with a mastery of mobile warfare, dazed units from the German First and Seventh Armies were captured, surrendered, or staggered back toward the Rhine, awaiting their destruction as they organized a hopeless last defence.[51] Then, on March 23, the withdrawal order came through. Scattered forces held perimeters at ferry sites, and those forces that could made a dash for the last remaining bridge across the Rhine—one at Germersheim, south of Speyer.[52] "The order," noted a US Nineteenth Infantry Division combat report, "that every village [be] a fortress, every house a pillbox had been replaced by 'every man for himself.'"[53] On March 24, the Germans, mindful of another Remagen, blew up this bridge too, leaving large numbers of forces trapped on the other side. In approximately ten days, Patton had enveloped the German Seventh Army, while he and Patch together enveloped the German First Army. Together, they captured over ninety thousand prisoners.[54] Importantly, they were on the Rhine.

On the morning of March 23, as the Fifth Division faced stiff resistance, Patton called Bradley: "I'm across." After a delay requested by Patton to avoid alerting the Germans, Bradley took great pleasure in giving the Third Army report at the army group briefing that morning: "without benefit of aerial bombing, ground smoke, artillery preparation, and airborne assistance, the Third Army at 2200 hours, Thursday evening, March 22, crossed the Rhine River."[55] It was a swipe at Montgomery over timing and over the British field marshal's dramatically staged assault on the river.

Patton's Rhine crossing must have been thrilling, but beating Montgomery to it mattered little. The most important point was that four armies had crossed the Rhine up the length of the front. The Western Allies were ready to pour into the heart of Germany. There, inside its homeland, the Wehrmacht—driven by fear, loyalty, and in some quarters, committed National Socialist sentiment and/or a genuine belief that the Allies' goal was not a victory over the Nazi regime but the total obliteration of the German nation—prepared to meet them. On March 30, Jodl issued a call for uncompromising resistance. "The enemy must be taught over the next days that he has stumbled into a country with a fanatical will to fight. He must suffer great material losses. . . . The Führer expects every commander and officer [*Oberbefehlshaber und Befehlshaber*] to throw every ounce of themselves into this task . . . and that they inspire a fanaticism against the swiftly moving [*in Bewegung geratenen*] enemy. Concern for the [civilian] population can play no role here."[56]

CHAPTER 17

HITLER RAGES

S PEER'S EFFORTS TO BLOCK Hitler's scorched-earth policy, which had begun back in September, continued into January 1945. On the nineteenth, he wrote to a Reichsleiter (the highest rank in the Nazi Party below Hitler) in the Party Chancellery in Munich to draw his attention to Hitler's support for disabling but not destroying industry.[1] Two days later, citing the authority of Schörner, one of Hitler's most loyal commanders, Speer wrote to the Blechhammer and Heydebreck synthetic oil and chemical factories, instructing them that disabling measures taken before the Russian occupation should only keep the factories out of operation for two to three weeks.[2] As before, his motivations were rational: he opposed purposeless destruction, not all destruction. The day after this intervention, Speer informed a Generalmajor Toppe that it was necessary to prepare Hungarian oil refineries for destruction because the Soviets could put these back into production too quickly.[3]

These efforts bought Speer time, but they did not make the problem go away. On February 22, an important order went out to the army groups. They were directed to appoint a "battle commander," an officer or civil servant who would be personally responsible for the evacuation of the local population and for the evacuation or destruction of industry; he would also be responsible for the distribution of food and heating supplies.[4] Officers who failed to make the right call and allowed goods or industry to fall intact into enemy hands would face a court martial.[5] The result would almost certainly be death: from late 1944, Himmler had assumed control of the Wehrmacht penal system.⁶ Orders on the destruction of bridges followed a similar logic: the local commanders of the engineer units were ordered to distinguish between the temporary disablement and permanent destruction of bridges, and to do so in close cooperation with civilian authorities.⁷ To the degree that it was respected, the last order was significant: it provided local authorities with a formal role in the defence and destruction and, by extension, in the refusal to destroy their localities.

As these orders were going out, Speer travelled through Germany to persuade Gauleiter and army commanders to respect them. He took eighteen trips in February alone and set up thirty-five meetings with Gauleiter, army commanders, industrialists, and public servants.⁸ Harried by Allied fighters and, on his trip to Silesia, within earshot of the guns on the front, Speer tried to convince them not to destroy Germany.⁹

March brought no respite. On March 1, 1945, Hitler ordered the Gauleiter and Reich Defence Commissioners (Reichsverteidigungskommissare) to prepare the Volkssturm for the final battle.¹⁰ Then another order went out, this one calling for the complete destruction of all road and rail bridges, rail tunnels, signal stations and signal boxes, train stations, and locomotives in Germany. It would have crippled Germany's transportation system indefinitely.¹¹ That same month, Hitler told Walter Rohland, a steel magnate and senior official on Speer's Ruhr staff, that "if the German people lacks the strength [Kraft] to end victoriously this war that the enemy powers have forced on them, then that people has no right to exist!"¹²

Speer responded by sending out orders designed to save what he could of Germany's dense and sophisticated road and rail networks. He contacted the undersecretary of the Reich Transportation Ministry, Albert Ganzenmüller, and asked him to revise the order. Ganzenmüller did so on March 14 and sent the revised order out the next day.¹³

Also on March 15, Speer sent out revised instructions to OKW. Writing to the army chief of staff section responsible for engineers and fortresses (Generalstab des Heeres, General der Pioniere und Festungen), he stated, "I amend the orders regarding destruction within Germany itself in the following way:"¹⁴

1. Operationally important road bridges may only be destroyed or rendered unusable following a specific order from the army. Operationally
   unimportant bridges may *only* be rendered unusable [*unterbrochen*
   werden].
2. Every manner of rail facility . . . may only be destroyed through the
   order of Wehrmacht or Army High Command [OKW or OKH].
   Locomotives that cannot be transported are only to be disabled . . .
3. Waterways [*Schiffahrtswege*] are under no circumstances to be destroyed;
   rather, when necessary, they are to be disabled.
4. Industry and companies are not to be destroyed but, rather, disabled . . .
5. Lodgings are only to be destroyed in exceptional circumstances, when
   the battle unconditionally demands it.[15]

The order ended with another qualification designed to limit destruction: "These measures are to be implemented with an eye to the coming
shortages of explosives and fuses . . . [which requires] the limitation [of
destruction] to militarily essential targets." The previous day, March 14,
Hitler had ordered that civilian evacuation was to be the lowest transportation priority: troops, coal, and food supplies were to be moved first.[16]

By March 1945, Speer was effectively in open rebellion. He expanded
his travel schedule, making thirty-one trips and arranging another thirty-
five meetings over the course of the month.[17] In mid-March, by his own
account, Speer also sent Hitler a memorandum that, for the first time,
made an argument against scorched earth without mentioning eventual
German victory. "Even if a re-conquest does not become possible. . . . It
cannot possibly be the purpose of warfare at home to destroy so many
bridges that . . . it will take years to rebuild this transportation network. . . .
Their destruction means eliminating all further possibility for the German
people to survive."[18]

As Speer ramped up his efforts, so did Hitler. On March 18, a Wehrmacht
communiqué announced the execution of four officers who had failed to
blow up the Remagen bridge before the Allies took it.

The following day, Hitler issued his clearest scorched-earth order,
known as the "Nero Order":

The struggle for the existence of our people forces us to employ even on Reich territory every means to weaken the fighting strength of our enemy and hinder his further advance. All possible methods must be utilized to inflict, directly or indirectly, severe and lasting damage on the striking power of the enemy. It is an error to believe that transportation, communications, industrial or supply installations that are not destroyed or only put out of action for a short time can be put in working order again for our own use when lost areas are re-conquered.

The enemy when he retreats will leave us only scorched earth and will abandon all consideration for the population. I therefore give the following orders:

1) All military, traffic, communications, industrial and supply installations and objects of value within Reich territory that the enemy can in any way turn to use for the continuation of battle, either now or within the foreseeable future, are to be destroyed.

2) *The military authorities are responsible for carrying out the destruction of military installations, including traffic and communications installations, the Gauleiter and Reich Defence Commissioners [are responsible] for all industrial and utility installations and miscellaneous objects of value. The troops are to give the Gauleiter and Reich Defence Commissioners the necessary help in carrying out their task.* [emphasis added]

3) This order is to be brought immediately to the notice of all commanders of troops. Orders that contradict the above are invalid.

Signed, Adolf Hitler.[19]

March 19, 1945, was also Speer's fortieth birthday. He used it as an excuse to see Hitler in person, attending a military conference between Hitler and his generals. After midnight on the preceding evening, Feldmarschall Albert Kesselring reported on the situation in the Saar. Kesselring had already observed that the local population was desperate for an end to the war, and civilians were begging the army not to destroy their villages by defending them against the Americans.[20] Hitler responded with fury. He ordered Keitel to have the entire population west of the Rhine evacuated.[21] The order went out the next day, and with it an order that all men between the ages of fourteen and fifty-five be given priority (presumably to re-establish a fighting front on the right side of the Rhine).²² If motor transportation for the evacuation was insufficient—the military had first priority on that anyway— civilians were to march. The evacuation would effectively have been an expulsion, and the millions trekking miserably westward from East Prussia and beyond would have been matched by similarly miserable columns moving east. When one of the generals objected to Hitler that evacuating people without food, without trains, and without prepared shelter would result in great misery for civilians, the dictator replied: "That can't be our concern any longer. Get them out."²³

With the war lost, Hitler followed his crude and murderous social Darwinism to its logical conclusion: German industry, infrastructure, culture, and lives were all to end in an orgy of destruction. As he told Speer in person, "If the war is lost, the people will also be lost [and] it is not necessary to worry about their needs for elemental survival. On the contrary, it is best for us to destroy even these things. For the nation has proved to be weak, and the future belongs entirely to the strong people of the East. Whatever [of Germany] remains after this battle is any case only the inadequates [Minderwertigen], because the good ones will be dead."²⁴

The Nero Order went out to both the eastern and the western fronts. At 9:00 on March 20, it was sent to Army Group G, Military District XII (Wiesbaden), Army Group H, Army Group B, and the Nineteenth Army.²⁵ Kesselring, who had succeeded Rundstedt as OB West on March 10, had every intention of obeying the order. He told his armies to make preparations for the destruction of all military installations, including traffic and communications installations, within their military districts and within the areas occupied by their troops. They were to see to it that the "destruction is carried out in good time."²⁶ On the eastern front, the navy reported on March 23 its plans to mine, destroy, and block the harbours of Gotenhafen, Hela, Pillau, Danzig, Königsberg, Stettin, and Swinemünde.²⁷ On the twenty-seventh, the head of naval armaments (Chef der Kriegsmarine-Rüstung) reported that his men had destroyed all shipyards, weapons factories, and related equipment in Danzig.²⁸

By the twenty-ninth, the order had gone out to all Gauleiter, to the Wehrmacht located in the Reich, and to occupied territories.[29] In a particularly chilling line, the orders to the army noted, "destruction is only useful if it occurs on the broadest possible basis."[30] It was, as historian Michael Geyer writes, a death sentence for Germany.[31]

Beyond its callous savagery, Hitler's order is noteworthy for three further reasons. First, Hitler overruled in it Speer's many instructions to "render unusable, not destroy" and attempted to transfer power from his Reichsminister to the military and, to a lesser extent, the Gauleiter. Second, Hitler felt the need to continue his argument with Speer. The line beginning "It is an error to believe . . ." was really an extension of his argument with Speer. It is a mark of the remaining strength of the curious relationship of these two men, divided by upbringing and class but united by an unquenchable thirst for power, that Hitler felt the need to explain himself. Third, as Order 3 makes clear, the German army was to be the key actor in implementing scorched earth. Whether cities lived or died; whether industry, bridges, airports, and signals communications went down in flames or survived the war; whether Germany itself emerged from the war ravaged but reparable or an utter wasteland came down to the decisions made by individual Wehrmacht, and above all army, commanders on all fronts.

In his account, Speer's next move was to meet the three Gauleiter of the Ruhr region—Florian, Hoffmann, and Schleßmann—who had firm plans to flood mines, blow bridges up, and destroy the Ruhr canals.[32] They had already tasked Hörner, one of Speer's technical assistants, with drawing up plans for destruction.[33] The plan involved flooding coal mines, destroying the mines' lift machinery, and sinking barges loaded with cement to block Ruhr ports and canals. Walter Rohland, the steel magnate, worked with Speer to ensure that no explosives were available to implement the order.[34] Speer then tried to use his powers of persuasion to convince Hoffmann and Schleßmann not to destroy the Ruhr.

Florian remained unmoved. He promised to set every building in Düsseldorf alight and to evacuate everyone from the city. "Let the enemy march into a burned out, deserted city!" he exclaimed.[35] As the next chapter will show, the actions of its citizens, not Speer's entreaties, would determine Düsseldorf's fate.

After seeing the Gauleiter, Speer went again to meet Feldmarschall Model. Speer claims in his memoirs that his persuasion carried the argument.[36] In fact, Model despaired in the face of Allied firepower.[37] But the important fact was that even this most fanatical of Hitler's field marshals, a committed National Socialist, was prepared to disobey. Although the orders were drawn up to implement the destruction, Model never passed them on.[38] He agreed to keep the fighting as far as possible from the industrial areas, thus avoiding the need for demolitions designed to slow advancing Allied armies.[39] After seeing Model, Speer stopped in Heidelberg. He collected orders to destroy water- and gasworks across Baden and deposited them in a letterbox in an area that was soon to be occupied by the Americans.[40] Speer credits himself with saving Heidelberg, but it was the German army's decision, under massive American pressure, to withdraw after destroying two bridges that placed the famous town outside harm's way (more on this below).[41] With the army out of the city, there was no one with the means to implement scorched-earth orders, and whether they arrived before or after the Americans was irrelevant. German civilians everywhere were desperate to surrender, and Heidelberg was no exception.

Speer then went to Würzburg and, using a now well-worn argument about German troops' needs after reoccupying territory temporarily lost to the Allies, persuaded the Gauleiter of Mainfranken, Otto Hellmuth, to spare the ball-bearing factories at Schweinfurt. The decisive argument for Hellmuth was the inevitably of defeat. He asked Speer when the vaunted miracle weapons would be deployed; Speer replied, "They're not coming." Only then did Hellmuth agree to spare the factories.[42]

After Würzburg, Speer headed to Berlin, where he arrived on March 29. Two days earlier, on March 27, at 16:00, Hitler had supplemented his March 19 Nero decree. The new order demanded the "total annihilation, by explosives, fire or dismantlement" of the entire railway system, the waterways, communications systems, and broadcasting, as well as all of the masts, antennas, and stocks of spare cable and wireless parts.[43]

This was not the only news greeting Speer. Bormann had reported on Speer's activities with the Gauleiter—who were Bormann's domain— and Hitler wanted to see him.[44] A heated argument resulted when Hitler demanded that Speer reaffirm his belief in ultimate victory.[45] When Speer continued to demur, Hitler gave him twenty-four hours to reconsider and then dismissed him. To add to the pressure, Speer returned to his quarters to find a March 29 telegram from the chief of transportation. "[The] aim," it read, "is creation of a transportation wasteland in abandoned territory. . . . [The] shortage of explosives demands resourceful utilization of all possibilities for producing lasting destruction."[46]

The next morning, Speer went to see Hitler. He had composed a lengthy justification of his actions, one that Gitta Sereny later described as "romantic waffling"; by then, 1978, even Speer admitted that it was "rubbish" (Quatsch).[47] But as it happened, Speer never delivered the letter.[48] Rather, he saw Hitler waiting for him as he went into the bunker below the Chancellery. The dictator looked at him coldly and said only, "Well?"

Speer replied, "My Führer, I stand unreservedly behind you."

Tears filled Hitler's eyes, and Speer, still this late in the war attached to his Führer, felt the emotion pass through him. "Then," Hitler replied, "all is well."[49]

Speer's account might well be embellished, or indeed falsified, but one element of it rings true: in the meeting, he was less inclined than Hitler to let emotion interfere with calculation. He saw the opportunity to increase his power. "If I stand unreservedly behind you," Speer replied, "then you must again entrust me rather than the Gauleiter with the implementation of your decree."[50] With Speer's mendacious assurance that he would draw up a list of important objects to be destroyed, Hitler agreed, and Speer drew up an order "amending" his March 19 scorched-earth order. Hitler signed it and ordered a glass of wine for Speer.[51]

After downing his wine, Speer dashed back to his offices, where the print shop was ready and waiting. Within thirty minutes, his staff had prepared several hundred copies of the order.[52] By 4:00 the next morning, the orders were being distributed across Germany. Keitel, meanwhile, forwarded Hitler's new order to the field commanders.[53] Speer sent it on

March 30 to all the Gauleiter. "On the suggestion of [Speer]," it read, "the Führer is issuing the following new order concerning the destruction of industry":

1. The destructive measures ordered were solely designed to prevent the enemy from using facilities and plants to increase his fighting capacity.

2. Under no circumstances should the measures weaken our own ability to prosecute the war. Production must be kept up to the last moment, even at the risk that the enemy's rapid advance might lead to a factory falling undestroyed into his hands. Industrial facilities of every kind, including utility plants [Versorgungsbetriebe], are only to be destroyed when the enemy DIRECTLY [unmittelbar] threatens them.

3. Whereas bridges and other transportation facilities [Verkehrsanlagen] can only be rendered useless to the enemy through destruction, industrial facilities, including utility plants, can be rendered useless through sustained disabling. The Reichsminister for Armaments and War Production will, under my directive, decide whether important industries (e.g, munitions factories, the most important chemical factories, etc.) will be destroyed.

4. The Gauleiter and Reich Defence Commissioners will oversee the implementation of destruction or paralysis of industrial facilities.

   The implementation [itself] will be carried out by agencies and organs under the Reich Minister of Armaments and War Production. All agencies of the party, the state, and the Wehrmacht will assist to that end.

5. *The decision on when and how the order will be implemented* [Durchführungsbestimmungen] *rests, with my approval, with the Reichsminister for Armaments and War Production.* He has the authority to give implementation and follow-up orders to the Reich Defence Commissioners [emphasis added].

6. These principles apply equally to firms and plants outside the battle zones.

Signed, Adolf Hitler.[54]

The order still left the Gauleiter in the picture, but radically reduced their power. Under point 4, "overseeing" is a highly passive and distant role. Under point 5, the order gave Speer the ability to continue his campaign against scorched earth. It was an illustration of the mutual dependence of the two men. As long as Hitler believed in victory, he needed Speer to pursue it; if Speer was to defy Hitler, he needed his authority and approval to do so.[55]

Speer's first order used point 5, the granting of implementing powers to him, to reinterpret the order as a restatement of his previous "dismantle, do not destroy" order. He made four essential points. First, Hitler's Nero Order (from March 19) and the March 30 order meant that Speer's line fully applied.[56] This was a particularly generous interpretation of the Nero Order in view of the fact that the order said exactly the opposite. Second, only Speer could implement an order for total destruction. Third, the course of the war, and not politics, would determine the timing of any destruction. Finally, on the ground, the Gauleiter and Reich Defence Commissioners could implement disabling and destruction orders only in cooperation with the Wehrmacht.

Speer was making an immense effort to transfer power on the Reich level from Bormann and the party to himself and on the local level from the Gauleiter and other party hacks to the army. It worked to a considerable degree. When Gauleiter Uiberreither from Graz wrote for clarification on what exactly had to be destroyed, he wrote to Speer rather than Bormann.[57] Speer replied that scorched earth was no more, and that Hitler had decisively come down in favour of disabling rather than destroying.[58] Others played along, including some otherwise uncompromisingly nasty figures. Hans-Joachim Riecke, first Reichsminister and later state secretary for food and agriculture, was, after Walther Darré and Herbert Backe, among the most important figures in the implementation of the hunger policy—that is, deliberate starvation—in eastern Poland, Lithuania, and Russia.[59] On March 30, he wrote to the heads of the regional food bureaus (*Leiter der Landesernährungsämter*), which were responsible for organizing agricultural production at the state level. Riecke passed on Speer's instructions, ordering the directors to opt for paralysis rather than destruction of agricultural industry whenever possible.[60] In the face of advancing Allied forces, they were to transport food back further into the Reich or to distribute it to the local population. Around this time, he also ordered ten to twelve trains to be loaded with food and dispatched them, without conductors, into the encircled Ruhr.[61]

Speer followed his general March 30 order with a series of specific ones. On April 3, he wrote to each of the waterway authorities (*Wasserstraßenamt*) in Hamburg, Hannover, Münster, Bremen, Magdeburg, Potsdam, Stettin, and Stuttgart, as well as to the Ministry of the Interior in Munich and Dresden-Neustadt: "Under the Führer order of March 30, 1945, the destruction without my express permission of locks, barrages, dams, canal bridges, and harbour installations is forbidden."[62] The next day, between 17:19 and 17:28, he fired off three more orders. The first went to Heinz Küppenbender, engineer at the optical firm Zeiss-Werk in Jena, and to the head of the armaments commission in Wehrkreis IX (which included parts of Thuringia and Hesse). "With reference to Hitler's order of March 30, 1945, . . . [r]oad and rail bridges running over the Saale River near Saalfeld, Grossheringen, Saalfeld-Jena-Halle [all towns on a roughly north–south line west of Leipzig] and eastwards thereof should be destroyed or paralyzed [*lähmen*] only at the last moment."[63] To do otherwise would harm troop movements. Although the order left open the possibility that widespread destruction could occur, he added a further condition that made it highly unlikely: "Paralysis and, for that matter, destruction are only to occur after consulting the director of German Imperial Railways and military units [*Militärdienststellen*]."[64]

In the context of rapidly advancing Soviet forces, such consultations could only result in the bridges and roads being captured intact. The same day, Armed Forces Operations Staff (Wehrmachtsführungsstab) sent a more comprehensive set of orders on rail lines, bridges, and communications to General August Winter, responsible since late 1944 for the details of operational planning (under Jodl).[65] It called for the delay until the last moment of all destruction or disabling measures for rail networks across Germany: from Vienna to Lundenburg (Břeclav in the Czech Republic); from Wesermünde-Bremen-Kreiensen and eastward; and from Erfurt-Nordhausen-Northeim-Kreiensen. When coupled with orders to coordinate all paralysis and destructive measures with an official at the Imperial

Railways who was himself hostile, the result was the preservation of essential rail nexuses across Germany and Central Europe.

Two days later, Speer followed up with still further orders. He sent to the military directives designed to preserve the Zeiss optical firm, as well as the road and rail lines leading to and from Jena.[66] He also instructed his eight Organization Todt Task Force leaders (OT-Einsatzgruppenleiter), who collectively oversaw 1.4 million workers, to continue their engineering and construction work until the last possible minute.[67] Literally interpreted, the orders might suggest that Speer intended to do everything possible to prolong the war. Whereas that may have been the effect, it was not the cause. All evidence suggests that even Speer had given up on victory by late March 1945.[68] The order to avoid destroying or even disabling factories until the last second was based on the hope that they would not be destroyed or disabled at all.

A third April 5 order—marked "top secret" and "extremely urgent!"—went out to Otto Hellmuth, the Gauleiter and Reich Defence Commissioner in Würzburg, giving official sanction to Speer's previous entreaties. "In preparing any demolitions, it is essential to note that the following are to be paralyzed but not destroyed: factories, traffic and communications, and energy suppliers. Distribute this order to the Kreisleiter of Schweinfurt, the Schutzbereichskommandeur, and the flak commander."[69] As ever keeping the Wehrmacht in the loop, Speer copied the order to the commander of Schweinfurt.[70] In developing these orders, Speer displayed his usual workaholic attention to detail. He ordered an auxiliary unit, the First Fahrbrigade (Transport Brigade), to loan its vehicles and trailers to local farmers or transportation firms in the event that they found themselves cut off behind enemy lines.[71]

Bormann sent out a related order. At the same moment that Speer sent his order to Jena, Bormann sent one to Austria, specifically to Reichsleiter Baldur von Schirach in Vienna and Hugo Jury, Gauleiter in the lower Danube region. "All destruction," Bormann ordered, "of oil refineries and oil wells is prohibited [unterbleiben]. There are only to be preparations for paralysis, and these are not to be initiated without the agreement of Army Group South." He then added a line designed to give credibility to Speer: "The Army Group has developed its instructions in close cooperation with

Reichsminister Speer."[72] As Bormann was a longstanding personal and institutional rival of Speer, as he had done everything he could to undermine Hitler's confidence in this Reichsminister, and because he had strongly supported scorched earth earlier, this intervention is difficult to explain. Either Bormann was such a sycophant that his change of mind simply followed Hitler's, or—a more promising line of thought—he, like Speer, was seeking to position himself as a player in postwar Germany.

After sending out these orders, Speer returned again to see Hitler. Hitler was once again fantasizing about a decisive attack on the Americans' flank, one that would expose their cowardice. As he did, Speer dryly noted, "If everything is destroyed, the recovery of these areas will do me no good at all."[73] To Speer's surprise, and for reasons that are not entirely clear, Hitler took it well and even reassured Speer that not all of the dictator's orders to blow up bridges had been implemented. Seizing the moment once again, Speer then presented to Hitler and Keitel yet another decree, this one focused on bridges. In Speer's account, Keitel exploded, yelling, "No war can be waged without destroying bridges!"[74] Indeed, no war could or has, but Speer's orders always left open the possibility of destruction at some later date. Keitel agreed to the draft, and the new Führer order went out on April 7. Citing the need for a "unified implementation of my [Hitler's] March 19 order on traffic and communications," the decree stated:

1) Operationally important bridges must be destroyed such that their use by the enemy is impossible. . . . The most serious punishments will follow if these bridges are not destroyed.

2) All other bridges may only be destroyed once the Reich Defence Commissioner, the responsible Reich Transportation departments, and the Reich Minister for Armaments and War Production determine that the enemy's approach or interference [*Feindeinwirkung*] makes paralysis [*Einstellung*] and evacuation impossible. In order to be able to continue production until the last moment in accordance with my March 30 order, traffic is to continue intact until the last moment.

3) All other transportation [infrastructure] and communications systems of the Reich Post, Reich Rail, and private companies are only to be paralyzed.

With the exception of 1), all destruction and disabling must be carried
out on the understanding that transportation and communications can be
easily rendered functional once lost territories are recaptured.[75]

Speer immediately dispatched the order to every significant player in
late Nazi Germany: the Wehrmacht, the Reich Defence Commissioners/
Gauleiter, the Organization Todt Task Forces, and the Reich Ministers for
Transportation, Post, and Agriculture.[76] To guard against rogue activity,
on April 7 Walter Rohland ordered businessmen and industrialists across
the Reich to report immediately any destruction of industry undertaken
without Speer's authorization.[77] Ten days later, Luftwaffe General Ludwig
Wolff, responsible for Hannover, Bremen, Hamburg, and Wismar, issued
another order countering scorched earth. Writing to the Eighth Flak
Division (Bremen), he ordered: "In the destruction of non-military installations, increased attention is to be paid to the requirements of the national
economy and traffic . . . In the destruction of [Luftwaffe] installations . . .
the same principles are to apply, first and foremost in respect of the essential
needs of the population."[78] In practice, this meant: destroying electricity
transformers and power stations just before they were occupied, leaving
water and drainage untouched, and disabling but not blowing up Luftwaffe
installations when their destruction would harm the civilian population in
any way. But not everyone was playing ball. On April 14, the Luftwaffe had
sent a call for volunteers for suicide missions against German infrastructure
and Allied troops behind "enemy lines."[79] There is no record of how many
volunteered, but in the context of what was by then mass desertion, there
were few if any. Speer was winning the argument.

He continued his efforts through to the end of the month. On April 16,
he wrote again to Richard Fischer and made him personally responsible for
both keeping electricity running to the last moment and for shutting down
the grid.[80] The next day, Speer sent instructions to Franz Xaver Dorsch, a
civil engineer and one of the most senior figures in the Organization Todt.
Speer's OT task forces were to keep the trains moving until the last moment,
even at the risk of ending up in enemy captivity. Speer's stated reason for
placing such importance on railways was their central role in supplying the

population with food and other essential supplies.[81] A cynic might inter-
pret these moves, as scholars indeed have, as an effort by Speer to save his
skin rather than that of German civilians. If so, a man as clever as Speer
would surely have known that a paper trail of protests against ill treatment
of POWs, forced labourers, or Jews (about whom he might have claimed
indignant last-minute knowledge) would have done him more good with
postwar prosecutors.

In his memoirs, Speer notes that the raft of orders sent out in March
and April of 1945 created an "unclear command" structure.[82] This was an
understatement. On April 7 alone, orders gave to the Wehrmacht the full
responsibility for the preparation of disabling measures for communication infrastructure within its own jurisdiction; to Himmler for paralysis
measures affecting the Waffen and regular SS's communication systems;
to Wehrmacht commanders (Oberbefehlshaber) in the east for their own
field units as well as for communication systems of Reich authorities within
their jurisdiction;[83] and to OKW and the Reich authorities for Berlin and
Military District III (Berlin/Brandenburg).[84] Orders sent by Rohland the
following day divided disabling and destruction tasks based on whether
they would primarily affect military or economic infrastructure: the army
was responsible for the former, and Speer's ministry was responsible for
the latter.[85] He also added a further order: any bridge that contained
economically essential infrastructure—such as water pipes or electricity
lines—was to be neither demolished nor prepared for demolition. This
order stood in direct conflict with Hitler's April 7 order on tactically important bridges.[86] To further add to the confusion, Keitel sent out a telegram
on the same day that ordered Oberbefehlshaber West and Northwest, as
well as Army Group B, to secure OKW's consent before any measures
were taken, except when all communications were severed. In each case,
Keitel ordered, all questions were to be directed to the Reich Defence
Commissioners and the relevant departments of the Reich Ministry for
Armaments and War Production.[87]

This complex mix of overlapping and at times contradictory orders
assigned multiple responsibilities and required both that multiple actors—the
Wehrmacht, Reich Defence Commissioners, Armaments Commissioners,

and Speer himself—be consulted before any action was carried out *and* that destruction be delayed until the last possible moment. Speer's hope, we can reasonably conclude, was that the result would be no destruction or even paralysis until it was too late.

Because Speer lied to so many people—his American interrogators and Allied prosecutors, his sympathetic biographer, his close friends, and the distant German public—it is tempting to conclude that he lied about, or at least vastly exaggerated, his role in blocking scorched earth. He did not. Virtually every significant claim made in *Inside the Third Reich* regarding scorched earth is verified by the original sources. Speer threw himself bravely, even recklessly, into the task of blocking these directives.

An obvious question is whether he succeeded. Speer would have us believe that his efforts were uniquely successful, that scorched earth ended with his definitive early-April interventions. The matter was neither this simple nor this flattering for Speer. The situation in early April 1945 was one that allowed a massive degree of individual discretion. The chain of command was breaking down, communications were poor, and many officers found themselves and their men isolated. Under such circumstances, the bar to disobedience lowered, and those who opposed the Nazi leadership, or at least the destructive orders emanating from it, felt more able to act. At the same time, existing orders assigned responsibility to multiple actors, and the orders demanded that each of those actors make judgments on what was essential (when was a bridge tactically important, and when was it just a bridge?) and when the last possible moment had in fact arrived. These orders also rested uneasily with the broader demands of fanatical resistance to the Allies' advance. If Germans failed to destroy essential German infrastructure, their refusal to surrender would likely lead the Allies to do so.

More broadly, orders mean nothing if they are not obeyed. There were many in Germany who wished to oppose or who would have only reluctantly implemented scorched-earth orders. Particularly for them, Speer's order may have been decisive. But there were many others who wished to fight fanatically to the end and who were more than prepared to exploit the orders' provisions on tactical necessity to unleash a campaign of destruction against Germany itself. Which group succeeded—those who wished to destroy or those who wished to preserve—depended on the balance of proponents and opponents in a particular jurisdiction; on the call made by local Wehrmacht officials; and, above all, on the opponents' guile, resources, and powers of persuasion. For all his ordering, Speer's reach did not include these local actors, and in crediting himself with stopping scorched earth, he seriously overclaimed and did further violence to the history of Germany in the last months of the war.[88] To understand it, we need to turn to the particular stories of obedience and disobedience themselves.

CHAPTER 18

THE SIEGE OF DÜSSELDORF

As the Allies closed in on Germany from all sides, the Wehrmacht faced shortages of men, equipment, and fuel. The German military, which had once dazzled and terrified the world with its speed, was grinding to a halt. The shortage of men and the inability to move them quickly both argued for one particular defensive position: cities. Cities had many advantages as strategic positions, as each house was a natural defence point; every few feet brought a corner around which one could hide; every tower was a sniper's nest; and cities could be defended with relatively fewer troops than were required on the open battlefield.[1] These considerations encouraged Churchill to think in 1939 and 1940 of London and Paris as great battle zones that would hold back the mighty German army. Now, with Allied armies in the Reich, German cities were to play this role. The strategic considerations underpinned Hitler's standard advice to hold all positions. No German city was to be surrendered until the army, SS, and/or Volkssturm troops defending it had fought to the last man. As OB West put it on February 11, 1945, "[T]he Führer has once again explicitly forbidden all evacuations of and retreats from defence positions [*Befestigungsanlagen*] or cities. The enemy might be able to storm the rubble of a city or a fortified position [*Bunkerlinie*], but we will under no circumstances retreat from them!"[2]

Hitler's order was nested within a larger late–National Socialist aim. After the failure of the Ardennes offensive, Hitler could no longer believe in a German victory. He had played with the idea of a Wagnerian end to German history since at least September 1944, when the western Allies reached German soil, but by January 1945 he was fully committed to it: he would destroy the German people, who he believed had betrayed him through their weakness, and ensure that Germany fell into Allied hands only as, to paraphrase his words on Paris, a heap of rubble.

Allied impatience made such an outcome more, not less, likely. The Americans and British were extremely frustrated with the slow movement of Allied armies in the Eifel, Ardennes, Hürtgen, and elsewhere and with continued casualties in a war that they knew they would clearly win. Whereas Eisenhower's armies passed through Italy under clear instructions to minimize damage to non-military targets, no such limitation existed for Germany. The Allies' strategy was simple: when they approached a German city they intended to occupy, they would give it the opportunity to surrender. If the opportunity was refused, they would throw everything they had at it by launching a mighty artillery barrage and, if deemed necessary, an area bombing raid before risking an occupation.[3] Once the city had been blasted to pieces, Allied soldiers would march in and clear out any remaining resistance. The result would be lower Allied casualties, but the destruction of architecture, culture, and civilian life would be massive.

With the exception of instances in which German troops conducted a tactical withdrawal, which allowed a city denuded of forces to be taken without a fight, the fate awaiting any particular city depended on the attitudes and actions of the army and civilians within it. Two conflicting attitudes were clear: (1) with a few exceptions, civilians wished to surrender to avoid the destruction of their beloved home cities and to prevent (further) loss of civilian life; and (2) the Waffen-SS, which was more fanatical than the army and which, unlike the army, had no tradition, logic, or future without the National Socialist Party, would defend any city it held to the end, killing without hesitation any civilians who opposed them or sought to surrender. For civilians across the Reich, the flying of a white flag was often a death sentence: on April 3, Himmler ordered that all men in any house displaying a white flag were to be shot.[4] The army, for its part, was more malleable. Almost all senior commanders—field marshals and high-ranking generals—fought to the last day, but lower down the chain of command, officers' reactions varied. Some decided, or were persuaded, to surrender cities without a fight and, under great risk, sought to secure the safe transfer of areas under their command to the Allies. In still other cases, commanders had the decision made for them: civilians were able to neutralize the army command and themselves surrender the city.

These choices were made in the context of what political scientists call institutional breakdown. The rapid disintegration of divisions, corps, and even whole armies placed an enormous strain on the chain of command. German commanders, given direct responsibility by Hitler for the estab-lishment of city defences and for the destruction of transportation,[5] found themselves isolated because they either lost, or could convincingly pretend that they had lost, contact with their superiors. Those superiors, in turn, often had only the vaguest idea of what was occurring in the areas of their command that they could not observe directly. The chain of command was disintegrating, and each new gap that resulted from that breakdown pre-sented German commanders with an opportunity to disobey their Führer's extremist orders. They faced a political, a military, and above all a moral choice: whether to defend cities, thus ensuring their destruction, or to surrender them without a fight. The fate of what was left of Germany's infra-structure and architectural heritage, along with the lives of many German civilians and soldiers on both sides, turned on these decisions.

AFTER THE FIRST US ARMY began breaking out of the Remagen bridge-head, Eisenhower ordered it to encircle and capture the Ruhr, stopping the still-beating industrial heart of Germany and entrapping four German armies in the process. By April 1, the Ninth and First Armies had cut Army Group B off from Army Group G and trapped three armies within the Ruhr pocket: the headquarters and supporting troops of Army Group B, all of the Fifth Panzer Army, the bulk of the Fifteenth Army, plus two corps from the First Parachute Army—a total of more than 400,000 men.[6]

Inside the Ruhr pocket, Düsseldorf remained in German hands. In February, the army had declared the city a stronghold to be fiercely defended.[7] For months, few of its citizens had displayed any confidence in the much-trumpeted final German victory. After the failure of the Ardennes offensive, they had even less, as the district attorney (Generalstaatsanwalt) reported to Berlin in early February 1945: "The mood, which lifted following the December 1944 attack in the west, is very depressed [*stark gedrückt*] as a result of recent events in the East and of the continued bombing, which a large portion of the population had believed we could successfully combat. According to reports I've received, people are increasingly expressing their anger openly in correspondence and in public conversation; only the smallest portion of these utterings is of course prosecuted."[8]

In the face of rapidly deteriorating morale, the regime responded the only way it knew how: the SS turned viciously on the local population. In late February, the SS seized a twenty-four-year-old soldier, "Felix K.," who was serving ten years in prison for observing from his hospital bed that the war was pointless. The SS shot him.[9] A few weeks later, in another example of how the regime eradicated its critics as the Allies approached, they came for a forty-three-year-old Communist Party member, Baltasar Sieberg, whom the Gestapo had picked up multiple times previously.[10] No one ever found his body. On April 13, the SS took seventy-one prisoners from the Lüttringhausen prison near Solingen and massacred them; ten were from Düsseldorf.[11]

The Gestapo concentrated much of its efforts on tracking down forced labourers who had used the bombings and artillery attacks as an opportunity to escape.[12] As the labourers hid in ruins and stole food, the Gestapo hunted them mercilessly.[13] The concentration camps at Ravensbrück (for women) and Buchenwald received new prisoners until the last days of the war, and torture and murder were as ever routine.[14] In early April, around ten Russian prisoners of war were taken to the Kalkumer Forest near Düsseldorf.[15] A detective (*Kriminalkommissar*) ordered the Russians out of the van. Once out, a shot went off, and the prisoners panicked, fleeing in all directions. The SS sprayed them with bullets, killing most of them instantly. The detective finished off the wounded personally.[16] The bodies were buried in a water-filled bomb crater.[17] Only one prisoner was left alive on the promise that he would identify other forced labourers in hiding.[18] For every prisoner shot, many more starved. One American prisoner of war, an airman held in a POW camp on the Bergischen highway (*Landstraße*), saw from early January 1945 one to three "Russians" (possibly Russians and Eastern Europeans) dying every day.[19] The Roma, with whom the Nazis had a more complicated relationship, continued to be sterilized until the last day of the war. One mother signed under threat of deportation to Auschwitz a sterilization consent form for her children (why, one wonders, did such thugs bother with consent?).[20] Only the arrival of the Americans spared them the operation.[21]

Foreigners were not the only targets. The SS and the Wehrmacht shot or hanged deserters, resisters, and even those who expressed "defeatist" attitudes.[22] In the face of such terror, the perspective of most Düsseldorfers—like their co-nationals across the country—narrowed: they sought to feed and to save themselves and their families, and above all to survive the wave of pitiless violence driven by a regime in panic. A few, however, managed to transform empathy into action. A monk hid first a German-Jewish couple, later French POWs and Russian forced labourers, and finally Volkssturm deserters in his monastery, saving some twenty-five people.[23]

The SS and the party also created institutions designed to increase terror. In early March, Kreisleiter Karl Walter placed Volkssturm Hauptmann August Kaiser at the head of a military patrol (*Heeresstreife*) tasked with the job of rooting out deserters.[24] Kaiser unleashed his men on the population of Düsseldorf. Those suspected of harbouring deserters were tortured; others were killed, despite the group's lack of jurisdiction to impose death sentences. Frequently drunk, Kaiser did nothing as torture devolved into routine murder.[25]

At the same time, Police Oberstleutnant Karl Brumshagen, commander of the police, appointed Major Walther Peiper head of a "military" court similarly charged with tackling acts of treason (for example, flying a white flag) and desertion. Screams of the tortured echoed through the streets of Düsseldorf, and some interrogations led to death.[26] Even by the standards of this group, one Feldwebel (sergeant), Adolf Stender, was particularly sadistic.[27] Responding to a tip, Stender tracked down a seventeen-year-old boy named Alwin who lay ill at home. He suffered from a heavy cough as well as foot and back pains—basic signs of a serious flu. The boy's father had dutifully registered him as ill with the army, but it made not a bit of difference. Stender's men stormed into Alwin's house, pushed his weeping and pleading mother aside, and dragged the boy out. She heard nothing from him until she received a letter stating that her son had been shot.

Those who harboured actual deserters fared no better. On April 11, a week before the Americans were to move into the city, a woman named Else Gores allowed two soldiers to hide in her house.[28] When Stender's men discovered them, she claimed that she did not know they were deserters. Not overly concerned about the principle of reasonable doubt, they took her to the Eller Forst on the southeastern edge of the city. Applying a technique perfected on the eastern front, one of the men placed a pistol at the point where her spine met her skull. He then fired. She lunged forward, and they left. Sometime later, another woman found her, seriously wounded but still alive. The soldier had not pointed the pistol high enough, and the bullet passed through her neck without killing her. The woman and two others took Else to a nearby pub. Before they could take her to the hospital, however, Stender's men, clearly tipped off, arrived. Else panicked. "Those are the men who took me before! . . . Mrs. Mü, come with me, I'm afraid that I'll fall into the hands of the Gestapo once more!" No one ever saw her again.

Having murdered a sick boy and a woman, Stender's men then turned their attention to an old man. On April 14, they found a seventy-two-year-old named Moritz Sommer and declared that he had provided deserters with food and civilian clothing.[29] When he was brought to Stender, the captain declared Sommer a "splendid catch" ("*prächtiger Fang*"), possibly because he was a half-Jew. Stender's men tortured him, smashing his face in. They then tied a sign around his neck reading, "I am a traitor," and hanged him by the neck from a transformer station on the Oberbilker Markt. The next day, Stender dissolved his patrol, and two days later, the Americans moved into the city. Sommer, who had survived the Nazis' murderous anti-Semitism for twelve years only to die within the last hours of their reign, was still hanging.

Düsseldorf's Gauleiter since 1930, Friedrich Karl Florian, fully supported these brutalities. Florian was a Nazi fanatic who refused all of Speer's entreaties against scorched earth and, indeed, was virtually intoxicated on visions of Düsseldorf's fiery downfall. He had welcomed the new year of 1945 with a pathos-filled call for continued fighting: "The community of war and community of fate stand on the threshold of a new year with unwavering loyalty to the flag of the National Socialist revolution. We will fly it through the storms of time and on to a free and victorious German future."³⁰ As mothers tried to protect their sons, Florian called up all men of Düsseldorf, young and old alike, for battle; even members of the Hitler Youth, aged fourteen to seventeen, were not exempt and were led to their deaths on the battlefield.³¹ He had long ago called all men from between sixteen and sixty to serve in the Volkssturm, and the Wehrmacht conscripted boys born in 1928 and 1929 starting in January 1945.³²

The front, meanwhile, was moving ever closer. On March 1, 1944, the US 329th Infantry Regiment, Eighty-Third Division reached Neuß, slightly south of Düsseldorf on the left side of the Rhine, and occupied it the next night against little resistance. On March 3, the Americans pushed northward to Oberkassel, a part of Düsseldorf also on the left side of the Rhine and directly opposite the old city. As the Americans reached it, the Germans pulled out: the 338th Infantry Division was ordered to retreat across the Rhine into Düsseldorf.³³ At 9:30, the last German troops retreated across the Skagerrak Bridge (before and after the Nazis, the Oberkassel Bridge), the last intact bridge across the river at Düsseldorf. When the first American tank touched the bridge, German engineers set off explosives in the middle of the structure. The bridge's huge arches heaved up into the air, then fell back into the Rhine.³⁴ Its upper girders protruded from the water, but it was impassable for vehicles. The Americans were not the only ones disappointed by the bridge's collapse. As it caved into the Rhine, electricity cables running along it were severed, leaving large numbers of Düsseldorfers without electricity until the end of the war.³⁵ On the eastern side of the Rhine, those who had made their way toward the bridge to welcome American occupiers into Düsseldorf watched as the explosives went off.³⁶

In the weeks before the Skagerrak Bridge was destroyed, thousands of civilians had fled with what they could carry across the bridge into the centre of Düsseldorf. Seeking refuge, what they in fact entered was a fortress under siege.[37] As the German 338th Infantry Division brought in thirty to forty flak guns to defend the right side of the Rhine, the Americans opened an artillery barrage. From Oberkassel and adjacent areas, the Americans lobbed shell after shell into Düsseldorf. The citizens cowered in cellars and crowded bunkers, rarely venturing into the street. When they did, because they had to work and/or look for scarce food, death awaited them. Forty died on March 4, twenty more the following day; by April, 1,073 civilians had been killed.[38] German artillery from the east side of the river returned fire on the Americans but had little effect. Their main contribution was to destroy houses and kill German civilians in Oberkassel. Some two hundred Düsseldorfers were killed by soldiers who were supposedly protecting them from the Americans.[39]

Florian and his second in command, Kreisleiter Karl Walter, were indifferent to those deaths. Together, they prepared Düsseldorf for Armageddon. Florian took Hitler's March 19 Nero Order—that "[a]ll military, traffic, communications, industrial and supply installations and objects of value within Reich territory" be destroyed—literally, and he chose to ignore all of Speer's subsequent orders to disable rather than destroy. It was a clear illustration, were one needed, of the fact that orders are meaningless unless they are obeyed. Florian ordered the city prepared for a street-by-street battle. Outside the city, antitank ditches were dug; inside it, trees were chopped down to form protection for machine guns, and concrete and rubble were used to form antitank obstacles.[40] Allied and, more specifically, British bombing meant that there was much loose material with which to work.[41] Florian ordered the destruction in the city of all rail bridges and of rail lines running between Duisburg in the north and Cologne in the south.[42] As they did, Nazi functionaries destroyed (or tried to destroy) even the smallest bridges crossing the Rhine, including those too small for tanks.[43] Finally, Florian ordered that all rail and road bridges in the city be mined with explosives that were to be detonated at the first sign of American troops; doing so would cut the city off and would also take out its water and electricity supplies.[44] Much of this work was done by forced labourers and prisoners of war. On March 6, hundreds of Russian women and girls were forced to dig defensive trenches. According to an eyewitness account, they came under direct artillery fire, and many were killed.[45]

In preparation for the final battle, the Nazi Party sought, as it had done in Aachen, to organize an evacuation of the city toward the east. Most civilians, facing the prospect of shattered roads and rail lines, long marches, and unimpeded Allied fighters strafing everything that moved, opted to stay where they were. On March 29, three days before the Ruhr pocket was sewn shut, Florian tried to expel them.[46] Nazi Party bureaucrats came to people's houses urging them to leave, but civilians responded with fury, hurling abuse at the them.[47] The publisher (*Verlagsleiter*) of the *Rheinische Landeszeitung*, Victor Muckel, refused to publish the evacuation order. When the Gauleiter's office called him to see why the order had not appeared, Muckel, employing a resister's typical dodge, claimed that he had run out of paper.[48]

Those civilians who tried to flee the city were in any case interested in moving west rather than east. Based on a false rumour, some civilians tried to raise the 1,200 marks that would buy passage by paddleboat across the Rhine and into American captivity.[49] There could be little doubt who were for German civilians the captors, who the liberators. Most, in any event, stayed in the city: of the 288,000 residents in Düsseldorf in early February 1945, 256,000 were still there in early March.[50] One of the few who left was the mayor. On the night of March 27–28, he donned a Red Cross uniform and slipped out of the city.[51]

The next day, Gauleiter Florian combined his scorched-earth and evacuation orders in a single leaflet distributed across the city.[52] It contained the usual Nazi bombast and anti-Semitism, along with a not-uninteresting reference to colonial subjects and North American Indians:

> The enemy, who has launched under Jewish leadership a pitiless war against us, lies in his words and actions as he has always lied. His urgings to rely on and to trust him are nothing but bait on a hook [*Speck in der Mausefalle*]. The American and English plan for us, as it has been and is for Indians, Africans, Boers, and Native Americans, is mass starvation. . . . Germans are to live as slaves. This Anglo-American death-by-starvation

[*Hungertod*] is every bit as gruesome as that of the Red Bolshevists. Anyone who believes the enemy is a traitor to his people and to himself.

The militarily necessary evacuation must therefore be respected. Anyone who resists is a traitor and will be treated as such. . . .

Comrades! Nothing can fall into the hands of the enemy, neither men nor material, that he can use to destroy us. Everyone is obligated to ensure that the necessary [destructive] measures are carried out. We believe nonetheless in Germany's immortality!

Long live the Führer!

Long live the German community of the people [*Volksgemeinschaft*]!

Long live our sacred homeland [*Heimat*]!

Not even Florian himself could take the claim of final victory seriously, hence its mystical packaging in the leaflet as "immortality"; we can be immortal in this world or in the next.

The forces that Florian had nominally under his command were an army-subordinated Kampfgruppe with seven companies, chiefly made up of police recruits taking orders from army soldiers, all of whom answered to the police commander, Brumshagen; a flak division with an uncertain amount of ammunition; and four thousand further policemen under the command of Oberstleutnant Franz Jürgens.[53] It was not a conspicuously impressive force, but it was more than enough, particularly with Jürgens's police force, to provoke a harsh American response. Faced with such a possibility, members of the resistance in Düsseldorf began to mobilize.

IN JANUARY 1945, a young Social Democrat named Otto Blumhoff got on his bicycle in Neuß.[54] Hundreds of flyers were hidden in a basket, sharing space with a rabbit (whether it was a pet or a meal is unclear). Blumhoff cycled the nine kilometres to Düsseldorf. He distributed the leaflets in bars, in tunnels, and on bridges. Blumhoff and others like him continued to do so throughout 1944 and into 1945. The leaflets urged people to join resistance groups, to sabotage the regime's policies, and to be prepared to report all Werewolves (that is, National Socialist guerrillas who would continue to wage war behind Allied lines and, indeed, after the war ended).

Blumhoff was part of a small group of resisters in Düsseldorf: the *Antifaschistische Kampforganisation* (the Antifascist Combat Organization), or the Antifako, which had come together in the summer of 1944. In addition to Blumhoff, its main members were the merchant Hermann Smeets and Willi Erkelenz; all three were friends.[55] Smeets was, it seems, the intellectual inspiration of the group. He was sympathetic to Communist principles and had second-hand knowledge of the concentration camps: a friend's brother-in-law had been interned at Buchenwald.[56] As a resister, Smeets positioned himself implicitly between the Tresckow military circle, which saw an overthrow of Hitler as a precursor to any change, and Moltke's aristocratic Kreisau Circle, which planned for the world after Hitler's inevitable and essential defeat. For Smeets, the time to act was *during* the regime's collapse, which he was convinced since Stalingrad was only a matter of time. "I am of the view, as are my friends, that when everything collapses, there must be people there who are prepared to take charge."[57]

The Antifako grew out of earlier resistance circles of workers and craftsmen from working-class Düsseldorf who were sympathetic to Social Democracy and Communism.[58] This alone was noteworthy, as the intellectuals within each of these parties generally detested each other to the point where they allowed the fatal left-wing split through which Hitler had slipped into power in the first place. The Düsseldorf conspirators were a tight-knit group that met increasingly frequently in workers' gardens and apartments and in raid shelters.[59] There, they spoke of the regime, what they could do against it, and, as a sort of working-class Kreisau Circle, what postwar Germany should be like.[60] As the war dragged on, their membership expanded. Despite this, the group was free of informants: they had not been part of the Communist or Social Democratic resistance groups ripped up by the Nazis after 1933, and without this history, the Gestapo possessed no files on them. Their close friendships and hardened, working-class suspicion of outsiders made subsequent Gestapo infiltration next to impossible.[61]

The group had about eighty members, even though most of them were passive, making it the strongest opposition group in Düsseldorf.[62] The role of the antifascist groups (*Antifa-Gruppen*) in the last months of the war merits brief comment. Such groups emerged in a number of German cities—Düsseldorf was one, Augsburg another—as the war drew to a close. They were not part of the earlier formations of Communist or Social Democratic resisters who had plans for the overthrow of the regime and the establishment of another form of government. Nor were they part of the military, whose members had to choose between obedience and disobedience. They were, rather, individuals who did not have any (remaining) sympathy for National Socialism but who had previously felt unable to act given the strength of the regime. A combination of factors lowered the bar for taking action: the obvious fact that the Nazi regime's days were numbered, the approach of the Allies, increasingly urgent fears for the loss of their cities, and (at least in Düsseldorf) a hope, inspired by Stauffenberg, that the military would listen to reason.

The Antifako's resistance activities in the last year of the war could be divided into four categories. The first, perhaps taking inspiration from the Scholls, who had been executed in 1943, was a leaflet campaign. The several hundred leaflets that Blumhoff crammed into his bicycle basket in January 1945 urged people to pick up where Stauffenberg had left off—itself an important example of the mutually reinforcing effects of military and civilian resistance. They defined the Antifako and its goals, and showed that, in contrast with the writers at Kreisau, they were working-class street fighters:

> The Antifako is the concentration of all anti-fascist energy and strength in the struggle against the Nazis and has only one goal: the defeat of Hitler and his clique who alone are responsible for this atrocious [*grausam*] world war. The Antifako is a paramilitary organization. Its members have to be fighters who draw strength from the belief that what the Nazis have taken from us should not be lost in a sea of misery, pain, and despair [*nicht in einen verlorenen Weltschmerz nachtrauern dürfen*] but rather that we must continue fighting [*sondern wieder erkämpfen müssen*]. . . . Support our work by organizing yourselves into small cells and being prepared for action when the hour arrives. Register the Nazis in your streets, companies [*Betrieben*], and offices, and above all determine those among you who might be inclined to join the murderous "Werewolf" squads. Ensure that any lists you draw up do not fall into the hands of the Gestapo. . . .[63]

The Antifako members left the leaflets under bridges and in tunnels, in pubs, cafés, restaurants, and post offices.

The second category of action involved providing aid to the victims of Nazism. The Antifako helped around a hundred Soviet forced labourers who had fled by hiding and feeding them.[64] In another case, the group learned of a father who had been called up to the Volkssturm in the last days of the war. A doctor who was a member of or at least sympathetic to the group fitted the man's leg with a cast.[65]

The third category of action involved actively and directly encouraging disobedience. Antifako members appealed directly to Volkssturm recruits and soldiers to desert. They urged engineers not to set off demolition charges on several bridges in the city; these road and rail bridges were essential to supplying Düsseldorf.[66] In one case around April 12, they heard that the large railway underpass on the Hüttenstraße was to be destroyed.[67] Smeets got together a few men, and they drove out to the bridge. There, they confronted the engineers and the sentries directly. "Men, forget this nonsense," Smeets said. "What are you going to achieve? You cannot stop an entire army by destroying this tunnel. But you will bring great misfortune on Düsseldorf!"[68] The engineers, "simple soldiers," were amenable; they accepted a half a pound of butter as a bribe and left the bridge intact.[69] The Antifako also informed civilian Helene Püster, a Social Democrat or Communist, of plans to blow up the Flehe Waterworks, an act of vandalism that would have cut off Düsseldorf's water supply. Püster, in turn, informed a Social Democratic resister who went to the waterworks and disabled the charge.[70] Both were examples of local resistance for which Speer claimed credit. These efforts were inevitably not all successful, but despite having taken place in public, even those who refused to help did not pass members' names on to the Gestapo. As in the run-up to July 20, doing nothing was doing something: resistance depended on the silence of the wider circle of individuals who knew of their plans and actions.

The final category of action went to the core of the Antifako's purpose: avoiding the total destruction of Düsseldorf by preventing a military defence against the final Allied assault. The plan was to make contact with the Americans, offer the surrender of Düsseldorf, and secure an Allied airdrop of hand grenades and automatic weapons.[71] They would then launch an insurrection as the Allies entered the city. Aiming high, Smeets drew up a letter for Eisenhower. It outlined the group's aims, promised close cooperation with the Allies, and requested that arms be supplied so that the group could launch an armed insurrection as the Americans invaded. "The point," Smeets said decades later, "was to say to the Allies: 'will you finally get over here, and put an end to this terror [*kommt endlich rüber und macht dem Spuk ein Ende*]? There's nothing here that can really threaten you!'"[72] Two men, Hermann Maaßen and Helmut Teppe, agreed to make the journey across the Rhine.[73]

They first tried to do so on March 26, but elaborate preparations they had made to cross the Rhine in an inflatable boat came to nothing when the boat was stolen, probably by someone who fled across the river to American captivity.[74] It took almost another three weeks, until April 12, to organize another boat (transportation was in short supply in Germany at this point). This time it was a paddleboat, which the men carried with some difficulty through backyards and fields. Once at the Rhine, they had to get past the patrols. Smeets told them in his strong working-class accent, "Now, boys, look. This is a father who has just got to get across the river to his kids in Neuß. Be a sport and let him cross!"[75] The men had brought a couple of pounds of butter to help convince the patrols; had that failed, they were ready to use their pistols.[76] The butter and the story were enough, though, and they managed to slip across the Rhine.

A further wrinkle in the plan was that neither of the men spoke English. Smeets could manage a little, and he told Maaßen: "When you meet the Americans, you point to your bag and say only 'Certification.' Got it? Also, when you make it over you mustn't whisper. You must speak loudly so that [the Americans] see that you're harmless, rather than shooting you straight away!"[77]

Once they reached Neuß, Maaßen began complaining in German, "I'm so hungry, let's first have some bread with butter!"[78] Almost immediately, a voice shouted, "Hands up!" and the men felt gun barrels in their backs. Maaßen shouted, "Certification! Certification!" but, as that did not really mean anything in that context, the Americans ignored him and loaded the two into a truck bound for Grimlinghausen, a section of Neuß.[79] There, a couple of soldiers held them in a duty room. Maaßen kept shouting the whole time, "Certification! Certification!" and eventually, the Americans could not take it any longer.[80] They took the letter addressed to Eisenhower. A soldier left with it, and a few minutes later, two officers arrived. The men were then transported to Grevenbroich, thirty kilometres southwest of Düsseldorf, where they were searched for weapons and then fed. The officers did not, however, open the letter, as it was addressed to Eisenhower; they instead had it delivered unopened to the most senior general in the American army. Maaßen was impressed with this respect for protocol. "They were as Prussian as we were!" he later said—and he meant it as a compliment.[81]

At the time, however, it meant that the effort had failed. The letter took two days to reach Eisenhower. The Americans did not send arms or men over the Rhine. They did, however, do the Antifako one favour. Anyone listening to the radio in Düsseldorf on April 15 heard a curious announcement: "the hat suits Veronika well" (*"der Hut kleidet Veronika gut"*).[82] It was a signal, drawn up by Smeets's group and broadcast by the Americans, to the Antifako members on the other side of the Rhine that their team had made it and the letter had been successfully delivered.

With the Antifako group sidelined for the moment, the spark of final resistance would have to be ignited by someone else. The task fell to the so-called Wiedenhofen Group. Finding itself notably higher up the social ladder than the largely working-class Antifako, the group took its name from a lawyer, Dr. Karl August Wiedenhofen, who chaired meetings of doctors, lawyers, merchants, and small businessmen in order to plan resistance activities. As ever, the group's members had contrasting motivations. Theodor Winkens's wife was Jewish, and his marriage to her had cost him his job with the police. Aloys Odenthal was an architect whose opposition to Nazism was rooted in his deep commitment to Christianity. Unlike so many Germans swept up in what was for many the genuine euphoria of 1933, Odenthal took the time to read *Mein Kampf*. In his postwar account, which might of course have been developed with hindsight, he objected particularly strongly to Hitler's attitudes toward Jews. But even before 1945,

Odenthal's refusal to join the party, his close friendship with Communists, and his critical remarks about the regime had led to two warnings from the Gestapo. There was to be no third warning—only delivery to a concentration camp. Winkens and Odenthal had met for years, and they included in their group Wiedenhofen, a cosmopolitan lawyer who maintained extensive foreign contacts, itself a mark of suspicion for the Nazis.

It was in 1943, the same year that Stauffenberg joined the rather larger military resistance, that Wiedenhofen came into contact with the group while in an air-raid shelter in the Bismarckstraße. There, hiding from British bombs, Wiedenhofen began chatting with an anti-Nazi master joiner named Ernst Klein.[83] Having identified themselves to each other as Hitler opponents, the two men revealed their respective networks of friends. Doing so brought Wiedenhofen into contact with Karl Kleppe, Josef Knab, and Dr. Karl Müller. Diehard defenders of area bombing might take note of the case. British Air Chief Marshal Arthur T. Harris had claimed that area bombing would drive the Germans into the arms of the resistance. It did not, but in this case, it facilitated the meeting of resisters in the same bomb shelter.

Once in the Düsseldorf resistance, Wiedenhofen acted like a sort of local civilian Stauffenberg: he was the driving force of the group, bringing more and more citizens into it and organizing the meetings. A key date for the group was February 12, 1945. At Wiedenhofen and Klein's urging, the men present agreed to develop a plan to protect Düsseldorf from total destruction.[84] To do so, they needed arms, and they therefore needed to contact a willing individual in the Nazi Party, the military, or the police. They ruled out the first two as pointless. That left the police. Someone suggested a name: Franz Jürgens.[85]

On the face of it, Jürgens was an unlikely resister. He had joined the Nazi Party in 1933, and postwar accounts are split on whether he did so out of professional opportunism or real sympathy for the Nazis' cause. Rumour at the time, however, spoke in Jürgens's favour: word had it that he had refused the Nero Order's directive to destroy the city's energy works.[86] Not without some risk, the Wiedenhofen Group decided to call on him. The policeman told them that Police Chief and SS-Brigadeführer August

Korreng had ordered him to organize a forced evacuation of the city's population. Jürgens claimed to have replied, "Every time you have something
particular dirty that has to be done, you give it to me. I refuse to organize
this operation."[87] Jürgens was their man.

By April, the time for action had come. The American encirclement
of the Ruhr on April 1 had trapped over 400,000 German soldiers in the
pocket, which the Americans immediately began to squeeze. At times, the
American advance was easy: there was no resistance in Essen, and contingents of the American Seventeenth Airborne Division walked into Duisburg
"almost without a fight."[88] The US Ninety-Fifth Infantry Division faced, by
contrast, an often heavy fight. In Dortmund, the mayor tried to surrender
his already flattened city, but Gauleiter Hoffmann prevented it.[89]

In some cases, continued military opposition to the Allies was combined with acts of disobedience, the provenance of which is not always clear:
in several towns south of the Ruhr, the First US Army found bridges intact
even though they had been wired with explosives.[90] Someone had refused
to flick the switch or had stopped someone else from doing so. Civilians
throughout the Ninety-Fifth Division's area, running from Dortmund to
Hamm, provided the Americans with information on German troop levels
and strongpoints.[91]

By April 13, the Ruhr pocket had shrunk to include only the area from
greater Düsseldorf to Wuppertal in the east.[92] Units disintegrated, and
soldiers deserted and surrendered in the thousands; many walked miles,
struggling to find an American sufficiently unoccupied to accept their surrender.[93] As command over his subordinate units slipped away, General von
Zangen surrendered his Fifteenth Army on April 13, as did General Köchling
his LXXXI Corps; what remained of the Panzer Lehr Division did the same
two days later.[94]

This left Feldmarschall Walter Model. General Karl Wagener, Model's
chief of staff, had urged the field marshal on April 7 to spare his troops and
Ruhr civilians by seeking permission from Hitler to surrender.[95] That permission would not be forthcoming, and Model felt bound by the vacuous
dictum that "a field marshal never surrenders." Recovering some degree of
moral worth, though, he decided on April 15 to give up without technically

surrendering: he dissolved Army Group B and ordered youth and old men discharged from the army. His men then streamed into American captivity over the next three days. Model moved toward Düsseldorf to go down with Florian in a glorious last stand.

As Army Group B disintegrated, Jürgens met the wider Wiedenhofen Group on April 14 and possibly again the next day. The air was thick with talk of resistance, and Jürgens agreed to help. He did so just in time, because events were beginning to move quickly. Having closed the Ruhr pocket, American troops were moving on Düsseldorf from all sides. On April 16, Gauleiter Florian called a "war council" (*Kriegsrat*) of party, Wehrmacht, and police leaders in his headquarters at the Park Hotel in the Königsallee (today, the Steigenberger Park Hotel). There, he, Model, and Police Chief August Korreng agreed to make their last stand: barricades were to be erected and explosives detonated. The NSDAP and the Wehrmacht prepared their fortifications. Korreng ordered Jürgens and Brumshagen to prepare the police for a defence of the city, while the Nero Order specifications went out to what was left of the Wehrmacht and the Volkssturm in the vicinity.

Kept constantly abreast of these developments by Jürgens, the Wiedenhofen Group mobilized. On April 15, Wiedenhofen, Odenthal, and Müller met in Odenthal's apartment at Lakronstraße 52.[96] Müller told them that there was a plan to surrender the city bloodlessly to the Americans. Odenthal agreed without hesitation and suggested a fourth figure, Theodor Andresen, for the handover.[97]

The next morning, April 16, at 9:00, Andresen arrived at Odenthal's office. Odenthal told him that "a number of Düsseldorf citizens have declared themselves ready to prevent this pointless terror that awaits us."[98] Andresen signed on, and what became the Wiedenhofen Group assembled at 11:00 in Wiedenhofen's apartment: Knab, Müller, Odenthal, Winkens, and Hermann Weill, a twenty-one-year-old half-Jewish student.[99] The men committed themselves to action with a handshake.[100] Wiedenhofen then called Jürgens, who was much closer to events than any of the other men.[101] Jürgens told them to come to his office in the Police Presidium at 13:00.[102]

Arriving at the bulky, interwar building, the Wiedenhofen Group, less Weill and Winkens, slipped past the large numbers of police and SS men in the Presidium and made their way to Jürgens's rooms. He expressed his delight that there were men who loved their city and were prepared to protect it. And, he continued, they had to act now: Korreng was prepared to mobilize all police officers under his command for a final defence of Düsseldorf.[103] Odenthal offered the first suggestion on how to act. He was an acquaintance of Korreng, and he could use that connection to get into his office. Armed with a pistol supplied by Jürgens, he would shoot Korreng. This way, Odenthal argued, they would avoid Stauffenberg's mistake at the Wolf's Lair.[104] As resisters often did, however, they decided against it, ostensibly because they wanted information about Werewolf groups in the city, but in all likelihood actually because they possessed a humanity that those whom they wished to stop lacked.

Jürgens then summoned his closest and most trustworthy colleagues and explained the plans to them. All but two agreed that it was necessary. The head of the criminal investigations department (*Leiter des Kriminalkommissariats*), Schlosser, was the only source of real opposition, describing the idea as "grotesque."[105] Odenthal won him over with some rough-and-tumble flattery and persuasion. "Come on, you big, tough fellow," Odenthal said as he hit Schlosser on the shoulder, "show some courage! The fate of Düsseldorf, of women, and of children hangs in the balance!"[106]

Armed with a pistol each, Wiedenhofen, Müller, Jürgens, Knab, and Odenthal moved down the corridors of the imposing Police Presidium. They pushed through the first three of Korreng's rooms and right into his office. Wiedenhofen spoke: "We come as five free citizens of Düsseldorf. You have told the commander that Düsseldorf must be defended. You will only bring more despair, agony, and ruin [*Not, Elend, und Verderben*] to our city. We are therefore obligated to protect her. You are under arrest!"[107] Korreng broke into a sweat and lunged for the pistol in his desk. Knab thrust a pistol in Korreng's chest and shouted, "You are under arrest! You need nothing from that desk!"[108] The group took Korreng to a jail cell. On the way, Jürgens told his senior officers, "Herr SS-Brigadeführer Korreng is under arrest. Anyone who resists my orders will be shot!"[109]

All agreed that Jürgens and the "odious" individual could not be left alone.[110] Müller agreed to guard him temporarily, while Jürgens sought replacements for him and as Odenthal and Wiedenhofen made for American lines.[111] Jürgens, Odenthal, and Wiedenhofen first went to the police officers' rooms while Müller stood guard with two of Jürgens's men. Multiple other police officers came by to ask, not unreasonably, why an armed civilian stood outside a cell containing their commander. When he told them, no one objected.[112] Indeed, the action had general police support; officers had nodded approvingly from their offices as the group led Korreng to his cell.[113]

While Müller guarded Korreng, Jürgens took Wiedenhofen and the others to his superior, Dr. Otto Goetsch.[114] Goetsch dictated a letter stating that Wiedenhofen had been authorized to surrender the city. Goetsch stamped the letter with the police president's official seal—stamps and seals being an unquestionable sign of official approval in virtually all aspects of German bureaucracy, even in these fraught hours—and Jürgens signed it.[115] Jürgens then supplied a Mercedes, and Wiedenhofen and Odenthal went to pick up the other members of the Wiedenhofen Group.[116]

Wiedenhofen, Odenthal, Weill, and the others made it back to the police headquarters by late afternoon. As they approached the building, Andresen met them and told them that Müller was no longer there.[117] Knab and Andresen went upstairs to look for Müller and the others, while Wiedenhofen and Odenthal waited in the courtyard. Then, rather suddenly, another member of the group flashed past on a bicycle and shouted, "We've been betrayed! Get out of here!"[118] Wiedenhofen and Odenthal did just that.

In planning their operation, the insurgents made a fatal mistake: they did not occupy the telephone exchange. Police loyal to the Nazis reported the revolt to the city's battle group commander, Brumshagen, who immediately dispatched troops.[119] Müller was the first to suspect something was up. He had been promised to be relieved in ten minutes, and no one was there after thirty.[120] He sent one of Jürgens's men to find his boss; he did not return, and the other policeman managed to slip off as well.[121] Ten minutes later, a desk officer tipped Müller off: "Herr Doktor, you are in a precarious situation here."[122] In great danger, Müller left the police cell and stepped into the courtyard. He saw twenty soldiers in SS uniforms at one entrance armed with guns.[123] Müller decided to play it cool.

"Why are you here?" he asked them.

"We don't know," one of them replied. "We just received an order to come here."[124] Another pointed to a man being led away at gunpoint. It looked like Jürgens.

Displaying a calm that would save his life, Müller slowly walked across the courtyard and up to Jürgens's rooms. Finding them empty, he made his way to the street, where he saw Jürgens being forced into an open truck on the other side of the Kavalleriestraße. As there was nothing he could do, and as he had freely identified himself to many police officers, he walked out of the building and east toward the neighbourhood of Gerresheim.[125]

Others were not so lucky. Kleppe, Andresen, Knab, and Weill were all arrested in the building, either because they were unlucky or because they panicked and drew attention to themselves. All four were taken to be shot. Gauleiter Florian, who had coincidentally come to the Police Presidium, personally released Korreng.[126] This otherwise disastrous turn of events had one positive consequence for the resisters: following the arrest of Jürgens, the Düsseldorf police moved en masse into the resisters' column, at least passively. Florian could not count on them to join a defence of the city.[127]

Once tipped off, Wiedenhofen and Odenthal made a dash for their car, put a pistol in the back of the driver, and ordered him to step on it. When he refused, Odenthal shouted, "Then I'll shoot you and drive myself!"[128] The threat worked, and the man drove them as far as the northeastern outskirts of the city. There, the driver, citing consequences for his family, begged to be released.[129] Wiedenhofen and Odenthal obtained a promise from him that he would speak to no one about what had just occurred and then let him go. The two men walked from there.[130] They crossed the last German lines with the improbable claim that Wiedenhofen was a veterinarian on his way help the "farmer" Odenthal's cow deliver a calf.[131]

The two men, flying a white flag, arrived at American positions at Mettmann, twenty kilometres east of the city, by 18:00. Odenthal and Wiedenhofen handed over their pistols as they approached an American tank, and they asked to be taken to the Americans' commanding officer.[132] Jürgens had provided them a document stating, "The holder of this document, Dr. August Wiedenhofen, is authorized to cross German lines in order to negotiate with Allied troops in the name of the city of Düsseldorf."[133] The American soldiers took them to their commander, and the two Düsseldorfers urged him to take the city.

The commander refused. It was not, he said, worth "precious American blood" when one thousand bombers were ready to launch a raid on Düsseldorf.[134] This was, at least in part, a bluff: tactical bombing raids were common, but it is unlikely that the Americans would have sent a thousand bombers to attack Düsseldorf. The threat nonetheless sent panic through the two men.[135] They begged him to call off the raid, arguing that there were only between four and five thousand poorly armed and poorly trained soldiers in the city. Citing the fate of their four comrades and their families, they urged the commander to make a dash for the Police Presidium in the centre of the city. "Whoever takes the Police Presidium," they argued, "takes Düsseldorf."[136]

The commander seemed impressed but replied, "I have to speak with my general. He will decide what happens. We won't take Düsseldorf today; we may take it tomorrow, we may only take it a week from now."[137] The commander then had a note written confirming that the two Germans could stay at headquarters "on my invitation" and that they were "to be treated with courtesy."[138] He ordered a lieutenant to look after them.

The next morning, Odenthal and Wiedenhofen were at breakfast when the lieutenant appeared. "The general has decided to take Düsseldorf. And you're going to help us do it."[139] The lieutenant had the men taken to divisional headquarters at Langenfeld, but by the time they arrived, the situation had changed. The commanding general told him that American tanks had been fired on in two of the city's outer districts, and that he "had no interest in spilling more American blood for the city of Düsseldorf." "We will have to hit this city," he said, "as we hit all large cities, with eight hundred bombers before taking it." The effect on both men was, in Odenthal's words, "indescribable."[140] They assured the commander that Düsseldorfers would put up no resistance and then, in an inspired move, Odenthal produced his official badge as an architect responsible for building air-raid shelters.[141] He promised to identify every tank obstacle in the city and to identify two routes into Düsseldorf. He backed up his claim to expertise by telling the

Americans that it would take thirty minutes to break through tank obstacles. The American commander paused, and then said, "Gentlemen, what
brought you to do this? Which positions do you want after the occupation?"[142] Odenthal replied, "We want to return to our old jobs. This is about
saving Düsseldorf, so that after this curse of National Socialism, our children will be able to wake up to a peaceful and safe world."[143]

The Americans were convinced. Large maps of Düsseldorf were laid
out on the tables. Wiedenhofen and Odenthal pored over them with the
American officers. The two men showed them the location of the police
headquarters, pinpointed tank barricades, and suggested two possible routes
into the city.[144] They decided to enter the city at 15:00. The Americans asked,
"How many tanks and how many infantrymen do you think you need?"

Rising to the occasion, Wiedenhofen said, "Give me two tanks and two
hundred men; I don't need any more."[145] Odenthal thought a figure twice
that would be necessary.[146]

The Americans doubled the last German offer: "We'll give you eight
hundred men and eight tanks, but we'll only take the city if you sit in the
first tank and guide us into the city."[147] Odenthal agreed to sit in the first
tank, Wiedenhofen the second.[148] At 15:00, the tanks and soldiers departed
for Düsseldorf; their orders were to storm and seize the Police Presidium.

After a few kilometres, a German-speaking American soldier asked
Odenthal, "Don't you want a weapon, so that you can defend yourself?"[149]

Odenthal replied, "I won't shoot another Düsseldorfer. My friends and
my family are probably dead. What does life have to offer me now? My task
is almost fulfilled."[150] The American took Odenthal's hand, put one arm
around him, and the tank rolled on toward Düsseldorf.

Within the city itself, order was breaking down. The arrest of Jürgens
had shaken whatever confidence in the regime was left among the police,
and there is evidence that, possibly at the solicitation of Jürgens himself,
police officers began deserting their posts. Florian and Korreng began to
panic, and they prepared to flee Düsseldorf, leaving its defence to others.
And above all, the Antifako, without any knowledge of Wiedenhofen and
Odenthal's activities, sprang into action, launching a campaign across the
city with thousands of leaflets:

The "Antifako" calls on you!

The Americans are on the borders of our city.

WHITE FLAGS OUT!

Block every effort at sabotage; put an end to any provocation, and beware of the Werewolf.

The Antifako Action Committee, signed Walter Jordan [i.e., Hermann Smeets].[151]

As Florian and Korreng fled the city, the defences collapsed. White flags sprang up everywhere. On the Germaniastraße, an Antifako member tied four large sheets together and hung the massive white flag on a dry cleaner's shop.[152] Members of the Antifako rushed out to the suburbs with their flyers in hand, trying to anticipate the direction of the American advance. As they did, civilians came out of their homes and grabbed bundles of leaflets from their hands, spreading them throughout their own neighbourhoods.[153] Otto Blumhoff and another resister ran straight into the advancing Americans. They were first put under arrest, but they were able to explain themselves and showed their flyers to some German-Jewish US soldiers.[154] The Americans immediately released them, and they continued to distribute the flyers.

The convoy passed along Kölner Straße, blew up a concrete tank barrier, and moved toward the main station.[155] On the Worringerplatz, a square not far from the station, they rammed through another tank obstacle.[156] As the tanks approached the main station, civilians came into the streets and ran alongside them, cheering and thanking their liberators.[157] One of them was Hermann Smeets, who was at the station with his bicycle.[158] The procession turned gently southward toward police headquarters on the Mackensenplatz—today, the Jürgensplatz.[159] As they did, Smeets and two other Antifako members followed them on their bicycles. American sentries were already guarding the building but, seeing the leaflets, let the men in. An American commander welcomed them with the words, "Your organization is well known to us," and, in a bit of role reversal, introduced Smeets and the others to the Wiedenhofen Group.[160] In the meantime, the Americans had dispatched a unit to place Odenthal and Wiedenhofen's

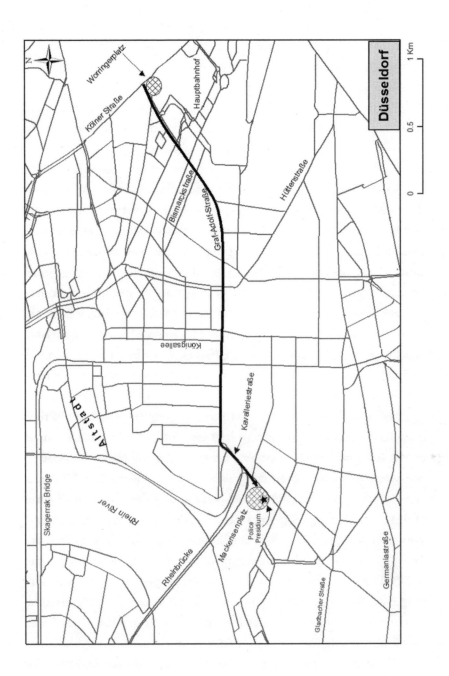

Düsseldorf

families under military protection. All policemen had by this point surrendered without any resistance, and the Americans ordered them to gather in
the courtyard. Brumshagen was among them. An American officer went up
to him and asked him, "Where is Jürgens?"

Brumshagen replied, "He's dead."[161]

AFTER THEIR ARREST, but before the Americans arrived, Florian
had informed Model of Jürgens, Kleppe, Weill, Knab, and Andresen's
actions. Model insisted that they be court martialled at the Park Hotel.[162]
Jürgens's trial took place on April 16. Model's court had three judges, with
Brumshagen presiding. Florian, already in hunting clothes in preparation
for his flight, was in the room with Model, but it is unclear whether he took
part in the trial.[163] The court found Jürgens guilty and sentenced him to
death by shooting. His subordinate, Gehrke, was also tried but found innocent as he was judged to have simply followed orders. Jürgens was taken to
a courtyard next to a school-cum-barracks in south-central Düsseldorf (in
Bilk's Färberstraße). Hauptwachtmeister Heinrich Gesell gave the order to
shoot. Before he did, Jürgens shouted, "Gesell, give my love to my wife, and
long live my Germany!" The hail of bullets cut him down.

The other four men were tried later that night, in the early hours of
April 17. The interrogators tortured Knab severely and smashed his right
arm. They crushed Andresen's skull. There is little reason to think Kleppe
or Weill, the half-Jew, escaped such attention, although the documents do
not provide details on their fates. Major Walther Peiper presided over a
"flying court" (*fliegendes Standgericht*) that had earlier sentenced deserters
to death. He found the four men guilty and ordered them executed on the
same spot as Jürgens. To speed the killings, Peiper dispensed with the tradition of executing men only by daylight. In an eerie repetition of the fate met
by Stauffenberg, Olbricht, Mertz, and Haeften, these four far less famous
men, both then and now, were brought to a courtyard lit by artificial light.
Whereas Fromm used cars, Gesell used flashlights. By their light, Peiper
had Kleppe, Weill, Knab, and Andresen executed.

The men's self-sacrifice was not in vain. Jürgens's disobedience, and
above all his arrest, moved the police of Düsseldorf into the resistance

column. Equally importantly, the silent, indeed unknown, partnership between the Wiedenhofen and Antifako groups ensured that when the Americans were guided into the city a few hours after Jürgens's death, they met only white flags and cheers.

CHAPTER 19

DYING SO THAT THEY MAY LIVE

Central Germany

A
s Hodges's First Army swung north to encircle the Ruhr,
Patton's Third Army guarded its right flank and rear by pushing
toward Thuringia.[1] By March 28, Lieutenant General Manton Eddy's XII
Corps had pushed almost as far north as Gießen. Joining the XX Corps
from the south, Eddy's men then moved on to Kassel. On March 30,
Lieutenant General Walker, XX Corps's commander, ordered Major
General Grow to make a dash with his Sixth Armored Division for the city.
Grow's division was six miles from Kassel before the end of the day, while
the Eleventh Armored Division took the high ground overlooking Fulda.
One battalion of the Twenty-Sixth Division would clear Fulda on April
2; Kassel, by contrast, required the full force of the Eightieth Division,
which fought for four days against automatic weapons, mortar, and direct
fire.[2] The German commander, Generalmajor Johannes Erxleben, finally
surrendered to the 318th Infantry Regiment on April 4.[3] Eisenhower had
originally wanted Patton to stop there in order to allow Hodges's First Army
to pull up on the left flank, allowing a joint advance farther into Germany.
The Fourth Armored Division, however, picked up a German officer,
a deserter, who informed them that a high-level German headquarters
or communications centre was located at Ohrdruf, just south of Gotha.
Patton thus had another excuse to push forward. Eisenhower allowed him
to advance on the town, and Patton predictably seized it. He dispatched

one combat command of the Fourth Armored Division for Gotha, the other for Ohrdruf.

In Gotha, the commander responsible for the defence of the city was an Austrian Luftwaffe officer, Oberstleutnant Josef Ritter von Gadolla. Gadolla was aristocratic (he was descended from Italian nobility) and deeply religious (his mother was a strict Polish Catholic).[4] His actions had shown an early disregard for National Socialist rules. In 1935, a young half-Jewish (by descent) soldier from Gotha named Hollaender was registered at the army registration bureau (Wehrmeldemamt), to which Gadolla had been transferred in 1943. Hollaender began receiving correspondence as a precursor to his expulsion: "You, as a Jew . . . ," one letter stated, while another demanded he turn over his service eyeglasses (*Dienstbrille*).[5] Someone at the registration bureau was notified of Hollaender's Jewish heritage, and he crossed the soldier's papers in red. Fearing for his life, Hollaender, who was (a probably converted) Christian, approached a priest in Gotha, Otto Linz, who in turn appealed to Gadolla. Gadolla agreed to remove the relevant papers from the bureau's files.[6] Doing so saved Hollaender's life. This might not have been Gadolla's only experience with resistance: according to some accounts, he had had contact with Erwin von Witzleben and had been interrogated by the Gestapo following July 20, 1944.[7]

In early April 1945, Gadolla had in his pocket an order from Hitler: the "fortress Gotha," an essential obstacle on the Allies' march through the Reich, was under no circumstances to surrender.[8] Hitler and Thuringia's Gauleiter, Fritz Sauckel, were singing from the same song sheet. In January, Sauckel had declared: "Neither threats nor blandishments will separate the German people from their Führer. . . . Every man and woman in our region [*Gau*], old and young, will together fulfill the great and difficult duty. . . . Shirkers [*Drückeberger*], cowards, deserters, and traitors have no place in our battle-hardened [*schwerringenden*] people's community [*Volksgemeinschaft*]."[9] Behind all the rhetoric lay a strategic consideration: Thuringia stood between the Western Allies and the Red Army. If Patton's troops pushed through and met the Soviets advancing from the east, the Reich would be sliced in two. Gotha, along with Weimar, Jena, and Erfurt, stood in the way of Patton's push eastward. Hitler ordered that the river

Saale (running north–south) be a new defence line and "that every yard of German soil . . . be contested."[10]

In January 1945, the previous commander of Gotha, an Oberst von Reckow, had been transferred to Mühlhausen.[11] Gadolla stood next in the chain of command, and on February 1, Generalmajor Kurt Hübner summoned him to Erfurt and appointed him combat commander of the city. Hübner gave him the following order: "I order you, as combat commander of Gotha . . . to ensure with all your soldierly honour and with life and limb [auf Leib und Leben] an unconditional defence of the city entrusted to you. You are to reject every offer of surrender from the enemy. For you and your unit [Besatzung], there shall only be a battle to the very end." Gadolla in turn had to state out loud, "I promise to defend Gotha to the very end. I accept the obligations as you have outlined and bind myself to them through my signature."[12]

On March 19, as Patton's Third Army was still fighting its way to the Rhine, two scorched-earth orders came through. Both were likely linked with Hitler's Nero Order. One, received by Gadolla, called for the usual destruction of all military, traffic, communications, industry, and supply stores in the Reich. The second, received by Erich Wendler, a captain in a Hungarian flying school unit transferred to the city in January, was much more precise. It ordered him to prepare for destruction the underpass in the city's eastern rail station, the city's viaduct supporting east–west train movements, residential accommodation in a military airfield, the administrative buildings of the Gothaer Waggonfabrik (which produced airplanes and railcars), and the Waffen-SS ration depot (Verpflegungslager) in an old porcelain factory.[13] Wendler reinterpreted the order rather generously: he gathered bombs and munitions on his airfield runway and set them alight.[14] He had his Hungarian recruits guard the runway, and ordered them to open fire in case anyone attempted to block the destruction.[15] Just over a week later, on March 29, as Third Army troops moved into Thuringia, Gadolla spoke with his adjutant, Major Graf Heinrich zu Brandis. Citing the bombing of Dresden and the early-March bombing of Gotha, Gadolla told Brandis that the defence of the city was pointless. He was not, he continued, going to "sacrifice countless refugees and defenceless civilians" for an obviously lost war.[16] On April 2, he took leave of his landlady with the words, "Dear lady, you must not worry about yourself or your children. I will see to it that Gotha is not defended."[17]

At 10:10 the next morning, April 3, sirens rang out across the city: the enemy was approaching, and the Volkssturm was to be called up.[18] Gadolla recorded in a log that Gotha could not be defended with weapons, flak, or the Luftwaffe.[19] That day or the next, he ordered white flags flown over the city castle, city hall, and the military hospital.[20] On April 3, a defence committee made up of Mayor Fritz Schmidt, Kreisleiter Wilhelm Busch, School Inspector (*Kreisschulrat*) Heinrich Magdlung, Council and Provincial Undersecretary (*Landrat und Ministerialrat*) Dr. Ernst Guyet, a Major Häussler (standing in for Gadolla), and SS-Obergruppenführer and Generalleutnant of the Police Paul Hennicke agreed to surrender the city without a fight.[21] This alone was quite incredible: it was extremely rare for a Kreisleiter, still less for a senior SS officer, to agree to surrender. Hennicke seems, however, to have been acting unilaterally—SS soldiers in and around the city were still insistent on defending Gotha.

As they did, Gadolla made his first attempt to reach American lines. Accompanied by City Treasurer Dr. Georg-Heinrich Sandrock, Gadolla drove with a white flag flying toward American lines. They did not make it very far. At Brühl, not far northeast of the city centre, SS soldiers—unaware of Hennicke's commitments, or not under his command—stopped them. Gadolla justified his actions with reference to the defence committee's decision; the SS threatened to shoot him if he tried something like this again, and Gadolla and Sandrock returned to Gotha.[22]

As he did, the NSDAP abandoned him. At 17:00, other members of the defence committee—Kreisleiter Busch, Mayor Schmidt, and Hennicke—fled eastward out of the battle zone.[23] Sandrock, to whom authority passed after the mayor left, retreated to his apartment. Either he shot himself or the SS shot him.[24] Gadolla pressed on alone. Defying threats by a Waffen-SS Obersturmbannführer to inform Himmler, Gadolla ordered the local Volkssturm troops to stand down.[25] He also ordered that all Wehrmacht troops within the city withdraw toward Arnstadt-Erfurt and, finally, that white flags be hoisted.[26] He then sought out civilian contacts that he could use to reach the Americans. The matter was pressing: the SS, who did not answer to Gadolla, had removed the white flags, and they got their hands on a lone flak gun and shot at Allied planes passing overhead.[27] Flak guns could be easily turned horizontally against advancing troops, and their use would have provided the American Third Army with more than enough justification for launching an air raid or artillery barrage, or both. Such a barrage, in turn, would have been devastating for Gotha: much of the city's firefighting equipment had been transferred to Bavaria in March, and the city would have been essentially defenceless against any ensuing fires.[28]

In Sandrock's absence, Gadolla worked with the next man down in the civilian chain of command: Stadtbaurat (city planner, roughly) Müller-Kirchenbauer.[29] After a long delay occasioned by their inability to find a driver, Gadolla set out with Müller-Kirchenbauer and Ernst Rudolph (the driver) to meet the Americans with the Führer order in his pocket.[30] It was the evening of April 3 between 21:00 and 22:00. Dodging the artillery fire that was raining down on the city, they took a detour and drove with white armbands and a white flag out of Gotha. After driving two kilometres, they saw troops from a distance and hoped they had reached the Americans.[31] They had not: Gadolla and Müller-Kirchenbauer had run right into a reserve company of Flak Battalion 59, stationed in the city. An informer had overheard the two men and reported to the army, which was waiting for them. The soldiers tore open the doors and yanked out the driver.[32] "You bastards [*Lumpen*]! You traitors!" screamed a sergeant. "You wanted to run to the Americans, you cowards!"[33] The men were interrogated and declared guilty by two young, fanatical lieutenants.[34] A sentence was not, however, carried out immediately. Bizarrely, given the way in which the country was collapsing around them, the army decreed that they be subjected to a court martial in Weimar, following loose, though wholly inadequate, standards of procedural justice. On their way, Allied forces fired on them, forcing them to dive for cover (the driver, Rudolph, used this as a chance to escape), and a truck accidently crashed into their car.[35] It was consequently a seriously wounded Gadolla who faced trial in Weimar.[36]

Without word from Gadolla, the rest of the civilian resisters waited nervously at the castle in Gotha.[37] Sometime later, they heard shots. Assuming that the SS had again removed the white flag, two of them went out to inspect the roof. The flag was there, but so was something else: bullets were flying just over their heads.[38] It seemed that the Americans were launching an artillery barrage in preparation for a full assault on the city. The resisters were determined to try again to make contact the next morning.

When the proposal was discussed, it was rather like paying taxes: most of the group thought the plan was sound as long as someone else executed it. One after another, those in the city hierarchy claimed they lacked the nerve. The job fell to the least senior city administrator: Günther Ewald.[39] Ewald led the group to the Rathaus, assuming the negotiations would take place there. The plan was for Ewald then to go with an interpreter to the Americans.[40]

He did not need to: they came to him. A junior German officer, who had been taken prisoner when the Americans overtook a military hospital in the Arnoldi School, had already committed treason by leading an American officer there.[41] The Americans had seen the white flag and were there to negotiate a truce.[42] The officer said that one of them could offer surrender terms. Taking a metaphorical step back in unison, the rest of the German delegation gladly elected Ewald. He accompanied the German soldier and the American to the military hospital, where an American soldier who spoke flawless German was waiting for him. The commanding officer was called, and Ewald offered to surrender.[43] Ewald then led the Americans back to the city hall, where the commanding officer demanded that he offer a written surrender. Ewald hastily had a typist prepare some text and presented it to the translator. The commanding officer demanded that the word "unconditional" be added to the text. Ewald, after some questions, agreed, and the city's surrender was officially signed. The commanding officer then said, "Now, we need to get immediately to headquarters [*Befehlsstand*]; if we're not back in time, the artillery barrage will start again." As the Americans left, the Germans waited nervously. No shells were to be heard; the delegation had made it in time. That night, Allied bombers bombed Nordhausen, eighty-five kilometres to the north, for the second consecutive night. According to local sources, the bombers were bound for Gotha and diverted to Nordhausen after the former's surrender.[44]

As the remaining resisters delivered Gotha into the hands of the Americans on April 4, Gadolla was judged well enough to face a trial, despite his declaration to the contrary. He appeared before a court martial held in the staff headquarters of the First Panzer Division in Weimar.[45] The army, not the SS, tried him. Gadolla made no apology for his actions and defended them with reference to the defence committee's decision to surrender the city. In what were among his last words, he also achieved the defiant eloquence that marked many resisters facing death. "I acted entirely as an idealist and did so to spare the city death and destruction [Verfall]. Others would have done the same if they had been in my shoes. I can only say, speaking as an old soldier, that I take full responsibility for my conduct."[46] Müller-Kirchenbauer claimed to have opposed the surrender of the city and said that Gadolla had ordered him to ride along on the attempt to surrender.[47] He pleaded for mercy. He received it: the court declared him innocent on the grounds that he had tried to resist Gadolla and was ignorant of the order to fight to the last man.[48] Gadolla received none. The court judged him guilty on two counts: failing to defend Gotha to the last man and attempting to surrender to the Americans.[49] The court sentenced him to death by firing squad. The trial, unsurprisingly, failed to meet even minimum standards of justice and due process: no members of the defence committee—Busch, Schmidt, or Hennicke—were brought as witnesses to corroborate Gadolla's story.[50]

Gadolla spent his last hours with a priest, Leo Schramm, who gave the wounded officer communion. "I only wanted to do the right thing," Gadolla told the priest. "I wanted to save Gotha from destruction. Is that a crime, Father?"[51] Accompanied by Schramm, Gadolla was taken out for execution at 7:00 on the morning of April 5, 1945.[52] He refused a blindfold.[53] His head bandaged and weak from his injuries, Gadolla uttered, with forgivable pathos, his last words: "I must die so that Gotha may live."[54] Then, with Father Schramm reciting the Lord's Prayer, the shots were fired.[55]

As Gotha surrendered, the second American combat command reached Ohrdruf, where they found a massive underground communications centre constructed as an army headquarters in the time preceding the 1938 Sudeten crisis.[56] It had never been used. The men of the Fourth Armored Division also made another, more horrifying discovery: the Ohrdruf concentration camp (a satellite of Buchenwald). There, in striped shirts, were haggard and emaciated prisoners, bare shells of humanity. The ground was covered with the thin bodies of the dead, piled on or next to each other. They had looks of horror of their faces. Others died after they tried to eat solid foods given to them by the Americans.[57] After seeing the camp, both Eisenhower and Patton vomited.[58] The town's mayor and his wife were also forced to see the camp; when they returned home afterwards, they hanged themselves.[59]

AFTER REACHING GOTHA and Ohrdruf, Patton's Third Army paused to allow the Ninth and the First Armies to catch up. The Ninth prepared to move north of the Harz Mountains toward the large cities of Hannover, Brunswick (Braunschweig), and Magdeburg, while the First would move south toward Leipzig and Chemnitz. In approaching Leipzig, Hodges's troops would run straight into "flak alley."[60] Attempting to protect synthetic-oil refineries around Leipzig from American attacks, which terrified the Nazi regime much more than the attacks by the British on their city centres, the Germans had installed as many as a thousand anti-aircraft guns grouped in batteries of twelve to thirty-six 75 mm to 128 mm guns.[61] After pointing vertically for most of the war, these great guns could be aimed horizontally, sending their ammunition slicing through American infantry and tanks.

Flak guns were not the only obstacles. After the Ninth Armored Division swung south of the guns and across the river Mulde on intact bridges at Colditz, the Second and Sixty-Ninth Divisions were sent into Leipzig itself.[62] They reached the outskirts of the city on April 16. As they approached, citizens and the police made a valiant effort to surrender the city. Explosives were defused on bridges over the Weiße Elster (a tributary of the river Saale), and the chief of police came to meet the Americans with a surrender offer.[63] A large, stubborn, and activist Communist resistance movement in the city provided a strong foundation of anti-Nazi sentiment, and civilians decked their houses in white flags.[64] The army, however, would not cooperate and put up a stiff resistance. Anti-aircraft auxiliary units again turned their flak guns on the Americans, who had to fight a hard, street-by-street battle for two days before the garrison commander surrendered the

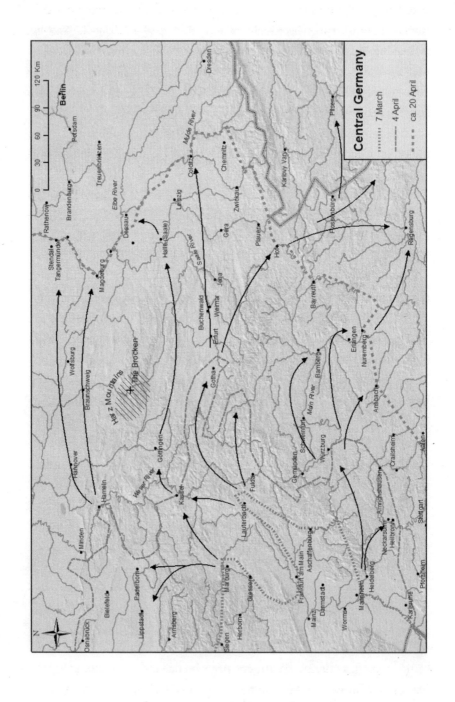

Central Germany

.... 7 March
------- 4 April
- - - - ca. 20 April

last, fanatical holdouts.[65] Before the commander surrendered, an ardent National Socialist and the director of a local *Panzerfaust* (bazooka) factory, a Herr Bundnis, held an unorthodox dinner party. He invited his closest colleagues to a lavish meal. After the last round of drinks had been served, the room exploded, killing everyone instantly. He had arranged for the room to be rigged with explosives.[66]

Before and while the Americans moved into Leipzig, the SS cut a swathe of murder through the city and its environs. The Gestapo arrested fifty-two men and shot them on the Exerzierplatz on April 12.[67] As the SS evacuated concentration and labour camps, they murdered many hundreds of prisoners. In one case, they pushed three hundred forced labourers into a barracks, doused the building in gasoline, and lit it aflame with a cannon shot.[68] Some seventy managed to escape, but the SS mowed them down with gunfire as they ran; the Americans discovered their bodies tangled in the surrounding barbed-wire fences.[69] The rest died from heat or asphyxiation.

With the Americans approaching, the SS unleashed a similar wave of murder in Weimar and elsewhere.[70] On April 6, the SS transported theologian Dietrich Bonhoeffer from Buchenwald, near Weimar, to Flossenbürg; like so many resisters before him, he was hanged. These eleventh-hour murders were designed to eliminate those who could testify to or otherwise provide evidence of Nazi crimes. Also on April 6, Gauleiter Fritz Sauckel, who had called on the people of Weimar to fight to the end on February 19, fled for his life toward southern Germany. That same day, Buchenwald guards sent three thousand Jews from the camp on a death march. As Buchenwald's Jews left the area, others arrived. On April 7, three columns containing thousands of prisoners were marched by the SS through Weimar and on to Buchenwald. Two days later, 4,800 prisoners, including presumably those who arrived on the seventh, were sent on death marches out of the camp. These marches were a small part of the forced evacuations of inmates from concentration and death camps across Germany and Eastern Europe.[71] Few survived them.

SOUTH OF THE FIRST ARMY, Patton spent almost a week in early April waiting for Simpson's Ninth Army to catch up. On April 10, Patton was finally free to go. He ordered his divisions forward into the inhospitable terrain of the steep, forested mountains of Thuringia. He had orders to capture the medium-sized but important cities of Jena, Erfurt, and Weimar.

On April 11, the Eightieth Infantry Division faced heavy resistance moving into Erfurt. The German defenders established positions along an east–west canal in the south of the city, and it took several hours of bitter fighting before the line was broken.[72] Two battalions of the 318th Infantry Regiment then had to fight their way house to house into the city centre; portions of the city were in flames.[73]

As the Fourth and Sixth Armored Divisions subsequently pushed into relatively open terrain, the task of clearing the cities—Weimar, Jena, and Gera—fell to the Eightieth Infantry Division, fresh from its fight in Erfurt. The first one went well. Perhaps fearing the American reaction to Buchenwald, the SS and army pulled out of Weimar before the Americans arrived. As the 319th Infantry Regiment approached the city, its commander commissioned the mayor of neighbouring Troistedt, Richard Weyde, with the task of delivering an ultimatum: surrender the city or suffer a heavy aerial and artillery bombardment.[74] With the battle commander and army gone, the decision fell to Weimar's mayor, Karl Otto Koch. Knowing the price of disobedience was death, and perhaps even knowing the fate of Gadolla, he was determined to spare the city of Goethe and Schiller. Koch, Weyde, and two English-speaking civilians drove out to meet the Americans.[75] Before the quick surrender formalities were completed, American tanks entered Weimar.[76]

The Second Battalion, 317th Infantry Regiment took over the occupation of Weimar the same day, and the 319th Infantry Regiment moved southeast toward Jena. The regiment neared the city via the steep approaches to the west.[77] In the city, two civilian resistance groups had emerged. The first included Armin Schmidt, Jena's mayor, and Hans Dittmer, head of the city's economics and agriculture office (*Ernährungs- und Wirtschaftsamt*).[78] The second group was made up of the university rector Professor Friedrich Zucker, medical Professor Wolfgang Veil, and other citizens who wished to prevent the city's destruction. Details on the relationship between the groups and the nature of their plans are vague.[79] It is fairly clear, though, that these middle-class resisters sought, following what was in March and April 1945 a fairly common pattern across the western Reich, to avoid the city's further destruction through its defence against the Third US Army. On April 6, according to their unverified account, Veil and Zucker went to the city's commander, Generaloberst Hermann Hoth, and urged him to surrender. Hoth responded furiously and ordered their court martial, though one never occurred.[80]

Hoth was subsequently replaced by an Oberst Hess, who, if anything, was more determined than his predecessor to defend Jena. He set up a defensive position in the eastern portions of the city, using an air-raid shelter as his headquarters.[81] On April 12, he ordered the destruction of all bridges crossing the river Saale, which had the effect of cutting his forces (east of the river) from the central administration of the city (west of the river).[82] Dittmer, meanwhile, made contact with the Americans, telling them that the city would not be defended.[83] The move very nearly cost him his life: SS-Sturmbannführer and Police Director Walter Schulze hauled him to army headquarters in east Jena and threatened him with execution.[84] Dittmer survived only because the army overruled Schulze. Oberst Hess warned Dittmer not to try contacting the Americans again, reminded him of the consequences of treason, and then concluded: "For all that, I'm going to let you go." Jena, Hess insisted, would be defended.[85]

In the end, both Hess and Dittmer were right. Hess's bridge-busting had cut the city in two: the western side, including the centre, surrendered when the Americans reached it on the thirteenth, whereas the eastern side resisted. Over the next two days, the Americans faced fanatical resistance on the outskirts and in the west of the city.[86] They responded with devastating artillery fire, obliterating resisting German units and all surrounding houses.[87] They faced no resistance when they moved from there into the centre. As in Erfurt, when the city fell, the Germans had suffered large numbers of pointless, eleventh-hour casualties.[88]

As the Eightieth Infantry Division surrounded Jena, the Third Army's next objective was Gera, which also fell only after bitter, house-to-house fighting on April 14, a day after Jena.[89] Patton hoped to make a dash for Berlin, but Eisenhower blocked it. Controversy has raged over this decision for decades, generally to Eisenhower's detriment, but the decision was a political rather than a military one. It had been made six months earlier, with Churchill leading the charge. Under the Allied agreement, the Americans would vacate Thuringia, and Berlin would be well within the Soviet zone.[90] The prime minister's rather erratic reversal of position won him many postwar admirers, but an occupation of Berlin solely by the Western Allies was never in the cards: it would have meant ripping up written agreements with the Soviets over Austria, and it would have risked war with the Red Army. An American attack on Berlin had no support among chiefs of staff on either side of the Atlantic.[91] If Churchill could not move this particular mountain, then neither could Eisenhower. The latter ordered Patton to stop on the Mulde, a tributary of the Elbe, fourteen miles west of Chemnitz. From there, he moved south into Bavaria and Czechoslovakia.

CHAPTER 20

NUREMBERG'S DESTRUCTION,
HEIDELBERG'S SALVATION

Southern Germany

A S THE FIRST AND NINTH US Armies were beginning their great encirclement of the Ruhr, Devers's Sixth Army Group made a dash for the east. Eisenhower assigned Devers the role of guarding the Twelfth Army Group's right flank through a northeastern push, followed by a push southeastward to cut off any German troops retreating toward the Alps.[1] Crossing the Rhine at Worms on March 26, the Third and Forty-Fifth Divisions, which had fought all the way from the beaches of the Mediterranean into the heart of Germany, moved on toward Aschaffenburg. The Forty-Fifth crossed the Main River just south of Aschaffenburg on March 28, the Third just north of the city two days later.

They met stiff, indeed uncompromising, resistance—further proof that there was nothing inevitable about the bloodless surrender of German cities. The Forty-Fifth Infantry Division opened up a massive aerial and artillery bombardment on Aschaffenburg. For six days, its 157th Infantry Regiment fought resistance from house to house, battling German soldiers, fanatical Hitler Youth who had learned to shoot and shave at roughly the same time, and, very unusually, armed citizens dropping grenades from rooftops.[2] "There was some of the hardest fighting of the war in that town," wrote an American officer. "Hitler had said that every man, woman, and child should fight . . . this town was the only place where that was really carried out."[3] The German combat commander ordered the hanging of

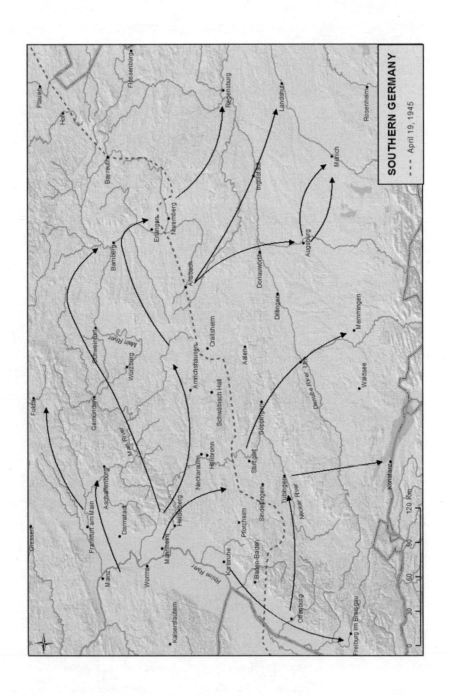

SOUTHERN GERMANY
--- April 19, 1945

Cologne's Hohenzollern Bridge, destroyed by retreating Wehrmacht, 1945.

May 1944: General Johannes Blaskowitz, Feldmarschall Erwin Rommel and Feldmarschall Gerd von Rundstedt in Paris. Blaskowitz had earned Hitler's undying enmity—and lost his chance of becoming a Feldmarschall—by protesting the murders of Jews on the eastern front.

Dietrich von Choltitz, 1940 or 1941: The focus on this one man as "the saviour of Paris" by journalists and Hollywood filmmakers obscures the role of other German officers.

October 1943, destruction of rail line on the eastern front to prevent its use by Soviet troops. Within Germany itself, the fairly systematic refusal to implement the "scorched earth" policy had important implications for the country's post-war recovery.

Dedication of a new bridge over the Elbe River at Tangermünde, September 1933.

May 1, 1945:
Civilians flee
across the badly
damaged bridge
at Tangermünde;
Captain J. McMahon
carries a child.
Thanks to the actions
of General Wenck,
thousands of civilians
crossed the river to
safety.

Düsseldorf's Skaggerak (Oberkassel) Bridge in 1938.

Heidelberg's Old Bridge (Karl-Theodor-Brücke), circa 1930: the German army agreed to surrender Heidelberg but destroyed this symbol of the city.

Berlin, April 13, 1945. "Now it's all or nothing – but we'll make it!"

Speer and Hitler, Berghof, 1938.: According to Speer, Speer alone saved Germany from its Wagnerian fate. Documents presented in this book prove that Speer exaggerated his role but was not, in the end, a complete charlatan.

civilians and soldiers who attempted surrender before finally giving up himself, on April 3; his sense of military honour apparently did not extend to self-sacrifice, and he walked safely into American captivity.[4] When the Americans entered the town, they saw civilians swinging from lampposts above the bodies of twelve- and thirteen-year-old boys on the ground below.[5]

Meanwhile, the Seventh Army ordered the Forty-Fourth Infantry Division south along the Rhine, with the goal of capturing Mannheim and then linking up with the French First Army. When the division reached Mannheim, a telephone call was put through to the city's mayor. He agreed to arrange a meeting between the local German army commander and the American assistant division commander.[6] When the American contingent, led by Colonel Robert Dulaney, arrived at the designated meeting point, they were received not by the mayor but, rather, with shellfire: the Germans opened a mortar barrage that resulted in American casualties. A German captain had refused to allow a civilian delegation from the city to meet the Americans.[7] No doubt livid, the division commander, Major General William F. Dean, called in an air strike and asked his artillery commander, Brigadier General William A. Beiderlinden, to unleash his fifteen battalions of artillery on Mannheim.[8]

On March 28, an intelligence officer came across a telephone connection in Mannheim's by then abandoned waterworks.[9] Following protocol strictly, he tested it. It worked. He was connected with the mayor of Mannheim, who was still trying to save his doomed city.[10] The call would not spare Mannheim the agonies of the assault, but it would provide salvation for another city, as the connection was used to reach Heidelberg. It was an example of how sparing infrastructure in one area allows its preservation in another; disobedience made more disobedience possible.

Following the barrage, civilians in Mannheim again made telephone contact with the Americans, claiming that they had finally persuaded the troops—mostly Volkssturm—to leave the city. Beiderlinden ordered the Seventy-First Infantry Regiment into the tortured city. As he did, German civilians streamed out of Mannheim, climbing into small boats to cross the river Neckar. The Germans responded by opening artillery fire on them.[11] But by then, it was almost over. The city's mayor continued to beg what was left of the German army to leave Mannheim, and, because it lacked ammunition or the will to continue a pointless battle, it finally relented.[12]

The next morning, the Americans moved across the river and into the city; by March 30, Mannheim was theirs. The city, ravaged by multiple air attacks and blown to pieces by artillery, was a wasteland.

After Mannheim fell, the Forty-Fourth Infantry Division followed the Neckar toward Heidelberg, with orders to capture the city. Heidelberg has long been a favourite among American tourists to Germany, and within the Forty-Fourth Infantry Division were several soldiers who knew the place.[13]

Heidelberg was not yet doomed, but things did not look good. Mayor Karl Neinhaus hoped to surrender his beautiful and famous city without a fight, and he invoked the oft-made argument that Heidelberg was a hospital city and, therefore, should not be defended. Kesselring responded on March 28 with an order stating that all wounded soldiers (some eight thousand) be evacuated from the city in preparation for its final defence.[14] There were no hospitals to which the wounded could be evacuated, no vehicles that could safely carry them, and many would have died en route.[15] The dean of the university medical faculty, Professor Achelis, refused to cooperate.[16]

But that did not remove the threat of Heidelberg's defence and destruction. Kesselring and fanatical Gauleiter Robert Wagner wished to establish the Neckar as a new front and Heidelberg as a major defence point.[17] The mayor, with the support of much of the university's medical faculty and of Heidelberg's citizens, responded with a dual effort: to make contact with the Americans and to persuade the Wehrmacht to spare the city's bridges. The former succeeded; the latter did not. On March 28, the mayor's office tried to make contact with US forces, but most telephone lines and postal routes were non-operational. One woman, Hildegard Egetmeyer, managed to find a single functioning telephone line and was able to make contact with city hall in Mannheim, which was by then in American hands.[18] Around the same time, a young German-speaking doctor from the Forty-Fourth Infantry Division asked the telephone operator in Mannheim's city hall, a Frau Alrichs, to pass on a message from US Brigadier General William Beiderlinden, artillery commander for the Forty-Fourth Division.[19] "According to information gathered by American troops, large numbers of

German batteries have been brought to Heidelberg. Unless these troops are immediately withdrawn and representatives of the city are prepared to discuss surrender, the thus-far intact city will be bombed tonight from 20:00 until every shred of resistance is broken."[20] This stark message certainly concentrated minds, and Mayor Neinhaus promised to send a surrender delegation.

But he had to convince the German army first. He begged the city's battle commander to spare Heidelberg and the lives of the civilians and wounded soldiers within it. Following the evacuation order, the medical faculty had made a similar appeal.[21] The battle commander relented: he would remove all troops and arms from a 200-metre perimeter around all military and civilian hospitals—a quick glance at the city's map confirmed that this area included all of the old city and most of the rest of the city.[22] The commander's decision was an act of disobedience masked as a humanitarian gesture. The commander—or someone else in the German army—also agreed to send a lieutenant colonel from the 197th Infantry Division as part of the delegation attempting to reach the Americans.[23] The delegation, made up of Oberstleutnant Dr. Dieter Brüggemann and three doctors, prepared to leave the city on March 29 at 21:00.[24]

A turn in events, however, meant that they would have to leave earlier. The army had shifted toward open disobedience—it was prepared to declare Heidelberg an open city—but possibly to save face, possibly with an eye to the Remagen death sentences, it went back on an earlier commitment to leave the city's remaining bridges intact.[25] A Feldwebel Schwarz ordered the destruction of the last two bridges across the Neckar: the Karl-Theodor Bridge (the "Old Bridge" that graces so many postcards) and the Friedrich Bridge (today, the Theodor Heuss Bridge).[26] An army engineer called late in the day to give the mayor the news: "Herr Oberbürgermeister, I have been ordered to destroy the Old Bridge at 21:00."[27] The mayor argued, then pleaded, but he got nowhere; the engineer kept repeating that he had his orders. Exasperated, the mayor demanded, "Then why are you calling to tell me this anyway?" The engineer replied: "My girl is from Heidelberg, and she thought I should at least phone you before I did it."[28] This motivation was curious, but the effect important: Neinhaus could dispatch the delegation before the bridge was gone. The delegation made for an ambulance with white flags and the word *"Parlamentäre"* ("emissaries") emblazoned on it and sped across the Friedrich Bridge at 20:45.[29] Engineers began demolitions soon after, and by 22:00, both the Karl-Theodor and Friedrich Bridges lay in the Neckar.[30]

The Germans soon reached a US post. American soldiers searched their vehicle for weapons, offered the men a cigarette, and escorted them past a long and intimidating column of American tanks to their commanders, Beiderlinden and Dean.[31] It did not go well. Beiderlinden was furious that the delegation was largely civilian and as such unable to offer the unconditional surrender of the city.[32] If the Wehrmacht wished to continue fighting, there was nothing he could do, and the matter of the hospitals was neither here nor there. "It remains regrettably the case," Beiderlinden said, "that the German army, which once earned honour and respect for its brave fighting skill, cannot see that it has lost this war and that it is pointless to destroy still more cities. . . . [The surrender of hospitals is irrelevant, since] we don't fire on hospitals."[33] One member of the delegation saved the situation by showing Beiderlinden a city map indicating the many hospitals in Heidelberg.[34] His point was that to fire on the city was to fire on the hospitals. Another Heidelberger assured the Americans that they would keep all armed soldiers a good distance from any hospitals, which, given the density of the hospitals, effectively kept them out of the old city.[35] The men's appeal, their obvious sincerity, and likely Beiderlinden's own desire to spare Heidelberg led him to relent. He then told them to return to the city, and warned them as they departed: "See to it that there are no battle-ready troops within five kilometres of Heidelberg. If a single American soldier is killed, we will destroy Heidelberg without mercy [*erbarmungslos*]."[36]

Under fire, the delegation hastened back to Heidelberg; two of the five men were wounded and had to be sent for medical attention on the left side of the Neckar.[37] With the bridges out, there was no easy way for the German negotiators to cross the river and ensure the formal surrender of the city. The German team asked several fishermen and ferryboat captains to carry them across the river, but all refused.[38] Then, at 3:30 the next morning, a sixteen-year-old girl named Anni Tham and two of her friends offered their

help. The girls broke into a boathouse and retrieved a paddleboat, the negotiators climbed in, and Anni paddled across the Neckar, the occasional shell
landing in the river as they went.[39] The delegation reported the results of the
meeting—and Beiderlinden's warning—to the army, and the commander
withdrew the remaining forces from the southern sections of the city.[40]

Within a few hours, on the morning of March 30, the first American
troops crossed the Neckar in boats and began building a pontoon bridge.
They met little resistance. The army was gone, the Volkssturm melted away,
and only a few remaining SS units shot off some rounds from a cemetery.[41]
White flags hung from almost every window. Thanks to the determination
of American soldiers and officers, to the courage of three young German
women, and to some much-needed luck, Heidelberg emerged from the war
virtually unscathed. Beyond the bridges, the only ruin was the imposing
castle, destroyed by French forces in the late 1600s, rising above the intact city.

THE STORY WOULD NOT BE such a happy one elsewhere. On March
31, the Twelfth Armored Division reached the river Tauber. On April 3,
to the northeast, VI Corps drew up to the Neckar north of Heilbronn.
Generalleutnant Friedrich Foertsch's German First Army had placed
its only remaining battle-worthy division, the Seventeenth SS Panzer
Grenadier, on the river. With great effort, he managed to position a sizable
agglomeration of other troops—two battalions of an engineering school,
several regular engineer battalions, Volkssturm troops, replacement artillery and anti-aircraft units, several hundred Hitler Youth, and several tanks
and assault guns—in Heilbronn itself.[42] The American VI Corps got troops
across the river, but they faced massive resistance, and there was no hope
of building a bridge and expanding the bridgehead. General Brooks, commander of VI Corps, responded imaginatively. Seeking to create a wide
envelopment, he sent combat commands north and south along the Neckar
in search of intact bridges. There, they were to cross, encircle Heilbronn
from the south and the north, and then link up.

The plan soon ran into trouble. On April 4, the 100th Infantry Division
faced heavy artillery fire in its attempt to cross the Neckar (the bulk of
the city is to the east of the river).[43] Those forces that made it across faced

stubborn resistance north of Heilbronn.[44] In Neckarsulm, twenty kilometres north of Heilbronn, civilians took American propaganda leaflets that had been fired into the city to the town's mayor, urging him to surrender.[45] When he tried, the SS murdered him and replaced him with a pro-Nazi. Civilians forcibly removed the new mayor from office, leading to what the 100th Infantry Division described as a "small scale civil war."[46]

Combat Command A (CCA), meanwhile, had managed to push all the way into Crailsheim, eighty kilometres east of Heilbronn and approximately the same distance northeast of Stuttgart, and took it against virtually no resistance on April 6. Starting on April 8, however, SS troops counterattacked ferociously, while Alpine troops (Gebirgsjäger, mountain infantry troops) prevented Combat Command R from moving southward to relieve CCA.[47] The ensuing battle resulted in the complete destruction of 300 houses in the Crailsheim area as well as of 570 of the 1,082 buildings making up the old city.[48] Many others were severely damaged, amounting to the destruction of some four-fifths of the city. At least one hundred (though probably many more) civilians were killed by the time Crailsheim fell again on April 21.[49] The death toll would have been far higher had large numbers of residents not fled between the two American occupations.[50] With the SS controlling the area, attempts at disobedience by civilians—and even a rare instance by a Nazi—led to a predictable result. In Brettheim, within the Crailsheim district, the SS sentenced a farmer to death for "defeatism," that is, doubting Germany's ultimate victory and/or urging surrender. When the local mayor and NSDAP branch leader refused to carry out the sentence, the SS had them hanged.[51]

A third combat command, CCB, had to fight its way down the same path travelled by CCA, while IX Troop Carrier Command flew to a captured airfield outside Heilbronn to bring supplies and to remove a growing number of American wounded.[52] All the while, CCA dodged sporadic (and at this point in the war, utterly rare) German air attacks, struggled around demolished bridges, and fought off German counterattacks. Holding the salient, the 100th Division crossed toward a small bridgehead north of the city and then turned to move into Heilbronn. There, with no armoured and only inadequate artillery protection from the west bank of the Neckar, the division fought house to house through the city under mortar, Panzerfaust, and light artillery fire.[53] Bridgeheads north of the city continued to come under artillery fire, as did positions west of the Neckar.[54] The Germans, taking advantage of the particular protection offered by urban warfare, generally surrendered only at riflepoint. One platoon of Hitler Youth, however, dropped their guns and ran screaming toward their newly arrived American saviours as their own officers shot at their backs as they fled.[55]

American engineers finally completed a bridge over the Neckar on April 7, but barely a company of tanks crossed before the Germans knocked it out. A heavy pontoon ferry met the same fate after transporting a few tanks and tank destroyers. But the battle nonetheless slowly began to turn. On April 12, after nine days of fighting, the Americans took rubble-strewn Heilbronn and built a bridge across the Neckar. The battle had cost VI Corps on average 230 casualties per day.[56] The one bright spot in the region was nearby Schwäbisch Hall. There, a delegation of citizens surrendered to the Americans, sparing their city Heilbronn's tortures.[57]

To the north of XV Corps, XXI Corps also had a fight on its hands. CCB from the Fourteenth Armored Division took Gemünden only after XII Tactical Air Command blew it to pieces, and even then, it required tanks to clear the town on April 5.[58] The Forty-Second Division, meanwhile, took several days to root out a force made up of soldiers, firemen, and policemen, who evidently thought there was something worth defending in Würzburg; RAF Bomber Command had completely destroyed the city on March 16. The bombing, which was far less strategically necessary than even the one on Dresden, had only one definite strategic benefit: it aided the German defence. Piles of rubble slowed the American advance and provided excellent cover for riflemen. The city fell only after the 222nd and 223rd Infantry Regiments liquidated the last pocket of resistance there.[59] "An emotional struggle raged inside me" ("*ein seelischer Kampf tobt in meinem Innern*"), wrote Würzburg's battle commander, Oberst Richard Wolf, after the war.[60]

From Würzburg, the Forty-Second Infantry Division moved on to relieve CCA, which had run into trouble in Schweinfurt. It took four days to take that city, and again only after the Ninth Bombardment Division sent its medium bombers to hammer it into submission.[61] On April 11, infantry

254 | DISOBEYING HITLER

cleared the remaining combative German soldiers from the rubble. Old Schweinfurt was no more.

On the same day, both XV and XXI Corps, which had made contact with the Third Army on April 7, turned southward. XV Corps moved toward a once endlessly charming city transformed after 1933 into the citadel of Nazism: Nuremberg. On April 16, XXI Tactical Command swept in overhead as the Third and Forty-Fifth Infantry Divisions attacked from the north and the east-southeast. As they came in, Germans turned the massive anti-aircraft guns horizontally onto the Americans. Once they broke through the flak ring, the Americans had to fight for every inch against fanatical resistance.[62] As the fighter-bombers screamed overhead and artillery blasted what was left of the city, the Americans moved between crumbling buildings and over shelled-out cellars, fighting off futile but brutal and often murderous counterattacks. On April 19, the city's Gauleiter, Karl Holz, an extremist to the last breath, launched a final counterattack in the old town. The Third Division's Thirtieth Infantry defeated it, and that finally crushed resistance in Nuremberg. Holz died in battle or killed himself.

As Nuremberg fell, XXI Corps moved to the southwest toward Ansbach. Within the city, a twenty-year-old university student led a one-man—or, rather, a one-boy—resistance movement. Robert Limpert circulated leaflets urging citizens to stand up to the "Nazi executioners" and to place white flags on their houses. On April 18, he convinced the mayor of the town to surrender the city to the Americans.[63] The city's battle commander was determined to defend Ansbach, however, so the next day, Limpert cut the communications wires linking the army headquarters with troops in the town. Two Hitler Youth denounced him, the battle commander ordered a drumhead court martial, and Limpert was hanged within minutes.[64] The battle commander ordered the body to hang until it began "to stink." He then fled the city. When American forces took Ansbach three hours later, they were so moved by the story that they recorded it in the official history of Seventh Army operations.[65]

The next great natural barrier facing the Seventh Army after Nuremberg and Ansbach was the Danube. As the Germans retreated behind this last defence, the Americans crossed at multiple points. On April 22, XXI Corps's

Twelfth Armored Division moved toward Dillingen on the Danube. The town's mayor made contact and informed the division that the town's bridge over the river was intact. In a minor second Remagen, the division's soldiers rushed the bridge, surprising German soldiers at lunch.[66]

As Dillingen surrendered, XX Corps's Sixty-Fifth and Seventy-First Divisions moved up the Danube toward Regensburg with orders to capture the city. They crossed at Donaustauf and Frengkofen without difficulty, but at Bad Abbach south of Regensburg, the Sixty-Fifth ran into resistance. The Seventeenth SS Panzer Grenadierdivision fought back bitterly, and the screams of American soldiers drowning in the Danube pierced the air. The Sixty-Fifth Division suffered heavy losses before it broke out of Bad Abbach and moved north.[67]

With the Americans approaching, the Germans prepared, and had then every intention of implementing, a defence of Regensburg. The city's Gauleiter and Reich Defence Commissioner, Ludwig Ruckdeschel, ordered the destruction of bridges in and around the city on April 23.[68] When word of this got out, thousands of women made for the central Moltkeplatz, where they demonstrated in favour of surrendering the city without a fight. Dr. Maier, a pastor (*Domprediger*) from the city's famous cathedral, addressed the crowd at 18:00. "We urge the surrender of this city for four reasons," he began. Then he was cut off: troops, most likely from the army, rushed toward him and arrested him. By 2:00 the next day, Maier was hanging in the square. Generalmajor Otto Amann also sacked the city's battle commander, an Oberst Babinger, who had turned a blind eye to the demonstration and expressed some agreement with Maier.[69] These demonstrations of loyalty served Amann poorly: the commanding general of LXXXII Army Corps ordered him sacked as well.

The next battle commander, Major Hüsson, had to sign five times when accepting his commission that he would, with the price of failure being his head, defend the city until "relieved by an attack from the Alpine fortress."[70] He had more than enough men and materiel to launch a defence of Regensburg. OB West transferred three infantry battalions, two flak units, and a company of engineers with some fourteen hundred men.[71] His soon-to-be-named deputy, Major Bürgers, who knew the city well, was no more

inclined than Babinger to defend it, and Bürgers put the matter to his superior, Generalleutnant Tolsdorff, based sixty kilometres away at Landshut.
Tolsdorff decided that it was madness to sacrifice both a city and a battle-
ready regiment.[72] At 23:00 on April 26, he dissolved all Volkssturm troops
and ordered all combat units out of Regensburg. The order ended with
the words: "following the withdrawal of the battle group, Regensburg is an
open city." The city's mayor, Schottenheim, a Nazi Party member, hastily
arranged buses to ship out the troops as quickly as possible; by 3:30 the next
morning, the soldiers were on their way out of the city.[73] The mayor then
sent an emissary to the Americans offering unconditional surrender.[74] The
battle commander, Bürgers, fled the city, leaving a retired general the job
of handing Regensburg over to the Americans. At 10:30 on April 27, Major
General Hermann Leythäuser, the former commandant of the Elsenborn
training grounds, formally surrendered the city.

The Seventh Army was now driving toward the Austrian border.
Armoured divisions pushed forward, while the infantry followed to mop
up resistance. As towns and villages were reached, German action determined the American reaction. Where white flags were displayed, American
troops took the city without firing a shot, but where the Germans made a
stand, artillery, tanks, and bombers ravaged the place.[75] Many of the towns
reached by advancing American columns were fairly small. Memmingen,
just east of the Iller River between Ulm and the Austrian border, had a population of some twenty thousand people. It was taken without a fight when
the Tenth Armored Division sent mayors from towns already captured to
warn that only white flags and an unconditional surrender would spare the
city.[76] Others were among Germany's most important cities: Munich and
Augsburg. In late April 1945, O'Daniel's Third Division, part of XV Corps,
pulled up to the latter.

CHAPTER 21

A CITIZENS' REVOLT

Augsburg

A UGSBURG, SIXTY KILOMETRES northwest of Munich, is Germany's second-oldest city after Trier (though Augsburg itself claims the first spot). Formerly one of the most important trade centres in Europe, it peaked economically in the fifteenth and sixteenth centuries. From then, it ceded regional prominence to Munich. During the Second World War, it remained an important communications centre and, in any case, RAF bombers spared few German cities. On February 25 and 26, 1944, British Bomber Command destroyed much of Augsburg. As the end of the war approached, what remained of the city faced further destruction: Augsburg was to be furiously defended. As ever, the price of disobedience would be death.

Augsburg's commander, Generalmajor Franz Fehn, was fully committed to such a defence. There is some uncertainty over the military means at his disposal. According to his postwar statement under interrogation, Fehn had only eighty soldiers under his command.[1] In the postwar account of Augsburg's Nazi mayor, Josef Mayr, Fehn could in fact call on between six and seven thousand troops outside Augsburg and had another twenty-four battalions of Volkssturm troops (totalling a few thousand) within the city itself.[2] Fehn's figure is massively deflated, and Mayr's figure is probably inflated, but it does not matter. Augsburg had multiple flak guns, and it only took a few dozen men firing them horizontally to provoke an American artillery or aerial assault, or both, on the city.

Fehn was opposed within Augsburg by a disparate group of teachers, doctors, clerics, and merchants who made up the Deutsche Freiheitsbewegung, or German Freedom Movement (GFM).[3] The movement was an umbrella organization containing three groups, all of middle-class background. Georg Achatz, a merchant and National Socialist bureaucrat who had switched sides, it seems, out of conviction rather than opportunism, and Rudolf Lang, a doctor, were the main actors.[4] They met in late 1944 and by December agreed that the city had to be saved from destruction.[5] Other members of the group included Anton Setzer, a Jesuit director of a school for the blind, and Hubert Rauch.[6] Rauch's father was a local prison guard who empathized with imprisoned dissidents and had told his son of resisters such as Alfred Delp, a Jesuit critic of National Socialism and member of the Kreisau group who was arrested and murdered after July 20, 1944.[7] The invocation of Delp is noteworthy: it was one of several instances in which those who opted for disobedience in the last months of the war connected their narrower actions to a longer tradition of German resistance.

In early March 1945, the various resistance groups came together for a meeting at Setzer's school. The choice of locale was deliberate: the blind students would not be able to identify the activists by appearance. Thus, the German Freedom Movement was formed.[8] It was, like the Wiedenhofen Group in Düsseldorf, a chiefly middle-class organization and possessed neither a long history of partnership nor strong material or psychological bonds that would justify it lasting beyond May 1945. But it did have a clear purpose: bringing the war to an end and saving Augsburg from total destruction.

It also had one important and unexpected asset: the support of the town's mayor. Among those cities that surrendered without resistance in the last weeks of the war, Augsburg stands out as one in which leading National Socialists tried to convince leading figures in the army of the pointlessness of struggle—it was usually the other way around. In Augsburg, that National Socialist was Mayor Josef Mayr, a purse-lipped, gaunt, and not terribly robust-looking man (features that were by no means uncommon among those leading the so-called master race). Mayr joined the party in 1922, a sign of the true believer were there one.[9] The Gauleiter of Swabia,

Karl Wahl, was on the face of it a similarly unreconstructed fanatic: on April 9, he wrote in a local newspaper of the "great miracle" of "belief in the Führer," whose own belief in victory would secure it for Germany; eleven days later, Wahl swore undying loyalty to Hitler on the Führer's last birthday.[10] But in subsequent weeks, both men tolerated the GFM and made no moves to have them arrested.[11]

There is some debate over what else they, and especially Mayr, did. In a report written after the war, Mayr claims to have singlehandedly saved the city and ignores completely the role played by the GFM.[12] The truth was more complicated and far less flattering to Mayr. To his credit, he listened to Rudolf Lang's appeal to spare the city, agreed not to destroy the bridges, and provided Lang with information on Augsburg's defences.[13] He may also have stalled on the calling up of Volkssturm troops; if so, both he and the local army commander must share credit, as the latter appears not to have objected.[14] That the Gestapo placed Mayr under surveillance (in Mayr's account, the Gestapo ordered his arrest) suggests that his actions had alienated him from the regime. Finally, Mayr also claims that he and Gauleiter Wahl appealed to Reichsstatthalter General von Epp on April 20 to declare Augsburg an open city.[15] Epp refused. Beyond that, Wahl and Mayr's claims that they issued counterorders and worked tirelessly to preserve infrastructure in the city can be dismissed. Until the last days, they parroted National Socialist rhetoric on the defence of the city; they collaborated in the establishment of defence points on bridges and roads across the city; and no significant body of postwar documentation or testimony attributes to them more than a passive role in preserving Augsburg.[16] The decisive role in blocking them was played by civilian actors: Lang, Achatz, and the other members of the GFM.

Although there is some competition in postwar recollections for hero status, Rudolf Lang appears to have been the leader of the group. As the Americans approached, he gathered information on the city's defences and defined two goals as paramount: (1) preserving bridges over the Lech and Wertach rivers, and (2) saving the city's factories from destruction, whether by the SS, the Wehrmacht, or the invading Americans.[17] Lang asked Achatz to put together a team to protect local industry from destruction. Achatz sought recruits from local men, and he dragooned French prisoners of war and forced labourers to undertake the job as well.[18] Industrialists responded with enthusiastic support.[19] As it was their factories facing destruction, this is in itself not surprising. But the price of disobedience remained death, so action beyond mere enthusiasm required some bravery. In one case, a fanatical National Socialist instructed an Augsburg munitions factory to manufacture more than a thousand machine guns; the majority was to be delivered to the Volkssturm.[20] Achatz's men succeeded in sabotaging production.[21] As they disarmed others, they armed themselves: Anton Setzer gathered weapons from Volkssturm troops who had switched sides.[22] Finally, the city's police force lent its support to the resistance. Police officers seized the city's main depot of explosives and ammunition and neutralized them. There would be no scorched earth in Augsburg.

In launching these and subsequent efforts, the GFM had to contend with the usual suspects both in the SS and Volkssturm as well as with the army. The city's commander, Fehn, took all orders seriously and literally. All attempts by Mayr, Lang, or anyone else to persuade him to surrender the city came to nothing. He provided passive support to the resistance—he arrested no one for their entreaties, and he turned a blind eye at a couple of crucial points to their activity—but if the Americans entered or fired upon the city, Fehn was determined to put up a robust defence. And a robust German defence would lead, as day does to night, to a massive American artillery barrage and possibly aerial bombardment.

The GFM had no luck with anyone else in the German chain of command. Multiple officers agreed that it was pointless to defend the city, but they were unwilling to risk their lives to stop it.[23] The GFM was twice on the verge of success when events conspired against them. They succeeded in convincing, after multiple appeals, a captain commanding six hundred men in a local military barracks to assist their resistance efforts; at the crucial moment, however, the captain and his men were called to the front.[24] After a Dr. Röck and his son of the same name put together a small armed group (the provenance of which is unclear), they received word that the Gestapo was on their tail.[25] They disappeared, and so did the armed group.

As the Americans closed in on the city, the GFM met once again. Anton Kaiser, a wounded soldier whose religious commitments got him into trouble with the Nazis, led the conversation, which covered both high principle—"Are we traitors?" asked one member—and simple practicalities—"Does anyone speak English?" asked another.[26] As so often in resisters' circles, debate was a substitute for decision: no firm plans were made.

But plans soon became urgently necessary: April 27 was Augsburg's D-Day. Another scorched-earth order came through from Berlin, stating that the city's bridges and industrial installations were to be destroyed. Weighing on the Wehrmacht were the executions following Remagen; disobedience meant death. Meeting in the Schillerstraße, southeast of the old quarter, Lang, Achatz, and the others decided to act.[27] A local pastor and member of the group took Lang's car and drove through the city's suburbs with a message for members of the GFM: they should all try to make contact with the Americans and tell them the GFM wanted to surrender the city; that the GFM could provide information on how to occupy the city; and that, should contact prove impossible, the GFM would lead the Americans into the city.[28] In all cases, they were to prevent a dreaded tactical bombing of the city.[29]

At 16:00, a call came through: someone had reached the American Fifteenth Infantry Regiment, Third Infantry Division commanded by Colonel Hallett Edson. An English-speaking Siemens engineer named Keller did the talking. Keller's first appeals got him nowhere. Edson told him that they had two thousand bombers ready to launch a raid on the city.[30] This was an exaggeration: the Americans were more than prepared to send in the bombers, but certainly not two thousand of them. And Edson, in any case, already knew about the resistance group. Early on April 27, Major General H. W. Blakeley of the nearby Fourth Division had phoned O'Daniel of the Third Infantry Division to tell him that two "industrialists" had reached him and were trying to arrange the surrender of the city.[31] One was actually a churchwarden (*Kirchenpfleger*); it is not clear who the other one was.[32] As Blakeley and O'Daniel spoke, Augsburg's flak batteries, manned no doubt by civilians, fired white pillowcases into the air. O'Daniel ordered a moratorium on American artillery fire until the matter was clarified.[33] Edson's threat was designed to concentrate German minds, and it

262 | DISOBEYING HITLER

certainly did. Keller told them everything his group knew about the position and nature of defences around the city. When Edson asked about Fehn, the army commander, the Germans promised to do everything they could to persuade him but conceded that he was not yet prepared to surrender the city without a fight.[34] Edson told the Germans to cease all shooting, to have the town's citizens mark sniper-free houses with white flags, and to make their way across the bridges in small surrender parties holding white flags.[35] And he gave them an hour to persuade Fehn.[36] Edson also extended the Germans a lifeline: he reported Fehn's willingness to surrender. Taking some liberty with the truth, Edson noted in his journal that the "commander of troops of the town wants to surrender but not formally."[37]

When Keller reported the conversation to Lang, the group moved. Hubert Rauch wrapped a white towel around his stomach, jumped on his bicycle, and, trying to avoid SS positions, cycled out of the city, hoping to find the Americans.[38] Rauch spoke no English, so Lang gave him a text to present to the Americans. He made it across the Wertach River and cycled until 3:00 the next morning, when an American soldier stopped him and placed him under arrest.[39]

At approximately the same time, another effort was being made to reach the Americans. The exact chain of events is disputed, but one thing is clear: as Franz Hesse spoke the best English, he received the commission.[40] As Hesse left, Lang and Achatz went to find Fehn. They travelled to the air-raid shelter in the Riedingerhaus, by then headquarters for both the city's civilian and military administrations. The building itself was a heap of rubble. Seeking Fehn, they found Mayr and reported their conversation to him instead.[41] Flustered and showing nothing of the cool resolve he later claimed in his postwar report, Mayr screamed at them: "You are insane to come here! God knows if you'll ever leave this room!"[42]

Ignoring this, Lang repeated his arguments for surrendering the city and told Mayr that all his efforts to convince Fehn of them had failed. "Where is Gauleiter Wahl?" Lang continued. "Bring me to him, and I will try to convince him."[43] The two men left together while Achatz remained behind, prepared to take charge of the operation if Lang failed to return.[44] When Lang and Mayr reached Wahl in his villa, Lang did the talking:

Herr Gauleiter, you can have me arrested or shot, but you would be doing yourself and the city a great disservice. We have made contact with the Americans, who are standing outside our city. They want to know within the hour whether or not General Fehn is going to defend the city. You must persuade General Fehn to surrender the city![45]

Wahl replied that it would be his head on the block: surrendering the city would expose him to the SS and Werewolves' revenge. Lang replied:

Indeed, it will be your head. But that is nothing more than results of the efforts to which you have devoted yourself for the last twelve years.[46] Of far greater importance is the fact that [the defence of the city] would mean the heads of 160,000 Augsburgers, most of them innocent women and children! If you manage to convince Fehn to abandon the pointless defence of this city against American occupation, you will have done in the twelfth hour a service to Augsburg that in the fullness of time will merit official and honourable mention [bei gegebener Gelegenheit zu Ihren Gunsten Erwähnung finden wird].

The last was a reference to postwar Allied and/or German prosecution.

Gauleiter Wahl first tried to stall. He pleaded for two days' time in the hope that the expected fall of Berlin would occur within that time and thus give him more freedom to manoeuvre. Lang, now speaking very much like the one with power, refused:[47] Wahl had to speak with Fehn immediately. The Gauleiter conceded defeat and accompanied Lang to Fehn's headquarters, where he made (by Lang's account) a powerful appeal to the commander to surrender.[48] Mayr added another, similar appeal, as did further members of the GFM.[49] They all failed. It was by now abundantly clear that Fehn would not budge. The GFM gave up on their efforts to secure a legal handover of the city to the Americans.

They decided instead to pursue an illegal one. Lang contacted local resisters and asked them to use the city's telephone lines to send out a call to residents of the areas about to be occupied by American troops: "Hang out your white flags; the city is surrendering!"[50] The men of the GFM jumped on bicycles and motorbikes and raced through the city, delivering the same message house to house. Anton Kaiser added authority by donning his full uniform and giving the same command to each house on the Ulmsstraße: "Order from Major Hörmann: fly the white flag immediately! The city is surrendering!"[51]

They were pushing at an open door. White flags sprung up across the city, and citizens—sometimes led by GFM men and sometimes acting alone—took to the streets and bridges to remove barricades.[52] Finally, members of the GFM appealed directly to soldiers and Volkssturm troops in the city's suburbs to lay down their arms. Call after call came through to the resisters' headquarters, a building deliberately close to American lines, confirming that the appeal had succeeded.[53]

As promising as these developments were, there remained the problem of Fehn, who could still order enough of a defence of the city to undo the entire effort. Over the course of the day, twenty-seven GFM men, armed with machine guns, rifles, hand grenades, and pistols, positioned themselves around the air-raid shelter in the destroyed Riedingerhaus, to which Fehn had returned, ready to block the commander's exit.[54] With Fehn surrounded, the GFM waited for the Americans.

They would soon arrive. Late in the night of the twenty-seventh, Franz Hesse was picked up by the Third Battalion, Fifteenth Infantry Regiment under the command of Major John O'Connell. Hesse promised O'Connell that he "could and would secure the advance of American troops into the city of Augsburg."[55] Hesse rushed back into Augsburg by car. Thirty minutes later, he was back and told O'Connell that everything was ready: the main entry points to the city—the major bridges crossing the Wertach and the Lech— were in GFM hands, as was the city hall.[56] A twenty-five-year-old Wehrmacht captain from Augsburg, Maximilian Wirsching, by his account spared the Hochzoller Bridge over the Lech (in southeast Augsburg).[57] SS troops had ordered him to prepare the bridge for destruction. As Wirsching approached the bridges, two civilians from nearby houses came out, begging him to preserve them. He did: Wirsching waited until the SS withdrew from the area, then ordered two engineers to defuse the bombs and then to disappear. They did so, and he never saw them again. As Hesse spoke with O'Connell, civilians were guarding the bridge lest the army or, worse still, the SS reappear. Hesse also told O'Connell that they had Fehn surrounded, and that now would be the time to arrest him. It was all coming together. The GFM men in front of Fehn's headquarters readied their weapons and prepared to open fire if Fehn attempted to leave the building. O'Connell, meanwhile, secured permission from regimental headquarters to take "K" company of three tanks and three trucks, all led by Hesse in his car, into the city.[58] Augsburgers had removed roadblocks in their path, and the armour drove past these and houses covered with white flags. GFM men stood at points all around the city with instructions to guide the Americans to Fehn's headquarters.[59]

As they approached the Wertach River, O'Connell saw approximately six civilians step out of the bushes; they were GFM men guarding the bridge.[60] O'Connell ordered his men across the bridge. Jumping off the tanks, they dashed across and fanned out into the neighbouring streets, securing positions.[61] With Hesse again in the lead, the company moved on to a railway overpass.[62] According to a number of local accounts, American tanks had to clear several railway cars before crossing.[63] O'Connell does not mention the cars in his report, which might suggest it was insufficiently significant to merit mention. This was not a coincidence. Earlier that day, one Wilhelm Martini, whose rank is unclear, received an order to block the bridges by filling three railway cars with rocks and tipping them over.[64] He used a bulldozer to arrange the cars in such a manner that their contents could easily be pushed into the river and the cars themselves pushed by a tank back to their original position.[65] The story is likely reliable, as O'Connell crossed without difficulty: with GFM members standing guard, Hesse led the Americans across the bridge.[66] Because his company was thinning as it spread across the city, O'Connell decided against taking the bridges over the Lech and, instead, decided to push into the centre of Augsburg.[67] Hesse, in the meantime, called someone from the GFM and learned that its men were holding Fehn.[68] He reported this to O'Connell, and with the commander's permission, the Augsburger led an armoured reconnaissance car and five jeeps toward Fehn's headquarters.[69]

The GFM were waiting for them. Major O'Connell ordered an immediate assault on the German headquarters. The American soldiers and the armed GFM civilians stormed the bunker together, quickly overwhelming the guards.[70] O'Connell demanded Fehn's surrender. Fehn asked to speak with a military operations office (*militärische Dienststelle*); O'Connell allowed him five minutes.

Lang, Keller, and Achatz drew short breaths. They knew that only twenty-one civilians and a few Americans guarded the headquarters, and that the hundreds of SS men under Fehn's command could easily overwhelm them. A shot then rang out: the acting Gauleiter, Anton Mündler, had killed himself. Confusion spread. The phone rang; Fehn answered it. Assuming the Americans spoke no German and the Germans no English, Fehn tried to call in SS reinforcements; a GI wrenched the phone from his hand.[71] Lang urged O'Connell to act immediately.

O'Connell shouted: "Two minutes' time!"

A German voice added, "No, one minute!" Fehn pulled out his pistol; it was knocked out of his hand.

After a moment's silence, O'Connell said, "Time is up! . . . General, get up!"[72] Fehn decided that the jig was finally up.

O'Connell led Fehn outside the building. The surprise on his face was obvious. Rather than the full regiment he expected, he saw a handful of American soldiers and another two dozen armed civilians. Two jeeps with white flags pulled up: Hubert Rauch had convinced a German-speaking American soldier of his story, and the unit commander sent the jeeps into the city.[73] As Fehn stared in shock, the telephone rang in the headquarters. A Wehrmacht unit wanted orders. A GFM man said into the phone: "General Fehn and his staff are under arrest. You are to abstain from any further military action and to inform your units of the situation."[74] Augsburg was liberated.

WITH WHITE SHEETS AND handkerchiefs still fluttering from virtually every building in Augsburg, the Seventh Army moved on to that second citadel of Nazism: Munich. Major General Harry Collins's Forty-Second and Major General Robert Frederick's Forty-Fifth Infantry Divisions, motorized with borrowed or captured vehicles, led the way, and the Third Division joined them on its exit from Augsburg.[75] Major General Orlando

Ward's Twentieth Armored Division and General Smith's Twelfth Armored Division of XXI Corps joined (the latter without authorization) what had become a divisional race toward the Bavarian capital.[76]

As they did, resisters within Munich launched an effort to ensure the city's bloodless surrender. Rupprecht Gerngross, the head of a Wehrmacht interpreters' unit, had been part of longstanding anti-Nazi circles in Munich and took inspiration from Stauffenberg and July 20.[77] Leading a group of some four hundred individuals known as the Freiheitsaktion Bayern (Freedom Action Bavaria, or FAB), Gerngross planned to arrest the Gauleiter and Reich Defence Commissioner, Paul Giesler; to prevent any defence of the city; and to seize the radio stations in order to call for a popular uprising.[78] On April 27, the FAB managed to seize one station and call for a revolt, but it failed to materialize.[79] The SS came for the putsch leaders, and Gerngross fled into the Alps. The SS murdered some forty members of the organization.

The FAB revolt inspired action elsewhere in Bavaria, with similarly tragic consequences. In Burghausen, factory workers launched a sympathy strike; the SS broke it up and executed three ringleaders.[80] In Penzberg, a mining town with a strong anti-Nazi working-class movement, workers launched a revolt with two aims: protecting the city's mines from destruction and preventing the defence of the town. Gauleiter Paul Giesler ordered the army to crush the revolt; sixteen men and women were executed.[81] In several other localities, civilians removed roadblocks and hoisted white flags, often with deadly consequences. It was not, however, all in vain. Civilian members of the FAB managed to defuse demolitions on bridges over the Isar, and a few of them guided the Americans as they moved through the streets of Munich.[82] As if the heavens wished to recognize the efforts of the city's citizens, thick clouds prevented the launch of a tactical bombing raid. When the Third and Forty-Second Divisions pushed into the centre on May 3, white flags hung from the buildings, and cheering crowds filled the streets.

Other units failed to meet such a warm welcome. The Forty-Fifth Division ran right into an SS school and barracks and had to attack with its three regiments abreast. The 180th Infantry Regiment was stopped at a railroad underpass, and the 179th Regiment met the same fate on the Munich–Ingolstadt Autobahn.[83] Lacking air support, they called in punishing 240 mm howitzer barrages to blast their way forward. The final battle was an "ugly room-to-room brawl" in the instalment.[84] Munich showed that there was nothing inevitable about a German surrender even in the last days of the war—a fact that casts important light on parallel developments playing out in Hamburg (discussed in subsequent chapters).

As awful as the Forty-Fifth Infantry Division's last fight with the SS in Munich was, the experience did not compare with that which had awaited Forty-Second "Rainbow" Division at Dachau a few days earlier. There, the Americans faced SS moral depravity. As hundreds of SS guards walked into captivity, the Americans entered rooms stacked almost to the ceiling with mangled and broken bodies.[85]

After Munich, the Seventh US Army moved on toward the Brenner Pass in order to hook up with advance units of the American Fifth Army, which had moved up through Italy. The Allies were on the edge of the Austrian and Italian borders, and they had sliced Germany in two. The destruction of the Wehrmacht on the western front—the encirclement of Army Group B and the shredding of Army Group G—had been chiefly, but not exclusively, an American achievement. Not for the first time in the history of American war, victory had a slight but noticeable French accent.

CHAPTER 22

"WE, THE WOMEN OF FREIBURG, BEG YOU"

The French Occupation of Southern Germany

THROUGHOUT 1944 AND 1945, the French First Army under de Lattre was waging two wars: a military one against the Germans and a political one against the Americans. The faster the French advance became, the more cities and territories its divisions conquered, the more convincing its claim to a role in governing postwar Germany and Europe would be. And of course, advances and victories had a non-quantifiable but nonetheless massive role to play in salvaging French pride. Such considerations informed de Gaulle's landing in Normandy, Leclerc's rush on Paris, de Monsabert's crossing of the Rhine at the end of March, and de Lattre's March-April thrust into southern Germany.

De Lattre's Rhine crossing took place between March 31 and April 2. The first troops of the Third Algerian Division set across the Rhine at Speyer in a single rubber assault boat, ten at a time, at 2:30 on March 31.[1] The Germans awoke to the crossing the next day and ordered shelling, but it was too late: an entire infantry company had already made it across. "Having made even Patton's surprise crossing at Oppenheim look like a deliberate, set-piece assault," writes the US official history, "the French were on the east bank to stay."[2]

Indeed they were. Backed up by troops from two other Rhine crossings and ever-fearful of American incursions into their assigned zone, French forces moved quickly on Karlsruhe, reaching the outskirts of the city on

April 3. De Lattre began his assault by launching a massive artillery barrage on the city, killing two dozen people. As the cannon fire shredded buildings and bodies, the police were practising defence exercises with Panzerfausts, an activity that only attracted more French artillery fire. Enraged civilians demanded that the chief of police end the exercise, which he did, but he remained determined to defend the police headquarters.[3] A group of police officers made plans to murder the chief, though nothing came of this.[4]

As the artillery rained down on Karlsruhe, the city faced another threat: the destruction by the army of the city's electricity grid, gas distribution system, and waterworks, all of which were threatened by the March 19 Nero Order.[5] The Kreisleiter was determined to implement it. The city's mayor, Dr. Oscar Hüssy, was equally determined to ensure that he did not: Hüssy mobilized to prevent both the defence of the city against French forces and its wilful destruction under the scorched-earth order.[6] He urged the city's chief engineer (*Baudirektor*), Konstantin Eglinger, to appeal directly to the Wehrmacht commander in Karlsruhe to spare the utilities. Eglinger urged the city's battle commander, Oberstleutnant Paul Marbach, to see the madness of destroying the city's infrastructure. He did. Among the infrastructure spared was a bridge, passing over the city's marshalling yard, which served to pipe in much of the city's water.[7]

Not all of Hüssy and Eglinger's efforts succeeded: as French troops entered the city on April 3, a railway bridge south of the city near the marshalling yard was blown up, though by whom is not clear.[8] That was the extent, however, of resistance encountered by the French. Marbach pulled the 257th Volksgrenadier Division out of the city. On April 3, mystified French officers and soldiers watched a sixty-seven-year-old in civilian clothes, a civil servant named Josef Heinrich, come toward them to offer the surrender of Karlsruhe.[9] German High Command was furious over the surrender of the city; on April 4, the Nineteenth Army ordered a court martial of Marbach.[10]

After Karlsruhe, de Lattre's forces entered Pforzheim on April 8. The local commander blew up all the bridges and retreated to a southern corner of the city.[11] To obey nominally Kesselring's order to make the city an essential defence point, the commander declared only this corner such a point.[12] The southern part of the city was taken without much trouble, though it took until April 18 for French forces to subdue stubborn resistance in the rest of Pforzheim.[13] From there, de Lattre moved within ten miles of Stuttgart, where, ignoring Devers's orders to hold his position, he ordered a double envelopment: of the southern half of the Black Forest and then, from the south and east, of Stuttgart.[14] This involved first seizing the important road junction at Tübingen and then moving north from there into Stuttgart itself, ideally trapping large numbers of German forces there.[15]

On April 18, de Lattre's men crossed the inter-army boundary with the Seventh US Army and made a plunge for Tübingen and its important road network. Within this university town, fabled for its imposing and beautiful half-timbered houses, there were in 1945 several military hospitals that housed six to seven thousand wounded men. One of the hospital's head physicians (*Oberfeldarzt*), Dr. Theodor Dobler, feared that the defence of the city would lead to both senseless destruction and loss of life, both among his patients and among civilians. Dobler urged his superior, a Dr. Penner, to make an appeal to the army to leave the city.[16] Penner agreed, and following a short consultation, so did the local battle commander, an Oberst Schütz.[17] He ordered all units, except those working directly for the military hospital, out of the city. This done, Dobler sent two of his men to French lines with the message that the city was theirs to occupy. SS forces withdrawing from Crailsheim made a push for the city, but American artillery cut them to pieces.[18] De Lattre's men moved into Tübingen on April 19 and, with that, were within striking distance of Stuttgart. Six days later, on April 25, German High Command declared that all deliberations on surrendering German cities with hospitals were "nullified" and "that no German town has or will be declared a hospital town."[19]

Within the battered city, Stuttgart's mayor, Karl Strölin, who had long if unclear ties to the resistance and who had urged Rommel to join it, was trying to save his city from further destruction. It did not look good. Gauleiter, Reichsstatthalter, and Reich Defence Commissioner Wilhelm Murr, a National Socialist fanatic who had helped get Rommel killed, ordered the destruction of all military, industrial, and utility facilities.[20] Almost immediately, the plundering of shops and warehouses began.[21] Strölin allied himself with the heads of industry, senior city administrators, representatives of the

Wehrmacht, and even some members of Murr's office in appealing to the Gauleiter to spare the city's infrastructure and to surrender without a fight.[22] Murr refused all entreaties but fled the city with his wife as French forces approached on the nineteenth.[23]

His departure handed the matter over to the army. Stuttgart's first battle commander, General Rudolf Veiel, was sacked and sentenced to death for trying to declare Stuttgart an open city.[24] The Wehrmacht commander, Oberstleutnant Paul Marbach, fresh from narrowly escaping his own court martial proceedings over the surrender of Karlsruhe, was disinclined to risk his life once again.[25] After a long standoff, however, he opted for a compromise. He saved face by blowing up all bridges along the Neckar in the early hours of April 21, but he spared the bridge (*Steg*) along which water pipes supplying the city ran.[26] He then ordered his troops to withdraw. With the army gone, the NSDAP leadership turned tail and ran, making for Kißlegg 170 kilometres to the south. French forces rushed into the city, easily sealing off pockets of Volkssturm resistance. By the end of the day on the twenty-first, Stuttgart was surrounded by French troops to the left of the Neckar and by American troops to the right. Strölin personally surrendered the city to the French commander on the morning of April 22. Veiel survived: the chaos of the last weeks of the war meant that his death sentence was never implemented.[27] Whether Veiel banked on such a development was unclear (and his decision remained a very brave one in any case), but the Stuttgart example shows how the confusion of the last months and weeks of the war expanded the discretion of commanders and encouraged the disobedient among them to attempt to save something of the country going down in flames around them.

Stuttgart was an impressive catch for French forces, and it had followed others. "In an imaginative, aggressive maneuver," writes US Army official historian Charles MacDonald, "de Lattre's First French Army in twelve days had swept the northern half of the Black Forest, trapped the bulk of the *LXIV Corps*, and seized Stuttgart, in the process taking some 28,000 prisoners at a cost of 175 French troops killed, 510 wounded."[28] This prisoner haul owes more to German disobedience than MacDonald allows, but the basic points stands.

As Stuttgart fell, other French forces were cutting southward to clear the southern half of the Black Forest. They moved along the eastern fringe of the forest, crossed the Danube, and took the northwestern tip of Lake Constance, thus cutting off any attempted escape of the Nineteenth Army's Eighteenth SS Panzer Corps through the forest.[29] As this occurred, another column moved up the east bank of the Rhine and turned to seize another university town (though one that had suffered during the war much more than Tübingen) and a major administrative and railway centre located along the old Paris–Vienna road: Freiburg.

Freiburg was subject to the usual fight-to-the-last-man orders, but OKW had also decided to transform it into a defence stronghold.[30] Himmler had published on April 13 an order in *Der Alemanne* stating, "[N]o German city will be declared an open city. Every village and every town must be defended and held with every means."[31] Feldmarschall Kesselring, behaving perhaps like an obedient commander but sounding very much like a fanatic, said much the same thing. On March 18, he had announced that army commanders were to fulfill their duty "to the last cartridge and the last drop of blood."[32] Two weeks later, he specified a number of fortress cities that were to be defended with particular vigour: Pforzheim, Ettlingen, Rastatt, Baden Baden, Calw, Horb, Offenburg, Lahr, Lörrach, Donaueschingen, Villingen-Schwenningen, Waldkirch, Furtwangen, Rottweil, Neustadt, and Freiburg.[33] These cities and towns were to be defended and held to the end (*bis zum Äußersten*). Any soldier who failed to implement this order, and any civilian who frustrated it, was to be executed.

In Freiburg, the city's Nationalist Socialist leaders were more than glad to follow it. From September, all fourteen- to sixty-five-year-old males and all sixteen- to fifty-year-old females had been called up for military service; the latter group was to bring its own spades, shovels, or picks for digging trenches and other defences. In early 1945, the Nazi rhetoric ratcheted up further, and Gauleiter Robert Wagner declared on behalf of a citizenry that very much wanted to surrender, "[W]e will never capitulate! . . . What we lack in material we must make up in faith, will, bravery, tenacity, and obedience." The city lacked plenty in material: the units defending it were an ill-equipped and ill-trained ragtag assemblage of police and security battalions, border guards, Volkssturm troops, and battle-shy Ukrainian recruits. But with some 1,779 fighting men, 72 light and 19 heavy machine guns, 1,166 rifles, and 550 Panzerfausts, there was more than enough to launch the sort of defence that would provoke a massive Allied artillery barrage.[34] Indeed, it did not take much at all.

Whether Freiburg would make up for any materiel shortcomings with will, tenacity, and obedience depended not on the Nazi Party but on the army. One thing is clear: the people themselves shared no such will. Freiburgers were relieved that the Western Allies were closing in on them, and with increasing frequency one heard throughout the streets, "Thank God the war will soon be over for us."[35] The city's commander was Generalmajor Rudolf Bader, a veteran of the battles of the Ardennes and a Freiburger himself. Kesselring's January order, and subsequent orders by Keitel, Bormann, and Himmler, had made the fortress city commanders personally responsible for its defence. As ever, the punishment for disobedience was death. To add to the pressure on Bader, he answered not to the Wehrmacht but to XVIII SS Army Corps.[36] The SS's penchant for murdering those who dared to hoist a white flag, or even to speak of surrender, was well known.

On Good Friday 1945, March 30, Bader arrived in the bomb-ravaged city of Freiburg and visited the city commander, Generalmajor Knörzer, whom he was replacing.[37] He found that Knörzer's adjutant and head of the reserves in the city, a Hauptmann der Reserve Freßle, was an old comrade from the First World War and himself also a Freiburger. Bader then went to see XVIII SS Corps and told its commander, Obergruppenführer Georg Keppler, that he would need at least a company of engineers and a battalion of battle-worthy infantry if he was to defend the city.[38] Keppler gave him not a single soldier. Instead, he gave Bader an order: the commander was to prepare the bridges over the Dreisam, the river running through the city, for demolition.

Bader ordered Freßle to contact the director of the city's gas and electricity works and find out the implications of bridge demolition for the city's utilities. The answer: devastating. If the demolition were carried out,

Freiburg would be without gas, electricity, and water. An order from the SS could not be ignored, so Bader found a way around it. He ordered the reserves to line the bridges with explosives wired with dud fuses. When the SS checked them, the bridges would appear prepared for demolition, but demolished they would never be. The question that remained was whether he would defend the city once the French crossed those bridges.[39]

In the midst of all of this, a middle-aged woman named Philomene Steiger decided to act. Having been rebuffed by the Kreisleiter several times, she went to see the mayor, Dr. Kerber.[40] She made a fearless, proto-feminist appeal to him to spare the city: "In the name of all decent women of Freiburg . . . [I] protest against [the defence of the city]. We will not be made into partisans and snipers [*Heckenschützen*]. We will not tolerate being degraded by becoming that which we have condemned in others [that is, terrorists]. . . . We women have not been consulted about this. . . . Where are the women of the Nazi Party? They've vanished, and we are supposed to defend Freiburg to the last?. . . . We must save our beloved Freiburg from this final, total annihilation!"

Kerber, although evidently sympathetic to civilians' plight,[41] told her it was out of his hands and that she should go see the Kreisleiter. As Steiger left to do so, Kerber's secretary took her hand and said, "You're the first woman who's had the courage to speak the truth."[42]

The truth, unfortunately, was not what Kreisleiter Karl Neuscheler wanted to hear. He was determined to defend Freiburg, and he wanted death sentences for anyone who sabotaged his efforts.[43] For days, Neuscheler had been trying to wrest from Bader control over the preparation of defences, including the mining of bridges.[44] In this case, Speer's division of responsi-bilities between the army and the Gauleiter/Reich Defence Commissioners sealed the matter. Bader told him that, as a party member, Neuscheler had no authority over the defensive measures; this responsibility rested solely in the hands of the army. Instead, Bader continued, the Kreisleiter should report on the French army's movement. They were close: the Ninth Colonial Infantry Division was moving toward southern Baden. Overwhelmed perhaps by this news or the realization of his powerlessness, Neuscheler called in sick.[45] He was out of the picture.

So was the SS. On April 20, as French forces reached Lake Constance (der Bodensee) on the Swiss border, XVIII SS Corps received permission to move eastward through the Black Forest with the goal of linking up with the Nineteenth Army. The fate of the city was now entirely in Bader's hands.

On April 21, the day after her unsuccessful appeal to the mayor, Steiger made her way with characteristic determination to the Kreisleiter's office. When she learned of his alleged illness, she demanded to see the city's commander and made much the same argument to the soldier greeting her. Her interlocutor was caught between horror and respect that a woman would speak that way to a soldier, much less demand to see a commander, but she would not go away. As French forces were opening artillery fire on the city, Bader appeared.

"What do you want?" he asked.

"Herr General," she replied, "when the French arrive, simply disappear. We, the women of Freiburg, beg you."[46]

A heated discussion continued for a few minutes. Bader argued that a general could not, as a coward would, hand over a city without a fight. Steiger replied that Freiburg would only be lost if its citizens had to abandon a destroyed city deprived of gas, water, and electricity. Then she made another appeal: "Herr General, I ask you again to please save our city. You must help us!"

Bader argued one last time, then paused. His expression seemed to change. "I will help you. You have been very brave. Go now and tell the people they should hide in the cellar. It will be over soon."[47]

As Bader and Steiger were arguing, French forces were advancing on the city from the north. Some loosely organized Werewolf and armed youths fired on the French units but to little effect.[48] Nonetheless, the scattered defence managed to hold the French up for two hours, with the result that artillery fire heard by Bader and Steiger was opened up on the northern portion of the old city and the streets just outside it: Zähringerstraße, Karlstraße, and Karlsplatz.[49] Then, around 14:00, engineers set off demolition charges against Bader's orders on two railway bridges. Civilians attempting to flee to safety were on the bridges when they collapsed; two were killed and several injured.[50] They also destroyed the Freiburg radio station's transmitter. These actions were, however, the extent of scorched earth in Freiburg. Bader organized no defence of the city. Volkssturm troops melted into the crowds or attempted to join the SS's flight into the Black Forest.

French troops quickly found intact road bridges into the city and crossed them against no resistance. The explosives underneath them were duds—and sabotaged duds at that. Unaware of Bader's own sabotage efforts, Freiburgers had cut the wires or removed and discarded the charges.[51] As the French pushed through the city gates in the afternoon, some Freiburgers fled; others held out white flags; a few even plundered with the justification that they should do it before the French did.[52] Bader himself received an order to report to XVIII SS Corps in Hammereisenbach, where he would take over the 719th Infantry Division.[53] He handed command of the city over to Generalmajor Richard Bazing, but this newly minted commander also retreated east.[54] Freiburg never formally surrendered, but it was—with most of its bridges (if not its buildings) intact—fully in French hands by April 22.

Elsewhere in southern Germany, the fate of cities, towns, and villages depended on the comparable choices and actions of army commanders, local politicians, and civilians. In Waldsee, just to the east of Freiburg, the local army commander remained determined to defend the commune, fearing for his life if he were to disobey. A large number of civilians stormed the town hall demanding that he surrender; when some of their number raised a white flag, cheers exploded from the crowd.[55] In Amrichshausen, northwest of Heilbronn and in the Americans' path, civilians also played the decisive role. When a short exchange of fire between the SS troops and American forces promised the city's destruction, the village's inhabitants ignored death threats and hoisted two white flags up the church tower, while a priest made for American lines and successfully persuaded US troops to take the city without a fight.[56] Yet in other cases, efforts came to nothing. In Sindelfingen, southwest of Stuttgart, several hundred women appeared in front of the town hall, begging the army commander to surrender the city. They had the support of the town's mayor, who argued against erecting tank barriers. It was all to no avail: the army commander insisted on obeying his orders, and the heavily bombed town suffered more destruction before it was all over.[57] Similarly, in Staufen, to the south of Freiburg, the Waffen-SS put up a defence. The small town was bombed accordingly, with heavy losses of life and property. The SS then withdrew, destroying a wayside crucifix, and shooting the local priest farther up the valley.[58] That disobedience was unsuccessful does not, of course, change the fact that it was disobedience. Rather, these cases make clear the stakes involved in surrendering a city without a fight.

In most German cities (there were a few in which the SS or the army pulled out without pressure from local politicians or civilians and a few in which they could not bother to muster any defence at all), whether the town surrendered or was defended (and destroyed) was a local story of urging, intrigue, and action. Many, as we have seen, paid for their choices with their lives.

There is, perhaps unsurprisingly, a western bias to these stories: most come from the territory of what would become West Germany (the "old" German states, Bundesländer, in today's parlance). The majority of towns and cities that surrendered did so to the Americans, British, or French. Even Gotha and Leipzig, which ended up in the Soviet zone, first surrendered to American troops. National Socialist propaganda regarding Allied intentions to destroy Germany and the atrocities that would accompany that destruction, chiefly because they were more accurate, fell on much more fertile ground in the east than in the west; predictions of an agonizing occupation proved true in the Soviet-controlled zones. More than a few Germans had an "Ahnung," a sense that rests at an indeterminate point between full knowledge and mere suspicion, of what the Germans had done to the Soviet Union (Speer delicately referred to his own knowledge of the Holocaust in this way). As a result, civilians in the east were more likely to flee before the Soviets arrived (meaning no civilians to urge surrender), and the army on the eastern front was far more likely to fight to the last man. By contrast, more than a few Germans by March and April 1945 viewed the British and Americans as what they were: liberators. And this fact, combined with the knowledge that defence meant destruction, explained the near universal enthusiasm among civilian populations for surrender in what became West Germany.

This uneven distribution makes the few cases of disobedience on the eastern front all the more intriguing, and it is to them that the book now turns. To do so, we briefly revisit the Soviets' long, brutal, and, above all, bloody road to Berlin.

CHAPTER 23

A HOUSE OF CARDS

The Soviet Assault on the Reich

A T THE BEGINNING OF 1945, the eastern front stretched 2200 kilometres, roughly from the mouth of the Niemen River (near Tilsit),
south through Poland, then southeast toward Lake Balaton in Hungary
and farther south into Yugoslavia.[1] In addition, two major positions were
cut off from the encircled Army Group North: on the Courland Peninsula
in western Latvia and in the Hungarian capital. In January 1945, over six
million Soviet soldiers were positioned along the long front. From east of
Königsberg in the north to east of Lake Balaton below Budapest in the south,
seven army groups stood along the front (the cities and landmarks mentioned represent latitude, not position): the Third Belorussian Front under
General Chernyakhovskii at Königsberg; the Second Belorussian Front
under Rokossovskii north of Warsaw; the First Belorussian Front under
Zhukov south of Warsaw; the First Ukrainian Front under Ivan Konev at
Sandomierz; the Fourth Ukrainian Front under Yeremenko on the same
latitude as Brno (German: Brünn); the Second Ukrainian Front under
Malinovsky northeast of Budapest; and the Third Ukrainian Front under
Fyodor Tolbukhin at Lake Balaton. These armies planned four thrusts along
this long front: toward the Baltic, Berlin, Prague, and Vienna.[2]

Such a massive buildup could not go unnoticed even to those who
so much wanted not to notice it. Army Chief of General Staff Heinz
Guderian, in a series of heated exchanges with Hitler, urged the dictator to

see the dangers of the Soviet buildup; to withdraw troops from the Courland
pocket for the defence of the Reich; to establish a forward line of defence
(*Hauptkampflinie*) that would serve as a buffer for the greater, second
defence line (*Großkampflinie*); and, above all, to prepare the Wehrmacht
for a Soviet onslaught predicted to occur "towards the middle of January"
at the latest.[3] Himmler dismissed the threat of a Soviet attack to Guderian's
face: "It's all an enormous bluff."[4] Guderian replied: "The Eastern Front is
a house of cards. If there is one breakthrough, it will collapse."[5]

ON THE MORNING OF JANUARY 12, at 4:00, that breakthrough occurred
with a ferocity and effectiveness that even Guderian failed to anticipate.

Konev opened the assault in the centre of the long front. As "fierce, rolling fire" rained down on the Fourth Panzer Army, forward battalions seized the first line of German trenches.[6] They dove to the ground before reaching the second, for Konev unleashed the great Soviet guns once more, pounding the Germans at a depth of ten kilometres for almost two hours.[7] The onslaught ripped through German defences. The frozen ground exploded everywhere. Bunkers collapsed, crushing their occupants. Bodies flew through the air as the wounded screamed below them.[8] Those who survived stumbled into Soviet captivity "ashen and trembling."[9]

The bombardment destroyed the Fourth Panzer Army headquarters, killed 25 percent of that army's men, and wrecked 60 percent of the German artillery.[10] And it was only the beginning. Three armies surrounded and captured Kielce, southeast of Warsaw, and Konev pushed home his advantage by ordering three armies and one tank corps to attack on a broad front toward Krakow. By the seventeenth, Konev's forces were pulling up to the city, which would fall two days later. The road to the river Oder was open.[11]

As Konev launched his offensive, Yeremenko's Fourth Ukrainian Front moved toward the Skawa River and the southern Polish city of Rybnik. Two weeks into the offensive, riflemen from the Thirty-Eighth Army stumbled upon a large, prison-like structure denuded of German troops. It was Auschwitz. They found 7,600 emaciated and traumatized survivors, a seven-ton pile of human hair, 348,820 men's suits, 836,255 women's coats and dresses, and the overpowering stench of death emanating from now-cold ovens.[12]

On January 14, two days after Konev had attacked, Zhukov launched what was in fact the main offensive. Within a day, his forces reached the Pilica River, and by nightfall, the bridgeheads on the western side were linking up along a three-hundred-mile front.[13] By January 17, the Germans had abandoned a Warsaw that they had so meticulously destroyed, and on January 19, the Soviet Eighth Guards Army captured Łódź (German: Lodsch). To the north of Łódź, Zhukov's forces gained speed along western Poland's good road network, while to the south, Zhukov's left flank hooked up with Konev's right in a concerted push.[14]

Words cannot capture the effect on the Germans: the Red Army destroyed the Ninth and Fourth Panzer Armies, part of Army Group A under the command of Generaloberst Josef Harpe, cutting through a mangled mass of broken machines and smashed bodies of what had once been the world's most effective military. Large numbers of the divisions' shattered and dazed remnants scrambled back toward the Reich.[15] Others drifted aimlessly, resigned to death or captivity. By January 20, just over a week into the offensive, the Soviets had blown the entire German front wide open.

To the north of Zhukov, Rokossovskii's Second Belorussian Front pushed approximately sixty kilometres into German positions before being ordered, to the commander's dismay, to swing north and northeast toward East Prussia, cutting it off from the Reich. East Prussia, particularly Königsberg, had been the focus of the Third Belorussian Front's efforts since January 13. Smashing his way though German defences in one battle after another, Chernyakhovskii pushed his way slowly toward Kant's city. Rokossovskii, once he had overcome his fury at the change in orders, threw himself into the attack and launched a rapid, brutal assault toward the same goal.[16]

As they pushed into the German Reich, Soviet soldiers combined hardened warfare with atavistic revenge. They burned villages and small towns, shot German officials in the back of the head, and mowed down civil servants, mayors, and even entire families at their dining tables with sudden bursts of machine-gun fire.[17] Soldiers raped German women. As columns of refugees attempted to flee west, Soviet tanks rolled over them, crushing horses and humans alike. Blood, exploded brains, and intestines seeped into the snow among the corpses and severed limbs. Families outside the tanks' direct path huddled whimpering at the roadside or in ditches, the father often brandishing a pistol with which he would shoot his wife, children, and then himself. When reports of Soviet behaviour drifted back to Keitel, he bemoaned the fact that the German civilian population had lost its valour.[18]

Rokossovskii's forces took Tannenberg on January 21; the Germans had withdrawn, taking the remains of Hindenburg and his wife with them and blowing up the massive memorial to Hindenburg's August 1914 victory as they withdrew. Before the end of the month, Rokossovskii's men reached the sea, cutting off East Prussia and trapping the German Third Panzer Army, the Fourth Army, and eight divisions (six infantry, two motorized) from the Second Army.

Hitler, whose meddling had helped ensure this military catastrophe, responded the only way he knew how: with fury and firings. Seething against every real or imagined tactical withdrawal, he sacked Generaloberst Georg-Hans Reinhardt, Commander of Army Group Centre, and Fourth Army commander Friedrich Hoßbach. He replaced them with Ferdinand Schörner and Lothar Rendulic, two generals who had previously established a record of stiffening morale and stabilizing fronts through the judicious shooting of German recruits, but neither of these men could change the outcome.[19]

In a move that reached even more brazenly for the absurd, Hitler created an "Army Group Vistula" ("Heeresgruppe Weichsel") under the command of Heinrich Himmler. It was a paper army made up of the wrecked fragments of the Second and Ninth Armies, and Commander Himmler's military expertise did not extend far beyond firing a gun — if even that far. The choice was ideological. "Hitler," writes military historian Albert Seaton, "was of the conviction that loyalty, reliability, and fanaticism outweighed military ability and experience. Of these latter qualities Himmler had none."[20] Added to these changes were a few tactical movements, but given the shortages that he had in large measure created, these involved robbing one beleaguered sector to reinforce another.[21] Rather predictably, Hitler also sought to shift the blame to his generals, implying that they had kept the truth from him in the run-up to the Soviet offensive. "I order," he said in the last week of January, ". . . that every report sent to me directly or through the usual channels contains the unvarnished truth. I will in future punish most severely any attempt to conceal the truth whether this has arisen intentionally, through slackness, or through neglect."[22]

Guderian continued to tell the truth to little effect. By now frequently shouting at Hitler, he demanded that troops in the Courland pocket, Italy, Norway, and the Balkans be withdrawn and gathered for a counterstrike against Soviet forces from the Cottbus-Glogau line. The Soviets' rapid advances, he argued, had opened gaps and left lead armies thinned out and short on supplies. Hitler refused, transferring instead the Sixth SS Panzer Army toward western Hungary.[23] That army, led by Sepp Dietrich, launched a counterattack in the southern sector on February 17. It succeeded in pushing the Soviets back over the Hron River running through central Slovakia, and the SS pushed several miles into Soviet lines. But in the end, it failed: after losing 500 tanks, 300 guns, and 40,000 men, the counterattack ground to a halt on March 15. The German front teetered, then collapsed as Soviet tanks surged forward, crushing the few tanks in their path, as the SS, including Dietrich himself, fled.[24] German resistance in Hungary collapsed, and by April 1, the Second and Third Ukrainian Fronts were at the gates of Vienna.

Even before the Sixth SS Panzer Army shed its lifeblood in the wrong sector, the Soviets launched the devastating assaults that Guderian had feared. On February 10, as Guderian endured a hysterical rant from Hitler, Rokossovskii launched an attack to destroy German forces in East Pomerania and to make a drive for Stettin (Szczecin).[25] Chernyakhovskii had already received orders a day earlier to destroy the Fourth Army in East Prussia. The two Soviet commanders launched their attacks simultaneously on the tenth to little immediate effect. General der Panzertruppe Walther Wenck launched a counterattack with the Third Panzer Army on February 15, but this got nowhere after Wenck crashed his car and temporarily incapacitated himself. The most notable Soviet success in February occurred in Posen (Poznań), where Chuikov's Eighth Guards Army took the city after a month-long battle that ended when they pushed the Germans, who defended every block, back toward the city's citadel.

Shortly before Posen fell, Guderian made another stab, if a futile one, at reason: he told Ribbentrop that an armistice had to be sought on at least one front.[26] Ribbentrop made his move on February 16. He sent a communiqué to the German Legation in Dublin and asked that it be passed on to the Americans and British.[27] The communiqué spoke of Germany's "iron determination" to fight on against the Allies, and assured that "Germany and her Allies cannot be conquered."[28] After outlining a not wholly inaccurate picture of Soviet designs on all of Eastern Europe, France, Italy, and Britain, Ribbentrop assured his would-be Anglo-American audience that Germany "desires freedom for all nations in Europe" and that the "Jewish question in other countries does not interest Germany." He then urged that the Americans and British join Germany against the Soviet Union. As evidence that this former champagne salesman's diplomatic skills had hardly improved since he was the laughingstock of London, Ribbentrop admitted that he was unaware of which "Englishmen and Americans are available at [the Irish] end." The ludicrous offer went nowhere, of course, not least because Ultra intercepts had told the Allies in August 1944 of plans by Ribbentrop to make peace with Stalin in order to concentrate all forces in the west![29] In the end, the sheer idiocy of the missive mattered little: no German appeal for an armistice had even the remotest chance of success at this point in the war.

Following the relatively poor February results, due in part to stretched supply lines following the huge early advances, the Soviets modified their plan, ordering Rokossovskii to turn east and attack Danzig (Gdańsk) on February 24 and Zhukov to move toward Kolberg (Kołobrzeg) on March 1.[30] Both fronts swept toward the Baltic Coast. Zhukov reached Kolberg on March 4, while Rokossovskii cleared Danzig by the end of March. Chuikov's forces, meanwhile, raced from Posen toward the Oder bridgeheads. On March 29, they launched an artillery assault on Küstrin (Kostrzyn), a fortress town straddling the Oder. After shells pounded the fortress, Soviet infantry-men stormed it, breaking in and engaging the defending Germans in close combat. At noon, the garrison surrendered, the bodies of its men strewn throughout the fortress.[31] Zhukov was across the Oder.

To the south, Konev, the only marshal giving Zhukov a serious run for his money in the race for military glory, launched on February 8 an assault north of Breslau (Wrocław). His First Ukrainian Front encircled Glogau (Głogów) and then did the same to Breslau, both of which had been declared fortresses. Silesians fled in conflicting directions: some of those who had begun escaping Breslau rushed back into the city, where they suffered the agonies of a siege that did not end until May 6, while almost all others fled west. The great flight and expulsion—*die Flucht und Vertreibung*, which would become the numerically greatest ethnic cleansing in human history, denuding Eastern Europe of German populations that in some cases had been there for centuries—was under way. By March 30, as Zhukov crossed the Oder, Konev had conquered Upper Silesia. These ambitious command-ers set their sights on the battered and desperate streets of Berlin.[32]

The great assault occurred in darkness on April 16. Facing the German-held Seelow Heights (Seelower Höhen), Zhukov's First Belorussian Front turned on great floodlights intended to blind the Germans.[33] Zhukov launched a massive artillery raid with bombing support, but the artillery too often missed its intended target, and the great lights blinded his own infantry instead of his enemy's.[34] The Germans responded with fierce resis-tance, and Zhukov was forced to report that the operation was not going according to plan.[35]

To the south, General Ivan Konev's First Ukrainian Front opened with a more conservative but more effective artillery barrage on German forma-tions on the river Neiße.[36] When his forces moved under a smokescreen, they were able to make a deep cut into the Fourth Panzer Army's lines; several divisions disintegrated, and Konev pushed north toward Berlin.[37] His advance panicked both the Germans and Zhukov, who feared that the commander of the First Ukrainian would enter the capital before he did. It was an entirely reasonable fear: the original plan had been to allow Zhukov to cover himself in glory by taking the capital, but it foundered on the fact that Konev's forces were also needed to get the job done. Stalin solved the problem by assigning the capital to whomever got there first.[38]

Driven partly by jealousy between the two great commanders (men in some of Zhukov's patrols got themselves killed trying to find out how far Konev had advanced), German defences were broken within three days. Zhukov was within firing range of Berlin. On April 20, Hitler's fifty-sixth birthday, the first shells landed in the capital, and British and American air forces marked the Führer's birthday with a particularly heavy raid on the city. By the next day, Soviet forces were advancing street by street. Zhukov's forces entered from the east, Konev's advanced from the south, and Rokossovskii's men of the Second Belorussian Front encircled Berlin from the north. By April 25, the city was entirely surrounded. Shells shattered buildings and

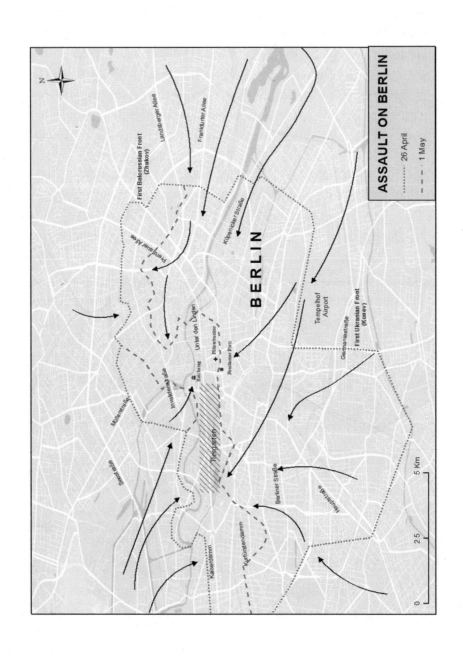

ASSAULT ON BERLIN

.... 26 April
– – – – 1 May

BERLIN

First Belorussian Front (Zhukov)

Landsberger Allee

Frankfurter Allee

Köpenicker Straße

Prenzlauer Allee

Unter den Linden

Reichstag

Führerbunker

Potsdamer Platz

Invalidenstraße

Müllerstraße

Seestraße

Tiergarten

Kaiserdamm

Kurfürstendamm

Berliner Straße

Hauptstraße

Gethaniastraße

Tempelhof Airport

First Ukranian Front (Konev)

0   2.5   5 Km

N

bullets sprayed through streets as Konev advanced toward Anhalter Station (near Potsdamer Platz) and Zhukov toward the Reichstag. All the while, bands of SS roamed the streets, hanging civilians and soldiers who showed any desire to surrender. On April 30, Hitler killed himself. The next day, Soviet troops were advancing through a storm of fire toward the Reichstag.

As Soviet forces were closing in on the very centre of Berlin, the bulk of the Second Belorussian Front, led by Rokossovskii, moved west across northern Germany to link up with British forces. Rokossovskii ordered the right spearhead to move through the Mecklenburg Lake District over Prenzlau, Waren, Rostock, and Wismar (the last within 120 kilometres of Hamburg). One corps split off and moved north toward Pasewalk and then northwest toward Anklam, not far from the Baltic Sea. From Anklam, the corps split again: the southern flank moved toward Schwerin, Wittenberge, and the Elbe. Two divisions with large numbers of tanks, heavy artillery, and bombers moved northwest toward Greifswald, a small Hanseatic city of approximately forty thousand inhabitants on the Baltic coast.

As they did, the commander of the city, Rudolf Petershagen, anticipating these movements on a map, raised his eyes and looked out the window. He imagined the city's ancient walls, medieval houses, and brick Gothic churches exploding into fragments and dust.[39]

CHAPTER 24

SAVING CASPAR DAVID FRIEDRICH'S CITY

O N APRIL 18, an order from Himmler arrived on Greifswald battle commander Rudolf Petershagen's desk. It concerned the "duty to defend all German cities and localities." The enemy, Himmler wrote, "is trying to intimidate mayors of cities and villages with the threat that, should they not surrender, they will be destroyed by tank or artillery fire. This ruse will not succeed. No German city will be declared an open city. Every village and every city will by all means be defended and held. Every German man who violates this clear national duty will lose his honour and his life."[1]

Goebbels urged Petershagen and all other battle commanders to take inspiration from the more immediate example of Breslau's "heroic struggle" under siege. Goebbels cited another example of unyielding resistance: Franz Schwede-Coburg, the unrelenting Gauleiter of a besieged Stettin.

Around that moment, the "defender of Stettin" knocked on Petershagen's door.[2] Schwede-Coburg, appearing haggard and depressed, told Petershagen of his relief that "in these dark [*ernsten*] hours there is at the helm in Greifswald a front-hardened bearer of the Knight's Cross [*Ritterkreuzträger*]." Petershagen paused and wisely replied, "Gauleiter, whatever happens, I will share this city's fate!" He did not specify which fate. Schwede-Coburg took his leave and fled to the west.

Documentation surrounding Greifswald's last days is relatively thin compared to that of Augsburg, Düsseldorf, Freiburg, or Hamburg. Nonetheless, it is clear that in Greifswald, as in so many other German cities, opposition to Hitler and Goebbels's calls for fanatical defence emerged from two main sources. One was military and centred on Petershagen himself. The main documentation of military disobedience in Greifswald is Petershagen's memoirs, which need to be treated with appropriate caution in two ways: as, by definition, an effort in self-justification (as all memoirs are) and as a manuscript drawn up with East German censors peering over Petershagen's shoulder. Occasional acidic comments about the Federal Republic of Germany,[3] whether made by Petershagen or added later by some governmental functionary, seem to have struck the right balance that made the memoir acceptable for publication in East Germany. In addition, there is some debate about whether the report was ghostwritten. His wife named a university professor as the real author, whereas others made the doubtful claim that Petershagen threatened to pull the manuscript unless more Communists were written into the story.[4]

The second source of resistance in Greifswald was civilian and was centred on the town's university. The key figure was the university's rector, Carl Engel, a specialist in early and pre-history in Europe. Engel joined the NSDAP in 1933 and in the coming years became ever more committed to National Socialist ideology.[5] The party rewarded his support: when the University of Greifswald expressed reservations about his candidature for a chair, the Reich education minister overruled the university and moved Engel from fourth place on the candidate list to first.[6] Engel oversaw the sacking of fourteen Jewish faculty members and the expulsion of the university's few Jewish students, including one who held American citizenship.[7]

Engel broke with National Socialism not over principle but, rather, over outcome: the disaster of Stalingrad marked the beginning of his break with the regime. As news of fallen sons arrived in Greifswald, opposition groups began to form in the city. They were made up of the usual Communist, Social Democratic, clerical, and bourgeois elements. Leading figures were Hugo Pfeiffer, a Communist who had come from Berlin to found a local chapter of the Nationalkomitee Freies Deutschland, and a Social Democratic lawyer named Hans Lachmund.[8] Somewhat unusually, although perhaps explicable given the city's small size, both Communists and conservatives — such as lawyer Walter Graul—worked together. Engel established ties to this hybrid group from 1943.[9] His own report on the last weeks in Greifswald, written in May and June 1945, corroborates in large measure Petershagen's memoirs. The story of both civilian and military action as the end of the war neared shares many similarities with the stories of Düsseldorf, Hamburg, Augsburg, Gotha, and many other German cities. This fact provides some measure of confidence in the history as reported by Petershagen and Engel.

Petershagen was appointed battle commander of Greifswald on January 1, 1945. In his account, he began by gently sounding out members of his staff and the other two services in and around Greifswald in order to determine who might serve as helpful partners in the surrender of the city. Inevitably, there was nothing direct in these conversations. Instead, Petershagen dropped a few negative comments about the course of the war, the chances of victory, or the prospect of defending Greifswald. He often heard in response recitations of Goebbels's propaganda, waffling about miracle weapons and final victory, and of course reaffirmations of the absolute need to follow orders. But in other cases, he found a sympathetic ear. Gradually, the core of what became a small military resistance in Greifswald emerged: Oberst Max Otto Wurmbach from the Luftwaffe, who was a doctorate holder and Russian speaker, and a retired Major von Winterfeld, who was responsible for the air defences of the city. Petershagen brought Wurmbach into his circle by telling an anti-Hitler joke; Winterfeld attracted Petershagen's attention by remarking that the air defence of the city would have been unnecessary "had July 20 worked."[10] When Petershagen told Wurmbach of his plans for surrendering the city, Wurmbach replied enthusiastically: "Dead or alive, I will be at your side at the surrender of Greifswald!"[11] Petershagen made him his second in command.

Whereas many German cities were denuded of inhabitants by this point in the war—especially in the east—Greifswald's population had doubled to a record 68,423 people as columns of refugees fled the Soviet onslaught.[12] Joined by local inhabitants, and above all by members of the NSDAP and the SS, they moved west. Petershagen allowed them to pass unmolested.[13]

As refugees passed through the town, civilian resistance groups organized. On April 23, Rector Carl Engel met one of the university's trustees,

Richard Schmidt, who would later serve as acting mayor after the city's Nazi mayor skipped town.[14] They discussed how they might secure the peaceful surrender of Greifswald.[15] They first contacted a Dr. Hatten, a military doctor, and urged him to lobby for surrender in the name of some ten thousand wounded soldiers in the city.[16] They won him over, and he planned to approach Army Group Vistula, one of Himmler's "armies" to which Hatten answered, on the next day together with a university trustee, Dr. Kuhnert. But nothing came of it: the army group's staff had withdrawn from Prenzlau and could not be found.[17] That left Petershagen. They went to see him, although not before Engel made a point of burning all papers that might have incriminated him after the war.[18]

In his account, Petershagen had taken decisive steps to prevent a defence of the city before the delegation arrived. On April 25, he spoke to his staff and told them the city would not be defended. As if to concentrate minds, an air raid on the city the next day left some two dozen dead.[19] Petershagen then took a series of steps designed to give flesh to his decision. Whereas Himmler had ordered that churches become defence points, Petershagen made them into hospitals. He ordered his men to collect sacred books and had them shipped by truck to Lübeck.[20] And he ordered Volkssturm troops that had concentrated at two defence points to spread out across the city, hoping to neutralize their fighting effectiveness. It was, in fact, a poor decision given his purposes: properly informed, an invading army can move successfully around concentrated defence points. Scattered defences, by contrast, encourage loose fire, and even scattered attacks on Allied forces could have provoked a massive military response.

His next problem was the presence of military divisions outside Greifswald. Petershagen's commanding general had ordered the division at Anklam to make a fighting retreat moving toward Greifswald and to establish a new position there. "Greifswald can and must be held," the general concluded the order. "It will serve as the launching point for a planned eastward operation."[21] The defence of the city by a division would be the end of Greifswald. Urged on by his adjutant, Petershagen gambled and simply ordered the divisions to avoid Greifswald.[22] It worked: the Soviets had savaged them at Anklam, and they had no desire to relive the experience.

When the troops retreated from a destroyed Anklam, only a few stragglers arrived in Greifswald.

On April 27, the civilian resisters secured their meeting with Petershagen. Accounts differ as to who was present. According to Petershagen, Engel, university trustee Dr. Kuhnert, and a third, unknown man came together.[23] Men with long, sad faces reprieved only by hopeful eyes, they begged Petershagen not to defend the city. With rhetorical flourish—at one point showing them Himmler's order to defend the city to the end—Petershagen eloquently promised to surrender Greifswald: "Gentlemen, you need not be afraid. These documents, like the words we have exchanged here, are safe with me. And be sure, your excellencies, that I will take your advice to heart!"[24] With that, Petershagen placed the papers in his safe and slammed it shut. In Engel's account, the university professor initiated the meeting; the Kreisleiter—Engel's "archenemy"—was there; and he, Engel (rather than Petershagen), did most of the talking and placed particular emphasis on the fate of the wounded and the cultural treasures in the city's still-intact university.[25] But they both agree on the essential point: Petershagen concurred that a defence of the city would be nasty, brutish, and short.[26]

To avoid it, Petershagen needed to neutralize forces within Greifswald and to make contact with the Soviets. There were two substantial pockets of opposition within the city, centred on Mayor Dr. Rickels and Kreisleiter Otto Schmidt. Rickels was responsible for the Volkssturm, which would be called to battle through a ringing of the churches' bells. According to Petershagen, the matter came to a standoff between the two men. Staring Rickels down, Petershagen coolly stated, "The bells of Greifswald will remain silent."[27] Although he was very keen for others to go to battle, Rickels himself had no interest in a fight with either Petershagen or the Allies. He had prepared a convoy of vehicles—including fire engines—that were loaded with, among other things, twelve cases of champagne. After a tearful protest that the military man Petershagen viewed with contempt, Rickels made one last appeal for the Volkssturm to fight on the edges of Greifswald. Then he boarded his convoy and travelled west.

With Rickels out of the way, that left the Kreisleiter. Late into the night of April 27, Otto Schmidt pleaded with Engel to abandon his efforts to surrender the city, to accept false papers, and to flee to the west.[28] Engel demurred and spent the next two days avoiding him. Schmidt turned instead to the one who could arrest Engel, have him shot, and launch the city's defence measures: Petershagen.

Meeting the Stadtkommandant in person, Schmidt began with a bombastic appeal: "We are on the cusp of a great turning point of destiny [*Schicksalswende*] in the war. We will hold fast, and then . . ."[29]

Petershagen cut him off: "Greifswald will not be held." Petershagen began to draw his pistol, tacitly giving Schmidt the choice of flight or death. Schmidt chose the former and handed over his orders.

Petershagen made a similar offer to an SS officer who arrived at the headquarters under the pretext of being wounded but, as it turned out, had been dispatched by Kreisleiter Schmidt to shoot Petershagen. After being found out, the officer switched horses and began disarming Hitler Youth in the city.[30] As these events unfolded, Greifswald's citizens joined the fight. Women appealed for a surrender of the city, and industrialists reported any efforts to sabotage industry.[31]

With the city largely under his control, it remained necessary to contact the Soviets. And this is where the civilians who had visited Petershagen on April 27 came in. "This visit was a gift from God," Petershagen said to Wurmbach afterwards.[32] The next day, Engel received a message from Gerhardt Katsch, a colleague professor of medicine at the university: "The third man from yesterday recalls your offer. He thinks the hour has arrived and wants to know if you stand by your word."[33] Engel replied: "Of course."

The next evening, Katsch phoned Engel to report that Soviet forces were at the Peene River, about forty kilometres south of Greifswald, and were likely to cross it in the coming night.[34] The Soviets did not make their move then, but the next morning, the situation in the city began to unravel. The telephone rang constantly: officials seeking orders, the Kreisleiter making last pleas before fleeing the city. By 18:00, Petershagen had summoned Engel to inform him that the Soviets had indeed crossed the Peene and were headed into the city. Petershagen and Wurmbach put together a hastily prepared delegation. Wurmbach, Engel, Katsch, and two interpreters made their way to Soviet lines.[35] With Engel providing directions, Wurmbach led the group out of the city shortly before midnight.[36]

Some ten kilometres south of Greifswald, the group heard the rumbling sound of tanks or trucks.[37] Engel called for the convoy to stop, and a few moments later, several trucks came around the corner. The question on everyone's mind was whether they were Russians or Germans. Chancing it, Engel jumped out of the car with a white flag. Wurmbach screamed, "For God's sake, man, put that flag away, they're Germans!" As Engel was hiding the flag, Wurmbach changed his mind: "Wait, take it back out! They're Russians!" Whether this display of German competence left any impression on the Russian interpreters is unclear. One shouted: "We are a delegation from Greifswald. Don't shoot!"[38]

Through the interpreter, Wurmbach explained the mission. The Soviets agreed to take them to the nearest troop commander, and they rushed past a longer column of tanks and motorized artillery toward the ravaged city of Anklam, itself a visible warning of Greifswald's fate if it were to be defended.[39] Wurmbach offered the unconditional surrender of the city to the young divisional commander, Major General Borstschew.[40] It was 2:17 on the morning of April 30, and the Soviet general claimed to have an order to launch a massive artillery barrage on Greifswald at 3:00.[41] In all accounts, though all were written while Greifswald was under Soviet occupation, General Borstschew treated the delegation with great respect.[42] The general agreed to call off his attack on the city and insisted only that Greifswald's commander formally surrender the city later that morning, at 11:00. "Tell your commander," he continued, "that not another shot is to be fired and everything is to be handed over undestroyed."[43] The clock struck three, and all remained quiet.

Within Greifswald itself, Petershagen's men prepared for what they hoped would be the bloodless Soviet arrival. The city was divided and restless. Civilians across Greifswald put out white flags of surrender; others, Volkssturm troops and/or Hitler Youth, attempted to prepare bridges, reservoirs, and industrial facilities with explosives. Petershagen credits one of his staff in particular, a Major Schönfeld, for blocking these efforts, while civilians stopped foolhardy youth from arming themselves with Panzerfausts.

But it was not quite over yet.[44] Borstschew had the delegation driven back to Greifswald in two cars, one, driven by a Soviet officer, containing Engel and Katsch. As they approached their destination, they met another car coming out of the city at great speed. The Soviet officer signalled it to stop, and it did. As the Soviet took a step toward the car, a burst of blood and skin exploded from his right hand. Someone had opened fire. Hand bleeding, the officer returned fire, spraying the Mercedes with bullets. When they approached the car, they found the bodies of Kreisleiter Schmidt, his adjutant, and two other soldiers.[45] Engel and the others could claim their first victory in the salvation of their city.

At 5:00, Wurmbach appeared before Petershagen. "It's done."

Six hours later, General Borstschew arrived at the city hall for the formal surrender. After accepting it, Borstschew stretched out his hand. "I thank you," he told Petershagen. "You are a worthy opponent."

Neither Petershagen's worthiness nor that of any other Greifswalder spared them the revenge that the Soviets meted out on Germany. Within the year, the Soviets arrested everyone involved in the surrender of Greifswald except Katsch.[46] Engel, Wurmbach, and former mayor Richard Schmidt all died in captivity. The university's first rector under the Soviets and a longtime critic of National Socialism who had urged the surrender of the city, Ernst Lohmeyer, was shot.[47] Soviet troops plundered the city, and there were reports of mass rapes. The director of a women's clinic, Günther Karl Friedrich Schultze, had a pistol held to his head while soldiers raped first the clinic's students and then female patients and staff.[48] Afterwards, he and his wife killed themselves.

CHAPTER 25

FINISHING THE JOB THAT
BOMBER HARRIS STARTED

Hamburg

FOLLOWING MONTGOMERY'S great Rhine crossing in March,
Eisenhower was conscious that his armies' halt on the Elbe opened the
possibility of a Soviet sweep across northern Germany and into Denmark. He
urged Montgomery therefore to "push across the Elbe without delay, drive
to the coast at Lubeck [*sic*] and seal off the Danish peninsula."[1] Eisenhower
tried to tempt the famously cautious field marshal into action by offering to
return Simpson's Ninth Army to the Twenty-First Army Group.[2] Trying to
ensure that no good deed went unpunished, Montgomery used the offer as
an opportunity to denounce both the Simpson transfer that Eisenhower was
prepared to reverse *and* the supreme commander's strategy generally.[3] By
his diplomatic standards, Eisenhower got tough, reminding Montgomery
of the chain of command: "You must not lose sight of the fact that during
the advance to Leipzig you have the role of protecting Bradley's northern
flank. It is not his role to protect your southern flank. My directive is quite
clear on this point."[4]

Montgomery, as ever when push came to shove, fell into line. He sent
the I Canadian Corps north to the IJsselmeer and the North Sea, from
which it was to cut both westward and eastward in order to liberate the
Netherlands. The Canadians took Arnhem on April 14 and from there made
their move northward. Fighting hard against the ubiquitous Generaloberst
Blaskowitz, the I Canadian Corps pushed its way through one canal or river

crossing after another, reaching the IJsselmeer on April 18.[5] The Canadians blasted the poorly armed German defenders with flame-throwing tanks. The Germans defended fiercely but were wiped out; only thirty men survived.[6]

As the II Canadian Corps attacked eastward, the I Corps turned west, launching the final push to drive the Germans out of Holland. They fought until April 22, when Reichskommissar Arthur Seyß-Inquart threatened to flood the countryside if the Canadians pushed past the Grebbe Line, a centuries-old line of defence, which could leave huge swathes of land flooded. This threat might have been a bluff. Seyß-Inquart, in a doomed effort to avoid the hangman's noose, had already worked with Speer to resist Hitler's orders to open the dikes.[7] The Canadians, in any case, stopped, and Seyß-Inquart lived up to his promise to allow some airdrops of food to the starving Dutch beginning on April 20. In late April, Blaskowitz also made contact with the deputy commander in chief of the First Canadian Army in order to relieve the food crisis in the Dutch fortresses.[8] These mildly conciliatory moves had no effect on the military course of events: Seyß-Inquart refused surrender negotiations until the Third Reich collapsed.[9]

As the Canadians pushed into the Netherlands, Montgomery sent his Second Army from the Wesel bridgehead northwest toward the Elbe. The first major city it reached was Bremen, and the German garrison there put up stiff resistance. The city's battle commander, Generalleutnant Fritz Becker, wanted to blow up all bridges leading into the city, including those supplying essential utilities. Playing it by the book, however, Becker sought Speer's permission in Berlin, but the breakdown of communications prevented him from getting through.[10] Johannes Schroers, head of the Bremen police, and Dr. Karl Bollmeyer, president of the local chamber of commerce, discussed the possibility of organizing a coup: they would shoot Becker and local Kreisleiter Max Schümann and then hand the city over to the British. The plan failed, however, when they could not persuade a working-class resister (and future head of IG Metall) to do the dirty work.[11]

The Gauleiter responsible for Bremen, Paul Wegener, asked the navy not to mine one area of the harbour, but otherwise he and Kreisleiter Schümann insisted on a final defence of the city.[12] Becker, a cliché of a Prussian officer, launched it. Charges on the cities' bridges went off, and they

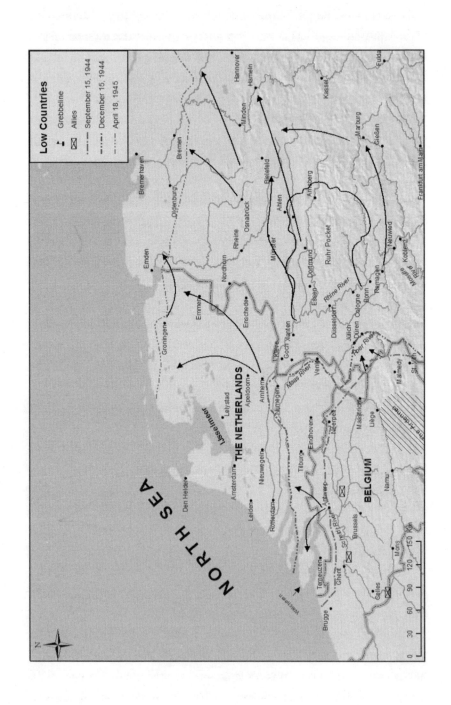

collapsed into the Weser.[13] Montgomery's men fought their way through the city and surrounded Becker and his men garrisoned in an air-raid shelter. Becker collapsed in indecision, and Oberst Ernst Müller, commander of Flak Group South, launched a minor mutiny by ordering a major to lead a surrender party out of the bunker with a white bed sheet and a British POW.[14] It was April 27.

After Bremen, Montgomery pulled up to the Elbe, crossed it, and made a dash for Lübeck.[15] That left Germany's second-largest city, its largest port, and the largest commercial centre in northwestern Germany: Hamburg. Two years earlier, Sir Arthur Harris had promised that his July–August 1943 bombing campaign would "destroy" the city. He destroyed much of it, but by May 1945, the familiar silhouette of five churches still graced what was left of the cityscape. Perversely but predictably, the Nazis were to finish the job that Harris had started.

THE MAYOR AND GAULEITER of the wealthy, elegant, and aloof city of Hamburg, Karl Kaufmann, was a non-Hamburger with a long history of right-wing radicalism and anti-Semitism.[16] Kaufmann joined the NSDAP in 1922 and received, very tellingly, membership number 95. Hitler rewarded him for his early faith and later work for the party with the appointment as Gauleiter of Hamburg in 1929.[17] During his tenure, he concentrated an immense amount of power in his office. By early 1945, Kaufmann was Gauleiter, Reichsstatthalter, head of the Hamburg government (*Landesregierung*), head of the Greater Hamburg Administration (*Staats- und Gemeindeverwaltung*), and Reich Defence Commissioner for Wehrkreis X.[18] Two characteristics in particular marked his rule of the Hanseatic city: cruelty and corruption.

When the National Socialists seized power in Hamburg in March 1933, Kaufmann unleashed a brutal wave of terror against his enemies: Social Democrats, Communist, Jews, and foreigners.[19] As the concentration camps filled with his victims, Kaufmann complained that the treatment of political prisoners was too lax.[20] For Hamburg's Jews, Kaufmann organized what a local newspaper chillingly termed in 1939 a "solution to the Jewish question."[21] Following a September 1941 air raid, Kaufmann urged Hitler to arrange the deportation of Hamburg's Jews to provide housing for the homeless. These actions may have inspired other Gauleiter.[22]

Kaufmann rewarded his friends with the same fervour with which he punished his enemies; his reign depended on a level of corruption and patronage that was "without parallel in the history of Hamburg."[23] Within two years, he had given city jobs to no fewer than ten thousand National Socialists, mostly embittered lower-middle-class failures seething with fury at their social and economic superiors—above all, of course, at Hamburg's wealthy Jews residing in their attractive and spacious turn-of-the-century apartments.[24] He created the "Hamburg 1937 Foundation," over which he had sole control. The so-called foundation raised ten million reichsmarks through donations, compulsory contributions from local businesses, and, above all, stolen Jewish property. Kaufmann spent the funds on the NSDAP and, not surprisingly, himself.[25] The level of corruption made most other Gauleiter appear by comparison to be paragons of moral and fiscal rectitude.

There is thus ample reason to view Kaufmann as an unreliable source. In his account, uncritically reproduced in the first, quasi-official postwar history of Hamburg's capitulation, he portrayed himself as the saviour of the city.[26] As he would have it, Kaufmann met Hitler, Bormann, Himmler, Keitel, Jodl, and Dönitz in the Reich Chancellery on April 3.[27] When Hitler was informed of the hopelessness of the situation in northwest Germany, he reacted in character: Hamburg was to be a fortress and would be defended to the last, and none of the 680,000 women and children in the city would be evacuated.[28] Artillery barrages, low-level bombing attacks, and house-to-house fighting were to be Hamburg's fate.

Roused to fury by Hitler's intransigence, Kaufmann then spent the next month heroically saving the city on the Elbe. "What was decisive for me," Kaufmann wrote after the war, "was my duty to the city and its people entrusted to my care. In the second half of the war, I saw it as my most essential duty to extend to Hamburg and Hamburgers all the help that I could and, if possible, to protect them from the final, difficult sacrifices."[29] If not the good, Kaufmann was at least the sincerely repentant Nazi, a sort of local combination of Collins and Lapierre's Dietrich von Choltitz and Albert Speer's Albert Speer. It was an incredible story and, indeed, is only partially true. Kaufmann did play a role in Hamburg's last days, but he exaggerated it, downplayed the role of other, more important actors, and generously predated his loss of faith in German victory.[30]

As for all German cities, Hitler's plan for the end of the war was a tragedy in two acts. The first involved applying scorched earth in Hamburg. On March 22, Hitler ordered the destruction of Hamburg's harbour.[31] It was still largely intact despite the firestorm of July and August 1943—another indication, were one needed, of the ineffectiveness of Arthur Harris's city-busting campaign. Under Hitler's order, passed on by Feldmarschall Ernst Busch, head of German Command Northwest (OB Nordwest), all quays and docks were to be destroyed, all ships sunk, all bridges and cranes blown up.[32] The sunken ships and newly laid mines would then block all entry to the harbour. Without the harbour, there is no Hamburg.

Kaufmann naturally claimed credit for preventing this destruction, but scorched earth was not in his jurisdiction to block. Under Speer's very deliberate drafting of regulations, the decision on paralysis and destruction fell to the Armaments Commissioners (under Speer) and the Wehrmacht, *not* to the Gauleiter. Hamburg's key figure in this regard was Konteradmiral (Rear Admiral) Hans Bütow, who received the March 22 order. Bütow responded by demanding 6,000 tons of explosives and an entire engineer regiment in order to do the job.[33] He was going to get neither, and he knew it; the deliberately inflated demands bought him time. He then developed an institutional arrangement that scuttled the scorched-earth orders entirely: following negotiations with the city administration, Bütow was given full authority over the preparation of all measures aimed at paralyzing or destroying the harbour.[34]

The harbour was saved, but industry and bridges remained under threat. Speer and the army, not Kaufmann, worked to save them. In fact, Speer's confidence in Kaufmann was in such short supply that he appealed directly to the newly appointed chief engineer under OB Northwest, Generalmajor Hubertus-Maria Ritter von Heigl.[35] Trying to determine what sort of man Heigl was, Speer asked him what he had done with the scorched-earth orders while serving in East Prussia. Heigl, uncertain of the drift, replied that the scorched-earth order could not be implemented;

the necessary munitions and explosives were just not available there.[36] The formulation was a deliberately careful one: saying that an order could not be implemented was safer than flatly refusing to implement it. Speer and Heigl recognized their common cause, and Speer came up with one of his time-buying bureaucratic regulations. Army Group North would implement scorched-earth orders only when it did not affect things that were essential for life. ("*wenn es sich nicht um lebensnotwendige Dinge handele*") and after both the party and the army had signalled agreement.[37] Then, Heigl made a dash for Hamburg.

Without reference to Kaufmann, Heigl worked with Bütow to have the detonation charges removed from Hamburg's bridges and to prevent any new ones from being added.[38] Heigl personally supervised the work in one case, and he ordered the preservation of other road and rail bridges. He then met the city's commander, Generalmajor Alwin Wolz. Wolz had been commander of the Third Flak Division stationed in Hamburg since May 1944. Before that, he had served in the African campaign, and then as commander of a brigade in Hannover.[39] In March 1945, Kaufmann suggested him as battle commander for the city.[40] OKW refused, as Wolz had no fighting experience on the eastern front and had also served the now disgraced Rommel.[41] The fact that his wife was a wealthy German American and the daughter of New York merchants probably did not help either.[42] Kaufmann nonetheless insisted, refusing to accept Berlin's alternative, and Wolz assumed the post on April 1, 1945.[43] Wolz readily agreed to leave the bridges over the Elbe River intact.[44] Finally, Heigl drew up preservation orders for specific industries—power stations, food-processing plants, and so on—and had them distributed, sometimes with the enthusiastic help of local industrialists.[45]

Then came Hitler's second act. With scorched earth more or less contained, the central issue became the defence of the city. On April 23, Feldmarschall Busch visited Hamburg to discuss the matter with Wolz. The commander spoke truth to power. Wolz told Busch that a defence of the city would have only one consequence: massive loss of civilian life before the inevitable surrender. Referring to a possible British tactical air raid, he said:

My flak division can get the warning out to the population . . . only ten minutes before the arrival of the enemy bombers. It takes at least twenty minutes for people to escape to the safety of air-raid shelters. The result is that for at least ten minutes, and probably longer, civilians will be defenceless against the air raid. Who, Herr Feldmarschall, will give me the vehicles to transport the dead and wounded? Where shall I take the wounded? How will I stop the epidemic that will almost certainly break out? . . . I, Herr Feldmarschall, cannot accept the responsibility [for these deaths]. If I am forced to take it, then I will put a bullet in my skull, for I cannot live with these victims on my conscience![46]

Wolz had hoped this dramatic stand would sway Busch. It did not. The field marshal smashed his hand against the table and ranted, "This is nothing but a cheap trick to shift responsibility. You have to arm yourself with a Panzerfaust and throw yourself into battle against the enemy's tanks. If you fall in battle, then the honour is yours. Hamburg will be defended. *That is my order!*"[47]

Wolz retreated, shrugging his shoulders. "You'll understand, Herr Feldmarschall, that as a soldier I feel I can state my view openly. [However,] Hamburg will be defended." Wolz gave his chief of staff a wink.[48]

As a reward for good behaviour, to steel his courage, or perhaps both, Busch gave him a copy of *Mein Kampf.*[49]

A WEEK BEFORE BUSCH'S VISIT to the port city, Gauleiter Kaufmann made his own rather belated move to save Hamburg. On April 17, he got in touch with Waffen-SS Generalleutnant and police head Georg-Henning Graf von Bassewitz-Behr. Together, they visited Gauleiter Wegener (responsible for the Weser-Ems area of northern Germany, including Bremen). On that day, Kaufmann informed the Danish consul general in Hamburg that he was prepared to surrender and asked for help in contacting the British.[50] The consul general pointed him toward two Swedish bankers and a German diplomat who were part of a larger group of civilians and consulate officials from Hamburg, Denmark, and Sweden seeking to block scorched earth and to prevent the defence of Hamburg and Denmark.[51] They got in touch with a close contact of the bankers, Sir Victor Mallet, an official from the British diplomatic service posted in Stockholm. Getting the intention right but the actors wrong, Mallet wrote, "Kaufmann has now come around to [Feldmarschall] Busch's view that the city must be surrendered unconditionally, but only after British troops have reached the Baltic coast."[52] The effort was only secondarily about Hamburg: they hoped to secure a surrender of northern Germany, Denmark, and Norway; keep fighting on the eastern front; and persuade the British to make a dash for the Baltic Sea east of Stettin, thus blocking the Soviets at the Oder.[53]

It was not the first Nazi effort to make contact with the Allies. Himmler had in fact been trying to position himself as an intermediary for months. From mid-March, he floated via the Swedish foreign minister the idea of using Jews as hostages, releasing some of them as a show of good faith.[54] In April, Himmler asked the vice president of the Swedish Red Cross, Count Folke Bernadotte, to approach the Allies and to mediate on the SS leader's behalf.[55] Bernadotte agreed under two conditions: that Himmler launch a coup, making himself leader of Germany, and dissolve the National Socialist Party.[56] Himmler made several more attempts leading right up to the end of April. One involved offering the release of the (greatly exaggerated) remaining Jews in camps; Himmler claimed that 150,000 were still in Auschwitz and 450,000 in Budapest.[57] Another attempt involved an offer to Charles de Gaulle of a German alliance with France against the Anglo-Saxons intent on making France a vassal state (coming from a senior Nazi, this was particularly rich).[58] None of these offers came to anything, and on April 29, Hitler learned of Himmler's efforts, flew into a rage, and expelled Himmler from the party and all offices of state.[59]

Kaufmann's comparable effort got no further. Although some Foreign Office officials and Churchill himself reiterated the importance of making a dash for the Baltic in order to cut off the Soviets should they make a surge toward Denmark, the British in the end dismissed the main players as unreliable and Kaufmann as of questionable influence.[60] As Mallet was entirely wrong about Busch's intentions, the call was a reasonable one. Moreover, selecting a senior SS figure and a Gauleiter to lead negotiations with the Allies did not constitute a high point of German diplomacy. The

British most likely also took a dim view of the almost vanquished Germans dictating Allied military strategy. In the end, this did not matter: other men had assumed mastery of events in Hamburg. As Mallet reported in his last telegram on the topic, "Hamburg has received an order to surrender from a 'Lyne.' Busch does not know who Lyne is or which rank he holds, but he would probably be prepared to capitulate if necessary . . . Busch wants to know who Lyne is."[61]

Major General Lewis Owen Lyne was, thanks in no small measure to the determination of a Captain Thomas Martin Lindsay serving under him, the saviour of Hamburg.

As BRITISH TROOPS moved on Harburg, a southern district of Hamburg, an unusual factory came under artillery fire: one that doubled as a military hospital. Under Kaufmann's orders, Dr. Hermann Burchard had agreed to transform the Phoenix Rubber Factory into a hospital and to accept wounded Volkssturm troops.[62] As British troops approached and the factory/hospital started taking hits, Burchard had a large red cross mounted on the roof.[63] The factory's director, Albert Schäfer, objected on two grounds: the acceptance of Volkssturm soldiers as patients implied support for the defence of Harburg and, as the factory was working in effect for the war effort, the use of a red cross violated the Geneva Conventions.[64] To placate Schäfer, Burchard agreed to send a delegation to British lines to explain the hospital and urge them to desist from artillery and air attacks.[65]

Schäfer leapt at the chance, for he saw within the request a larger possibility: the peaceful surrender of Hamburg.[66] Burchard put the plan to the city's commander, Wolz.[67] He was pushing at an open door; Wolz agreed readily to the plan to approach the British.[68] He designated Burchard as the military leader of the delegation and sent along Schäfer as the factory owner and local expert.[69] Wolz also sent an interpreter, Leutnant Otto von Laun, who spoke imperfect but passable English.[70] Wolz gave them no authorization to enter into any negotiations with the British, but he also made no effort to forbid it. Whether the delegation recognized it or not, this could only have meant one thing: Wolz hoped to make contact with the Allies.

On April 27, Burchard, Schäfer, and Laun drove to the front near Lürade, south of Hamburg.[71] They got out of their vehicle, and Laun waved the large white flag that they had flown as they drove.[72] As they approached an open field on foot, a blast of artillery fire shattered the silence—an SS unit bearing a white flag had passed through the night before, so the British were not taking any chances this time.[73] Burchard shouted at them in English: "We are here to negotiate!" Several British soldiers burst from the bushes and surrounded them, as Laun furiously tried to explain in broken English that they were a delegation seeking to negotiate a surrender of the city.[74] Eventually, Burchard convinced a skeptical officer of their intentions, and the British took them blindfolded to the battle headquarters of the First/Fifth Battalions, Queen's Royal Regiment, Seventh Armoured Division.[75]

The negotiations, such as they were, went badly at first. Burchard and Laun had come armed, which hardly highlighted the pacific character of the visit, and Burchard gave the Hitler salute as he entered an office (and was immediately thrown out).[76] Laun tried to save the situation but had limited initial success. The British were unimpressed by his plea regarding the wounded at Schäfer's factory. If the Germans wanted to save the wounded, a major replied, they could move them elsewhere. Laun only convinced him to act when, showing him letters from British POWs, he told them that British soldiers were also present at the hospital.[77]

Laun, Burchard, and Schäfer were blindfolded and transported to a guesthouse on the Lüneburg Heath (Lüneburger Heide).[78] Captain Thomas Martin Lindsay, an intelligence officer of the Seventh Armoured Division, was waiting for them. Charming and gentle, Lindsay led the negotiations. He quickly agreed to halt the shelling of the hospital.[79] Lindsay then moved on to what he wanted to talk about: the surrender of Hamburg. He got nowhere with Burchard or Laun, who took a narrow view of their orders.[80]

Giving up on the military men, Lindsay went to see Schäfer, the factory chief. He began by playing hardball. Lindsay told Schäfer about the British surrender offer to Bremen, its refusal, and the final battle that flattened what was left of the city. If Hamburg wished to avoid this fate, it had to surrender. Lindsay then softened his pitch: he asked about the mood in the city and the position of the Gauleiter. Schäfer replied that Hamburgers feared nothing more than a final defence of their city; that they only wanted a quick surrender; and that, based on his last words in the Gauhaus, Kaufmann was ready to surrender.[81]

Captain Lindsay had what he wanted. Keeping the military men under arrest (against their loud protests), Lindsay had Schäfer delivered on April 30, with a letter from General Lyne hidden in his shoe, across British lines. Before leaving, Lindsay and Schäfer raised a glass of whisky to Hamburg's capitulation.[82] The military men got a somewhat rougher treatment. The British showed Laun and Burchard pictures of Bergen-Belsen. Burchard assured them that the Führer could have known nothing about it.[83]

After making his way through no man's land and past German mines, Schäfer reported to the commander of an air-raid shelter in Wilhelmsburg, south of Hamburg, and a major accompanied him to Wolz's headquarters.[84] Schäfer handed the letter to Wolz.[85] Citing Bremen's fate following its commander's refusal to capitulate, and threatening the city with a bombing raid, the letter urged Wolz to surrender: "In the name of humanity, Herr General, we demand the surrender of Hamburg."[86] Wolz put down the letter, smiled, and said in a strong southern German accent, "Herr Engländer will have his reply soon."[87] He then gave Schäfer a warm handshake and dismissed him.

Wolz then immediately set about replying and wrote two letters to Lyne. The first thanked the British general in effusive terms for sparing the hospital and let him know that a Major Andrae had been commissioned with the task of delivering further, highly confidential letters to him.[88] The second letter dealt directly with the issue of surrender. It referenced the "extensive military and political consequences for the still-fighting portions of the Reich," then stated that he was prepared to meet the British to discuss surrender terms.[89]

The next day, Schäfer saw Gauleiter Kaufmann. "How dare you," the Gauleiter asked, "pose as a negotiator and go see the British?"[90] Maintaining his cool, Schäfer told him what had happened. When he finished, he concluded, "Now, under existing laws, Herr Gauleiter, you can have me hanged." Kaufmann smiled, stood up, came out from behind his desk, and shook Schäfer's hand. The Gauleiter was on side.

Not everyone else was. On April 30, Kaufman had asked Großadmiral—and by then, President of the Reich—Karl Dönitz for permission to surrender Hamburg to the Allies, arguing that continued resistance would force the Western Allies to unleash complete destruction upon Hamburg and would give the Soviets the chance to overrun the rest of the north.[91] Surrendering cities without a fight, he continued, would allow German troops to be transferred to the eastern front. Dönitz rejected the request and made exactly the opposite point: that the Soviets could be held in Mecklenburg only if the struggle continued in the west.[92]

On May 1, Captain Lindsay accompanied the blindfolded Burchard and Laun to German lines and instructed them to ask General Wolz to meet them at the same spot within the next twenty-four hours. If he failed to show, Lindsay continued, the Seventh Armoured Division would order a devastating bombing raid and hand the city over to the Red Army for street-by-street fighting.[93]

The pressure on Wolz ratcheted up further: an officer of the Eighth Parachute Division appeared the same day at Wolz's office and declared that his division was still preparing to defend Hamburg to the bitter end.[94] In addition, the navy in Hamburg was also refusing to surrender. To top it all off, Wolz learned that he was to be replaced. Dönitz's appointee, General der Flieger Joachim Köhler, was making his way to Hamburg.

As he did, Wolz acted on Lindsay's request: he sent Major Andrae and his interpreter, a Hauptmann Link, back toward British lines. At 19:00, they crossed the front at Meckelfeld and were subsequently transported—blindfolded, of course—to Lyne's headquarters. Lyne was waiting for them.[95] Andrae handed the British general the letters. Lyne read them, put them down, and informed the Germans that he had been authorized to negotiate the surrender of Hamburg. He told the Germans that he expected Wolz to be at the British line at Meckelfeld by 21:30 the next day. The Germans requested a twenty-four-hour extension of their deadline. Lyne consulted Montgomery and then agreed. Andrae and Link returned to Hamburg and reported the news to Wolz.

By the morning of May 2, three obstacles of stubborn German military persistence stood in the way of Hamburg's surrender: naval forces in

Hamburg's ports, further armed forces inside and outside the city, and Dönitz in Flensburg. Wolz dealt with all three.

The commander first neutralized his would-be successor. Launching an eleventh-hour coup, he prepared to arrest Köhler upon his arrival.[96] He then dealt with the army. Wolz ordered his forces to avoid enemy contact and to retreat from the front slowly. He gave the same order to the Waffen-SS and ordered that anyone who wished to defend the Reich should do so outside the city limits.[97] As he did, the threat from another division was removed. The commander of the Eighth Parachute Division, a Major Bode, had shown up just as the general had given his order to the SS. As it happened, Bode had served on Wolz's staff previously, and the general easily convinced the major of the merits of surrendering Hamburg.[98] With the army and Waffen-SS secure, that left the navy. Here, Konteradmiral Bütow, who had spared the harbour, again came to Hamburg's aid: he ordered all marine units out of the city.[99]

An hour later, Wolz's named successor, Köhler, arrived in Hamburg. Wolz delayed for an hour, saying he had urgent business. He then invited the general to a briefing, where he outlined the chaos engulfing Hamburg. Köhler declined to assume command, so Wolz had no need to order his arrest.[100]

Another hour later, at noon, the *Hamburger Zeitung* published an appeal by Kaufmann to Hamburgers. Referring to the announcement on the same day that Hitler had "fallen in battle," the Gauleiter urged the city to "trustingly place your fate and your future in my hands. Follow me with unshakable faith and discipline on this difficult journey. I will act in the interests of the city and its people." Kaufmann also included a passage rarely quoted by his apologists: "what [Hitler] has left us is the eternal idea of the National Socialist Reich."[101] The important thing for Wolz was that the Gauleiter was no longer in the way.

As word about Kaufmann's appeal and rumours about a surrender drifted back to Berlin, the telephones in Wolz's and Kaufmann's offices started ringing.[102] Dönitz called Kaufmann immediately, but the Gauleiter stood his ground. Speer, a confidant of Kaufmann, phoned Dönitz and threatened to resign from the government if Dönitz did not agree to

Hamburg's capitulation.[103] When it became clear to Dönitz that Kaufmann and Wolz would go ahead anyway, he tried to claim the decision as his own. Dönitz was still labouring under the delusion that he would have a leading role in Germany's postwar government. In the late afternoon of May 2, he called Kaufmann and stated that Hamburg would be declared an open city; at 20:30, Busch sent out the order.[104]

But that order had long been overtaken by events. At 21:00 that evening, Wolz left Hamburg with Major Andrae, the interpreter Link, and, at Kaufmann's request, a retired mayor from the pre-Nazi era (and brother of Hermann Burchard), Wilhelm Amsinck Burchard-Motz.[105] After crossing British lines, they were taken first to Major General John Michael Kane Spurling. After a rough start attributed by Wolz to language problems, the German general indicated his willingness to surrender unconditionally.[106] The mood improved immediately, and Spurling took him to General Lyne. The two men agreed on the basic conditions: British troops would march into Hamburg at 13:00 the next day; Hamburg's police would secure bridges and maintain order; flak guns would not be destroyed; the Volkssturm would assemble and prepare to surrender; and Kaufmann, the head of the police, and the mayor would wait for Spurling at the city hall from 13:00.[107]

After the meeting, Lyne allowed Wolz to return to Hamburg only to call him back again. Dönitz was making his own, characteristically ham-fisted intervention. Generaladmiral Hans Georg von Friedeburg (Dönitz's successor as Chief of the Naval Staff) and General Hans Finzel (Chief of Staff of OB Northwest) had made contact with the British to discuss peace. As a surrender in the northwest obviously implicated Hamburg, Lyne recalled Wolz and forced him to join the delegation, which was sent to the Second Army Tactical Air Command headquarters near Lüneburg. The head of Second Army, General Miles Dempsey, had the senior officers dispatched to see Montgomery and kept Wolz with him.

Dempsey took Wolz to a large room and sat with his back to a window. He had Wolz and his staff officer placed directly in front of him, staring into the light. As soon as everyone was seated, Dempsey said to the interpreter, "I am commander of the Second Army. I understand he is prepared to surrender Hamburg. I make these conditions": that no documents be destroyed; law and order be maintained; stocks of food, fuel, and stores of all kinds must be protected; the radio station be handed over intact; no airplanes be flown; and Allied prisoners of war and displaced persons by war be controlled and provided for.[108] Wolz agreed, and the two sides worked out the details of the surrender. Dempsey, his voice firmer, added a final condition: "[General Wolz] will precede the British troops."[109]

At noon, Wolz, "a large, florid man of sinister appearance" according to Commodore Hugh T. England, signed the surrender of Hamburg. At the end of the proceedings, Dempsey remarked to the commodore, "This has been a *very* satisfactory morning."[110]

While Wolz spoke with Dempsey, Dönitz's men—Friedeburg and Finzel—arrived at Field Marshal Montgomery's headquarters just outside the village of Wendisch Evern, on the Lüneburg Heath. "Who are these men?" asked Montgomery. "What do they want?" The commanders offered the surrender of three German armies then facing the Russians. Montgomery refused: he would accept only the surrender of the forces facing his own. Otherwise, Montgomery continued, "I shall go on with the war and will be delighted to do so. . . . All your soldiers will be killed."

The men left around noon to report back to Dönitz and returned to Montgomery by 17:30. Within the hour, they surrendered all German forces in Holland, Denmark, and northwest Germany. It was May 3, 1945. Wolz had bought enough time to deliver the city to the Allies.

CHAPTER 26

ESCAPING THE SOVIET NET

Walther Wenck and the Flight across the Elbe

IN LATE APRIL 1945, General Simpson's Ninth US Army pushed toward the last remaining great river in Germany: the Elbe. He still hoped to jump the river, move toward Berlin, envelop Potsdam to the southwest, and then take the capital itself. Despite several near misses, all efforts so far to establish a bridgehead had failed.[1] Those stepchildren of the bombing war, flak guns, again performed their by then customary role. Anti-aircraft guns from the flak ring around Magdeburg sprayed the Elbe, shredding a bridge that had come within two dozen metres of completion.[2] German forces in Magdeburg itself held out to the last, only surrendering on April 17–18 following a devastating bombing raid by 350 airplanes.[3]

As German artillery held the Americans on the west side of the river, on Hitler's orders General der Panzertruppe Walther Wenck's new Twelfth Army pulled up to the Elbe at Dessau.[4] This army officially had nine divisions, but most of these existed on paper only.[5] Wenck and Simpson would soon meet on the same side of the river, but for the moment, Simpson was stuck on its left banks.

Hitler had invested great faith in General Wenck, who had served under Guderian and suggested the idea of creating a militia to defend Germany.[6] Perhaps emboldened by Roosevelt's death on April 12 (apparently a sign that providence, which had been less than kind to him since July 20, 1944, was again on his side), Hitler ordered Wenck on April 15 to jump the Elbe

south of Dessau, smash through Simpson's Ninth Army, and then relieve
the Eleventh Army, which was trapped in the Harz.[7] What was left of XXXIX
Panzer Corps did launch an attack with two under-strength divisions, but it
resulted only in their total destruction five days later.[8]

The Eleventh Army was, in any case, not terribly interested. Kesselring
had given it several orders over the last few days: first to break out west,
then to defend itself until Wenck broke through, and then to cut northeast
toward Magdeburg.[9] The army's commander, General der Artillerie Walter
Lucht, judged the orders impossible to implement and ignored them.[10]
Then a final order came through: slow the Americans' advance by making
a last stand.[11] To the palpable relief of his men, Lucht instead redefined
his task as holding his units together until the inevitable end.[12] From April
15 to April 20, with the exception of the Brocken (the highest point in the
Harz), Eleventh Army forces fought only a delaying action against the US
First Army's First and Ninth Infantry Divisions.[13] By April 16, the Americans
captured between one thousand and two thousand prisoners a day as one
town or village after another fell; by the twentieth, German units were surrendering en masse.[14] Over the next three days, the remaining stragglers
and General Lucht himself walked quietly into captivity. Lucht's surrender
saved hundreds, perhaps thousands, of lives and allowed several beautiful cities in this underrated part of Germany—Quedlinburg, Goslar, and
Wernigerode, among others—to emerge from the war intact.

As forces in the Harz surrendered, only Wenck's Twelfth Army stood
between Simpson's Ninth Army and Berlin.[15] Everyone, including Wenck,
assumed the Americans would cross the Elbe and move on the capital. But
Hitler, as ever building castles—or, perhaps, fortresses—in the sky, had more
ambitious plans than defence for Wenck's army. Before the Ruhr pocket collapsed, Oberst Günther Reichhelm and other key officers had been flown
out; Reichhelm landed at Jüterbog airfield south of Berlin and was driven
to OKH headquarters at Zossen.[16] His old friend and Guderian's former
deputy, Walther Wenck, was there to greet him. Wenck had good news—
Reichhelm was to be his deputy—and bad—he was to see Jodl and Hitler.[17]

At the Reich Chancellery in Berlin, Hitler got into an argument with
the usually emollient Jodl over the value of downed trees and partisan

warfare in the Harz before ordering Reichhelm to join Wenck.[18] The only value added to this diversion was the promise of two hundred Volkswagen trucks. When Reichhelm went to Döberitz (just west of Berlin) to collect the vehicles, the logistics officer had only a tenth of that figure available and would only release them to Reichhelm after a lengthy bureaucratic battle. Rightly guessing that Wenck would establish a makeshift head-quarters at an army armour school (*Panzerschule*) at Roßlau, some 125 kilometres southwest of Berlin near Dessau, Reichhelm succeeded in his rendezvous with Wenck.[19]

Shortly after Reichhelm arrived at Roßlau, an order to break out to the west had become an order to attack to the east: Hitler ordered him and Wenck to launch an assault toward Potsdam and Jüterbog and to link up with General der Infanterie Theodor Busse's Ninth Army, after which a further attack toward Berlin would occur.[20] Keitel came to them and gave the order in person on April 23, which he did with much waving of his field marshal's baton.[21] The order, and a related order to SS General Felix Steiner to drive his "army" south from Mecklenburg to cut off Zhukov's advancing spearheads, was evidence of two types of disintegration: of Hitler's mind, and of the regime he had governed for twelve years.[22] The day before, Hitler had exploded in a deranged and hysterical fit when he learned that Steiner had neither the forces nor the will needed for an attack from the north.[23]

The question was whether Wenck and Reichhelm would lead the charge on Berlin. According to Reichhelm's postwar account, the two men agreed early on that an assault on Berlin was impossible. They also agreed that all orders emanating from Berlin were utopian fantasies that were not worth implementing or altering. Reichhelm wrote after the war:

> [It was a matter] of officers using what was left of the best of Germany's youth . . . to save what could be saved and to prevent a collapse into total chaos . . . We instead used mobile battle tactics that used our troops for a temporary [*zunächst*], robust defence of the Elbe and limited, partial attacks, all with two goals: (i) controlling civilian panic in cities, on the roads, and among the fleeing refugees from the East and (ii) achieving some order for the imminent end of the war. [After restoring order on the

Elbe,] an attack toward Berlin would allow us to save the largest number of Germans from the eastern enemy . . . and to prevent the planned destruction of those industries, businesses, and cultural monuments that had so far survived the bombing war.[24]

In his own account, Wenck had ordered an end to all offensive operations against the Americans on the Elbe on April 22 — the day before Keitel saw him.[25]

After his meeting with Keitel, Wenck ordered one division to maintain its position at Barby, but he also sent battle-ready troops to positions along the Elbe between Coswig and Dessau, with orders to block movements from the south.[26] He then ordered two further divisions to defend a bridgehead from movements from the east and northeast, and to secure the Elbe from Wittenberg and Coswig.[27] This resulted in two fronts meeting in Coswig: one running east to Wittenberg, and another running west to Dessau. Both roughly followed the Elbe. Wenck then took the rest of the Twelfth Army northeast toward Beelitz, home of a military hospital at which one Corporal Hitler had been treated for wounds sustained at the Somme. As Wenck turned his forces east from Wittenberg toward Beelitz, he left only a "light screen" of forces facing the Americans.[28]

Now turned east, Wenck ordered an attack. His forces launched a furious assault between April 26 and 28 on the area between Wittenberg and Niemegk.[29] Two strategies were at play: pushing into Berlin if Soviet resistance proved surmountable or, if it did not, pushing the Soviets back, forcing open a corridor from the Elbe, and allowing soldiers and civilians to stream westward.[30] By April 27, the Twelfth Army reached the peak of its success. Its forces, trying to break toward Potsdam and Berlin, were blocked by General Dmitry Lelyushenko's Sixth Mechanized Corps, which was throwing itself at Wenck's forces near Brandenburg on the Havel.[31] In the southeast, positions at Wittenberg were collapsing. On April 26, Twelfth Army forces, seeking to prevent the loss of life and the destruction of Martin Luther's city, retreated from Wittenberg.[32] Within the city, women hastily hid ammunition and weapons in their back gardens so that nothing would give the Soviets the impression that anyone in the city wanted a fight.[33]

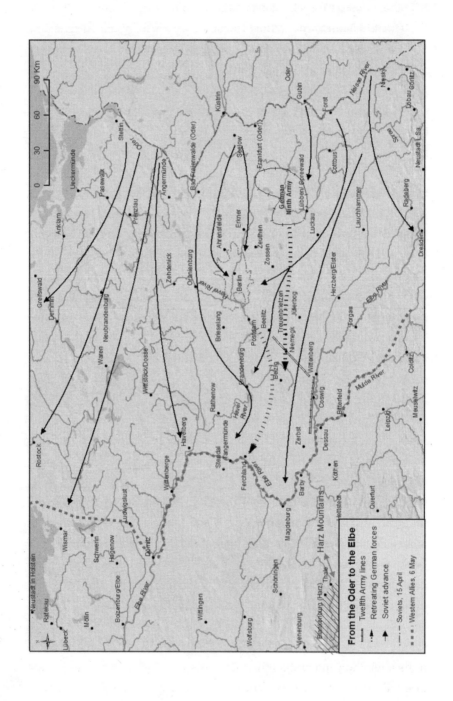

From the Oder to the Elbe

	Twelfth Army lines
	Retreating German forces
	Soviet advance
	Soviets, 15 April
	Western Allies, 6 May

Whether General Wenck intervened personally to save Luther's city—also the general's hometown—is unclear.

For a time, the Twelfth Army managed to hold and, to some degree, even threaten Soviet forces, particularly the Fifth Mechanized Corps, to the point where it desperately called in reinforcements.[34] Because his recruits were young and because Wenck commanded a particular respect among them, Twelfth Army soldiers' morale was unusually high at this late point in the war. One of the soldiers, future German foreign minister Hans-Dietrich Genscher, later said "[We had] a feeling of loyalty, a sense of responsibility and comradeship."[35] Wenck himself praised their "outstanding fighting spirit" (*"einen hervorragenden Kampfgeist"*), a compliment that we might be tempted to dismiss as instrumental were it not for the fact that German generals often blamed inadequate troops for their defeats in the last year of the war.[36] In one particularly daring move, XX Corps moved back toward the military hospital at Beelitz-Heilstätten, surprising Soviet forces there and rescuing three thousand wounded German soldiers, who were transported back west to be handed over to the Americans.[37] The rescue was possible only, as the Germans noted, because the Soviets had spared them—a degree of respect that the Germans had rarely accorded to Soviet prisoners of war.[38] These German successes, however, could only be short-lived. By April 29, the Twelfth Army was exhausted and without direction. After April 30, no more orders arrived from Berlin.[39] Throughout this period, forces under Wenck's command committed at least one unadulterated act of disobedience: the general refused to destroy one of Berlin's most important power stations, the Kraftwerk Zschornewitz south of Dessau.[40] Reichhelm also indicated after the war that the commanders of the larger cities within the area under the Twelfth Army were each ordered to maintain their defences "only as long as necessary for planned operations and movements." This contributed to Wittenberg, Brandenburg (on the Havel), and Rathenow escaping the fate to which Hitler had consigned them.[41]

THE CAPITAL WAS BY THEN under a full Soviet siege. The Soviets had pushed their way into the centre and surrounded the Gestapo headquarters in the Prinz-Albrecht-Straße. The Führer bunker near the Wilhelmstraße was just a few short blocks away. Throughout the capital and the Reich, any shred of a will to resist on the part of the civilian population—and there had only been a shred since at least January—completely vanished, and this in turn led to what the National Socialists delicately called "a disintegrating influence on the troops."[42] Reports of Himmler's entreaties to the Allies made their way, via British or American wireless, back to Sipo and SD chief Ernst Kaltenbrunner. Himmler, about to be sacked for treason, was forced to denounce the "malicious perversions" and to assure Kaltenbrunner that he, Himmler, was committed to fighting on.[43]

Two days later, on May 1, rumours of Hitler's death began to circulate with immediate effects on the ground.[44] Doctors at army hospitals felt sufficiently emboldened to expel wounded SS officers to make room for Wehrmacht soldiers.[45] In the west, naval war staff sent out some of their last orders countering scorched earth: it ordered that German harbour installations west of Swinemünde (Polish: Świnoujście) were to be crippled only if directly threatened by the British and the Americans; otherwise, no demolition of quay walls or equipment and no mining of the harbours was to occur.[46] The same order went out for Danish ports, with the exception of the West Jutland harbours, which were to be destroyed as ordered.[47]

With the Twelfth Army repulsing Soviet attacks at Beelitz, Wenck was preparing the evacuation.[48] He hoped to hold the front until what was left of the Ninth Army could retreat across it and then to pull the entire front back toward the Elbe.[49] His orders to his troops were clear: they were to fight the Soviets to the last bullet, launch a fighting retreat of the Twelfth and Ninth armies, and open negotiations with the Americans.[50] In the middle of all of this, a plane from Berlin arrived with propaganda leaflets urging the defence of the capital and the Führer. Wenck had the papers burned.[51]

In preparation for the Ninth Army's arrival, and to care for the tens of thousands of civilians who were streaming west, Wenck set up field kitchen units that were feeding some 25,000 soldiers in addition to thousands of civilians. On May 1, the Ninth Army finally arrived. The 25,000 to 30,000 troops who made it had been thoroughly ravaged by the Red Army. They had lost all their heavy weapons as well as most of their light ones. Worse still, they were so exhausted, apathetic, and disoriented that even harsh orders and threats often failed to persuade them to take a single step farther.[52] "Sometimes we even had to beat them [to get them into the trucks]," Reichhelm later remarked. "It was terrible."[53] Wenck had them transported toward the Elbe.

With Ninth Army soldiers loaded into anything that would move, the fighting withdrawal was on—and not a moment too soon. On May 2, Red Army forces broke into Havelberg. A regiment of Infantry Division Hutten rushed into the city, but it was not to be retaken.[54] Fighting hard, the regiment made a tactical retreat, hooked up with the northern flank of XXXIX Panzer Corps, and moved in a fighting retreat back toward the Elbe.[55] On May 3, Wenck ordered General der Panzertruppe Maximilian von Edelsheim to relinquish command of XLVIII Panzer Corps and to report immediately to Twelfth Army headquarters.[56] Wenck then told him to go to Tangermünde, a small city on the Elbe north of Magdeburg and directly west of Berlin, and to make an offer of capitulation to General Simpson.[57]

At noon on May 3, a delegation crossed the Elbe in an amphibious truck; they were taken to a Lieutenant Colonel Fresner.[58] Edelsheim said a capitulation decision would be made at Stendal on the morning of May 4 at 8:00. The next morning, the chief of staff of the American Ninth Army met the German delegation. Edelsheim requested assistance in transferring Germans across the Elbe in this order: sick and wounded soldiers (mostly from the Ninth Army) and civilians, refugees from the east, and finally Twelfth Army fighting troops.[59] Edelsheim also requested technical assistance in building a bridge across the Elbe and in transferring refugees.[60] Citing agreements with the Soviets and the limits of territory under its control, the Americans denied all assistance and civilian access but allowed the Twelfth Army to use a damaged bridge at Tangermünde for pedestrian traffic as well as ferries at Tangermünde, Schönhausen, and Ferchland.[61] At this point, 90,000 to 100,000 troops and many more civilians were within Wenck's Twelfth Army perimeter.

The evacuation began the next morning. The perimeter was at this point less than twenty-five kilometres long and some eighteen kilometres deep.[62] Wenck ordered the evacuation of wounded troops, chiefly from the Ninth Army, first.[63] With Soviet shells and artillery hammering the perimeter on all sides, killing soldiers and civilians alike, Twelfth Army soldiers ferried the wounded across the Elbe at Ferchland, helped them across the heavily damaged railway bridge between Stendal and Schönhausen, and carried them across what was left of the bridge at Tangermünde.[64] There is no record of civilian reaction within the perimeter, but it must have been one of total panic.

By May 6, forces guarding the perimeter were running out of ammunition.[65] The perimeter had now shrunk to eight kilometres. Wenck issued a second evacuation order: to withdraw the fighting troops.[66] Tens of thousands of soldiers made for the ferries and tattered bridges. Civilians, including women wearing helmets given to them by soldiers, Soviet-born Wehrmacht soldiers, and members of the SS tried to slip into the crowds, but the Americans often caught them, particularly the women.[67] On the eastern side of the Elbe, many of those who could not cross killed themselves.[68]

Then luck intervened. As the perimeter shrank, Soviet fire raked not only Germans but also Americans, particularly those checking the identities of Germans on the eastern side of the Elbe. Simpson ordered them back across the river and, for good measure, pulled all his forces back from the Elbe.[69] One suspects that both sentiment and strategy informed the second order, but at the very least he could not have been unaware of the humanitarian consequences. The refugees surged toward the water. With the strong swimming and the weak and children pulling themselves across on makeshift lines, they tugged themselves over the river.[70] In a sort of mini German Dunkirk, people boarded dinghies, canoes, skiffs, and every other craft available. Some soldiers shot themselves; strong currents swept others, along with many women and children, away.[71]

On May 7, the perimeter collapsed, and Wenck ordered an end to the evacuation.[72] It was now every man for himself. German soldiers destroyed their guns and made for the river. Before crossing, the men of the Division Scharnhorst shouted a "thundering" *Sieg Heil*, pathos and bitter defiance mingling as the last of the Twelfth Army disintegrated.[73] Wenck stayed in his headquarters at Schönhausen to the very last minute, perhaps contemplating how the town's famous son, Otto von Bismarck, would view Germany's decision to tangle with the Soviet Union. Wenck was among the last to get into the boats, and he, Reichhelm, and a few officers crossed the river under fire.[74] Soviet bullets hit two of his NCOs, one fatally.[75] Once across, they walked calmly into captivity. On the other side of the Elbe, Soviet forces enveloped the tens of thousands of refugees and thousands of Soviet "Hiwis" (volunteers) who had not made it across in time.[76] Many of the refugees had trekked hundreds of kilometres ahead of the Red Army only to be a captured by it within a few metres of safety. But 100,000 soldiers and an unknown number of civilians had made it.[77]

The next day, the man who had ordered Wenck to Berlin, Feldmarschall Wilhelm Keitel, travelled to a former Wehrmacht officers' mess hall at Karlshorst, in the southeast of the capital. A few minutes after midnight, he signed Germany's unconditional surrender.

CONCLUSION

O N MAY 9, 1945, the most destructive war in Europe's history— indeed, when measured in total deaths, in any history—was finally over. A staggering sixty million people had been killed and millions more displaced. The Jews of Central and Eastern Europe had been obliterated. Hundreds of cities had been levelled, and two thousand years of cultural history—palaces, museums, opera houses, and monuments, as well as commercial and residential buildings—were gone. In over a millennium of warfare, Europe's cities, which count among them some of the most beautiful in the world, had never suffered such a degree of devastation.[1] They would never fully recover from it.

It is profoundly depressing to recognize that there was nothing inevitable about old Europe's awful final act. Had the stock market not crashed in 1929, the Nazis would have been a footnote. Had Hitler lingered longer in a Munich pub in 1939, the war would have been over that year. And had the weather in East Prussia been cool rather than hot on July 20, 1944, which resulted in the conference's move from an airtight bunker to an open-windowed hut, Stauffenberg's bomb would have killed Hitler, Keitel, and all others in the room.[2] As late as the July 20 attempt was, it might have spared millions of lives and prevented the Soviets from colonizing Eastern Europe.

After the last attempt on Hitler's life—on July 20, 1944—German generals and field marshals were given the opportunity to participate in what

Gerhard Weinberg has playfully called united Germany's last election before 1990.[3] They were asked to choose between one "ticket" made up of Stauffenberg, Goerdeler, Witzleben, and Beck and another made up of Hitler, Göring, Goebbels, and Himmler. The vast majority opted for the latter, and over the next nine and a half months, they fought a brutal defensive war that led to the deaths of more Germans and the destruction of more German cities than had the previous five years of war combined.[4] Such was the "colossal price," writes Ian Kershaw, that was paid by Germany for its leaders' willingness to continue the war "to its bitter end."[5]

The German army fought on until the end, invariably at the army group, army, and corps levels and with almost as great consistency at the divisional level. But there were important exceptions further down the chain of command. That disobedience was the exception rather than the rule makes it particularly intriguing. Why, given that the vast majority of commanders followed orders, did a few actors—Choltitz in Paris, Wolz in Hamburg, Gadolla in Gotha, Petershagen in Greifswald, and to a degree Schäfer and Ruhfus in southern France—refuse to do the same?

As so often in history, generalization is difficult. Common structural factors link some or all these cases: all these commanders thought the defence of their positions was impossible and ultimately futile. In addition, all three French cities examined here constituted isolated positions abandoned by armies that had retreated. Yet in many other instances—the Colmar pocket, Breslau, Cherbourg, and Brest—commanders defended similarly isolated positions brutally and with great loss of life. Personality, that great black box, especially for social scientists, played a basic role: had Ramcke (who destroyed the French city of Brest) been the commandant of Paris, Florian (who tried to destroy Düsseldorf) the Gauleiter in Augsburg, or Karl Holz (who launched the final battle-to-the-death in Nuremburg) the commander in Greifswald, the outcome in these cities would have been markedly different. In the last months of the war, the German army was composed of fanatics and realists. Whatever their protestations after the war, most fell into the former camp, but a significant minority was to be found among the latter.

Timing was also determinative. From March 1945, the chain of command within the Wehrmacht began to break down. Communications were unreliable, and commanders could credibly claim not to have received orders. Desertion rates increased, units crumbled, and calls for reinforcements went unanswered. As military control weakened, individual discretion increased, and opportunities opened for commanders to ignore or reinterpret orders. Doing so was not without risk, as the example of Gotha makes clear. Plenty of army and, above all, SS officers were prepared to set up flying courts martial that inevitably led to death sentences.

Timing was as crucial in the civilian sphere as it was in the military one. Much has been made of the great upsurge in support for Hitler after the July 20, 1944, attempt on his life. Surge it did, but this is not particularly surprising.[6] Assassination attempts invariably bolster a leader's support, whether in a dictatorship or a democracy. US president Ronald Reagan's public support surged after the failed 1981 attempt on his life, and that support drew on a much broader base than registered Republicans. Reagan and many others also explained his survival with reference to providence. In Hitler's case, however, the post-assassination bounce in the (figuratively speaking) polls did not last. As Ian Kershaw notes, "Apart from [a] brief resurgence [after Stauffenberg's assassination attempt], Hitler's popularity had been on the wane since winter 1941 and by 1944–5 was in free fall."[7]

Opposition is not the same thing as action, but the latter also became ever more common as the war drew to a close. It did so for two closely related reasons: the costs of action fell as the Nazi regime crumbled, and the costs of inaction rose—civilians faced the destruction of their homes, villages, towns, or cities, and the death of their loved ones. Under these circumstances, two different types of civilians responded: civilians in positions of power, such as mayors, and civilians without any particular political position. The latter included both working-class and middle-class circles associated with separate and often unconnected organizations. There was, quite simply, much more active opposition to the National Socialist regime in the last year of the war than much of the literature, transfixed by the horrifying and enchanting image of a Wehrmacht in its death throes, allows.

Power and gender relations being what they were, men led the informal organizations that launched resistance efforts as Allied armies approached, but women played a fundamental role across the country in the last months of the war. They urged commanders to refrain from defending their cities, and in a few cases they verbally and physically abused commanders who did not; they hid weapons and soldiers; and they persuaded their sons and husbands to refrain from reporting for Volkssturm duty.[8]

The extent of civilian opposition and its success is remarkable: likely one half of German cities surrendered without a fight, often following very brave action on the part of civilian resistance groups who used the power of persuasion and, when that did not work, the power of force: they organized local coups against army, police, and SS leadership. Many other civilians assisted by removing barricades, putting out white (or, more accurately, grey) sheets of surrender, and pleading with soldiers to move on. All of these lesser acts were punishable by death. It is only a slight exaggeration to suggest that German civilians throughout the Reich were in open revolt against the regime in March and April of 1945. They were also in revolt against the prevailing majority of the German army leaders that continued to pursue the war. By April 1945, the army had, as Blumentritt himself admitted, utterly lost the support of the German people, who in large portions of the western part of the country positively looked forward to the Allies' arrival.[9] In at least one case, army commanders reported that civilians had fired on German soldiers.[10]

There was some debate during the 1990s about whether 1945 was for Germany a defeat or a liberation; for the civilians discussed in this book, there was no question. For them, the German army (to say nothing of the SS) signified conscription, violence, and murder; the Western Allies brought an end to all three. In more than a few cases, American and British soldiers met cheers, whistles, and white flags of both surrender and joy as they occupied German cities. Despite the complete absence of a free press (to say nothing of social media), German civilians were able to come to a reasonable judgment about the various armies descending upon them. They viewed the British and the Americans with relatively little fear and in many cases with anticipation. They expected the Soviets to avenge themselves on the civilian population.

Civilian disobedience was the more common variant, followed, at some distance, by military disobedience. The rarest form, however, occurred among committed National Socialists, and the most famous case of such disobedience was centred on Albert Speer. As the documents presented in chapters 15 and 17 attest, Speer threw himself into a determined and, it must be said, brave effort to subvert scorched-earth decrees. There were two elements to his strategy. The first and most obvious was issuing counterorders. The second, and more interesting, involved the institution of a decision-making process designed to buy time. By involving numerous actors — himself, the army, and the Armaments Commissioners — in decision making leading up to scorched earth, Speer removed crucial powers from the Gauleiter, introduced what political scientists call multiple veto points, and at all stages built more time into the process. In the context of rapidly moving Allied troops, this layered decision process would often mean that bridges, railroads, or factories fell into Allied hands before either paralysis or destructive measures could be implemented. Speer, true to form, shamelessly exaggerated his effect while trivializing the role of others, above all the silent army of civilians who joined in the effort. But there is no doubt that he, in the end, acted to save what was left of Germany from Hitler.

The question is why he did so. Some have concluded that Speer sought to save his own life.[11] This is doubtful, and not only because Speer could have chosen the objects of his concern more wisely. Speer did not seek to save his life because he did not think it was in danger. His comportment as a minister in Germany's absurd post-Hitler, pre-capitulation government led by Dönitz, as a polite and helpful subject during Allied interrogations, and even as a contrite and self-critical defendant at Nuremberg all paint a picture of a man convinced that he would at the very least live to see a postwar Europe. Speer's charm and (social) class had served him immensely well in the past; he had no doubt that they would do so again.

His efforts to block scorched-earth policies were rooted not in concerns for his *Leben* (life) but, rather, for his *Lebenslauf* — his curriculum vitae. Germany's industrial complex and its impressive output (famously on the rise up until September 1944) was in large measure his empire: in addition to the Ministry for Armament and War Production at large, he also controlled the Organization Todt, the construction and engineering body supported by an army of forced labourers under his command. It was German industry and industrial output, Speer's creation, that Hitler wished to destroy. Speer was determined that his work would have a life after the Nazis because he would have a life after them too. From early 1945, he looked toward a Germany after Hitler, and he was convinced that he, as the most cultured and sympathetic of the senior Nazis, would play a role in it. In preparation, Speer began organizing from late 1944 his workers from the Germania project (the planned rebuilding of Berlin) for postwar work and in February suggested setting up three architectural firms in the future British zone so that they could start rebuilding the country immediately after the war.[12] Such a motivation is fully consistent with what we know of Speer: more than anything, he wanted power.[13]

THE LAST ISSUE TO CONSIDER is the effect these multiple but often unconnected events had during the last year of war. Simply put, how much did disobedience matter? The answer is that it had a modest but nonetheless real effect. The early capture of Toulon and Marseille, which was a function of Allied speed and of the refusal of these cities' commanders to sacrifice their men, as well as of the isolated actions of officers lower down the chain of command, had the largest measurable effect. The continued armed struggle against the German army was quite literally unthinkable without Allied control of these harbours, which for a time provided more supplies to Western Allied armies than any other port in Europe. There was nothing inevitable about their surrender: in northern France, fully twelve ports and the Channel Islands were defended for months after the Normandy landings, some into the autumn of 1944 and others into 1945.[14]

Choltitz's actions in Paris had both immediate and long-term effects. In the former, the general's refusal to destroy bridges, utilities, railroads, or factories enabled Paris to recover relatively quickly. Indeed, life was harder for longer and the city more scarred in London than it was in the French capital. Over the longer term, the return of an intact capital to the French was a seldom-recognized precondition for Franco-German reconciliation, itself the anchor of a peaceful, prosperous postwar Europe. It would have been impossible to achieve such reconciliation on the ruins of an obliterated or even scarred Paris; the French would never have forgiven the Germans for it. The liberation of an unscathed Paris thus contributed to what one author cheekily referred to as the second, successful collaboration.[15]

Within Germany itself, the fairly systematic refusal to implement scorched earth had important implications for the rebuilding of the country after the war. Intact industries, railways, bridges, and roads all contributed to making German economic recovery far easier than it would have been had these things been destroyed according to Hitler's vision. In late April 1945, Japanese diplomats predicted that Germany's recovery from the ravages of war would take 100 years.[16] Economically, if not morally, it took ten, and the speed and completeness of that recovery owe something to the scores of resisters who ignored, neutralized, or disobeyed Hitler's destructive orders in 1944 and 1945.

Those who disobeyed acted alone or in small groups, but their actions had important collective effects. Although they were working in isolation from each other, they were working toward the same end. But more importantly, their actions had positive feedback effects. The sparing of bridges allowed resisters to cross them and to make contact with Americans. The preservation of telephone lines allowed civilians and soldiers to make contact with the Americans to alert them of their plans. And the first peaceful surrenders of German cities made the Allies sensitive to the possibilities of peaceful surrender in the future; in multiple cases, such as Hamburg, Heidelberg, and Gotha, it made them willing to make additional efforts to help citizens save their cities.

At the municipal level within Germany, the refusal to defend cities meant, quite simply, that those cities emerged from the war intact or in far better shape than those that were defended. Disobedience saved roads, railways, and factories, but also architecture, culture, and beauty. Among the smaller cities spared (or mostly spared) by Allied bombers before the invasion of Germany, there is a close correlation between whether the city emerged from the war as it entered it and whether the Germans defended it. It is no coincidence that some of Germany's most attractive small and medium-sized cities—Heidelberg in the west, Regensburg in the southeast, Göttingen and Gotha in the centre, and Greifswald in the north—all surrendered to the Allies without a fight.

In Germany's larger cities, Allied bombing had in all cases destroyed all or most of their centres by early 1945, although the degree of destruction varied according to the intensity and number of raids. Cologne, for example, was bombed far worse than Dresden, as was Hamburg. But as extensive as that destruction was, it would have been far worse had Augsburg, Düsseldorf, or Hamburg been subject to artillery barrages and/or further aerial bombing raids. It is a credit to the citizens of these and other cities that they succeeded in preventing such pointless, eleventh-hour destruction. It is, or should be, to the shame of postwar planners and architects that they in so many cases squandered the heritage bequeathed to them by often less exalted citizens. Much postwar architecture in Germany ranges from the banal to the offensively ugly. The latter dominated from the 1960s, after the excuse that cities needed to be rebuilt quickly had long tired. Dreadful postwar planning in Stuttgart, Hannover, Frankfurt, and West Berlin is referred to by Germans, accurately, as the "second destruction."[17]

The surrender of German cities also had a strategic effect, though one that is hard to quantify. Every bloodless surrender of a city or town meant that the Allied division, regiment, or battalion responsible for capturing it was free to move on to another battle. The reverse was also the case: the fact that the Americans had to recapture, for instance, Crailsheim and Soest slowed their advance. It is conceivable that, cumulatively, these actions helped hasten the end of the war, a war in which thousands, often tens of thousands, of people were dying every day. Such a conclusion is, however, only tentative; so many factors were in play on so many fronts, and within Germany itself, that it is almost impossible to attribute direct causal effect. What can be definitively concluded is that surrenders cost the Allies less in terms of life, materiel, and time, all of which enabled the fight to continue elsewhere.

Finally, and most important, these acts of disobedience saved lives. The refusal in Toulon and Marseille to fight on to the end saved thousands of German and French lives. Ruhfus and Schäfer are owed some credit here, but even more is owed to the lower-ranking officers who walked into French captivity and who, rather incredibly, provided the French with intelligence on the location of German defences. In both cities, French forces acted with chivalry and even generosity toward an army that had conquered and occupied their country. Why they did so is unclear. Perhaps it was that, being Europeans, the French were better than the Americans at flattering German commanders' vanity and need to pay homage to antiquated conceptions of military honour. Elsewhere, the refusal to defend towns and cities saved in each case dozens, hundreds, or even (low) thousands of lives. Over the course of the last year, cumulatively, thousands became tens of thousands, perhaps even hundreds of thousands, though we will likely never know exactly how many.

As ever in studies of resistance, it is important not to exaggerate the extent and effect of disobedience. Many commanders who surrendered their positions, including Choltitz, first launched a pointless token fight. The numbers could have been much higher, but several thousand German and French soldiers nonetheless died in Paris, Toulon, and Marseille. Given the outcome, which should have been obvious to everyone, these deaths were unnecessary. All that can perhaps be said in mitigation is that asking a commander, especially a commander answerable to a fanatical dictator, to surrender before time is difficult in a manner that civilian observers find hard to understand.

Like everything else after July 20, 1944, the events described in this book occurred because of the failure of Stauffenberg's conspiracy. It does no disservice to the bravery of the July 20 plotters—and even their critics, who are legion, concede their bravery—to recognize that Stauffenberg's coup did not save a single life. Indeed, it resulted in many people, not least the plotters themselves, being killed. By contrast, the less well-known and less august group of individuals described in this book (few have "*von*" before their names, and none "*Graf*") saved many lives. Although they had no contact, there was a connection between the two groups. The July 20 resisters gave the postwar Federal Republic a normative anchor it desperately needed: a basis for the thinnest sliver of German pride and, more importantly, a moral framework of reference for postwar political life in Germany.[18] The post–July 20 disobeyers helped ensure that there was a Germany that could be economically, physically, and morally rebuilt. Collectively, they played a great and largely unrecognized role in the recovery of Germany and, therefore, of Europe.

NOTE ON APPROACH, SOURCES, AND ACKNOWLEDGEMENTS

THROUGHOUT, this book focuses on disobedience as a category distinct from two more generally known forms of resistance: resistance-as-regime-change and daily resistance. Within the scholarly literature, a focus on disobedience places this manuscript between positions articulated by, respectively, Martin Broszat and Klaus-Jürgen Müller.

Broszat, in a series of famous studies, argued that the concept of *Resistenz* should be added to our traditional understanding of resistance (*Widerstand* in German).[1] According to Broszat, who pioneered social history of the Third Reich, *Resistenz* included every passive and active decision that implied rejection of the regime and that entailed risk.[2] Examples of such include refusing to give the mandatory "Heil Hitler" greeting, not displaying the swastika, or knowingly entering a Jewish shop.[3] The difficulty with the concept of *Resistenz* is twofold: first, it is very hard to measure and, second, it counts under the umbrella of resistance acts that not only failed to affect the regime's fortunes but acts that the regime would not even have noticed.

The military historian Klaus-Jürgen Müller argued that the category becomes so broad as to be of little explanatory use, and that a proper definition of "resistance" (*Widerstand*) should include a desire to overthrow the system.[4] This book positions itself between these poles by focusing on the narrowing category of *disobedience*. Although falling short of regime change (implied by *Widerstand*), "disobedience" is a preferable category to *Resistenz* in that it captures actions intended to have a measurable impact on the course of the war.

READERS OF THIS BOOK should note a couple of conventions followed throughout. First, I use 24-hour time (14:30, etc.). Second, German ranks are left in the original German (to minimize confusion given their non-intuitive correspondence with US ones). A glossary translates all the important ranks.

In terms of sources, this book relies on extensive archives in four countries and in three languages. In the United Kingdom, the National Archives (until recently, the Public Record Office) served me well. The National Archives "HW" class contains the transcripts of all Ultra intercepts (that is, intercepts of German codes broken by the British) from the war. The collection is a treasure trove. First, it provides a comprehensive view of the war as the Germans themselves saw it. Second, it contains transcriptions of documents that no longer exist on the German side. This is particularly important given the paucity of German-language documents from the final year of the war: the Germans deliberately destroyed many; the Soviets carted many others off to Moscow; and often those responsible for writing reports or recording communications had other, rather more pressing concerns. Finally, these documents provide an invaluable basis to cross-reference claims made by Germans and others (but especially Germans) after the war. Also in London, the Liddell Hart archives contain corps, divisional, and regimental reports, as well as extensive private papers.

For all the shortages of documentation, Germany's military archives in Freiburg contain important files on the liberation of Paris, the background to July 20, 1944, and the movement of some divisions, corps, and armies in 1944 and 1945. The Bundesarchiv photo collection in Koblenz contains a wealth of images related to military operations and Germany's cities during the war. The Paris police prefecture archives fill out the story of that city to a great extent: well over a thousand pages of police reports present an almost minute-by-minute overview of the final week of the German occupation.

In the United States, the National Archives at College Park and the US Army Military History Institute at Carlisle provided extensive source material on the American war in Europe: battle plans and orders, intelligence reports, divisional histories and reports, after-action reports, personal memoirs, and, at Carlisle, the German Foreign Military Series. I am grateful to archivists from all these collections for their assistance in retrieving and advising on documents.

The last source includes reports written by German generals under the auspices of a US-funded military history study running from 1946 to 1947 (under Colonel S. L. A. Marshall) and from 1948 to 1961 (under Generaloberst Franz Halder).

German generals were hardly disinterested observers, and their recollections need to be read with caution. As one historian put it, the Germans' reports suffer from "selective memory syndrome," leading to a body of work "characterized by the absence of war crimes (with the exception of those committed by the Red Army), an unquestioning admiration of the skills of the German soldier, and an explanation of the loss of the war that is almost invariably linked to Allied material strength and/or the interference of a certain Austrian corporal."[5] The first-hand accounts contributed to the myth—never taken terribly seriously within the English-speaking world—of an innocent, apolitical Wehrmacht that did its job and had nothing to do with the crimes of the SS.[6] This background should be borne in mind when these documents are cited, but two factors mitigate their problems for the purposes of this study. First, the documents cited were all drafted in 1946 and 1947 while the program was under American rather than German control. Second, in an early postwar context in which the July 20 resisters were still widely viewed as traitors within the Wehrmacht, the incentive to inflate one's hostility to the Nazis in order to please the Americans was checked by the desire to appear a loyal, patriotic soldier. The myth of the apolitical Wehrmacht portrayed generals who obeyed orders, not ones who questioned them.[7]

The final major primary sources come from local archives across Germany: Augsburg, Düsseldorf, Freiburg, Greifswald, Gotha, Heidelberg, Jena, and Hamburg. City archives in Germany contain a wealth of reports on the last days or weeks of the war drawn up by those who lived through them. In most cases (Freiburg is something of an exception), they wrote these reports within a year of the war's end; there are invariably multiple reports that can be cross-referenced against each other; and many local historians have reviewed and provided a ruling on these documents' reliability. Historians have used these sources for local studies, often appearing on anniversaries, but they have not yet been incorporated into a national narrative that connects widespread local disobedience to debates about the German army's conduct in the last stages of the war.

Bookshelves are sagging—nay, collapsing—under the weight of the secondary literature on World War II. One would quite literally die trying to get through it all. For this book, I have selected several books as my core reference texts for the history of the war: Gerhard Weinberg's *A World at Arms* for the whole war, Russell F. Weigley's *Eisenhower's Lieutenants* for the western front, and John Erickson's *The Road to Stalingrad* and *The Road to Berlin* for the eastern front. Added to this is *Germany and the Second World War*, the German Military History Institute's comprehensive ten-volume study of the war, a monument to both scholarship and the Germans' determination to shed light on every corner of their dark history. For the events of July 20 and the German military resistance generally, I have relied on Peter Hoffmann's magisterial *History of the German Resistance*.

Multiple institutions and individuals have made this book possible. My first thanks goes to my London agent, Andrew Lownie, for providing extensive advice and encouragement, and to John Pearce in Victoria, who provided many comments on the book proposal and who met in person to discuss the work multiple times. An equally warm word of thanks goes to my editor at Doubleday Canada, Tim Rostron, for his comments and suggestions. Without him, there would be no book.

For research support, I am grateful to the Social Science and Humanities Research Council (SSHRC) Standard Research Grants program and the Canada Research Chair I hold. I owe a great debt to Gerhard Weinberg, who discussed the outlines of the project with me in its earliest stages and suggested I examine the course of events in Toulon and Marseille. Doris Bergen had multiple conversations with me on issues important to this book: Wehrmacht war crimes on the eastern front; the Holocaust in France; and the role of the military oath to Hitler in explaining, or rather excusing, German commanders' loyalty to the regime. Winfried Heinemann read and provided extensive written comments on this project's initial proposal as well as drafts of the resulting manuscript. Jeffrey Kopstein, Phil Triadafilopoulos, and David Wolfe read and provided comments on a SSHRC grant proposal that formed the basis of this book. Portions of this book were presented in Potsdam and Jena, and I am grateful to John Zimmermann (Zentrum für Militärgeschichte und Sozialwissenschaften der Bundeswehr / Bundeswehr Centre for Military History and Social Sciences) and Norbert Frei (Friedrich Schiller University, Jena) for organizing these events and for their comments at them. An earlier draft was also presented at the Council of European Studies meeting in Barcelona, June 20–21, 2011, at which Konrad Jarausch provided extensive comments. Finally, a first draft of the manuscript was presented at a workshop at the Munk School of Global Affairs, Toronto, on "Germany and the Transatlantic Relationship: World War II and Beyond." My sincere thanks go to the participants at that event: Doris Bergen, Richard Bessel, Peter Hoffmann, James Retallack, Gerhard Weinberg, and David Yelton. The German Academic Exchange Service (DAAD) and the Canada Centre for Global Security Studies provided the funding that made the workshop possible. Jonathan Beard also read the entire manuscript and provided many helpful comments. For research assistance, I am grateful to Matthias Karl and Joseph Hawker. Mr. Hawker in particular logged many hours of work and discussed the manuscript with me at length. I am immensely grateful for his help. Finally, Murat Yasar provided indispensible assistance in creating maps.

The bulk of this book was written during a sabbatical leave in Berlin, and most of the writing was done at the Staatsbibliothek at Potsdamer Platz. Berliners, and Germans generally, take a curious view of libraries. They view them not as video rental outlets, dating services, or community centres but, rather, as places of quiet study. The "Stabi" is an ideal place for writing and research, and I am very grateful to its staff.

During my time in Berlin, I was also a Visiting Research Fellow from early 2012 at the Bundeswehr's Centre for Military History and Social Sciences in Potsdam. The centre has an outstanding library, and thanks go once again to John Zimmermann and Winfried Heinemann for welcoming me to Potsdam and for many conversations whilst I was there.

I am also very grateful to the Department of Political Science at the University of Toronto for granting me sabbatical leave. The department is a place of great methodological pluralism and lively, often passionate debates on contemporary history and politics. The Munk School of Global Affairs, which houses the university's Centre for European, Russian, and Eurasian Studies, is an outstanding place to do research. I owe a great debt to David Cameron and Louis Pauly, Departmental Chairs, and Janice Stein, Director of the Munk School, for ensuring the vitality of these research and teaching units.

My last word of thanks goes to my family. My wife, Katja, has for almost two decades been my favourite critic. It would be a stretch to suggest that military history stands at the centre of her intellectual interests, but she steeled herself impressively and showed great patience when I returned from the archives excitedly determined to explain, over an hour or so, how a particular bridge or factory survived the war. I am also very thankful for and to my son, Kieran, to whom I dedicate this book. His presence constantly reminds me that, although I enjoy writing about the period covered in this and my last book, I am immensely grateful that he did not live through it. For the better world that followed, at least in Western Europe, I owe a last word of gratitude and respect to the men and women who led the Western Allied war effort. I doubt that we will see such resolve again.

NOTES

INTRODUCTION

1. "Räumung des Kuban-Brückenkopfes und Verteidigung der Krim vom 4. 9. 1943," OKW/Gen St d H/Op. Abt (IS/A), September 4, 1943. Reproduced in Percy Ernst Schramm, ed., *Kriegstagebuch des Oberkommandos der Wehrmacht*, 4 vols. (Frankfurt: Bernard & Graefe Verlag für Wehrwesen, 1961), III(2):1455–6; Karl-Günter Zelle, *Hitlers zweifelnde Elite: Goebbels—Göring—Himmler—Speer* (Paderborn: Ferdinand Schöningh, 2010), 330; Christian Hartmann, "Verbrecherischer Krieg—verbrecherische Wehrmacht?" *Vierteljahrshefte für Zeitgeschichte* 52, no. 1 (2004): 60–1.
2. Quoted in Albert Speer, *Erinnerungen* (Berlin: Propyläen Verlag, 1969), 412. Also see Zelle, *Hitlers zweifelnde Elite*, 330.
3. Zelle, *Hitlers zweifelnde Elite*, 330; Peter Longerich, *Heinrich Himmler* (Oxford: Oxford University Press, 2012), 712.

CHAPTER 1: WAR, ATROCITIES, RESISTANCE

1. Gerhard L. Weinberg, *A World at Arms: A Global History of World War II*, 2nd ed. (Cambridge: Cambridge University Press, 2005), 51, on the Polish air force.
2. Quotation and statistics from ibid., 57.
3. Statistics from Richard C. Lukas, *The Forgotten Holocaust: The Poles under German Occupation 1933–1944* (Lexington: University Press of Kentucky, 1986), 3, drawing on Polish sources.
4. One study concludes that, over the last three hundred years of warfare, civilians have made up 50 percent of the casualties. William Eckhardt, "Civilian Deaths in Wartime," *Security Dialogue* 20, no. 1 (1989), 90.
5. For a discussion of the evolution of intentions, see Christopher Browning with

Jürgen Matthäus, *The Origins of the Final Solution: The Evolution of Nazi Jewish Policy, September 1939–March 1942* (Lincoln: University of Nebraska Press, 2004), chapter 2.

6. For a discussion of the central place of violence in National Socialism, see the work of Richard Bessel, *Germany 1945: From War to Peace* (New York: HarperCollins, 2009). On violence, destruction, and expansion in Hitler's worldview, see Ian Kershaw, *Hitler 1936–1945: Nemesis* (London: Penguin, 2000), especially chapters 1–3 and 8. On death in Hitler's worldview and in National Socialist ideology, see Michael Geyer, "There is a Land Where Everything is Pure: Its Name is Land of Death," in *Sacrifice and Belonging in Twentieth-Century Germany*, ed. Greg Eghigian and Matthew Paul Berg (Arlington: University of Texas Press, 2002) and "The Stigma of Violence, Nationalism, and War in Twentieth-Century Germany," *German Studies Review* 15 (Winter 1992): 75–110.

7. See Christopher R. Browning, *Ordinary Men: Reserve Police Battalion 101 and the Final Solution* (New York: Harper Perennial, 1998), 9–10.

8. Browning, *Origins of the Final Solution*, 16. The Einsatzgruppen operated in the following areas: Einsatzgruppe I under Bruno Streckenbach in Krakow and southern Poland; Einsatzgruppe II under Emanuel Schäfer first in Czestochowa and then in Radom; Einsatzgruppe III under Hans Fisher in Łódź; Einsatzgruppe IV under Lothar Beutel (later replaced by Josef Albert Meisinger) from West Prussia and Bydgoszcz to East Prussia and Białystok; Einsatzgruppe V under Ernst Damzog out of East Prussia toward Warsaw; Einsatzgruppe VI under Erich Naumann in Poznań; and Einsatzgruppe VII under Udo von Woyrsch primarily in Upper Silesia but also for a short time in Tarnów. Ibid., 438n11.

9. Browning, *Origins of the Final Solution*, 16.

10. Helmut Krausnick and Hans-Heinrich Wilhelm, *Die Truppe des Weltanschauungskrieges: die Einsatzgruppen der Sicherheitspolizei und des SD, 1938–1942* (Stuttgart: Deutsche Verlags-Anstalt, 1981), 34.

11. Richard Rhodes, *Masters of Death: The SS-Einsatzgruppen and the Invention of the Holocaust* (New York: Alfred A. Knopf, 2002), 7.

12. Details on Eimann and the mass grave from Henry Friedlander, *The Origins of the Nazi Genocide: From Euthanasia to the Final Solution* (Chapel Hill: University of North Carolina Press, 1995), 137.

13. Longerich, *Heinrich Himmler*, 429–32.

14. Ibid., 429.

15. For the details, see Browning, *Origins of the Final Solution*, 15–24, and Jürgen Förster, "Operation Barbarossa as a War of Conquest and Annihilation," in *Germany and the Second World War* (hereafter, GSWW), vol. 4, *The Attack on the Soviet Union* (Oxford: Clarendon Press, 1998), 491–507.

16. Raul Hilberg, *The Destruction of the European Jews*, vol. 1 (New Haven: Yale University Press, 2003), 305.

17. 3.3 million troops. Hartmann, "Verbrecherischer Krieg," 5.

18. Russell F. Weigley, *Eisenhower's Lieutenants: The Campaign of France and Germany 1944–1945* (Bloomington: Indiana University Press, 1981), 14–7.

19. Along with Panzer Group 1.

20. Christian Streit, *Keine Kameraden: die Wehrmacht und die sowjetischen Kriegsgefangenen 1941–1945* (Bonn: Verlag J. H. W. Dietz Nachf., 1997), 119.

21. Ibid.; Hans Mommsen, *Alternatives to Hitler: German Resistance under the Third Reich*, trans. Angus McGeoch (Princeton: Princeton University Press, 2003), 270.

22. Because the source — Ereignismeldung UdSSR – Nr. 10 vom 2. Juli 1941 — was a Soviet report of the sort used for propaganda purposes, we cannot be sure of its reliability without further evidence. On *Selbtsreinigungsaktionen*, see David Gaunt, "Reichskommissariat Ostland," in Jonathan C. Friedman, ed., *The Routledge History of the Holocaust* (New York: Routledge, 2010), 214.

23. On Soviet generals, see Förster, "Securing 'Living-space'" in GSWW, vol. 4, 1195. On the Seventeenth Army's anti-partisan measures, see ibid., 1200.

24. Streit, *Keine Kameraden*, 119.

25. Quoted in Förster, "Securing 'Living-space,'" 1200–1.

26. Winfried Heinemann, "Military Resistance Activities and the War," in GSWW, vol. 9, bk. 1, *German Wartime Society 1939–1945: Politicization, Disintegration, and the Struggle for Survival*, ed. Jörg Echternkamp (Oxford: Clarendon Press, 2008), 808.

27. Hilberg, *Destruction of the European Jews*, 1:308, citing the Seventeenth Army war diary. Browning identifies the unit as Sonderkommando "EK 4a" in *Origins of the Final Solution*, 292. Additional evidence for "4b" is found at the Yad Vashem Killing Sites Project website at http://www.yadvashem.org/yv/en/about/institute/killing_sites_catalog_details_full.asp?region=Poltava (accessed July 17, 2013).

28. Browning, *Origins of the Final Solution*, 292. Oberstleutnant Helmuth Groscurth, who would later die in Soviet captivity, was one of the few who sharply protested these killings. On this, see Mommsen, *Alternatives to Hitler*, 270–1.

29. Comments by Peter Hoffmann, workshop on German resistance in the last year of World War II, Munk School of Global Affairs, University of Toronto, September 21, 2011.

30. Ibid. Original German: *"Du musst anständig bleiben."*

31. Thus, in Simferopol, the Crimean capital, the Eleventh Army urged Einsatzgruppe D to complete the shootings by December 1941. With the assistance of army personnel, trucks, and gasoline, all of the Jews of Simferopol were dead by Christmas. Hilberg, *Destruction of the European Jews*, 1:311.

32. At the end of the war, Hastings Ismay described the city as "absolutely flat: there are certainly not twenty houses habitable." Ismay to R. G. Casey, February 28, 1945. Liddell Hart Centre for Military Archives (LH), Ismay Papers, 4/6/8a.

33. Michael Jones, *Leningrad: State of Siege* (London: John Murray, 2008), 192–3. For several chilling examples, see 215–9.

34. Timothy Snyder, *Bloodlands: Europe between Hitler and Stalin* (New York: Basic Books, 2010), 173.

35. John Erickson, *The Road to Berlin: Continuing the History of Stalin's War with Germany* (Boulder, CO: Westview Press, 1983), 61.

36. Ernst Klink, "The Conduct of Operations" in GSWW, vol. 4, 671; Kershaw, *Hitler: Nemesis*, 433; John Erickson, *The Road to Stalingrad: Stalin's War with Germany* (London: Weidenfeld & Nicolson; repr. London: Cassell Military Paperbacks, 2003), 214–5.

37. Weinberg, *World at Arms*, 274. Also see Hartmann, "Verbrecherischer Krieg," 5–6.

38. Klink, "Conduct of Operations," 702–3; Weinberg, *World at Arms*, 292.

39. See Weinberg, *World at Arms*, 295–6 for details.

40. Ibid., 293.

41. See Omer Bartov, *Hitler's Army: Soldiers, Nazis, and War in the Third Reich* (repr. New York: Oxford University Press, 1992), 16–7.

42. Ibid., 19.

43. Weinberg, *World at Arms*, 415.

44. Ibid., 410.

45. Gerhard L. Weinberg, *Visions of Victory: Hopes of Eight World War II Leaders* (Cambridge: Cambridge University Press, 2005), 19.

46. Gerhard L. Weinberg, "Some Myths of World War II," *The Journal of Military History* 75 (July 2011), 703. See also Klaus-Michael Mallmann and Martin Cüppers, *Nazi Palestine: The Plans for the Extermination of the Jews in Palestine*, trans. Krista Smith (New York: Enigma, 2010).

47. Weinberg, *World at Arms*, 415.

48. Ibid., 467, 601–4.

49. Ibid., 604.

50. Ibid.

51. Ibid., 667–71.

52. I owe the imagery of dual bulges to Erickson, *Road to Berlin*, 192.

53. German Ninth and Fourth Armies, respectively. Weinberg, *A World at Arms*, 704–5.

54. Figures from Erickson, *Road to Berlin*, 224.

55. Weinberg, *World at Arms*, 705. See also Karl-Heinz Frieser, "Der Zusammen-bruch der Heeresgruppe Mitte im Sommer 1944," *Das Deutsche Reich und*

der Zweite Weltkrieg (hereafter, DRZW), vol. 8, *Der Krieg im Osten und an den Nebenfronten* (Munich: Deutsche Verlags-Anstalt, 2007), 526–7, 537–48.

56. Frieser, "Zusammenbruch der Heeresgruppe Mitte," 552; Erickson, *Road to Berlin*, 227.

57. Weinberg, *World at Arms*, 708.

58. Ibid. Lublin-Majdanek was a storage depot for booty from Operation Rheinhard (also known as Aktion Rheinhardt) killings. All of the machinery and some of the shoes and hair found by the Soviets at the camp came from Operation Rheinhard activities. I am grateful to Professor Peter Black, Senior Historian, United States Holocaust Memorial Museum, for this information.

59. United States Holocaust Memorial Museum Encyclopedia article on Lublin/Majdanek, available at: http://www.ushmm.org/wlc/en/article.php?ModuleId=10007299. The Soviets would also liberate the killing centres of Belzec, Treblinka, and Sobidor (all of which had been closed down and abandoned) in late July 1944; the killing centre at Auschwitz-Birkenau in January 1945; and the concentration camp at Stutthof in April 1945.

60. Erickson, *Road to Berlin*, 244; Weinberg, *World at Arms*, 707.

61. Rüdiger Overmans, *Deutsche militärische Verluste im Zweiten Weltkrieg* (Munich: Oldenbourg, 2000), 278 (142,079 in June, 169,881 in July, and 277,465 in August). Battle deaths on the eastern front in the third quarter of 1944 were 517,907. Ibid., 279. The vast majority of these losses would have occurred during the Soviet summer offensive.

62. Streit estimates 3.3 million (*Keine Kameraden*, 10). Hartmann cites a lower figure of "about 3 million" (Christian Hartmann, *Unternehmen Barbarossa: der deutsche Krieg im Osten 1941–1945*. [Munich: Verlag C. H. Beck, 2011]), 65 and "Verbrecherischer Krieg," 11).

63. Hartmann, "Verbrecherischer Krieg," 11.

64. See the story of the relationship between the soldier Dr. Konrad Jarausch and a Soviet POW painter in Konrad H. Jarausch, ed., *Reluctant Accomplice: A Wehrmacht Soldier's Letters from the Eastern Front* (Princeton: Princeton University Press, 2011).

65. On this, see Snyder, *Bloodlands*, 5.

66. For a discussion of German plans for starvation and population transfer, see Christopher Browning and Jürgen Matthäus, "Economic and Demographic Preparations for 'Operation Barbarossa,'" in Browning, *Origins of the Final Solution*, 234–43.

67. For the details on who was informed and how, see Felix Römer, *Der Kommissarbefehl: Wehrmacht und NS-Verbrechen an der Ostfront 1941/42* (Paderborn: Ferdinand Schöningh, 2008), 50–8 and 67–8.

68. Quoted in Hilberg, *Destruction of the European Jews*, 1:287; Förster, "Operation Barbarossa," 491.

69. Römer, *Kommissarbefehl*, 69. OKH was subordinate to OKW. See Glossary for further explanation.

70. Förster, "Operation Barbarossa," 492.

71. Heinemann, "Military Resistance Activities," 812–3. According to Feldmarschall Erwin Rommel's chief of staff, Hans Speidel, Wagner came into contact with the resistance in 1942. See Speidel's answers to a questionnaire drafted by Elisabeth Wagner on her husband's role in the resistance, n.d., BArch N 510–64, fol. 1.

72. Römer, *Kommissarbefehl*, 71–5; Förster, "Operation Barbarossa," 499–507.

73. The Commissar Decree applied the logic of the jurisdiction decree—that is, encouraging the army to murder safe in the knowledge that it was free from prosecution—to Soviet commissars. Römer, *Kommissarbefehl*, 75.

74. Förster, "Operation Barbarossa," 507–13; "Richtlinien für die Behandlung politischer Kommissare," reproduced in Römer, *Kommissarbefehl*, 77.

75. Römer, *Kommissarbefehl*, 551, based on an exhaustive examination of the Wehrmacht's official war records held by the German Military Archives in Freiburg.

76. Stalin responded in kind. In a July 3, 1941, broadcast, he argued that the war was no "ordinary war," that the struggle against "Fascist Germany" was a matter of life and death, and that the Soviets should "have no pity for the enemy." Förster, "Securing 'Living-space,'" 1196.

77. Browning, *Origins of the Final Solution*, 260.

78. Ibid., 260–1.

79. Details ibid., 261.

80. Quoted ibid.

81. Wehrmachtbefehlshaber Ostland Abt. Ia Nr. 500/43, "Meldewesen über Banditenlage," March 1, 1943, BArch RH 19 III/489, quoted in Winfried Heinemann, "Der Widerstand gegen das NS-Regime und der Krieg an der Ostfront," *Militärgeschichte* 8 (1998):52.

82. Longerich, *Heinrich Himmler*, 193–6.

83. Heinemann, "Military Resistance Activities," 821–3.

84. Michael Burleigh, *The Third Reich: A New History* (London: Pan Books, 2001), 672.

85. Peter Hoffmann, *The History of the German Resistance, 1933–1945*, 3rd English ed., trans. Richard Barry (Montreal: McGill-Queen's University Press, 1996), 198.

86. Peter Hoffmann, ed., *Behind Valkyrie: German Resistance to Hitler; Documents* (Montreal: McGill-Queen's University Press, 2011), 67.

87. Heinemann, "Military Resistance Activities," 774.

88. Hugh Trevor Roper, "Admiral Canaris: 'The Hamlet of Conservative Germany,'" *Listener*, June 12, 1980, quoted in Klemens von Klemperer, *German Resistance against Hitler: The Search for Allies Abroad, 1938–1945* (Oxford: Clarendon Press, 1992), 23.

89. Ibid., 22–3.

90. The most active of Canaris's men was Oberst Hans Oster, who used his position to launch numerous resistance activities: supplying false papers, working with the military on coup plans, passing information on to the Allies, and aiding Canaris in providing safe passage for Jews. Ibid.

91. Heinemann, "Military Resistance Activities," 774 on the link with Christianity.

92. Ibid., 775 on the group's isolation.

93. Heinemann, "Widerstand gegen das NS-Regime," 49.

94. Heinemann, "Military Resistance Activities," 776.

95. Ibid., 783.

96. The pogrom is discussed above. On the equation of Judaism and Bolshevism, see Streit, *Keine Kameraden*, 118–9, and Manfred Messerschmidt, "Motivationen der nationalkonservativen Opposition und des militärischen Widerstandes seit dem Frankreich-Feldzug," in *Der deutsche Widerstand 1933–1945*, ed. Klaus-Jürgen Müller, 2nd ed. (Paderborn: F. Schöningh, 1990), especially 67–71.

97. "Ulrich von Hassell's Reactions to the 9 November 1938 Pogrom," in Hoffmann, *Behind Valkyrie*, 189.

98. "Carl Goerdeler's Plan to Protect the World's Jews, 1941/1942" in Hoffmann, *Behind Valkyrie*, 200.

99. See Hoffmann's discussion of *Das Ziel*, ibid., 192–210. See also Hoffmann, *Carl Goerdeler and the Jewish Question, 1933–1942* (Cambridge: Cambridge University Press, 2011).

100. Hoffmann, *Behind Valkyrie*, 196.

101. Ibid.

102. "Johannes Popitz, Prussian Minister of Finance, Protest against the 9 November 1938 Pogrom," in Hoffmann, *Behind Valkyrie*, 182–5.

103. Ibid., 183.

104. See for instance Christian Gerlach, "Männer des 20. Juli und der Krieg gegen die Sowjetunion," in *Vernichtungskrieg: Verbrechen der Wehrmacht 1941–1944*, ed. Hannes Heer and Klaus Naumann (Hamburg: Hamburger Edition, 1995), 427–46. For a critique, see Heinemann, "Der Widerstand gegen das NS-Regime," 49. Reading Gerlach's work, one is left with the impression that he is chiefly interested in playing a game of "gotcha."

105. "July 20 1944: The German Resistance to Hitler," in Gerhard L. Weinberg, *Germany, Hitler, and World War II* (New York: Cambridge University Press, 1995), 246.

106. By July 1944, Helldorf was firmly in the anti-Hitler column. As such, he was among the most morally ambiguous of the July plotters. Helldorf declared himself a National Socialist in 1924, was elected to the Prussian Landtag as a National Socialist in 1924, encouraged an anti-Jewish demonstration (and quasi-pogrom) on the Kurfürstendamm in 1931 and again, before Kristallnacht, in September 1938. But he was also a natural joiner in putsches: he took part in the 1920 Kapp putsch, encouraged Hitler's 1923 putsch, and it seems considered both a 1932 putsch against Papen and a 1938 putsch against Hitler. Once it became clear that Hitler was leading Germany to disaster, he joined yet another one. Ted Harrison, "'Alter Kämpfer' im Widerstand: Graf Helldorff, die NS-Bewegung und die Opposition gegen Hitler," *Vierteljahrshefte für Zeitgeschichte* 45, no. 3 (July 1997):386, 423.

107. As Michael Burleigh notes, most authors write Nebe out of the resistance entirely. Burleigh, *Third Reich*, 681. On Nebe, see Walter Kiess, *Der Doppelspieler: Reichskriminaldirektor Arthur Nebe zwischen Kriegsverbrechen und Opposition* (Stuttgart: Gatzanis Verlag, 2011).

108. Heinemann, "Military Resistance Activities," 788–91.

109. See Stauffenberg's comments on "senseless orders to stand firm" and another resister's reaction to SS-Gruppenführer Sepp Dietrich's amateurism and willingness to "senselessly" sacrifice "ideologically misguided young men." Heinemann, "Military Resistance Activities," 794.

110. On this, see also Peter Steinbach, "The Conservative Resistance," in *Contending with Hitler: Varieties of German Resistance in the Third Reich*, ed. David Clay Large (Cambridge: Cambridge University Press, 1995), 93.

111. See Heinemann, "Military Resistance Activities," 810–20 for details and names.

112. On the Röhm putsch, see Heinemann, "Military Resistance Activities," 781. On Kristallnacht, see Bodo Scheurig, *Henning von Tresckow: eine Biographie* (Oldenburg: Gerhard Stalling Verlag, 1973), 64–5. On the atrocities, see Hoffmann, *History of the German Resistance*, 264, 267–9.

113. For a full list and discussion, see Hoffmann, *History of the German Resistance*, 264–7.

114. Ibid., 267.

115. Ibid., 271.

116. Ibid.

117. Ibid., 273–5.

118. Ibid., 282–3.

119. See Peter Hoffmann, *Stauffenberg: A Family History*, 2nd ed. (Montreal: McGill-Queen's University Press, 2003), 86, 192, 197, 202.

120. Peter Pulzer, *Germany, 1870–1945: Politics, State Formation, and War* (Oxford: Oxford University Press, 1997), 160. On February 11, Olbricht finalized the

combat formations, based on infantry regiments, for Operation Valkyrie. Hoffmann, *History of the German Resistance*, 304.

CHAPTER 2: THE COUP AGAINST HITLER

1. Hoffmann places the time between 12:40 and 12:50; I have taken the midpoint. Hoffmann, *Stauffenberg: A Family History*, 266.
2. See Hoffmann, *History of the German Resistance*, 402–5.
3. This fact and details on the three men's injuries from ibid., 404–5.
4. Heinemann, "Military Resistance Activities," 839.
5. Without Olbricht's permission, Mertz von Quirnheim had sent out some alert orders just after 14:00. Hoffmann, *History of the German Resistance*, 416.
6. Quoted ibid., 419.
7. Ibid.
8. Ibid., 419–20.
9. Until recently, little was known about Oertzen. Thanks to a recent biography, based on 240 letters from Oertzen to his then young wife that she only recently made public, we now have a fuller picture. See Lars-Broder Keil, *Hans-Ulrich von Oertzen: Offizier und Widerstandskämpfer* (Berlin: Lukas Verlag, 2005).
10. Hoffmann, *History of the German Resistance*, 422–3.
11. Ibid., 429.
12. In Cottbus, 160 kilometres south of Berlin, Oberstleutnant Hans-Werner Stirius received an order to occupy the National Radio station near Herzberg, the radio transmitters in Königs Wusterhausen, and all major road junctions and bridges in the Cottbus area. By 18:45, Stirius's men had occupied the Herzberg National Radio station; the Königs Wusterhausen transmitters were theirs by 20:00. In the Infantry School at Döberitz, twenty-five kilometres west of Berlin, Major Friedrich Jakob, a highly decorated officer and tactics instructor who was not privy to the conspiracy, received orders to occupy the Broadcasting House. He ordered his men, fully armed with mortars and machine guns, into trucks. They occupied the building without difficulty, and Jakob ordered the superintendent to stop all broadcasts. The superintendent agreed, took Jakob to the main switch room, and assured the major that everything had been turned off. What Jakob, who knew nothing about radio, could not know was that the central switch room had been moved from the Broadcasting House to an adjacent bunker; broadcasts, including those by Keitel denouncing the coup, continued all night. Ibid., 430–5.
13. Ibid., 431–2.
14. Ibid., 435.
15. I owe this point to Winfried Heinemann.

16. A view also held by Hoffmann, *History of the German Resistance*, 483–4.
17. Ibid., 482–3.
18. Hoffmann, *History of the German Resistance*, 483.
19. Graf von Kanitz to Elisabeth Wagner, April 14, 1964, BArch N 510-82, fol. 1–2.
20. Hoffmann, *History of the German Resistance*, 497. "*Schöne Schweinerei, das*" in German. Translated sometimes as "a fine mess," this gentlemanly phrase hardly conveys the anger and passion that must have consumed Witzleben that night.
21. Ibid., 498.
22. "*Wie verhält er sich jetzt? Wir sind bemüht, hier reinen Tisch zu machen.*" Dialogue recounted by Graf von Kanitz, letter to Elisabeth Wagner, April 14, 1964, BArch N 510-82, fol. 1–2.
23. Hoffmann, *History of the German Resistance*, 501–2.
24. Ibid., 502.
25. Generaloberst Erich Hoepner was also there, and Ludwig Beck was either there or arrived shortly. Ibid., 503.
26. Adapted from ibid., 507.
27. Ibid., 508.
28. Quoted in letter from Elisabeth Wagner to Graf von Kanitz, April 5, 1964, BArch N 510-82, fol. 4–6.

CHAPTER 3: FROM FAILING HANDS

1. Otto Stülpnagel succeeded Alfred Streccius, who was head of the military administration in France from late June until August.
2. Allan Mitchell, *Nazi Paris: The History of an Occupation, 1940–1944* (New York: Berghahn Books, 2008), 17. Also see the memoires of the Swedish consul general to France: Raoul Nordling, *Sauver Paris: Mémoires du consul de Suède* (Paris: Petite Bibliothèque Payot, 2012), 96.
3. Jean Texcier, "Conseils à l'Occupé" (August 1940), point 1, available at: http://www.museedelaresistanceenligne.org/doc/flash/texte/2616.pdf.
4. Story from diary of Madame Talbot, Mémorial de Caen (MdC) Archives, TE 133, 32.
5. Ibid.
6. Mitchell, *Nazi Paris*, 15–6.
7. Ibid.
8. On de Gaulle, see Maurice Larkin, *France since the Popular Front: Government and People, 1936–1986* (Oxford: Oxford University Press, 1988), 110.
9. See Mitchell, *Nazi Paris*, chapter 6.
10. Ibid., 52. For an exchange between Stülpnagel and Keitel, see Walter Bargatzky, *Hotel Majestic: ein Deutscher im besetzten Frankreich* (Freiburg: Verlag Herder, 1987), 91–2.

11. Ulrich Herbert, *Hitler's Foreign Workers: Enforced Foreign Labor in Germany under the Third Reich,* trans. William Templer (Cambridge: Cambridge University Press, 1997), 1.

12. Oberg's first name is sometimes written as "Karl."

13. Bargatzky, *Hotel Majestic,* 95.

14. Michael R. Marrus and Robert O. Paxton, *Vichy France and the Jews* (Stanford, CA: Stanford University Press, 1995), 251–3.

15. Ibid., 252–5.

16. Ibid., 251.

17. Ibid., 263–9.

18. Richard Vinen, *The Unfree French: Life under the Occupation* (London: Penguin, 2007), 108.

19. Marrus and Paxton, *Vichy France and the Jews,* 225.

20. Gerald Reitlinger, *The SS: Alibi of a Nation, 1922–1945* (1957; repr. New York: Viking Press, 1968), 346. For a discussion of the German army's role in the Nazis' anti-Jewish policies, see Gaël Eismann, *Hôtel Majestic: Ordre et sécurité en France occupée (1940–1944)* (Paris: Éditions Tallandier, 2010), 187–91.

21. On the first point, see Bargatzky, *Hotel Majestic,* 106, quoting fellow resister Friedrich von Teuchert.

22. Jackie Metzger and Yael Weinstock Mashbaum, "From Democracy to Deportation: The Jews of France from the Revolution to the Holocaust," available at: http://www.yadvashem.org/yv/en/education/newsletter/24/main_article.asp (accessed September 1, 2013).

23. For a discussion of statistics from French sources, see Marrus and Paxton, *Vichy and the Jews,* 343–4.

24. Marrus and Paxton, *Vichy France and the Jews,* 270–9.

25. Ibid., 326.

26. Ibid., 325.

27. I owe the tripartite distinction to Mitchell, *Nazi Paris,* 93.

28. Ibid.

29. Julian Jackson, *France: The Dark Years, 1940–1944* (Oxford: Oxford University Press, 2003), 531.

30. Matthew Cobb, *Eleven Days in August: The Liberation of Paris in 1944* (London: Simon & Schuster, 2013), 84.

31. Mitchell, *Nazi Paris,* 142.

32. Wilhelm von Schramm, *Aufstand der Generale: der 20. Juli in Paris* (Munich: Kindler, 1964), 82.

33. Ibid., 83.

34. Hoffmann, *History of the German Resistance,* 470.

35. Ibid.

36. Wilhelm von Schramm, *Conspiracy among Generals*, trans. R. T. Clark (London: George Allen & Unwin, 1956), 24.

37. Schramm, *Aufstand der Generale*, 84.

38. *"Also doch"* in German. Ibid.

39. Ibid., 85.

40. Günther Blumentritt to a historian, January 31, 1959, BArch N 252. Blumentritt makes the remark at page 10 in the manuscript.

41. Schramm, *Conspiracy among Generals*, 27.

42. The latter position (German: *Oberbefehlshaber West*) meant that Kluge was Blumentritt's superior.

43. Schramm, *Aufstand der Generale*, 87–8.

44. On Hofacker, see Ulrich Heinemann, "Caesar von Hofacker—Der Vermittler," in Klemens von Klemperer, Enrico Syring, and Rainer Zitelmann, eds., *"Für Deutschland" Die Männer des 20. Juli* (Frankfurt: Ullstein, 1993), 108–9, and Alfred von Hofacker, *Cäsar von Hofacker: ein Wegbereiter für und ein Widerstandskämpfer gegen Hitler, ein Widerspruch?* (Wallstein: Haus der Geschichte Baden Württemberg/Baden-Württemberg Stiftung gGmbH, 2009).

45. Klaus-Jürgen Müller, "Carl-Heinrich von Stülpnagel: Die 'Zentralfigur' in Paris," in Klemperer, Syring, and Zitelmann, *"Für Deutschland" Die Männer des 20. Juli*, 262.

46. Schramm, *Aufstand der Generale*, 99–100; Pierre Galante, *Operation Valkyrie: The German Generals' Plot against Hitler* (New York: Harper & Row, 1981), 19; Bargatzky, *Hotel Majestic*, 131.

47. Hoffmann, *History of the German Resistance*, 471.

48. Heinrich Bücheler, *Carl-Heinrich von Stülpnagel. Soldat—Philosoph— Verschwörer. Biographie.* (Berlin: Verlag Ullstein, 1989), 303.

49. Quoted in von Schramm, *Aufstand der Generale*, 101; Bargatzky, *Hotel Majestic*, 132.

50. Bargatzky, *Hotel Majestic*, 132.

51. Ibid., 133.

52. Ibid.

53. Schramm, *Aufstand der Generale*, 102; Hoffmann, *History of the German Resistance*, 471.

54. Hoffmann, *History of the German Resistance*, 471; Vinen, *The Unfree French*, 109.

55. Schramm, *Aufstand der Generale*, 102.

56. Bücheler, *Carl-Heinrich von Stülpnagel*, 304.

57. Hoffmann, *History of the German Resistance*, 471; Ernst Jünger, *Sämtliche Werke*, Erste Abteilung, Tagebücher III (Stuttgart: Ernst Klett, 1979), 288–9;

Dankwart Graf von Arnim, *Als Brandenburg noch die Mark hieß* (Munich: Goldmann Verlag, 1995), 223–4.

58. Arnim, *Als Brandenburg noch die Mark hieß*, 224.
59. Ibid.
60. Ibid.
61. Details in this paragraph from ibid., 224–5.

CHAPTER 4: PARIS, JULY 20, 1944
1. Arnim, *Als Brandenburg noch die Mark hieß*, 225.
2. Schramm, *Aufstand der Generale*, 138.
3. Galante, *Operation Valkyrie*, 29; Arnim, *Als Brandenburg noch die Mark hieß*, 225.
4. Hoffmann, *History of the German Resistance*, 475.
5. Schramm, *Aufstand der Generale*, 139.
6. Hoffmann, *History of the German Resistance*, 475.
7. Schramm, *Aufstand der Generale*, 139.
8. Ibid.
9. Schramm, *Conspiracy among Generals*, 68.
10. Schramm, *Aufstand der Generale*, 139; Bargatzky, *Hotel Majestic*, 134.
11. Schramm, *Aufstand der Generale*, 140; Bargatzky, *Hotel Majestic*, 134.
12. Hoffmann, *History of the German Resistance*, 475.
13. Schramm, *Aufstand der Generale*, 140.
14. Ibid.
15. Ibid.
16. Hoffmann, *History of the German Resistance*, 475.
17. Ibid.
18. Bargatzky, *Hotel Majestic*, 127.
19. Details in this paragraph from Arnim, *Als Brandenburg noch die Mark hieß*, 227.
20. Hoffmann, *History of the German Resistance*, 476.
21. Bargatzky, *Hotel Majestic*, 134.
22. Details in this paragraph from Arnim, *Als Brandenburg noch die Mark hieß*, 227–8.
23. Hoffmann, *History of the German Resistance*, 473; "Blumentritt: July 20, 1944," August 19, 1945, UK National Archives (UKNA), WO 208/4170, SRGG 134.
24. Hoffmann, *History of the German Resistance*, 473.
25. Arnim, *Als Brandenburg noch die Mark hieß*, 227.
26. Schramm, *Conspiracy among Generals*, 99.
27. Ibid., 100; Hoffman, *History of the German Resistance*, 478.
28. Schramm, *Conspiracy among Generals*, 105.
29. "Blumentritt: July 20, 1944," August 19, 1945, UKNA, WO 208/4170, SRGG 134.

30. Ibid.; Schramm, *Conspiracy among Generals*, 106.

31. Schramm, *Conspiracy among Generals*, 107–8.

32. *"Da muß nach oben eine Sprachregelung gefunden werden!"* quoted in Schramm, *Aufstand der Generale*, 188. The English version of Schramm's book translates *Sprachregelung* as "formula," meaning a crafty wording that would allow them to save face. The important point here, though, is that they were all on the same page in explaining themselves to their superiors.

33. "Blumentritt: July 20, 1944," August 19, 1945, UKNA, WO 208/4170, SRGG 134.

34. Ibid.

35. Ibid. See the note on the translation of *"Sprachregelung," supra*. Emphasis in the original.

36. Schramm, *Conspiracy among Generals*, 109–10.

37. Arnim, *Als Brandenburg noch die Mark hieß*, 228; "Blumentritt: July 20, 1944," August 19, 1945, UKNA, WO 208/4170, SRGG 134. According to Blumentritt, Stülpnagel and Oberg "were getting on famously."

38. Details in this paragraph from Arnim, *Als Brandenburg noch die Mark hieß*, 228–9.

39. Schramm, *Conspiracy among Generals*, chapter 4.

CHAPTER 5: THE RESISTANCE'S LAST HOPE

1. The details on Rommel's journey in the following three paragraphs come from "Bericht über die Verwundung des Oberbefehlshabers der Herresgruppe B, Generalfeldmarschall Rommel, durch Tiefffliegerangriff am 17.7," August 21, 1944, BArch N 117–28. Also see Manfred Rommel, "Rommels Tod," in the *Südkurier*, September 8, 1945, BArch RH N 117–25.

2. Hans Speidel, "Gedanken des Oberbefehlshabers der Herresgruppe B GFM Rommel über die Abwehr und die Operationen im Westen 1944," [prepared for the US Historical Division, Operational History Section], March 31, 1947, BArch RH 20-7-149. Also see my *Fire and Fury: The Allied Bombing of Germany, 1942–45* (Toronto: Doubleday Canada, 2008), chapter 20. Although it refers to a later period in the year, also see "Tätigkeitsbericht für die Zeit von Schramm 1.7. bis 31.12.44: Feindlage," BArch RH 19 IV/136, fol. 20-1.

3. According to Lang's report, the second aircraft tried to "bomb" them, but is more likely that it strafed the road. Desmond Young, *Rommel: The Desert Fox* (repr. New York: Quill/William Morrow; New York: Harper 1950), 187; Samuel W. Mitcham, Jr., *Rommel's Last Battle: The Desert Fox and the Normandy Campaign* (New York: Stein and Day, 1983), 158; Charles F. Marshall, *Discovering the Rommel Murder: The Life and Death of the Desert Fox* (Mechanicsburg, PA: Stackpole Books, 1994), 147–8.

4. Young, *Rommel*, 187; Marshall, *Discovering the Rommel Murder*, 148.

5. B. H. Liddell Hart, *The German Generals Talk: Startling Revelations from Hitler's High Command* (repr. New York: Harper, 2001), 45.
6. On Dietl, see Winfried Heinemann, "Eduard Dietl: Lieblingsgeneral des 'Führers,'" in *Die Militärelite des Dritten Reiches: 27 biographische Skizzen*, ed. Ronald Smelser and Enrico Syring (Berlin: Ullstein, 1995), 99–112.
7. Dennis Showalter, *Patton and Rommel: Men of War in the Twentieth Century* (New York: Berkley Caliber, 2005), 26.
8. John Keegan and Andrew Wheatcroft, *Who's Who in Military History* (London: Routledge, 2002), 253.
9. See Showalter, *Patton and Rommel*, chapter 1.
10. Keegan and Wheatcroft, *Who's Who in Military History*, 253.
11. Ibid.
12. Liddell Hart, *German Generals Talk*, 47.
13. Young, *Rommel*, 111–2.
14. Ibid., 118. See also Showalter, *Patton and Rommel*, 3, 43–6.
15. Liddell Hart, *German Generals Talk*, 50.
16. Showalter, *Patton and Rommel*, 31, 43, 52, 141–6.
17. Maurice Philip Remy, "Rommel und der militärische Widerstand" in *Erwin Rommel: Geschichte und Mythos* [produced by the Haus der Geschichte Baden-Württemberg] (Karlsruhe: G. Braun, 2009), 109; Showalter, *Patton and Rommel*, 147.
18. I owe my thanks to Colonel Dr. Winfried Heinemann for the ideas in this paragraph.
19. For a thorough analysis of existing sources on Rommel and war crimes orders, see Peter Lieb, "Erwin Rommel: Widerstandskämpfer oder Nationalsozialist?" *Vierteljahresheft für Zeitgeschichte* 61, no. 3 (July 2013): 313–28, 342. Lieb concludes, "Rommel absolutely came into contact with war crimes in the Second World War and was even structurally implicated in several measures taken in northern Italy in 1943 [that would be considered war crimes]. But at the same time, he disobeyed criminal orders in North Africa and [later] France in 1944 on several occasions." Ibid., 328.
20. See Omer Bartov, *Hitler's Army*, and Bartov, *The Eastern Front, 1941–1945: German Troops and the Barbarisation of Warfare* (Houndmills: Palgrave, 2001).
21. Jon Latimer, *Alamein* (London: John Murray, 2002), chapter 3.
22. Quoted in Richard Holmes, ed., *The Oxford Companion to Military History* (Oxford: Oxford University Press, 2001), 783.
23. Quoted in Young, *Rommel*, 152.
24. Showalter, *Patton and Rommel*, 291.
25. John Keegan, *The Second World War* (London: Hutchinson, 1989), 343.

26. Showalter, *Patton and Rommel*, 329.
27. Mitcham, *Rommel's Last Battle*, 158; Remy, "Rommel und der militärische Widerstand," 115.
28. Rommel had disagreed with Kesselring even while in Africa. He felt Kesselring was too pro-Italian and, as a Luftwaffe officer, had no understanding of ground mobile warfare. My thanks to Winfried Heinemann for this point.
29. Holmes, *Oxford Companion to Military History*, 784; Showalter, *Patton and Rommel*, 335–6.
30. Showalter, *Patton and Rommel*, 336.
31. Ibid.
32. Holmes, *Oxford Companion to Military History*, 789–90.
33. Ibid., 784.
34. Keegan, *Second World War*, 374.
35. Hans Speidel, "Gedanken des Oberbefehlshabers," March 31, 1947, BArch RH 20-7-149.
36. Keegan, *Second World War*, 372.
37. Quoted ibid.
38. See Weinberg, *World at Arms*, 679–82.
39. Speidel, "Gedanken des Oberbefehlshabers." Also see Keegan, *Second World War*, 374.
40. "Eberbach: Bericht 7. Armee 22.-31. August 1944," BArch RH 20-7-149, fol. 4.
41. Speidel, "Gedanken des Oberbefehlshabers."
42. Weinberg, *World at Arms*, 686–7.
43. Quoted in Max Hastings, *Finest Years: Churchill as Warlord 1940–45* (London: HarperPress, 2009), 487.
44. I owe this image to Keegan, *Second World War*, 382.
45. On this, see Weigley, *Eisenhower's Lieutenants*, chapter 1.
46. Keegan, *Second World War*, 383.
47. Weinberg, *World at Arms*, 688.
48. Dr. Hans Speidel to Herr Müller, April 16, 1947, BArch N 24-33, fol. 77.
49. Weinberg, *World at Arms*, 681–2.
50. Ibid. See also Speidel, "Gedanken des Oberbefehlshabers."
51. Willis Thornton, *The Liberation of Paris* (New York: Harcourt, Brace & World, 1962), 115. The sentiment, if not the direct quotation, is confirmed by General der Panzertruppen Eberbach in UKNA, WO 208/4170, SRGG 1347, August 19, 1945.
52. Ralf Georg Reuth, *Rommel: The End of a Legend*, trans. Debra S. Marmor and Herbert A. Danner (London: Haus Publishing, 2005), 174, 176.
53. Ibid., 72–3; Marshall, *Discovering the Rommel Murder*, 138–9.
54. Reuth, *End of a Legend*, 185.

55. Mitcham, *Rommel's Last Battle*, 134–5. Rommel never forgave him.

56. Erwin Rommel, "Abschrift. Betrachtung zur Lage," July 15, 1944, Museum to the German Resistance, Berlin.

57. The colleague was Oberstleutnant Elmar Warning, who had served with Rommel in North Africa. Heinemann, "Military Resistance Activities," 901.

58. To Rommel's great disappointment, he was not appointed OB West— Commander in Chief West—when Hitler fired Rundstedt; rather, Kluge was.

59. See Young, *Rommel*, 196–7.

60. Sönke Neitzel, *Tapping Hitler's Generals: Transcripts of Secret Conversations, 1942–1945*, trans. Geoffrey Brooks (St. Paul, MN: Frontline Books, 2007), 101. For references to Rommel, see Documents 37, 155, and 157 in both the German and English versions of this source.

61. Lieb, "Rommel: Widerstandskämpfer oder Nationalsozialist?," 337–8.

62. Remy, *Mythos Rommel* (Munich: List Verlag, 2002), 274–7; Remy, "Rommel und der militärische Widerstand," 118.

63. Reuth, *End of a Legend*, 177–8. Reuth goes perhaps somewhat too far in stating, "Even if Hofacker had spoken about a violent upheaval in Berlin, it would not have occurred to Rommel that the elimination of Hitler was implied." He attributes, in part, this "obtuseness" to the "political *naiveté* of the simple soldier." This supposition seems hard to believe—Rommel was hardly naive— but the basic point that Rommel could have supported a coup but opposed an assassination stands. On the likelihood that Rommel was, at most, a marginal figure in the conspiracy, see Heinemann, "Military Resistance Activities," 900, especially n159.

64. Quoted in Reuth, *End of a Legend*, 177.

65. Marshall, *Discovering the Rommel Murder*, 225.

66. Remy himself notes this. "Rommel und der militärische Widerstand," 118.

67. Marshall, *Discovering the Rommel Murder*, 238.

68. Heinemann notes the questionable nature of Speidel as a source, "Military Resistance Activities," 897-8n145. Heinemann also points out that Speidel's position on whether Rommel knew about the assassination plot is inconsistent in Speidel's memoirs. Ibid., 901n166.

69. Reuth, *End of a Legend*, 195–6; Remy, "Rommel und der militärische Wider-stand," 121–2, 127–9.

70. See Peter Hoffmann's introduction to Hans Bernd Gisevius, *To the Bitter End: An Insider's Account of the Plot to Kill Hitler, 1933–1944* (New York: Da Capo Press, 1998).

71. Reuth, *End of a Legend*, 211.

72. See, for example, the recollections of Gotthard Freiherr von Falkenhausen and Friedrich Freiherr von Teuchert, which were written in summer 1945 and

January 1946, respectively. These statements are based on the individuals' inter-actions with Hofacker, not Rommel. Remy, "Rommel und der militärische Widerstand," 119–20.

73. See, for example, the recollections of Elmar Michel, ibid., 121.

74. Quoted in Heinemann, "Military Resistance Activities," 901. Confirmed by General der Panzertruppe Heinrich Eberbach: Neitzel, *Tapping Hitler's Generals*, 260 (Document 155).

75. Neitzel, *Tapping Hitler's Generals*, 260 (Document 155). Also see Heinemann, "Military Resistance Activities," 901 and General Heinrich Eberbach's com-ments on Dietrich in Neitzel, *Tapping Hitler's Generals*, 266 (Document 159). There is also some evidence that Rommel reported his conviction that the war had to be brought to an end to Gauleiter Karl Kaufmann of Hamburg. See Frank Bajohr, "Gauleiter in Hamburg: zur Person und Tätigkeit Karl Kaufmanns," *Vierteljahrshefte für Zeitgeschichte* 43, no. 2 (April 1995): 293-4n132.

76. Lieb, "Rommel: Widerstandskämpfer oder Nationalsozialist?," 342.

77. Ibid., 343.

78. In his private and secretly recorded conversations with other German generals in captivity, Eberbach expressed strong support for the resistance, referring to it once as "the cause." UKNA, WO 208/4363, GRGG 196, September 18–19, 1944, 5.

79. Though he had not been in any formal sense a member of the July 20 plot. Heinemann, "Military Resistance Activities," 902.

80. On this, see Bernd Freiherr von Freytag-Loringhoven, "Secrets of the July 20 Plot," originally published in the *Observer*, July 21, 1946, BArch N 362/3, fol. 10–12.

81. Joachim Fest, *Plotting Hitler's Death: The Story of the German Resistance*, trans. Bruce Little (New York: Metropolitan Books, 1996), 291.

82. Ibid.

CHAPTER 6: HITLER'S REVENGE

1. Hoffmann, *History of the German Resistance*, 484.

2. Heinz Guderian, *Panzer Leader* (London: Michael Joseph, 1952), 348; Hoffman, *History of the German Resistance*, 485.

3. On this, see Russell A. Hart, *Guderian: Panzer Pioneer or Myth Maker?* (Washington: Potomac Books, 2006), chapter 8. For Guderian's version, see Guderian, *Panzer Leader*, 338–50.

4. Hoffmann, *History of the German Resistance*, 509.

5. Quoted ibid., 514.

6. Ibid.

7. Ibid.

8. Ibid., 515.

9. Ibid. After the war, Praun published a number of tributes to Fellgiebel (in 1951 and 1955). They, as well as detailed information on Fellgiebel's World War I service and his work on German radio communications before and during World War II, can be found in Albert Praun, "Erich Fellgiebel: der Meister operativer Nachrichtenverbindungen," handwritten date given as February 5, 1969, BArch N 591/83.

10. Hoffmann, *History of the German Resistance*, 515.

11. Ibid.

12. The Bundeswehr signals school barracks in Feldafing is named after Fellgiebel. Also see Oberst a.D. Rolf Göhring, "General Erich Fellgiebel zum 4. Oktober 1971," BArch N 633-3-015, and Winfried Heinemann, "General Erich Fellgiebel und die Rolle der Kommunikationsmittel am 20. Juli 1944," in *Führung und Führungsmittel*, ed. Heinemann (Potsdam: Militärgeschichtliches Forschungsamt, 2011), 57–66.

13. Hoffmann, *History of the German Resistance*, 515–6.

14. Philipp Freiherr von Boeselager, *Valkyrie: The Story of the Plot to Kill Hitler by Its Last Member* (New York: Alfred A. Knopf, 2009), 169.

15. Ingrid Oertzen interviewed by NDR 1 for the radio program "Gescheiterter Tyrannenmord—der 20. Juli 1944," available at: http://www.ndr.de/geschichte/chronologie/nszeitundkrieg/tyrannenmord100.html (accessed July 22, 2013). Mrs. Oertzen knew something was terribly wrong but did not have the foggiest idea why he would not be home that night.

16. Hoffmann, *History of the German Resistance*, 512.

17. Ralf Georg Reuth, "Das Schweigen meines Mannes hat mir das Leben gerettet," interview with Ingrid Simonsen (previously Ingrid Oertzen), *Bild*, July 19, 2008.

18. Hoffmann, *History of the German Resistance*, 512.

19. In Boeselager's version, Oertzen pulled the pin while in the bathroom. Boeselager, *Valkyrie*, 169. As Hoffmann cites original reports, I have opted to retell his version of events. Fest, *Plotting Hitler's Death*, 293 is consistent with the Hoffmann narrative. After describing Oertzen's death, Fest adds a (for him unusual) judgmental comment: "suicides such as this only extended the circle of suspects to include friends, relatives, and colleagues." The Gestapo clearly already suspected Oertzen and anyone connected with him; he had already incriminated himself under questioning; and, as he no doubt himself knew, it was by no means clear that he would incriminate fewer under torture than he would through suicide. In fact, we know so relatively little about Oertzen and his role in the resistance (thus making it easier to dismiss it) because he left such a small paper trail: in some 240 letters to his wife over several years, he made only the vaguest references to his links with the resistance; he told her nothing

of the plans for July 20; and his suicide prevented the Gestapo from interrogating him. It is, however, true that the suicides, attempted or successful, of those in the highest echelons of army command drew attention to those below them.

20. Hoffmann, *History of the German Resistance*, 512.

21. Theodore S. Hamerow, *On the Road to the Wolf's Lair: German Resistance to Hitler* (Cambridge, MA: Belknap Press, 1999), 369.

22. Boeselager, *Valkyrie*, 166.

23. Quoted ibid.

24. Quoted ibid., 168.

25. Peter Steinbach and Johannes Tuchel, eds., *Lexikon des Widerstandes 1933–1945* (Munich: Beck, 1994), 193.

26. *Revolt against Hitler: The Personal Account of Fabian von Schlabrendorff* (London: Eyre and Spottiswoode, 1948), 145. I have mostly quoted directly from the English translation of Schlabrendorff's book, adjusting only a few words for clarity of expression. For a different translation, see Klemperer, *German Resistance against Hitler*, 385.

27. Hoffmann, *History of the German Resistance*, 513. Wagner's wife, Elisabeth, makes passing reference to the visit in a letter to Graf von Kanitz, April 5, 1964, BArch N 510-82, fol. 3–6.

28. Graf von Kanitz to Elisabeth Wagner, April 14, 1964, BArch N 510-82, fol. 1–2.

29. Gerd Riedel to Elisabeth Wagner, April 9, 1956, BArch N 510-64, fol. 4. Well into the 1970s, Elisabeth Wagner was still looking for her husband's diary. See letter from David Irving to Elisabeth Wagner, July 5, 1973, BA, N 510-66, fol. 2. Revealingly, Irving's letter was written in response to one from Wagner in which she complained that he had broken his promise to return original documents within a few days. See letter from Elisabeth Wager to David Irving, July 31, 1973, BArch N 510-66, fol. 1. Irving returned the documents but backdated his letter to July 5, 1973.

30. The story of Stülpnagel's journey is taken from Schramm, *Conspiracy among Generals*, chapter 5. For a more abbreviated version of the story, see Ernst Jünger, *Sämtliche Werke*, Erste Abteilung, Tagebücher III, 289.

31. "Blumentritt: July 20, 1944," August 19, 1945, UKNA, WO 208/4170, SRGG 134.

32. Quoted in Alfred Hofacker, *Cäsar von Hofacker*, 24.

33. Thirteen other death sentences were enacted elsewhere. Johannes Tuchel, "Die Verfahren vor dem 'Volksgerichtshof' nach dem 20. Juli 1944," in *Der Umgang des Dritten Reiches mit den Feinden des Regimes*, Königswinterer Tagung February 2009, ed. Manuel Becker and Christoph Studt (Münster: Lit Verlag, 2010), 143–4.

34. "Zum 25. Jahrestag des 20. Juli 1944," June 2, 1969 [originally published in the *Nachrichtenblatt der Baltischen Ritterschaften*], BArch N 362/3, fol. 31.

35. Section on July 20, 1944. My thanks to Winfried Heinemann for drawing my attention to this fact.

36. Hoffmann, *Stauffenberg: A Family History*, 279.

37. Longerich, *Heinrich Himmler*, 697. For the story of the Hofacker family, see Alfred Hofacker, *Cäsar von Hofacker*, 24–7.

38. See Alfred Hofacker, *Cäsar von Hofacker*, chapter 2.

39. Letter from Heinrich Himmler, September 26, 1944, BArch N 362/3, fol. 46.

40. Reitlinger, *The SS*, 275.

41. Longerich, *Heinrich Himmler*, 720.

42. One can deduce this conclusion from Himmler's treatment of remaining Jewish prisoners of concentration camps. By March 1945, as part of his efforts to seek an audience with the Allies, he returned to an old idea of using Jewish prisoners as hostages, and he went so far as to issue an order to camp commandants not to kill any more Jewish prisoners and to reduce mortality among them. Ibid., 724.

43. Winfried Heinemann, "Selbstreinigung der Wehrmacht? Der Ehrenhof des Heeres und seine Tätigkeit," in *Der Umgang des Dritten Reiches*, ed. Becker and Studt, 117–29.

44. Guderian, *Panzer Leader*, 346.

45. Richard J. Evans, *The Third Reich in Power, 1933–1939* (New York: Penguin, 2005), 68.

46. Joseph Goebbels was another. On this, see Alexander Dallin, *German Rule in Russia, 1941–1945: A Study of Occupation Policies*, 2nd rev. ed. (Boulder, CO: Westview Press, 1981), 10.

47. Hitler also suspended court martial proceedings against indigenous populations in occupied territories; "'terrorists and saboteurs' caught in the act were to be 'crushed on the spot.'" Longerich, *Heinrich Himmler*, 705.

48. Tuchel, "Die Verfahren vor dem 'Volksgerichtshof,'" 139; Kershaw, *Hitler: Nemesis*, 692.

49. Quoted in Hoffmann, *Stauffenberg: A Family History*, 279.

50. Adapted from ibid., based on the original German.

51. On this, see Hamerow, *On the Road to the Wolf's Lair*, 382–3.

52. Hoffmann, *History of the German Resistance*, 526.

53. Quoted ibid.

54. As distinct from the Abwehr.

55. Quoted in Hamerow, *On the Road to the Wolf's Lair*, 371.

56. Kershaw, *Hitler: Nemesis*, 692.

57. I owe this turn of phrase to Gerhard L. Weinberg, "The Plot to Kill Hitler," *Michigan Quarterly Review* 10, no. 2 (spring 1971): 129.

58. Quoted in Kershaw, *Hitler: Nemesis*, 688.

59. Unless otherwise specified, details in this paragraph are from a statement by Manfred Rommel on the circumstances surrounding his father's death, published as "Rommels Tod," September 8, 1945, BArch N 117/25, fol. 1–4.
60. Generals Ernst Maisel and Wilhelm Burgdorf. "Rätsel um Rommels Tod," *Die Welt*, November 23, 1948, BArch N 54/70, fol. 11.
61. Quoted in Manfred Rommel, "The Last Days," in *The Rommel Papers*, ed. B. H. Liddell Hart, 15th ed. (repr. Da Capo; New York: Harcourt, Brace, 1953), 502.
62. Unless otherwise specified, details in this paragraph are from Manfred Rommel, "Rommels Tod," BArch N 117/25, fol. 1–4.
63. Manfred Rommel's statement has him meeting his father coming out of his mother's room; according to the account he gave Liddell Hart after the war, he went in after his father. Cf. "Rommels Tod," BArch, N 117/29 fol. 3, and "The Last Days," 503.
64. Rommel, "The Last Days," 503.
65. Rommel, "Rommels Tod," BArch N 117/25, fol. 4.
66. Rommel, "The Last Days," 503.
67. Reuth, *End of a Legend*, 200; Marshall, *Discovering the Rommel Murder*, 1.
68. Heinrich Doose of the Waffen-SS. For his report on the day's events, and the story of what happened to Rommel's marshal baton, see "Niederschrift über die Aussage des Heinrich Doose vor C I C 101," May 30, 1945, BArch N 117/29 fol. 12.
69. Doose, "Niederschrift," 2; Reuth, *End of a Legend*, 201–2, 209.
70. Reserve-Lazarett "Wagnerschule."
71. Young, *Rommel*, 204; Reuth, *End of a Legend*, 182–3.
72. Manfred Rommel, "Rommels Tod," BArch N 117/25, fol. 4.
73. Reuth, *End of a Legend*, 183, 191. Rahtgens was hanged at Plötzensee on August 30, 1944. His name is often given as "Rathgens," but I defer here to the spelling established in the short biography provided by the Gedenkstätte Deutscher Widerstand, available at http://www.gdw-berlin.de/nc/de/vertiefung/biographien/biografie/view-bio/rahtgens/ (accessed July 23, 2013).
74. Reuth, *End of a Legend*, 184.
75. Ibid., 185, 188.
76. Ibid., 192.
77. Ibid., 185.
78. Quotations in this paragraph from Young, *Rommel*, 206.
79. Ibid.
80. Ibid., 207.
81. "Notiz für Herrn Reichsleiter Bormann," September 19, 1944, BArch N 117/29, fol. 2.

82. "Aktenvermerk für Pg. Friedrichs," September 28, 1944, BArch N 117/29, fol. 4.

83. "Notiz für Herrn Reichsleiter Bormann," September 19, 1944, BArch N 117/29, fol. 2.

84. Ibid.

85. Ibid.

86. Walkenhorst, "Kreisleiter Maier, Ulm/Generalfeldmarschall Rommel," October 16, 1944, BArch N 117/29, fol. 8.

87. Hansen, *Fire and Fury*, chapter 16.

88. Walkenhorst, "Kreisleiter Maier, Ulm/Generalfeldmarschall Rommel," October 16, 1944, BArch N 117/29, fol. 8.

89. Ibid.

90. "Notiz für Herrn Reichsleiter Bormann," September 19, 1944, BArch N 117/29, fol. 2.

91. Reuth, *End of a Legend*, 193, citing Bormann "Aktenvermerk für Pg. Friedrichs," September 28, 1944, BArch N 117/29.

92. Reuth, *End of a Legend*, 192–5.

93. On reconstructing the *Ehrenhof* proceedings, see ibid., 193–6. Speidel "all his life firmly denied the accusation that he had implicated Rommel" and protected himself with the assertion that Hofacker later retracted the relevant part of his confession. Ibid., 195. Statements from 1947 by Kirchheim and Guderian, both of whom were present at the Ehrenhof proceedings, state plainly that Speidel claimed to have dutifully passed information from Hofacker on to Rommel, thus implicating the field marshal. Ibid., 194–5. Moreover, Speidel did not contradict Kirchheim's recollections when he wrote them down in 1945. Keitel, who, according to all parties, sought a guilty verdict for Speidel, stated rather surprisingly at his Nuremburg trial that Speidel had not implicated Rommel. Reuth suggests that this was due to Speidel's favourable—and, later, powerful—postwar stature among the Allies. Speidel's share of responsibility for Rommel's fate therefore remains, at best, in question.

94. Bormann, "Aktenvermerk," September 28, 1944, BArch N 117/29, fol. 2.

95. Rommel wrote: "You, *mein Führer*, know how I have exerted my whole strength and capacity, be it in the Western campaign 1940 or in Africa 1941–43 or in Italy 1943 or again in the west 1944. One thought only possesses me constantly, to fight and win for your new Germany." Quoted in Liddell Hart, *The Rommel Papers*, 501.

96. Liddell Hart, *Rommel Papers*, 502.

97. Reuth, *End of a Legend*, 196–8.

98. Ibid., 198.

99. Private papers of General William J. Donovan, Cornell University, Nuremberg Trials Collection, "Office of the US Chief of Counsel for the Prosecution of

Axis Criminality. Interrogation Division Summary. Interrogation of Wilhelm Keitel by Colonel J H Amen," September 28, 1945.

100. Circular from Ribbentrop to all Stations, July 29, 1944 (drafted July 25), UKNA, H1/3150: "Through the elimination from the Wehrmacht of all not absolutely reliable and determined men, a process which is now in course, the will to victory of soldiers and leaders will take on quite a different aspect. . . . [T]here cannot be the slightest doubt that certain trends in the Higher Command, which became apparent now and again in difficult situations in the past and which undoubtedly contributed to our set-backs, will now finally and completely disappear. In this way the German armed forces will regain to the full their historic ability to resist and their power of attack which, in the past and indeed to the present day, enabled our troops to accomplish mighty deeds and which was only temporarily affected by the refusal of a military leadership to face up to a critical situation. They will now be able to crown their achievements with success and will ensure that final victory is ours."

101. Ian Kershaw, "'Working Towards the Führer': Reflections on the Nature of the Hitler Dictatorship," in *The Third Reich: The Essential Readings*, ed. Christian Leitz (London: Blackwell, 1999), 245. Hans Mommsen developed the thesis on polycratic structures in the Third Reich. See Mommsen, "Die Auflösung des Dritten Reiches," in *Zur Geschichte Deutschlands im 20. Jahrhundert: Demokratie, Diktatur, Widerstand* (Munich: Deutsche Verlags-Anstalt, 2010), 194–213.

102. Circular from Ribbentrop to all Stations, July 29, 1944, UKNA, H1/3150.

CHAPTER 7: DID A PRUSSIAN SAVE PARIS?

1. "Karl" referred to anti-concrete weapons first produced in 1939. There were two versions: one with a 60 cm Mörser Gerät 40 (which mounted a 60 cm barrel), the other with a 54 cm Mörser Gerät 041. The former had a range of 4500 metres, the latter of 6240 metres, and both could penetrate between 2.5 and 3.5 metres of concrete. The Karls were used successfully during the siege of Sevastopol (at which Choltitz was present) and, during the Warsaw uprising, to crush Polish underground fighters and to demolish the centre of Warsaw. Chris Bishop, ed., *The Encyclopedia of Weapons of World War II*, rev. ed. (New York: MetroBooks, 2002), 114–5.

2. On this, see Klaus-Jürgen Müller, "Die Befreiung von Paris und die deutsche Führung an der Westfront," in *Kriegsjahr 1944: im Großen und im Kleinen*, ed. Michael Salewski and Guntram Schulze-Wegener (Stuttgart: Franz Steiner, 1995), 43–60.

3. For the most recent statement of this view, see Cobb, *Eleven Days in August*, 364–6.

4. UKNA, WO 208/4363, GRGG 189, September 8–9, 1944, 2. Emphasis in the original.

5. "Kommentar von Timo von Choltitz, Sohn von General Dietrich von Choltitz," available at http://www.choltitz.de/Kommentar.html. Choltitz refers to a "photocopied summary." It is a summary, but it is an original typescript.

6. UKNA, WO 208/4364, GRGG 204, September 27–29, 1944. Emphasis in the original. Commanders Broich, Rassene, Wahle, and Reimann generally agreed that a Jewish brigade was intolerable, while Oberst Reimann added that "the business with the Jews in Germany was quite right, only it should have been done quietly." Only Generalleutnant Schlieben (who defended and destroyed Cherbourg) declined to join the anti-Semitic and self-pitying rants: "Well, we've known for a long time that the enemy won't present us with any bouquets."

7. Hitler seems not, at this point, to have given the order to destroy Paris, as is often claimed. According to Choltitz, it only arrived once he was in Paris. UKNA, WO 208/4363, GRGG 217, 3.

8. Hans Speidel, "Gedanken des Oberbefehlshabers," March 31, 1947, BArch RH 20-7-149.

9. Thornton, *Liberation of Paris*, 121.

10. There is also some evidence that Choltitz disliked Paris and the French. See Adrien Dansette, *Histoire de la libération de Paris* (Paris: Perrin, 1994), 117. This evidence, however, is based on interrogations by the Americans, which occurred shortly after Choltitz surrendered, saw one of his officers gunned down in the streets, and was kicked and spat on by civilians. Those statements should be interpreted in that context.

11. "General von Choltitz" (Report of a British officer), August 31–September 3, 1944, UKNA, WO 208/4363, GRGG 185, 15.

12. Arnim, *Als Brandenburg noch die Mark hieß*, 231.

13. Steven J. Zaloga, *Liberation of Paris 1944: Patton's Race for the Seine* (Oxford: Osprey Publishing, 2008), 19; Samuel W. Mitcham, *Retreat to the Reich: The German Defeat in France, 1944* (Mechanicsburg, PA: Stackpole Books, 2000), 185.

14. Thornton, *Liberation of Paris*, 121.

15. Details in this paragraph based on Larry Collins and Dominique Lapierre, *Is Paris Burning?* (New York: Simon and Shuster, 1965), 48.

16. Fritz-Dietlof Graf von der Schulenburg was executed on August 10, 1944, Ulrich Wilhelm Graf Schwerin von Schwanenfeld and Heinrich Graf von Lehndorff-Steinort in September.

17. Dankwart Graf von Arnim, MdC TE 819, 240.

18. Ibid.

19. Ibid.

20. See Choltitz's comments on Stauffenberg while in British captivity in Neitzel, *Tapping Hitler's Generals*, 257–67 (Documents 153, 154, 158, and 161). In these last two documents, Choltitz states that Stauffenberg was the *"ideal* of the coming German generation" and that Hitler should "be killed and the whole world should be told about it; he should be photographed pleading for his life . . . He should be made to wear just a pullover [author's note: that is, stripped of all political and military garb and regalia], and to stand there as a criminal, with his hair cropped and so on." Emphasis in the original. Choltitz went so far as to claim that Stauffenberg approached him with the offer of a post, but I have seen no evidence confirming such a meeting. UNKA, WO 208/4363, GRGG 181 (c), August 25, 1944, 7. This report was made the day of Choltitz's arrest, when he was in an agitated and likely fearful state.

21. Ulrike Pretorius, "Der Retter von Paris hatte manchen Helfer: NRZ Gespräch mit Dankwart von Arnim," *Neue Rhein-Zeitung*, November 12, 1966.

22. "Stammtafel: Sicherungs-Regiment 1," July 1944, BArch RH 26/325, fol. 1; Zaloga, *Liberation of Paris*, 26; Müller, "Die Befreiung von Paris," 43.

23. Ernst von Krause, "Military Commander France (July–September 1944)," n.d., USAMHI, B 612, 2; Zaloga, *Liberation of Paris*, 26.

24. Müller, "Die Befreiung von Paris," 43.

25. Dansette, *Histoire de la libération de Paris*, 119.

26. Ibid.

27. Müller, "Die Befreiung von Paris," 43.

28. Zaloga, *Liberation of Paris*, 1944, 27; Müller, "Die Befreiung von Paris," 46.

29. USAMHI, B 015, Freiherr von Boineburg, "Organization for the Defence of Greater Paris," May 1945, 6.

30. Dansette, *Histoire de la libération de Paris*, 119. Zaloga, *Liberation of Paris*, 27, gives a higher figure of 20,000.

31. Thornton, *Liberation of Paris*, 126; Müller, "Die Befreiung von Paris," 44.

32. Thornton, *Liberation of Paris*, 127.

33. Ibid.

34. Müller, "Die Befreiung von Paris," 44.

35. Robert Aron, *Histoire de la Libération de la France* (Paris: Fayard, 1959), vol. 2, 11–2.

36. Roger Bourderon, *Rol-Tanguy* (Paris: Tallandier, 2004), chapters 5–7; Thornton, *Liberation of Paris*, 120. Bourderon published works with Rol-Tanguy, and his book should be read as an official biography. See, for example, Colonel Rol-Tanguy and Roger Bourderon, *Libération de Paris: les cents documents* (Paris: Hachette, 1994).

37. Henri Rol-Tanguy obituary, *Daily Telegraph*, September 28, 2002.

38. Ibid.

39. Dansette, *Histoire de la libération de Paris*, 148.

40. See Thornton, *Liberation of Paris*, 136.

41. Jackson, *France: The Dark Years*, 543.

42. Cobb, *Eleven Days in August*, 13; François Marcot, *Dictionnaire historique de la résistance: résistance intérieure et France libre* (Paris: Éditions Robert Laffont, 2006), 386.

43. Jackson, *France: The Dark Years*, 521.

44. Ibid., 562.

45. Aron, *Histoire de la Libération de la France*, vol. 2, 22.

46. Quoted in Larkin, *France since the Popular Front*, 109.

47. Marcot, *Dictionnaire historique de la résistance*, 440–1. The Parisian Liberation Committee (CPL) was set up in 1943. Of the eighteen organizations that joined the CPL, seven were Communist. Jackson, *France: The Dark Years*, 519.

48. Jackson, *France: The Dark Years*, 521.

49. Cobb, *Eleven Days in August*, 35.

50. Ibid., 36.

51. Thornton, *Liberation of Paris*, 128.

52. "Rôle de la Police Parisienne dans les Combats de la Libération du 19 au 26 Août 1944," n.d., Archives de la Préfecture de Police de Paris (APPP).

53. Le Commandant de la Région de Paris des Forces Françaises de L'Interieur, "Appel.," Archives de Paris, D 38 Z/4.

CHAPTER 8: TO DESTROY THE CITY OF LIGHT

1. West Europe, August 15, 1944, UKNA, HW/1 3194, TOO 0930.

2. Zaloga, *Liberation of Paris*, 51, 54.

3. Dansette, *Histoire de la libération de Paris*, 121.

4. Zaloga, *Liberation of Paris*, 54.

5. Thornton, *Liberation of Paris*, 132–3.

6. Ibid.

7. Dansette, *Histoire de la libération de Paris*, 121.

8. Implied ibid.

9. Nordling, *Sauver Paris*, 153–4.

10. Michael Neiberg, *The Blood of Free Men: The Liberation of Paris, 1944* (New York: Basic Books, 2012), 159. In another version, Bender might have been a double agent. See Fabrice Virgili, introduction to *Sauver Paris*, 24–5.

11. Dansette, *Histoire de la libération de Paris*, 130; Nordling, *Sauver Paris*, 154–5.

12. Nordling, *Sauver Paris*, 155.

13. Dansette, *Histoire de la libération de Paris*, 129–30; Nordling, *Sauver Paris*, 157–8.

14. Nordling, *Sauver Paris*, 156.

15. Quotation from ibid.
16. Nordling, *Sauver Paris*, 156.
17. Ibid.
18. Ibid., 157.
19. Ibid.
20. Nordling notes in his memoirs that this pointless negotiation was done to save some face for the Germans by creating the illusion that they had received a better deal than the French. Ibid.
21. "Contrat passé entre Nordling, Consul de Suède, et l'Administration allemande de l'hôtel Majestic," reproduced in Dansette, *Histoire de la libération de Paris*, Annex XIV.
22. Dansette, *Histoire de la libération de Paris*, 131. Matters then took a turn for the worse. The Germans had already packed their official seal, and they refused to regard the contract as valid without it. Nordling, Huhm, and Bender furiously tore open boxes and packages until they found one. Nordling, *Sauver Paris*, 158.
23. Dansette, *Histoire de la libération de Paris*, 132.
24. Ibid., 131; Nordling, *Sauver Paris*, 161.
25. Nordling, *Sauver Paris*, 161–2.
26. Ibid., 168; Dansette, *Histoire de la libération de Paris*, 131.
27. Nordling, *Sauver Paris*, 168. In Dansette's account, Heigen threatened to form a company and take the camp by force. *Histoire de la libération de Paris*, 132.
28. Nordling, *Sauver Paris*, 169.
29. Dansette, *Histoire de la libération de Paris*, 131.
30. Nordling, *Sauver Paris*, 159 and 207–8. Also see the introduction by Fabrice Virgili, ibid., 26–7.
31. Ibid., 208.
32. Dansette, *Histoire de la libération de Paris*, 143.
33. Quoted ibid., 144.
34. Quoted ibid.
35. Thornton, *Liberation of Paris*, 136.
36. Ibid.
37. "Rôle de la Police Parisienne dans les Combats de la Libération du 19 au 26 Août 1944," n.d., APPP.
38. Dansette, *Histoire de la libération de Paris*, 145.
39. UKNA, HW 1/3179, SX 943, August 18, 1944.
40. Dansette, *Histoire de la libération de Paris*, 124–5; Cobb, *Eleven Days in August*, 135.
41. Dansette, *Histoire de la libération de Paris*, 124.
42. Ibid., 125.

43. Müller, "Die Befreiung von Paris," 44.

44. Ibid.

45. "Rôle de la Police Parisienne dans les Combats de la Libération du 19 au 26 Août 1944," n.d., APPP.

46. Thornton, *Liberation of Paris*, 138.

47. "Rôle de la Police Parisienne dans les Combats de la Libération du 19 au 26 Août 1944," n.d., APPP; "Historique: Résumé des journées glorieuses d'insurrection à la préfecture de police (19 au 26 Août 1944)," n.d., APPP.

48. Thornton, *Liberation of Paris*, 139.

49. "Rôle de la Police Parisienne dans les Combats de la Libération du 19 au 26 Août 1944," n.d., APPP. There is some debate about whether the tricolour went up above the Hôtel de Ville or the Prefecture first.

50. "Libération de Paris: Historique," April 14, 1946, APPP.

51. "Résumé des journées glorieuses d'insurrection à la préfecture de police (19 au 26 Août 1944)," n.d., APPP. N.B.: this is different document to the one of the same title preceded by "Historique."

52. "Historique: Résumé des journées glorieuses d'insurrection à la préfecture de police (19 au 26 Août 1944)," n.d., APPP.

53. Francis Crémieux, *La vérité sur la libération de Paris* (Paris: Messidor, 1984), testimony of Rol-Tanguy, 37.

54. "Historique: Rôle de la Police Parisienne dans les Combats de la Libération du 19 au 26 Août 1944," n.d., APPP.

55. Ibid.

56. Thornton, *Liberation of Paris*, 139; "Allocution prononcée par Monsieur Pisani," n.d., APPP.

57. Dansette, *Histoire de la libération de Paris*, 151. Bussière was condemned in July 1946 to a lifetime of forced labour. He was released in 1951 and died two months later. Nordling, *Sauver Paris*, 172.

58. Antony Beevor, *D-Day: The Battle for Normandy* (London: Viking, 2009), 486. According to Cobb, drawing on French sources, Choltitz learned of the seizure of the Prefecture *before* he sent Arnim out and ordered the liquidation "of all important points of resistance." *Eleven Days in August*, 148. Arnim, who was there, maintains that neither Choltitz nor anyone else under his command knew what was happening on the nineteenth. *Als Brandenburg noch die Mark hieß*, 243.

59. Remaining details in the paragraph from Arnim, *Als Brandenburg noch die Mark hieß*, 243–4.

60. Thornton, *Liberation of Paris*, 139.

61. Ibid.

62. Beevor, *D-Day*, 486.

63. "Résumé des journées glorieuses d'insurrection à la préfecture de police (19 au 26 Août 1944)," n.d., APPP.

64. Ibid.; Thornton, *Liberation of Paris*, 139.

65. "Résumé des journées glorieuses d'insurrection à la préfecture de police (19 au 26 Août 1944)," n.d., APPP.

66. Dansette, *Histoire de la libération de Paris*, 154.

67. Thornton, *Liberation of Paris*, 140.

68. Ibid.

69. "Résumé des journées glorieuses d'insurrection à la préfecture de police (19 au 26 Août 1944)," n.d., APPP.

70. Dietrich von Choltitz, *Soldat unter Soldaten* (Konstanz: Europa Verlag, 1951), 254; Arnim, *Als Brandenburg noch die Mark hieß*, 245. Arnim corroborates the story, though a few details differ: he mentions two SS men rather than three, and he quotes Choltitz slightly differently.

71. UKNA, WO 208/4363, GRG 184, August 30, 1944, 3.

72. Ibid.; Arnim, *Als Brandenburg noch die Mark hieß*, 245.

73. UKNA, WO 208/4363, GRG 184, August 30, 1944, 3.

74. Ibid.

75. Ibid.; Arnim, *Als Brandenburg noch die Mark hieß*, 245.

76. Antony Beevor and Artemis Cooper, *Paris after the Liberation 1944–1949*, rev. ed. (New York: Penguin, 2004), 35.

77. Müller, "Die Befreiung von Paris," 44–5.

78. See Günther Blumentritt, "Aufruf an die Pariser Bevölkerung," August 20, 1944, BArch RH 19 IV/141, fol. 94.

79. Zaloga, *Liberation of Paris*, 66–7.

80. Dansette, *Histoire de la libération de Paris*, 174–5. For a different wording but the same effect, see Nordling, *Sauver Paris*, 176–7.

81. Nordling, *Sauver Paris*, 178–9. For a different wording, see Dansette, *Histoire de la libération de Paris*, 174–5.

82. Dansette, *Histoire de la libération de Paris*, 175.

83. Ibid.; Nordling, *Sauver Paris*, 177.

84. Nordling, *Sauver Paris*, 179.

85. Ibid.

86. Dansette, *Histoire de la libération de Paris*, 177; Nordling, *Sauver Paris*, 181.

87. Nordling, *Sauver Paris*, 180.

88. Ibid., 182.

89. Cobb, *Eleven Days in August*, 162.

90. It worked: Pisani later reported that the Germans were "impressed by the battle we led . . . [and] recognized our authority over everything we occupied." "Allocution prononcée par Monsieur Pisani," n.d., APPP.

91. "Rôle de la Police Parisienne dans les Combats de la Libération du 19 au 26 Août 1944," n.d., APPP; "Allocution prononcée par Monsieur Pisani," n.d., APPP.

92. "Rôle de la Police Parisienne dans les Combats de la Libération du 19 au 26 Août 1944," n.d., APPP.

93. Zaloga, *Liberation of Paris*, 62.

94. "Rôle de la Police Parisienne dans les Combats de la Libération du 19 au 26 Août 1944," n.d., APPP. The document puts the figure at 3,000. It is unclear where they were coming from, but multiple sources confirm large numbers of SS troops in the capital.

95. Dansette, *Histoire de la libération de Paris*, 179; Nordling, *Sauver Paris*, 189.

96. Nordling, *Sauver Paris*, 190 and 192; Crémieux, *La vérité sur la libération de Paris*, testimony by Hamon, 69–70.

97. "Historique: Résumé des journées glorieuses d'insurrection à la préfecture de police (19 au 26 Août 1944)," n.d., APPP.

98. Beevor, *D-Day*, 487.

99. "Résumé des journées glorieuses d'insurrection à la préfecture de police (19 au 26 Août 1944)," n.d., APPP. There are great inconsistencies in times recorded for various actions during the last weeks of August. In the case of conflict, I report the time found in the primary documents. For Hamon's account of events, see Crémieux, *La vérité sur la libération de Paris*, testimony by Hamon, 70–1.

100. Zaloga, *Liberation of Paris*, 54.

101. Quoted in Thornton, *Liberation of Paris*, 146.

102. Last two sentences from Dansette, *Histoire de la libération de Paris*, 184.

103. Vincent Wright, *The Government and Politics of France* (London: Hutchinson, 1978), 209, 214–5.

104. Dansette, *Histoire de la libération de Paris*, 216–8.

105. "Résumé des journées glorieuses d'insurrection à la préfecture de police (19 au 26 Août 1944)," n.d., 72, APPP.

106. Ibid. These recorded statistics of mortality come from French sources. They are a good guide, but they need to be treated with caution: there is generally a tendency to exaggerate the casualties one inflicts.

107. Thornton, *Liberation of Paris*, 148.

108. Story from Dansette, *Histoire de la libération de Paris*, 232. The source is not specific about the type of soldiers they were, but the method suggests they were from the SS.

109. Story from Thornton, *Liberation of Paris*, 147–8.

110. Ibid., 149.

111. "Résumé des journées glorieuses d'insurrection à la préfecture de police (19 au 26 Août 1944)," n.d., 73, APPP.

112. Nordling, *Sauver Paris*, 187.

113. Madeleine Betts-Quintaine, "Le Journal de Guerre d'une jeune Normande," June 6–August 29, 1944, MdC TE 361, 73; Jackson, *France: The Dark Years*, 563; Nordling, *Sauver Paris*, 194.

114. André Gisoni, "Avis à la Population," n.d., Archives de Paris.

115. Dansette, *Histoire de la libération de Paris*, 193.

116. Details in this paragraph from *Libération de Paris: Historique. Main Courante des Journées d'insurrection (20 au 26 Août 1944)*, "Journée du 20 Août, 1944," 2, APPP.

117. Particularly around the Île de la Cité. Betts-Quintaine, "Journal de Guerre," MdC TE 361, 72.

118. See Thornton, *Liberation of Paris*, 140.

119. Ibid.

120. Betts-Quintaine, "Journal de Guerre," MdC TE 361, 76.

121. Transmit from Group Captain Jones to Group Captain Winterbotham, August 25, 1944, UKNA, HW 1/3187. The same day, Philippe Pétain drafted his last message to the French, claiming he had "always sought to serve the best interests of France loyally and without compromise" and that he "had sought to protect [the French] from the worst." The Germans arrested him that day; Pétain instructed his subordinates to distribute the message as widely as possible. "Ultime message du Maréchal de France, Chef de l'État, aux Français," August 20, 1944, Archives de Paris, D 38/Z.

CHAPTER 9: PARIS IN REVOLT

1. Barricades also sprang up all over southern France in reaction to the Allied landings at Normandy. See Max Hastings, *Das Reich: Resistance and the March of the 2nd SS Panzer Division through France, June 1944* (London: Michael Joseph, 1981), 75.

2. Dansette, *Histoire de la libération de Paris*, 236.

3. Ibid.

4. "Rôle de la Police Parisienne dans les Combats de la Libération du 19 au 26 Août 1944," n.d., 74, APPP.

5. Dansette, *Histoire de la libération de Paris*, 236.

6. "Rôle de la Police Parisienne dans les Combats de la Libération du 19 au 26 Août 1944," n.d., 74, APPP.

7. The story about the passageway was related to me by a longtime official at the hotel who had met Choltitz when he and his men came back for a reunion banquet. The Hotel Continental is now the Westin Paris–Vendôme. On the prisoners: the French believed that the police officers would be shot. *Libération de Paris: Historique. Main Courante des Journées d'insurrection (20 au 26 Août 1944)*, "Journée du 21 Août, 1944," 5, APPP.

8. "Rôle de la Police Parisienne dans les Combats de la Libération du 19 au 26 Août 1944," n.d., 74, APPP. Later in the day, at 12:25, a less robust approach bore results: five French prisoners at the Hotel were traded for four Germans.

9. There is some debate about the number of tanks at Choltitz's disposal. Rumours at the time suggested as many as two hundred, but this was clearly too high a figure. Early postwar accounts suggested fifty. More recent research put the figure at twenty, but this is perhaps too low. Archival French sources from the time recorded fifteen tanks at different locations at 14:00 on August 21, 1944. See *Libération de Paris: Historique. Main Courante des Journées d'insurrection (20 au 26 Août 1944)*, "Journée du 20 Août, 1944," 8, APPP. It is hard to imagine that Choltitz had only five more tanks in the entire city of Paris. Another eyewitness noted a strong presence of German tanks around Place de la Concorde and the Jardin des Tuileries on August 20. Betts-Quintaine, "Journal de Guerre," MdC TE 361, 73.

10. *Libération de Paris: Historique. Main Courante des Journées d'insurrection (20 au 26 Août 1944)*, "Journée du 21 Août, 1944," 7, APPP. According to this source, the tanks fired "without provocation" after "being stopped." Presumably the Germans viewed being stopped as the provocation.

11. Ibid.

12. Ibid., 8.

13. Ibid., 10.

14. For the attack on the Prefecture, see "Résumé des journées glorieuses d'insurrection à la préfecture de police (19 au 26 Août 1944)," n.d., 74, APPP.

15. Ibid., 75.

16. *Libération de Paris: Historique. Main Courante des Journées d'insurrection (20 au 26 Août 1944)*, "Journée du 22 Août, 1944," 15, APPP.

17. Ibid., 18.

18. "Résumé des journées glorieuses d'insurrection à la préfecture de police (19 au 26 Août 1944)," n.d., 77, APPP.

19. Ibid., 75.

20. *Libération de Paris: Historique. Main Courante des Journées d'insurrection (20 au 26 Août 1944)*, "Journée du 21 Août, 1944," 9, APPP.

21. Besprechungen, Erwägungen, Entschlüsse, August 21, 1944, BArch RH 19 IX/18, fol. 66–7; Müller, "Die Befreiung von Paris," 46.

22. Choltitz, *Soldat unter Soldaten*, 256; Müller, "Die Befreiung von Paris," 47. The order was issued on August 21 but was apparently received by Choltitz the next day. According to Hans Speidel, the order ended with "even if residential areas and artistic monuments are destroyed thereby." Hans Speidel, *Invasion 1944: Rommel and the Normandy Campaign* (repr. Westport, CT: Greenwood Press, 1971; Chicago: Henry Regnery Co., 1950), 143.

23. Besprechungen, Erwägungen, Entschlüsse, August 21, 1944, BArch RH 19 IX/18, fol. 66, 68.
24. Ibid., fol. 72–3.
25. Dansette, *Histoire de la libération de Paris*, 195.
26. *Libération de Paris: Historique. Main Courante des Journées d'insurrection (20 au 26 Août 1944)*, "Journée du 21 Août, 1944," 7, APPP.
27. Ibid., 11.
28. *Les fusillées de la Cascade du bois de Boulogne 16 août 1944* (Paris: Marie de Paris, 2004).
29. *Libération de Paris: Historique. Main Courante des Journées d'insurrection (20 au 26 Août 1944)*, "Journée du 21 Août, 1944," 27, APPP.
30. Story of the SS atrocities from Dansette, *Histoire de la libération de Paris*, 242.
31. Ibid.
32. Nordling, *Sauver Paris*, 218.
33. On the avenue de Selves. Dansette, *Histoire de la libération de Paris*, 243.
34. One is on display at the Militärhistorisches Museum der Bundeswehr, Dresden.
35. The police reported the Grand Palais on fire at 10:45. *Libération de Paris: Historique. Main Courante des Journées d'insurrection (20 au 26 Août 1944)*, "Journée du 23 Août, 1944," 24, APPP.
36. Ibid.
37. Cobb, *Eleven Days in August*, 230–1 on the animals; Neiberg, *Blood of Free Men*, 197 on the prostitutes.
38. *Libération de Paris: Historique. Main Courante des Journées d'insurrection (20 au 26 Août 1944)*, "Journée du 23 Août, 1944," 24, APPP.
39. Cobb, *Eleven Days in August*, 231.
40. *Libération de Paris: Historique. Main Courante des Journées d'insurrection (20 au 26 Août 1944)*, "Journée du 23 Août, 1944," 24, APPP; Dansette, *Histoire de la libération de Paris*, 243.
41. Ibid. On the baron, see Collins and Lapierre, *Is Paris Burning?*, 202–3 and Neiberg, *Blood of Free Men*, 197.
42. Nordling, *Sauver Paris*, 218.
43. Transmit from Group Captain Jones to Group Captain Winterbotham, August 25, 1944, UKNA, HW 1/3187. This communication is an Ultra intercept.
44. Details in this paragraph from Zaloga, *Liberation of Paris*, 66–7. The main source for this story is Choltitz himself, but primary sources confirm Luftwaffe activity west of Paris on August 24, 1944, suggesting that a bombing raid would have been possible. "Summary: GAF Report," August 24, 1944, UKNA, HW 1/3187. And, indeed, after the German surrender, Deßloch ordered a bombing raid on the northern suburbs of Paris that caused substantial damage and killed two hundred people. A similar raid on the centre of Paris would have caused

great damage to the city's historic core. For the details of the late raid, see Cobb, *Eleven Days in August*, 334–6.

45. Besprechungen, Erwägungen, Entschlüsse, August 13, 1944, BArch RH 19 IX/87, fol. 226.
46. Nordling, *Sauver Paris*, 199.
47. Besprechungen, Erwägungen, Entschlüsse, August 16, 1944, BArch RH 19 IX/18, fol. 11.
48. BArch RH 19 IX/88, fol. 90. Quoted in Müller, "Die Befreiung von Paris," 48.
49. Zaloga, *Liberation of Paris*, 65.
50. Besprechungen, Erwägungen, Entschlüsse, August 23, 1944, BArch RH 19 IX/18, fol. 95.
51. Müller, "Die Befreiung von Paris," 49.
52. Quotations in this paragraph from Wehrm.Bef. Paris um 22.15 Uhr; Lageorientierung an HGR B, BArch RH 19 IX/9, fol. 106, quoted ibid., 49.
53. Ibid.
54. Nordling, *Sauver Paris*, 209.
55. UKNA, WO 208/4364, GRGG 210, October 11–12, 1944, 6 (Choltitz's testimony to a British interrogator).
56. Information and quotations in this paragraph from Dansette, *Histoire de la libération de Paris*, 260–1.
57. Ibid., 260.
58. Quoted ibid., 261.
59. Quoted ibid. Choltitz claimed after the war to have known nothing about the meetings. Ibid., 260.
60. Leclerc was a *nom de guerre*. His real name was Philippe de Hauteclocque.

CHAPTER 10: PARIS LIBERATED, PARIS SPARED

1. Details from Dansette, *Histoire de la libération de Paris*, 274–5.
2. Quoted ibid., 284.
3. Zaloga, *Liberation of Paris*, 63; Beevor, *D-Day*, 493–4.
4. Nordling, *Sauver Paris*, 221.
5. Ibid., 222.
6. Ibid.
7. Beevor, *D-Day*, 494; Nordling, *Sauver Paris*, 224–5.
8. Beevor, *D-Day*, 494. For the details on Gallois, see Cobb, *Eleven Days in August*, 205–6 and 221–4. It appears that both men were sent by Patton to appeal to Bradley.
9. Beevor, *D-Day*, 494.
10. Ibid.
11. Ibid., 494–5.

12. Rev. Père Roger Fouquer [Second Division's chaplain], "Journal de Marche," n.d., MdC TE 825, 33–4.

13. As suggested by Zaloga, *Liberation of Paris*, 67–8.

14. Fouquer, "Journal de Marche," n.d., MdC TE 825, 32.

15. Beevor, *D-Day*, 499–500; Zaloga, *Liberation of Paris*, 68.

16. Zaloga, *Liberation of Paris*, 68–9.

17. Müller, "Die Befreiung von Paris," 54.

18. Beevor, *D-Day*, 501.

19. Fouquer, "Journal de Marche," n.d., MdC TE 825, 34.

20. "Summary," August 26, 1944, UKNA, HW 1/3188.

21. Quoted in Müller, "Die Befreiung von Paris," 54.

22. Ibid.

23. Beevor, *D-Day*, 501.

24. Fouquer, "Journal de Marche," n.d., MdC TE 825, 37.

25. Ibid., 28.

26. Quoted in Beevor, *D-Day*, 502.

27. Ibid.

28. Bourderon, *Rol-Tanguy*, 446, and USAMHI, B 015, Boineburg, "Organization for the Defence of Greater Paris," May 1945, 8.

29. Marc de Possesse, "Souvenirs d'un ancien de la France Libre de la 9ème C.ie la 'NUEVE,'" MdC TE 361, 72–3.

30. Ibid., 73–4.

31. Ibid.

32. Zaloga, *Liberation of Paris*, 68.

33. Beevor, *D-Day*, 503.

34. Possesse, "Souvenirs d'un ancien de la France Libre," 73.

35. Beevor, *D-Day*, 503.

36. Betts-Quintaine, "Journal de Guerre," MdC TE 361, 78.

37. Dankwart Graf von Arnim, MdC TE 819, 261.

38. Zaloga, *Liberation of Paris*, 72.

39. Müller, "Die Befreiung von Paris," 55.

40. West Europe, August 25, 1944, UKNA, HW 1/3189, TOO 0800.

41. Ibid.

42. It is doubtful that Model thought much of it. He had by this point given up on Paris and was rebuilding the front north of the French capital. Müller, "Die Befreiung von Paris," 53.

43. Dankwart Graf von Arnim, MdC TE 819, 262.

44. Müller, "Die Befreiung von Paris," 55.

45. Beevor, *D-Day*, 504–5.

46. Fouquer, "Journal de Marche," n.d., MdC TE 825, 37.

47. Ibid.

48. Beevor, *D-Day*, 507.

49. Ibid.

50. Fouquer, "Journal de Marche," n.d., MdC TE 825, 37.

51. Or, "Here they come."

52. Fouquer, "Journal de Marche," n.d., MdC TE 825, 40.

53. Zaloga, *Liberation of Paris*, 73.

54. Mitcham, *Retreat to the Reich*, 195. According to Zaloga, he replied, "Of course I speak German!" Zaloga, *Liberation of Paris*, 73.

55. Fouquer, "Journal de Marche," n.d., MdC TE 825, 40; Arnim, *Als Brandenburg noch die Mark hieß*, 253–4.

56. Arnim, *Als Brandenburg noch die Mark hieß*, 254; Cobb, *Eleven Days in August*, 307.

57. Arnim, *Als Brandenburg noch die Mark hieß*, 254.

58. Photo in Collins and Lapierre, *Is Paris Burning?*

59. Conventions de reddition conclués entre le Colonel Rol, General de Division Leclec, et le General von Choltitz, August 25, 1944, Archives de Paris, D 38/Z.

60. Müller, "Die Befreiung von Paris," 56.

61. Betts-Quintaine, "Journal de Guerre," MdC TE 361, 79.

62. Ibid.

63. Fouquer, "Journal de Marche," n.d., MdC TE 825, 38.

64. Dansette, *Histoire de la libération de Paris*, 120. The hypothesis on Kluge is mine.

65. Ibid., 119. These were possibly the explosives that Boineburg and Choltitz refused to deploy, but I have not confirmed this possibility.

66. Longerich, *Heinrich Himmler*, 705.

67. For the most recent effort, see Cobb, *Eleven Days in August*.

68. On this, see Nordling, *Sauver Paris*, 230–1.

69. Dankwart Graf von Arnim, MdC TE 819, 240.

70. UKNA, WO 208/4364, GRGG 215, 4–5, October 24–26, 1944, Appendix, 3–4.

71. In another passage, Choltitz expresses regret over what he believed was the coming destruction of "Fortress Utrecht" and Holland in general. UKNA, WO 28/4364, GRGG 218, November 1–4, 1944.

CHAPTER 11: NORMANDY SOUTH

1. Mitcham, *Retreat to the Reich*, 9. Blaskowitz was not appointed to a Heeresgruppe—translated in this book as "army group"—but, rather, an Armeegruppe, which constituted an "ad hoc headquarters" corresponding to a force between army (Armee) and army group (Heeresgruppe) size. The appointment of

Blaskowitz to an army group command would have required his being named a field marshal, which Hitler would not countenance given Blaskowitz's open opposition to eastern front atrocities.

2. General der Infanterie Ferdinand Neuling's LXII Army Corps controlled the area from the Italian border to Toulon. This corps included two infantry divisions. Generalmajor Otto Fretter-Pico's 148th Infantry (Reserve) Division guarded a line running from the Italian border to Antheor Cove and including the small ports at Cannes and Nice. Generalleutnant Johannes Baeßler's 242nd Division covered the area from Antheor Cove to Toulon, including the important harbour in the latter city. General der Infanterie Baptist Knieß's LXXXV Army Corps covered the area between Toulon and Marseille. It also had two divisions: the 338th and the 244th. The 338th Division under (German) Generalleutnant René de l'Homme de Courbière had redeployed one regiment, and the rest were pulled back to Arles in anticipation of a transfer north. The southern coast was thus left to Generalleutnant Hans Schäfer's 244th Division, tasked with defending both the coast and the great port at Marseille. Finally, General der Flieger Erich Petersen's IV Luftwaffe Field Corps held the area between the Rhône delta and the Spanish border. This corps included the 198th and 716th Infantry Divisions, and the weak 189th Reserve Division. Jeffrey J. Clarke and Robert Ross Smith, *Riviera to the Rhine* (Washington, DC: Center for Military History, United States Army, 1993), 65–6.

3. "Order of the Battle Notes," G-2 Periodic Report N. 274, March 1945, National Archives at College Park, MD (NACP), RG 407, 101-2.1.

4. Walter Botsch, "Nineteenth Army (June 43–15 Sep 44)," US Army Military History Institute, Carlisle, PA (USAMHI), B 515, 11.

5. Ibid. (on the duds); Weigley, *Eisenhower's Lieutenants*, 225 (on the landmines).

6. Botsch, "Nineteenth Army," USAMHI, B 515, 14.

7. Ibid., 6–7; Johannes Blaskowitz, "German (OB West) Estimate of the Situation Prior to Allied Invasion of Southern France," 1947, USAMHI, B 421, 3. There is some disagreement on this point. See Clarke and Smith, *Riviera to the Rhine*, 67.

8. H. Paul Jeffers, *Command of Honor: General Lucian Truscott's Path to Victory in World War II* (New York: NAL Caliber, 2008), v.

9. "XII Air Force Service Command in Operation 'Dragoon,'" May 15, 1945, USAMHI, D 790, 22.

10. *The Invasion of the South of France: Operation "Dragoon", 15th August, 1944* (London: HMSO, 1994), 11.

11. "Directive: Commanding Officer, 1st Special Service Force," July 18, 1944, USAMHI, D 762.P7 o 37.

12. Operation Dragoon, "Popping the Cork," 1984, USAMHI, William B. Breuer Papers (hereafter, Breuer Papers).
13. Details in this paragraph from Willard Sterne Randall, "The Other D-Day," *Quarterly Journal of Military History* 6, no. 3 (spring 1994): 75.
14. Joseph D. Antrim diary, August 15, 1944, USAMHI, Breuer Papers, Operation Dragoon.
15. Sterne Randall, "The Other D-Day," 75; letter from Major "Pappy" Hermann, Battalion S-3, USAMHI, Breuer Papers, Operation Dragoon.
16. Interview with T/Sgt, Ralph Wenthold, n.d., USAMHI, Breuer Papers, Operation Dragoon.
17. Interview with Captain Jud Chalkley, n.d., USAMHI, Breuer Papers, Operation Dragoon.
18. Interview with Staff Sergeant Jim Stevens, n.d., USAMHI, Breuer Papers, Operation Dragoon.
19. Interview with Sergeant Martin Kangas, n.d., USAMHI, Breuer Papers, Operation Dragoon.
20. Interview with Sergeant "Hedy" Lamar, n.d., USAMHI, Breuer Papers, Operation Dragoon.
21. Ibid.
22. USAMHI, Oscar Reeder Papers, 143.
23. Clarke and Smith, *Riviera to the Rhine*, 104.
24. Sterne Randall, "The Other D-Day," 75.
25. Quoted in William B. Breuer, *Operation Dragoon: The Allied Invasion of Southern France* (Novato, CA: Presidio Press, 1987), 168.
26. South Europe, August 16, 1944, UKNA, HW 1/3177, TOO 1800/16/8.
27. Jeffrey J. Clarke, "The Champagne Campaign," *The Quarterly Journal of Military History* 20, no. 2 (Winter 2008): 39.
28. USAMHI, A 878, Major General [Generalleutnant] von Schwerin, Report, April 19, 1946.
29. Clarke, "Champagne Campaign," 42.
30. Clarke and Smith, *Riviera to the Rhine*, 122.
31. South Europe, August 16, 1944, UKNA, HW 1/3177, TOO 1800/16/8.
32. Weigley, *Eisenhower's Lieutenants*, 226.
33. Wend von Wietersheim, "Eleventh Panzer Division in Southern France (15 Aug–14 Sept 44)," 1953, USAMHI, A 880, 3.
34. Ibid., 4.
35. South Europe, August 16, 1944, HW 1/3176, untitled intercept contained in C410317, n.d., UKNA, HW 1/3177, TOO 1800/16/8.
36. South Europe, August 16, 1944, UKNA, HW 1/3177, TOO 1800/16/8.
37. Wietersheim, "Eleventh Panzer Division," USAMHI, A 880, 13.

38. South Europe, August 16, 1944, UKNA, HW 1/3177, TOO 1800/16/8.
39. Verlauf, August 16, 1944, BArch RH 19 IX/18, fol. 1–2. See also Besprechungen, Erwägungen, Entschlüsse, August 15, 1944, BArch RH 19 IX/87, fol. 241.
40. Steven J. Zaloga, *Operation Dragoon 1944: France's Other D-Day* (Oxford: Osprey Publishing, 2009), 51, 55.
41. On the question of Hitler's military competence, see Weinberg, "Some Myths of World War II," 704.
42. UKNA, HW 1/3177, TOOO 1730, August 17, 1944.
43. On a line running along the rivers Seine–Yonne–Canal de Bourgogne, which meet in Burgundy.
44. UKNA, 3177, TOO 1730, August 17, 1944.
45. Wietersheim, "Eleventh Panzer Division," USAMHI, A 880, 9–10.
46. Zaloga, *Operation Dragoon*, 57.
47. South Europe, August 17, 1944, UKNA, HW 1/3177, TOO 0930.
48. "Signed Blaskowitz," August 23, 1944, UKNA, HW 1/3189, TOO 1030.
49. Wietersheim, "Eleventh Panzer Division," USAMHI, A 880, 17–18.
50. Ibid., 18.
51. UKNA, HW 1/3189, TOO 0030, August 26, 1944.
52. UKNA, HW 1/3193, CX/MSS/T291/63, August 28, 1944, and West Europe, August 28, 1944, TOO 2300.
53. South Europe, August 15, 1944, UKNA, HW 1/3174, TOO 1800.
54. Between Bonlieu and Sauzet. UKNA, HW 1/3193, CX/MSS/T291/63, August 28, 1944.
55. UKNA, HW 1/3193, TOO 0800, August 28, 1944.
56. UKNA, HW 1/3193, CX/MSS/T291/63, August 28, 1944 (on the blocking position), and UKNA, HW 1/3193, TOO 0800, August 28, 1944 (on the tank thrust north).
57. Wietershcim, "Eleventh Panzer Division," USAMHI, A 880, 18.
58. Ibid., 22. Wietersheim refers to Roman le Bourg, but there is no such town north of Valence; given his description of events and the chronology, Bourg-lès-Valence is likely the town, although Romans-sur-Isère is located about twenty kilometres to the northeast of Valence.
59. Von Gyldenfeldt, Army Group G, orders, August 30, 1944, UKNA, HW 1/3195, TOO 1200.
60. Wietersheim, "Eleventh Panzer Division," USAMHI, A 880, 24–8.
61. Ibid., 29.
62. Ibid., 34.
63. Ibid., 34–5.
64. Zaloga, *Operation Dragoon*, 88.
65. At La Coucourde, north of Montélimar; on the Drôme, and east of Lyon on the way to Belfort. Wietersheim, "Eleventh Panzer Division," USAMHI, A 880, 37.

66. Zaloga, *Operation Dragoon*, 88.

67. Naval Headlines 1141, August 18, 1944, UKNA, HW 1/3177.

68. UKNA, HW 1/3177, TOO 1730, August 17, 1944; Naval Headlines 1139, August 16, 1944, UKNA, HW 1/3174. The smaller Mediterranean harbours at Port de Bouc, Port Saint-Louis, Port Vendres, and Sète were also to be destroyed. Naval Headlines 1144, August 21, 1944, UKNA, HW 1/3181.

69. UKNA, HW 1/3173, CX/MSS/T277/76, August 15, 1944, and Naval Headlines 1139, August 16, 1944, UKNA, HW 1/3174. The order to destroy Le Havre's port followed on August 29, 1944, though Allied bombing did much of the work. West Europe, August 29, 1944, UKNA, HW 1/3193, TOO 1300, and UKNA, HW 1/3201, TOO 9730, August 29, 1944.

70. UKNA, HW 1/3177, TO 0930/17/8/44, August 18, 1944.

CHAPTER 12: FORTS AND FORTRESSES

1. Mitcham, *Retreat to the Reich*, 212.

2. *The Invasion of the South of France: Operation "Dragoon,"* 46.

3. Heinrich Ruhfus, "Toulon: Naval Commander," n.d. [late 1940s], USAMHI, Foreign Military Studies (FMS), B 556, 6–7.

4. Mitcham, *Retreat to the Reich*, 212–3.

5. Zaloga, *Operation Dragoon*, 61.

6. Mitcham, *Retreat to the Reich*, 212. These included 5,500 naval troops and 2,800 naval troops. Clarke and Smith, *Riviera to the Rhine*, 138.

7. Mitcham, *Retreat to the Reich*, 212.

8. Naval Headlines 1140, August 17, 1944, UKNA, HW 1/3176, SX 937.

9. South Europe, August 17, 1944, UKNA, HW 1/3177, TOO 0930.

10. Zaloga, *Operation Dragoon*, 60.

11. For the details, see Paul Gaujac, *La Bataille et la Libération de Toulon*, rev. ed. (Paris: Nouvelles Éditions Latines, 1994), chapter 8.

12. Zaloga, *Operation Dragoon*, 60–1.

13. Naval Headlines 1146, August 23, 1944, UKNA, HW 1/3184.

14. Ruhfus, "Toulon: Naval Commander," USAMHI, FMS, B 556, 13.

15. Details from Gaujac, *Bataille et Libération de Toulon*, 260.

16. Ibid.

17. Ibid., 260–1.

18. Ibid., 261.

19. Ibid., 262.

20. Ibid.

21. The story of Gauvin comes from ibid., 264.

22. Ibid.

23. Ibid.

24. Ibid., 264–5.
25. Ibid., 265–8.
26. The town was home to many German émigrés in the 1930s, including Thomas Mann.
27. Gaujac, *Bataille et libération de Toulon*, 287.
28. Ibid.
29. Ibid., 292.
30. Ibid.
31. This paragraph is based on ibid., 292–3.
32. Ibid., 293–4.
33. Ibid., 294.
34. Ibid.
35. The story of Malbousquet's surrender is taken from ibid., 295–9.
36. "Ça c'est du travail!" Ibid., 301.
37. Ibid., 303.
38. Ibid.
39. Ibid., 307.
40. Ibid., 307–8.
41. Ibid., 308.
42. This paragraph is based on ibid., 311–8.
43. Ibid., 312.
44. Ibid.
45. Ibid., 313.
46. Ruhfus, "Toulon: Naval Commander," USAMHI, FMS, B 556, 25.
47. Quoted in Gaujac, *Bataille et libération de Toulon*, 316.
48. Ruhfus, "Toulon: Naval Commander," USAMHI, FMS, B 556, 25.
49. Gaujac, *Bataille et libération de Toulon*, 316.
50. Zaloga, *Operation Dragoon*, 63 and Clarke and Smith, *Riviera to the Rhine*, 140.
51. Gaujac, *Bataille et libération de Toulon*, 319.

CHAPTER 13: EUROPE'S LIFELINE
1. Pierre Guiral, *Libération de Marseille* (Paris: Hachette Littérature, 1974), 80–1.
2. Naval Headlines 1139, August 16, 1944, UKNA, HW 1/3184.
3. Guiral, *Libération de Marseille*, 81.
4. Ibid.
5. Guiral, 81, says they were young; Hans Schäfer, "244 Infantry Division Marseille, 19–28 August 1944," n.d. [likely 1947], USAMHI, A 884, 10, says they were old.
6. Clarke and Smith, *Riviera to the Rhine*, 203.
7. Schäfer, "244 Infantry Division Marseille," 5.
8. Ibid., Guiral, *Libération de Marseille*, 84.

9. Schäfer, "244 Infantry Division Marseille," 13.
10. Hans Schäfer, "The German Defence of Marseille," August 1944, USAMHI, B 420, 8.
11. Ibid., 9.
12. Guiral, *Libération de Marseille*, 81.
13. Schäfer, "244 Infantry Division Marseille," 10.
14. Ibid., 2.
15. Besprechungen, Erwägungen, Entschlüsse, August 15, 1944, BArch RH 19 IX/87, 240.
16. Schäfer, "244 Infantry Division Marseille," 9. Emphasis in the original.
17. Ibid., 15.
18. Ibid., 20.
19. Ibid.
20. Ibid.
21. Naval Headlines 1146, August 23, 1944, UKNA, HW 1/3184.
22. Proc 6911 PKA, August 21, 1944, UKNA, HW 1/3181: "Strong indications that demolition of Marseilles port installations ordered."
23. Schäfer, "244 Infantry Division Marseille," 21.
24. See Schäfer's comments on the "80,000" rebels in the city. Ibid., 14. This was a vast exaggeration; the figure was closer to a paltry 500. Zaloga, *Operation Dragoon*, 63.
25. Ibid., 23–4. Spiegel made further attempts. See Guiral, *Libération de Marseille*, 102. Schäfer claims that Spiegel was a hostage at this point. Guiral, who researched the matter at length, concludes that he only pretended to have been taken hostage and did so three days later, on the August 23. I have followed Guiral's chronology (see below).
26. Schäfer, "244 Infantry Division Marseille," 24.
27. Guiral, *Libération de Marseille*, 84, 90.
28. Ibid., 90.
29. Quoted ibid.
30. Ibid., 85
31. Ibid.
32. Schäfer, "244 Infantry Division Marseille," 24.
33. Guiral, *Libération de Marseille*, 85.
34. Schäfer, "244 Infantry Division Marseille," 25.
35. Guiral, *Libération de Marseille*, 85.
36. Quoted ibid.
37. Schäfer, "244 Infantry Division Marseille," 25–6.
38. Guiral, *Libération de Marseille*, 90.
39. Ibid.; Schäfer, "244 Infantry Division Marseille," 27.

40. Guiral, *Libération de Marseille*, 90.
41. Ibid.
42. Schäfer, "244 Infantry Division Marseille," 26.
43. Ibid.
44. Guiral, *Libération de Marseille*, 91–2.
45. Story from ibid.
46. Ibid., 92.
47. Ibid.
48. For the French version, see ibid. For the German, see Schäfer, "244 Infantry Division Marseille," 27–8.
49. Schäfer, "244 Infantry Division Marseille," 28; Guiral, *Libération de Marseille*, 92.
50. Schäfer, "244 Infantry Division Marseille," 28.
51. Ibid.
52. Guiral, *Libération de Marseille*, 94.
53. Ibid., 95.
54. Ibid.
55. Schäfer, "244 Infantry Division Marseille," 29.
56. Ibid., 33.
57. Ibid. Emphasis in the original.
58. Ibid.
59. Quoted in Guiral, *Libération de Marseille*, 96.
60. It is unclear from Schäfer's account where the battalion was located.
61. Schäfer, "244 Infantry Division Marseille," 33.
62. Guiral, *Libération de Marseille*, 96.
63. Schäfer, "244 Infantry Division Marseille," 30–1.
64. Ibid., 31.
65. Ibid., 31–2.
66. Guiral, *Libération de Marseille*, 97.
67. Description of harbour defences from Schäfer, "244 Infantry Division Marseille," 32. "AA guns" in the document.
68. Ibid.
69. Still intact and visible on Google Earth just northeast of the position "Cap Janet, Marseille."
70. Schäfer, "244 Infantry Division Marseille," 35.
71. Ibid., 36; Guiral, *Libération de Marseille*, 97.
72. Quoted in Guiral, *Libération de Marseille*, 98.
73. Schäfer, "244 Infantry Division Marseille," 36.
74. Ibid.; Guiral, *Libération de Marseille*, 98.
75. Guiral, *Libération de Marseille*, 99.

76. Ibid., 102.
77. Archives historiques de la Chambre de Commerce et d'Industrie Marseille-Provence (CCIMP) photo collection, 966 A/14, photos nos. 1048–69, September 1944.
78. Guiral, *Libération de Marseille*, 102.
79. Captain Jean Croisa. Guiral, *Libération de Marseille*, 83.
80. Story from ibid., 102–3.
81. The Marseille Chamber of Commerce has photos of the crane unloading equipment in early 1945. CCIMP photo collection, 966 A/14, photos nos. 1036–7, March 1945.
82. Guiral, *Libération de Marseille*, 104.
83. Roland G. Ruppenthal, *The U.S. Army in World War II: The European Theater of Operations*, vol. 2: *Logistical Support of the Armies: September 1944–May 1945* (Washington: Office of the Chief of Military History, 1959), 124.
84. Ibid.
85. Ibid., 121–3.
86. The standard criticism of Dragoon is that it diverted great human and material resources from the more important battle in northern France to little effect, given Army Group G's withdrawal. Thus a recent review concludes, "Dragoon clearly had no discernable impact on the fighting in Normandy." Anthony Tucker-Jones, *Operation Dragoon: The Liberation of Southern France 1944* (Barnsley, UK: Pen & Sword, 2009), 174. For a detailed examination of Dragoon's impact, see ibid., chapter 12.
87. Weinberg, *World at Arms*, 761.

CHAPTER 14: VIOLENCE COMES HOME

1. Steven J. Zaloga, *The Siegfried Line 1944–45: Battles on the German Frontier* (Oxford: Osprey, 2007), 10–1.
2. Weigley, *Eisenhower's Lieutenants*, 327.
3. Ibid.
4. Ibid.
5. Martin Blumenson, *The Patton Papers* (Boston: Houghton Mifflin, 1974), 2:588–9.
6. Weigley, *Eisenhower's Lieutenants*, 399–401.
7. Ibid., 406.
8. Ibid., 409.
9. Christoph Rass, René Rohrkamp, and Peter M. Quadflieg, *General Graf von Schwerin und das Kriegsende in Aachen: Ereignis, Mythos, Analyse* (Aachen: Shaker Verlag, 2007), 29–48.
10. Quoted ibid., 48.

11. Ibid., 49.
12. Ibid., 50–3.
13. Details on the battle from Weigley, *Eisenhower's Lieutenants*, 360–4.
14. Rass, Rohrkamp, and Quadflieg, *Schwerin und das Kriegsende in Aachen*, 58.
15. Max Hastings, *Armageddon: The Battle for Germany 1944–45* (London: Macmillan, 2004), 204–5.
16. Zaloga, *Siegfried Line*, 53.
17. Lieutenant William Devitt, a twenty-two-year-old Minnesotan, of the 330th Infantry, quoted in Hastings, *Armageddon*, 206.
18. Zaloga, *Siegfried Line*, 76.
19. For the statistics and the argument, see Hastings, *Armageddon*, chapter 7.
20. Zaloga, *Siegfried Line*, 91.
21. Hastings, *Armageddon*, 217–8.
22. The Schlieffen Plan was Feldmarschall Graf Alfred von Schlieffen's plan for a decisive blow against France, which would subsequently enable an attack on Russia. The core of the plan was to allow the Germans' left wing to fall back, pulling the French forces into the trap. Once the French army was crushed and Paris surrendered, the German army could then throw its western armies against Russia, causing it to sue for peace. Holmes, *Oxford Companion to Military History*, 808.
23. "Market" referred to the airborne portions of the operation, "Garden" to the accompanying land assault. Weinberg, *World at Arms*, 701.
24. "21 Army Group: Personal Message from the C-in-C," September 17, 1944, LH, Pyman Papers.
25. Omar N. Bradley, *A Soldier's Story* (New York: Modern Library, 1999), 416. "SHAEF" stands for "Supreme Headquarters Allied Expeditionary Force," Eisenhower's headquarters from the planning stages of the Normandy invasion through the end of the war.
26. See Weinberg, *World at Arms*, 701–2; Martin Gilbert, *Second World War* (London: Weidenfeld and Nicolson, 1989), 593.
27. UKNA, HW 1/3195, TOO 1000, August 28, 1944.
28. West Europe, September 23, 1944, UKNA, HW 1/3227, TOO 1600.
29. J. L. Granatstein, *The Generals: The Canadian Army's Senior Commanders in the Second World War* (Calgary: University of Calgary Press, 2005), 83.
30. Naval Headlines 1215, October 31, 1944, UKNA, HW 1/3302.
31. Bradley, *Soldier's Story*, 425.
32. Ibid.
33. Letter from Ismay to "Dick," December 11, 1944, LH, Ismay Papers, 4/6/7.
34. West Europe, November 5, 1944, UKNA, HW 1/3311, TOO 1700.
35. Ibid.

CHAPTER 15: TO DESTROY GERMANY

1. I owe the comparison to Gerhard Weinberg, "Some Myths of World War II," 705.
2. Longerich, *Heinrich Himmler*, 700.
3. See, for example, Andreas Kunz, "Die Wehrmacht in der Agonie der national-sozialistischen Herrschaft 1944/45: eine Gedankenskizze," in *Kriegsende 1945 in Deutschland*, ed. Jörg Hillmann and John Zimmermann (Munich: R. Oldenbourg, 2002), 103–4.
4. David K. Yelton, *Hitler's Volkssturm: The Nazi Militia and the Fall of Germany, 1944–1945* (Lawrence: University Press of Kansas, 2002), 7.
5. David K. Yelton, *Hitler's Home Guard: Volkssturmmann Western Front, 1944–1945* (Westminster, MD: Osprey, 2006), 7–8.
6. Ibid., 8.
7. Yelton, *Hitler's Volkssturm*, 13.
8. Ibid., 43.
9. Quoted ibid.
10. Ibid., chapters 3–4. On Kreisleiter independence vis-à-vis Bormann, see in particular 60–4.
11. As Martin Bormann complained. See "General," December 1, 1945, UKNA, HW 1/3462, TOO 0400.
12. See Yelton, *Hitler's Home Guard*, 17, 22.
13. Zelle, *Hitlers zweifelnde Elite*, 330. Scorched-earth policies in general became known in the bureaucratic jargon as "ARLZ-Maßnahmen," an acronym standing for disassembly (*Auflockerung*), evacuation/removal (*Räumung*), paralysis (*Lähmung*), and destruction (*Zerstörung*) measures.
14. See ibid., chapter 6.
15. Dan van der Vat, *The Good Nazi: The Life and Lies of Albert Speer* (London: Weidenfeld and Nicolson, 1997), 241.
16. Quoted in Albert Speer, *Inside the Third Reich* (repr. London: Phoenix, 2003; Weidenfeld & Nicolson, 1970), 541.
17. See Zelle, *Hitlers zweifelnde Elite*, 331.
18. Gitta Sereny, *Albert Speer: His Battle with Truth* (New York: Alfred Knopf, 1995), 457.
19. Speer, *Inside the Third Reich*, 542.
20. Speer to Bormann, September 15, 1944, BArch R 3/1623, fol. 30–34. German: "*Lähmungen*."
21. Speer, *Inside the Third Reich*, 542.
22. Speer to Bormann, September 15, 1944, BArch R 3/1623, fol. 30–5.
23. See Speer, *Inside the Third Reich*, 543.
24. Communication from Speer to Chairmen of Armaments Commissions,

BArch R 3/1623, fol. 64; Willi A. Boelcke, "Hitlers Befehle zur Zerstörung oder Lähmung des deutschen Industriepotentials 1944/45," *Zeitschrift für Firmengeschichte und Unternehmerbiographie* 13, no. 6 (1968): 307–8.

25. Communication from Speer to Bormann, September 15, 1944, BArch R 3/1623, fol. 30–5.

26. Speer, *Inside the Third Reich*, 543.

27. Communication from Bormann to Speer, September 16, 1944, BArch R 3/1623, fol. 47.

28. Ibid., fol. 45.

29. Schreiben Reichsminister RuK, October 23, 1944, BArch R 3/1623, fol. 44 [summarizing events in September].

30. Communication from Bormann, forwarded by Liebel, n.d., BArch R 3/1623, fol. 49–52.

31. David M. Crowe, *Oskar Schindler: The Untold Account of His Life, Wartime Activities, and the True Story behind the List* (Cambridge: Westview Press, 2004), 79–80.

32. Communication from Speer to Goebbels, September 18, 1944, BArch R 3/1623, fol. 61, 66.

33. Communication from Speer, "very urgent" (*"eilt sehr!"*), September 21, 1944, BArch R 3/1623, fol. 74.

34. Communications from Schulze-Fielitz, October 23, 1944, BArch R 3/1623, fol. 100–1.

35. Oliver Werner, "Garanten der Mobilisierung: Die Rüstungskommissionen des Speer-Ministeriums im 'totalen Krieg,'" in *Mobilisierung im Nationalsozialismus: Institutionen und Regionen in der Kriegswirtschaft und der Verwaltung des 'Dritten Reiches' 1936 bis 1945*, ed. Werner (Paderborn: Ferdinand Schöningh, 2013), 218–21.

36. Ibid., 219.

37. Communication from Hörner to coal mines in Wehrkreis VI, September 21, 1944, BArch R 3/1623, fol. 75.

38. Communication from Speer to the Directors of Rüstungskommissionen Vb, VIa and VIb, X, XIIa, XIIb, General Schindler, and western Gauleiter September 22, 1944, BArch R 3/1623, fol. 77–8.

39. Ibid.

40. Communication from Speer to the Gauleiter, October 2, 1944, BArch R 3/1623, fol. 82–3. See also Zelle, *Hitlers zweifelnde Elite*, 332.

41. Communication from Fischer to Bezirkslastverteiler V, VIa, VIb, X, and XIII, October 5, 1944, BArch R 3/1623, fol. 86.

42. Communication from Speer to the western Gauleiter, October 17, 1944, BArch R 3/1623, fol. 95.

43. Order on the Paralyzing of Energy Supplies (Electricity, Gas, Water) from Commander in Chief West, October 21, 1944, BArch R 3/1623, fol. 111–14.

44. Implied by communication from Speer to multiple parties, October 12, 1944, BArch R 3/1623, fol. 90–1.

45. For the development of this theme in relation to food supplies, see Zelle, *Hitlers zweifelnde Elite*, 335.

46. From Bormann: communication from Bormann to Schindler, sent by Liebel, n.d., BArch R 3/1623, fol. 49–52, and communication from Bormann to Speer, September 16, 1944, BArch R 3/1623, fol. 47. From the Wehrmacht, see: Order on the Paralyzing of Energy Supplies (Electricity, Gas, Water) from Commander in Chief West, October 21, 1944, BArch R 3/1623, fol. 111–14.

47. Communication from Keitel to Speer, December 6, 1944, BArch R 3/1623, fol. 124.

48. Communication from Speer to Armaments Commissioner Kelchner, December 6, 1944, BArch R 3/1623, fol. 125.

49. Keitel's order to Heeresgruppe G, December 12, 1944, BArch R 3/1623, fol. 126.

50. Communication from Speer to Dönitz, December 12, 1944, BArch R 3/1623, fol. 127.

51. See Speer, *Inside the Third Reich*, 468 on the war being over in May 1944 and chapter 30 on his motivations.

52. For a different interpretation, see Zelle, *Hitlers zweifelnde Elite*, 335.

53. Zelle, *Hitlers zweifelnde Elite*, 298–300. Zelle places particular emphasis on the idea of war as sport for Speer. On Speer's commitment to victory into 1945, see Alfred C. Mierzejewski, "When Did Albert Speer Give Up?" *Historical Journal* 31, no. 2 (1988): 391–7.

54. John Powell, ed., *Magill's Guide to Military History* (Pasadena: Salem Press, 2001), 1:238.

55. R. V. Gersdorff, "The Ardennes Offensive," n.d., USAMHI, D 379.F6713.

56. Ibid.

57. David Jordan and Andrew Wiest, *Atlas des Zweiten Weltkriegs* (Vienna: Tosa, 2005), 166.

58. Kershaw, *Hitler: Nemesis*, 742.

59. Ibid.

60. Weinberg, *World at Arms*, 766.

61. Gersdorff, "The Ardennes Offensive," n.d., USAMHI, D 379.F6713.

62. West Europe, December 12, 1944, UKNA, HW 1/3378, TOO 0745.

63. Donald L. Miller, *Masters of the Air: America's Bomber Boys Who Fought the Air War against Nazi Germany* (New York: Simon & Schuster, 2006), 373.

64. Charles B. MacDonald, *The Last Offensive*, part of *United States Army in World War II: European Theater of Operations* (Washington: Office of the Chief of

Military History, 1973), chapter 2; "The Winter Crossing of 1944/45 on the Western Front," n.d., LH, Pyman Papers.

65. Weigley, *Eisenhower's Lieutenants*, 574.
66. Ibid.
67. "The Winter Crossing of 1944/45 on the Western Front," n.d., LH, Pyman Papers.

CHAPTER 16: FIGHTING TO THE LAST MAN

1. Tagesbefehl für Neujahr 1945, BArch RH 20-7-146, fol. 2.
2. Alfred D. Chandler, Jr., ed., *The Papers of Dwight David Eisenhower: The War Years* (Baltimore: Johns Hopkins Press, 1970), 4:2408–9.
3. Bradley, *Soldier's Story*, 398–9.
4. Quotation and review of strategic considerations from Stephen G. Fritz, *Endkampf: Soldiers, Civilians, and the Death of the Third Reich* (Lexington: University Press of Kentucky, 2004), 19–20.
5. Bradley, *Soldier's Story*, 420, 436.
6. On the defensive value of the West Wall, see Manfred Groß, *Westwallkämpfe: Die Angriffe der Amerikaner 1944/45 zwischen Ormont (Rheinland-Pfalz) und Geilenkirchen (Nordrhein-Westfalen). Eine Dokumentation* (Aachen: Helios, 2008).
7. This description draws on MacDonald, *Last Offensive*, 58–9.
8. Story of O'Daniel and Neuf-Brisach from Weigley, *Eisenhower's Lieutenants*, 599.
9. C. P. Stacey, *Official History of the Canadian Army*, vol. 3, *The Victory Campaign: The Operations in North-West Europe, 1944–1945* (Ottawa: Department of National Defence, 1960), 467; Samuel W. Mitcham, Jr., *German Order of Battle* (Mechanicsburg, PA: Stackpole Books, 2007), 1:142.
10. Stacey, *Official History of the Canadian Army*, 3:468.
11. Ken Ford, *The Rhineland 1945: The Last Killing Ground in the West* (Oxford: Osprey, 2000), 29; "The Winter Crossing of 1944/45 on the Western Front," n.d., LH, Pyman Papers.
12. "Boniface" report, February 10, 1945, UKNA, HW 1/3516.
13. Quoted in Weigley, *Eisenhower's Lieutenants*, 595.
14. G-2 Period Report, March 26, 1945, NACP, RG 407, 101-2.1.
15. For the details, see MacDonald, *Last Offensive*, 138–9.
16. Weigley, *Eisenhower's Lieutenants*, 614.
17. Ibid., 615.
18. "Ground Situation, 7pm/22/2," February 22, 1945, UKNA, HW 1/3539.
19. Weigley, *Eisenhower's Lieutenants*, 626. Myth has it that British bombers spared the cathedral because it provided a marker guiding them to the city. This is nonsense. British radar was more than capable of identifying cities by 1942,

but British bombing was not precise enough to destroy a city while sparing a church. Furthermore, the British had no interest in doing so. The cathedral owes its survival to its size, solidity, shape—the long, thin steeples meant that many bombs would have bounced off of them—and to that great saviour of cultural sites in the bombing war: pure chance.

20. "First Impressions of Cologne," Annex No. 2 to First U.S. Army G-2 Period Report No. 275, March 1945, NACP, RG 407, 101-2.1.

21. Aktennotiz "Speer," March 7, 1945, BArch R 3/1623a, fol. 19.

22. Details from MacDonald, *Last Offensive*, 212–3. Combat Commands were armed task forces roughly the size of brigade or regiment (3,000 to 5,000 troops); Combat Commands A and B contained the primary fighting elements in a division, and Combat Command R was the reserve, though the last was often actively engaged in operations. See Don M. Fox, *Patton's Vanguard: The United States Fourth Armored Division* (Jefferson, NC: McFarland & Co., 2003), 26.

23. This section on Bad Godesberg draws on Klaus-Dietmar Henke, *Die amerikanische Besetzung Deutschlands* (Munich: R. Oldenbourg, 1995), 357–61.

24. MacDonald, *Last Offensive*, 215.

25. Weigley, *Eisenhower's Lieutenants*, 627.

26. Ibid.

27. Hermann Janowski, "Army Group B, Engineer Staff 113 (March 1945)," n.d., USAMHI, D793.F6713, B 072.

28. Weigley, *Eisenhower's Lieutenants*, 627.

29. Janowski, "Army Group B, Engineer Staff 113 (March 1945)," n.d., USAMHI, D793.F6713, B 072.

30. MacDonald, *Last Offensive*, 230. For a review of the possibilities, see Ken Hechler, *The Bridge at Remagen: The Amazing Story of March 7, 1945—The Day the Rhine River Was Crossed*, rev. ed. (1957; repr. Missoula, MT: Pictorial Histories Publishing Company, 1995), chapter 21, "Facts and Fiction."

31. Quotations from Bradley, *Soldier's Story*, 510.

32. Weigley, *Eisenhower's Lieutenants*, 628.

33. Ibid., 628–9.

34. Ibid., 629.

35. West Europe, March 7, 1945, UKNA, HW 1/3580, CX/MSS/T482/75.

36. West Europe, March 11, 1945, UKNA, HW 1/3591, TOO 2100. It was thanks, once again, to American air superiority that the Luftwaffe was only able to attack with two to three airplanes at a time and lacked any fighters for horizontal attacks. With them, the Germans might have destroyed the bridgehead. Albert Kesselring, "Ludendorff Bridge at Remagen," 1954, USAMHI, D 739.F6713.

37. West Europe, March 11, 1945, UKNA, HW 1/3591, TOO 2100.

38. Naval Headlines 1349, March 14, 1945, UKNA, HW 1/3601; UKNA, HW 1/3616, TOO 1800, March 16, 1945; West Europe, March 19, 1945, UKNA HW 1/3586, TOO 0100. The Americans report dive-bomb attacks but no suicide attacks. G-2 Periodic Report, March 10, 1945, NACP, RG 407, 101-2.1. On the Germans' anticipation of American moves after Remagen, see West Europe, March 9, 1945, UKNA, HW 1/3583, TOO 0030.

39. MacDonald, *Last Offensive*, 229–30. I owe the imagery of rising dust and the trembling bridge to MacDonald.

40. "Conduct of the War in the West," Annex No. 2 to G-2 Periodic Report No. 265, March 1945, NACP, RG 407, 101-2.1.

41. West Europe, March 7, 1945, UKNA, HW 1/3580, CX/MSS/T482/22. One captain was sentenced in absentia. Kesselring showed no contrition for the action after the war: USAMHI, D 739.F6713, Kesselring, "Ludendorff Bridge at Remagen," 1954.

42. West: Military, March 15, 1945, UKNA, HW 1/3611.

43. Ibid.

44. Naval Headlines 1344, March 9, 1945, UKNA, HW 1/3583. "Unbowed" was "undismayed" in the original translation, but "unbowed" captures Dönitz's meaning more accurately.

45. West Europe, March 15, 1945, UKNA, HW 1/3614, TOO 2000. On the divisions at this point, see Mitcham, *German Order of Battle*, 1:247 and 2:156 for the 198th Infantry Division and the 559th Grenadier Division, respectively.

46. West Europe, March 16, 1945, UKNA, HW 1/3611, TOO 1400.

47. West Europe, March 19, 1945, UKNA, HW 1/3603, TOO 0930.

48. West Europe, March 16, 1945, UKNA, HW 1/3617, TOO 1400.

49. Ops Orders for the night of 20–21/3, March 20, 1945, UKNA, HW 1/3624, TOO 1230/20/3/45.

50. West Europe, March 14, 1945, UKNA, HW 1/3614, TOO 1400.

51. For the details, see MacDonald, *Last Offensive*, 262–4.

52. Ibid., 264.

53. 94th Infantry Division G-2 After Action Reports, 1 March 1945 to 31 March 1945, NACP, RG 407, 394–2.

54. Weigley, *Eisenhower's Lieutenants*, 639.

55. These quotations from ibid., 643.

56. Order from Jodl transmitted by Bormann to all Gauleiter, Reichsleiter, and Reichsjugendführer, March 30, 1945, BArch R 3/1623a, fol. 72.

CHAPTER 17: HITLER RAGES

1. Communication from Speer to the Party Chancellery, January 19, 1945, BArch R 3/1623a, fol. 3.

2. Communication from Speer to the Blechhammer and Heydebreck works, January 21, 1945, BArch R 3/1623a, fol. 4.

3. Communication from Speer to OKH Gen. Qu. General Toppe, January 22, 1945, BArch R 3/1623a, fol. 5.

4. Order from Oberkommando Heeresgruppe Weichsel regarding ARLZ-Maßnahmen (Lager und Bestände), February 22, 1945, BArch R 3/1623a. The order was reaffirmed in late March: "Befehl für Verteidigungsmaßnahmen im Armeegebiet rückwärts des Hauptkampffeldes," BArch RH 20-19/180, 3(d), fol. 86.

5. Order from Oberkommando Heeresgruppe Weichsel regarding ARLZ-Maßnahmen (Lager und Bestände), February 22, 1945, BArch R 3/1623a.

6. Longerich, *Heinrich Himmler*, 703.

7. Order from Oberkommando des Heeres, General der Pioniere und Festungen on bridge detonations [*Brückensprengungen*], February 28, 1945, BArch R 3/1623a, fol. 16.

8. Sereny, *Albert Speer*, 482, citing the diary of Manfred von Poser.

9. Ibid., 482–3.

10. Order from Hitler to the Gauleiter and Reichsverteidigungskommissare, March 1, 1945, BArch R 3/1623a, fol. 17.

11. Communication from Ganzenmüller to Speer, March 15, 1945, BArch R 3/1623a, fol. 36.

12. "... *dann ist dieses Volk nicht wert, weiterzubestehen!*" Walter Rohland, *Bewegte Zeiten: Erinnerungen eines Eisenhüttenmannes* (Stuttgart: Seewald Verlag, 1978), 99.

13. Ganzenmüller to Speer, March 15, 1945, BArch R 3/1623a, fol. 36. One week earlier, Speer had already made an effort to save the transportation system. He wrote to Reichsbahn (Imperial Rail) President Lammertz on March 7: "I must once again clearly state that Hitler's orders—that the paralysis of industry is only implemented to the extent that we can easily bring it back into pro-duction—are for us unambiguous directives [*eindeutige Richtlinien*]. Every violation of this order must be brought to my immediate attention. We need, above all at this moment, unity of command over such matters and we cannot tolerate instances in which orders are violated. When they are, there must be the harshest consequences." Aktennotiz Speer, March 7, 1945, BArch R 3/1623a, fol. 18.

14. "*Dem Befehl über Zerstörungen im eigenen Lande bitte ich folgende Fassung zu geben.*"

15. Order from Speer to Generalstab des Heeres—General der Pioniere und Festungen [multiple drafts], March 15, 1945, BArch R 3/1623a, fol. 31–5.

16. Order from Hitler, March 14, 1945, BArch R 3/1623a, fol. 29[a].

17. Sereny, *Albert Speer*, 482.
18. Speer, *Inside the Third Reich*, 583–4.
19. "Zerstörungsmaßnahmen im Reichsgebiet," March 19, 1945, BArch R 3/1623a, fol. 46; West Europe, March 20, 1945, UKNA, HW 1/3624, TOO 0900. Emphasis added. The translation follows the latter document with small adjustments.
20. Sereny, *Albert Speer*, 485.
21. Ibid.
22. "Räumung im Westen," March 19, 1945, BArch R 3/1623a, fol. 42; telegram from Chief of the General Staff, OB West to the 19th Army, March 20, 1944, BArch RH 20-19/180.
23. Quoted in Sereny, *Albert Speer*, 485.
24. Quoted ibid., 485–6.
25. The Chief Quartermaster West, the Inspectorate of the German Air Force West, the Chief Naval Command West, Military Districts VI, XII, V, and the Special Emissary of the Party Chancellery with Commander in Chief West were also informed. West Europe, April 20, 1945, UKNA, HW 1/3624, TOO 0900/20/3/45.
26. West Europe, March 20, 1945, UKNA, HW 1/3624, TOO 0900.
27. Telegram of March 26, 1945, BArch R 3/1623a, fol. 65–71.
28. Telegram from OKM/Chef Mar Rüst 1098/45, March 27, 1945, BArch R 3/1623a, fol. 64.
29. "Anordnung: Aufnahme der unquartierten Volksgenossen usw. aus Räumungs-gebieten," March 23, 1945 [from Bormann to all Gauleiter], BArch R 3/1623a, fol. 50; "Telegram KR," March 29, 1945 [orders for the army], BArch R 3/1623a, fol. 59–61; "KR Telegram," March 19, 1945 [orders for the northern coast and Denmark], BArch R 3/1623a, fol. 55–58.
30. Fernschreiben KR, March 29, 1945, BArch R 3/1623a, fol. 59–61, point 4.
31. Geyer, "There is a Land Where Everything is Pure," 139.
32. Corroborated by Manfred von Poser. Sereny, *Albert Speer*, 487; Speer, *Inside the Third Reich*, 595.
33. Speer, *Inside the Third Reich*, 595.
34. Rohland, *Bewegte Zeiten*, 101.
35. Speer, *Inside the Third Reich*, 597.
36. Ibid., 598.
37. Ian Kershaw, *The End: Hitler's Germany, 1944–45* (London: Allen Lane, 2011), 305.
38. On the implementing orders, see BArch R 3/1623a, fol. 59.
39. Kershaw, *The End*, 290.
40. Speer, *Inside the Third Reich*, 599.
41. Ibid.

42. Ibid., 291; Robert Gellately, *Backing Hitler: Consent and Coercion in Nazi Germany* (Oxford: Oxford University Press, 2001), 232.

43. Sereny, *Albert Speer*, 489.

44. Kershaw, *The End*, 291.

45. Sereny, *Albert Speer*, 491–2; Elke Fröhlich, ed., *Die Tagebücher von Joseph Goebbels*, pt. 2, vol. 15 (Munich: K. G. Saur, 1995), March 31, 1945, 643.

46. Speer, *Inside the Third Reich*, 605.

47. Sereny, *Albert Speer*, 494.

48. Kershaw, *The End*, 291.

49. Speer, *Inside the Third Reich*, 607–8.

50. Ibid., 608. In his conversations with Sereny, Speer claimed he had said, "But then it will help if you will immediately reconfirm my authority for the implementation of your March 19 decree." Sereny, *Albert Speer*, 497.

51. Sereny, *Albert Speer*, 498.

52. Ibid.

53. "Zerstörungsmaßnahmen im Reichsgebiet," March 30, 1945, BArch R 3/1623a, fol. 95.

54. Führer's Order, March 30, 1945, BArch R 3/1623a, fol. 81.

55. Sereny, *Albert Speer*, 492.

56. "Durchführungsbestimmungen zum Führererlass vom 30.3.1945 über Lähmungs- und Zerstörungsmaßnahmen," March 30, 1945, BArch R 3/1623a, fol. 87; telegram on "Zerstörungsmaßnahmen im Reichsgebiet," April 1, 1945, BArch R 3/1623a, fol. 101-2.

57. Telegram from Uiberreither [rendered as "Ueberreither"] to Speer, April 3, 1945, BArch R 3/1623a, fol. 106.

58. Radio message from Speer to Uiberreither, April 4, 1945, BArch R 3/1623a [missing folder no. on document, likely 107 or 108].

59. See Andreas Dornheim, "Rasse, Raum und Autarkie Sachverständigengutachten zur Rolle des Reichsministeriums für Ernährung und Landwirtschaft in der NS-Zeit," commissioned by the German Federal Ministry for Food, Agriculture, and Consumer Protection (March 2011): 66, http://www.bmelv.de/SharedDocs/Downloads/Ministerium/RolleReichsministeriumNSZeit.pdf?__blob=publicationFile.

60. Communication from Riecke to the Leiter der Landesernährungsämter, Abteilung A, March 31, 1945, BArch R 3/1623a, fol. 92-3.

61. Speer to Riecke and Ganzenmüller, March 30, 1945, BArch 3/1623a, fol. 90; Sereny, *Albert Speer*, 499, citing testimony from Manfred von Poser.

62. Telegram from Speer, April 3, 1945, BArch R 3/1623a, fol. 110.

63. German police decodes No. 1 Traffic, April 5, 1945, UKNA, HW 16/43.

64. Ibid.

65. Communication from OKW/WFSt to General Winter, April 5, 1945, BArch 3/1623a, fol. 130–1.

66. Communication from Speer to OKW/WFSt General Winter, April 5, 1945, BArch R 3/1623a, fol. 139–40.

67. Speer to all OT-Einsatzgruppenleiter (radio message), April 3, 1945, BArch R 3/1623a, fol. 111.

68. Mierzejewski, "When Did Albert Speer Give Up?," 391–7.

69. German police decodes No. 1 Traffic, April 5, 1945, UKNA, H16/43.

70. Communication from Speer to Hellmuth, April 4, 1945, BArch R 3/1623a, fol. 116. On Speer's fear that the Wehrmacht had not been brought into anti–scorched earth orders in Jena, see telegram from Speer to the Reich Ministry of Transportation, April 5, 1945, BArch R 3/1623a, fol. 140.

71. Communication from Speer to the commander, 1. Fahrbrigade, April 4, 1945, BArch R 3/1623a, fol. 115.

72. German police decodes No. 1 Traffic, April 5, 1945, UKNA, H16/43.

73. Speer, *Inside the Third Reich*, 614.

74. Ibid.

75. Führer order, April 7, 1945, BArch R 3/1623a, fol. 152.

76. "Lähmung bezw. Zerstörung von Verkehrsanlagen und Nachrichtenmitteln," April 7, 1945, BArch R 3/1623a, fol. 151.

77. Weisung an alle Betreibsführer, April 7, 1945, BArch R 3/1623a.

78. No. 252 From AOC Gelip, signed by Gen. der Flieger Wolff to 8 Flak Divisions, April 17, 1945, UKNA, HW 1/3709, TOO 0700/17/4/45.

79. West Europe, April 14, 1945, UKNA, H1 1/3709, TOO 1130.

80. Communication from Speer to Fischer, April 16, 1945, BArch R 3/1623a, fol. 194.

81. Communication from Speer to Dorsch, "Zentrale [Bau]verwaltung," April 17, 1994, BArch R 3/1623a, fol. 195.

82. Speer, *Inside the Third Reich*, 615.

83. Telegram from Praun, April 7, 1945, BArch R 3/1623a, fol. 157–8.

84. "Durchführungsbestimmungen betr. die Zerstörung der Nachrichtenanlagen im Raum von Berlin," April 7, 1945, BArch R 3/1623a, fol. 158a–b.

85. Rohland "an die Direktionen unserer Mitgliedswerke," n.d. [likely April 8 or 9, 1945], BArch R 3/1623a, fol. 165–6.

86. It seems, though the reference by Rohland is a bit vague, that an "army group" (*Heeresgruppe*) agreed to Speer's interpretation of the order. Radio message (*Funkspruch*) from Rohland to Speer, April 7, 1945, BArch R 3/1623a. [missing fol. no., possibly 160].

87. "KR-Blitz-Fernschreiben" from Keitel, April 8, 1945, BArch R 3/1623a [missing fol. no. on document]. Speer falsely claims in his memoirs that Keitel "refused

to issue new instructions on the basis of Hitler's latest decree." Speer, *Inside the Third Reich*, 615.

88. On this point, see Sereny, *Albert Speer*, 473.

CHAPTER 18: THE SIEGE OF DÜSSELDORF

1. On this, see MacDonald, *Last Offensive*, 139.

2. Telegram from General der Infanterie Rasp, 19th Army, February 12, 1945, BArch RH 20-19/180, fol. 52–3. Himmler had said much the same thing in November: "Our enemies must be taught to understand that every kilometre they advance into our country will cost them rivers of their own blood. Every building in the town, every village, every farm, every forest will be defended by men, young and old, and—if necessary—by girls and women too." Longerich, *Heinrich Himmler*, 712.

3. Henke, *Die amerikanische Besetzung Deutschlands*, 781.

4. "Befehl des Reichsführers-SS Himmler über Maßnahmen gegen Zivilbevölkerung im Westen," March 28, 1945, BArch RH 20-19/196. This order, referred to as the *"Flaggenbefehl"* ("Flag Order"), is sometimes cited with the date of April 3, 1945.

5. See "Befehl für Verteidigungsmaßnahmen im Armeegebiet rückwärts des Hauptkampffeldes," March 25, 1945, BArch RH 20-19/180, fol. 86, 3(d). Hitler's last scorched-earth orders, issued toward the end of March, assigned responsibility for the destruction of industry to the Gauleiter and Reichsverteidigungskommissare and responsibility for the destruction of military installations to the Wehrmacht. Military installations included transportation and communications, including bridges and railways. See the chapters on scorched earth above and Nineteenth Army telegram of March 23, 1945, and Army Group G telegram of March 21, 1945, BArch RH 29–19, fol. 212.

6. MacDonald, *Last Offensive*, 359.

7. West Europe, February 22, 1945, UKNA, HW 1/3556, TOO 0930.

8. Volker Zimmermann, *In Schutt und Asche: Das Ende des Zweiten Weltkrieges in Düsseldorf* (Düsseldorf: Grupello Verlag, 1995), 28.

9. Ibid., 63.

10. Ibid.; *Unvollständige Liste der nicht-jüdischen NS-Opfer*, Archiv der Mahn- und Gedenkstätte Düsseldorf.

11. Zimmermann, *In Schutt und Asche*, 64.

12. Uwe Kaminsky, "Fremdarbeiter in Ratingen während des Zweiten Weltkriegs," *Ratinger Forum: Beiträge zur Stadt- und Regionalgeschichte* 1 (1989), 200.

13. Ibid.

14. Zimmermann, *In Schutt und Asche*, 64.

15. Kaminsky, "Fremdarbeiter in Ratingen," 200.

16. Zimmermann, *In Schutt und Asche*, 64.

17. Kaminsky, "Fremdarbeiter in Ratingen," 201.

18. Zimmermann, *In Schutt und Asche*, 64.

19. Ibid., 65; Hildegund and Bobo Schmidt, "Ein Stein kommt ins Rollen. Spuren sowjetischer Kriegsgefangener auf dem Gallberg in Düsseldorf-Gerresheim," in *Augenblick: Berichte, Informationen und Dokumente der Mahn- und Gedenkstätte Düsseldorf* 3 (1992), 17.

20. Karola Fings and Frank Sparing, *"Z. Zt. Zigeunerlager": die Verfolgung der Düsseldorfer Sinti und Roma im Nationalsozialismus* (Cologne: Volksblatt Verlag, 1992), 78–9.

21. Ibid., 79.

22. Andreas Kussmann, "Sieben Wochen in der Front: Kriegsende in Düsseldorf," 26, Stadtarchiv Landeshauptstadt Düsseldorf (SLD).

23. Ibid.; Zimmermann, *In Schutt und Asche*, 67.

24. Zimmermann, *In Schutt und Asche*, 61.

25. Ibid., 62.

26. Ibid., 61–2.

27. Ibid., 62. Stender, like Kaiser, was an injured veteran of the First World War.

28. The story of Else Gores is found ibid., 62.

29. Ibid., 62–3.

30. Published in the *Düsseldorfer Nachrichten*, December 31, 1944.

31. Zimmermann, *In Schutt und Asche*, 33–4.

32. Kussmann, "Sieben Wochen in der Front," 24.

33. Zimmermann, *In Schutt und Asche*, 36. The commander of the 338th Infantry Division from January 1945 was Wolf Ewert. Mitcham, *German Order of Battle*, 2:46–7.

34. Interview with Paul Hilberath, 1988, SLD, Kussmann Nachlass, 4-63-0-21. There is some debate about where precisely the charges were laid. See the interviewer's comments in this file.

35. Kussmann, "Sieben Wochen in der Front," 23.

36. Zimmermann, *In Schutt und Asche*, 36.

37. Kussmann, "Sieben Wochen in der Front," 22.

38. Zimmermann, *In Schutt und Asche*, 39.

39. Ibid., 41.

40. Kussmann, "Sieben Wochen in der Front," 24.

41. Zimmermann, *In Schutt und Asche*, 48.

42. Kussmann, "Sieben Wochen in der Front," 25.

43. Zimmermann, *In Schutt und Asche*, 52.

44. Kussmann, "Sieben Wochen in der Front," 25.

45. Statement by Dr. Victor Muckel, September 27, 1948, SLD XXIII, 192.

46. Kussmann, "Sieben Wochen in der Front," 25.

47. Ibid.

48. Statement by Dr. Victor Muckel, September 27, 1948, SLD XXIII, 192.

49. *Rheinische Landeszeitung*, March 15, 1945.

50. "Liste des Ernährungsamtes mit Bevölkerungszahlen von März 3, 1945," SLD IV, 1578.

51. Private Papers of Walther Hensel, Band 23, SLD.

52. Florian, Gauleiter and Reichsverteidigungskommissar, "Räumungsbefehl," March 29, 1945, SLD XXIII, 192.

53. Kussmann, "Sieben Wochen in der Front," 26–7.

54. Story from "Gespräch mit Herrn Hermann Smeets," November 5, 1984, SLD, Kussmann Nachlass, 4-63-0-12, 3.

55. Others included Peter Hupperts, Hermann Maaßen, Matthias Metzmacher, Willi Tewes, and Helmut Walter. "Gespräch mit Herrn Hermann Smeets," 1.

56. Zimmermann, *In Schutt und Asche*, 71.

57. ". . . *wenn alles zusammenbricht, sofort Leute da sein müssen, die das Ganze in die Hand nehmen.*" Ibid.

58. All but one of the main members came from Bilk; Willi Erkelenz was from Oberbilk. "Gespräch mit Herrn Hermann Smeets," 1.

59. Ibid., 2.

60. Kussmann, "Sieben Wochen in der Front," 26.

61. Zimmermann, *In Schutt und Asche*, 72.

62. Ibid. In addition to those named above, Zimmerman also identifies Hans van der Weiden and Ludwig Weingarten as members of the group.

63. Quoted ibid., 73.

64. In, among others, the cellars in the Völklingerstraße and in another cellar on the Gladbacherstraße. "Gespräch mit Herrn Hermann Smeets," 4.

65. Ibid.

66. According to Smeets, they were successful in preventing destruction of bridges in the Hüttenstraße, Bachstraße, Volmerswerther Straße, and Martinstraße. Zimmermann, *In Schutt und Asche*, 74.

67. "Gespräch mit Herrn Hermann Smeets," 3.

68. Ibid., 4.

69. Ibid.

70. "Folgende Beschreibung der KP-Widerstandsstrukturen und -aktionen in Düsseldorf stüz sich auf einem Zeitzeugenbericht von Helene Biebler, née Püster," SLD, Sammlung Kussmann, 4-0-63, 44a/1.

71. Details on the plan from "Gespräch mit Herrn Hermann Smeets," 5.

72. Ibid., 6.

73. Ibid., 5.

74. Ibid.

75. Ibid.

76. Ibid.

77. Ibid., 6.

78. Ibid.

79. Ibid.

80. Ibid., 7.

81. Ibid.

82. Zimmermann, *In Schutt und Asche*, 76.

83. Report by Wiedenhofen, April 12, 1946, SLD XXIII 192, 1; Schreinermeister Ernst Klein, "Bericht über meine Erlebnisse zur Übergabe der Stadt Düsseldorf," n.d., SLD XXIII, 192.

84. Report by Bäckermeister Josef Lauxtermann, n.d., SLD XXIII 192; Klein, "Bericht über meine Erlebnisse."

85. Josef Knab apparently made the suggestion. Report by Wiedenhofen, 1–2.

86. Karl Müller, "Bericht über die Vorgänge, welche zur Einnahme Düsseldorfs führten," April 12, 1946, SLD XXIII, 192.

87. Ibid.

88. MacDonald, *Last Offensive*, 364.

89. G-2 Journal, 95th Division, April 12, 1945, NACP RG 407, 395-2.3.

90. MacDonald, *Last Offensive*, 365.

91. See the 95th Division's combat reports in NACP RG 407, 395-2.3.

92. Specifically, between Ratingen, Velbert, Remscheid, and Langenfeld.

93. MacDonald, *Last Offensive*, 370.

94. Ibid.

95. Ibid., 368.

96. Aloys Odenthal, "Bericht über die Übergabe der Stadt Düsseldorf 16–17 April 1945," SDL XXIII 192, 1; Report by Wiedenhofen, 2.

97. Odenthal, "Bericht über die Übergabe der Stadt Düsseldorf," 1.

98. Ibid.

99. Report by Wiedenhofen, 2.

100. Odenthal, "Bericht über die Übergabe der Stadt Düsseldorf," 1.

101. Report by Wiedenhofen, 2.

102. Odenthal, "Bericht über die Übergabe der Stadt Düsseldorf," 1; Report by Wiedenhofen, 2.

103. Odenthal, "Bericht über die Übergabe der Stadt Düsseldorf," 1.

104. Ibid.

105. Ibid.

106. Ibid., 2. In the original German: *"Sie großer, schwerer Kerl, zeigen Sie Mut, es geht um Düsseldorf und um Frauen und Kinder!"*

107. Ibid. According to Wiedenhofen's recollection, the phrasing varied slightly but conveyed the same meaning. Report by Wiedenhofen, 3.
108. Odenthal, "Bericht über die Übergabe der Stadt Düsseldorf 16–17 April 1945," 2.
109. Ibid.
110. Ibid.
111. Ibid.
112. Müller, "Bericht über die Vorgänge," 1–2.
113. Odenthal, "Bericht über die Übergabe der Stadt Düsseldorf," 3.
114. Actually "Dr. Dr. Goetsch," as the man had two doctorates, but the rendering is absurd in English.
115. Odenthal, "Bericht über die Übergabe der Stadt Düsseldorf," 2; Report by Wiedenhofen, 2.
116. Odenthal, "Bericht über die Übergabe der Stadt Düsseldorf," 2.
117. Ibid.
118. Report by Wiedenhofen, 3–4.
119. In Wiedenhofen's account, Florian dispatched the troops. See also Odenthal, "Bericht über die Übergabe der Stadt Düsseldorf," 2.
120. Müller, "Bericht über die Vorgänge," 1–2.
121. Ibid., 2.
122. Ibid. *Sie stehen hier auf einem gefährlichen Posten.* The desk officer's name was Neuss.
123. Ibid.
124. Ibid.
125. Ibid.
126. Kussmann, "Sieben Wochen in der Front," 28.
127. Report by Wiedenhofen, 4.
128. Odenthal, "Bericht über die Übergabe der Stadt Düsseldorf," 3.
129. Report by Wiedenhofen, 4.
130. Ibid.
131. In Odenthal's version, they pushed past a German guard with guns drawn. Odenthal, "Bericht über die Übergabe der Stadt Düsseldorf," 3.
132. Report by Wiedenhofen, 4.
133. Authorization for Wiedenhofen signed by Jürgens, April 15, 1945, SLD XXIII, 192.
134. Report by Wiedenhofen, 4–5. Eight hundred bombers were mentioned, according to Odenthal's account. "Bericht über die Übergabe der Stadt Düsseldorf," 3.
135. Odenthal, "Bericht über die Übergabe der Stadt Düsseldorf," 3.
136. Report by Wiedenhofen, 4–5.
137. Ibid.

138. Letter signed by lieutenant, April 16, 1945, SLD XXIII, 192.
139. Report by Wiedenhofen, 4–5.
140. Odenthal, "Bericht über die Übergabe der Stadt Düsseldorf," 3.
141. Ibid.
142. Ibid.
143. Ibid. Original German: ". . . *damit nach diesem Fluch des Nationalsozialismus Deutschland und unsere Kinder wieder aufwachen können.*"
144. Report by Wiedenhofen, 6.
145. Ibid.
146. Odenthal, "Bericht über die Übergabe der Stadt Düsseldorf," 4.
147. Ibid.
148. Zimmermann, *In Schutt und Asche*, 90.
149. Odenthal, "Bericht über die Übergabe der Stadt Düsseldorf," 3.
150. Ibid.
151. Zimmermann, *In Schutt und Asche*, 91.
152. Helmut Walter. "Gespräch mit Herrn Hermann Smeets," 8.
153. Ibid., 5.
154. Ibid.
155. Report by Wiedenhofen, 6.
156. Odenthal, "Bericht über die Übergabe der Stadt Düsseldorf," 3.
157. G-2 Periodic Report, April 18, 1945, NACP RG 407, 101-2.1, 2.
158. "Gespräch mit Herrn Hermann Smeets," 5.
159. Ibid., 8. The convoy followed the Graf-Adolf-Straße and the Kavalleriestraße.
160. Ibid.
161. Report by Wiedenhofen, 6.
162. Kussmann, "Sieben Wochen in der Front," 28.
163. Zimmermann, *In Schutt und Asche*, 87. Zimmermann concludes that Florian was only there as an observer.

CHAPTER 19: DYING SO THAT THEY MAY LIVE

1. This paragraph draws on MacDonald, *Last Offensive*, chapter 17.
2. 80th Infantry Division G-2 After Action Report, 1–30 April 1945, Part II: "The Battle of Kassel," NACP, RG 407, 380-0.3.
3. 80th Infantry After Action Report: European Theatre of Operations 1944–1945, report of April 1945, USAMHI; Wilhelm Frenz, "Zusammenbruch—Stunde Null?" in *Volksgemeinschaft und Volksfeinde: Kassel 1933–1945, Band 2: Studien*, ed. Frenz, Jörg Kammler, and Dietfrid Krause-Vilmar (Fuldabrück: Hesse, 1987), 415–6.
4. Inge Smith, "Der Mensch Josef von Gadolla—persönliche Erinnerungen 50 Jahre danach," in *Gotha 1945: Erlebnisberichte von Zeitzeugen und Autoren*

aus Australien, Frankreich, Gotha, Ohrdruf, Polen, Remstädt, Russland, Waltershausen, Wechmar (Wechmar: Gotha Druck und Reproduktion, 1995), 9. Smith, born Inge von Gadolla, was Josef von Gadolla's only daughter.

5. Egon Ehrlich and Helga Raschke, "Ein Grazer Offizier im militärischen Widerstand," in *Jahrbuch 2003: Schwerpunkt Exil*, ed. Christine Schindler (Dokumentationsarchiv des österreichischen Widerstandes: Vienna, 2003), 174–5.

6. Helga Raschke, Protokolle und Korrespondenz "Gotha 1945," B. 98, Erklärung von Hans Hollaender, Gotha, Hohe Straße 11, n.d., Museum für Regionalgeschichte und Volkskunde Gotha, Inventarnummer 17920.

7. Ehrlich and Raschke, "Grazer Offizier," 176n48.

8. Günther Ewald, "Das Ende des Zweiten Weltkrieges in der Stadt Gotha," in *Die letzten Kriegstage Anfang April 1945 in Gotha* (Stuttgart: Drückerei Schäuble, 1988), 8.

9. Helga Raschke, "Die letzten Tage faschistischer Herrschaft in Gotha," in *Die letzten Kriegstage Anfang April 1945 in Gotha*, 22. This text was clearly written with an eye to GDR censors, but the narrative is corroborated by the other reports.

10. West Europe, April 4,1945, UKNA, HW 1/3462, TOO 1000.

11. Officially because of illness. Standortbefehl, January 1, 1945, Universitäts- und Forschungsbibliothek Erfurt/Gotha (UFEG) [copy of original held in the Bundesarchiv Freiburg].

12. Both quotations from Ehrlich and Raschke, "Grazer Offizier," 181.

13. Raschke, "Die letzten Tage faschistischer Herrschaft in Gotha," 23.

14. Ehrlich and Raschke, "Grazer Offizier," 182.

15. Ibid.

16. Smith, "Der Mensch Josef von Gadolla," 10.

17. Quoted in Ehrlich and Raschke, "Grazer Offizier," 182.

18. On the sirens: Abschrift des Berichtes vom 15. 6. 1965 des ehemaligen städtischen Rechtsrates Günther Ewald, *Gadolla und die Stadt Gotha*, UFEG (hereafter, Ewald Bericht).

19. Ehrlich and Raschke, "Grazer Offizier," 183.

20. Egon Ehrlich, *Josef Ritter von Gadolla: ein österreichisches Offiziersleben in der k.u.k. Armee, im Bundesheer und der Wehrmacht*, 2nd ed. (Vienna: Bundesministerium für Landesverteidigung, 2000), 37. In one account, a city official named Ritter gave the order. Ernst Rudolph, "Die letzten Tage des Faschismus in Gotha," *Gadolla und die Stadt Gotha*, February 20, 1946, UFEG. In a third account, SS-Obergruppenführer and Generalleutnant of the Police Paul Hennicke and the city's mayor ordered the white flag flown on the castle.

21. Rudolph, "Die letzten Tage des Faschismus in Gotha," UFEG; Ehrlich and Raschke, "Grazer Offizier," 184; "Weisse Fahnen über Gotha," March 1965, UFEG 8/14/8.

22. Ehrlich, *Josef Ritter von Gadolla*, 37.

23. Raschke, "Die letzten Tage faschistischer Herrschaft in Gotha," 24; Ewald Bericht, UFEG.

24. Kurt Dobler [founder of the Gotha CDU after the war], "'Damit Gotha leben kann, muss ich sterben!,'" in *Die letzten Kriegstage Anfang April 1945 in Gotha*, 18; Helga Raschke, "Gotha kapitulierte kurz nach 9 Uhr," *Allgemeiner Anzeiger*, April 5, 1995; Ewald Bericht, UFEG.

25. Dobler, "'Damit Gotha leben kann, muss ich sterben!,'" 18.

26. Ehrlich and Raschke, "Grazer Offizier," 184.

27. Ibid.

28. Ibid., 185–6. The Landestheater and surrounding buildings consequently burned unchecked because of the insufficient firefighting equipment.

29. Ewald, "Das Ende des Zweiten Weltkrieges in der Stadt Gotha," 8.

30. "Abschrift des ehem. Fahrbereitschaftsleiters Ernst Rudolph," February 20, 1946, *Gadolla und die Stadt Gotha*, UFEG. The longer version of this report, "Die letzten Tage des Faschismus in Gotha," contains a transparent effort to write himself more fully into the history and an equally transparent one to ingratiate himself to new Soviet masters.

31. Ehrlich and Raschke, "Grazer Offizier," 186.

32. Ernst Rudolph [the driver], "Gotha und Gadolla," April 4, 1965, *Gadolla und die Stadt Gotha*, UFEG; "Abschrift des ehem. Fahrbereitschaftsleiters Ernst Rudolph," February 20, 1946, ibid.

33. Ibid.; Ewald, "Das Ende des Zweiten Weltkrieges in der Stadt Gotha," 12; Statement by Otto Stier, Standgericht der Wehrmachtkommandantur Weimar, April 4, 1945, Thüringisches Staatsarchiv Gotha (TSG).

34. Rudolph, "'Gotha und Gadolla," April 4, 1965, UFEG.

35. Ehrlich and Raschke, "Grazer Offizier," 187; Pastor Leo Schramm, "Bericht über die Erschießung des Oberstleutnants Josef von Gadolla am 5. April 1945," February 24, 1967, *Gadolla und die Stadt Gotha*, UFEG.

36. Schramm, "Bericht über die Erschießung des Oberstleutnants Josef von Gadolla," UFEG.

37. This paragraph is taken from Ewald, "Das Ende des Zweiten Weltkrieges in der Stadt Gotha," 10–11.

38. Ewald Bericht, UFEG. The two who climbed the roof were Ewald and Martin.

39. "Parlamentäre kehren nicht züruck," n.d., UFEG. The order was: Sandrock, Müller-Kirchenbauer, Ritter, Martin, and then Ewald. Ewald Bericht, UFEG.

40. Ewald Bericht, UFEG.

41. Ibid.

42. Ibid.; "Abschrift aus dem Artikel: 'Parlamentäre kehren nicht züruck,'" n.d., *Gadolla und die Stadt Gotha*, UFEG.

43. Remaining details in this paragraph from Ewald Bericht, UFEG.

44. Ibid. Bombers were also reported over Gotha, then turning north toward Nordhausen. "Abschrift aus dem Artikel: 'Parlamentäre kehren nicht züruck,'" UFEG. Nordhausen was hit for the second night in a row. Martin Middlebrook and Chris Everitt, *The Bomber Command War Diaries: An Operational Reference Book, 1939–1945* (Harmondsworth: Viking, 1985), 690–1.

45. "Abschrift des ehem. Fahrbereitschaftsleiters Ernst Rudolph," February 20, 1946, UFEG; Ehrlich, *Josef Ritter von Gadolla,* 39. Oberst von Drebber presided, and Major von Achterberg acted as prosecutor. "Erschießung von Oberstleutnant von Gadolla im April 1945 durch SS-Einheiten in Gotha," December 13, 1963, TSG, 315.

46. Statement by Josef Ritter von Gadolla, April 4, 1945, Standgericht der Wehrmachtkommandantur Weimar, TSG, 315.

47. Statement by Stadtbaurat Müller-Kirchenbauer, April 4, 1945, Standgericht der Wehrmachtkommandantur Weimar, TSG, 315.

48. Urteil in der Strafsache gegen den Stadtbaurat Adolf Müller-Kirchenbauer, April 7, 1945, TSG, 315.

49. Standgericht der Wehrmachtkommandantur Weimar, April 4, 1945, TSG, 315. A copy is on display at the Militärhistorisches Museum der Bundeswehr, Dresden, section on military resistance.

50. Ermittlungsverfahren gegen Oberst von Drebber u. A. wegen Mordes bzw. Beihilfe zum Mord an dem Oberstleutnant Ritter von Gadolla, November 23, 1946, TSG, 315. An effort was made here by the Soviets to charge the members of the defence committee. The effort may have been serious, but it was most likely an effort to embarrass West Germany, to which the relevant members had moved.

51. "Für Gotha ist der Krieg am 4. April zu Ende," *Gadolla und die Stadt Gotha,* UFEG [abstract from Ursula Höntsch and Alfred Harendt, *Die Stunde Null: Tatsachenberichte über Erlebnisse aus den letzten Tagen des 2. Weltkrieges* ([East] Berlin: Verlag der Nation, 1966), 111].

52. Pastor Leo Schramm, Erklärung, December 10, 1945, Militärhistorisches Museum der Bundeswehr, Dresden, section on military resistance.

53. "Für Gotha ist der Krieg am 4. April zu Ende."

54. Schramm, "Bericht über die Erschießung des Oberstleutnants Josef von Gadolla am 5. April 1945"; Schramm, "Der letzte Gruß," in *Die letzten Kriegstage Anfang April 1945 in Gotha,* 21. It was not until the 1960s that Gadolla received recognition for his actions. Like the survivors of the more famous July 20, 1944 resisters, his wife struggled to secure a pension for her and her daughter, and the GDR declared him a "career-militarist," not an anti-fascist, and thus unworthy of honour. Matthias Wenzel, "Ein Mann kann eine ganze

Stadt erretten, aber die Stadt nicht zwei Menschen helfen," in *Gotha 1945*, 18. Gadolla himself was not posthumously rehabilitated until 1997. Enrico Brissa, "Josef Ritter von Gadolla," *Zeitschrift für Thüringische Geschichte* 65 (2011), 235.

55. Ewald Bericht, UFEG. The execution order might well have come from high up the chain of command: the day before the army executed Gadolla, General der Infanterie Schultz of Army Group G bemoaned the surrender of Gotha and Karlsruhe and ordered that the "harshest measures be taken against those responsible for the defence of these cities." Telegram from Army Group G to the 19th Army, April 4, 1945, BArch RH 20-19/180, fol. 149.

56. MacDonald, *Last Offensive*, 377.

57. "Jim Sanders sah Befreite elend sterben," *Gothaer Tagespost*, April 5, 1995.

58. See the account of one of Patton's soldiers, David Cohen, at http://www.americancenturies.mass.edu/centapp/oh/story.do?shortName=cohen1945.

59. "The Nazi Mayor of Ohrdruf," annex no. 3 to First US Army G-2 Periodic Reports, April 1945, NACP RG 407, 101-2.1. On May 1, Eisenhower ordered that all those who died in concentration camps within Twelfth Army Group's jurisdiction be reburied, ideally with the appropriate chaplain present. German men were assigned the task of disinterring or otherwise collecting the bodies, digging fresh graves, and keeping the plots in acceptable condition. Local civilians were required to attend the ceremonies. "Burial of Victims of Nazi Atrocities," May 1, 1945, NACP RG 407, 103-0.18.

60. G-2 Periodic Report, April 15, 1945, NACP RG 407, 101-2.1.

61. Weigley, *Eisenhower's Lieutenants*, 694.

62. Ibid., 717.

63. Ibid.

64. Gerhard Steinecke, *Drei Tage im April: Kriegsende in Leipzig* (Leipzig: Lehmstedt Verlag, 2005), 26–53; Henke, *Die amerikanische Besetzung Deutschlands*, 701–2.

65. G-2 Estimate of the Enemy Situation, April 27, 1945, NACP RG 407, 369-2.1; G-2 Periodic Report, April 15, 1945, NACP RG 407, 101-2.1; G-2 Periodic Report, 69th Infantry Division, April 19, 1945, NACP RG 407, 369-2.1

66. G-2 Periodic Report, 69th Infantry Division, April 19, 1945, NACP RG 407, 369-2.1.

67. Henke, *Die amerikanische Besetzung Deutschlands*, 702.

68. Details from ibid.

69. Ibid.; G-2 Periodic Report, 69th Infantry Division, April, 20 1945.

70. Details on the death marches in this paragraph from Walter Steiner, Renate Wagwitz, Frank Funke, and Anke Bickel, *Weimar 1945: ein historisches Protokoll* (Weimar: Stadtmuseum Weimar, 1997), 12–3.

71. See Martin Gilbert, *The Holocaust: A History of the Jews of Europe during the Second World War* (New York: Holt, Rinehart and Winston, 1985), chapter 40.

72. 80th Infantry After Action Report: European Theatre of Operations 1944–1945, report of April 1945, USAMHI.
73. Henke, *Die amerikanische Besetzung Deutschlands*, 670; 80th Infantry Division G-2 After Action Report, 1–30 April 1945, NACP RG 407, 380-0.3.
74. Ibid.; Steiner et al., *Weimar 1945*, 14–6.
75. Steiner et al., *Weimar 1945*, 15.
76. Ibid., 16.
77. Jens Fügener, "Amerikanisches Intermezzo: Jena zwischen Drittem Reich und Sowjetischer Besatzungszone," in *Macht und Milieu: Jena zwischen Kriegsende und Mauerbau*, ed. Rüdiger Stutz (Jena: Verein für Jenaer Stadt- und Universitätsgeschichte, 2000), 31; 80th Infantry After Action Report: European Theatre of Operations 1944–1945, report of April 1945, USAMHI.
78. The group also included a businessman named Carl Schmidt, a police major named Zürtz, and a Dr. Eisenhut. Fügener, "Amerikanisches Intermezzo," 31–2.
79. Ibid., 32.
80. Ibid., 32n19.
81. The details in this paragraph are from ibid., 31–2.
82. Ibid., 31; Jörg Valtin, "Die Übergabe der Stadt Jena an die amerikanischen Streitkräfte am 13.04.1945," Stadtarchiv Jena, MS ge Ic/5.
83. Hans Dittmer, "Meine Mitwirkung bei der Besetzung der Stadt," June 2, 1945, Stadtarchiv Jena, MS ge Ic/5. In Dittmer's account, the Americans contacted him.
84. Ibid.
85. Ibid.
86. 80th Infantry After Action Report: European Theatre of Operations 1944–1945, report of April 1945, USAMHI.
87. Fügener, "Amerikanisches Intermezzo," 31.
88. The chronology on Jena's official city website states that the war ended when the city was "occupied without a fight" (*kampflos*) on April 13. "Chronik der Stadt Jena," April 1945, available at http://www.jena.de/de/stadt_verwaltung/stadtportraet/chronik/1945/236315 (accessed August 31, 2013). This example makes clear that using a binary categorization—"defended" or "surrendered"—sometimes glosses over greater complexities in the manner in which the war ended. In this book, I have tried to reserve the use of the label "surrendered" for cities and towns in which there was little or no defence leading up to the actual act of surrender.
89. 80th Infantry After Action Report: European Theatre of Operations 1944–1945, report of April 1945, USAMHI; G-2 Periodic Report, April 15, 1945, NACP RG 407, 101-2.1.
90. On this, see Weinberg, *World at Arms*, 812–3 and 829–30.
91. Ibid., 830.

CHAPTER 20: NUREMBERG'S DESTRUCTION, HEIDELBERG'S SALVATION

1. MacDonald, *Last Offensive*, 407.

2. Ibid., 410.

3. Quoted in Hastings, *Armageddon*, 500.

4. MacDonald, *Last Offensive*, 410.

5. Hastings, *Armageddon*, 500; Charles Whiting, *America's Forgotten Army: The Story of the U.S. Seventh* (Rockville Centre, NY: Sarpedon, 1999), 169–71.

6. Lt. Gen. Robert E. Coffin, "The Demonstration at Heidelberg—Guts, Good Sense, Great Timing," *Army* 45, no. 4 (April 1995): 56.

7. G-2 Journal, 44th Infantry Division, March 27, 1945, NACP RG 407, 344-2.2.

8. Coffin, "Demonstration at Heidelberg," 56. Coffin incorrectly cites Dean as commander of the Sixty-Third Infantry Division, later brought in to relieve the Forty-Fourth. Louis E. Hibbs was the Sixty-Third's commander.

9. *Zusammenbruch 1945 und Aufbruch: eine Dokumentation der letzten Kriegstage vom Neckar zum Odenwald* (Heidelberg: Rhein-Neckar-Zeitung, 1995), 5.

10. Ibid., 8.

11. "Mannheim," 44th Division website, http://www.efour4ever.com/44thdivision/mannheim.htm (accessed July 31, 2013).

12. Coffin, "Demonstration at Heidelberg," 56.

13. *Zusammenbruch 1945 und Aufbruch*, 8.

14. Oberstarzt Dr. Eugen Niessen, "Die Nacht vom 29.–30. März 1945 in Heidelberg," n.d. [likely October 1953], Stadtarchiv Heidelberg, B 128 g, 2; Günter Weber, "Heidelbergs Schicksal hing am seidenen Faden," in *Heidelberg zur Stunde Null*, ed. Werner Pieper (Heidelberg: N. Grubhofer Verlag, 1985), 41. Some five thousand had already been evacuated on March 23.

15. "Bericht über meine Tätigkeit (Achelis)," n.d. [early 1950s], Stadtarchiv Heidelberg, B 128 g, 1.

16. Ibid.

17. Ibid. The role of Kreisleiter Wilhelm Seiler is unclear. Some reports claim that he wished to evacuate and defend the city; others suggest that he worked with Neinhaus to secure its surrender.

18. Dr. Dieter Brüggemann to Oberverwaltungsdirektor Dr. Fritz Schlipphak, May 6, 1981, Stadtarchiv Heidelberg, B 128 g, 3; Rüdiger Schubert to May Reinhold Zundel, February 5, 1983, 1.

19. There is no agreement within the archives about who called whom first, but there is agreement that the communication between the Americans and Heidelberg went through Mannheim. Friederike Reutter, *Heidelberg 1945–1949: zur politischen Geschichte einer Stadt in der Nachkriegszeit* (Heidelberg: Verlag Brigitte Guderjahn, 1994), 39 claims the Americans made the first call, but no source is given.

20. *Zusammenbruch 1945 und Aufbruch*, 6.

21. "Bericht über meine Tätigkeit (Achelis)," 1.

22. Ibid., 3; "So war das vor zehn Jahren: Heidelbergs letzte Kriegsstunden—Augenzeugen berichten—Mutiges Verhalten rettete die Stadt," *Rhein-Neckar-Zeitung*, March 26, 1955.

23. Brüggemann to Schlipphak, May 6, 1981, 2.

24. Military doctors Eugen Niessen and Dahmann, Dean of the Medical Faculty Professor Achelis, and driver and translator Fritz Grimm.

25. "Die Nacht vom 29. zum 30. März 1945. Bericht Dr. Niessen," n.d., Stadtarchiv Heidelberg, B 128 g, 4.

26. Schwarz had been attempting to blow up the bridge since March 18, but large numbers of engineers refused to cooperate. On this and the bridge's eventual destruction, see "Beitrag zu den Vorgängen bei der Sprengung der Alten Brücke in Heidelberg am 28. 3. 1945," n.d., Stadtarchiv Heidelberg, Z 651/399. The document dates the destruction one day early.

27. *Zusammenbruch 1945 und Aufbruch*, 8.

28. Ibid.

29. "Bericht Dr. Niessen," 5.

30. Ibid.

31. Ibid.; Brüggemann to Schlipphak, May 6, 1981, 4–5.

32. "Bericht über meine Tätigkeit (Achelis)," 5; "Bericht Dr. Niessen."

33. "Bericht über meine Tätigkeit (Achelis)," 5; "Und wurde so der Retter Heidelbergs," *Heidelberger Tageblatt*, April 8 [?], 1953.

34. Günter Weber, "Heidelbergs Schicksal hing am seidenen Faden," *Heidelberger Tageblatt*, March 30, 1955.

35. "Bericht über meine Tätigkeit (Achelis)," 5.

36. Weber, "Heidelbergs Schicksal," *Heidelberger Tageblatt*, March 30, 1955.

37. "Bericht Dr. Niessen," 7–9.

38. Ibid., 9.

39. Ibid.

40. Rüdiger Schubert to May Reinhold Zundel, February 5, 1983, Stadtarchiv Heidelberg, B 128 g, 1.

41. Reutter, *Heidelberg 1945–1949*, 41.

42. MacDonald, *Last Offensive*, 415.

43. 100th Division S-2 Report, April 4, 1945, NACP RG 407, 3100-2.2.

44. 100th Division G2 Telegram, April 4, 1945, NACP RG 407, 3100-2.2.

45. Telegram to G-2 from Artillery Division, April 12, 1945, NACP RG 407, 3100-2.2.

46. Ibid.

47. Folker Förtsch, "Warum Crailsheim 1945 zerstört wurde," in *Kriegsende in Crailsheim und Umgebung*, ed. Förtsch (Crailsheim: Baier BPB Verlag, 2008), 187.

48. Henke, *Die amerikanische Besetzung Deutschlands*, 784–5.

49. Ibid.

50. Armin Ziegler, *Crailsheim 1945/46: Überleben und Neuanfang* (Crailsheim: Baier, 1999), 13.

51. Jill Stephenson, *Hitler's Home Front: Württemberg under the Nazis* (London: Hambledon Continuum, 2006), 330.

52. This sentence and details on Heilbronn and Crailsheim from MacDonald, *Last Offensive*, 415–8.

53. 100th Division G2 Summary, April 6, 1945, NACP RG 407, 3100-2.2.

54. 100th Division G 2 Periodic Report, April 6, 1945, NACP RG 407, 3100-2.2.

55. MacDonald, *Last Offensive*, 417.

56. Ibid., 418.

57. Förtsch, "Warum Crailsheim 1945 zerstört wurde," 200–1.

58. MacDonald, *Last Offensive*, 418–9; *The Seventh United States Army in France and Germany, 1944–1945: Report of Operations* (Heidelberg: Aloys Gräf, 1946), 767.

59. *Seventh U.S. Army: Report of Operations*, 769.

60. Quoted in Karl Kunze, *Kriegsende in Franken und der Kampf um Nürnberg im April 1945* (Nürnberg: Selbstverlag des Vereins für Geschichte der Stadt Nürnberg, 1995), 32.

61. MacDonald, *Last Offensive*, 420.

62. On the organization of the city's defences, see Generalleutnant Benignus Dippold, "Defence of Nuremberg (12–16 April 1945)," n.d. [likely 1947], USAMHI, B 145.

63. Gellately, *Backing Hitler*, 234.

64. Ibid., 235.

65. Fritz, *Endkampf*, 157.

66. Joachim Brückner, *Kriegsende in Bayern: der Wehrkreis VII und die Kämpfe zwischen Donau und Alpen* (Freiburg: Rombach, 1987), 99–101.

67. Details in this paragraph from ibid., 152–3.

68. Ibid., 150.

69. Details from ibid., 150–1.

70. Ibid., 151.

71. Ibid.

72. Ibid., 153–4, in particular n53.

73. Ibid., 154.

74. Ibid.

75. MacDonald, *Last Offensive*, 435.

76. Ibid.

CHAPTER 21: A CITIZENS' REVOLT

1. Stadtarchiv Augsburg, *Bewahrt Eure Stadt . . . Kriegsende und Neuanfang in Augsburg 1945–1950* (Augsburg: Wißner-Verlag, 2005), 12.

2. Josef Mayr, "Tatsachenbericht über die Vorgeschichte und Durchführung der Übergabe der Stadt Augsburg," June 1, 1955, Stadtarchiv Augsburg, Dok. 822.

3. In contrast with Düsseldorf, in which eyewitness reports were collected, collated, and officially evaluated within a year of the war's end, some of the documents from Augsburg date to the 1990s and 2000s. This outcome was, it seems, intentional. The city archives attempted in 1949 to fill in the details behind the city's liberation by publishing a newspaper call for witnesses ("Zur Übergabe der Stadt Augsburg an die amerikanischen Truppen am 28. April 1945: ein Aufruf des Stadtarchivs an die Augsburger Bevölkerung," *Amtsblatt der Stadt Augsburg*, April 14, 1949), but only Georg Achatz replied. The others kept silent (Engelbert Schraudy, "Eine wahre Begebenheit am 28. April 1945," May 28, 2002, Stadtarchiv Augsburg, Dok. 818; Prof. Dr. Karl Filser, "Als die Amerikaner kamen: Der 28. April 1945 in Augsburg," April 28, 1995), and it seems that the archive did not release the Achatz report. The motivation appears to have been Christian humility: a pastor, Dr. Josef Hörmann, had sworn the group to secrecy, saying after Augsburg's liberation: "We need neither heroes nor saints; we are grateful to God that everything worked out" (Schraudy, "Eine wahre Begebenheit"). There was a certain irony in this, as Hörmann himself sent in a report after a further appeal from the city's archivist. (Letter from Stadtarchivdirektor to Augsburg's Oberbürgermeister, April 24, 1950, Stadtarchiv Augsburg, Dok. 818.) A newspaper article ten years after the event bemoaned the refusal of any witnesses to discuss what happened ("Vor zehn Jahren marschierten US-Truppen in Augsburg ein," *Schwäbische Landeszeitung*, April 28, 1955). Rudolf Lang had written a report in May 1945, but it was likely held by the Americans at this point. Some eyewitness reports thus come from the 1970s, and even 1990s and 2000s. This naturally raises the usual concerns about memory and its reliability, but the reports are broadly consistent and can be compared with three others—the two mentioned above and one by an American major—that were published shortly after the war.

4. On Achatz, see the correspondence solicited by the city archivist, in particular the letter to Dr. Deininger, Director of the Archive, May 12, 1965, Stadtarchiv Augsburg, Dok. 503. The second resistance cell was led by another doctor, Röck (junior), and a businessman from Aachen named Franz Hesse (Hubert Rauch, "Mein Beitrag zur kampflosen Übergabe von Augsburg am 28. 4. 1945," March 21, 1995, Stadtarchiv Augsburg, Dok. 818; Anton Kaiser, "Widerstand zur kampflosen Übergabe der Stadt Augsburg," n.d. [1981 or 1982]). Friedrich Rüggeberg, a soldier and concert singer with contacts in the UK, led the third

group (Georg Achatz, "Bericht über die Tätigkeit der Freiheitsbewegung 1945," April 20, 1949, Stadtarchiv Augsburg, Dok. 820).

5. Achatz, "Bericht über die Tätigkeit der Freiheitsbewegung 1945," April 20, 1949. Other figures drawn into the Achatz-Lang group were Bishop Dr. Josef Kumpfmüller and lawyer Dr. Franz Reisert. The last had had some contact with the Kreisau Circle and was eventually arrested because of his links to July 20 conspirators. See Prof. Dr. Karl Filser, "Als die Amerikaner kamen: der 28. April 1945 in Augsburg," April 28, 1995, Stadtarchiv Augsburg, Dok. 818; Engelbert Schraudy and Dr. Marianne Schuber, "'Wie die Einnahme Augsburgs durch die Amerikaner am 28. April 1945—fast—ohne Blutvergießen verlief,'" April 28, 2008, Stadtarchiv Augsburg, Man 228.

6. Hubert Rauch, "Mein Beitrag"; Anton Kaiser, "Widerstand zur kampflosen Übergabe."

7. "Mit weisser Fahne im Jeep: Hubert Rauch führte Amerikaner in die Stadt," n.d. [newspaper clipping likely from 1995], Stadtarchiv Augsburg, Dok. 818.

8. Filser, "Als die Amerikaner kamen."

9. Karl-Ulrich Gelberg, "Einleitung," in *Kriegsende und Neuanfang in Augsburg 1945: Erinnerungen und Berichte*, ed. Gelberg (Munich: R. Oldenbourg, 1996), 12.

10. Solia, "Sie logen bis zum bitteren Ende. Der ehemalige Gauleiter verfasste noch am 9. April 1945 Durchhalte-Aufrufe," *Augsburger Rundschau*, April 25, 1970, Stadtarchiv Augsburg, Dok. 819.

11. Filser, "Als die Amerikaner kamen."

12. Mayr, "Tatsachenbericht."

13. Achatz, "Bericht über die Tätigkeit der Freiheitsbewegung 1945"; Rudolf Lang, "Bericht über die Tätigkeit der Deutschen Freiheitsbewegung in Augsburg," May 1945.

14. Mayr, "Tatsachenbericht."

15. Stadtarchiv Augsburg, *Bewahrt Eure Stadt*, 22. The source for this report is Mayr himself, "Tatsachenbericht."

16. For a measured discussion of Mayr and Wahl's role, see Filser, "Als die Amerikaner kamen."

17. Lang, "Freiheitsbewegung in Augsburg."

18. Ibid.

19. Filser, "Als die Amerikaner kamen."

20. Lang, "Freiheitsbewegung in Augsburg."

21. Lang, "Die Übergabe der Stadt Augsburg," 127.

22. Lang, "Freiheitsbewegung in Augsburg."

23. Ibid.

24. Lang, "Die Übergabe der Stadt Augsburg," 127.

25. Lang, "Freiheitsbewegung in Augsburg."
26. Report by Engelbert Schraudy, May 28, 2002, Stadtarchiv Augsburg, Dok. 818. On Kaiser's religious commitments: Schraudy and Schuber, "Einnahme Augsburgs," April 28, 2008, Stadtarchiv Augsburg, Man 228. The nature of Kaiser's wounds was unclear, but they seem to have been serious enough to keep him out of the army but not serious enough to keep him from active disobedience.
27. Rüggeberg, and Karl Eckl, a resister from the postal service. Hubert Rauch, "Mein Beitrag"; Kaiser, "Widerstand zur kampflosen Übergabe."
28. Lang, "Freiheitsbewegung in Augsburg." The suburbs were Aystetten, Gessertshausen, Zusmarshausen, and Langweid.
29. Filser, "Als die Amerikaner kamen."
30. Rauch, "Mein Beitrag"; Lang, "Die Übergabe der Stadt Augsburg," 129.
31. Weigley, *Eisenhower's Lieutenants*, 713.
32. The churchwarden was Ludwig Emmerling. Filser, "Als die Amerikaner kamen."
33. Weigley, *Eisenhower's Lieutenants*, 713.
34. Lang, "Freiheitsbewegung in Augsburg."
35. Lang, "Die Übergabe der Stadt Augsburg," n16.
36. Lang, "Freiheitsbewegung in Augsburg."
37. Lang, "Die Übergabe der Stadt Augsburg," n16.
38. Rauch, "Mein Beitrag"; Kaiser, "Widerstand zur kampflosen Übergabe."
39. Ibid.
40. In one account, clerics Josef Hörmann and Alois Vogg agreed with Franz Hesse that they would try to reach American lines without informing Achatz or Lang. Report by Engelbert Schraudy, May 14, 2005, Stadtarchiv Augsburg, Dok. 818. In Achatz's own account, he gave the order. Achatz, "Bericht über die Tätigkeit der Freiheitsbewegung 1945."
41. Achatz, "Bericht über die Tätigkeit der Freiheitsbewegung 1945."
42. Lang, "Freiheitsbewegung in Augsburg."
43. Ibid.
44. Achatz, "Bericht über die Tätigkeit der Freiheitsbewegung 1945."
45. Quotations in this paragraph from Lang, "Freiheitsbewegung in Augsburg."
46. *"Das ist aber letzten Endes eine der Konsequenzen, die sich aus den letzten 12 Jahren für Sie ergeben."*
47. Lang, "Freiheitsbewegung in Augsburg."
48. Ibid.
49. The cleric Dr. Josef Hörmann, a colleague of Anton Setzer, and Bishop Josef Kumpfmüller.
50. Lang, "Freiheitsbewegung in Augsburg." The men were Karl Eckl, an engineer, and his son of the same name.

51. Kaiser, "Widerstand zur kampflosen Übergabe." The "major" was in fact a cleric.
52. Lang, "Die Übergabe der Stadt Augsburg," 132.
53. Lang, "Freiheitsbewegung in Augsburg."
54. Lang, "Die Übergabe der Stadt Augsburg," 132–3.
55. Major John O'Connell, "Franz Hesse und die Einnahme Augsburgs durch das Third Battalion 15th Infantry Regiment," April 30, 1945, Stadtarchiv Augsburg, Dok. 818.
56. Ibid.
57. Wirsching's story from a letter to the mayor, May 17, 1995, Stadtarchiv Augsburg, Dok. 818.
58. O'Connell, "Franz Hesse und die Einnahme Augsburgs."
59. Achatz, "Bericht über die Tätigkeit der Freiheitsbewegung 1945."
60. O'Connell, "Franz Hesse und die Einnahme Augsburgs."
61. Ibid.
62. The Gögginger Bridge.
63. Report by Wilhelm Martini, May 5, 1970, Stadtarchiv Augsburg, Dok. 818; Kaiser, "Widerstand zur kampflosen Übergabe."
64. Report by Wilhelm Martini, May 5, 1970.
65. Ibid.
66. O'Connell, "Franz Hesse und die Einnahme Augsburgs."
67. "German Citizen Prevented Fierce Battle," The SACom Scene, April 29, 1955 [English original of O'Connell's report], Stadtarchiv Augsburg, Dok. 819.
68. Lang, "Freiheitsbewegung in Augsburg."
69. O'Connell, "Franz Hesse und die Einnahme Augsburgs."
70. Lang, "Freiheitsbewegung in Augsburg."
71. Weigley, Eisenhower's Lieutenants, 713. Lang gives the credit for grabbing the phone to Achatz. Lang, "Freiheitsbewegung in Augsburg."
72. Lang, "Freiheitsbewegung in Augsburg."
73. Rauch, "Mein Beitrag"; Kaiser, "Widerstand zur kampflosen Übergabe."
74. Friedrich Rüggeberg. Quoted in Lang, "Die Übergabe der Stadt Augsburg," 135.
75. Weigley, Eisenhower's Lieutenants, 713.
76. Ibid.
77. Brückner, Kriegsende in Bayern, 190.
78. Heinemann, "Military Resistance Activities," 910–1.
79. Ibid., 910.
80. Gellately, Backing Hitler, 236.
81. Ibid.
82. Weigley, Eisenhower's Lieutenants, 713.

83. Ibid., 714.
84. Ibid.
85. Ibid., 713.

CHAPTER 22: "WE, THE WOMEN OF FREIBURG, BEG YOU"

1. MacDonald, *Last Offensive*, 322.
2. Ibid.
3. Josef Werner, *Karlsruhe 1945: Unter Hakenkreuz, Trikolore und Sternenbanner*, 2nd ed. (Karlsruhe: G. Braun, 1986), 68.
4. Ibid.
5. Ibid., 69.
6. Ibid., 68.
7. Ibid., 69.
8. Ibid. The railway bridge was on the Mittelbruchstraße.
9. Ibid., 70.
10. Telegram from Army Group G, April 4, 1945, BArch RH 20-19/180, fol. 148.
11. Ibid.
12. Although all the bridges had been detonated. Telegram from the 19th Army, April 6, 1945, BArch RH 20-19/180, fol. 106. The city had been declared an essential defence point (*Ortsstützpunkt*) in early April. See the telegram from Oberstlt. Klett, April 1, 1945 and telegram from Army Group G to the 19th Army, April 4, 1945, BArch RH 20-19/180, fol. 143 [text unclear, possibly 123].
13. MacDonald incorrectly states that Pforzheim was "quickly captured." My thanks to Dr. Christian Groh of the Stadtarchiv Pforzheim for clarifying this fact in e-mail correspondence. See also Hans Georg Zier, *Geschichte der Stadt Pforzheim: von den Anfängen bis 1945* (Stuttgart: Konrad Theiss Verlag, 1982), 352–6.
14. For the details, see MacDonald, *Last Offensive*, 427–8.
15. Ibid., 428.
16. This paragraph is based on Hermann Werner, *Tübingen 1945* (Stuttgart: Konrad Theiss Verlag, 1986), 52–63.
17. Oberst Schütz, who had arrived to assume his post on April 5, had recently sustained a head wound from which he had not recovered. According to Werner, Schütz viewed a defence of Tübingen as pointless and was prepared to ignore certain orders. Ibid., 26, 53.
18. Stephenson, *Hitler's Home Front*, 328.
19. West Europe, April 25, 1945, UKNA, HW 1/3732, TOO 1030.
20. Roland Müller, "'Make Democracy Work': Verwaltung und Politik in Stuttgart 1945," in *Stuttgart 1945: Anfang nach dem Ende*, ed. Wulf D. von Lucius (Stuttgart: Lithos-Verlag, 1995), 14.

21. Ibid. By whom is not perfectly clear. It may have been Wehrmacht soldiers and NSDAP officials, though the latter were more than busy burning documents.
22. Ibid.
23. Stephenson, *Hitler's Home Front,* 333. Murr and his wife later killed themselves.
24. Werner, *Karlsruhe,* 89.
25. On the court martial and Marbach's successful defence, see Werner, *Karlsruhe,* 84–9.
26. Müller, "'Make Democracy Work,'" 14.
27. Werner, *Karlsruhe,* 89.
28. MacDonald, *Last Offensive,* 429.
29. Ibid., 431.
30. Gerd R. Ueberschär, "Freiburgs letzte Kriegstage bis zur Besetzung durch die französische Armee am 21. April 1945," in *Endlich Frieden! Das Kriegsende in Freiburg 1945,* ed. Thomas Schnabel and Ueberschär (Freiburg: Schillinger Verlag, 1985), 20.
31. The order is reproduced in ibid.
32. Ibid., 26.
33. Telegram of April 1, and telegram from the Nineteenth Army, April 6, 1945, BArch RH 20-19/180, fol. 23 [possibly 123] and 104.
34. Ueberschär, "Freiburgs letzte Kriegstage," 22.
35. Ibid., 28.
36. Ibid., 26; Rudolf Bader, "1945: Freiburgs letzte Kriegstage," *Freiburger Almanach* 26 (1975), 51.
37. Bader, "1945: Freiburgs letzte Kriegstage," 51. Knörzer's name is often rendered as "Knoerzer," but I defer here to the spelling given by Bader.
38. Ibid.
39. Ibid., 51–2; Ueberschär, "Freiburgs letzte Kriegstage," 32, 34.
40. Quotations in this paragraph from Max Bruecher, *Freiburg im Breisgau 1945: eine Dokumentation* (Freiburg: Verlag Rombach, 1980), 10–2.
41. Kerber wished to work with Bader in saving the city. See Bader, "1945: Freiburgs letzte Kriegstage," 52–3; Werner Köhler, *Freiburg i. Br. 1945–1949: politisches Leben und Erfahrungen in der Nachkriegszeit* (Freiburg: Stadtarchiv Freiburg im Breisgau, 1987), 12.
42. Bruecher, *Freiburg im Breisgau 1945,* 11.
43. Köhler, *Freiburg i. Br. 1945–1949,* 12.
44. This paragraph draws on Bader, "1945: Freiburgs letzte Kriegstage," 52.
45. Bruecher, *Freiburg im Breisgau 1945,* 12.
46. Quotations in this paragraph from ibid., 13.
47. Ibid.
48. Köhler, *Freiburg i. Br.,* 13.

49. "Bilder aus Freiburg im Breisgau," July 15, 1945, Stadtarchiv Freiburg B1, 328/7, unpaginated [p. 3].

50. Pastor Nörbers, "Kurze Darstellung wie das Ende des unglücklichen Krieges in Freiburg-Zähringen erlebt und empfunden wurde," September 10, 1945, Stadtarchiv Freiburg B1, 328/7, unpaginated [p. 3].

51. Heiko Haumann and Hans Shadek, eds., *Geschichte der Stadt Freiburg im Breisgau*, vol. 3, *Von der badischen Herrschaft bis zur Gegenwart* (Stuttgart: Theiss, 2001), 368.

52. Köhler, *Freiburg i. Br.*, 14–5.

53. Bader, "1945: Freiburgs letzte Kriegstage," 55.

54. Haumann and Shadek, *Geschichte der Stadt Freiburg*, 3:370.

55. Stephenson, *Hitler's Home Front*, 328.

56. Ibid., 335.

57. Ibid., 328.

58. Helmut Moll, ed., *Zeugen für Christus: das deutsche Martyrologium des 20. Jahrhunderts*, 2 vols., 4th ed. (Paderborn: Ferdinand Schöningh, 2006), 224–5. The priest was Father Willibald Strohmeyer. See also Wilhelm Weitzel, "Ereignisse in Staufen am Kriegsende," in *Staufen vor und nach dem Fliegerangriff*, ed. August Villinger (Staufen im Breisgau: Verlag A. Villinger, 1986), 373–4.

CHAPTER 23: A HOUSE OF CARDS

1. Specifically from Tukums (Latvia) south to Memel-Klaipeda-Augustów, cutting southwest to Warsaw, somewhat southeast to Sandomierz, and then following a line through Jasło-Košice-Esztergom-Balaton and ending on the Drava River.

2. Albert Seaton, *The Russo-German War 1941–45* (London: Arthur Baker Limited, 1971), 522.

3. Erickson, *Road to Berlin*, 432.

4. Ibid., 430, 447.

5. From Hastings, *Armageddon*, 279, with a slight altering of the translation.

6. Erickson, *Road to Berlin*, 456.

7. Seaton, *Russo-German War*, 534.

8. Imagery in this paragraph drawn from Hastings, *Armageddon*, 280–1, and Erickson, *Road to Berlin*, 456.

9. Erickson, *Road to Berlin*, 456.

10. Hastings, *Armageddon*, 280.

11. Erickson, *Road to Berlin*, 458.

12. Statistics from Hastings, *Armageddon*, 285, and Weinberg, *World at Arms*, 801.

13. Hastings, *Armageddon*, 281.

14. Erickson, *Road to Berlin*, 460.

15. Weinberg, *World at Arms*, 800.

16. Erickson, *Road to Berlin*, 464–6.
17. Details in this paragraph from ibid., 466–7.
18. Seaton, *Russo-German War*, 546.
19. Weinberg, *World at Arms*, 801.
20. Seaton, *Russo-German War*, 539.
21. Ibid., 535.
22. West Europe, January 24, 1945, UKNA, HW 1/3483, TOO 1750.
23. Seaton, *Russo-German War*, 536.
24. Erickson, *Road to Berlin*, 510–4.
25. Ibid., 518–9.
26. Seaton, *Russo-German War*, 540.
27. Communiqué from Ribbentrop to the German Legation, Dublin, February 16, 1945, UKNA, HW 1/3539.
28. "Iron mood" in the text, but this is a slightly loose translation of what must have been the original German.
29. Japanese Plan for German-Soviet Peace: Ambassador Oshima's enquiries, August 28, 1944, UKNA, HW 1/3191.
30. I am grateful to Richard Bessel for drawing my attention to the point on supply lines.
31. Erickson, *Road to Berlin*, 524.
32. Ibid., 526, 528; Hastings, *Armageddon*, 299.
33. Seaton, *Russo-German War*, 567.
34. Richard Lakowski, *Seelow 1945: die Entscheidungsschlacht an der Oder*, 3rd ed. (Berlin: Brandenburgisches Verlagshaus, 1996), 75–7.
35. Ibid., 78.
36. Erickson, *Road to Berlin*, 556.
37. Ibid., 564, 567.
38. See ibid., 568–72.
39. Rudolf Petershagen, *Gewissen in Aufruhr* ([East] Berlin: Verlag der Nation, 1966), 34.

CHAPTER 24: SAVING CASPAR DAVID FRIEDRICH'S CITY

1. Original in German reproduced in Petershagen, *Gewissen in Aufruhr*, appendix.
2. Details in this paragraph from ibid., 41.
3. See the comments on Adenauer as well as the crudely contrived symbolism contrasting a young, sturdy female socialist peasant and the old, wizened reactionary militarist. Ibid., 42 and 51–3, respectively.
4. See Helge Matthiesen, "Das Kriegsende 1945 und der Mythos von der kampflosen Übergabe," in *Greifswald: Geschichte der Stadt*, ed. Horst Wernicke (Schwerin: Thomas Helms Verlag, 2000), 135–40.

5. Günter Mangelsdorf, ed., *Zwischen Greifswald und Riga: Auszüge aus den Tagebüchern des Greifswalder Rektors und Professors der Ur- und Frühgeschichte, Dr. Carl Engel, vom 1. November 1938 bis 26 Juli. 1945* (Stuttgart: Franz Steiner Verlag, 2007), 3–4.

6. Ibid., 5.

7. Wolfgang Wilhelmus, *Geschichte der Juden in Greifswald und Umgebung* (Kückenshagen: Scheunen-Verlag, 1999), 66, 68.

8. Historian Ernst-Joachim Krüger quoted in Jantje Hannover, "Zerstörung und Rettung in letzter Minute: das Kriegsende in den Nachbarstädten Anklam und Greifswald," *Deutschlandradio Kultur*, April 29, 2005, available at: http://www.dradio.de/dkultur/sendungen/laenderreport/368478/ (accessed August 7, 2013).

9. Ibid.

10. Petershagen, *Gewissen in Aufruhr*, 37 and 35, respectively.

11. Ibid., 37.

12. Mangelsdorf, *Greifswald und Riga*, 35.

13. See Petershagen, *Gewissen in Aufruhr*, 43 (on the SS) and 44 (on the refugees).

14. Carl Engel, "Erinnerungen an die letzten Kriegstage und die kampflose Übergabe Greifswalds," May 19–June 3, 1945 [exact date unclear], in Mangelsdorf, *Greifswald und Riga*, 318. Richard Schmidt, who only briefly served as acting mayor, should not be confused with the local Kreisleiter, Otto Schmidt. Other civilians who sought the surrender of the city included Stadtrat Siegfried Remertz and Ernst Lohmeyer, who would become the university's first rector after the war, albeit only briefly. Both men were arrested and died in Soviet camps.

15. Mangelsdorf, *Greifswald und Riga*, 36.

16. Engel, "Erinnerungen," 318.

17. Ibid. On Himmler's undistinguished command, see Longerich, *Heinrich Himmler*, 715–9.

18. Mangelsdorf, *Greifswald und Riga*, 36.

19. Ibid.

20. Petershagen, *Gewissen in Aufruhr*, 45.

21. Ibid., 49–50.

22. Ibid., 50. Major Schönfeld was the adjutant.

23. Ibid., 54.

24. Ibid., 55–6.

25. Engel, "Erinnerungen," 319–21.

26. It is possible that Petershagen confused two different meetings: one with Engel and another with Acting Mayor Schmidt and a group of men from the Communist National Committee for a Free Germany, although if so the error

was genuine as he would have had every interest in remembering. For the details, see ibid., 324.

27. Details in this paragraph from Petershagen, *Gewissen in Aufruhr*, 59–61.
28. Engel, "Erinnerungen," 320–1.
29. Details from Petershagen, *Gewissen in Aufruhr*, 62–3.
30. Petershagen, *Gewissen in Aufruhr*, 67.
31. Ibid., 63–6.
32. Ibid., 56.
33. Engel, "Erinnerungen," 322.
34. Ibid.
35. Ibid., 325.
36. Ibid. Engel states the time as being shortly before 23:40.
37. Petershagen, *Gewissen in Aufruhr*, 70.
38. Ibid.; Engel, "Erinnerung," 326.
39. Engel, "Erinnerung," 326–7.
40. This is the German transliteration of the general's name as it appears in the original sources.
41. Petershagen, *Gewissen in Aufruhr*, 71.
42. Ibid.; Engel, "Erinnerungen," 329.
43. Petershagen, *Gewissen im Aufruhr*, 71.
44. The rest of the narrative draws on Petershagen, *Gewissen in Aufruhr*, 72–6.
45. Schmidt's motivations were unclear. See Hans Georg Thümmel, *Greifswald — Geschichte und Geschichten: die Stadt, ihre Kirchen, und ihre Universität* (Paderborn: Ferdinand Schöningh, 2011), 210.
46. Ibid., 211.
47. Ibid. According to a memorial plaque at the university, he was hanged.
48. Ibid., 212.

CHAPTER 25: FINISHING THE JOB THAT BOMBER HARRIS STARTED

1. Chandler, *Papers of Eisenhower*, 4:2568.
2. Weigley, *Eisenhower's Lieutenants*, 719.
3. Ibid., 719–21.
4. Ibid., 721. Churchill shared these concerns. See UKNA, FO 954/23, cited in Leif Leifland, "Hamburgs Kapitulation im Mai 1945: Querverbindungen nach Schweden," *Zeitschrift des Vereins für Hamburgische Geschichte* 78 (1992), 247.
5. Weigley, *Eisenhower's Lieutenants*, 721.
6. West Europe, April 18, 1945, UKNA, HW 1/3713, TOO 1330.
7. Sereny, *Albert Speer*, 499–501.
8. Report from Commander in Chief Netherlands, Blaskowitz, to OKW, May 1, 1945, UKNA, H1/3744.

9. Seyß-Inquart attempted in the last days to secure permission to negotiate with the Allies, writing to the already dead Führer on May 2. Telegram from Seyß-Inquart to Hitler, May 2, 1945, BArch R 3/1623.

10. Ludwig Plate, "Überschwemmungen zur Verteidigung Bremens im April 1945," in *Kriegsende in Bremen: Erinnerungen, Berichte, Dokumente*, ed. Hartmut Müller and Günther Rohdenburg (Bremen: Ed. Temmen, 1995), 20.

11. Hartmut Müller, "'Es waren schöne warme Frühlingstage': Bremen am Vorabend der Einnahme durch britische Soldaten," in *Kriegsende in Bremen*, ed. Müller and Rohdenburg, 16; Charles Whiting, *Bloody Bremen: Ike's Last Stand* (London: Leo Cooper, 1998), 138–9.

12. Herbert Schwarzwälder, *Bremen und Nordwestdeutschland am Kriegsende 1945*, vol. 3, *Vom "Kampf um Bremen" bis zur Kapitulation* (Bremen: Carl Schünemann Verlag, 1974), 87.

13. Naval Section: Naval Headlines, 1398, May 2, 1945, UKNA, HW 1/3744.

14. Peter Groth, "'Bremen war nur noch ein Wrack': die Einnahme Bremens durch die Engländer im April 1945," in *Kriegsende in Bremen*, ed. Müller and Rohdenburg, 44; Schwarzwälder, *Bremen und Nordwestdeutschland am Kriegsende 1945*, 3:65.

15. Weinberg, *World at Arms*, 815.

16. See Frank Bajohr, "Gauleiter in Hamburg," 271–5. Kaufmann was born in Krefeld.

17. Jan Heitmann, *Das Ende des Zweiten Weltkrieges in Hamburg: die kampflose Übergabe der Stadt an die britischen Truppen und ihre Vorgeschichte* (Frankfurt: Peter Lang, 1990), 39.

18. Bajohr, "Gauleiter in Hamburg," 270.

19. Ibid., 274–5.

20. Ibid., 276.

21. *Hamburger Fremdenblatt*, January 7, 1939, quoted ibid., 291.

22. Ibid., 291–2.

23. Ibid., 277.

24. Ibid., 278; Bajohr, "Die Zustimmungsdiktatur: Grundzüge nationalsozialistischer Herrschaft in Hamburg," in *Hamburg im "Dritten Reich,"* ed. Forschungstelle für Zeitgeschichte in Hamburg (Göttingen: Wallstein Verlag, 2005), 88–9.

25. Bajohr, "Gauleiter in Hamburg," 279.

26. Kurt Detlev Möller, *Das letzte Kapitel: Geschichte der Kapitulation Hamburgs* (Hamburg: Hoffmann and Campe Verlag, 1947). For a discussion of the history of and problems associated with Möller's book, see Joist Grolle, "Schwierigkeiten mit der Vergangenheit: Anfänge der zeitgeschichtlichen Forschung in Hamburg der Nachkriegszeit," *Zeitschrift des Vereins für Hamburgische Geschichte* 78 (1992): 1–66.

27. Karl Kaufmann, "Die Kapitulation von Hamburg," June 1946, Staatsarchiv Hamburg, III.9, fol. 98 [p. 2].

28. Ibid.

29. Ibid., fol. 97 [p. 1], quoted in Manfred Asendorf, "Karl Kaufmann und Hamburgs langer Weg zur Kapitulation," in *Kriegsende und Befreiung: Beiträge der nationalsozialistischen Verfolgung in Norddeutschland*, ed. Detlef Garbe, Heft 2 (Bremen: Ed. Temmen, 1995), 12.

30. Kaufmann traces his realization that the war was lost all the way back to 1943. "Kapitulation von Hamburg," fol. 97 [p. 1]. In making this claim, he attempted to hitch his wagon to Speer's star, citing the armament minister's own 1943 loss of faith (ibid.). More recent evidence has shown that Speer did not cease believing in final German victory until early 1945. Mierzejewski, "When Did Albert Speer Give Up?," 392. In his report, Kaufmann claims to have been "entirely in agreement" with the city's battle commander, General Alwin Wolz, over the need to preserve Hamburg throughout 1945. Kaufmann, "Kapitulation von Hamburg," fol. 99 [p. 3].

31. Möller, *Das letzte Kapitel*, 51.

32. Ibid., 50–1.

33. Ibid., 51.

34. Ibid., 52–3.

35. "Bericht des Generalmajors a. D. Ritter von Heigl über seine Tätigkeit in Nordwestdeutschland vom April bis Juni 1945," Staatsarchiv Hamburg, III.23.

36. Ibid.

37. Ibid., 2.

38. Ibid., 2–3.

39. Details from Möller, *Das letzte Kapitel*, 46.

40. Wolz, "Die Übergabe Hamburgs an die 7. englische Panzerdivision am 3. 5. 1945," Staatsarchiv Hamburg, III.9, fol. 71–7, p. 1.

41. Ibid.; Möller, *Das letzte Kapitel*, 47.

42. Dr. Ascan Klée Gobert [soldier under Wolz's command in the Third Flak Division], "Ein Beitrag zur Kapitulation Hamburgs," 1945 [likely March], Staatsarchiv Hamburg, III.9, fol. 139 [p. 2] verso.

43. Wolz, "Übergabe Hamburgs," 1; Möller, *Das letzte Kapitel*, 47.

44. "Bericht von Heigl," 3.

45. Ibid.

46. Report by Major Nietmann, September 9, 1946, Staatsarchiv Hamburg, III.9, fol. 137.

47. Ibid. Emphasis in the original.

48. Ibid.; Wolz, "Übergabe Hamburgs," 1–2.

49. Report by Major Nietmann.

50. Leifland, "Hamburgs Kapitulation," 245, citing original Danish Foreign Ministry sources.

51. Dr. Heinrich Riensberg, a shipping official (*Schiffahrtssachverständiger*) of the German representation in Stockholm, and Swedish bankers Jacob and Marcus Wallenberg. The papers are held in the Staatsarchiv Hamburg, III.9: report by Dr. Karl-Henz Krämer, June 4, 1945, with cover letter from May 12, 1947, fol. 162; report by Dr. Heinrich Reinsberg, May 9, 1945, fol. 64–70; and "Unterhaltung mit Direktor Bertram vom Norddeutschen Lloyd Bremen," January 9, 1947, fol. 168.

52. Telegram from Mallet to the Foreign Office, April 18, 1945, UKNA, FO 188/487.

53. Asendorf, "Karl Kaufmann," 21.

54. See Longerich, *Heinrich Himmler*, 724–5. Himmler "issued notification" of the release of 2,700 Jewish prisoners at this point. Whether they were actually released is unclear.

55. Ibid., 726.

56. Ibid., 726–7.

57. Ibid., 727.

58. Ibid., 728–9.

59. Ibid., 729.

60. Leifland, "Hamburgs Kapitulation," 248–50. The official records cited by Leifland are UKNA, FO 371/46748 and FO 188/487.

61. Quoted ibid., 250–1. The quotation has been translated back into English from German and likely differs from the original. I have not consulted it, but it can be found in UKNA, PRO, FO 188/487.

62. Albert Schäfer to the Hamburg Senate, January 21, 1947, Staatsarchiv Hamburg, III.9, fol. 154 [p. 2]; Miles Hildyard, *It Is Bliss Here: Letters Home 1939–1945* (London: Bloomsbury, 2006), 312. Schäfer refers to Burchard as "Prof. Burghard."

63. Schäfer to Hamburg Senate, 2.

64. Ibid., 3.

65. Evidently on the suggestion of a doctor responsible for the Volkssturm, Werner Lochmann. Heitmann, *Ende des Zweiten Weltkrieges in Hamburg*, 80.

66. Schäfer to Hamburg Senate, 3.

67. Heitmann, *Ende des Zweiten Weltkrieges in Hamburg*, 81.

68. Wolz, "Übergabe Hamburgs," 2.

69. Heitmann, *Ende des Zweiten Weltkrieges in Hamburg*, 81.

70. Schäfer to Hamburg Senate, 3.

71. Heitmann, *Ende des Zweiten Weltkrieges in Hamburg*, 83.

72. Schäfer to Hamburg Senate, 3.

73. Heitmann, *Ende des Zweiten Weltkrieges in Hamburg*, 83–4.

74. Ibid.; Schäfer to Hamburg Senate, 3–4.

75. Heitmann, *Ende des Zweiten Weltkrieges in Hamburg*, 84–5.

76. Schäfer to Hamburg Senate, 4.
77. Heitmann, *Ende des Zweiten Weltkrieges in Hamburg*, 86.
78. Schäfer to Hamburg Senate, 4.
79. Heitmann, *Ende des Zweiten Weltkrieges in Hamburg*, 87
80. Ibid., 88–91.
81. Details in this paragraph from Schäfer to Hamburg Senate, 4–5.
82. Heitmann, *Das Ende des Zweiten Weltkrieges in Hamburg*, 99.
83. Details from this paragraph ibid., 95–9. See also Schäfer to Hamburg Senate, 6–7.
84. Heitmann, *Ende des Zweiten Weltkrieges in Hamburg*, 100.
85. He also handed him a letter from Lindsay explaining that the two others had been kept back because they had not been blindfolded the entire time. Lindsay to Wolz, April 29, 1945, Staatsarchiv Hamburg, III.9.
86. Hildyard, *It Is Bliss Here*, 31. English translation of letter from Lyne to Wolz, April 29, 1945, Staatsarchiv Hamburg, III.9.
87. Schäfer to Hamburg Senate, 7.
88. Wolz to Lyne, April 30, 1945, Staatsarchiv Hamburg, III.9 [letter beginning, *"Für die liebenswürdige Berücksichtigung . . ."*].
89. Wolz to Lyne, April 30, 1945, Staatsarchiv Hamburg, III.9 [letter beginning, *"Die Gedanken . . ."*].
90. Quotations in this paragraph from Schäfer to Hamburg Senate, 8.
91. Letter from Kaufmann to Dönitz and Busch, April 30, 1945, Staatsarchiv Hamburg, III.9, fol. 9.
92. Telegram from Dönitz to Kaufmann, April 30, 1945, Staatsarchiv Hamburg, III.9, fol. 10.
93. Heitmann, *Ende des Zweiten Weltkrieges in Hamburg*, 112.
94. Details in this paragraph from Wolz, "Übergabe Hamburgs," 4.
95. Details in this paragraph from Heitmann, *Ende des Zweiten Weltkrieges in Hamburg*, 123–4.
96. Wolz, "Übergabe Hamburgs," 4.
97. Ibid., 4, and Heitmann, *Ende des Zweiten Weltkrieges in Hamburg*, 127.
98. Ibid.
99. Ibid.
100. Wolz, "Übergabe Hamburgs," 5.
101. Kaufmann, "Drahtfunkansprache des Gauleiters an die Hamburger am 1. Mai 1945, 23:00 Uhr," Staatsarchiv Hamburg, III.9, fol. 12.
102. Heitmann, *Ende des Zweiten Weltkrieges in Hamburg*, 130–1.
103. Ibid., 131.
104. Order from OB Nordwest (Busch) to Kauffmann [*sic*], Wolz, and others, May 2, 1945, Staatsarchiv Hamburg, III.9, fol. 35.

105. Dr. W. A. Burchard-Motz, "Bericht über die Teilnahme an den Kapitulations-verhandlungen für Hamburg am 2./3. Mai 1945," Staatsarchiv Hamburg, III.9, fol. 144–51.

106. Wolz, "Übergabe Hamburgs", 5.

107. Ibid., 6; letter to Polizeipräsident, "Einmarsch der Besatzungstruppen in Hamburg," May 3, 1945, Staatsarchiv Hamburg, III.9, fol. 38.

108. Hugh T. England, Commodore, "Surrender of Hamburg," n.d., Pyman Papers, Liddell Hart Centre for Military Archives (LH).

109. Ibid.; act of surrender signed by Alwin Wolz, n.d. [night of May 2–3, 1945], Staatsarchiv Hamburg, III.9, fol. 22–3.

110. England, "Surrender of Hamburg." Emphasis in the original.

CHAPTER 26: ESCAPING THE SOVIET NET

1. Weigley, *Eisenhower's Lieutenants*, 688–90.

2. For the details, see ibid., 690–1.

3. Kershaw, *The End*, 297.

4. Walther Wenck, "Bericht über die 12. Armee für 'Historical Division US Army,'" April 20, 1945, USAMHI, B 394, 2.

5. Günther Reichhelm, "Das letzte Aufgebot: Kämpfe der deutschen 12. Armee im Herzen Deutschlands zwischen West und Ost vom 13.4.1945–7.5.1945," May 31, 1947, USAMHI, B 606, 5.

6. Yelton, *Hitler's Volkssturm*, 12.

7. Wenck, "Bericht über die 12. Armee," 2–3; "Walter Wenck: General der Panzer Truppe," n.d., USAMHI B 394; Reichhelm, "Das letzte Aufgebot," 9.

8. Reichhelm, "Das letzte Aufgebot," 9–10.

9. Fritz Estor, "Kämpfe der 11. Armee April 1945 in Mitteldeutschland," January 3, 1947, USAMHI, B 581.

10. Ibid.

11. Ibid.

12. Ibid., 24; Walter Lucht, "Stellungnahme zu dem Bericht des Oberst Estor," May 19, 1957, USAMHI, B 581.

13. MacDonald, *Last Offensive*, 404.

14. Ibid., 405; Estor, "Kämpfe der 11. Armee," 45–7.

15. The Twelfth Army was made up of nine divisions, including Divisions Ulrich von Hutten, Scharnhorst, and Potsdam. "Walter Wenck: General der Panzer Truppe," USAMHI, B 394.

16. Antony Beevor, *Berlin: The Downfall 1945* (London: Viking, 2002), 200.

17. Ibid., 201.

18. Ibid.

19. Reichhelm, "Das letzte Aufgebot," 9.

20. Wenck, "Bericht über die 12. Armee," 3; Reichhelm, "Das letzte Aufgebot," 22.

21. Erickson, *Road to Berlin*, 586. The official order came out on April 24. Reichhelm, "Das letzte Aufgebot," 23–4.

22. On both orders, see Weinberg, *World at Arms*, 823.

23. Erickson, *Road to Berlin*, 586. The scene was portrayed with some brilliance by Swiss actor Bruno Ganz in the 2004 film *Downfall* and has since been parodied in countless YouTube videos.

24. Reichhelm, "Das letzte Aufgebot," 5–6.

25. "Walter Wenck: General der Panzer Truppe," USAMHI, B 394.

26. Reichhelm, "Das letzte Aufgebot," 24. Division Scharnhorst.

27. Ibid. Division Hutten and Division Körner.

28. Ibid.; Beevor, *Berlin*, 285.

29. Reichhelm, "Das letzte Aufgebot," 29.

30. Ibid., 26. On the corridor, see Beevor, *Berlin*, 285.

31. Reichhelm, "Das letzte Aufgebot," 29; Erickson, *Road to Berlin*, 601.

32. Reichhelm, "Das letzte Aufgebot," 29. Reichhelm incorrectly cites the date of Wittenberg's fall as April 28. Although most troops pulled out, some scattered resistance remained, which the Soviets had to fight "street by street." Gottfried Herrmann, ". . . *Wittenberg brennt* . . ." *1945: das Kriegsende in der Lutherstadt Wittenberg, den Städten und Dörfern des Flämings und der Elbaue* (Wittenberg: Drei Kastanien Verlag, 1999), 131–2.

33. Herrmann, "*Wittenberg brennt*," 128.

34. Erickson, *Road to Berlin*, 601.

35. Beevor, *Berlin*, 286, quoting an interview with Genscher.

36. Wenck, "Bericht über die 12. Armee," 3. "Poor forces" is a consistent term among the general's reports in the USAMHI's Foreign Military Studies' archives.

37. Reichhelm, "Das letzte Aufgebot," 30.

38. Ibid.

39. Wenck, "Bericht über die 12. Armee," 6.

40. Reichhelm, "Das letzte Aufgebot," 15. The forces were of the Infantry Division Hutten. Reichhelm notes that this was apparently only one example and that, under Wenck's command, the scorched-earth orders were hindered "almost everywhere" in the Twelfth Army's area.

41. Ibid.

42. "Boniface" report, April 24, 1945, UKNA, HW 1/3720.

43. Telegram from Himmler to Kaltenbrunner, April 30, 1945, UKNA, H1/3741.

44. Telegram from Commander in Chief, Naval Chief Command West to Commander in Chief, Navy, May 1, 1945, UKNA, H1/3541. Also see the telegram from Himmler to Kaltenbrunner, April 30, 1945, H1/3741.

45. Telegram from Berger to Himmler, May 1, 1945, UKNA, H1/3744.

46. Naval Headlines 1398, May 2, 1945, UKNA, H1/3544.
47. Ibid.
48. Beevor, *Berlin*, 377.
49. Reichhelm, "Das letzte Aufgebot," 31.
50. Ibid., 31–2.
51. Ibid., 30.
52. Ibid., 33.
53. Quoted in Beevor, *Berlin*, 378.
54. Reichhelm, "Das letzte Aufgebot," 34.
55. Ibid., 34–5.
56. Maximilian von Edelsheim, "Surrender of the Twelfth Army," May 4, 1945, USAMHI, B 220.
57. Ibid.
58. Ibid.
59. Edelsheim, "Surrender of the Twelfth Army"; Reichhelm, "Das letzte Aufgebot," 37.
60. Edelsheim, "Surrender of the Twelfth Army."
61. Ibid.
62. Beevor, *Berlin*, 396.
63. Ibid.
64. Reichhelm, "Das letzte Aufgebot," 37.
65. Ibid., 39.
66. Ibid.
67. Beevor, *Berlin*, 396.
68. Ibid.
69. Ibid., 397.
70. Ibid., 397–8.
71. Ibid., 398.
72. Reichhelm, "Das letzte Aufgebot," 39; Beevor, *Berlin*, 398.
73. Ibid.
74. Edelsheim, "Surrender of the Twelfth Army." Wenck's boat was a rubber raft according to Reichhelm, "Das letzte Aufgebot," 39.
75. Beevor, *Berlin*, 398.
76. Edelsheim, "Surrender of the Twelfth Army."
77. Reichhelm, "Das letzte Aufgebot," 40.

CONCLUSION

1. This takes Charlemagne's wars as the starting point. Michael Howard, *War in European History* (Oxford: Oxford University Press, 2009).
2. Most popular accounts attribute Hitler's survival to the movement of the bomb

away from him. Of far greater significance was the movement of the entire conference Hitler attended from an airtight bunker to a wood hut with open windows. In the former, the full force of the blast would have ricocheted, killing everyone instantly; in the latter, its impact was diminished by the open windows.

3. Weinberg, *World at Arms*, 754.

4. Overmans, *Deutsche militärische Verluste im Zweiten Weltkrieg*, 238.

5. Kershaw, *The End*, 379. Also see Kunz, "Die Wehrmacht in der Agonie der nationalsozialistischen Herrschaft 1944/1945."

6. One counterexample, however, shows how difficult it is to generalize. When Generalmajor Bock von Wülfingen passed through Stuttgart immediately after the July 20 coup, civilians, seeing his army uniform, clapped, saluted, and came to shake his hand. UKNA, WO 208/4363, GRGG 199, 5.

7. Kershaw, *The End*, 389.

8. See Fritz, *Endkampf*, 120 (on Ochsenfurt) and 139–50 (on the *Weibersturm* [women's storm] of Bad Windsheim).

9. "'Armee Blumentritt,' 8. 4. 45—Kapitulation," June 29, 1946, Staatsarchiv Hamburg, III.9, fol. 115 [p. 5].

10. Chemnitz. West Europe, April 18, 1945, UKNA, HW 1/3713, TOO.

11. See van der Vat, *The Good Nazi*.

12. Zelle, *Hitlers zweifelnde Elite*, 334–5; Sereny, *Albert Speer*, 503.

13. Thus, although Speer was shocked by and opposed the July 20 attempt on Hitler's life, he would have accepted the resisters' offer to become armaments minister (*Rüstungsminister*) in a post-Hitler government of Carl Goerdeler. Zelle, *Hitlers zweifelnde Elite*, 299. On Speer's pursuit of power, see Sereny, *Albert Speer*, 489–90. On another, more psychological interpretation that understands Speer's actions against scorched earth as an "ultimate expression of his despair and disillusion," see Karl Hettlage's comments in Sereny, *Albert Speer*, 473.

14. Weinberg, *World at Arms*, 696–7.

15. Mitchell, *Nazi Paris*, 154–5. Charles de Gaulle made a point of driving in Choltitz's 1936 Horch 830 BL Cabriolet for ceremonial events such as those commemorating his June 18, 1940, appeal. De Gaulle viewed Choltitz's refusal to obey Hitler as a moral cornerstone of French-German reconciliation. Militärhistorisches Museum der Bundeswehr, Dresden, section on "1945–Heute."

16. Report from Japanese Minister Berne to Minister for Foreign Affairs, Tokyo, April 27, 1945, UKNA, HW/1 3744.

17. On this and on the disasters of postwar West German planning, see Wolf Jobst Siedler and Elisabeth Niggemeyer, *Die gemordete Stadt: Abgesang auf Putte und Straße, Platz und Baum*, rev. ed. (Berlin: Sammlung Siedler, 1993). For an

exhaustive survey of architectural loss and postwar reconstructions, see Hartwig Beseler and Niels Gutschow, *Kriegsschicksale deutscher Architektur: Verluste, Schäden, Wiederaufbau*, 2 vols. (Neumünster: K. Wachholtz, 1988).

18. See, for example, Chancellor Dr. Ludwig Erhard, "Der Aufstand gegen Hitler vor 21 Jahren," July 19, 1965, BArch N 362–3, fol. 51–2.

NOTE ON APPROACH AND SOURCES

1. Martin Broszat, Elke Fröhlich, and Falk Wiesemann, eds., *Bayern in der NS-Zeit*, 6 vols., Institut für Zeitgeschichte (Munich: Oldenbourg, 1977–83).
2. Ian Kershaw, *The Nazi Dictatorship: Problems and Perspectives of Interpretation*, 3rd ed. (London: Edward Arnold, 1993), 158.
3. Ibid., 159.
4. Ibid., 159–60; Klaus Tenfelde, "Soziale Grundlagen von Resistenz and Widerstand," in *Der Widerstand gegen den Nationalsozialismus: die deutsche Gesellschaft und der Widerstand gegen Hitler*, ed. Jürgen Schmädeke and Peter Steinbach (Munich: Piper, 1985), 799–812. For a similar critique, see Klaus-Michael Mallmann and Gerhard Paul, "Resistenz oder loyale Widerwilligkeit? Anmerkungen zu einem umstrittenen Begriff," *Zeitschrift für Geschichtswissenschaft* 41 (1993): 99–116.
5. James A. Wood, "Captive Historians, Captive Audience: The German Military History Program, 1945–1961," *Journal of Military History* 69, no. 1 (2005): 126–7. Wood's article provides a useful overview of the collection and its problems, with sensitivity to the relative strengths and weaknesses of the various portions. He reveals, however, his own biases in suggesting that American policy during the Cold War was a function of American ideology rather than Soviet aggression.
6. Rolf-Dieter Müller and Hans-Erich Volkmann, eds., *Die Wehrmacht: Mythos und Realität* (Munich: R. Oldenbourg, 1999), 17.
7. Thus see the efforts by General Hans Schäfer to deny that units within greater Marseille surrendered after only a token fight. USAMHI, A 884, Schäfer, "244 Infantry Division Marseille."

THE DEFENSE AND SURRENDER OF GERMANY CITIES IN 1945

T̲H̲E̲ following chart provides an overview of the cities in Germany that were defended and those that surrendered in 1945. It is not a comprehensive list but, rather, a preliminary survey based on the research done for this project. With the exception of those examples discussed at length in the book, it is based on secondary literature. A comprehensive work, especially one taking into account a wide breadth of local archives, would be a valuable asset.

A few considerations should be borne in mind when reading the list:

- The distinction between defense and surrender is not perfectly clear. In some cases, there was a token defense; in other cases, the majority of the city surrendered while pockets continued to resist.
- Many cities (as evidenced by their official histories online) claim a "peaceful surrender". It seems that in some cases, this is a rather narrow view, meaning that the act of surrender itself was peaceful, but that it followed a prolonged and bloody defense. I have coded such cities as "defended." When "surrendered" is indicated, it means that there was little to no defense before the surrender occurred.
- The actors named here should not universally be regarded as heroes. There are, for example, NSDAP mayors among these listed. The only criterion was action: did they act in a manner that contradicted military and political (NS) directives, either to defend and/or to carry out destructive measures?

- The success of disobedience is not a prerequisite for being on this list (an uprising in Munich failed, for instance, but it still deserves mention). There is nonetheless an unavoidable selection bias in that successful disobedience was more frequently recorded than disobedience that failed to ensure the surrender of a city.
- The Volkssturm has been considered a civilian organization.

City/Town	surrendered or defended	civilian or military disobedience	Main actor(s)
Aachen	defended		see Chapter 14
Ahlen	surrendered	military	Oberfeldarzt Dr. Paul Rosenbaum
Altenberge (Münsterland)	surrendered	civilian	Mayor Bohn and other residents
Altenstadt (Bavaria)	surrendered	military	Oberst Kretschmann
Amrichshausen	surrendered	civilian	Local residents
Ansbach	surrendered	civilian	Robert Limpert
Aschaffenburg	defended	both	unidentified soldiers and civilians hanged for attempting to surrender
Aub	defended	military	Alfred Eck (soldier)
Augsburg	surrendered	civilian	*Deutsche Freiheitsbewegung* (German Freedom Movement); see Chapter 21
Aurich	surrendered	both	Friedrich van Senden, Heinrich Alberts; Kampfkommandant Jaehnke
Bad Godesberg	surrendered	both	see Chapter 16
Baden Baden	surrendered		
Baldersheim (Unterfranken)	surrendered	both	Robert Limpert (see entry for Aub), two unnamed German soldiers
Beckum	surrendered	military	Maj. Rudolf Dunker (after being convinced by Dr. Paul Rosenbaum of Ahlen)
Berlin	defended		
Bielefeld	defended	civilian	deputy mayor of Brackwede district; Bielefeld Mayor Budde

Binswangen	defended		
Bonn	surrendered		
Borghorst	defended	civilian	Mayor Reinbrecht, Pastor Kaup, unidentified factory owner, citizens (who deterred German soliders by keeping them drunk!)
Braunschweig (Brunswick)	defended		
Braunsdorf	defended		
Bremen	defended	military	unidentified Oberst
Bad Brückenau	defended	civilian	Mayor Dr. Trost, Deputy Mayor Karl Müller, Karl Schöppner, other residents
Brettheim	defended		Friedrich Hanselmann, Friedrich Uhl, Leonhard Gackstatter, Leonhard Wolfmeyer, other residents
Butzdorf	defended		
Chemnitz	defended	civilian	Otto Schmerbach, Erich Gatsche, various city officials and anti-fascist activists
Cologne (Köln)	partially defended		
Coswig (Anhalt)	surrendered	civilian	local women, Acting Mayor Briedenhahn
Cottbus	defended		
Crailsheim	surrendered once, defended once		See Chapter 20
Demmin	surrendered (abandoned)	civilian	Dr. Achterberg. Mass suicides also occurred.
Dillingen	surrendered	civilian	local mayor
Donauwörth	defended		
Dortmund	defended (some districts surrendered)	civilian	local miners/engineers, Mayor Dr. Willi Banike
Dresden	surrendered (abandoned)		

Duisburg	surrendered (mostly)	civilian	Volkssturm units (refused to report for duty)
Düsseldorf	defended	civilian	See Chapter 18
Emden	defended	civilian	Mayor Carl Renken
Emsdetten	surrendered	civilian	Mayor Hülsmann
Erfurt	defended		
Erlangen	defended	both	City commander Werner Lorleberg finally convinced by local mayor to surrender
Essen	surrendered		
Frankfurt (am Main)	defended	both	Peter Fischer and other residents; Generalmajor Friedrich Stemmermann and a Major Umbach withdrew troops against orders
Freiburg	surrendered	both	Philomene Steiger, local commander Rudolf Bader; see Chapter 22
Freising	surrendered		
Füssing	surrendered	civilian	two groups of civilian negotiators
Gallin	surrendered (abandoned)	civilian	Volkssturm disbanded and fled
Garmisch	surrendered	civilian	unidentified civilian envoys
Gemünden	defended		
Gera	defended	both	Wehrmacht and Volkssturm units (quickly dispersed)
Gollhofen	defended	civilian	local residents
Gotha	surrendered	military	Oberstleutnant Josef Ritter von Gadolla
Göttingen	surrendered		
Greifswald	surrendered	both	see Chapter 24
Halle (Saale)	defended		
Hamburg	surrendered		see Chapter 25
Hannover	surrendered		
Heidelberg	surrendered		see Chapter 20
Heilbronn	defended		see Chapter 20
Herbolzheim	defended		

Hillmitzheim	defended		
Holzheim	surrendered		
Ingolstadt	defended	military	local commander Maj. Paul Weinzierl
Iserbegka	surrendered (abandoned)	civilian	Volkssturm disbanded
Jena	half surrendered, half defended	civilian	see Chapter 19
Karlsruhe	surrendered	both	see Chapter 22
Kassel	defended		see Chapter 19
Kellmünz	defended		
Kerzendorf	surrendered (abandoned)		
Kiel	surrendered (undefended)		Kapitänleutnant Otto Schlenzka, Charlotte Helen Rodewald, Kapitän zur See Wolfgang Kähler, commander Victor Petersen
Koblenz	defended		
Königshofen (ob der Tauber)	defended		
Konstanz	surrendered	both	Mayor Mager, Major Brune
Kolberg	defended		
Köpnick	defended	civilian	local residents (prevented erection of tank barricades)
Külso	surrendered	civilian	Volkssturm fled
Leipzig	defended	both	many unidentified residents, large numbers of anti-fascist activists (incl. Nationalkommitee "Freies Deutschland"), soldiers of the 662th Motorized Flak Regiment
Lemgo	defended	civilian	Mayor Wilhelm Gräfer
Lippstadt	surrendered	civilian	Franz Engelhardt and other union organizers/anti-fascists
Lohr	defended	civilian	six influential (but "defeatist") local citizens
Lörrach	surrendered		
Lübeck	surrendered		

Luko	surrendered	civilian	unidentified stove maker (Ofensetzermeister)
Magdeburg	defended		Cathedral Pastor (Domprediger) Martin, local lawyer named Ackermann, other local residents
Mainz	defended		
Mannheim	defended (then abandoned)	civilian	local mayor and other residents; see Chapter 20
Memmingen	surrendered	both	Mayor Berndl (convinced to surrender at last minute; Wehrmacht allowed retreat)
Mühlanger	surrendered (abandoned)	civilian	Volkssturm fled
Münster	surrendered	civilian	unidentified city officials
Munich	defended	both	Hauptmann Rupprecht Gerngross, Freiheitsaktion Bayern; see Chapter 21
Nennig	defended		
Nienborg	surrendered	civilian	Jop Horstmöller, other local residents
Nuremburg	defended	both	see Chapter 20
Oberstdorf	surrendered	military	Oberleutnant Karl Richter and other local soldiers
Ochsenfurt	defended	civilian	local women
Oldenburg	surrendered	both	Mayor Dr. Heinrich Rabeling and Oberstleutnant H.-H. Sander
Orscholz	defended		
Osnabrück	surrendered (mostly)		
Paderborn	defended (in suburbs)	military	unidentified soldiers
Passau	defended	civilian	Deputy Mayor Dr. Carl Sittler, Volkssturm commander Friedrich Stuis
Penzberg		civilian	Local miners
Pforzheim	defended		
Pfullingen	defended	civilian	local women

Potsdam	defended		
Regensburg	surrendered	both	local women; Cathedral Pastor (Domprediger) Dr. Maier; Major Hüsson, Major Bürger, Gen. Tolsdorff; see Chapter 20
Rostock	surrendered	civilian	Wilhelm Hörning and other anti-fascist activists, other local residents
Saarbrücken	defended (then abandoned)	civilian	Remaining Volkssturm disbanded
Schwäbisch Hall	surrendered	both	Mayor Wilhelm Prinzing und Police Captain Bulling, Leutnant Hüfner (convinced commander not to defend the city)
Schwäbisch Gmünd	surrendered	both	local Wehrmacht and Volkssturm commanders
Schweinfurt	defended	civilian	Speer (convinced Gauleiter to prevent destruction)
Schwerin	surrendered		
Sindelfingen	defended		
Soest	defended	civilian	local residents
Straach	defended		
Stralsund	defended	civilian	Paul Reetz and other local residents
Staufen	defended	civilian	Mayor and local farmer
Stuppach	defended		
Stuttgart	surrendered	both	Mayor Dr. Karl Strölin, Oberstleutnant Paul Marbach and General Kurt Hoffmann, local industrialists and residents
Treuenbrietzen	defended		
Trier	surrendered		
Tübingen	surrendered	both	Dr. Theodor Dobler, Oberst Schütz
Ulm	surrendered	both	Karl Eychmüller, local commander Oberst Fritz Teichmann
Ummeln	surrendered	civilian	three local women and an unidentified carpenter

Urlau (im Allgäu)	surrendered	military	Maj. Günter Zöllner, Sanitätsoffizier Friedrich Jung
Waldkirch	surrendered	military	soldiers assigned locally
Weimar	surrendered	civilian	Mayor Karl Otto Koch, Troistedt mayor Richard Weyde, other unidentified civilians
Wiesbaden	surrendered	both	Hermann Roos and other local resisters, commander Oberst Wilhelm Karl Zierenberg
Wittenberg	defended	both	local women, Leutnant Hermann Puhlmann and his units
Woltersdorf	surrendered	civilian	local residents, including a Frau Dorn
Würzburg	defended		
Zerbst	surrendered		
Zörnigall	surrendered (abandoned)		
Zwickau	surrendered	civilian	Luftschutzpolizist Arno Rau, church caretaker (Kirchendiener) Fritz Schubert, and Schubert's son

GLOSSARY

Abwehr	German military intelligence organization
ARLZ	acronym for disassembly (*Auflockerung*), evacuation/removal (*Räumung*), paralysis (*Lähmung*), and destruction (*Zerstörung*) measures
Einsatzgruppe	special task force (murder squad)
Gauleiter Nazi	regional Nazi Party governors
Gestapo	*Geheime Staatspolizei*, Nazi Party secret state police
Heeresgruppe	army group
Kampfkommandant	battle commander
Kreisleiter	local Nazi Party officials (subordinate to Gauletier)
Kripo	*Kriminalpolizei*, Nazi Party criminal police
NSDAP (or NS)	*Nationalsozialistische Deutsche Arbeiterpartei*, National Socialist German Workers' Party (the Nazi Party)

Oberbefehlshaber	military commander (usually used in conjunction with the name of the units over which the command is held)
Oberbürgermeister	mayor
OB West	*Oberbefehlshaber West*, referring to German High Command West and/or its commanding officer, Commander in Chief West
OKH	*Oberkommando des Heeres*, Army High Command (compare OKW)
OKW	*Oberkommando der Wehrmacht*, Wehrmacht High Command. "Wehrmacht" refers to the combined German armed forces, including the army (*Heer*), air force (*Luftwaffe*), and navy (*Marine* or *Kriegsmarine*). Each component organization had its own High Command: OKH, OKL, and OKM, respectively.
Orpo	*Ordnungspolizei*, Nazi Party order police
Reichsstatthalter	regional Reich government deputy; title often held concurrently by Gauleiter
Reichsverteidigungskommissar	Reich Defense Commissioner, a title granted to most Gauleiter in connection with their duties regarding the final defense of Germany
Rüstungskommission	regional armament commission, created by Speer for streamlining of armament and other infrastructural matters
Sipo	*Sicherheitspolizei*, Nazi Party security police
Sippenhaft	retaliatory Nazi policy under which penalization (in theory, including execution) of family of individuals who were deemed to have disobeyed orders
SD	*Sicherheitsdienst*, Nazi Party secret security service

SS	*Schutzstaffel*, Nazi Party paramilitary wing	
Stadtkommandant	city commander; see also *Kampfkommandant*	
Volkssturm	German militia, called up as the Allies entered the Reich	
Waffen-SS	SS combat troops	
Wehrkreis	military defense district	

COMPARATIVE MILITARY RANKS

US Army	German Army	SS
General of the Army	(General)Feldmarschall	—
General	Generaloberst	Oberstgruppenführer
Lieutenant General	General	Obergruppenführer
	der Artillerie (artillery)	
	der Infanterie (infantry)	
	der Kavallerie (cavalry)	
	der Panzertruppe (tank troops)	
	der Pioniere (engineer)	
	der Flieger (Luftwaffe)	
Major General	Generalleutnant	Gruppenführer
Brigadier General	Generalmajor	Brigadeführer
—	—	Oberführer
Colonel	Oberst	Standartenführer
Lieutenant Colonel	Oberstleutnant	
Obersturmbannführer		
Major	Major	Sturmbannführer
Captain	Hauptmann	Hauptsturmführer
First Lieutenant	Oberleutnant	Obersturmführer
Second Lieutenant	Leutnant	Untersturmführer
Technical Sergeant	Oberfeldwebel	Hauptscharführer
Staff Sergeant	Feldwebel	Oberscharführer
Sergeant	Unterfeldwebel	Scharführer
Corporal	Unteroffizier	Rottenführer
Private	Gefreiter	Sturmmann

WORKS CITED

PRIMARY SOURCES

Archiv Mahn- und Gedenkstätte Düsseldorf
Archives de Paris (city archives)
Archives de la Préfecture de Police de Paris (APPP)
Bundesarchiv (BArch): Berlin, Freiburg, Koblenz
Chambre de Commerce et d'Industrie Marseille Provence (CCIMP)
Liddell Hart Centre for Military Archives (LH)
Mémorial de Caen Archives (MdC)
Militärhistorisches Museum der Bundeswehr, Dresden
The National Archives, London, UK (UKNA)
Staatsarchiv Hamburg
Stadtarchiv Augsburg
Stadtarchiv Freiburg
Stadtarchiv Greifswald
Stadtarchiv Heidelberg
Stadtarchiv Jena
Stadtarchiv Landeshauptstadt Düsseldorf (SLD)
Thüringisches Staatsarchiv Gotha (TSG)
Universitäts- und Forschungsbibliothek Erfurt/Gotha (UFEG)
US Army Military History Institute (USAMHI), Carlisle, Pennsylvania
US National Archives at College Park, Maryland (NACP)

SECONDARY LITERATURE

Arnim, Dankwart Graf von. *Als Brandenburg noch die Mark hieß*. Munich: Goldmann Verlag, 1995.

Asendorf, Manfred. "Karl Kaufmann und Hamburgs langer Weg zur Kapitulation." In *Kriegsende und Befreiung: Beiträge der nationalsozialistischen Verfolgung in Norddeutschland*, Heft 2, edited by Detlef Garbe, 12–23. Bremen: Ed. Temmen, 1995.

Bader, Rudolf. "1945: Freiburgs letzte Kriegstage." *Freiburger Almanach* 26 (1975): 51–5.

Bajohr, Frank. "Gauleiter in Hamburg: Zur Person und Tätigkeit Karl Kaufmanns." *Vierteljahrshefte für Zeitgeschichte* 43, no. 2 (April 1995): 267–95.

———. "Die Zustimmungsdiktatur: Grundzüge nationalsozialistischer Herrschaft in Hamburg." In *Hamburg im "Dritten Reich"*, edited by the Forschungsstelle für Zeitgeschichte in Hamburg, 69–121. Göttingen: Wallstein Verlag, 2005.

Bartov, Omer. *The Eastern Front, 1941–1945: German Troops and the Barbarisation of Warfare*. Houndmills: Palgrave, 2001.

———. *Hitler's Army: Soldiers, Nazis, and War in the Third Reich*. Reprint, New York: Oxford University Press, 1992.

Becker, Manuel and Christoph Studt, eds. *Der Umgang des Dritten Reiches mit den Feinden des Regimes*. Königswinterer Tagung February 2009. Münster: Lit Verlag, 2010.

Becker, Rolf O. *Niederschlesien 1945: die Flucht - die Besetzung*. Bad Neuheim: Podzun-Verlag, 1965.

Beevor, Antony. *Berlin: The Downfall 1945*. London: Viking, 2002.

———. *D-Day: The Battle for Normandy*. London: Viking, 2009.

——— and Artemis Cooper. *Paris after the Liberation 1944–1949*, rev. ed. New York: Penguin, 2004.

Beseler, Hartwig and Niels Gutschow. *Kriegsschicksale Deutscher Architektur: Verluste, Schäden, Wiederaufbau*. 2 vols. Neumünster: K. Wachholtz, 1988.

Bessel, Richard. *Germany 1945: From War to Peace*. New York: Harper Collins, 2009.

———. "The Shadow of Death in Germany at the End of the Second World War" in *Between Mass Death and Individual Loss: The Place of the Dead in Twentieth-Century Germany*, edited by Alon Confino, Paul Betts, and Dirk Schumann. New York: Berghahn Books, 2008.

Bishop, Chris, ed. *The Encyclopedia of Weapons of World War II*, rev. ed. New York: MetroBooks, 2002.

Blumenson, Martin. *The Patton Papers*. 2 vols. Boston: Houghton Mifflin, 1972–74.

Boelcke, Willi A. "Hitlers Befehle zur Zerstörung oder Lähmung des deutschen Industriepotentials 1944/45." *Zeitschrift für Firmengeschichte und Unternehmerbiographie* 13, no. 6 (1968): 301–16.

Boeselager, Philipp Freiherr von. *Valkyrie: The Story of the Plot to Kill Hitler by Its Last Member*. With Florence and Jérôme Fehrenbach. Translated by Steven Rendall. New York: Alfred A. Knopf, 2009.

Bohl, Hans-Werner, Bodo Keipke, and Karsten Schröder, eds. *Bomben auf Rostock: Krieg und Kriegsende in Berichten, Dokumenten, Erinnerungen und Fotos 1940–1945*. Rostock: Konrad Reich Verlag, 1995.

Bradley, Omar N. *A Soldier's Story*. New York: Modern Library, 1999.

Breuer, William B. *Operation Dragoon: The Allied Invasion of Southern France* Novato, CA: Presidio Press, 1987.

Brissa, Enrico. "Josef Ritter von Gadolla." *Zeitschrift für Thüringische Geschichte* 65 (2011): 229–43.

Broszat, Martin, Elke Fröhlich, and Falk Wiesemann, eds. *Bayern in der NS-Zeit*. 6 vols. Produced by the Institut für Zeitgeschichte. Munich: Oldenbourg, 1977–83.

Browning, Christopher R. *Ordinary Men: Reserve Police Battalion 101 and the Final Solution*. New York: Harper Perennial, 1998.

———. *The Origins of the Final Solution: The Evolution of Nazi Jewish Policy, September 1939–March 1942*. With Jürgen Matthäus. Lincoln: University of Nebraska Press, 2004.

Brückner, Joachim. *Kriegsende in Bayern: Der Wehrkreis VII und die Kämpfe zwischen Donau und Alpen*. Freiburg: Rombach, 1987.

Bruecher, Max. *Freiburg im Breisgau 1945: eine Dokumentation*. Freiburg: Verlag Rombach, 1980.

Burleigh, Michael. *The Third Reich: A New History*. London: Pan Books, 2001.

Busch, Dieter. *Der Luftkrieg im Raum Mainz während des Zweiten Weltkrieges 1939–1945*. Mainz: v. Hase & Koehler Verlag, 1988.

Buske, Norbert, ed. *Das Kriegsende in Demmin 1945: Berichte, Erinnerungen, Dokumente*. Landeszentrale für Politische Bildung Mecklenburg-Vorpommern, 1st ed. Schwerin: Helms, 1995.

Chandler, Alfred D., Jr., ed. *The Papers of Dwight David Eisenhower*. 21 vols. Baltimore: Johns Hopkins Press, 1970–2001.

Clarke, Jeffrey J. "The Champagne Campaign." *The Quarterly Journal of Military History* 20, no. 2 (Winter 2008): 37–45.

——— and Robert Ross Smith, *Riviera to the Rhine*. Washington, DC: Center for Military History, United States Army, 1993.

Cobb, Matthew. *Eleven Days in August: The Liberation of Paris in 1944*. London: Simon & Schuster, 2013.

Coffin, Robert E. "The Demonstration at Heidelberg—Guts, Good Sense, Great Timing." *Army* 45, no. 4 (April 1995): 55–7.

Collins, Larry and Dominique Lapierre. *Is Paris Burning?* New York: Simon and Schuster, 1965.

Crémieux, Francis. *La vérité sur la libération de Paris*. Paris: Messidor, 1984.

Dahrendorf, Ralf, Margarete Mitscherlich, and Ralph Giordano. *Hamburg 1945: Zerstört. Befreit. Hoffnungsvoll?* Hamburg: Christians Verlag, 1995.

Dallin, Alexander. *German Rule in Russia, 1941–1945: A Study of Occupation Policies*. 2nd rev. ed. Boulder, CO: Westview Press, 1981.

Dansette, Adrien. *Histoire de la libération de Paris*. Paris: Librairie Arthème Fayard, 1958.

Das Deutsche Reich und der Zweite Weltkrieg. 10 vols. [13 bks.] Militärgeschichtliches Forschungsamt. Stuttgart: Deutsche Verlags-Anstalt, 1979–2008.

Dobler, Kurt. "'Damit Gotha leben kann, muss ich sterben!'" In *Die letzten Kriegstage Anfang April 1945 in Gotha*.

Dopheide, Renate. *Kiel, Mai 1945: Britische Truppen besetzen die Kriegsmarinestadt*. 2nd ed. Kiel: Verlag Ludwig, 2007.

Eckhardt, William. "Civilian Deaths in Wartime," *Security Dialogue* 20, no. 1 (1989): 89–98.

Ehrlich, Egon. *Josef Ritter von Gadolla: ein österreichisches Offiziersleben in der k. u. k. Armee, im Bundesheer und der Wehrmacht*. 2nd ed. Vienna: Bundesministerium für Landesverteidigung, 2000.

——— and Helga Raschke, "Ein Grazer Offizier im militärischen Widerstand." In *Jahrbuch 2003: Schwerpunkt Exil*, edited by Christine Schindler, 162–91. Dokumentationsarchiv des österreichischen Widerstandes: Vienna, 2003.

Engel, Carl. "Erinnerungen an die letzten Kriegstage und die kampflose Übergabe Greifswalds," May 19–June 3, 1945. In *Zwischen Greifswald und Riga: Auszüge aus den Tagebüchern des Greifswalder Rektors und Professors der Ur- und Frühgeschichte, Dr. Carl Engel, vom 1. November 1938 bis 26 Juli. 1945*, edited by Günter Mangelsdorf, 317–29 [Anhang 3]. Stuttgart: Franz Steiner Verlag, 2007.

Erickson, John. *The Road to Berlin: Continuing the History of Stalin's War with Germany*. Boulder, CO: Westview Press, 1983.

———. *The Road to Stalingrad: Stalin's War with Germany*. London: Weidenfeld & Nicolson, 1975. Reprint, London: Cassell Military Paperbacks, 2003.

Evans, Richard J. *The Third Reich in Power, 1933–1939*. New York: Penguin, 2005.

Ewald, Günther. "Das Ende des Zweiten Weltkrieges in der Stadt Gotha." In *Die letzten Kriegstage Anfang April 1945 in Gotha*.

Fest, Joachim. *Plotting Hitler's Death: The Story of the German Resistance*. Translated by Bruce Little. New York: Metropolitan Books, 1996.

Fings, Karola. "Kriegsenden, Kriegslegenden: Bewältigungsstrategien in einer deutschen Großstadt." In *Kriegsende 1945: Verbrechen, Katastrophen, Befreiungen in nationaler und internationaler Perspektive*, edited by Bernd-A. Rusinek, 219–38. Göttingen: Wallstein Verlag, 2004.

——— and Frank Sparing. *"Z. Zt. Zigeunerlager": die Verfolgung der Düsseldorfer Sinti und Roma im Nationalsozialismus*. Cologne: Volksblatt Verlag, 1992.

Fischer, Torsten. *Kriegsende an Rhein, Ruhr und Weser* (Begleitbuch zur WDR-Dokumentation). Gudensberg-Gleichen: Wartberg Verlag, 2005.

Ford, Ken. *The Rhineland 1945: The Last Killing Ground in the West*. Oxford: Osprey, 2000.

Förster, Jürgen. "Operation Barbarossa as a War of Conquest and Annihilation." In *Germany and the Second World War*. Vol. 4, *The Attack on the Soviet Union*, 481–521.

———. "Securing 'Living-space.'" In *Germany and the Second World War*. Vol. 4, *The Attack on the Soviet Union*, 1189–1244.

Förtsch, Folker, ed. *Kriegsende in Crailsheim und Umgebung*. Crailsheim: Baier BPB Verlag, 2008.

———. "Warum Crailsheim 1945 zerstört wurde." In Förtsch, *Kriegsende in Crailsheim und Umgebung*, 175–202.

Fox, Don M. *Patton's Vanguard: The United States Fourth Armored Division*. Jefferson, NC: McFarland & Co., 2003.

Frenz, Wilhelm. "Zusammenbruch – Stunde Null?" In *Volksgemeinschaft und Volksfeinde: Kassel 1933–1945, Band 2: Studien*, edited by Frenz, Jörg Kammler, and Dietfrid Krause-Vilmar, 415–24. Fuldabrück: Hesse, 1987.

Friedlander, Henry. *The Origins of the Nazi Genocide: From Euthanasia to the Final Solution*. Chapel Hill: University of North Carolina Press, 1995.

Frieser, Karl-Heinz. "Der Zusammenbruch der Heeresgruppe Mitte im Sommer 1944." In *Das Deutsche Reich und der Zweite Weltkrieg*. Vol. 8, *Die Ostfront 1943/44: Der Krieg im Osten und an den Nebenfronten*, 526–603.

Fritz, Stephen G. *Endkampf: Soldiers, Civilians, and the Death of the Third Reich*. Lexington: University of Kentucky Press, 2004.

Fröhlich, Elke, ed. *Die Tagebücher von Joseph Goebbels: Diktate 1941–1945*. 15 vols. Munich: K. G. Saur, 1993–96.

Fügener, Jens. "Amerikanisches Intermezzo: Jena zwischen Drittem Reich und Sowjetischer Besatzungszone." In *Macht und Milieu: Jena zwischen Kriegsende und Mauerbau*, edited by Rüdiger Stutz, 25–51. Jena: Verein für Jenaer Stadt- und Universitätsgeschichte, 2000.

Galante, Pierre. *Operation Valkyrie: The German Generals' Plot against Hitler*. With Eugène Silianoff. Translated by Mark Howson and Cary Ryan. New York: Harper & Row, 1981.

Gaujac, Paul. *La bataille et la libération de Toulon*. Rev. ed. Paris: Nouvelles Éditions Latines, 1994.

Gaunt, David. "Reichskommissariat Ostland." In *The Routledge History of the Holocaust*, edited by Jonathan C. Friedman 210–20. New York: Routledge, 2010.

Gehling, Dominik, Volker Gehling, Jonas Hofmann, Holger Nickel, and Christopher Rüther, eds. *Paderborner Zeitzeugen berichten 1933–1948: "--das müssen Sie mir alles aufschreiben"*. Paderborn: Ferdinand Schöningh, 2005.

Gellately, Robert. *Backing Hitler: Consent and Coercion in Nazi Germany*. Oxford: Oxford University Press, 2001.

Gerlach, Christian. "Männer des 20. Juli und der Krieg gegen die Sowjetunion." In *Vernichtungskrieg: Verbrechen der Wehrmacht 1941–1944*, edited by Hannes Heer and Klaus Naumann, 427–46. Hamburg: Hamburger Edition, 1995.

Germany and the Second World War [=GSWW]. English translation of *Das Deutsche Reich und der Zweite Weltkrieg*. [9 of 13 books translated so far]. Oxford: Clarendon Press, 1990–2008.

Geyer, Michael. "The Stigma of Violence, Nationalism, and War in Twentieth Century Germany." *German Studies Review* 15 (Winter 1992): 75–110.

———. "There is a Land Where Everything is Pure: Its Name is Land of Death." In *Sacrifice and Belonging in Twentieth Century Germany*, edited by Greg Eghigian and Matthew Paul Berg, 118–47. Arlington: University of Texas Press, 2002.

Gilbert, Martin. *The Holocaust: A History of the Jews of Europe during the Second World War*. New York: Holt, Rinehart and Winston, 1985.

———. *Second World War*. London: Weidenfeld and Nicolson, 1989.

Gisevius, Hans Bernd. *To the Bitter End: An Insider's Account of the Plot to Kill Hitler, 1933–1944*. Translated by Richard and Clara Winston. New York: Da Capo Press, 1998.

Gotha 1945: Erlebnisberichte von Zeitzeugen und Autoren aus Australien, Frankreich, Gotha, Ohrdruf, Polen, Remstädt, Russland, Waltershausen, Wechmar. Wechmar: Gotha Druck und Reproduktion, 1995.

Granatstein, J. L. *The Generals: The Canadian Army's Commanders in the Second World War*. Calgary: University of Calgary Press, 2005.

Gräser, Hans, Horst Boog, and Wilhelm Ehrmann, eds. *Die Schlacht um Crailsheim: Das Kriegsgeschehen im Landkreis Crailsheim im 2. Weltkrieg*. Crailsheim: Verlag Robert Baier, 1997.

Grolle, Joist. "Schwierigkeiten mit der Vergangenheit: Anfänge der zeitgeschichtlichen Forschung in Hamburg der Nachkriegszeit." *Zeitschrift des Vereins für Hamburgische Geschichte* 78 (1992): 1–66.

Groß, Manfred. *Westwallkämpfe: die Angriffe der Amerikaner 1944/45 zwischen Ormont (Rheinland-Pfalz) und Geilenkirchen (Nordrhein-Westfalen): eine Dokumentation*. Aachen: Helios, 2008.

Guderian, Heinz. *Panzer Leader*. London: Michael Joseph, 1952.

Guiral, Pierre. *Libération de Marseille*. Paris: Hachette Littérature, 1974.

Hamerow, Theodore S. *On the Road to the Wolf's Lair: German Resistance to Hitler*. Cambridge, MA: Belknap Press, 1999.

Hannover, Jantje. "Zerstörung und Rettung in letzter Minute: Das Kriegsende in den Nachbarstädten Anklam und Greifswald." *Deutschlandradio Kultur*, April 29, 2005, http://www.dradio.de/dkultur/sendungen/laenderreport/368478/.

Harrison, Ted. "'Alter Kämpfer' im Widerstand: Graf Helldorff, die NS-Bewegung und die Opposition gegen Hitler." *Vierteljahrshefte für Zeitgeschichte* 45, no. 3 (July 1997): 385–423.

Hart, Russell A. *Guderian: Panzer Pioneer or Myth Maker?* Washington, DC: Potomac Books, 2006.

Hartmann, Christian. "Verbrecherischer Krieg – verbrecherische Wehrmacht?" *Vierteljahrshefte für Zeitgeschichte* 52, no. 1 (2004): 1–75.

Hartung, Hans Rudolf. *Soest im Krieg.* Hamm: Emil Griebsch Verlag, 1995.

Hastings, Max. *Armageddon: The Battle for Germany 1944–45.* London: Macmillan, 2004.

———. *Finest Years: Churchill as Warlord 1940–45.* London: HarperPress, 2009.

———. *Das Reich: Resistance and the March of the 2nd SS Panzer Division through France, June 1944.* London: Michael Joseph, 1981.

Hechler, Ken. *The Bridge at Remagen: The Amazing Story of March 7, 1945 — The Day the Rhine River Was Crossed.* Rev. ed., Missoula, MT: Pictorial Histories Publishing Co., 1995. First published 1957 by Ballantine Books.

Heidelmayer, Alfred. "Magdeburg 1945: zwischen Zerstörung und Kriegsende - ein Bericht." In *"Dann färbte sich der Himmel blutrot . . .": die Zerstörung Magdeburgs am 16. Januar 1945.* (Exhibit in the Kulturhistorisches Museum Magdeburg, 15 January 1995 to 14 May 1995), edited by Matthias Puhle, 2nd ed., 112–44. Magdeburg: Magdeburger Museen, 1995.

Heinemann, Winfried. "Eduard Dietl: Lieblingsgeneral des 'Führers.'" In *Die Militärelite des Dritten Reiches: 27 biographische Skizzen*, edited by Ronald Smelser and Enrico Syring, 99–112. Berlin: Ullstein, 1995.

———. "General Erich Fellgiebel und die Rolle der Kommunikationsmittel am 20. Juli 1944." In *Führung und Führungsmittel*, edited by Heinemann, 57–66. Potsdam: Militärgeschichtliches Forschungsamt, 2011.

———. "Military Resistance Activities and the War," in *Germany and the Second World War.* Vol. 9, bk. 1, *German Wartime Society 1939–1945: Politicization, Disintegration, and the Struggle for Survival*, 771–925.

———. "Selbstreinigung der Wehrmacht? Der Ehrenhof des Heeres und seine Tätigkeit." In Becker and Studt, *Der Umgang des Dritten Reiches*, 117–29.

———. "Der Widerstand gegen das NS-Regime und der Krieg an der Ostfront." *Militärgeschichte* 8 (1998): 49–55.

Heitmann, Jan. *Das Ende des Zweiten Weltkrieges in Hamburg: die kampflose Übergabe der Stadt an die britischen Truppen und ihre Vorgeschichte.* Frankfurt: Peter Lang, 1990.

Henke, Klaus-Dietmar. *Die amerikanische Besetzung Deutschlands.* Munich: R. Oldenbourg, 1995.

Herbert, Ulrich. *Hitler's Foreign Workers: Enforced Foreign Labor in Germany under the Third Reich*. Translated by William Templer. Cambridge: Cambridge University Press, 1997.

Herrmann, Gottfried. ". . . *Wittenberg brennt . . ." 1945: das Kriegsende in der Lutherstadt Wittenberg, den Städten und Dörfern des Flämings und der Elbaue*. Wittenberg: Drei Kastanien Verlag, 1999.

Herrmann, Hans-Walter. "Saarbrücken unter der NS-Herrschaft." In *Geschichte der Stadt Saarbrücken: von der Zeit des stürmischen Wachstums bis zur Gegenwart*, edited by Rolf Wittenbrock, vol. 2, 243–338. Saarbrücken: Saarbrücker Druckerei und Verlag, 1999.

Hilberg, Raul. *The Destruction of the European Jews*. 2 vols. New Haven: Yale University Press, 2003.

Hildyard, Miles. *It is Bliss Here: Letters Home 1939–1945*. London: Bloomsbury, 2006.

Hofacker, Alfred von. *Cäsar von Hofacker: ein Wegbereiter für und ein Widerstands-kämpfer gegen Hitler, ein Widerspruch?* Wallstein: Haus der Geschichte Baden Württemberg/Baden-Württemberg Stiftung gGmbH, 2009.

Hoffmann, Peter, ed. *Behind Valkyrie: German Resistance to Hitler: Documents*. Montreal: McGill-Queen's University Press, 2011.

———. *The History of the German Resistance, 1933–1945*. 3rd English ed., translated by Richard Barry. Montreal: McGill-Queen's University Press, 1996.

———. *Stauffenberg: A Family History, 1905–1944*. 2nd ed. Montreal: McGill-Queen's University Press, 2003. Originally published as *Claus Schenk Graf von Stauffenberg und seine Brüder* (Stuttgart: Deutsche Verlags-Anstalt, 1992).

Hoffmeyer, Ludwig and Heinrich Koch. *Chronik der Stadt Osnabrück*. 5th ed. Osnabrück: Meinders & Elstermann, 1985.

Holmes, Richard ed. *The Oxford Companion to Military History*. Oxford: Oxford University Press, 2001.

Höntsch, Ursula and Alfred Harendt. *Die Stunde Null: Tatsachenberichte über Erlebnisse aus den letzten Tagen des 2. Weltkrieges*. [East] Berlin: Verlag der Nation, 1966.

Hoser, Paul. *Die Geschichte der Stadt Memmingen*. Vol. 2, *Vom Nebeginn im Königreich Bayern bis 1945*. Edited by Hans-Wolfgang Bayer and Uli Braun. Stuttgart: Konrad Theiss Verlag, 2001.

Howard, Michael. *War in European History*. Oxford: Oxford University Press, 2009.

The Invasion of the South of France: Operation "Dragoon", 15th August, 1944. London: HMSO, 1994.

Jackson, Julian. *France: The Dark Years, 1940–1944*. Oxford: Oxford University Press, 2003.

Jahnke, Karl Heinz. "Von der Novemberrevolution bis zur Befreiung vom Faschismus. 1917–1945." In *Geschichte der Stadt Stralsund*, edited by Herbert Ewe. Weimar: Hermann Böhlaus Nachfolger, 1984.

Janßen, Dietrich. *Emden geht unter: Zerstörung und Kriegsende 1944–45*. Gudensberg-Gleichen: Wartberg Verlag, 2004.

Jones, Michael. *Leningrad: State of Siege*. London: John Murray, 2008.

Jordan, David and Andrew Wiest. *Atlas des Zweiten Weltkriegs*. Vienna: Tosa, 2005.

Jünger, Ernst. *Sämtliche Werke*. 18 vols. Stuttgart: Ernst Klett, 1978–83.

Kaminsky, Uwe. "Fremdarbeiter in Ratingen während des Zweiten Weltkriegs." *Ratinger Forum: Beiträge zur Stadt- und Regionalgeschichte* 1 (1989): 90–212.

——— . "Die Gestapo in Ratingen 1943–1945." *Ratinger Forum: Beiträge zur Stadt- und Regionalgeschichte* 2 (1991): 136–63.

Kanther, Michael A. "Duisburg und der Nationalsozialismus: zur Entstehung lokaler Formationen der NSDAP und zur politischen Geschichte der Stadt im 'Dritten Reich.'" In *Nationalsozialismus in Duisburg 1920–1945: eine Einführung mit Bibliografie und Fotografien der Zeit*, edited by Jan-Pieter Barbian, Hans Georg Kraume, and Sigurd Praetorius, 21–58. Essen: Klartext Verlag, 2009.

Keegan, John. *The Second World War*. London: Hutchinson, 1989.

——— and Andrew Wheatcroft. *Who's Who in Military History*. London: Routledge, 2002.

Keil, Lars-Broder. *Hans-Ulrich von Oertzen: Offizier und Widerstandskämpfer*. Berlin: Lukas Verlag, 2005.

Kershaw, Ian. *The End: Hitler's Germany, 1944–45*. London: Allen Lane, 2011.

———. *Hitler 1936–1945: Nemesis*. London: Penguin, 2000.

———. *The Nazi Dictatorship: Problems and Perspectives of Interpretation*. 3rd ed. London: Edward Arnold, 1993.

———. "'Working Towards the Führer': Reflections on the Nature of the Hitler Dictatorship." In *The Third Reich: The Essential Readings*, edited by Christian Leitz, 231–52. London: Blackwell, 1999.

Klemperer, Klemens von. *German Resistance against Hitler: The Search for Allies Abroad, 1938–1945*. Oxford: Clarendon Press, 1992.

Klink, Ernst. "The Conduct of Operations." In *Germany and the Second World War*. Vol. 4, *The Attack on the Soviet Union*, 525–763.

Koch, Fritz. *Oldenburg 1945: Erinnerungen eines Bürgermeisters*. Oldenburg: Heinz Holzberg Verlag, 1984.

Köhler, Werner. *Freiburg i. Br. 1945–1949: politisches Leben und Erfahrungen in der Nachkriegszeit*. Freiburg: Stadtarchiv Freiburg im Breisgau, 1987.

Krausnick, Helmut and Hans-Heinrich Wilhem. *Die Truppe des Weltanschauungskrieges: die Einsatzgruppen der Sicherheitspolizei und des SD, 1938–1942*. Stuttgart: Deutsche Verlags-Anstalt, 1981.

Kunz, Andreas. "Die Wehrmacht in der Agonie der nationalsozialistischen Herrschaft 1944/45: eine Gedankenskizze." In *Kriegsende 1945 in Deutschland*, edited by Jörg Hillmann and John Zimmermann, 97–114. Militärgeschichtliches Forschungsamt. Munich: R. Oldenbourg, 2002.

Kunze, Karl. *Kriegsende in Franken und der Kampf um Nürnberg im April 1945.* Nürnberg: Selbstverlag des Vereins für Geschichte der Stadt Nürnberg, 1995.

Ladowski, Richard. *Seelow 1945: Die Entscheidungsschlacht an der Oder.* 3rd ed. Berlin: Brandenburgisches Verlagshaus, 1996.

Larkin, Maurice. *France since the Popular Front: Government and People, 1936–1986.* Oxford: Oxford University Press, 1988.

Latimer, Jon. *Alamein.* London: John Murray, 2002.

Leifland, Leif. "Hamburgs Kapitulation im Mai 1945: Querverbindungen nach Schweden." *Zeitschrift des Vereins für Hamburgische Geschichte* 78 (1992): 235–52.

Die letzten Kriegstage Anfang April 1945 in Gotha: Augenzeugenberichte, Erinnerungen, Forschungen. Stuttgart: Drückerei Schäuble, 1988.

Liddell Hart, B. H. *The German Generals Talk: Startling Revelations from Hitler's High Command.* Reprint, New York: Harper, 2001.

———, ed. *The Rommel Papers.* 15th ed. Reprint, New York: Da Capo, 1982.

Lieb, Peter. "Erwin Rommel: Widerstandskämpfer oder Nationalsozialist?" *Vierteljahresheft für Zeitgeschichte* 61, no. 3 (July 2013): 303–43.

Longerich, Peter. *Heinrich Himmler.* Oxford: Oxford University Press, 2012.

Lukas, Richard C. *The Forgotten Holocaust: The Poles under German Occupation 1933–1944.* Lexington: Kentucky University Press, 1986.

MacDonald, Charles B. *The Last Offensive.* Part of *United States Army in World War II: European Theater of Operations.* Washington, DC: Office of the Chief of Military History, 1973. Also reprinted as *Victory in Europe, 1945: The Last Offensive of World War II.* Mineola, NY: Dover, 2007.

Mallmann, Klaus-Michael and Martin Cüppers. *Nazi Palestine: The Plans for the Extermination of the Jews in Palestine.* Translated by Krista Smith. New York: Enigma, 2010.

——— and Gerhard Paul. "Resistenz oder loyale Widerwilligkeit? Anmerkungen zu einem umstrittenen Begriff." *Zeitschrift für Geschichtswissenschaft* 41 (1993): 99–116.

Marcot, François. *Dictionnaire historique de la résistance: résistance intérieure et France libre.* With Bruno Leroux and Christine Levisse-Touzé. Paris: Éditions Robert Laffont, 2006.

Marrus, Michael R. and Robert O. Paxton. *Vichy France and the Jews.* Stanford, CA: Stanford University Press, 1995.

Marshall, Charles F. *Discovering the Rommel Murder: The Life and Death of the Desert Fox.* Mechanicsburg, PA: Stackpole Books, 1994.

Matthiesen, Helge. "Das Kriegsende 1945 und der Mythos von der kampflosen Übergabe." In *Greifswald: Geschichte der Stadt,* edited by Horst Wernicke, 135–40. Schwerin: Thomas Helms Verlag, 2000.

Messerschmidt, Manfred. "Motivationen der nationalkonservativen Opposition und des militärischen Widerstandes seit dem Frankreich-Feldzug." In *Der deutsche Widerstand 1933–1945*, edited by Klaus-Jürgen Müller, 2nd ed., 60–78. Paderborn: F. Schöningh, 1990.

Middlebrook, Martin and Chris Everitt. *The Bomber Command War Diaries: An Operational Reference Book, 1939–1945*. Harmondsworth: Viking, 1985.

Mierzejewski, Alfred C. "When Did Albert Speer Give Up?" *Historical Journal* 31, no. 2 (1988): 391–7.

Miller, Donald L. *Masters of the Air: America's Bomber Boys Who Fought the Air War against Nazi Germany*. New York: Simon & Schuster, 2006.

Mitcham, Samuel W., Jr. *German Order of Battle*. 2 vols. Mechanicsburg, PA: Stackpole Books, 2007.

———. *Retreat to the Reich: The German Defeat in France, 1944*. Mechanicsburg, PA: Stackpole Books, 2000.

———. *Rommel's Last Battle: The Desert Fox and the Normandy Campaign*. New York: Stein and Day, 1983.

Mitchell, Allan. *Nazi Paris: The History of an Occupation, 1940–1944*. New York: Berghahn Books, 2008.

Moersch, Karl and Reinhold Weber. *Die Zeit nach dem Krieg: Städte im Wiederaufbau*. Stuttgart: Kohlhammer, 2008.

Moll, Helmut, ed. *Zeugen für Christus: das deutsche Martyrologium des 20. Jahrhunderts*. 2 vols., 4th ed. Paderborn: Ferdinand Schöningh, 2006.

Möller, Jürgen. *Die amerikanische Besetzung des Leipziger Südraumes durch das V. US Corps im April 1945*. Weißenfels: Arps-Verlag, 2006.

Möller, Kurt Detlev. *Das letzte Kapitel: Geschichte der Kapitulation Hamburgs; von der Hamburger Katastrophe des Jahres 1943 bis zur Übergabe der Stadt am 3. Mai 1945*. Hamburg: Hoffmann und Campe, 1947.

Mommsen, Hans. *Alternatives to Hitler: German Resistance under the Third Reich*. Translated by Angus McGeoch. Princeton: Princeton University Press, 2003.

———. "Die Auflösung des Dritten Reiches." Chap. 12 in *Zur Geschichte Deutschlands im 20. Jahrhundert: Demokratie, Diktatur, Widerstand*. Munich: Deutsche Verlags-Anstalt, 2010.

Müller, Hartmut and Günther Rohdenburg, eds. *Kriegesende in Bremen: Erinnerungen, Berichte, Dokumente*. Bremen: Ed. Temmen, 1995.

Müller, Helmut. *fünf vor null: die Besetzung des Münsterlandes 1945*. 4th ed. Münster: Aschendorff, 1972

Müller, Klaus-Jürgen. "Die Befreiung von Paris und die deutsche Führung an der Westfront." In *Kriegsjahr 1944: im Großen und im Kleinen*, edited by Michael Salewski and Guntram Schulze-Wegener, 43–60. Stuttgart: Franz Steiner, 1995.

Müller, Roland. "'Make Democracy Work': Verwaltung und Politik in Stuttgart

1945." In *Stuttgart 1945: Anfang nach dem Ende,* edited by Wulf D. von Lucius, 13–95. Stuttgart: Lithos-Verlag, 1995.

Müller, Rolf-Dieter, Gerd R. Ueberschär, and Wolfram Wette, eds. *Wer zurück-weicht wird erschossen! Kriegsalltag u. Kriegsende in Südwestdeutschland 1944/45.* Freiburg i.Br.: Dreisam Verlag, 1985.

—— and Hans-Erich Volkmann, eds. *Die Wehrmacht: Mythos und Realität.* Munich: R. Oldenbourg, 1999.

Nachtmann, Walter. "Das Ende des Zweiten Weltkrieges in Stuttgart." In *Stuttgart im Zweiten Weltkrieg,* edited by Marlene P. Hiller, 493–99. Gerlingen: Bleicher Verlag, 1989.

Neiberg, Michael. *The Blood of Free Men: The Liberation of Paris, 1944.* New York: Basic Books, 2012.

Neitzel, Sönke. *Tapping Hitler's Generals: Transcripts of Secret Conversations, 1942–1945.* Translated by Geoffrey Brooks. St. Paul, MN: Frontline Books, 2007. Originally published as *Abgehört: deutsche Generäle in britischer Kriegsgefangenschaft 1942–1945* (Berlin: Propyläen, 2005).

Nordling, Raoul. *Sauver Paris: mémoires du consul de Suède, 1904–1905.* Edited by Fabrice Virgili. Brussels: Éditions Complexe, 2002.

Ott, Wilhelm. "Erinnerungen an die Tätigkeit als geschäftsführender Bürgermeister Augsburgs." In *Kriegsende und Neuanfang in Augsburg 1945: Erinnerungen und Berichte,* edited by Karl-Ulrich Gelberg, 19–106. Munich: R. Oldenbourg, 1996.

Overmans, Rüdiger. *Deutsche militärische Verluste im Zweiten Weltkrieg.* Munich: Oldenbourg, 2000.

Pelc, Ortwin, ed. *Kriegsende in Hamburg: eine Stadt erinnert sich.* Hamburg: Ellert & Richter Verlag, 2005.

Petershagen, Rudolf. *Gewissen in Aufruhr.* [East] Berlin: Verlag der Nation, 1966.

Petzold, Heinz. *Als für Cottbus der 2. Weltkrieg endete.* Cottbus: REGIA Verlag, 2005.

Powell, John, ed. *Magill's Guide to Military History.* Vol. 1. Pasadena: Salem Press, Inc., 2001.

Pulzer, Peter. *Germany, 1870–1945: Politics, State Formation, and War.* Oxford: Oxford University Press, 1997.

Randall, Willard Sterne. "The Other D-Day." *Quarterly Journal of Military History* 6, no. 3 (Spring 1944): 70–9.

Raschke, Helga. "Die letzten Tage faschistischer Herrschaft in Gotha." In *Die letzten Kriegstage Anfang April 1945 in Gotha.*

Rass, Christoph, René Rohrkamp, and Peter M. Quadflieg. *General Graf von Schwerin und das Kriegsende in Aachen: Ereignis, Mythos, Analyse.* Aachen: Shaker Verlag, 2007.

Rauscher, Hans. *1945: Die Wiedergeburt Österreichs: die dramatischen Tage vom Kriegsende bis zum Anfang der Republik.* Vienna: Böhlau, 1995.

Reitlinger, Gerald. *The SS: Alibi of a Nation, 1922–1945.* Reprint, New York: Viking Press, 1968.

Remy, Maurice Philip. *Mythos Rommel.* Munich: List Verlag, 2002.

———. "Rommel und der militärische Widerstand." In *Erwin Rommel: Geschichte und Mythos.* Published by the Haus der Geschichte Baden-Württemberg. Karlsruhe: G. Braun, 2009.

Reuth, Ralf Georg. *Rommel: The End of a Legend.* Translated by Debra S. Marmor and Herbert A. Danner. London: Haus Publishing, 2005.

Reutter, Friederike. *Heidelberg 1945–1949: zur politischen Geschichte einer Stadt in der Nachkriegszeit.* Heidelberg: Verlag Brigitte Guderjahn, 1994.

Rhodes, Richard. *Masters of Death: The SS-Einsatzgruppen and the Invention of the Holocaust.* New York: Alfred A. Knopf, 2002.

Rickling, Matthias, ed. *Osnabrück 1945: zwischen Krieg und Frieden.* Gudensberg-Gleichen: Wartberg Verlag, 2005.

Rockenmaier, Dieter W. *Das Dritte Reich und Würzburg: Versuch einer Bestandsaufnahme.* Würzburg: Mainpresse Richter Druck, 1983.

Rohland, Walter. *Bewegte Zeiten: Erinnerungen eines Eisenhüttenmannes.* Stuttgart: Seewald Verlag, 1978.

Rol-Tanguy, Colonel [Henri] and Roger Bourderon. *Libération de Paris: les cent documents.* Paris: Hachette, 1994.

Römer, Felix. *Der Kommissarbefehl: Wehrmacht und NS-Verbrechen an der Ostfront 1941/42.* Paderborn: Ferdinand Schöningh, 2008.

Rommel, Manfred. *1944 – Das Jahr der Entscheidung: Erwin Rommel in Frankreich.* Stuttgart: Hohenheim Verlag, 2010.

———. "The Last Days." In *The Rommel Papers,* 495–506.

Ruppenthal, Roland G. *Logistical Support of the Armies: September 1944–May 1945.* Vol. 2 of *United States Army in World War II : European Theater of Operations.* Washington: Office of the Chief of Military History Department, 1959.

Sander, Ulrich. *Mörderisches Finale: NS-Verbrechen bei Kriegsende.* Published by the Internationales Rombergparkkomitee. Cologne: PapyRossa Verlag, 2008.

Sax-Demuth, Waltraut. *Weiße Fahnen über Bielefeld: Untergang und Neubeginn 1945.* Herford: Bussesche Verlagshandlung, 1981.

Scheurig, Bodo. *Henning von Tresckow: eine Biographie.* Oldenburg: Gerhard Stalling Verlag, 1973.

Schlabrendorff, Fabian von. *Revolt against Hitler: The Personal Account of Fabian von Schlabrendorff.* London: Eyre and Spottiswoode, 1948.

Schmidt, Armin. *Frankfurt im Feuersturm: die Geschichte der Stadt im Zweiten Weltkrieg.* Frankfurt am Main: Societäts-Verlag, 1984.

Schnabel, Thomas, ed. *Formen des Widerstandes im Südwesten 1933–1945: Scheitern und Nachwirken.* Published by the Landeszentrale für politische Bildung

Baden-Württemberg and the Haus der Geschichte Baden-Württemberg. Ulm: Süddeutsche Verlagsgesellschaft, 1994.

———. "'Die Leute wollten nicht einer verlorenen Sache ihre Heimat opfern.'" In Schnabel, *Formen des Widerstandes*, 165–79.

——— and Gerd R. Ueberschär. *Endlich Frieden! Das Kriegsende in Freiburg 1945*. Freiburg: Schillinger Verlag, 1985.

Schramm, Leo. "Der letzte Gruß." In *Die letzten Kriegstage Anfang April 1945 in Gotha*.

Schramm, Percy Ernst, ed. *Kriegstagebuch des Oberkommandos der Wehrmacht*. 4 vols. Frankfurt: Bernard & Graefe Verlag für Wehrwesen, 1961–65.

Schramm, Wilhelm von. *Conspiracy among Generals*. Translated by R. T. Clark. London: George Allen & Unwin, 1956. English translation of *Aufstand der Generale: der 20. Juli in Paris* (Munich: Kindler, 1964).

Schultheiß, Hans, ed. *Die Männer von Brettheim: Lesebuch zur Erinnerungsstätte*. Villingen-Schwenningen: Neckar-Verlag, 1994.

Schwarzwälder, Herbert. *Bremen und Nordwestdeutschland am Kriegsende 1945*. Vol. 3, *Vom „Kampf um Bremen" bis zur Kapitulation*. Bremen: Carl Schünemann Verlag, 1974.

Seaton, Albert. *The Russo-German War 1941–45*. London: Arthur Baker Limited, 1971.

Sereny, Gitta. *Albert Speer: His Battle with Truth*. New York: Alfred Knopf, 1995.

Seventh U.S. Army. *The Seventh United States Army in France and Germany, 1944–1945: report of operations*. Heidelberg: Aloys Gräf, 1946.

Siedler, Wolf Jobst and Elisabeth Niggemeyer. *Die gemordete Stadt: Abgesang auf Putte und Straße, Platz und Baum*. Rev. ed. Berlin: Sammlung Siedler, 1993.

Smith, Inge. "Der Mensch von Gadolla – persönliche Erinnerungen 50 Jahre danach." In *Gotha 1945*, 9–10.

Snyder, Timothy. *Bloodlands: Europe between Hitler and Stalin*. New York: Basic Books, 2010.

Sollbach, Gerhard E. *Dortmund: Bombenkrieg und Nachkriegsalltag 1939–1948*. Hagen: Lesezeichen Verlag, 1996.

Specker, Hans-Eugen, ed. *Ulm im Zweiten Weltkrieg*. Ulm: Stadtarchiv Ulm, 1995.

Speer, Albert. *Inside the Third Reich*. Reprint, London: Phoenix, 2003. First English version published 1970, Weidenfeld & Nicolson. Originally published in German as *Erinnerungen* (Berlin: Propyläen Verlag, 1969).

Speidel, Hans. *Aus unserer Zeit: Erinnerungen*. Berlin: Propyläen, 1977.

———. *Invasion 1944: Rommel and the Normandy Campaign*. Reprint, Westport, CT: Greenwood Press, 1971. First published 1950, Chicago: Henry Regnery Co.

Stacey, C. P. *Official History of the Canadian Army*. Vol. 3, *The Victory Campaign: The Operations in North-West Europe, 1944–1945*. Ottawa: Department of National Defence, 1960.

Stadtarchiv Augsburg. *Bewahrt Eure Stadt . . . Kriegsende und Neuanfang in Augsburg 1945–1950*. Augsburg: Wißner-Verlag, 2005.

Steinbach, Peter. "The Conservative Resistance." In *Contending with Hitler: Varieties of German Resistance in the Third Reich*, edited by David Clay Large, 89–98. Cambridge: Cambridge University Press, 1995.

——— and Johannes Tuchel, eds. *Lexikon des Widerstandes 1933–1945*. Munich: Beck, 1994.

Steinecke, Gerhard. *Drei Tage im April: Kriegsende in Leipzig*. Leipzig: Lehmstedt Verlag, 2005.

Steiner, Walter, Renate Wagwitz, Frank Funke and Anke Bickel. *Weimar 1945: ein historisches Protokoll*. Weimar: Stadtmuseum Weimar, 1997.

Steinkamp, Peter. "Individuelle und organisierte Kampfeinstellung durch Soldaten der Wehrmacht im Zweiten Weltkrieg." In Förtsch, *Kriegsende in Crailsheim und Umgebung*, 42–54.

Stephenson, Jill. *Hitler's Home Front: Württemberg under the Nazis*. London: Hambledon Continuum, 2006.

Streit, Christian. *Keine Kameraden: Die Wehrmacht und die sowjetischen Kriegsgefangenen 1941–1945*. Bonn: Verlag J. H. W. Dietz Nachf., 1997.

Szokoll, Carl. *Die Rettung Wiens 1945: mein Leben, mein Anteil an der Verschwörung gegen Hitler und an der Befreiung Österreichs*. Vienna: Amalthea Molden, 2001.

Tenfelde, Klaus. "Soziale Grundlagen von Resistenz and Widerstand." In *Der Widerstand gegen den Nationalsozialismus: die deutsche Gesellschaft und der Widerstand gegen Hitler*, edited by Jürgen Schmädecke and Peter Steinbach, 799–812. Munich: Piper, 1985.

Thornton, Willis. *The Liberation of Paris*. New York: Harcourt, Brace & World, Inc., 1962.

Thümmel, Hans Georg. *Greifswald – Geschichte und Geschichten: die Stadt, ihre Kirchen, und ihre Universität*. Paderborn: Ferdinand Schöningh, 2011.

Tietmann, Lutz. "'. . . die Stadt vor dem Schlimmsten bewahren.'" In *Die anderen Soldaten: Wehrkraftzersetzung, Gehorsamsverweigerung und Fahnenflucht im Zweiten Weltkrieg*, edited by Norbert Haase and Gerhard Paul, 174–88. Frankfurt a. M.: Fischer Taschenbuch Verlag, 1995.

Tuchel, Johannes. "Die Verfahren vor dem 'Volksgerichtshof' nach dem 20. Juli 1944." In Becker and Studt, *Der Umgang des Dritten Reiches*, 131–46.

Tucker-Jones, Anthony. *Operation Dragoon: The Liberation of Southern France 1944*. Barnsley, UK: Pen & Sword, 2009.

Ueberschär, Gerd R. "Freiburgs letzte Kriegstage bis zur Besetzung durch die französische Armee am 21. April 1945." In Schnabel and Ueberschär, *Endlich Frieden!*, 8–40.

———. "Krieg auf deutschem Boden: der Vormarsch der Alliierten im Südwesten." In Müller, Ueberschär, and Wette, *Wer zurückweicht wird erschossen!*, 59–69.

——— and Rolf-Dieter Müller, *1945: Das Ende des Krieges*. Darmstadt: Primus Verlag, 2005.

Viertel, Gabriele, Uwe Fiedler, and Gert Richter, eds. *Chemnitzer Erinnerungen 1945*. Pt. 3, *Die Vororte der Stadt Chemnitz*. 2nd ed. Chemnitz: Verlag Heimatland Sachsen, 2006.

Vinen, Richard. *The Unfree French: Life under the Occupation*. London: Penguin, 2007.

Wagner, Christoph. *Entwicklung, Herrschaft und Untergang der nationalsozialistischen Bewegung in Passau 1920 bis 1945*. Berlin: Frank & Timme, 2007.

Weber, Günter. "Heidelbergs Schicksal hing am seidenen Faden." In *Heidelberg zur Stunde Null*, edited by Werner Pieper, 35–60. Heidelberg: N. Grubhofer Verlag, 1985.

Weigley, Russell F. *Eisenhower's Lieutenants: The Campaign of France and Germany 1944–1945*. Bloomington: Indian University Press, 1981.

Weinberg, Gerhard L. *Germany, Hitler, and World War II*. New York: Cambridge University Press, 1995.

———. "The Plot to Kill Hitler." *Michigan Quarterly Review* 10, No. 2 (Spring 1971): 125–30.

———. "Some Myths of World War II." *The Journal of Military History* 75 (July 2011): 701–18.

———. *A World at Arms: A Global History of World War II*. 2nd ed. Cambridge: Cambridge University Press, 2005.

Weitzel, Wilhelm. "Ereignisse in Staufen am Kriegsende." In *Staufen vor und nach dem Fliegerangriff*, edited by August Villinger, 373–4. Staufen im Breisgau: Verlag A. Villinger, 1986.

Wenzel, Matthias. "Ein Mann kann eine ganze Stadt erretten, aber die Stadt nicht zwei Menschen helfen." In *Gotha 1945*, 11–19.

Werner, Hermann. *Tübingen 1945*. Tübingen: Kulturamt, 1986.

Werner, Josef. *Karlsruhe 1945: unter Hakenkreuz, Trikolore und Sternenbanner*. 2nd ed. Karlsruhe: G. Braun, 1986.

Wette, Wolfram. "Durchhalte-Terror in der Schlußphase des Krieges: das Beispiel der Erschießungen in Waldkirch am 10./11. April 1945." In Müller, Ueberschär, and Wette, *Wer zurückweicht wird erschossen!*, 70–3.

Weyr, Thomas. *The Setting of the Pearl: Vienna under Hitler*. New York: Oxford University Press, 2005.

Whiting, Charles. *America's Forgotten Army: The Story of the U.S. Seventh*. Rockville Centre, NY: Sarpedon, 1999.

———. *Bloody Bremen: Ike's Last Stand*. London: Leo Cooper, 1998.

Wichers, Hermann. "Möglichkeiten und Grenzen des Widerstandes von Sozial-demokraten und Kommunisten in Baden und Württemberg." In Schnabel, *Formen des Widerstandes*, 26–52.

Wilhelmus, Wolfgang. *Geschichte der Juden in Greifswald und Umgebung*. Kückenshagen: Scheunen-Verlag, 1999.

Wood, James A. "Captive Historians, Captive Audience: The German Military History Program, 1945–1961." *Journal of Military History* 69, no. 1 (2005): 123–47.

Wright, Vincent. *The Government and Politics of France*. London: Hutchinson, 1978.

Yelton, David K. *Hitler's Home Guard: Volkssturmmann*. Westminster, MD: Osprey, 2006.

———. *Hitler's Volkssturm: The Nazi Militia and the Fall of Germany, 1944–1945*. Lawrence: University Press of Kansas, 2002.

Young, Desmond. *Rommel: The Desert Fox*. First published 1950 by Harper New York. Reprint, New York: Quill/William Morrow.

Zaloga, Steven J. *Liberation of Paris 1944: Patton's Race for the Seine*. Oxford: Osprey Publishing, 2008.

———. *Operation Dragoon 1944: France's Other D-Day*. Oxford: Osprey Publishing, 2009.

———. *The Siegfried Line 1944–194: Battles on the German Frontier*. Oxford: Osprey, 2007.

Zelle, Karl-Günter. *Hitlers Zweifelnde Elite: Goebbels – Göring – Himmler – Speer*. Paderborn: Ferdinand Schöningh, 2010.

Zelzer, Maria. *Stuttgart unterm Hakenkreuz: Chronik aus Stuttgart 1933–1945*. 2nd ed. Stuttgart: Alektor-Verlag, 1984.

Ziegler, Armin. *Crailsheim 1945/46: Überleben und Neuanfang*. Crailsheim: Baier, 1999.

Zier, Hans Georg. *Geschichte der Stadt Pforzheim: von den Anfängen bis 1945*. Stuttgart: Konrad Theiss Verlag, 1982.

Zimmermann, Volker. *In Schutt und Asche: das Ende des Zweiten Weltkrieges in Düsseldorf*. 1st ed. Düsseldorf: Grupello Verlag, 1995.

Zusammenbruch 1945 und Aufbruch: eine Dokumentation der letzten Kriegstage vom Neckar zum Odenwald. Heidelberg: Rhein-Neckar-Zeitung, 1995.

INDEX